JERRY WHITE

Jerry White is Emeritus Professor of London History at Birkbeck, University of London. He is the author of an acclaimed trilogy chronicling life in the capital from the eighteenth to the twentieth century. His other books include *Mansions of Misery: A Biography of the Marshalsea Debtors' Prison* and *Zeppelin Nights*, a social history of London during the First World War. He is a winner of The Wolfson History Prize and is a Fellow of the Royal Historical Society.

JERRY WHITE

The Battle of
London 1939–45

Endurance, Heroism and
Frailty under Fire

VINTAGE

1 3 5 7 9 10 8 6 4 2

Vintage is part of the Penguin Random House group of companies
whose addresses can be found at global.penguinrandomhouse.com

First published in Vintage in 2023

First published in hardback by The Bodley Head in 2021

Copyright © Jerry White 2021

Jerry White has asserted their right to be identified as the author of this
Work in accordance with the Copyright, Designs and Patents Act 1988

penguin.co.uk/vintage

Printed and bound in Great Britain by Clays Ltd, Elcograf S.p.A.

The authorised representative in the EEA is Penguin Random House
Ireland, Morrison Chambers, 32 Nassau Street, Dublin D02 YH68

A CIP catalogue record for this book is available from the British Library

ISBN 9780099593294

Penguin Random House is committed to a sustainable future
for our business, our readers and our planet. This book is made
from Forest Stewardship Council® certified paper.

For
Esther, Sam, Amelia, Theo and Lucas

CONTENTS

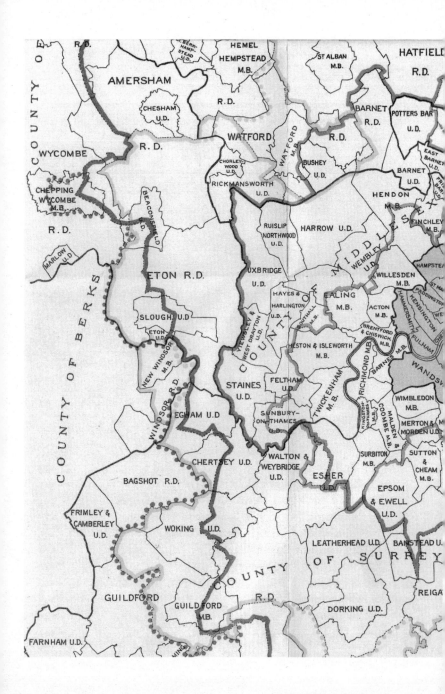

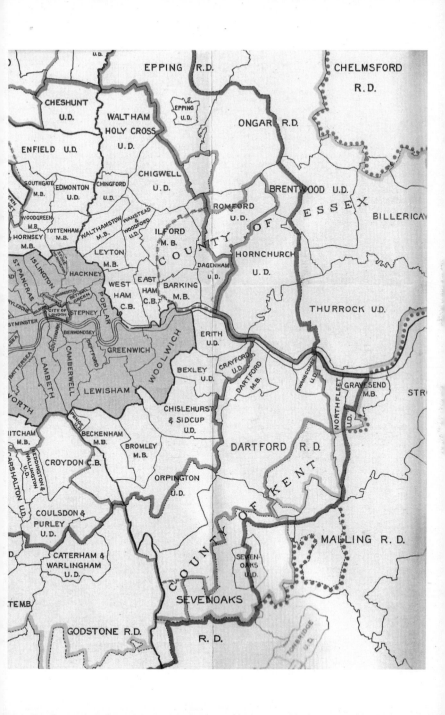

PREFACE

London and the nation were at war with Germany from 3 September 1939 to 8 May 1945. The war against Japan would continue for another three months until 15 August. These were almost six years of intermittent anxiety, disruption, deprivation and sacrifice. The moments of agony were not continuous. Even so, for eight months from September 1940 to May 1941, and again for much of the period from December 1943 to March 1945, London was under sustained, sometimes unrelenting, aerial bombardment by night and by day. In 1939 one in five of the population of England and Wales lived in London. By the spring of 1945 one in two of the nation's civilian war dead had been Londoners, nearly 30,000 people. Throughout the war, London was the nation's front line, and London and its people bore the brunt of the nation's suffering.

The history of these six years has been generally overborne by the intense savagery of the air war against London. No doubt the bombing defined the era for those who lived through it, and the blitz and the V-weapons must surely take centre stage in any retelling of this tempestuous period. But the air war can't be allowed to overshadow the medley of pain and pleasure that underpinned the rhythm of life in these six years. The months of terror were outnumbered by those spent knitting together the skein of daily life at work, in the home, on the allotment, in the cinema or theatre and, not least, standing in those interminable queues for daily necessities that were such a feature of London's war. Nor did the war's place in the history of London in the twentieth century end with the last of the V-weapons on 28 March 1945. The war would go on to define the trajectory of London history for a generation to come, casting a dense shadow over the city's future that did not begin to lift, in many ways, until the 1980s. The Second World

War would be the fulcrum on which London history in the twentieth century turned.

I've tried to tell the story of London at war with this bigger back-drop in mind. It is a scene-set that stretches back to the First World War as well as forward in time, for the experiences of Londoners between 1914 and 1918 helped stiffen resolve in 1940 and after. Although I've kept one eye on that wide canvas I've also got close up to the daily lives of ordinary Londoners, often telling the story through their own voices recorded in diaries and memoirs or cited in local newspapers. I've privileged the experience of those people who lived in one or two rooms in London's endless vistas of terraced houses rather than those of the rich and famous who have frequently populated the narratives of these years, though occasionally they make an appearance too. Much has been written about 'the Myth of the Blitz', but I've sought to unearth what actually happened at the time, giving promin-ence to the role of London's local civil defence forces, in my view unfairly neglected in previous accounts of the war. They were London's backbone. In doing so, however, I've told the story of the Londoner warts and all. This, after all, was a city with a wartime civilian popu-lation of some 6.5 million people. Some were heroes, some were villains, and some were both at different moments in time. Most fell between these extremes and just made do as best they could. None, though, were able to escape the drama which beset them. For every Londoner who stayed in the capital it was the time of their lives: 'I would rather have been in London under siege between 1940 and 1945 than anywhere else,' recalled the literary critic John Lehmann some years later, 'except perhaps Troy in the time that Homer celebrated.'[1]

Jerry White
Birkbeck, University of London

AUTHOR'S NOTES

Casualty Figures

There is frequently minor disagreement in the sources over casualty figures, especially for individual incidents. Where these inconsistencies exist, I've followed the figures given in the official histories, or in official files if the information is given after a suitable time lag. Otherwise I've followed secondary sources found to be trustworthy.

London

'London' and 'London Region' refer to Greater London, an area coterminous with the London Civil Defence Region, operational from 1938, and with the then Metropolitan Police District. Since 2000, with minor adjustments, it has been the area governed by the Greater London Authority. 'Inner London' and the 'County of London' are used interchangeably; they refer to the London County Council area (then comprising twenty-eight metropolitan boroughs, now eleven London boroughs) and the City; for the avoidance of doubt, inner London here excludes Newham, which has been sometimes added to the definition in later contexts. I have also tended to use 'borough' as shorthand for every local authority in Greater London, rather than complicating the text with the niceties of urban and rural district councils, and municipal, county and metropolitan boroughs; where the distinctions are important I've tried to draw them out.

Money

Before decimalisation the pound sterling comprised twenty shillings (20s) and a shilling comprised twelve pence (12d); so a shilling was equivalent to today's 5p and 1p to about 2d. The Bank of England inflation calculator estimates £10 in 1939 to be worth £659 in 2019 (the latest data available at the time of going to press); and the value of £10 in 1946 as £422 in 2019, some indication of the pound's loss of value during the war. I have not followed the distracting practice of translating prices and wages cited in the text by these modern comparators. Those readers for whom this is of interest will be able to check values online.

ABBREVIATIONS

AA	anti-aircraft
ABCA	Army Bureau of Current Affairs
AEU	Amalgamated Engineering Union
AFS	Auxiliary Fire Service
ARP	Air Raid Precautions
ATS	Auxiliary Territorial Service
AWOL	absent without leave
BBC	British Broadcasting Corporation
BEF	British Expeditionary Force
BUF	British Union of Fascists
CEMA	Committee for the Encouragement of Music and the Arts
CLP	County of London Plan
CO	conscientious objector
CP or CPGB	Communist Party of Great Britain
GLP	Greater London Plan
GWR	Great Western Railway
HE	high explosive
LAP	London Aircraft Production
LCC	London County Council
LCDR	London Civil Defence Region
LDV	Local Defence Volunteers
LFB	London Fire Brigade
LMS	London, Midland and Scottish Railway
LNER	London North Eastern Railway
LPTB	London Passenger Transport Board
LRE	London Repairs Executive
LWP	London Women's Parliament

MAGNA	Mutual Aid for Good Neighbours' Association
MAP	Ministry of Aircraft Production
NFS	National Fire Service
NUR	National Union of Railwaymen
PLA	Port of London Authority
POW	prisoner of war
RASC	Royal Army Service Corps
ROF	Royal Ordnance Factory
USAAF	United States Army Air Forces
UXB	unexploded bomb
WAAF	Women's Auxiliary Air Force
WHD	Women's Home Defence
Wrens	Women's Royal Naval Service
WVS	Women's Voluntary Services
YMCA	Young Men's Christian Association

I

THE GREATEST TARGET IN THE WORLD:
11 NOVEMBER 1918–31 AUGUST 1939

THE September crisis dawned only slowly on most Londoners. True, there had been undertones since German troops began to mass on their eastern borders in August, and at the end of the month Gladys Langford, an elementary school teacher in Hoxton, noted anxiously in her diary how 'Papers, wireless news and every placard full of hints of trouble in Czecho-Slovakia. I do get terrified with all this talk of war.' By 12 September 1938 almost everyone was aware that war of some sort was possible, even likely, in central Europe and that Britain once again might be dragged in. The mood wasn't helped by a heatwave striking London that week. Langford wrote from her bedsit in Highbury to her married sister in rural Essex 'a long screed ... saying I was contemplating suicide'; she blamed Hitler for her low state of mind. Tensions eased with Prime Minister Neville Chamberlain's first flight to see the Nazi leader on Thursday 15 September, which offered fresh hope of a diplomatic settlement: '"Hurrah for Neville,"' Pamela Wilsdon told her fellow Hampstead boarders crowded round the radio for the evening news the night before.[1]

Despite this public optimism, however, plans began to be implemented behind the scenes from 15 September to coordinate the defence of Britain should it come under attack from the air. Wisely so, for on Chamberlain's second flight to Germany, 22 September, he was met by Hitler's fresh demands: not just the self-determination of the German-speaking Sudetenland but the total dissolution of Czechoslovakia as a state. Even for Chamberlain, that was a demand too far. Britain moved rapidly and publicly to protect itself from attack should war be inescapable.

The nation's civil defence centred on London, and Londoners bore the brunt of what by now were frantic measures to protect a population of some 8.75 million citizens. Announcements were made on 22 September that plans were in place to evacuate the London hospitals should hostilities begin, that air raid precautions (ARP) booklets were being posted to every home, and that volunteers were needed in their tens of thousands for the emergency and other services. All these were overshadowed, though, by announcements from local councils that everyone was now to be provided with a gas mask. Measuring and fitting would begin that very day.

From Thursday 22 September to Friday 30 September the huge task of preparing London for war cranked falteringly into gear, but it was the gas mask that brought the perils of modern warfare vividly into every living room. The numbers involved were enormous. The masks were delivered to councils in pieces and had to be assembled by volunteer council staff or in some places 'factory girls' volunteered by their employers. Westminster City Council marshalled 1,900 volunteers to measure and fit 120,000 residents with gas masks, over 324,000 were distributed in Wandsworth, over 115,000 were fitted with masks in Croydon in three days and nearly everyone else in that borough of over 230,000 people by the 30th. In Bethnal Green, one of the smallest metropolitan boroughs, 67,000 masks were issued in just two days, 28 and 29 September, and in suburban Brentford and Chiswick 58,000. Everywhere there were queues outside town halls and other fitting centres of people waiting to be matched to their gas masks, which came in three sizes, small, medium and large. Thousands of home visits were made to arrange fitting and distribution. Pamela Wilsdon's boarding house in Belsize Square was knocked up at 9.30 on a Sunday night by the council's 'chirpy, talkative young man, very matey, lower middle class. Everybody sat on arms of chairs in the lounge, including me in my dressing gown [she had a cold] ... I tried on a medium one, which was much too big; the small one was a good fit, except that I couldn't see out of it. "I'd better put you down for a medium one," he said.' The masks were delivered two days later.[2]

In Dagenham, where over 100,000 masks were assembled, fitted and given out, the council's 'Borough Charter celebrations' planned for that week were postponed in the 'feverish tearing work of getting up protection'. There and elsewhere hundreds of thousands of sandbags were filled and piled round vulnerable or important buildings. There was insufficient sand for all of them so topsoil was often used instead: in the spring of 1939 dormant seeds would germinate and destroy both bags and the walls built with them. Most visible of all was the digging of trenches for air raid shelters for those caught in the open should bombing begin. These were the first public air raid shelters to be built in the capital. No London open space was too sacred for desecration by pick and shovel – in only a few cases were mechanical diggers available. 'Trenches have been dug in Hyde Park, St James's Park, and the Green Park,' *The Times* reported the day after 'A.R.P. Sunday' (25 September), and some were already roofed in with corrugated iron. The same was true of Kensington Gardens and Hampstead Heath, and indeed everywhere from Ravenscourt Park in the west to Hackney Marshes in the east and beyond. Shelters for lawyers were hurriedly dug in Lincoln's Inn Fields, all by volunteers working in their collars and shirtsleeves under the direction of council engineers. Elsewhere the unemployed were hired to work alongside volunteers. Everywhere the numbers were prodigious – 2,500 men in Wandsworth, 1,200 with three mechanical diggers in St Pancras, often working round the clock 'by the light of flares and lorry headlights' – 'like so many grave-diggers,' one observer thought.[3]

Householders too were encouraged to make their homes as safe as possible, by digging trench shelters in their gardens if they had them – 'When I got out of bed,' Pamela Wilsdon recorded on 27 September, 'I saw two people in the next garden digging a trench' – and by constructing gas-proof rooms where they could. These were especially important for families with young children for no gas masks were yet available for babies and toddlers and anxious mothers clamoured for advice at London's town halls. In Belsize Square on Saturday 24 September:

N.I., (spinster, journalist, aged 40) urged Mrs. Cook, our landlady, to make a gas proof room. It just seemed fantastic to me; whether sensible or not, it would never have occurred to me to do it. We spent much of the day surveying and discussing various rooms, and decided on the basement kitchen. We got hold of a diagram, and sat on the kitchen table, reading it out loud. Mrs. Cook went up to the Hampstead Town Hall on Monday, but everybody there was too busy to pay any attention to her. She went to the local Gas Proof House, where there was a lady who was very nice but who seemed to know nothing. She said: 'Of course, this is considered to be a perfect example of a gas proof room, and ordinary people couldn't be expected to do it.'

So far, (Sept. 28) we have done nothing about our gas proof room, but I believe a man is coming to put wooden beading round the wainscoting.

Others could fare better: the writer J. B. Priestley, then almost at the apex of his fame, instructed builders to make a bomb-proof (and presumably gas-proof) room in the cellar of his grand London house at 3 The Grove, Highgate.[4]

While police and council officers in loudspeaker vans toured London streets alerting residents to gas mask fitting centres and seeking labour for trench digging, the biggest call-up was for ARP volunteers – as wardens, first aid attendants, stretcher-bearers and rescue parties. The Home Secretary announced that he was seeking no fewer than half a million volunteers nationwide. Thirty thousand men and women were called for to staff London's Auxiliary Fire Service (AFS) and tens of thousands of others, even boys as young as fourteen to act as messengers, were asked to enrol at their local town halls. Not all were forthcoming, but in this moment of crisis many were. Before September, Wandsworth had enrolled 3,882 volunteers; by the end of the month the number had jumped to 6,154. In the twenty-eight metropolitan boroughs and the City of London, ARP recruitment almost doubled during the crisis, from 34,000 at the beginning to 65,000 at the end; even so, this was barely 60 per cent of the numbers sought.[5]

The dislocation of daily life in these tempestuous days was immense, and not just the queueing for gas masks, or the unwelcome toil for butter-palmed clerks and shop men of digging trenches, or facing an agonising decision to take on new public duties alongside the burdens of work and home. The journey to work for many was made even more nerve-racking than usual with the closure of eight underground stations for emergency gates or 'plugs' to be fitted to prevent flooding in the event of bombs breaching tunnels under the river. Long queues of City workers formed at south London stations on 28 and 29 September, commuters only vaguely aware of how to work their way round the blockage. And there was the gnawing anxiety deep in the stomach, the wondering whether tonight or tomorrow might bring some devastating aerial attack that would shake London to its core. 'My own condition was deteriorating fast,' wrote Lady Diana Cooper, one of London's leading socialites and a woman not lacking in courage. 'Fear did more harm to my physique than to my morale. Sleep was murdered for ever. My heart quaked … My hands shook …' 'It still seems "touch and go" for war. I can't get peace of mind,' Gladys Langford, alone in her Highbury bedsit, confided to her diary. 'If only I could summon the courage to gas myself!'[6]

When *The Times* wrote in a leader of London's 'calm but intense activity' in that crisis week of late September calmness was apparent only on the surface. And many abandoned the need for calmness altogether by getting out of London as fast as they could. Evacuation was a recognition that those who stayed in London could not be adequately protected by the authorities. Official plans for the evacuation of London's children had been rushed into place in early September. They were not implemented – thankfully, given their half-baked unreadiness – though children with physical and other disabilities in London County Council (LCC) schools were evacuated to the country on 28 September, some 3,000 of them bussed out of London to a camp in Kent. But it was the voluntary unofficial flight from London that marked the depth of people's fears. They left in uncountable numbers. By that same day a 'great exodus' from London's hotels of people rich enough to live in them all year round had begun – foreigners leaving for the seaports (Americans were formally advised by their ambassador on 27 September to get out of London) and others 'to the country'. On 29 September the exodus reached full flood. The roads were crowded, as many left by car or coach, but it was rail that shouldered the brunt. Trains for the West Country, for Scotland (where four London mothers with their young children joined their friend Naomi Mitchison in her Argyllshire hideaway) and the Irish boat trains had to be duplicated to meet the unparalleled demand. But really it was an escape to anywhere but London: 'A surprisingly large number of people took tickets for small villages in East Anglia.'[7] As *The Times* made plain on 30 September, this was a flight pre-eminently of the well-to-do:

At all the main line railway termini the scene was much the same – crowded trains, thronged departure platforms, husbands bidding farewell to wives and children, piles of trunks and perambulators, mothers and nurses carrying babies, buffets full to overflowing, hurrying porters and harassed officials, soldiers, sailors and airmen equipped with full packs. Many people took their pets with them. Dogs on leads, cats in baskets and even canaries and parrots were to be seen. As each train steamed out, those left standing on the platforms were mostly men.

Ironically, by the time the newspapers reported on scenes like this the crisis had passed its peak. Neville Chamberlain's third visit to Hitler on 29 September had at last secured something that looked like a promise of peace. Following his return to Heston Aerodrome in west London on the last day of September, the Prime Minister felt able to announce that the Munich Agreement was 'peace for our time'. Relief was felt in almost every home in the land, perhaps especially so in London, where people knew they had been hauled back from the very brink of disaster. Relief was tarnished for many by the feeling that British security had been won at the cost of the dismemberment of Czechoslovakia and German annexation of the Sudetenland, and by the betrayal of a brave and blameless nation; but it was relief nonetheless. That afternoon of 30 September, in Labour Fulham, just 10 per cent of people surveyed in an opinion poll declared themselves 'Anti-Chamberlain'; 54 per cent were 'Pro' and the rest unsure.[8]

There were two consequences of Munich for London that are worth noting here. First, the exodus of late September led some Londoners to reappraise their connection to the city. This impacted on all classes, though generally it needed a little money to make it happen, and two contrasting instances might be left to represent many. Middle-class V. S. Pritchett, a successful freelance writer, and his wife decided to abandon their flat near Little Venice, Maida Vale: 'Our daughter was a year old; my wife was pregnant again. We wisely went to live in the country,' taking a farmhouse near Newbury, west Berkshire, where they remained till near the end of the war. And Arthur Newens, a small-time haulage contractor from Bethnal Green with a young family, 'frantic with the general talk about air raids,' used his wife's inheritance to build a bungalow at North Weald, near Epping, moving there in April 1939.[9]

Second, even among those who stayed, the feeling that war was increasingly likely in the foreseeable future began to penetrate the thinking of all classes of Londoner. Munich made ARP a living reality. Before Munich, ARP numbers were low and it was only the enthusiast who had volunteered for a service that most people were doubtful would be needed. After, even though the numbers in ARP dropped away somewhat once the crisis had passed, few could doubt that it was something worth putting effort into. Now there was a general realisation that families and individuals needed to consider the consequences for themselves and their loved ones of protection against air raids.

The Munich crisis of September 1938 has often been described since as a 'dress rehearsal' for the real show that would later break on London and the Londoner. Well, this was a dress rehearsal where almost none of the actors had learned their lines and where most of the scenery failed to turn up. This great crisis of unreadiness would need to focus minds wonderfully.[10]

ON ARP Sunday, with the Munich crisis in full spate, the East Acton branch of the Association of Old Contemptibles held their annual parade on Shepherd's Bush Green. The irony of these men in their forties and fifties who had fought in one war, while preparations were advancing all around them for their sons and daughters to fight in another, was not lost on their friends and supporters. Now, indeed, these same men were urged by the Mayors of Hammersmith and Acton to 'do their bit' once more, this time by volunteering for the ARP services and other arms of civil defence, and many no doubt did so.[11]

The shadow of one war thus overlay the approach of another. For Londoners who had lived in the capital for thirty years or more, the memories of war and London's place in it were fresh in every mind. Thought of a new war inevitably drew memory back to what the previous conflict had meant on the home front – the endless queues, shortages, rationing, air raids and the perils of the blackout. But the war lay not just in the past. In many ways the First World War had helped make London the extraordinarily thriving city that it had become by 1938. The great manufacturing districts of west London that sprang up to make munitions and aeroplanes from 1915 to 1918 had not lain fallow long after the Armistice. Thousands of new jobs in west London especially, but also in north-east London along the Lea Valley and in south-west London along the Wandle, helped draw labour to London in unprecedented numbers. London in the twenty years before 1938 had been the brightest star in the nation's economic firmament, rivalled (but not matched) only by the West Midlands manufacturing belt centred on Coventry and Birmingham. With the demand for labour came demand for housing, and then the reciprocal requirement for commodities to fit out new homes, most of those consumer durables assembled in London factories. It was a virtuous circle that seemed to know no bounds.

The figures charting London's prosperity in the interwar period were stupendous. In the twenty years from 1918 to 1939 London doubled in size on the ground, the built-up area now thirty-four miles across from east to west. In these years some 860,000 homes were built in Greater London; in the peak year of 1934 they were being run up at 1,500 every week. The population growth was staggering – double the rate of the rest of the country. London's net increase of 1,228,000 people was equivalent to one third of the growth of the national population as a whole. In suburban London outside the LCC boundary, 810,000 were added in the 1920s (equivalent to the population of Manchester) and 900,000 more in the 1930s (like adding Birmingham's population to London). In 1939 more than one in every five persons resident in England and Wales was a Londoner. In that year the capital's population reached 8,728,000 – a figure not attained again until 2015. Fundamentally this was growth in outer London rather than in London's centre as the capital rapidly became a city of new suburbs. Most Londoners, over 4.7 million people, now lived in suburban London, many in houses less than twenty years old. One effect of this urban expansion was not just to bring people to London but also to draw people away from the older centre, the LCC area, whose population shrank by some 470,000 over the same period.[12]

This extraordinary period of growth would have important consequences for London as it faced the prospect of another war. One was the impact of an inchoate maze of local government bodies whose functions were now transformed and magnified by London's relentless growth, with formerly rural districts becoming urban townships within a decade or two. Greater London (as defined by the Metropolitan Police District) contained ninety-five local authorities responsible for most day-to-day functions safeguarding public health, local roads and lighting, refuse collection and so on. Above them, with some overreaching powers, lay six county councils – London, Middlesex, and parts of Hertfordshire, Essex, Kent and Surrey. Each authority, directly elected by the residents, clung tightly to its own domain. The resulting confusing patchwork was generally acknowledged to be a preposterous and obsolete mess.[13]

Second, there were very few who thought that London's growth was a cause for celebration. On the contrary, this modern megalopolis provoked much wrath, and for many reasons. Its size was a problem, because Londoners had to travel long distances both to work and to open countryside. Its tendency to grow yet further was a problem because its restless appetite for building land meant it would swallow even more rural scenery. Its suburbs were a problem because their terraced houses were repetitive and dull and because the people who lived in them were thought to be small-minded, materialistic, selfish and unimaginative. Its economic dynamism was a problem because it siphoned industry from other parts of the country and seized more than its fair share of the few new jobs created in these years of general depression; and because it sucked the vitality from more needy parts of Great Britain by encouraging young and talented people of both sexes to abandon their home communities to seek a life of glitter in the metropolis. In all these ways, London was a threat to the nation and – so was the pretty universal consensus in the late 1930s that crossed party-political boundaries but was especially strong on the centre left – it needed to be cut down to size: not just stopped from growing further but actively diminished.[14]

Even worse, London threatened the nation in one more way that might, indeed, prove fatal. Here was London, the seat of government and of the crown and empire, the hub of the nation's rail and road network, the greatest port in Europe if not the world, the prime location of courts and the law, of print media and broadcasting, of the best teaching hospitals in the country and much of the nation's electrical engineering and aircraft production. Yet London was also the biggest bombing target on earth, where air raids would not just distemper the lives of Londoners but might paralyse the nation's capacity to defend itself in war.

This was not just the worry of an overwrought imagination. London had already suffered under bombing and had suffered for a time quite badly. The Zeppelin raids of 1915–16 had been episodically frightening, but most Londoners had taken them in their stride. The daylight raids of the summer of 1917 had been an affront to national pride and caused considerable loss of life, but they were few and daylight eliminated many terrors. But the night raids by huge biplanes in the autumn and winter of 1917–18 had badly shaken Londoners' nerves. Deadly panic around places of shelter, the evacuation from London of those who could afford to leave, with trekking to bed down in forests and open spaces on London's edge for those who could not, the rush to the tube – over 300,000 sheltering underground one night in September 1917, far more than at any time in the war to come – all these raised question marks over how London would react in a new war where modern bombers with greater ordnance might cause catastrophic damage.[15]

These fears of a modern air war were stoked higher and higher during the years that followed the Armistice. There were some notable contributing factors. First was a forensic analysis in the 1920s and 1930s of the impact of bombing on London in the First World War that measured the grim effectiveness of German high explosives on property and people and calculated what it might do in future. Second, bombing entrenched itself as an alarming feature of modern warfare, especially in the 1930s: Italy used mustard gas and high explosives to overrun Abyssinia in 1936, and German- and Italian-backed rebel forces under General Franco used bombing to devastating effect in the Spanish Civil War of 1936-9. Third, a fascination with bombing in fiction and film was an important strand in British popular culture that reached its apogee in H. G. Wells's science fiction novel of 1933, *The Shape of Things to Come*. Filmed unforgettably by Alexander Korda in 1936, it showed great cities laid waste and popularised the notion of mass air attack destroying for ever the fragile trappings of contemporary civilisation.[16]

Official views of the likely casualties per ton of bombs dropped grew more and more pessimistic in the interwar period. In 1924 Whitehall estimated that the first week of bombing would produce 55,000 casualties of which one third would be fatal; but in 1937 a week's likely casualties were now estimated to be 200,000 of whom 66,000 would die.[17] Added to this were fears of a great super-raid at the beginning of an air war in which the aggressor threw everything at the target, aiming for a 'knockout blow'. Official casualty estimates were kept secret. But well-informed anxieties were brought home to the public by commentators who had long been trusted as experts on warfare, chief among them Basil Liddell Hart, a Great War army officer critical of Allied frontal attacks on the Western Front. Hart was a man of his class and expected the worst of those beneath him. He kept pulses racing with forecasts of the effects of attacks on London: 'Business localities and Fleet Street wrecked, Whitehall a heap of ruins, the slum districts maddened into the impulse to break loose and maraud, the railways cut, factories destroyed.' That was in 1924. Nine years later, writing in the *Daily Telegraph*, he predicted that four out of ten Londoners would flee the city after a gas attack and eight out of ten within a week. And in 1935, amid much more of the same, Tom Wintringham, a communist and Spanish Civil War veteran, wrote that under air attack 'massive fires would render London uninhabitable and result in the deaths of several hundred thousand citizens'.[18]

Hindsight allows us to see these forecasts as grossly exaggerated, but who could think so at the time? Winston Churchill for one was haunted from 1933 on by fears of what might happen to his beloved London, should standing up to Hitler's aggression actually lead to war. This is how he saw London, and its position as the strategic weakness for the nation in the event of war from the air, in speeches in the House of Commons in February and July 1934:

> This cursed, hellish invention and development of war from the air has revolutionised our position. We are not the same kind of country we used to be when we were an island, only twenty years ago ... We are a rich and easy prey. No country is so vulnerable and no country would repay better pillage than our own. With our enormous Metropolis here, the greatest target in the world, a kind of tremendous fat cow, a valuable fat cow tied up to attract the beasts of prey, we are in a position in which we have never been before, and in which no other country in the world is at the present time.[19]

It is worth stressing at this point that for Churchill, as for others, it was the sheer size of London that was considered its greatest vulnerability. London was the unmissable bullseye.

The 'passive defence' of Britain's cities and ports had been a matter of concern in Whitehall since the early 1920s. Of all the nation's defensive difficulties, though, London was the most intractable: that enormous size for one thing and its keystone position in the national arch for another, which meant that London's vulnerability undermined national security as a whole. London's defence was made most difficult of all by the confusing plethora of local authorities who would be called on as London's front line in the event of bombardment, and so the problem of coordination and leadership was in the front of defence planners' minds from the beginning.

In fact, there was an apparent solution to the coordination problem ready to hand. The fraught years of civil and industrial unrest after the First World War had spawned a Civil Emergency Organisation, which divided the country into regions to coordinate civilian and military responses to a national emergency. It had been blooded in the General Strike of May 1926 and was thought to have worked well. Greater London, as defined by the Metropolitan Police District, would become Civil Defence Region No. 5 in an eventual twelve-region structure for Great Britain. London Civil Defence Region (LCDR) would be led by one senior 'regional commissioner' with two more regional commissioners to assist.[20]

The arduous task of readying the country for civilian defence against an air war proceeded by way of a Whitehall steering group, the Air Raid Protection Committee, set up under the chairmanship of the country's most brilliant civil servant, Sir John Anderson, in 1924. The rise of Hitler to power in Germany during 1933 heightened the urgency with which the committee began to address its work. The first public step to define the responsibilities of local government – the front line of ARP – was a Home Office circular issued in July 1935 which told councils what would be expected of them but failed to indicate who would pay for the work to be done. In these early years the government's major achievement was the design and production of gas masks from 1936 to 1937. Though the programme was incomplete for young children, here was tangible evidence of at least some state of readiness when the Munich crisis hit home.[21]

An Air Raid Precautions Act of 1937 put local authorities under the statutory obligation to prepare and implement ARP schemes from 1 January 1938. The content of the schemes depended on the services which each of the ninety-five lower-tier councils and the six counties were already running. London's county councils included the LCC, the premier local government organisation in the country, with the spending power and bureaucratic expertise of a small European country. Its political leader was Herbert Morrison, not just a councillor on the LCC but MP for Hackney South, a key figure in the Parliamentary Labour Party and an ex-Minister of Transport.[22] The council governed what would later be known as inner London with a population in 1939 of just over 4 million, including many of the country's richest, and not a few of its poorest, among its citizens. The LCC, Middlesex County Council (whose area north of the Thames was wholly within Greater London) and the remaining four counties which governed far wider areas than the London authorities within their remit, all provided major services needed in the event of an air attack.

The most important of all was the LCC. It was the fire authority for its area in charge of the London Fire Brigade (LFB), once again the most prestigious firefighting organisation in the country, perhaps the world. The LCC also ran the ambulance service for inner London and, with the other counties, was a major provider of hospitals and social welfare, including subsistence payments for the very poor. And the council had responsibility for schools and children's welfare, including planning for the evacuation of children from London should that become necessary. Now, from New Year 1938, the LCC was given the additional tasks of providing rescue services (including shoring up and demolishing buildings damaged beyond repair by bombing) and establishing 'rest centres' for people made temporarily homeless by air attack; as plans developed some counties, notably Middlesex, devolved rest centre provision to local boroughs while paying the costs involved.

The ninety-five remaining London councils were not all equally constituted. Three county borough councils – West Ham and East Ham in the Essex portion of outer east London, and Croydon in outer south London, in the county of Surrey – were stand-alone authorities carrying out all local government functions. They ran their own fire brigades, ambulance services, hospitals, schools and so on and thus were given total responsibility for ARP functions normally split between counties and the lower tier. To make matters even more complicated, the lower tier itself was as variegated as rainforest foliage. First among equals were the twenty-eight metropolitan borough councils and the City Corporation, some governing populations that would dwarf many British cities: Wandsworth was home to 50,000 more people than Bradford, for instance, and Islington's population was greater than that of Huddersfield, Halifax and Doncaster put together. Although compli-cated hugely by the size of their populations, these boroughs had similar functional responsibilities to the smaller semi-rural authorities on London's outer edge, like Sunbury-on-Thames (Middlesex, 16,000) or Chigwell (Essex, 23,000). But in Middlesex and the other county areas, large urban authorities, like Ealing and Tottenham, ran their own fire services – there were some sixty-six fire brigades in London Region outside the LCC area, some covering more than one local authority's district; they also ran ambulance services, primarily for casualties of street accidents. On all of these authorities fell the new responsibilities of providing air raid wardens, stretcher parties, first aid posts, the distribution of gas masks and decontamination after gas or chemical attack, the billeting of homeless persons in local housing, the repair of bomb-damaged dwellings and the salvaging and storing of property of those who had lost their homes. And they were also given the most contentious and difficult responsibility of all: to provide shelter from air raids for their residents.[23]

The manpower and other resources for all these requirements had now, from 1938, to be detailed in a local ARP scheme submitted to the Home Office. Not all of London's 101 councils needed to make schemes – just forty had to do so, some submitting on behalf of others. But each submission would then be the subject of negotiations over the financial aid that would be forthcoming from central government. The submission process proved grindingly slow, the recruitment of ARP volunteers and their training haphazard and costly, and the arguments over what type of public shelter would be adequate in the circumstances of war unending. Everything was bedevilled too by politics. London's Labour authorities (which included seventeen of the twenty-eight metropolitan boroughs) were all in some way out of sympathy with Chamberlain's National Government and many were unwilling readily to do its bidding, offering numerous excuses for foot-dragging. Even boroughs with Conservative (Municipal Reform as they were known at the time) majorities had to contend with the general apathy of residents unwilling to convince themselves that air raid protection was either necessary or capable of implementation. Thus things stood at the Munich crisis of September 1938, when the country's – especially London's – unpreparedness was exposed for all to see.

It was as the crisis emerged on 15 September that the Senior Regional Commissioner for Greater London (Civil Defence Region No. 5) was established in post. This was the ubiquitous Sir John Anderson, drafted in at every crisis but specially qualified for this as having previously led ARP work in Whitehall. He was no longer a civil servant but a National Independent MP for the Scottish Universities, though his knowledge of government machinery remained unrivalled; in the months before Munich he had been dusting off evacuation plans for London. His appointment was testimony to the alarm felt in Cabinet over the chaos laid bare by Munich and the need for an urgent overhaul of ARP in London. Anderson helped set up an invigorated machinery to manage the interface between Whitehall and London's crazy-paving government. Within a month or two he found himself with new duties for ARP nationwide that would land him a seat in the Cabinet, leaving the senior regional commissioner's post vacant. But progress in coordinating key London services moved apace again once two new regional commissioners (the senior post remaining vacant) were installed in April 1939. These were Sir Ernest Gowers, a brilliant and experienced civil servant in the Anderson mould, and Admiral Sir Edward Evans, compact and charismatic, a household name as a hero in arms in the First World War.[24]

Progress was fastest where services could be centrally led and where the fractured nature of London government had least effect. The LFB, under the aptly named Aylmer Firebrace, shouldered the burden of coordinating all brigades in London Region and of recruiting the 30,000 AFS men and women needed in London County alone. Each of the sixty London County fire stations identified six substations for AFS pumps and crews and similar arrangements were made in the rest of the London fire services. Other chief officers of the LCC were given the task of coordinating rescue and demolition squads, all locally based and so in close contact with borough ARP services. From this time too, the recruitment of a Metropolitan Police War Reserve of 20,000 officers would more than double the normal strength of London's police force. Among the new intake was War Reserve PC John Reginald Halliday Christie, stationed at Harrow from early 1939; he would begin his murderous career against women in Notting Hill while still in uniform.[25]

Integration of the new civil defence services with existing arrangements proved difficult, none more so than in London's fire brigades. The AFS were set apart from the regular London brigade. They had grey Home Office tenders, not the well-known red fire engines, and hoses which would connect to LFB hoses only by an adaptor. AFS men – AFS women were employed in fire stations only and not on pumps and ladders – were further distinguished from their regular colleagues by being issued with only one uniform (a problem when wet) and rubber wellington boots rather than the 'lovely leather boots' of the LFB. The AFS men complained they had lower pay and 'no conditions of service ... No sick leave. No annual holidays'. Injuries on duty entitled men to two weeks' pay only. 'Many of the old professional firemen were bitterly opposed to the Auxiliary Fire Service. The newcomers were snubbed. The regulars were loath to take on the responsibility of instructing them.' All these obstacles would take time and shared danger to overcome. There was also work to be done in coordinating the sixty-six fire brigades in outer London. These were now to be grouped in five districts managed by an Assistant Regional Fire Officer; rivalries between the old brigades would have to be overcome here too.[26]

There were similar difficulties of rivalry and mutual distrust in the arrangements made for London's hospital services from 1938. Hospital planning for war in the LCDR was based on sector arrangements, with London as a cake and ten slices meeting at the centre. Each slice was based on a London voluntary teaching hospital which took on responsibilities for hospital facilities in the rest of the sector. So Sector VIII, for instance, was based on St Thomas's Hospital on the south bank of the river in north Lambeth and included fifty-eight local authority and voluntary hospitals and nursing homes in south-west London and adjoining parts of Surrey and even Hampshire. This nominal unification had somehow to cope with different traditions, cultures, training methods, pay and conditions, all with the need to transfer staff, often urgently, between one institution and another.[27] No doubt similar difficulties on a smaller scale were experienced when the Port of London Authority (PLA) put together a River Emergency Service in the months after Munich. Seven Thames pleasure steamers were fitted out as 'ambulance ships' to rescue casualties from wharves and rivercraft, and private boat owners and their craft were enlisted to assist. The service set up a medical team of doctors and nurses – the latter famed for their good looks, according to the writer Anthony Powell, whose wife, Violet, was one of them.[28]

All these tasks of central coordination and leadership paled to nothing, however, before the difficulties of herding 101 local authorities to face the same way and move at the same pace in planning and implementing an ARP programme for London. Munich had given Londoners a great fright and, although the immediate danger of attack had receded, probably most now thought that war was likely in the short or medium term. As a consequence, the ARP took its place alongside the actively rearming navy, army and air force as the fourth arm of national defence. That alone had unblocked recruitment to the local ARP services run by both the boroughs and the counties, and although they were still 40 per cent under strength in October 1938 it seemed clear that the numbers and training would both be forthcoming.[29]

Shelters of the right type and in the right place presented a more intractable problem. Even here, though, there was one rapid step forward. A month or so after Munich, Sir John Anderson commissioned a design for a cheap but effective domestic shelter that could be installed in back gardens. The Anderson shelter, as it became generally christened, was the brainchild of an old friend of his, a Scottish engineer called William Paterson. He designed and patented the structure in three weeks, it took another three weeks to test the prototype and it was then rapidly put into production. The first shelters were installed from February 1939, six curved steel sheets providing a tunnel some six and a half feet long by four and a half feet wide and capable of sheltering six people; they had to be dug two or three feet into the ground and then covered with soil. Provided by local councils, they were free to all households where the main breadwinner earned less than £5 a week (so free to the large majority of working-class families) and available to buy for £7 for those who were better off.[30]

If, however, where you lived had no garden – the case for most residents of Holborn, south Finsbury, south Shoreditch and other congested parts of inner London – then the Anderson was irrelevant and shelter needs had to be met in other ways. Many houses in such areas and elsewhere had basements and these, perhaps strengthened with timber beams, might be able to provide reasonable shelter. But if not then people had to rely on a public shelter of one sort or another. These proved generally problematic. Local authorities who had dug trenches in parks and open spaces during the Munich crisis were encouraged to complete the deepest of them and were given government aid to line and roof them in concrete; they were not, though, to be provided with duckboards (to keep shelterers off the wet floors) or with seating and were to be sealed until needed in wartime. In fact, progress in London was slow and many of the Munich trenches were abandoned and backfilled. So the trench programme was supplemented by strengthening the basements of public buildings – these years coincided with a flurry of town hall building in London, so shelters could be incorporated into the new structures, as at Barking, for instance – and some steel-framed industrial and commercial buildings were earmarked for use as public shelters, as had happened in the First World War.[31]

Though the eleven months between Munich and the declaration of war offered a 'breathing space', the result, in terms of shelter accommodation available to the public, seemed inadequate to most Londoners. Even before Munich, campaigns in London were under way to produce 'bomb-proof' shelters dug deep underground, and after the crisis there was a clamour that proved almost impossible to resist. The deep-shelter campaign had much popular support and was loudly voiced by a broad coalition of forces that included the Metropolitan Borough of Finsbury, architectural firms with designs to sell, the crypto-communist scientist J. B. S. Haldane in his best-selling book of 1938, *A.R.P.* (he advocated 1,000 miles of brick-built tunnels seven feet wide, buried sixty feet deep under London), and the Communist Party, the Labour Party and the Liberal Party. But deep shelters were rejected by the government following advice from an expert committee reporting in February 1939. The practical difficulties of such a programme were immense – not just the formidable cost in money or the time they would take to excavate, but their inexhaustible demand for concrete, steel and labour at the expense of rearmament and other vital building programmes. There was also the class-based fear that the London worker, once safe underground, would not be tempted up again to keep the city running. This argument also militated against the use of London's underground railways as a deep shelter network, as they would be needed to transport people safely to and from work and also, it was thought, for the movement of casualties. Even so, the popular desire for deep shelters in London would not go away.[32]

With the difficulty of keeping Londoners safe from air attack only too evident, attention was turned to the parallel policy of evacuation as a means of removing Londoners from danger altogether. Evacuation plans had been in place at the time of Munich, but they were rushed, not thought through and luckily not tried out. The crisis over, however, new efforts, again led by Anderson, were made to perfect the means by which children and others thought to be a burden during attack could be removed. Greater London was divided into 'evacuation areas', including the whole of London County and all inner suburbs north and south of the river, and 'neutral areas' in the outer suburbs. Vulnerable people – children, mothers with young children and pregnant women, the frail elderly and people with disabilities – would be encouraged to leave the evacuation areas voluntarily, with transport laid on by the local authorities and the state taking responsibility for their billeting in the 'reception areas' beyond Greater London. The evacuation areas in London were home to nearly 7 million people. Dagenham Urban District, with a population of over 100,000 clustered around the giant Ford Motor Works, was unaccountably missed off the list of evacuation areas but was added after 'a vigorous protest'. The neutral areas (including, for instance, Wembley and Southgate in Middlesex, Chigwell in Essex, Bromley in Kent and Carshalton in Surrey) had a total population of 1.8 million. These districts were not officially to receive people evacuated from the centre but neither would evacuation from them be assisted by the state, other than in exceptional cases.[33]

The main principles of evacuation – voluntary not compulsory, billeting in private homes in the reception areas enforced by law, the costs of billeting (rent and board) to be borne by the government but with parents and others who could afford it having to pay a contribution – were all in place before Munich. But the practical means of making possible this great movement of people (500,000 children in Greater London alone) were not in place when the September crisis struck. Now, during the months till August 1939, the finishing touches were put to the complex arrangements for transport by rail, road and riverboat; to the planning and publicity needed by schools, parents and health services; and to the reception of town children and their mothers in quiet country districts up and down the land. Matters were eased in London by the LCC taking responsibility for the transport arrangements of all evacuees in Greater London. Even so, the planning was fraught with fears, made worse by the sort of gloomy prognostications in respect of casualties that had bedevilled ARP planning throughout: in January 1939 it was confidently forecast that 3,000 children would be injured or killed – 'run over' or 'get wet through and die from pneumonia' – when being evacuated from London, even without an air raid in progress. In the spring and summer of 1939, school planning and training became almost non-stop. 'Air Raid Precautions swamped me,' Gladys Langford wrote in April, fretting nervously over her prospects at Hamond Square School, Hoxton: 'I'm almost distraught at the thought of being sent anywhere from "The Wash to Land's End" with children from whom I might not escape for years.'[34]

It wasn't just the schools who were planning for evacuation in the months following Munich. The London hospitals made plans to move all but critically ill patients away from London. Many government departments worked up arrangements to shift staff to safe country berths in the event of war. So too did London businesses, faced not just with the uncertain risk of destruction by bombing but, if they employed more than fifty people, with the certain costs if they stayed put of providing safe shelter for staff. Some were too big to move – Standard Telephones and Cables at New Southgate, for instance, had to provide shelter for 5,000 staff, driving concrete tunnels seven feet wide into an embankment at one end of the works. But for those more flexible, the *Estates Gazette* noted a huge demand for country houses from the middle of 1939: 'The list of historic mansions that have found a use by banks, insurance companies, shipping companies, and official bodies is an incredibly long one.' Similarly, when London industries vital to rearmament sought to expand to meet government requirements they did so far from London: Napiers of Acton, in the process of developing a new aero engine in early 1939, moved its production to a site near Liverpool, Greater London's vulnerability as a target putting it wholly out of bounds. This followed a well-worn pattern of 'shadow factories' emerging from 1935 on, where London engineering firms identified plant in the countryside to enlarge production in the event of war: Fairey Aviation (Hayes) developed a shadow near Stockport, Ford (Dagenham) assembled Merlin engines at Trafford Park near Manchester, Handley Page (Cricklewood) built Halifax bombers outside York and so on. All this was the reverse of tendencies in the First World War, when munitions industries had flocked to London to be close to labour supplies and communications networks.[35]

IN March 1939 Hitler invaded Czechoslovakia, ripping up the agreement he had made with Chamberlain just six months before. He looked unlikely to stop there. A war waged by Britain and France to stop Germany's ruthless ambitions appeared to many as both necessary and inevitable. For the next five months the work of constructing – it would be an exaggeration to say perfecting – air raid precautions in London quickened noticeably. How did things stand in London's localities by the end of the summer of 1939?

The first thing to note is that everywhere was at a different stage. Some (including Labour boroughs like Finsbury and Bermondsey) had embraced the need for ARP only reluctantly, either through disagreement with the National Government's defence policies or through a latent pacifism. Others (like Labour Hackney and Conservative Kensington, for instance) had been energetic from the start. Residents in some boroughs (Finsbury, Holborn, parts of Westminster and Southwark) had only a restricted ability to take advantage of the Anderson shelter. The tube network, out of bounds at this stage to ARP planners, still gave some comfort to Londoners with sharp memories of 1917–18, but it was of little help to the millions living south of the Thames. All this meant that where in London you lived and worked was critical in determining how safe you might feel should the air war eventually come, and these local differences could not be overcome by even the most energetic central coordination from London's regional commissioners.

Even so, progress had been made everywhere since Munich, though nowhere could it be said to be complete.

Poplar, for instance, a working-class borough with deep Labour and pacifist roots, might have been thought a likely laggard in response to ARP propaganda. Not so. In unpromising terrain, vulnerable to mass bombing because of its proximity to the docks and with parts of the borough easily cut off should roads and bridges be destroyed, Poplar had provided shelter for 80,000 in trenches or Andersons (for a peace-time population of some 140,000) and had all its thirty-five wardens' posts staffed, by paid wardens and volunteers. Next-door Stepney, covering much of the politically turbulent Jewish East End and some disorderly riverside districts around Cable Street, had rejected LCDR's advice that the borough ARP controller should be a council officer like the town clerk. Instead it had put a councillor into the position, the leader of the Labour group, M. H. 'Morrie' Davis. That would even-tually prove problematic, but by July 1939, after a door to door canvass, some 89 per cent of an ARP establishment of 6,559 paid staff and volunteers had been enrolled; even so, only 53 per cent of wardens, the council's front line, were at their scheduled posts.[36]

Indeed, wardens' posts were cropping up all over London and in the unlikeliest places. There were 117 in Wandsworth, including a concrete blockhouse on a Streatham roundabout; others were made of prefabricated sheet steel, mass-produced as a commercial venture and sold to local authorities in Middlesex and Essex; others were more homely – Dickens House Museum at 48 Doughty Street was Post No. 36 for St Pancras Metropolitan Borough Council, with the Dickens Fellowship's assistant secretary, Miss Minards, as post warden. Bethnal Green's warden service could do with just eleven posts staffed by 239 paid workers and 300 part-time volunteer wardens, many women among them – its stretcher parties comprised 241 men and 142 women. Paddington had enrolled an ARP staff of 2,140 of whom 342 were paid full-timers, in twenty wardens' posts; 31 per cent of the staff were women, a typical proportion, with women frequently in senior positions as post wardens. As for shelters, at this point the Anderson played a big part. One third of Fulham's houses had them, for instance, and they were ubiquitous in the suburbs – there were some 30,000 Andersons in Lewisham for a peacetime population of around 230,000, a fair proportion of the borough if each could fit six persons. Even so, public confidence in the availability and suitability of air raid shelters remained low. Gallup public opinion surveys in the first half of 1939 found that 72 per cent could not reach a shelter within seven minutes of a warning, and a majority (53 per cent) continued to call for the deep shelters that the government had said it would not provide.[37]

ARP in London was still very much work in progress as the final days of peace began to give out. Improvisation, quick thinking, making do with what came to hand and making the best of a bad job were still the watchwords of the hour. Because of London's size and administrative complexity, the twenty-eight metropolitan boroughs and the City were divided into five groups for purposes of mutual assistance and coordination, providing a subregional structure on top of the local warden arrangements. In Group 3 (the City, Holborn, Finsbury, Bethnal Green, Shoreditch, Stepney, Hackney and Poplar) – home between them to some 750,000 in peacetime – the scratch headquarters were not set up till mid-August 1939, in a basement office behind Shoreditch parish church used by the LCC's Weights and Measures Department. Group ARP staff 'cleared aside the packing-cases filled with glasses, mugs and measures sent for testing, scales and instruments undergoing examination, and a variety of general stores. Within that little space they disentangled from their trailing wires, and arranged in order the dusty, newly installed telephone instruments, and laid out maps, tally-boards and message pads ... Then, for over an hour, the new London operational network was tried for the first time. It worked successfully.' There was no canteen in the building but there were compensations because the local pub provided beer and sandwiches, served by 'a big, blonde barmaid, who must surely have been on the music-hall stage in an earlier life' if her wit and good cheer were anything to go by.[38]

Who were these people in ARP? Many were local government staff, especially those working in the ARP control rooms in town hall basements and annexes; the rest were a more or less representative cross-section of Londoners. Mass Observation, the social survey organisation established in 1937 by anthropologist Tom Harrisson and Charles Madge, a South African-born poet and journalist, interviewed a thousand ARP volunteers in Fulham in April 1939. The proportion of men (69 per cent) and women (31 per cent) was precisely the same as Paddington's but Mass Observation was interested in class too: 13 per cent, they concluded, were upper class, 23 per cent middle class,

54 per cent 'artisan' or upper working class and just 10 per cent unskilled working class. This was skewed towards the better-off and better-educated – perhaps the bossier classes – but it is important to remember that the rescue and demolition squads employed by the LCC, counties and county boroughs were of a different class altogether. Joan Wyndham, firmly one of the 13 per cent, was a student actress at the Royal Academy of Dramatic Art in Bloomsbury and about eighteen years old in 1939. She lived with her divorced mother and her mother's female companion in South Kensington. All three joined up to serve at the local first aid post. At an ARP concert later that year, 'My mother was down with the nobs, I was in the gallery with Decontamination and Demolition – the most awful collection of toughs and villains.'[39]

Besides all these advances in the boroughs, progress had been made in other directions too. The London fire services had geared up since Munich. The London AFS had received 2,000 extra pumps by the autumn of 1939, many drawn by 2,381 adapted London taxicabs, their tight turning-circle thought to be especially handy; thirty extra fire boats for the river were delivered or commissioned, the LCC now made responsible for fire services to the mouth of the Thames at Holehaven; and many water mains had been uprated to twenty-four-inch diameter and connected to the river and the Grand Union Canal.[40]

How to build esprit de corps in these variegated ARP services in London, around some 200,000 strong in all, was a puzzle. Uniforms and specialist equipment would eventually help, but they were in short supply in the summer and autumn of 1939. One way was to organise public exercises and reviews – bringing home to Londoners the value and civic status of services still seeking volunteers. The LFB and London AFS organised a review in Hyde Park before the Duke and Duchess of Kent on Saturday 3 June, with 20,000 men and women on parade in front of a vast crowd, many relatives and friends no doubt among them. The spectacular show included a 'turntable ladder drill in which three steel ladders shot 100 ft. into the air with firemen at their heads, making an arch of water high above'. And in early July the King and Queen reviewed a march past of 20,000 ARP men and women: when the Lambeth contingent passed, a crowd of onlookers 'broke spontaneously into laughing cries of "Oi" and hummed the "Lambeth Walk"', from *Me and My Gal*, the West End stage hit of that year. A month later there would be a trial blackout in the early morning of 10 August, its usefulness dented by the numbers of car drivers coming into central

London to see the effects, and there were local dry runs, imagining bombing raids with casualties caught in the open. Frances Faviell, a thirty-four-year-old painter, was an ARP volunteer in Chelsea, a mixed borough but one boasting many artists in residence. Chelsea organised a full-scale public exercise on 19 June 1939, ARP workers dressed in a uniform of local Chelsea design, where the official wailing air raid siren sounded for the first time in London. Frances was a casualty and spent much time lying down until eventually comprehensively bandaged. The longueurs got the better of some:

> Old Granny from Paradise Row left her allotted place and started away determinedly in the direction of her home. 'Raid's still on, come back!' shouted a warden at her. 'Call of nature, can't do nothing about that, raid or no raid,' she retorted, and marched resolutely away ... Next day we read in the Press that it had been an unqualified success.

And a month later, on 19 July, an evacuation rehearsal of 5,000 schoolchildren and their teachers took place, also in Chelsea.[41]

BY the middle of August it became apparent that the 'breathing space' won by the shabby capitulation at Munich was at last running out of puff. As Hitler had long planned, German claims for a land passage across the Danzig corridor separating East Prussia from the rest of 'the Reich' were now escalated into demands to recover all territory lost to Poland at Versailles in 1919. The British and French governments reiterated their commitment to defend Polish independence. After days of ever-tightening tension and escalating border clashes, Neville Chamberlain returned to London from his holidays on Monday 21 August.

That evening the staggering news broke that Hitler and Stalin had agreed a mutual non-aggression pact. Rhona Little, a shorthand typist at the Euston Tax District in Bloomsbury, saw the news on a paper-seller's placard on her way into work next morning and the day after signed on for ARP duties. Training began that same day: 'I had a head-ache on the way back to 22 [Canonbury Park North, Highbury, where she lodged] from taking sniffs of phosgene, mustard and lewisite gases.' On Thursday 24 August Parliament was recalled and an Emergency Powers Act giving the crown draconian powers over property and people passed all its stages that same day. At the Nag's Head Corner, Holloway, that evening Rhona watched 'a lot of men busy painting the kerbs black and white'. Senior civil servants were summoned to London from their holidays and all leave was cancelled at the BBC, where the entrance hall of Broadcasting House in Portland Place 'looked like King's Cross on Christmas Eve' as staff packed for evacuation to the country. Air raid drills were becoming commonplace everywhere. At the Euston tax office it took just three minutes for everyone to be hustled into the basement shelter; Mr Bartlett, the office air raid warden, declared himself 'very pleased'. In the streets, sandbags were again piled in great walls round government buildings and more trenches were dug by day and night in the parks. Blackout shades were fitted to traffic lights, blinds to shop windows and brown paper pasted over fanlights. The trams ran with shaded light bulbs. Treasures were being moved by pantechnicon from the British Museum, which buried the Elgin Marbles and more in the disused Aldwych tube tunnels, and from the National Gallery, which closed on 24 August as staff evacuated pictures to deepest Wales. Those who could afford it stocked their larders with dried foods and tins, and the prudent bought lots of candles because 'when the bombing starts ... the lights will all fail'. Trenches were being dug in back gardens as Anderson shelters were now hastily installed at what seemed like the last minute. Great silver barrage balloons, tethered in the gardens of squares and any other available open space, floated in the bright sunshine. Gas masks were issued to those without them and for the first time these were available for babies – toddlers still had to go without. For many, though, all this seemed less of a shock to the system compared to Munich. Virginia Woolf, removing her things from one Bloomsbury house to another, thought London responded with 'indifference almost', Londoners adapting to a fatalistic feeling that this time there was no escape from war. Others felt the tension more acutely: at the Euston tax office Rhona Little, still in her teens, a newcomer to London and perhaps missing her family in Northern Ireland, thought, 'Everyone felt out of sorts. Two were feeling physically sick and I didn't feel quite A1 myself, so there was deep gloom.'[42] On Monday 28 August, the London schools were opened for an evacuation practice on a mass scale, the children armed with gas masks, luggage and a packed lunch; they were reported to have had great fun, the teachers one imagines less so – Gladys Langford was one of those who had already (on 25 August) been temporarily signed off work with nervous ill health. Perhaps there should have been a practice in Whitehall, for Wednesday 30 August proved a day of confusion in government as the order to trigger the evacuation of London was given by the Prime Minister but then retracted with some difficulty; fortunately, the perplexed Minister of Transport noted, the confusion was kept from the press. Then, on Thursday 31 August, the order to evacuate Greater London's schoolchildren, mothers with young children and pregnant women was finally passed by the Ministry of Health to the LCC for implementation on the following day. The London Passenger Transport Board (LPTB) announced that all London's rail network, above ground and below, would be needed for evacuation on Friday and some days after and most Green Line suburban coaches stopped running at 7 p.m. on Thursday evening to help with evacuation next day. That day too Scotland Yard announced emergency changes to the London road network next morning to give those wishing to leave London by car a clear run. Nine main routes were made one-way out of London and sealed to incoming traffic, including Western Avenue, Finchley Road and Hendon Way to the north and west, Clapham Road to the south, King's Road in Chelsea to the south-west and dozens more.[43]

It was all just in time. Without warning, in the early hours of Friday 1 September, Germany invaded Poland by land and by air.

2

OH! WHAT A LOVELY WAR:
1 SEPTEMBER 1939–9 APRIL 1940

LONDON was on a war footing from Friday 1 September, two days before Britain declared war on Germany. The great movement of people fleeing 'the greatest target in the world' was under way from early morning. The official evacuation overseen by the LCC had to deal with astonishing numbers: 393,700 unaccompanied children in school parties; 257,000 mothers and their children under five years old; 5,600 pregnant women; 2,400 'Blind persons, cripples and other special classes'; and around 48,250 teachers and helpers – over 700,000 people from Greater London. Nearly 6,000 London buses and Green Line coaches moved the children from 1,600 assembly points to 172 tube stations and then ninety-eight London railway stations, including all the main termini and many in the suburbs. Some journeys proved more exciting than others. From the Ford jetty at Dagenham nearly 17,000 were lifted off by pleasure steamer from 8 o'clock on a beautiful morning to the East Anglian ports of Great Yarmouth, Lowestoft and Felixstowe.[1]

The original plan had been to move these huge numbers in four days, but at the last minute it was decided to complete the exercise in three. Whatever the justification, the outcome was dire, for rather than keep school parties together it became vital to fill every train as it stood on the platform irrespective of destination. Euan Wallace, the Minister of Transport, watched the 9.27 a.m. leave Hornsey station, in his constituency: 'Everyone seemed cheerful and even the effort of pushing 825 people into a train only scheduled for 800 at the rate of 14 per compartment did not unduly depress them.' The task was made easier by the numbers transported being well short of what had been expected. Despite schools' best efforts to enlist parental support over many months just 49 per cent of London County's schoolchildren turned up at the assembly points compared to the 80 per cent expected. On the Ford jetty, 'Many changed their minds even on the point of embarkation', and no doubt similar stories played out at every one of the LCC's gathering points and on station platforms.[2]

The task of getting the children and those adults identified as vulnerable out of London was generally thought to have gone 'without a hitch'. 'This Evacuation Business Has Shown the World' what a free people might achieve when they put their mind to it, enthused the *Daily Herald* on 4 September, and indeed in those early days there seemed much to crow about. It was an even more impressive achievement given the uncountable private evacuations of children from London going on in these same three hectic days. There were whole schools, from the grandest, like Westminster School, which removed to Lancing College in Sussex and later to Exeter – there would be no boys' voices in the Abbey choir for the duration – to the humblest, like a small Orthodox Jewish day school in West Hampstead, shipped out to 'sleepy' Little Houghton near Northampton, where 'The villagers had never set eyes on Jews before' and were astonished to find that 'the children wouldn't eat' until kosher meals were sent from London. And there was a host of individual migrations of children of all classes: Maurice Goymer, his father a motor engineer with a business in East Ham, was sent to a farming uncle in rural Essex; Dolly Scannell left Goodmayes, Ilford, with her sister and her children to stay in Wales with a relative; and Bryan Magee, his father a gent's outfitter in Hoxton Street, Shoreditch, was dispatched to his grandmother in Worth, Sussex, though his school had moved to Market Harborough, Leicestershire. There were untold moves of this kind, some purely temporary and others lasting till the war's end.[3]

The London diaspora beginning from 1 September had numerous other components, as we shall see, but one of the features of that day and the next was the evacuation of the central London hospitals. All patients fit enough to move and many staff clambered aboard Green Line coaches, specially fitted to receive stretcher cases, and travelled out to the receiving hospitals in their sectors. The policy imperative was to free up as many beds as possible in central London for the casualties expected from bombing and to adapt the hospitals for use in air raids. St Thomas's, for instance, had installed emergency operating theatres in the hospital's basement and transformed itself into a 'casualty clearing station' of 330 beds (reduced from some 680), of which 200 were reserved for raid victims; upper wards were closed and the casualty ward was abandoned because of its glass roof and relocated in outpatients, the latter's services for a time suspended altogether from 1 September. Staff and around 500 patients were evacuated to sector hospitals at Woking, Chertsey and Epsom. Similar plans were implemented at the London in Whitechapel, King's College at Camberwell, the Middlesex in Fitzrovia and so on. Patients in Guy's in Southwark could count themselves luckier than many: on 1 September they were bussed in gorgeous weather to Brighton.

Some of London's specialist hospitals now found themselves generalists awaiting air raid casualties. Moorfields Eye Hospital in Finsbury sent home all the patients it could on 1 September and made eighty-two beds available for bombing victims; the borough council took over part of the hospital as a first aid post for walking wounded and a decontamination centre for gas cases. In outer London some of the LCC's enormous asylums were cleared of patients (moved elsewhere or sent home) and opened as general hospitals to receive casualties patched up by London's clearing stations – Horton Hospital in Epsom was equipped with 2,000 beds for casualties sent on from King's College Hospital, for instance. These were drastic measures and, like the evacuation of schools, had unintended consequences. Some two thirds of maternity beds in central London were closed, so were many of the children's hospitals, and the numbers of specialist tuberculosis beds were cut wholesale; the first of these would have serious consequences for pregnant women in London right through the war and even beyond.[4]

LONDON was readied for war in other ways than evacuation on 1 September. It was 'Mobilisation Friday' for those men and women enrolled in the capital's civil defence services. Albert Turpin heard the order given over the wireless as he was sitting down to his tea in Temple Street, Bethnal Green; he bundled his shaving gear, blankets and food for two nights into a rucksack and ran off to the local AFS headquarters in Globe Road. The novelist Henry Green, also a London AFS man, attended the call-up 'fully dressed in tin hat, dark blue uniform, shiny black gas trousers, rubber boots, with axe and spanner in a blue belt'; he was overeager – he should have worn his uniform cap and black shoes, slinging the tin hat on his belt and carrying those annoying boots. Verily Anderson, who had enrolled in the First Aid Nursing Yeomanry (the FANYs) after Munich, was called up, put in uniform and told to drive cars fresh off the Ford assembly line at Dagenham to Aldershot. At first there were more FANYs than motors, but soon she was shunting backwards and forwards between Essex and Hampshire. The River Emergency Service was called up too, Alan Herbert, MP, attending with his boat *Water Gypsy* at Lambeth pier. And on that same Friday ARP wardens and control room staff took to their posts in their thousands in readiness for what now seemed certain war.[5]

Evacuation and civil defence call-up affected hundreds of thousands of Londoners. But one other development on 1 September, that first real day of London's war, affected everyone. The blackout would be one of the worst nightmares of the long war years to come. There had been a blackout in London from September 1914 too, but it was nothing like this, a mere 'dim-out' compared to the dungeon darkness of 1939. It transformed London at night and though people grew accustomed to it to a degree, it never lost its terrors or its dangers: 'there were many accidents in the streets those first days – a man heard moaning but not seen – a tin-hatted policeman running into a pub to telephone for an ambulance – it seemed fantastic not to use light on such occasions, but the discipline held everyone in its grip'. An early blackout victim on 5 September was Richard Gray, eighteen, of Poplar, who died when an AFS taxicab driven too fast mounted the kerb and crushed him against a pile of sandbags in the Highway, Shadwell.[6]

Pocket torches and torch batteries presented one of the war's first consumer shortages in London. Olivia Cockett, twenty-seven, a payroll clerk at Scotland Yard and living at Brockley, Deptford, complained as early as 12 September, 'Called at Boots for a battery for hand torch – no luck. That's the tenth shop in four days.' Even with a torch, London at night racked the nerves. On 4 September Nellie Carver, thirty-eight, a supervisor at the GPO telegrams office near Newgate Street in the City, left work to get a train home to West Norwood, Lambeth. A workmate had bought a torch for her at 'Woollies' that afternoon:

Once outside, I couldn't persuade myself to take a step forward. I'd never known real darkness before … & for the moment I was paralysed and lost all sense of direction. I stood still, panic-stricken … After a few seconds fight with myself I did venture along & came to Holborn [Viaduct station] safely, but when I made the train (in pitch darkness) I felt damp with perspiration & quite exhausted.[7]

The blackout held terrors just as alarming for the car driver and householder too. The lighting regulations for car drivers were byzantine in their complexity, requiring the off-side headlamp bulb to be removed and cardboard discs fitted on the driver's lamp 'so as to cover the glass except for a two-inch semi-circular gap at the bottom', with further requirements for reflectors, sidelights and indicators; the lazy driver could cheat by buying a police-approved 'headlamp mask'. The regulations requiring homes to be blacked out were even more draconian. A single glimmer could rouse shouts of 'Put out that light!' from air raid wardens – 'How they love their momentary holding of power,' thought Gladys Langford – from policemen and from any pedestrian worried the Luftwaffe might be hovering. It took Raymond Postgate, the socialist historian, thirty minutes each evening to cover the windows of his house in Finchley with blackout material, in his case 'thick cardboard lined with black', simple curtains being insufficient. The same duties, often more difficult to comply with, were imposed on business owners. Rowton Houses, the charity providing bedsit cubicles for single working men, had 6,500 windows to black out every evening, with 13,000 shutters made from over 60,000 square feet of plywood. All these efforts would never be enough. Before the war was over tens of thousands of Londoners were brought before the magistrates for lighting infringements – the first in the East End, at a flat in West Ferry Road, Isle of Dogs, led to an arrest when the occupier objected to the police constable removing four of his six light bulbs.[8]

AFTER these hectic days in London, the declaration of war by Great Britain against Germany, announced to the nation in a broadcast by Neville Chamberlain at 11.15 a.m. on Sunday 3 September, came as something of an anticlimax. It had been advertised by earlier bulletins and so wireless sets in London had a bigger than usual audience that morning. Everyone wanted to listen, it seems, but no one wanted to listen alone. Chiang Yee, a Chinese artist and writer living in Tasker Road, Hampstead, answered the door at 10.50 to a Chinese friend and they were joined by 'a lady who lives above my little flat' and her brother to listen in at 11.15. At Temple Street, Bethnal Green, 'a small crowd of people gathered in front of the open door of one of the houses … The place was directly opposite the [AFS] Post', where Albert Turpin was on duty, 'so we trooped over … No one uttered a word. Not a jingo song or sentiment. Not a single curse was flung at the enemy.'

There were no cheering crowds either, in Downing Street or outside Buckingham Palace; the contrast with 4 August 1914 could not have been more stark, as many Londoners noted at the time.[9]

Chamberlain's broadcast was received generally with resignation. But London's first air raid siren of the war, minutes after the Prime Minister had stopped speaking, was a shock to everyone, Chamberlain himself apparently 'visibly shaken when the sirens blew'. Beyond 10 Downing Street reactions varied. George Beardmore, an insurance clerk in his early thirties and living in north Harrow, thought he and everyone else responded 'with utter panic', the scenes of devastation in Korda's *The Shape of Things to Come* brought too sharply to mind. In Rhona Little's boarding house, 'We were all scared stiff. We all dashed upstairs for our gas masks and then spent a lot of time flying around collecting coats etc.' Arthur Buddell, forty-four, a senior civil servant and Great War veteran with a Military Cross to his name, was caught on a Croydon golf course in mid-round, unaware of the Prime Minister's broadcast: 'we decided to carry on although some people shouted to us excitedly from nearby houses telling us to take cover.' Vivienne Hall, thirty-two and single, a performer in a Putney amateur dramatics company and now working part-time in ARP, 'looked from my window and found everyone down the road hanging out of theirs. – In my loud carrying voice I shouted "That's the warning, you know" and it was most comical to see the heads disappearing and the windows slamming as they all hurried to the shelter.' In sedate South Kensington, at 26 Thurloe Street, Hilda Neal, fifty-nine, a spinster with her own secretarial business in the Strand, had listened in silence to Chamberlain's message with her downstairs neighbour, Mrs Turing-Mackenzie. When the siren went they put on their gas masks 'ready to go downstairs to the hall', which they had decided was the safest place to shelter. But 'Bedford', Mrs Turing-Mackenzie's maid, had left her mask at home in Wembley, so they soaked a towel and wrapped it round her head as the next best thing. In the hall Mrs Turing-Mackenzie and Bedford 'lay on their tummies … and I sat on the stairs. Feeling guilty at Bedford not having a mask to put on I took mine off and put it on her, and wrapped the towel round my own head'; perhaps too well, for she didn't hear the all clear when it sounded half an hour later. Robert Barltrop, seventeen, out in Walthamstow High Street, remembered years later a near panic: 'a young woman in a white ARP helmet passed us, whimpering and shaking with fright'. Barltrop and others trooped into a school set up as an

ARP post, where 'A middle-aged man in air-raid warden's uniform let us in grudgingly, saying it was not a shelter and he was not supposed to do this.' And in a Croydon shelter, the borough librarian and chronicler of Croydon in the First World War felt a deep unease:

> sitting underground in semi-twilight, breathing heavily through a gas mask and completely uncertain as to what form the impending attack would take or how severe it might be, and that immediately after the hope of peace had been shattered, was something that all who had the experience will never forget.

There would be a couple of further alarms, triggered like this one by a friendly plane identified late or some other nervousness, but after the first couple of days of war no siren would wail in anger over London until the following summer.[10]

Reporting on scenes in Lewisham that day, the local paper noted 'no panic' from the mid-morning siren but also remarked that 'One effect was to hasten the evacuation of private individuals, for among the motor traffic on the main roads many cars with luggage – the perambulator being seen in numerous cases – were soon in evidence.' The exodus from London did not begin and end with the great movement beginning on 1 September but continued well into the month. The BBC moved its music staff and orchestras, the features, drama, variety and religious broadcasting departments to Bristol, with schools broadcasting (including *Children's Hour*) sent to Evesham. Many City firms moved staff and business to the Home Counties – Morgan Grenfell to Berkhamsted and Rothschilds to Tring, both in Hertfordshire, Hambros to Bedfordshire, Barings to Hampshire and the London Central Clearing House went further afield to Staffordshire. The Bank of England moved its accounts department to Whitchurch in Hampshire; there would be over 2,000 Bank employees there, including hundreds of smart young women consigned to a slow-pulsed rural existence for the duration, or much of it. Scores of other firms did likewise: the Prudential Assurance Co. moved 4,000 staff from Holborn to Torquay; the Hulton Press, publishers of *Picture Post*, moved from the City to Watford; the main railway companies moved all or part of their headquarters, involving thousands of staff, from London to Aldermaston (Great Western Railway), Watford (London, Midland and Scottish), Hitchin (London North Eastern) and Dorking (Southern). Offices proved easier to relocate than factories, so it became safer for the pen-pusher than the machine minder in these first months of anxious flight.[11]

It would be the pen-pushers of Whitehall who were moved fastest and furthest. The numbers of civil servants moved out are difficult to quantify accurately, but they were substantial, some 15,000 or so at least. So the Board of Trade statistics division moved to Bournemouth, the Assistance Board headquarters to Southport, Lancashire, the Board of Inland Revenue to Llandudno, the Ministry of Food to Colwyn Bay, the Ministry of Health to Blackpool, the GPO to Harrogate – not all the staff of any of these, but thousands of those whom it was inessential to retain in the capital. London University joined this rush, following a pre-war plan, its colleges generally turning their backs on the metropolis for the rest of the war. University College reopened its doors to students that October not in Gower Street but in Aberystwyth, Bangor, Swansea and elsewhere; King's College moved to Bristol, its Faculty of Medicine finding a home in Glasgow; Bedford College, the London School of Economics, Queen Mary College and the School of Oriental and African Studies moved to Cambridge, Goldsmiths' and the Institute of Education to Nottingham; the University of London's headquarters staff at Senate House moved to Royal Holloway College in Egham, Surrey, its giant Malet Street building turned over to the new Ministry of Information. Only Birkbeck College off Fetter Lane on the borders of the City kept higher education's flame burning by day and by night in London, though even here the opening of the autumn term was delayed.[12]

Of London's private residents, the most noticeable migrations were from the middle-class districts and above. In Brompton on 3 September, 'Little groups of Kensingtonians are evacuating their aunts, their canaries and their small dogs', 'cars laden with luggage' filling the streets, and in the following weeks it felt as though well-off 'London is half-deserted', 'closed offices and West End mansions with "TO LET" notices' on boards and in windows. In Marylebone, 'the occupiers of more expensive houses seem to have evacuated themselves. House after house is boarded up and sandbagged.' Harley Street physicians were left twiddling their stethoscopes 'as all their patients had either gone away or stayed away' at their summer holiday destinations. Five or six miles to the north-west, 'The number of well-to-do people who have just upped and gone' from Wembley, leaving their rates bills unpaid, 'is astonishing.' In all, it has been estimated that Greater London lost 1,444,000 people or 16.5 per cent of its pre-war population between September 1939 and the summer of 1940. Taking into account enlistment in the fighting services, it seems likely that as many people (some 700,000) evacuated voluntarily or through their employment as through the official scheme.[13]

Many Londoners remarked on the strange atmosphere that followed the evacuation of so many schoolchildren, now absent from the city's streets, for a time at least. But there were other things missing too. Those Kensington lapdogs were the lucky ones. For in the first week or so of war occurred what one recent historian has called the 'great cat and dog massacre'. An estimated 400,000 animals were killed in London 'in a few days from 3 September 1939', including London Zoo's collection of 'poisonous snakes and insects' and spiders and scorpions, and all its saltwater fish, the aquarium deemed a great hazard in the event of a bomb blast. But the rest were pets – cats, dogs and birds from every class of home in London. Generally, this was killing through kindness, owners fearing pets would be left starving as homes were blasted or as food supplies ran out. A Lewisham RSPCA inspector had to kill hundreds of pets, the council disposing of the corpses; and in Leyton a vet complained of having to kill on their owners' instructions '1,200 small animals' in a matter of days, 'an experience I never wish to have again'. The cause, he thought, was 'sheer panic'.[14]

London changed in many other ways in these first few days of war. In the streets of course there were many more people in uniform, women as well as men; indeed, women in uniform with men on their arms wearing civvies was a reversal of the years from 1914 to 1918 and strange to many. From 4 September police officers wore black or blue tin hats; with gas masks slung on shoulder straps it 'gave quite a sinister touch to poor old London,' Nellie Carver thought. London's pillar boxes were decorated 'in squares of yellow detector paint, which change colour if there is poison gas in the air' and London's monuments – Eros at Piccadilly Circus, Charles I's equestrian statue at Charing Cross and more – disappeared under sandbags and timber, and were roofed in corrugated iron.[15]

Even worse, it seemed that London had shut down. From 3 September cinemas were closed countrywide, opening once more in rural areas from 11 September and in towns from the 15th. All cinemas had to close at 10 p.m. except in the West End, where they closed at 6 p.m. From 4 October some cinemas in the West End could also close at 10, but only on a weekly rota. The position was fully equalised from 4

November, when all cinemas could open till 11. This ban on entertainments applied to music halls and theatres too, a special nuisance to Anthony Heap, twenty-nine, an accounts clerk in Peter Robinson's Oxford Street store, a dedicated first-nighter and opinionated amateur critic. When the ban was lifted on suburban theatres but retained on West End evening shows, he thought that the Golders Green Hippodrome 'looks like becoming London's No 1 wartime theatre'. Covent Garden Theatre was closed to opera for the duration, the house eventually finding a new role as a dance hall.[16]

There was no consolation to be had from staying indoors. Television closed down on 1 September and though this was a service available only to 20,000 consumers nationally, most of those lived in London. Far worse, BBC radio broadcasting was cut to just one channel on a wavelength that some listeners couldn't obtain, an innovation designed to stop the Luftwaffe using wireless signals as a homing device. 'Looks like we'll have to invest in a new radio,' Anthony Heap concluded in the flat he shared with his widowed mother in St Pancras, their 'old worn-out set' unable to tune reliably to the new wavelength. Many could, though, listen to numerous foreign (including German) stations, where the fascist William Joyce, 'Lord Haw-Haw', provoked much comment and some anxiety; but this was no compensation for the reduction in BBC programmes, whose dull repetitive output in the first months of the war aroused much criticism.[17]

Even moving around London in daylight suddenly became more difficult. Nineteen tube stations were closed for anti-flood works left undone from the Munich crisis. They remained shut for weeks, the complex interchange between lines at King's Cross not finally open until the New Year. Green Line coach services to the suburbs were withdrawn from 1 September and bus routes curtailed from the 16th. Petrol rationing was introduced that same day. All these restrictions caused great crushes at bus and tram stops and uncomfortable crowding on all public transport that never abated as long as the war lasted; there was soon a noticeable bicycle boom in London. There were other things that only got worse as the war went on. London's enormous housing problem in the inner boroughs was primed to deteriorate further as many building contracts were precipitately ended and councils were told not to demolish places even though they had been condemned as slums two or three years earlier. And rent control, applied by new legislation on 1 September, combined with shortages of building materials to remove incentives and opportunities for landlords to make their tenants' lives more bearable.[18]

Much of London looked as though it had shut up shop, but one area at least was given a boost. The holes in ARP were even more evident now that war had been declared. Some things were in place. The London Civil Defence Regional Headquarters had been installed in great secrecy at the Geological Museum in Exhibition Road, South Kensington, and connected by telephone to all the London ARP control centres, though these arrangements were only completed in a rush in the last few days of peace at the end of August. Local control rooms were kitted out and staffed, though the full complement of paid wardens and volunteers was not even approximately up to establishment until the end of the year, four months or so after war was declared. The numbers were substantial: over 9,000 paid wardens (about nine per post) in the metropolitan boroughs alone, with over 10,000 full-time stretcher-bearers; the LCC's rescue service had 12,000 paid personnel. The paid wardens were greatly outnumbered by volunteers, 'part-timers carrying on their normal occupations by day or night'. To these must be added volunteers and paid staff in first aid posts, the 30,000 or so firemen and support workers in the London AFS, the 8,500 working in the London Auxiliary Ambulance Service (with their 900 green ambulances – white LCC ambulances being retained for ordinary civilian work – and their 700 ambulance cars), the boy volunteers who acted as ARP and fire service messengers, the decontamination squads and more. In addition, extra borough council mortuary staff were recruited and trained, and tradesmen's delivery vehicles were translated into temporary mortuary vans for collecting bodies and the remains of bomb victims.[19]

All this involved a great transformation in the functions of London's local public buildings: town hall basements were now control centres and sometimes shelters, public baths were first aid posts, local offices on housing estates were wardens' posts, and so to a great extent were wardens' own houses, at least in the early days. The left-wing journalist John Strachey, who wrote a wartime journal of his time in ARP, was a warden at 'Post D' in Chelsea in 1940; it was located in the five-storey house of 'Miss Sterling', the post warden, with only the basement passage strengthened with wooden props. Most versatile of all were the schools, now closed to children and recruited as AFS and auxiliary ambulance stations, council rest centres for people made homeless by bombing, and yet more wardens' posts, sometimes serving two or three of these functions together. The basements of many schools, along with church crypts – much favoured by the superstitious – and the cellars of factories and office blocks whose basements were requisitioned for shared public use at night, also doubled as shelters. All would eventually be identified by indicator arrows and a bold white 'S' stencilled onto walls.[20]

It was in these miscellaneous buildings that Londoners came together in ways and to an extent that had never happened before. At an auxiliary ambulance station in a school in Invicta Road, Greenwich, shared with the AFS, Michaela Wareham, twenty-six, a dance teacher living nearby, was a full-time ambulance driver paid £2 a week 'less insurance' – men doing the same job were paid £3. The crews worked seven days on one shift, then had a rest day, then worked a further seven days on another shift and so on. Most workers in the ambulance station were women, in the ratio three to two; all the women were in their twenties or thirties, middle class or above (driving, then, a pursuit for better-off women), the men middle class or below, including one 'lower-class. Very deaf. Looks like, & is mischievous as a monkey'. Their time was spent in practices, including timed 'turn outs', in keeping the ambulances and cars clean and filled with petrol, and in relaxation – ping-pong, reading, knitting, chatting and listening to the wireless, a rich source of dispute over which stations to tune to and how loud it should be. This was inner London, with its constant churn of population, and though all were locals none seem to have known each other before, apart from the 'perpetually bickering' married couple on Wareham's shift. Perhaps there was a more neighbourly feel in suburban areas: Frederick and Kathleen Bodley, both approaching forty, and 'Joan "next door"', all enrolled in the Borough of Sutton and Cheam's warden service on 17 September to '"do our bit"'. Their post in Worcester Park was purpose-built with brick walls fourteen inches thick and 'a 1 ft. concrete roof … It is very comfortable for we have a radio, shove ha'penny board, playing cards & an electric kettle. The heating is supplied by two electric radiators …' There were eight wardens attached to the post with just two on duty at any time in late 1939. When the Bodleys first enrolled the post had been in the senior warden's house.[21]

Whether people knew each other or not, all had to find ways of rubbing along together and for some, like gregarious Vivienne Hall, making new acquaintances in ARP was full of interest. She was a volunteer telephone operator at a local report centre in Putney, Wandsworth, working there some weekends and evenings while earning a daytime living as a clerk in an insurance firm in the City; she had more time for ARP from mid-September, when her firm decided no longer to open on Saturday mornings.

> There is one good thing, and one only, about this war – it is an instant and complete leveller of 'classes.' Everyone mixes and talks to anyone and I think we all find that the other is really quite a normal and interesting person and not a bit different from ourselves. About thirty of us are in the Centre, taken from widely divergent walks of life and we all get along very well indeed [4 September]. It really is the most amazing section of humanity that centre – one spends hours a day in the company of the butcher's wife, the carpet-maker's wife, a general's wife, a 'real' Lady, a hairdresser's assistant, the Major – in fact 2 'Majors' – me and many others and we all get along quite nicely [1 October].[22]

Her evenings of dull routine at the centre were varied by singing – 'the others fired songs at me ... and I sang it, if I happened to know it, while I knitted away', and 'Mrs Edgar every now and then rose and gave us a rendering of a Marie Lloyd song or an impersonation' – and practice alerts. Only once did her shift have a fright in those long months of waiting between September 1939 and April 1940:

> To the centre in the evening and was just settling down to knitting and the others to sausage and chips when the yellow warning [preliminary caution] was given. Instant activity and violent 'phoning to the wardens – the difference between the 'practice' raids we had had and this real warning was very clear – there was an urgency and tenseness about us all and although we were very calm we all became irritated by the apparent slowness of getting through to our numbers. Twenty minutes after we were given the white signal [cancel caution] and the tension lifted.[23]

While the men and women in ARP continued to practise endlessly for raids and emergencies that never came, it seemed as though among the general public preparedness was beginning to slip. The inelegant encumbrance of the gas mask in its cardboard box had been brightened in the first weeks of war by refashioning the container to make it more individual, even eye-catching. Vivienne Hall noticed among women that 'the most fantastic and colourful covers are appearing everywhere' in mid-September and Anthony Heap was glad to receive a 'black soft leather container' from his mother around the same time; perhaps she bought it from Prince Monolulu, the well-known 'African' racing tipster who now sold them in the streets, racing business curtailed by war. But by the beginning of October Heap noted that 'gas masks are definitely out of fashion', as fewer and fewer Londoners carried them. A count on Westminster Bridge by Mass Observation showed a drastic falling off from 71 per cent of men carrying masks on 6 September, and 76 per cent of women, to 24 per cent and 39 per cent on 9 November. This was matched too by a growing feeling that autumn that there wouldn't be raids on London at all, two thirds of working-class women thinking so and 40 per cent of working-class men; hopefulness was less apparent among the middle classes.[24]

THE biggest ARP worry that autumn and winter was the shelter question. The presence of shelters in the few new blocks of flats and offices able to finish building in the West End were major selling points – Bolton House, a new shop and office block in Curzon Street, Mayfair, was marketed in October 1939 as complete with a 'specially designed' basement shelter 'offering the best possible protection for all occupants of the building'. In older blocks, landlords had to provide a shelter if more than half the occupiers demanded it, but there were difficulties in doing so, especially if it meant evicting a tenant to remodel a basement. In the absence of a safe refuge in a block, then tenants were forced to rely on public shelters and even in September 1939 these were still in short supply. The main programme everywhere relied on completing trench shelters left unfinished from Munich or begun anew in August 1939. The main concern was to provide shelter for those caught in shopping streets during the day, domestic sheltering relying on the staple of the Anderson.[25]

Problems, however, for both trench shelters and Andersons emerged as the winter progressed. Flooding was apparent in shelters everywhere in London. In October heavy rain caused the River Ravensbourne to burst its banks, flooding Andersons in Ladywell, Lewisham, and as the weeks went by complaints of flooded shelters mounted. In November 5,000 Andersons were said to be flooded in Lewisham and 7,000–8,000 needed to be lined in concrete (6,200 of them were fixed by May 1940). Over the same period the council provided shelter for 30,000 in the main shopping streets, but here too problems arose: a subway shelter at Forest Hill provoked complaints in January 1940 because of its 'obnoxious smell due to the damp' and the 'befouled and rotting sandbags' protecting it. Lewisham was not alone. At Leyton a trench shelter for 450 at Wanstead Flats let in water and despite pumping could not be kept dry. Barking Council was having to concrete numerous Andersons. West Ham's trench shelters were said to have been dug in ground 'full of springs; small boys sailed boats in one', and others needed frequent pumping by fire engines to keep them usable. Every borough struggled to keep its existing shelters dry while adding new ones to its supply. Even so there was progress. In Westminster shelters were said to be available for over 160,000 people by the end of 1939, mainly in commercial buildings (60,000) and 'vaults' (probably beneath public buildings, another 60,000); schemes in the pipeline from owners of offices, shops and factories would provide shelter for a further 137,000. By January 1940 Stepney too could claim shelter accommodation for 190,000, including 40,000 in public basements, 5,000 in trenches and 6,000 under railway arches.[26]

Stepney's provision in January included public surface shelters in streets for some 4,000 people and from the beginning of 1940 surface shelters formed the major building programme in London as a whole. They were designed to offer shelter where Andersons were impractical, either through ground conditions or because multiple occupation of a house would render them too small to be of use. The usual design was a square brick box with a concrete roof, built with internal cross walls dividing the shelter usually into four, each cubicle capable of sheltering around twelve persons, so forty-eight or fifty in all. The buildings were generally low: 'the average person has to stoop to enter them.' This street shelter programme across London was immense and 'proceeded at an enormous rate: the shelters seemed to spring up almost overnight' in great numbers. Stepney Borough Council, for instance, advertised its intention on 11 April 1940 to build fifty-three shelters in nineteen streets for some 2,500 people as part of an extensive programme already under way: in Repton Street, Limehouse, five shelters would be built in mid-carriageway outside numbers 2–8, 10–14, 18–24, 28–32 and 34–42, offering shelter to occupiers on both sides of the road. In this way they were designed to become 'our shelters' for a small number of houses.[27]

These structures were greeted with some scepticism by the people who would have to use them. If they had no other option – no Anderson or reliable internal protection – then people recognised that they would have to shelter there and did so. But the very speed with which they were run up did not inspire confidence. An 'artisan class' woman told Mass Observation in July 1940: 'Well, they spring up so quickly. I suppose they're proof against splinters and that, but Christ, anything like a direct hit would bring a load of concrete down on their heads. The jerry-built things.'[28]

In truth, few if any shelters available to the public in London at this time were proof against a direct hit – even tube stations would prove vulnerable to an unlucky strike – but fears for the robustness of street shelters were not misplaced. A badly worded ARP leaflet issued to local authorities in April 1940 led to many shelters, some 5,000 in London alone, being built using a mortar made just of lime and sand without cement. This was corrected in July, but eventually, under fire, some had to be demolished or cased afresh in concrete. And a penny-pinching attitude by the Chamberlain government left no room for creature comforts: West Ham's architect ordered that street shelters be built with damp-proof courses and an eaves overhang to keep walls dry, luxuries which the Home Office would not fund – eventually it had to pay for damp-proof courses to be cut into the walls at a far greater cost.[29]

AMIDST all these efforts to keep Londoners safe, a furore had arisen out of what had seemed the one big success of the home front – evacuation. The stories, real or inflated, from reception areas reeling from the shock of meeting for the first time the products of Britain's slum schools staggered the nation. There resulted 'a spasm of horror', a 'thunderous storm', a 'scandal', an 'outcry'. Half the nation's 1.4 million evacuees were from London, and London children – and, worse it was said, their mothers – were high up the list of people complained about. In fact, when evidence was collected and weighed, the picture of bad and good was a very mixed one, but it was the anecdotes of filth and vermin, of 'animal' and 'uncivilised' behaviour, that circulated far and fast and came to define evacuation as a window on the British working classes, condemning them as a caste of untouchables. It is important to note here the key elements of the evacuation scandal, because they had an immediate impact on just how London would face up to war in the following six years.

The worst of the complaints can be summarised briefly. Some children, from Bethnal Green for instance, 'were simply crawling with lice, etc., and actually *never* used a lavatory; the children simply sat down in the house anywhere to relieve themselves and actually one woman who was given the guest room ... always sat the baby in the bed for this purpose'. Head lice, discovered in one out of six LCC schoolchildren in 1938, seem to have come as a complete shock to middle-class country dwellers who considered lice the nadir of uncleanness. Worse than everything was thought to be bed-wetting among evacuee children (and some mothers, apparently), a fact that 'has caused more harm to England than anything yet accomplished by the enemy', a middle-class Women's Voluntary Services (WVS) organiser at Guildford thought in early 1940. The very different culture of mealtimes in working-class London and the middle-class countryside also generated a litany of moans – of children eating with their fingers, of not sitting at table but wandering about with a 'piece' of bread and jam, of non-existent table manners when they did sit down, of not eating vegetables or home-cooked food at all but demanding tinned salmon and fish and chips. The source of many of these complaints lay in the gulf between, say, a Shoreditch slum tenement and a country vicarage in any one of the 476 local authority areas to which London children were dispatched. The ignorance of slum life – families sleeping six or eight to a bed, no access to running hot water or a bathroom, water having to be carried up many flights of stairs in jugs, lavatories shared with three or four other families and sometimes situated in the backyard – was astonishing given the exposés in books and news films and in the daily papers of the national slum scandal in the late 1930s. So too was the lack of sympathy that enabled parents and authorities in the reception areas to complain of the evacuees' poverty, their inadequate footwear (boots often an autumn purchase, plimsolls generally worn in summer), their shortage of underwear and warm outer coats. And so was the failure to empathise with the child's traumatic experience of evacuation – a lengthy and weary journey by train, the arrival often late in the day, the confusion (sometimes the humiliation) of being chosen for a billet, the foster family met for the first time, the pangs of homesickness on a first night alone, however inadequate that home might be. All these points would eventually be made by social workers and teachers and other commentators. But they had by then been drowned out in a cacophony of indignation.[30]

When the dust had settled a little and mature consideration was able to find a voice in social surveys published as early as 1940, then a more rounded picture emerged. 'The children [from Finsbury] billed in this village were well-behaved and on the whole quite healthy and clean'; 'Clean, well cared for and well behaved' (Fulham and Hammersmith); 'On the whole parents had been good in sending clothes and taking them away and mending' (Leytonstone) and many more. Some London children even shone in their new surroundings: 'At our Christmas party they [children from Lambeth] seemed more alive, quicker to play games and help entertain, than our country children.' And 'Their quick wits and ready interest have done much for the country children' (Bethnal Green).[31] On the whole, though, the impact of the chorus of contempt erupting from September through to December 1939 on those London families whose children had been sent away can only have been bitter and resentful; and some of London's communities harboured a collective sense of grievance over the way mothers and children were thought to have been treated by individual reception areas.

Just how much that resentment contributed to the steady stream of unaccompanied children and mothers with babies and toddlers who moved back to London in those same months cannot be quantified. It was probably significant because both children and mothers were no doubt demeaned and discomfited by the reception they might have received or by the row in the press. In any event, there were numerous factors contributing to what became a mass movement. Most important of course was the absence of bombing, which appeared to render evacuation not just unnecessary but foolish, even cowardly. Evacuation also had adverse consequences for many of the London schools shipped out. It had been the intention as far as possible to evacuate schools en bloc and keep them intact in the reception areas. Cramming evacuation into three days rather than four, with the resulting imperative to fill trains and move them as fast as possible, dislocated these arrangements and often led to the 'disintegration' of London schools, some of which found themselves spread over a number of villages (in one Norfolk case twenty-three), often miles apart. Sometimes this could be corrected by movements of children after evacuation, but that caused further disruption and the first accidental result often had to be accepted. Teachers billeted with children in a single location might find themselves having to teach all subjects to a mixed age group and it was often impossible for schools to reconnect completely. In these circumstances no doubt many parents thought their children's education would fare no worse if they, like so many others, headed back to London.[32]

An additional factor was cost. Families might have to comply with foster parents' pressure to meet perhaps exceptional requirements for footwear and outer garments. And from late October parents found themselves liable, after a means test, to contribute 6s per week per child to reimburse the government some of the cost of billets. The poorest paid nothing, some paid less than 6s and the best-off were 'invited' to pay the full cost of 9s. Finally, even for those children and mothers who had settled well outside London, in places where the education on offer was reasonable and for whom the contribution demanded was affordable, the lure of a family Christmas at home brought many back in the third week of December 1939. Some no doubt planned for a temporary holiday together but ended up making the arrangement long-term.[33]

Any attempt to bring children home, even just for the holiday, was frowned upon by the government and local education authorities, the LCC taking every opportunity to tell parents they were recklessly putting their children's lives at risk. But across London parents and children would not be deterred. 'Almost as soon as Wood Green children and parents reached the destination points the return movement began' and the drift back had become palpable on London's streets, at least to Gladys Langford's trained eye, as early as 22 September. By Christmas 80 per cent of evacuated mothers with babies and toddlers had returned to London, alongside almost 79,000 unaccompanied children in London County alone. It was estimated that in the LCC area two thirds of elementary school children had never left in the first place or were back in the capital by 8 January 1940. That was around 200,000 children in London who should have been in school. What education was provided for them?[34]

Those children left behind in London by the 1–3 September exodus had no education to go to at all. The schools were closed. Some two thirds had been taken over for new public purposes of civil defence. Those who drifted back to London through September to mid-October were similarly served. The government and most local education authorities were adamant that children were not wanted in the greatest target on earth and that making any provision for them would merely encourage them to stay and others to join them. Slowly, though, it dawned on the authorities that the reality of London life and the pressing needs of a whole generation of London children had to be listened to. From September a haphazard attempt to arrange home tuition for a few hours a day got under way, using any available space including private living rooms if parents had them, though with winter approaching there was no budget for heating or room hire. By early October a clamour among parents and children for schools to be reopened was audible in many areas, but local education authorities had their hands tied by the government refusing to sanction schools reopening in the evacuation areas. In Plaistow, West Ham, a former church school not used since 1905 was reopened by the vicar – nearly 500 children wanted to attend but there was capacity for far fewer. West Ham, Leyton and other councils lobbied for schools to be reopened and reluctantly the government permitted the opening of 'emergency schools' from 11 November 1939. In the LCC area, with 200,000 elementary school children to cater for, just thirteen schools were open by January 1940. They worked on a half-time basis so that two shifts of children aged from eleven to fourteen, but not younger, could attend either morning or evening classes. By March 1940, around 143,000 children were receiving schooling part-time in LCC schools or alternative premises like church halls, often shared with ARP or AFS crews. Even so, 70,500 London children received no education at all and were left to 'run wild', as it was put at the time.[35]

THE comprehensive disruption to Londoners' lives was apparent in every direction. Working life for many was turned upside down. The closure of cinemas and theatres and the emptying of hotels in London threw many out of work overnight and 'a general slaughter of magazines' did the same for freelance writers and printers. George Beardmore, working in insurance, was told by his boss that many in the firm would lose their jobs so found temporary work with the BBC, only to be laid off within the month. 'Lydia has been "shut out" of work for the time-being and Minnie Sudbury, after 20 odd years at H.M.V. [His Master's Voice gramophone works in Hayes, Middlesex] has been dismissed with most of the Head Office staff,' Dorothy Wells, working for Sankey's, a builders' merchants, in Aldwych, Holborn, noted on 10 September, adding: 'Doris Finch is sacked too. So many firms are closing down.' The building industry as a whole suffered greatly at the outset as council building contracts were suspended and landlords and developers grew wary of investing where they might not be able to recover their money. There were victims too at the fringes of the London economy: London's lively second-hand motorcar market became a ghost trade almost overnight after petrol was rationed. Within a month unemployment nationally rose by 200,000. 'We are at war. And what has happened to me, a lad of nineteen years?' complained Norman Bailey of Birkbeck Road, Acton, to *Picture Post*. 'I have been fired from my job. The Army does not want me, there are no civilian jobs vacant, and I'm refused A.R.P. work on account of my age.' There was one bright spot, though. The East London rag trade, memories of the boom-time on 'the khaki' in the Great War still fresh, began investing in plant and people for a war needing more men and women in uniform than ever before: Rego of Bethnal Green advertised for 500 workers to fill an extension factory within a week of the declaration of war.[36]

But in the run-up to the first Christmas of the war in London the greatest single disruption to life was the blackout. The blackout times announced daily in the newspapers were a tyranny. As the flood of prosecutions for blackout offences mounted in their hundreds, special sittings were needed at the North London Police Court just to hear lighting cases from February 1940 on. Despite an extension of summer time to mid-November, shops and some offices closed early as winter drew on, crowds emerging as the light failed to struggle for a bus, tram or train home. It was only the aesthetically minded who could dispel these practical worries to marvel at London's newly revealed beauties: under September's bright harvest moon 'the streets become rivers of light. The houses become feathery, soft, undefined, aspiring, so that any part of this town might be the most beautiful city in the world, sleeping amongst silk and water,' thought Stephen Spender, the poet. That was rather an acquired taste. 'Coming home in the pitch dark,' wrote George Beardmore after a visit to the cinema in suburban north Harrow, 'was an experience. All the streets were deserted as though plague had struck and the death-cart had made its daily collection ... It all seems very humiliating, this cowering down in expectation of death falling from the heavens.' 'Are you in favour of the blackout being made less severe?' asked a Gallup poll in December, and 75 per cent answered yes. Before Christmas there was some relaxation for vehicles and 'pin-prick' lighting was introduced in the streets, but still 'much below the standards permitted in the Great War'.[37]

Many people carried blackout bruises home with them. In the first four months of the blackout, road deaths by night in London more than doubled compared to the same period in 1938, 390 against 170. Some 322 of these were pedestrians. The figures for the first months of 1940 showed some improvement, evidence perhaps that people were adjusting their habits to the new conditions, although the ferocious frost and snow of the first two months kept many off the streets altogether. The more trivial injuries where vehicles were not involved were uncounted – indeed uncountable. 'Had a tumble on the way home,' Dorothy Wells, living in Hanwell, Ealing, noted in her diary in November. 'Striding along, singing to myself, when my toe caught in something and down I went. Leg a bit bruised, but no damage otherwise.' Vivienne Hall was at her ARP centre a couple of weeks later when an aunt phoned to say 'that poor old M [her mother, fifty-nine years old and a nurse] had forgotten there was a curb [sic] in the High Street [Putney] and had fallen and dislocated her thumb and cracked her nose, poor thing she was very badly shaken …' 'Took a toss last night in the blackout at Hyde Park Corner,' Hilda Neal wrote in January 1940 after one of her long walks home from the Strand to South Kensington, 'cut one knee and banged both badly; hole as big as an orange in a new pair of stockings[.] Went into the public convenience there and girl gave me hot water, so bathed both knees; all right today but stiff and aching. Attendant so nice and sympathetic.' 'Have you suffered any physical injury because of the blackout?' enquired Gallup that month, and 18 per cent said they had. The figure would mount: that April Arthur Christiansen, editor of the *Daily Express*, 'stumbled in the black-out, fell and broke my leg in five places'; he was in plaster till August.[38]

The blackout held other terrors too. Fifty-nine IRA bombs exploded in London in 1939, less than a pinprick compared to what was to come but disconcerting enough. The 'campaign' continued into 1940. In February Godfrey Clarke, forty-four, a retail seed and pet food merchant in Golborne Road, a shopping street in seedy North Kensington, heard a 'big "bang" at 10.30pm' on one of his weekly rambles by night; it 'turned out to be the I.R.A. bomb at Marble Arch!! Home by 11pm. Rather tired.' And on 17 March a bomb exploded at 3.30 a.m. outside Paddington Town Hall, where off-duty ARP staff awoke 'covered with debris'.[39]

Other anxieties were more attributable to rumour and anecdote. Recorded crime in London had been rising steadily in 1938 and continued to do so in the last months of peace in 1939. In the first three months of war, however, despite the blackout, it fell. This was attributed, fancifully or not, to evacuation removing juvenile offenders and hardened thieves taking stock of the new circumstances of a pitch-black London at night. In December, however, recorded crime reached a new seven-year peak and stories of elderly Londoners being bumped on the head and robbed circulated wildly. In fact, reports of robbery with violence were lower by nearly a third in 1939 than they had been the year before. The most serious problems occurred in the West End and in south London in the early months of 1940 with a systematic campaign of smash and grab raids against jewellers' and other shops. 'Shop after shop in Camberwell and Walworth-rd. is being robbed by smash-and-grab raiders in the black-out', and so were shops in Lewisham High Street later in the month. Around the same time in south London the '"Elephant Gang" of youths' were said to be connected especially to a 'protection racket', blackmailing shopkeepers under the threat of wrecking their shops; also in January an 'Epidemic of Shoplifting Charges' in south London police courts was remarked upon. The cinemas too noted a deterioration of patrons' behaviour in the blackout with cars and bicycles stolen from car parks, cinema seats slashed, lavatory fittings vandalised, windows broken and 'stills and lamps removed'. But little of this was out of the ordinary and the statistics show that even with the blackout recorded offences fell for several months after New Year 1940, the peak of the previous December not sustained.[40]

DESPITE the dangers of the blackout, real and imagined, London struggled back to a new normal from the full reopening of cinemas, theatres and music halls in November 1939. But the bright lights of the pre-war West End and scores of suburban shopping streets were stifled and some old consolations had to be revived or revalued. London's borough librarians reported that people were reading more, or at least borrowing more books, even though libraries now closed at 7 p.m. rather than 9 p.m.; and the wireless's one BBC channel had now improved and at least had the virtue of capturing most of the available audience, providing a talking point for everyone: '"Band Waggon" again – what a delight those silly comedians are, everyone looks forward to them and listens carefully – they are such a tonic,' thought Vivienne Hall in October 1939. For the particularly venturesome there was more than tonic available – at the pub, for instance, which maintained its staple place in London's evening culture throughout the war, often the last place of call after a night out. The cinema increased in popularity during the war years, not least because of the spread of Technicolor and some wartime blockbusters which every Londoner seems to have seen at least once. The theatre too stood up to the strain of call-up for actors and stage technicians, but three big West End houses had not reopened by Christmas – the Duke of York, the Playhouse (Northumberland Avenue) and the Haymarket. Covent Garden remained closed but opera and ballet flew their flags at Sadler's Wells, offering weekly, then twice-weekly, then nightly performances by the summer of 1940 'to record houses'.[41]

By Christmas 1939 the West End was thriving, with many pantomimes and reviews offering a comic take on the war, including Max Miller in *Haw-Haw!* at the Holborn Empire, although according to Mass Observation sex was what made people laugh most: 'sexual war references very well received'. Spring in the West End would bring a crop of new shows, chief among them Eric Maschwitz's revue *New Faces* at the Comedy Theatre, opening in April 1940; its hit, 'A Nightingale Sang in Berkeley Square', was one of the great songs of the war. But the surprising success of the winter was the revival of *Young England*, which followed *Haw-Haw!* at the Holborn Empire. Phyllis Warner, a keen theatregoer, reported the unlikely success for American readers:

When this play was first put on, the critics agreed that it was the worst show London had seen in twenty years, and wouldn't run a week. It ran to packed houses for over a year. Written in all sincerity it is a patriotic fantasy of Boy Scouts, Girl Guides, V.C. heroes, conscientious objector villains, and all the machinery of a Victorian melodrama. Word went round that here was a supreme subject for barracking, and soon the audiences were playing a more active part than the cast; indeed the audiences were so noisy that often when the players are seen on the stage gesticulating and moving their lips, not a sound can be heard. Those who have seen the play try to beat the actors to their lines whilst the actors attempt to come back with an alternative. Thus the villain will enter, and members of the audience will cry "Foiled," "Frustrated," "Stymied," "Checked," "Outwitted," etc., until he is quick enough to get in a variation of his own. Apart from this diversion, the parts are played straight. A high light is the camp song "Boy Scouts, Boy Scouts, Keep the Party Clean."[42]

For the well-off, London maintained its traditional luxuries in fine dining, the Savoy Grill a favourite; and now dinner was often combined with dancing to a jazz band and sometimes a cabaret. The well-known

American journalist Ed Murrow reported to a US audience that London nightlife was doing good business, 'in fact, improved since war came'. There were more West End dance bands than previously because 'Customers want to dance ... Places like the Embassy Club, Quaglino's, the Paradise, Café de Paris, and that padded room called the Four Hundred are jammed nearly every night.' 'Prices have gone up,' he noted, 'but that doesn't seem to matter.' Indeed, the war spawned new nightclubs offering floor shows and finding a way temporarily around the liquor licensing laws. 'Bottle parties', where nightclub guests ordered in booze from an associated high-price wine merchant, were all the rage from October 1939. The Florida and the Cabaret, the latter somewhere 'off Regent Street', offered a floor show 'as undressed as the Folies Bergères'.[43]

Some other new wartime attractions were more sedate, chief among them the weekday lunchtime concerts at the National Gallery. They opened with a recital by its most assiduous and popular performer, the pianist Myra Hess (then forty-nine, Jewish, Hampstead-born) on 10 October 1939. Tickets cost 1s, including tea and a sandwich, and audiences were at first restricted to 200. But even from the first day there were long queues in Trafalgar Square and eventually musicians were playing to over a thousand, many sitting on the floor between the rows of seats or standing at the back of the hall.[44]

Other things, though, were not available. Guy Fawkes Night was cancelled, as it would be throughout the war, and the 11 November Armistice commemoration that first autumn of the war was another damp squib. There were poppy sellers in the streets but no ceremony at the Cenotaph, no crowds, 'no maroon' heralding the two-minute silence and bringing it to a close, 'no bowing of a thousand heads,' recorded Walter Musto, sixty years old and working for the Crown Agency at Millbank; but he took 'ten truanted minutes' to stand in Parliament Square and as Big Ben struck 11 a.m., 'with one accord every scattered vehicle stopped dead, every pedestrian halted in his stride and stood still, every soldier, sailor and airman remained quietly at the salute and the silence was of the stars on a still night'.[45]

THAT Christmas of 1939 was the last to be relatively unaffected by those straitened circumstances that would so blight the next five years. The shops were full of things to buy, though most were a little more expensive than before – 'I'm spending a lot too much on presents,' thought Vivienne Hall, but 'Christmas is in the air and although we all felt earlier on that we could not celebrate it seems to be much the same as ever.' She had a family Christmas with her mother at her aunt's flat, nearby in Putney, with turkey and plum pudding as usual. At their more modest flat in Sinclair House, Hastings Street, St Pancras, Anthony Heap and his mother sat down at 3 p.m. to 'roast duck, apple sauce, potatoes, cauliflower and Christmas pudding and a glass of port'; that was all good, but the afternoon was let down by 'the King's Empire broadcast. A hesitating speech, uninspired and uninspiring.' A few days later and most people seem to have spent New Year's Eve quietly too. Ivan Maisky, the Soviet ambassador:

> drove around the city to see how the English were seeing in the New Year. The streets were shrouded in the usual black-out gloom. The pavements were white with snow: the week has been uncommonly cold and snowy for England. There were people in the streets, but immeasurably fewer than in former years. At Piccadilly, where huge, noisy crowds, singing and dancing, always flood the square on New Year's Eve, there were now only a few sparse, silent groups. At St Paul's Cathedral, where there is always a sea of human beings, shouting, laughing and dancing, there was nobody to be found. It was the same all over. Only Whitechapel was noisier, but perhaps that was due to the character of the locals [many Jewish, like Maisky himself].

Certainly, things were pretty quiet with Anthony Heap, who spent the evening at a friend's in Muswell Hill: 'Saw the New Year in, in the most quiet and sober fashion ... So ended 1939. And good riddance too.' Further west even lively Joan Wyndham, eighteen and eager to sacrifice her virginity to artistic Chelsea, had to be content with a small party at home. 'Then Alfred played "Auld Lang Syne" and we all sang, and kissed each other. I just hope 1940 turns out to be a bit more exciting than 1939.'[46]

It would, but not at first. The beginning of 1940 was unremittingly bleak for Londoners. The very poorest, as always, would have it hardest. The plight of women struggling to raise a family single-handedly – as soldiers' wives scraping by on a War Office allowance, or as widows and mothers abandoned by their men – was brought to public attention by Sylvia Pankhurst, just as she had done in similar circumstances in the First World War. Among others she raised the case of Mrs Lowe, of Custom House, Poplar, who would have had just 15s a week to live on had not her son in the army sent her an allowance. It's from now too that stories of abandoned babies become more common in local newspapers: a twenty-six-year-old thrown out by her parents left her baby on the steps of Plaistow Nurses' Home, for instance, and a still-born baby was discarded on the muddy foreshore by Stepney Borough Council's wharf on the Thames.[47] But in the first months of 1940 all Londoners faced deprivation of a kind, and for two reasons.

First, food. A German submarine blockade of merchant shipping, the revival of an effective strategy first tried in the Great War, led to inevitable scarcities from time to time of imported food. There had been intermittent shortages before Christmas – sugar and fish in September and October, bacon, eggs and butter in October and November – but with the New Year shortages became permanent and official. On 8 January sugar, butter and bacon were rationed. Butter was not such a problem for the poorest, because it had long been expensive and margarine was a traditional substitute, but sugar and bacon affected everyone. On 11 March butchers' meat was also rationed and further foods would be added in the summer. In general the system was smoothly rolled out and widely accepted as fair on everyone, but there were enormous burdens put on local council 'food offices' to distribute ration books and to enforce an increasingly complex bureaucracy of punitive laws affecting shopkeepers and consumers alike.[48]

In order to compensate for shortages and a lack of variety caused by rationing, the government had initiated a 'Dig for Victory' campaign in October 1939. Like food rationing, this resurrected policies trialled in the First World War. Old blueprints were now dusted off. Within a week or two of the campaign opening Leyton Borough Council thought it would need to arrange for the cultivation of 'Wanstead Flats and the Lammas lands' as it had in the Great War. Within a month every local authority in London was enthusiastically putting in hand allotment schemes in parks and gardens: Lewisham, for instance, by mid-November, in conjunction with the LCC, a major landholder in every metropolitan borough, had identified places to be divided up for allot-ment holders at 9d per rod. In association with the Lewisham and District Horticultural Society, it established a 'panel of experts' to answer growers' questions and provide general advice, and gardeners' columns bloomed in every local paper. Advice was needed for there were allotments and allotments. The builders' merchants' clerk Dorothy Wells, who had seen so many friends lose their jobs at the outset of war, lived with her mother and elder brother, Ken, forty-one, a warehouseman in the West End. Ken took a piece of ground from Ealing Council not too far from their home. 'Went up to help Ken at his allotment,' she wrote in March 1940, 'and found it the stoniest bit of land between here and Chesil Beach ... Every inch has to be chiselled out with a fork.' She concluded, 'I don't think we shall ever make anything out of it, as there is no possibility of digging.' Time would tell. And in another direction the cultivation of animals for food became a cottage industry even in urban Middlesex – Tottenham dustmen's 'Pig Club' became so well known that the men were 'almost becoming national figures' by February 1940.[49]

Added to the deprivations of rationing that winter, and cruelly frustrating all those keen to add to London's food supplies, came a ferocious frost. As Ivan Maisky indicated, there had been a harbinger before New Year but it struck with a vengeance in January. It heralded three consecutive winters that would be among the harshest in recent European history. Londoners reckoned that early 1940 was the worst winter since 1894, though January was the worst since reliable records began in 1841. The average temperature for the whole month was below freezing and for much of it snow lay thick on the ground. February proved little better and snow, sleet and rain washed out March. It was all made worse by the papers failing to report the country's privations until the worst was over, weather a state secret during the war. But everyone in London knew what everyone else was going through because the cold was the main topic of conversation everywhere and because many had to call on neighbours and friends for help.[50]

We can take Godfrey Clarke's winter at 68 Golborne Road, North Kensington, as typical of many, perhaps most. He lived over the seed and pet food shop with his sister Laurie, forty-eight, a civil servant; they had inherited the business from their father and they seem not to have paid too much attention to running repairs. They had trouble from the very start of 1940. Their pipes froze and left them without water on New Year's Day: 'However am able to get supplies in my jug & pail from Ewart Freeston [bootmakers] across the way at "69".' On 5 January, still without water, another neighbour, a young handyman who did odd jobs for a few shillings, came in and fiddled with the cistern which had been playing up and on 8 January did the same to the lavatory cistern, though both remained frozen; he 'also "cemented in" the crack on flats above the Kitchen window – so do hope we shall be free from water coming in now'. Next day he put some slates back on the roof 'so do hope by now the top bedroom ceiling will be water-proof ...' On 12 January, 'As cold as ever & still no water in Kitchen or lavatory!'; on the 16th, 'Bitterly cold & a heavy fall of snow in the afternoon'; and on the 17th, 'As cold as ever – in fact worse I think!' Two days later there had been some progress: 'Just as cold & still no water except on landing tap. Still,' reflected Godfrey, a devout Methodist, 'we must be thankful for that!' So it went on. 'One of the coldest day's I think ever remember!' (20th, the cold affecting his grammar), but on the 25th there was a thaw after twenty-four days – 'Such a blessing to have the water at the Kitchen tap "on" again.' Next day he fell off his stepladder cleaning the shop windows, cutting his head and spraining his writing arm. It had not been a good month. February was not much better: 'bitterly cold & ice & snowy slush lying about' (8th); 'One cannot seem to get warm anywhere' (9th); 'water coming through in Laurie's room and pouring down in Dining room! Such a mess' (10th); 'to every-one's dismay snow again in the evening. It is the worst winter we have had for years. No wonder people are ill! – there seems no end to it' (16th); then a thaw but 'A burst water-pipe to add to our discom-forts' (20th). The introduction of 'permanent summer time' at the end of February, giving lighter evenings all year round, must have seemed a grim joke from the jesters of Whitehall.[51]

March was warmer, though it started badly: 'Bitterly cold' on 1 March, 'Feeling really very queer with bad liver & back ache'. And complaints of illness and 'the flu' were general in London through all those miserable first months of 1940. Arthur Buddell, the Great War veteran and civil servant living in Croydon, also had a bad time. He, his wife (May) and daughter (Mary, not yet seven) were all laid up with flu or something like it. He took a couple of days off work in mid-March but 'Back to office' on the 12th, 'though not yet fit. Foolish perhaps. Heavy epidemic of influenza in London. Mary very trying.' There was a fresh fall of snow and a week later Arthur was worse, running a temperature and losing his voice. The doctor diagnosed pharyngitis and signed him off work – 'Hacking cough & feeling very weak ... May has not completely recovered from her attack of flu!' – she seems to have been ill since early February and this was the end of March. He was not cheered by the doctor's opinion of his daughter: 'Doctor says Mary has adenoids. Not surprised.'[52]

None of this – the inability to get warm, the general ill health and tetchy temper – was helped by a coal and coke shortage that hit London especially hard. The bad weather played a part in interrupting supplies and so did the U-boat threat that cut the coastal coal trade to London. By the end of January there was a 'crisis' that lasted for the whole of February. All classes of Londoner were affected. F. Tennyson Jesse lived in Pear Tree Cottage, Medina Place, St John's Wood, and in early February her husband was in bed with the flu; 'so you may imagine,' she wrote to friends in America, 'how terrified I was when we could get no coke' for their central heating – a rare luxury indeed in the London of 1940. They managed to scrape by, bailed out by her husband's theatrical contacts. Nellie Carver, at Idmiston Road, West Norwood, Lambeth, noted on 6 March, 'Have run short of coal – lorries unable to run on late bad roads ... Must see if I can get some from Fred at the oil shop – don't fancy freezing for another month.' Next day, 'Got 2 Bags of coal from Fred! Good boy, he managed to collect a little – will make do with Logs.'[53]

Nellie lived in south London and the coal crisis seems to have struck there hardest. By early February coal merchants in Camberwell, Streatham, Walworth and Wandsworth were complaining of low stocks, despite complying with the government's request to ration householders to two hundredweight a week. A few days later in Battersea, 'queues form daily at the coal offices and wharves. As soon as supplies are received they are distributed and the yards are emptied within an hour of delivery.' The town hall stocked some coal for the sick and needy but the council was running low too. 'A crowd waiting at the New Wandsworth depot at Battersea Rise on Wednesday ran into the yard when they were told there was no coal and began taking lumps from sacks and under the [railway] trucks. They left without trouble, however, when an official explained that the coal was meant for hospitals.' The need for further direct action faded as supplies began to pick up from late February.[54]

THIS dreadful winter added to London's scars. By the spring of 1940, without a bomb being dropped, London looked as though it really had been in the wars. Despite the return of many who had left last September, many houses were still empty and everywhere seemed to need a lick of paint after the winter's privations. It was a lick that would not be available for years to come. Anthony Weymouth, a Harley Street physician living in Marylebone, thought 'half the pleasure has gone from a London walk. The houses are either boarded up, or show other signs of being uninhabited. As you pass one derelict house after another, you get the impression that you are living in a beleaguered city,' and in many ways he was. The newly formed London Traders' Defence League claimed that countless shops had closed, with 'thousands of London traders ... facing ruin' from a combination of evacuation, blackout and public transport restrictions. Virginia Woolf, admittedly low in spirit but a profound lover of London, always ready to find the best in it, thought it 'a great dumb ox lying couchant ... the streets tunnels of gloom'.[55]

Dishevelled London seemed to be matched by the Londoner, chilled to the marrow, all care for appearance abandoned in the battle with frost, especially, many thought, London women: '*how* ugly London is now,' Gladys Langford complained in January. 'Cold weather causes women to wear most hideous garments, hoods round moon-faces, kerchiefs around the hatchet type. Fat females and lean hags in trousers, greasy suede jackets. Oh Eve! Where are thy charms?' 'The War Has Made Women Careless About Their Looks', a *South London Press* 'woman reporter' declaimed in a headline: 'Women are spending less money on their personal appearance, owing to the war and the absence of the menfolk, and a great many are definitely neglecting their hair.' South London hairdressers of her acquaintance told her their takings had 'dropped 50 per cent'.[56]

ARP in early 1940 was also in the doldrums. It had enjoyed a good Christmas, like many, and there were signs that a significant camaraderie might be in the making. This had been growing from the start and we see it as early as October 1939, when twenty of Vivienne Hall's ARP colleagues went on a beano to the Victoria Palace theatre to see *Me and My Girl* with Lupino Lane – 'I laughed until my jaws ached'. And goodwill took a more focused turn as Christmas approached: 'The present shift – B – has adopted a little child whose father has been killed in a trawler – they are undertaking to keep him clothed from top to toe and to send him things occasionally – really people are very good-hearted and it takes a war to find out about it.'

In fact the war tapped deep seams of associational life in working-class communities based on trade unionism and workplace solidarity, and on lower-middle-class mutual assistance in Freemasonry, Rotary Clubs and so on. There were many traditions to draw upon. Whatever the roots, the haphazard coming together in ARP sowed the seeds of a lively collective benevolence during that first Christmas of the war and the following months. All over London ARP workers organised parties for groups of children: a joint social club of AFS and ARP men and women at Stewart Headlam School, Brady Street, Whitechapel, gave a treat for 250 local children; Gascoigne ARP Depot's Sports and Social Club, Barking, entertained 260 and similar bashes were organised by other local depots; 'Personnel of the decontamination squads and the stretcher parties attached to St. Peter's Crypt ARP Depôt in De Beauvoir Town', Hackney, treated some 400 children to a New Year party at the church hall and so on. The very particular identity of the people who came together to put on these events is striking and by the beginning of 1940 there were attempts to cement a borough-wide collective fellow feeling among ARP staff. The Working Men's Club and Institute Union was the model here, with a Hackney ARP club opening in Homerton in January and a similar one in New North Road, beginning 'A new chapter in the history of Shoreditch AR.P.', as it was rather grandly described in the local paper.[57]

Some morale boosting was badly needed. '"Oh! What a lovely war",' wrote W. B. Williams of Gurney Road, West Ham, to the *Stratford Express*: 'What amount of remuneration do the Corporation clerks ... receive for doing "control room" duty at the various A.R.P. control centres throughout the Borough?' Some were volunteers or, if seconded full-time, then just their usual salaries, was the answer apparently, but sceptical voices inferring that ARP was merely just another kind of racket were audible from the very beginning. By early 1940 they had become a deafening chorus. The problem, of course, was the absence of bombing, and no amount of public drilling with mock casualties swaddled in bandages and fire crews putting out manufactured blazes could convince the public that ARP time was well spent or its personnel gainfully employed. The *Daily Express* and the *Daily Mirror* led the charge, with the AFS and ARP renamed the Darts Brigade, Duckers, Parasites, Idlers and '£3 p.w. Army Dodgers'. AFS men were especially vulnerable to these jibes because many were young or youngish men: 'Boys, riding bikes on errands, called out to them "Why don't you join the army?"' and many did. By April 1940 the whole of ARP was tarred with the same brush.[58]

Things weren't helped by stories in the local papers of ARP members caught with their hands in the till. A London thief did not stop being a thief just because he donned ARP overalls. Three members of an Islington demolition squad were jailed for stealing lead from a derelict house on which they had been practising, for instance. A particularly egregious case from Southwark raised a question mark over the selection process for ARP staff and how fit they would be to carry out their duties in any real emergency: an LCC woman ambulance driver was fined 40s for being drunk and incapable at Elephant Road; she had over twenty previous convictions for drunkenness.[59]

In this climate of press ridicule and growing public scepticism it became easy for the government to initiate retrenchment in ARP numbers from January 1940. London Region, with its huge ARP establishment, became a key target of austerity measures, the government generally demanding a cut in wardens from nine per post to six, any shortfall being made up by recruiting more volunteers as part-timers. There was universal council resistance to the cuts, but Paddington, for instance, had to reduce the warden service from 342 to 262 by the end of March, and Lewisham from 237 to 210; some, like Poplar, were told to cut ARP wages. Similar reductions were imposed on the London AFS. Eventually London Region 'dug our toes in and refused to make further cuts', but with these reductions, and with wastage in numbers as ARP volunteers and paid workers drifted away to do other things, London's civil defence was noticeably weakened by the spring of 1940.[60]

BUT did Londoners need to worry? On the face of it they didn't. For nearly the whole of the eight months following 3 September war news was almost eerily silent. There had been just one moment when the war had seemed close to London. The Battle of the River Plate and the scuttling of the *Graf Spee* in mid-December brought to London as victors the crews of HMS *Ajax* and *Exeter*. On 23 February 1940, 760 officers and men from the ships' companies marched from Waterloo Station to the City's Guildhall through packed crowds – the Londoners' first collective joy of the war. The excitement lasted a couple of hours at most. Londoners returned to their winter of self-absorption – battling with the deep freeze, the flu and the blackout, eking out what pleasure they could from cinema and theatre, from the wireless and their books. The war seemed far away again. But with spring in London at last, things began to stir. Early in the morning of Tuesday 9 April, again without warning, Germany invaded Denmark and Norway. 'My God,' wrote an excited Vivienne Hall, 'we said the war was going to start in the spring and it has.' But for Anthony Heap, an opponent of the war and a closet admirer of Adolf Hitler and Nazi Germany, twenty-nine years old and not in any reserved occupation, this was the moment he had been dreading:

Here we have the government's long awaited opportunity to sacrifice the lives of Britain's young manhood without stint. The more the merrier – for the armament makers. Now, more than ever with me it will be a case of eating, drinking and getting all the damned fun I can out of such uncertain span of life now left to me – for the morrow we get maimed, mutilated or murdered for the glory of democracy and all else that's rotten in the state of England today. So be it.[61]

3

THE LAST BARRICADES OF EUROPE:
10 APRIL–6 SEPTEMBER 1940

LONDONERS' 'Phoney War', 'Bore War', 'Sitzkrieg', whatever they had called it, ended on 9 April 1940. That day Denmark surrendered but Norway resolved to fight and Britain and France weighed in to help. The war news gleaned from wireless and newspapers, these last now shrinking before readers' eyes as Scandinavian newsprint supplies began to dry up, was eagerly followed by many. The dangers to Britain were apparent from the start. Olivia Cockett, at Scotland Yard's payroll office temporarily relocated to a school in Putney, recorded how this first dramatic twist of the war was eagerly discussed. From the outset, Hitler's next steps were a matter of anxiety, even if wrapped in black humour: '"You'd better put on your best make-up to welcome the Germans, Gussie,"' a young woman was ribbed. '"Oh well,"' she replied, '"it'll make a change."'[1]

Over the next week or so, some good news of Allied efforts against the German invaders did come out of Norway, but soon it became clear there were difficulties. 'A few remarks that "we don't seem to be doing so well"' were noted by Cockett on 17 April. But if people needed a fillip they were given one: next day the first great Hollywood hit of the war, *Gone with the Wind*, opened simultaneously in three London cinemas, including the Empire, Leicester Square – by the end of the war few Londoners had failed to sit through its three hours forty minutes at least once. Escapism was helpful because a week later the April budget piled the mounting cost of the war on everyone's shoulders with beer, whisky, tobacco, cigarettes, even matches all up in price and an extra 6d on income tax to 7s 6d in the pound (37.5 per cent). 'And there won't be a murmur of dissatisfaction from the poor bloody British

Public,' complained Anthony Heap. 'After all, it's to save liberty and democracy etc. Bah!'[2]

Liberty and democracy, however, really were in peril. On 6 May British troops had to be hurriedly evacuated from southern Norway and two destroyers were sunk in the action. It was a blow for which people had hardly been prepared, the news from Norway bowdlerised by government censors. A political storm blew up overnight. Labour forced a vote on the Chamberlain administration's handling of the war at the end of a two-day debate on 7–8 May in which the limp-wristed pursuit of the Norway campaign and much else was savaged from all sides. Chamberlain asked for a vote of confidence and won it but his majority was severely dented and his authority was shattered. With the opposition refusing to serve under him in a cross-party administration, Chamberlain resigned and Winston Churchill was appointed Prime Minister on 10 May, now leading a coalition in which the three main parties were represented. That same day, Hitler hurled a lightning strike at Luxembourg, Belgium, Holland and France in a move that would bring the war dramatically closer to London.

There followed an eerie echo of London's war in 1914. Once again, Londoners found themselves faced with a sudden inrush of hapless Belgian refugees needing shelter and the other necessities of life. They began to arrive from 13 May, many with stories of terror to tell. Déjà vu was not all on the Londoners' side. Eugène Steers, thirty-one, a motor mechanic from Antwerp, had been first brought to London in 1914 when he was four; now he and his wife had escaped on bicycles to Ostend and were machine-gunned by German planes with the rest of the refugee column. This time, he thought, the Germans were worse than ever. Most refugees, like the Steers, had little more than the clothes they wore, but many carried bundles and some had babies in prams, like the van den Bergs, also from Antwerp, he a Dutch shipping clerk, his wife Irish, from Dublin. Couples like these were given a government dole of 35s a week, single persons 21s.[3]

Reception centres were organised in the County of London by the LCC and the boroughs, often in municipal baths, where the refugees could clean themselves up. In Tottenham, Middlesex, the Jewish Hospital was 'used as a cleansing depôt and for medical examinations', Jews often in significant numbers among those fleeing the Germans. Metropolitan Police detectives were also part of this initial screening, rumour rife of German uniforms under refugee clothing and other giveaway signs of spies and 'fifth columnists'. Interpreters were sought through the local press and borough refugee committees were set up by those councils given responsibility for billeting; the inner boroughs (Southwark, Bermondsey and Deptford in south-east London, for instance) were excluded because of their vulnerability to bombing, now expected any day. Where billets were needed they seem to have been generously forthcoming: Wandsworth had 5,000 residents who offered their homes to the refugees, and in Chelsea women of all classes went out of their way to help people settle in, scrubbing out empty homes before they were occupied by the newcomers.[4]

In 1914 the refugees had been well received at first but their presence in London had eventually palled. Something similar happened in this war too, only faster. Everything was complicated by Britain's own risks, especially from invasion, and the behaviour of its allies was critically scrutinised. On 13 May the Dutch royal family fled to London. Not everyone saw this panicky flight in a positive light: 'Wilhelmina, her fat daughter Julianna, the grandchildren and Boche son in law Bernard Lippe Von Bisterfield [sic] as well as the Dutch cabinet "rat" to London,' Arthur Buddell ungallantly recorded in his diary. But worse was to come. The French defences proved far shakier than her allies had expected. On 17 May the US Embassy in London advised all Americans in the country to leave 'as soon as possible and in the meantime' make for Eire to await repatriation. That same day the government announced that all evacuees from London and elsewhere on the south-east coast would now be re-evacuated to Wales. Then, on 27 May, the heaviest blow so far: King Leopold of Belgium ordered his army to lay down arms and surrender, even while British and French forces were fighting alongside it. The news was received in London with shock and bitterness. In the tax office at Euston Rhona Little had arrived at work that morning as usual:

> We had hardly started work before someone told us that someone had heard on the wireless in French that King Leopold had betrayed us and given in to the Germans. Miss Dall [the emphatic head of the typing pool] got into a great state on this and went round the office telling off everyone for spreading rumours. At lunch time we had the rumour confirmed and Miss Dall spent the rest of the time explaining how much she had thought of Leopold. Apparently a lot of people thought he was wonderful. To be quite honest I never thought of the man at all.[5]

'It is incredible!' wrote Hilda Neal next day. 'We were all stunned and shocked beyond words ... Conjecture seems useless, for what could excuse such a betrayal?' That evening she listened to Duff Cooper's broadcast from the Ministry of Information spelling out the consequences: 'Our British Expeditionary Force [BEF] is in grievous plight, we are told tonight.'[6]

There seems to have been an immediate backlash against the Belgian refugees in London. The Home Office intelligence reports, gleaned from a network of contacts across the capital, had picked up some reservations soon after their first arrival: 'Influx of Dutch and Belgian refugees not regarded with favour,' they recorded on 21 May. Now, on the 29th, it reported 'Some bitterness against Belgium even to the extent of saying the Belgian refugees should be sent back'. A few days later they noted, 'A growing feeling against Belgian refugees,' this time in part fuelled by their allegedly favourable billeting rates when compared to those of evacuees and their generous allowances compared to British pensioners'. Great War moans of the Belgians' butter- and cheese-gluttony were revived once more. But one new grievance was also laid at their door: that Belgian refugees were taking up cross-Channel berths that should have been used to evacuate the BEF from Dunkirk.[7]

The surrender of Belgium and the accelerated German advance into France that followed pushed the British and French forces almost into the sea. The near-fatal position of the BEF was kept largely hidden from public view, but the necessity for a hasty evacuation by every available boat gained wide currency. In the First World War the results of such a crisis would have been immediately felt in the capital, with casualties brought from France to central London's railway termini and hospitals. Now, though, the central hospitals were kept empty, still waiting for air raid casualties, and the drama of Dunkirk would at first be a near calamity that took place largely behind Londoners' backs. They knew that something was happening nonetheless. 'Laurie rather late coming in,' wrote an anxious Godfrey Clarke about his civil servant sister, 'as trains were delayed at Addison Road – owing to troop trains & Hospital trains passing through.' That was 29 May. Next day Nellie Carver, on her way to work in the City, recorded that she:

Had a most wonderful experience this morning as I was waiting on Dulwich Station. Down the line, towards the coast, ran many empty trains – GWR LNER LMS as well as Southern. While I was gazing in amazement at them, on the up line came train after train of Troops – carriages simply bulging with them – one after another, the men, tired-looking & dirty. Those near the windows were hanging out & cheering. The porter told me this had been going on for hours today & all through the previous night. There were several elderly business men on my platform & as the trains passed they rose from their seats & took off their hats to these marvellous boys. They were looking back at us as though they had never expected to see England again. [At work she found the Telegraph Office] absolutely flooded with B.E.F. Traffic, hundreds & hundreds must have been brought back! In the Evening Papers were full accounts, pictures of the Evacuation from Dunkirk. It seems like a Miracle, all the little boats to Volunteer. What a triumph for Britain! Cannot think of this as a defeat.[8]

'Except in Kent,' the historian of Britain's wartime railways has written, 'the people of Britain knew little of what was going on until the afternoon of June 4,' when the Prime Minister announced the astonishing success of the evacuation to the House of Commons. But Londoners in the south-east suburbs had a plain view and so did the Emergency Medical Service staff in the outer reaches of London's hospital sectors. Mary Mulry, from County Galway in Eire, a nurse in training at Guy's, had been evacuated to the Kent and Sussex Hospital near Tunbridge Wells, where beds were cleared for the incoming wounded. The casualty ward was filled with 'wet, dirty and injured people' laid out in stretchers on the floor. Mary helped nurse the victims of oil burns like Private Brian Mullins, who was about eighteen:

my age. His face and hands have been sprayed with tannic acid, which has set into a hard black cement. His arms are propped up in front of him on a pillow, the fingers extended like claws and his naked body hangs loosely on straps just clear of the bed. His eyelids are coated with a thick layer of gentian violet and we give him morphia every three hours.

Even hospitals to the north of London were affected, High Barnet Hospital taking in 'French soldiers & moroccans,' as Nurse Gwen Rennie later recalled. On 3 June, at the height of the crisis, nursing staff hours in London Region were increased from forty-eight per week to fifty-eight, night staff's to sixty: 'We are all prepared to do what we can,' a nursing sister at Highgate Hospital noted in her diary.[9]

London helped out in other ways too. Among the small ships and boats that had sailed to France, the LFB's fire boat the *Massey Shaw*, named after the brigade's founding chief, made three trips to Dunkirk, returning to Ramsgate each time with ninety-six men and transferring 500 more to larger vessels. She returned to London on 12 June to a heroine's welcome from cheering crowds on the riverbanks. Other small boats, the procession led by vessels pulled in convoy by a tug, had had a similar rousing reception the Sunday before.[10]

George Orwell visited Waterloo Station in the midst of the evacuation expecting to find the BEF, but there were 'very few', with far more French and Belgian soldiers and yet more refugees, 'mostly middling people of the shop-keeper-clerk type, and ... in quite good trim, with a certain amount of personal belongings'. There were a few sailors and 'naval types' too; these were 'enthusiastically cheered', while the 'refugees were greeted in silence'. The undercurrent of hostility to people welcomed before their king 'deserted the British' was palpable, Orwell thought. Perhaps too there was a feeling that these refugees were coming into a city that did not need strangers in its midst when Londoners themselves appeared to be in mortal danger. For once the Dunkirk crisis had ended, a new phase of evacuation of mothers and children from London was organised. Some 61,000 schoolchildren were evacuated from London County between 13 and 18 June. That was not as many as had been hoped and a lot of these were soon brought back by their parents, some as early as July. There was a feeling, popular among London mothers, that their city was as safe as anywhere now that the whole country, and especially the coasts, were in peril. And in some places – Islington, for instance – mothers remembered how they and their children had been treated during the September 1939 evacuation and were reluctant to try it again.[11]

Although the official domestic scheme was hardly a success, others were making haste to get their children as far away as possible. Americans had begun to leave after the embassy called for their return – not all, by any means, although it looked like that to the US journalist Ben Robertson as he saw off the 'last train' from Euston 'for the last American ship ... Practically every American in London was there,' taking 'mountains of baggage with them; they had practically everything, including dogs and canary-birds'. In mid-June the War Cabinet endorsed a similar escape route for parents who wanted to send their children to safety in Canada and other Dominion countries. There was a rush to take advantage. The Children's Overseas Reception Scheme, run from Thomas Cook's former headquarters in Berkeley Square, had some 3,000 parents queueing round the block by 10 a.m. on the day the scheme opened. Around 210,000 children were nominated, of whom it was thought some 94 per cent were from working-class families. In the end the scheme shipped out just 2,662, 1,530 of them to Canada; a further 838 left for the USA 'unofficially'. Selection seems to have favoured the well-heeled, or perhaps the rich just found their own way out. 'Chips' Channon, the American-born socialite Tory MP, sent his son Paul, not quite five, with a nanny to Canada: at Euston 'there was a queue of Rolls-Royces and liveried servants and mountains of trunks. It seemed that everyone we knew was there ...' There were risks, of course. A Dutch vessel, *Volendam*, carrying 321 children, was torpedoed off Ireland; all were saved. But on the *City of Benares*, sunk in mid-September, some ninety children were lost, effectively bringing the scheme to an end.[12]

Paul Channon's mother and father remained in London, but others among the middle classes and above moved out altogether. From May through the summer there was a replay of the previous September, reversing the pattern of the pre-Christmas period when many had come back from the country. Anxious people with the necessary funds were keen to take themselves off, but now things were complicated. Just where would be safe? Hilda Neal's friend Mabel – 'the thought of bombs worries her to death' – risked the less certain of two evils and went to Exmouth but F. Tennyson Jesse's friend, who had sent a daughter to Wales, had now heard that 'was very unsafe' and 'didn't know what to do for the best'. But whatever the destination, the wealthier parts of London were looking deserted once more. 'I shopped a little in an almost deserted Harrods,' Colonel Raymond Lee, military attaché at the US Embassy, recorded in June; Eaton Square, where he'd lived before the war, 'is practically uninhabited except for Queen Wilhelmina'. 'Curzon and Clarges Streets struck me as very derelict, as many houses unoccupied,' thought Hilda Neal when she went to Mayfair to deliver a typescript to a client, and Anthony Weymouth 'noticed shop after shop in the Hanover Square neighbourhood which was empty. Where there used to be rows of cars lined up by the pavements, today there are none – or very few.' Even in the Savoy Grill the tables had been reduced in number and those which remained were half empty. This new evacuation of the London rich had benefits for those left behind. Theodora Fitzgibbon, a Chelsea painter with not too much cash in her purse, could rent a four-roomed mansion flat, 'fully, if drably, furnished', for £2 a week: 'Rents had dropped considerably owing to the evacuation of many people to the country ...' And the journalist Robert Henrey, who had brought his wife and baby son from France in a rush and was now looking for somewhere larger to live, found 'West-End flats were at a discount.' He rented a bargain in 'a great cement and steel building just off Piccadilly' with lifts and a roof garden; many flats were empty there.[13]

MOST Londoners, through choice or necessity, stayed on. The population in June 1940 was thought to be over a million fewer than before the war, but that was still some 89 per cent of the peacetime number. It meant that around 7.5 million people were having to face up to the likelihood of bombing and the possibility of invasion. Some resolved to stand and fight. On 14 May, Anthony Eden, the War Minister, had broadcast for volunteers to help repel an airborne invasion, should one come. In London, as in many other places, enrolment in the Local Defence Volunteers (LDV), as they were quickly named, was rapid and keen. Like ARP, the LDV was an intensely local affair. It was frequently based on the workplace. The London Passenger Transport Board was able to mobilise six battalions in May 1940 for the defence of bus and tube stations; the BBC's Broadcasting House formed its own LDV for the security of the building; the Metropolitan Water Board's LDV companies looked after reservoirs, the PLA's the docks and wharves and so on. But fundamentally the LDV was based on the neighbourhood. George Orwell, one of the Spanish Civil War veterans whose expertise was especially valued in the LDV, was made a sergeant in C Company, 5th London Battalion (St John's Wood). 'What I do not yet know,' he wrote at the end of June, 'is whether there has been any tendency to avoid raising L.D.V. contingents in very poor districts where the whole direction would have to be in working-class hands.' He needn't have worried. London's poorer boroughs were full of patriotic Great War veterans who sped to join the battalions of Bermondsey, Kennington, Shoreditch and so on. At first arms were in very short supply, but they arrived for distribution in St John's Wood and elsewhere in early July, ageing US army rifles still coated in the grease of 1918. They were intended for use: 'You may rest assured,' wrote Winston Churchill to an MP, 'that we should fight every street of London and its suburbs. It would devour an invading army, assuming one ever got so far.'[14]

By the time the guns arrived, the second great shock of the war so far brought the threat of invasion uncomfortably nearer. On 17 June, Hilda Neal:

Met Sallie for lunch at Army & Navy Stores. When we came out we saw the staggering news on placards:
THE FRENCH HAVE STOPPED FIGHTING!!!
It seemed unbelievable after all they had been through ... People seemed thunderstruck. Men's faces looked grey, worn, haggard; their eyes staring unbelievably in distance ... England is now left to fight the Battle of the World against Hitler & the evil forces that he has in his train. Long live the King! Each day now we wonder if it will be our last.[15]

Hilda put her faith in God, but for Nellie Carver the astonishing news had some consolation:

The very worst has happened. France asks for an Armistice – so now – what? The predominant feeling is one of relief. Now we know where we are. I'm absolutely sure that we can do better if we have nobody with us. They have let us down time & time again – now we can really get on with the job. Am afraid to say this aloud, at first, as it sounds so awful, but as the day goes on, I hear it again & again from our own folk all over the office. They are fighting mad but not in the least afraid.[16]

That same day in North Kensington, Godfrey Clarke noted, 'Air Raid Shelters now being erected in the streets here with feverish haste', for London Region's ARP – despite the panic of Munich, the declaration of war and two months or so of hot conflict – still had much catching up to do. In February a survey had revealed that the shelters at London's mainline railway stations were 'totally insufficient' for the numbers likely to need them. In May the relevant borough councils were asked to expand them with railway company help, but work only got under way in July, five months after the problem was identified; it was far from finished by September. In the boroughs themselves progress was uneven, but all in the right direction. Go-ahead Hackney began a shelter-building programme for its housing estate tenants in April, sophisticated structures with electric air conditioning and lighting, wooden seats, water supply and first aid rooms. Poplar claimed in August that shelter was available for 97 per cent of the borough's population; street shelters were provided with chemical closets, although the government thought these an unaffordable luxury and refused to pay for them. *Picture Post* advised its readers that 'Civilians can club together to buy' chemical closets at 50s a time, each one adequate for twenty persons, and suggested they do so. There were similar problems putting lights and seats in public shelters: Camberwell was refused permission by the Home Office to install them; under pressure, the government relented in shelters for over fifty persons. The Home Secretary – still Sir John Anderson, reappointed by Winston Churchill on 12 May – said, 'it was not thought probable that the shelters will be occupied for hours at a time, but he would be prepared to reconsider the question of seating if experience proves it necessary.' West Ham had been considered by London Civil Defence Region its 'weakest spot', but even here an official inspection in early July recorded progress, with 'good accommodation' for ARP depots and first aid posts. In mid-August the borough claimed to have shelters in place for over 200,000, with more being built. But the bulk of provision in West Ham, some 80 per cent, was in Andersons, even though ground conditions were often very wet; of some 29,000 Andersons just 6,000 had been concreted by the council.[17]

In only a few boroughs were large bomb-proof shelters available and, ironically given the government's approach to using the underground for shelter, these were in tunnels or stations under construction for the unfinished Central Line, from Bethnal Green through Leyton to Ilford, and in a disused tube tunnel, half a mile long and seventy feet deep, entered from Borough High Street, Southwark. The 'Southwark Tunnel' was planned from December 1939 and intended to shelter 14,000 people 'without crowding'. These tunnels would be available from the summer of 1940, and only just in time. In all, at the beginning of August, the shortfall in shelters left over a million Londoners unprovided for.[18]

At the end of July, Home Secretary Anderson ordered householders to take out all movable objects from lofts and attics used for storage as a precaution against incendiaries; the enforcement of this instruction, impossible to police in London, was put on the shoulders of already overburdened local authorities. And it was only about now that some people began to take seriously their own shelter needs. The Cockett family at Brakespears Road, Deptford, began clearing out the cellar at the end of June: 'Looks quite good now,' Olivia thought, 'one end clear, two very strong wooden uprights in ... and lots of whitewash.' It had electric lighting and they planned to bring up folding chairs from their holiday chalet near Southend. At the home of Doreen Bates, thirty-four, a tax inspector living with her mother and sister at Riddlesdown, Croydon, 'a man and a boy' began making an air raid shelter in early August; though the walls weren't up yet her mother was 'beginning to feel a sense of security which is ample compensation for the cost'. And on Dorothy Wells's fortieth birthday – 'not a very cheerful one' – her next-door neighbour in Osterley Park View Road, Hanwell, had 'built a wall to reinforce our [shared] shelter and padded it with "Sisalkraft" sandbags', Sisalkraft being the building paper that her employers, Sankey's, manufactured. 'It looks so good we are rather afraid the Council will commandeer it as a defence post.' And all over working-class London handymen laboured to make their Andersons homely, with seats or bunks and duckboard flooring, and running in electric light from the mains.[19]

Others were gearing up too. In July a force of 1,000 AFS 'messenger boys' on motorcycles was established in London to run messages during raids. That same month borough ARP services were encouraging a new spirit of solidarity by organising local parades with flags and music. Some 1,700 'men and women volunteers paraded to the music of four bands' at Peckham Rye and at Deptford 1,000 volunteers and eighty cars formed a procession a mile long: ARP, AFS and the auxiliary ambulance service were joined by 'the Mayor's own Home Guard Company', as the LDV were now called. These resources were boosted by the WVS (Women's Voluntary Services, this a war of acronyms), organised on a borough by borough basis since May 1938 and growing ever since. Established by Lady Reading, the WVS frequently had an upper-middle-class make-up but that didn't stop them getting their hands dirty and by 1940 they were everywhere. In proletarian West Ham, for instance, the WVS were ensconced in the council's ARP head-quarters, knitting pullovers and socks for evacuated children; Beckenham WVS had 'adopted' West Ham and were helping in the task. In another poor and vulnerable borough, Stepney, the WVS opened a centre in Commercial Road that June.[20]

Also in the East End, civilian resources were coming together in new ways. East Ham's Mutual Aid for Good Neighbours' Association (MAGNA – 'magnanimous' was perhaps in someone's mind) was formed in July, inspired by 'the little boats of Dunkirk', to 'band people together in each road so that in the event of air attack they can give simple first aid, quench fires, report damage and casualties, guide and comfort those whose homes have been wrecked', and so on; 'it is hoped that the spirit will remain when raids are a thing of the past'. Within a fortnight 6,522 had signed up to be 'guardians one of another'.[21]

No doubt MAGNA would have been mobilised in the event of invasion, for as it was formed there was another scare, with 19 July the favoured date for Hitler's forces to land in England. There had been many such danger signals sounded since the invasion of France and they multiplied and grew louder with her fall. From the beginning of those tense weeks, Hilda Neal expressed what many were thinking: 'The world seems full of evil; subversive forces seem to be impelling us on to destruction.'[22]

This notion of subversion, of the 'Trojan Horse' or 'Fifth Column', had roused widespread anxiety through the activities of the Norwegian fascist leader, Vidkun Quisling, who had unsuccessfully attempted a coup to establish a pro-German government on the night of 9 April, just hours after the German invasion. Quisling's treachery may have brought a new word into the English language but in Britain the lexicon was already full enough, the capacity for subversion multilayered. There were many suspects.

First and largest came the group of 'enemy aliens', German- or Austrian-born people living in Britain, the bulk of whom, perhaps 70,000 strong, were Jewish refugees who had fled Nazism from 1933 and especially since 1938. The large majority of these lived in the northwest London suburbs of Hampstead, Golders Green, Swiss Cottage and Finchley and were predominantly middle-class professionals, often well-to-do. There was also a relatively small number of non-Jewish political refugees from fascism and some other German and Austrian nationals who were politically neutral or actively pro-Nazi. This substantial number of enemy aliens was increased by some 10,000 Italians when Mussolini joined the war against Britain and France on 10 June.[23]

There were also many British nationals whose loyalty was suspect. They fell into three groups. First, Nazi sympathisers, including members of fascist parties, the biggest of which was Sir Oswald Mosley's British Union of Fascists (BUF), with many members in London, especially in the East End. There were also fellow travellers with similar views if less outspoken – we might put Anthony Heap among their number. Second, members of the Communist Party of Great Britain (CPGB), who at this time opposed what they called an 'imperialist war' as a direct result of the Hitler–Stalin pact of August 1939. Lastly, pacifists of many complexions who opposed any war as offending their conscience, often for religious convictions or a socialist belief in the brotherhood of man. Many fascists, communists and pacifists actively campaigned against the war through propaganda of one kind or another – newspapers, pamphlets and leaflets, street meetings, chalking or whitewashing slogans on walls and pavements and so on. This anti-war coalition had been widespread and highly visible in London since September 1939.

With an energetic and united coalition government in place from 10 May 1940, possessed of the urgency of Britain's vulnerability to invasion, the position of all these potentially subversive elements came under close scrutiny. In the First World War there had been an unflagging agitation from the very beginning to intern all 'alien enemies' irrespective of sex or age which many, in hindsight, viewed with a deep sense of shame. The Second World War had begun very differently. Sir John Anderson, as the first wartime Home Secretary, established a series of tribunals to review the allegiance of over 73,000 enemy aliens: just 569 were interned. Even so, among them were Jewish refugees who had attracted security service interest, apparently because they were active anti-fascists and so seen as politically suspect. These 600 or so 'Category A' aliens, seen for whatever reason as a threat and interned, were dwarfed by Category B (some 6,800 whose loyalty could not be guaranteed) and Category C, over 62,000 exempted from internment, their allegiance to Britain not in doubt; 55,457 of these were 'refugees from Nazi oppression', mainly the Jews of north-west London.[24]

That was the position still on 9 May 1940. In the next few days everything would change when stories of fifth column activities in Holland circulated in the press and among Dutch refugees. Fears of an immediate invasion (Churchill anticipated German paratroopers would land from 15 May, apparently) prompted the internment of male enemy aliens living along the east and south-east coasts and then, in an escalation of anxiety, of all men in Categories B and C aged eighteen to seventy and some women. Italian enemy aliens were added from 10 June. In all, in this hectic month, some 4,000 women and 23,000 men were seized and interned without trial, most of them refugees from Nazi Germany and Austria or, in the case of Italians, men and women who had lived in London sometimes for a generation and more. Of these numbers around 7,000 were sent abroad, the rest held in camps, most notably on the Isle of Man.[25]

In general the arrest, processing and imprisonment of internees were all markedly more humane in 1940 than in the First World War. There were, though, discomforts. Eugen Spier, a religious Jewish refugee, was arrested by two Scotland Yard detectives on 1 September 1939 for reasons that were entirely unclear to him. He was denied access to a lawyer and rushed to Olympia, entering through a guard of soldiers with rifles and fixed bayonets. There he was told he was 'Prisoner of War No. 2', though war had not yet been declared; he discovered that No. 1 was a staunch Nazi who introduced himself as Baron von Pillar. In the morning Spier woke to find himself amid a hundred or so Germans. Most were Nazis but there were Jews among them, mainly left-wingers. Within a few days they were moved by train to the former Butlin's holiday camp at Clacton, invasion at that time not thought likely. After a spell at another camp in England, Spier was shipped to Canada in the summer of 1940; released in 1941, he returned to London. Eva Maierhof, born in 1914 to a Jewish family in Frankfurt, fled to London just after Hitler's rise to power in 1933. She was interned in July 1940 as part of the great round-up and felt well treated by the women police officers who arrested her. She was taken to Holloway Prison, where she was made at home by fellow Jewish internees and was allowed to use the down-filled sleeping bag sent by her mother. In the autumn she was taken to Rushen Internment Camp on the Isle of Man, along with the rest of the Holloway contingent.[26]

Most Jewish refugees remained undisturbed in London. Klara Modern, born in Vienna in 1913, came to London in 1936, though most of her family emigrated to America. In mid-1938 she moved to Belsize Park, Hampstead, at the heart of the refugee community, and by Christmas 1939 had been awarded Category C status. From April 1940 she and her Dutch-born lover, Otto van der Sprenkel, a post-graduate student at the London School of Economics, rented the attic floor of 44 Belsize Park Gardens. Klara was part of an Austrian refugee elite who had established before the war a vibrant cultural centre in Paddington, known especially for its musical life. Klara worked as a freelance in the book trade during her pre-war days in London. From early 1940 she was a volunteer social worker with the Charity Organisation Society, assisting poor families with financial and other support, including the evacuation of toddlers to foster homes in the country. She was not untroubled by internment because a friend, Hans Striesow, an 'Aryan German' though with a Jewish wife, was nabbed and sent away early in 1940; he became suicidal at the turn of events. Klara agitated for his release through the Society of Friends, and perhaps wondered if she was vulnerable to arrest herself. But in July she rejected the opportunity offered by her absent family to move to New York: 'I have at present not the slightest intention to leave this country,' she wrote to them. 'As long as the war lasts, and it may be many years, I will stay here and do everything I can possibly do, to the extent of my meagre abilities, to help England and smash Hitler.'[27]

Otto, Klara's lover, worked in ARP and, as a naturalised British subject educated in London, was above suspicion. Enemy aliens, though, were summarily thrown out by many authorities after May 1940 on receipt of government advice that they should be suspended pending investigation. Even before that, Marylebone dismissed all enemy aliens (eleven Germans, six Austrians and five stateless persons) from its ARP services; Paddington followed suit soon afterwards and there were doubtless many more.[28]

There was no collective violence against Germans and Austrians in London, in sharp contrast to the anti-German riots of 1915. But when Mussolini hitched himself to the swastika on 10 June 1940, an outburst of indignation that evening expressed itself in window-breaking in Soho, the main Italian restaurant district of London. Though distressing for those on the receiving end, it was brief and not extensive – just three businesses attacked, it seems. There was also some window-breaking in Poplar, and in Cable Street, Stepney, a man of Italian extraction was abused by a crowd for posting pro-Italian posters – he was fined 10s. London was gratifyingly free from the anti-Catholic sympathies that drove much nastier and more prolonged episodes against the Italians in Liverpool and in Scotland. The rioting did, though, hasten a roundup of London Italians. Elena Salvoni was born in 1920, her immigrant parents living on Eyre Street Hill, Holborn, then the epicentre of London's old-established Little Italy. Her father, originally an asphalter, was interned in July 1940 despite having two sons in the British Army. 'Our English neighbours', in south Islington, where they had lived since 1933, 'never shunned or distrusted us, they were kind and concerned, but the newspapers were horrible with constant references to "the Fifth Column in our midst."'[29]

A backlash against the indiscriminate imprisonment without trial of so many people who had fled Nazi oppression to seek refuge in Britain began to make itself heard as early as July 1940. Protests and lobbying came too late for some. Among the 7,000 or so interned aliens shipped to the dominions were 734 Italian and 479 German internees who sailed on the *Arandora Star*, bound for Canada. It was torpedoed on 2 July 1940 with the loss of 805 passengers and crew; 868 were rescued, but deaths among the Italians were particularly severe. Among them were said to be no fewer than 'a score' of former waiters from the Savoy, the managers of the Savoy and Ritz restaurants, numerous prominent restaurant owners, the general manager of the Piccadilly Hotel and more. A (British) Savoy director summed it up: 'Most of the best brains in the English hotel business, managers and head waiters have been drowned. They were, almost to a man, kindly, inoffensive beings.' 'West End Will See Them No More' was the headline over Hannen Swaffer's influential column in the *Daily Herald*. The internment pressure relented within days. Release of non- and anti-fascist alien internees was speeded up through July and August 1940 and after.[30]

Home-grown fascists would have longer to wait. Fascists had been active in London ever since the declaration of war. Their platform was anti-Semitism and their propaganda was urged in chalking slogans on walls and pavements ('It's a Jew's War' was a favourite), pasting leaflets on walls and lamp posts, selling the BUF newspaper, *Action*, and public meetings, usually in the streets. These last were especially common in Dalston, Hackney, at Ridley Road (where a lively street market was held with many Jewish traders) and nearby John Campbell Road, where (one case among many) Frederick Young, forty, a fish fryer from Walthamstow, was arrested for claiming that Jews 'are all tucked away in nice safe A.R.P. jobs at home'. Sir Oswald Mosley's message was much the same: 'We were fighting for the investments of Jewish financiers,' he told a meeting at the Public Hall, Canning Town, in February 1940. That was during the Silvertown, West Ham, by-election, which gave the BUF a rare opportunity to field a candidate and raise their profile nationally. They polled disastrously, with just 151 votes against the Labour candidate's 14,343.[31]

Mosley and the BUF leadership, not just anti-war but actively pro-Nazi, were interned on 23 and 24 May with a number of other enthusiasts for Hitler, including a Scottish Tory MP; a couple of weeks later *Action* was shut down. Fascists represented a genuine fifth column threat, in the mould of Quisling and the Dutch collaborators, and their internment was an immensely popular move. Although Anthony Heap complained of a 'great democratic sham', he was in a small minority: 'quite time, too!' thought Hilda Neal in South Kensington, herself no lover of the Jews. Yet surreptitious fascist activity was continued in London by the smaller fry so far left alone, or by activists not yet found out. In the summer of 1940 there was a rash of prosecutions for advertising the 'New British Broadcasting Station', a German propaganda network, by means of 'sticky-back' leaflets. Prison sentences were handed out at the Old Bailey in July, including a mother and son living in Kynaston Road, Stoke Newington – she received twelve months; Wilfred Freeman, twenty-one, a railway porter, was given five years. Another man, a twenty-seven-year-old accountant from Whetstone in north London, was more repentant and got six months.[32]

A communist had also stood with the fascists against Labour in the Silvertown by-election earlier in the year. This was not just any communist but Harry Pollitt, formerly (and soon to be again) CPGB general secretary. He also ran on an anti-war ticket, just like the BUF man, because Stalin was actively aiding and abetting Hitler at this stage of proceedings: Pollitt's claim that the Soviets were 'liberating Finland', having invaded it in November 1939, must have infuriated many. Despite the CPGB having deep roots in east London, Pollitt polled fewer than a thousand votes. When the invasion scares multiplied from May, communists were seen as less of a fifth column threat than the fascists if only because they knew what would happen to them should Hitler invade. Even so, party members continued to pursue an active anti-war agenda which landed many agitators in hot water. To give one example among many, two communists were sentenced to one and two months for distributing anti-war leaflets to tenants on the LCC's Downham Estate in Lewisham in July 1940; they generated an angry crowd – 'I don't want papers like that put in my doors in these times,' one man told them, and 'Put them in the front line,' suggested another.[33]

Communist opposition to the war infected the left wing of the Labour Party in some London boroughs. A local Labour councillor stood against his own party at the Southwark parliamentary by-election in February 1940 on a 'Stop the War' ticket. Councillor Searson admitted communist aid for his campaign; he split the Southwark Labour Party and succeeded in siphoning off a number of similarly minded councillors from the Labour group in nearby north Lambeth. Stop the War polled 1,550 against Labour's 5,285, a National Independent candidate coming third with 1,382. Searson's vote was seen as a great blow to 'the "Stop-the-War" Movement' as peace campaigners had come from all over the country to canvass for him, besides the help he received from local Labour rebels and communists.[34]

Pacifism had always received a sympathetic hearing within the Labour movement. Boroughs like Bermondsey, where nationally renowned coun-cillors Alfred and Ada Salter had long opposed war, had great difficulty adopting an ARP programme, even after Munich and the declaration of war, because of the powerful pacifist lobby within the council's ranks. Pacifism had not been an easy option in the First World War, when some conscientious objectors (COs) had been treated with great brutality. Even in this war, many pacifists had their objections discountenanced by tribunals and ended up in prison or a military glasshouse. Attitudes hardened after 10 May and an intolerant press and public – with whom 'conchies' had never been popular – grew punitive in their demands for action to be taken against them as fifth columnists. On 24 May 200 workers at a Bermondsey council depot threatened to strike unless a temporary worker, 'said to be a conscientious objector', was dismissed. At first the council pledged not to discriminate against COs, but next month, in a vociferous anti-pacifist reaction fuelled by the state of the war, resolved to sack them all. Wandsworth had already done so, and Deptford and Southwark would have done but said they didn't employ any as far as they knew. North of the river, Kensington, Shoreditch and Stoke Newington, among others, did the same. The LCC, where its long-time leader Herbert Morrison had been a famous CO during the First World War, took no action against them: 'LCC Conchies Keep Their Jobs' ran a headline in the South London Press. But in general, the climate everywhere in London was now seen as actively hostile to the peace message: 'Anti-War organisations of South London made a strategic withdrawal this week because of public intolerance of pacifist propaganda,' it was said at the beginning of June. Paper sellers and open-air speakers now risked violence from locals and were arrested and charged for causing a breach of the peace: two young Peace Pledge Union activists were given five weeks in prison for handing out 'Stop the War' leaflets in Paddington, for instance, in one case among many.[35]

THROUGHOUT the tense months of May and June 1940, and despite Hitler's astonishing victories across continental Europe, it seemed as though most Londoners never wavered in their confident belief that Britain and its empire would win the war against Nazi Germany. Not everyone, of course: Olivia Cockett, talking over prospects with her married lover, 'agreed, quite cheerfully, that we expect an awful time and couldn't see how we could possibly win: but that we must keep cheerful'. Most people, though, seem to have felt like Nellie Carver and her colleagues, 'fighting mad but not in the least afraid'. Verily Anderson, briefly in London after the fall of France, found 'an extraordinary mood of exultation', a 'strange soaring of spirits … The combined sense of danger and of unity was exhilarating.'[36]

On the evening before 17 June, according to Home Office intelligence, many in London 'generally anticipated the capitulation of France. The West End was filled with people last night going to cinemas, with a general air of expectancy.' And once it had happened Londoners continued to go about their pleasures uninhibited by the turn of events. On the day France fell, Godfrey Clarke took in a whist drive at Kilburn on his afternoon off and that evening 'Laurie & I went & saw "Chu Chin Chow"', one of the great hits of the First World War, 'up at Golders Green Hippodrome. Most enjoyable Sydney Farebrother [sic] still playing the original part!!' That June, Walt Disney's *Pinocchio* was another of those films that Londoners saw at least once: 'The little cat Figaro was lovely and Monstro the Whale was marvellous,' Rhona Little thought. Though Anthony Heap felt these were 'dire days for theatre-goers', with just ten houses open and new productions on hold, and although both Whitsun and August bank holidays were cancelled for workers to focus on the war effort, Heap found Hampstead Heath heaving on what would have been Bank Holiday Monday, 5 August: 'The fair in full swing with people everywhere.' Dorothy Wells was made a little nervous by invasion scares forecast at intervals through June, July and August – 'We have never known invasion, and we have a ghastly time before us' – but she found her Ealing tennis club 'crowded with light-hearted youngsters' the day after France capitulated; she too soon became preoccupied by her tournament progress that summer. August also would see the first of the big savings campaigns, encouraging people to buy war bonds and so lend the government money to win the war. They were run on a borough by borough basis that would become such a feature of London's war. Poplar's 'Savings Week', for instance, netted £25,000, enough, it was thought, to build five Spitfires.[37]

*

AFTER Dunkirk and the fall of France, the *Daily Express* journalist Hilde Marchant noted how 'an unusual word came into our language. We were "citizens". It was a change from being the public – it had a ring of defiance about it. We were at the barricades, the last barricades of Europe.' By late June 1940 London had indeed become the capital of Free Europe. The governments in exile of Czechoslovakia and Holland were settled in London by the end of May. Days before France asked for an armistice they were joined by Norway, its king and government brought by HMS *Devonshire* from Tromsø on 10 June. A week later and General Charles de Gaulle escaped to London on 17 June and broadcast on the BBC to France the day after Pétain's radio announcement of his country's surrender. The Polish government in exile had established itself in Paris, where it had never been formally recognised by the French. It now found itself threatened once more by the German juggernaut. As France capitulated, the Polish government, under General Sikorski, made its way to London on 18 June; the remnants of its army fled to Britain, mainly to Scotland, many Polish airmen already fighting with the RAF. Over the next twelve months all these would be joined by the governments in exile of Belgium, Yugoslavia and Greece and, according to the *New Yorker* correspondent in London at the time, by 'a half-dozen semi-recognized national movements, free Danish, free Rumanian, free Bulgarian and free Austrian'.[38]

It was not just Free Europe that found itself assembled in London. Dominion troops and related services from Canada, New Zealand and Australia were all highly visible from that summer of 1940; and some of those Americans who had defied their ambassador's urgings to flee had organised themselves in London's defence in an American Home Guard, their uniforms sporting 'red eagles on their arms'. The general dislocation in Europe had also brought in more refugees: from France, especially Jews fleeing a Nazi invasion bringing with it certain persecution and perhaps death; and 11,000 Gibraltarians, brought to London in the mistaken notion that they would be safer there than on their rock fortress, were moved into flats in Kensington and Fulham.[39]

All these movements filled to some extent the vacuum left by evacuation in the great town houses and apartment blocks of west London, areas favoured by embassies pre-war. So the Polish Embassy in Portland Place – 'our own neighbourhood,' as the ambassador put it – now became the centre of the government in exile, though many Poles had to put up with a 'reception camp' in the Fulham Road on first arrival;

later the Polish government would fill many mansions in Kensington, Belgravia and elsewhere. The Norwegians – besides King Haakon, who stayed for a time at Buckingham Palace – settled in the City at Cornhill, where they had a shipping and trade mission; when they were bombed out in the autumn they took over half a dozen flats in a modern block (Kingston House) at Knightsbridge, eventually occupying forty-five flats there. When the administration expanded to 2,500 employees they spilled out into Bloomsbury hotels and Kensington mansions. The Dutch government in exile was 'administered by hundreds upon hundreds of Netherlanders in Stratton House, Arlington House and other impressive government buildings' around Piccadilly, while Queen Wilhelmina moved from Eaton Square to a town house in Chester Square, Belgravia. Free French London was also firmly based in west London, from Soho to Earl's Court, Kensington, its headquarters in 4 Carlton Gardens, north of St James's Park; de Gaulle himself moved to a modest suburban house, 41 Birchwood Road, Petts Wood, Orpington. In October, the Belgian government arrived after sojourns in France and Spain, settling in Eaton Square, home to its embassy before the war.[40]

These momentous movements of power and people altered the face of London. They brought new colour to the streets and fresh zest to the Londoner. 'London is an extraordinary place in this pause between battles,' thought the critic and publisher John Lehmann in early July. 'On the streets and in the pubs you see Canadian, Australian, New Zealand soldiers; French sailors, air-officers, legionnaires; Dutch officers, Norwegian and Dutch sailors; Poles and Czechs ... It quickens one's interest and excitement in the moment; it seems almost impossible to contemplate that one should fail them all.' 'Last night I mouched around the West End,' wrote Colin Perry, a Wandsworth teenager, at the end of that month. 'Czech, French, Polish, Dutch, Norwegian uniforms, with pilots, sailors and soldiers everywhere. Yes, it was all gay.'[41]

BUT gay for how much longer? Not long, surely, for by the time Perry wrote, the Battle of Britain, with Luftwaffe attacks on RAF airfields, had already brought the war to London's door. The first bombs on Greater London fell on the outskirts of the village of Addington, Croydon, 'in the early hours' of Wednesday 19 June – six high-explosive (HE) bombs thought to be '50kg or larger. The damage done was negligible', with some windows blown out and roof tiles dislodged. This appears to have been random misfortune or an unsuccessful effort to bomb Croydon Airport some four miles away. Not far from Addington, on 25 June, the air raid siren – or 'Dismal Jimmy', as Arthur Buddell called it – sounded just after midnight: 'We got up "according to plan" and took up "air raid station" in cupboard under stairs. Mary was in good fettle & played Tiddly winks & Ludo. Her doll, of course, took refuge with us. Warning lasted until 3.45am. No bombs, no guns audible.' That was a false alarm, but the edge of London would be peppered with light bombing through July – at Kenley airfield (Caterham), Enfield, Banstead, Barking, Walton-on-Thames, Dagenham, Thames Ditton and elsewhere. London Region's first fatalities of the war through enemy action were an AFS man, Jim Roberts, and Mrs Jane Page, seventy-six, in the same incident at Loughton, Epping Forest, on 26 July.[42]

In early August there was a variation. Instead of bombs, leaflets containing a translation of Hitler's recent Reichstag speech, in which he had raised the possibility of peace negotiations, were dropped in the Waltham Abbey area and St Mary Cray in Kentish London. When Hitler's gesture was contemptuously rejected by Churchill, then the bombing began again, but this time with more serious intent. The first violent attack of London's war was on Croydon Airport and the nearby aeroplane and other factories on the evening of 15 August. Some sixty-two were killed and others seriously injured, though rumours of much higher casualties swept the capital, a frequent occurrence in the years to come. First reports from the scene recorded that '"major parts" of human bodies had been retrieved, which confirmed the old view that bombs did not kill cleanly'. On the following Saturday, Colin Perry cycled over with a friend to see the damage for himself, a habit of blitz-tourism that many other Londoners would adopt in subsequent months. There then followed what were considered in these early days to be 'heavy raids' against outer London on the 16th (Merton and Colliers Wood), 18th (Woolwich and Eltham), 23rd (Edmonton, Woodford, Willesden and Dollis Hill, which received London's first oil bomb) and 24th (a light raid on Chigwell and Barkingside).[43]

On the night of 24/5 August, bombs were dropped for the first time on central London, apparently in error as the target was meant to be Rochester and the Thames estuary. Incendiaries and HE bombs fell on the City (where the church of St Giles Cripplegate was a prominent early casualty) and inner suburbs, with nine deaths and over a hundred made homeless in Bethnal Green. There was an immediate reply from the RAF, which bombed the outskirts of Berlin the following night. The

Luftwaffe's revenge quickly followed. Next night (26/7 August), central London received its first all-night raid, lasting from 11.20 p.m. to 5.20 a.m.; here, then, was the first inkling that shelters would indeed 'be occupied for hours at a time'. With the exception of 2 and 4 September, there would then be raids on London of varying severity by day and by night. Bombs fell mainly on the suburbs but also on three further occasions on central London and the inner East End. Through one of history's little ironies, 1 Allison Grove, Dulwich Common (Camberwell), was partly demolished in a raid on 29 August. It was occupied by 'Mr and Mrs Michael Joyce'; their son William was Lord Haw-Haw.[44]

This late summer of 1940 provided an important period of preparation for Londoners. Through much of July, all of August and the first week of September, they grew accustomed to the sound of the siren – or 'sireen' as many pronounced it – and to responding accordingly. The heavy raids of 26/7 August and after prompted the authorities to bring into use for the first time the deep shelters in old tube tunnels (Southwark) and new ones still being built for the Central Line and not yet used by trains (Liverpool Street, Bethnal Green, Leyton, Leytonstone, Gants Hill and Ilford, though in the last an entrance to some still-locked tunnel workings had to be broken open by an excited crowd). This was all useful preparation. It enabled too a refinement in the system of warning lights or coloured discs to yellow (preliminary caution), purple (exempted lights to be extinguished, raid might shortly occur), red (action warning), white (raiders passed). And industry adapted to avoid as far as possible loss of output during alerts: Ford at Dagenham developed teams of roof spotters to give a red alert when planes were seen to be coming their way.[45]

Everyone also began to adjust themselves to new routines. The first was to decide where to shelter. Despite the widespread availability of public shelters, most Londoners stayed at home. Often, like the Buddells in Croydon, they hunkered down under the stairs or somewhere even more flimsy: 'I heard Jean's heart beating within the sounding-board of the pantry's wooden walls,' George Beardmore wrote of his family's arrangements in north Harrow. Hilda Neal, on an upper floor of a large house in Kensington, took herself downstairs to the ground-floor hall, where she sat on the stairs. Her friend Follie was getting a room in her Wimbledon house 'reinforced so that she will feel safer. Poor Follie; never thought she would lose her nerve so.' Godfrey and Laurie Clarke moved down to the basement of their Golborne Road shop when things got noisy. At Ealing, Dorothy Wells, her elderly mother and brother Ken shared a stout garden shelter with their next-door neighbours, though they would eventually erect their own Anderson. In contrast to Hilda Neal's view of Follie, Dorothy wrote, 'I am very struck by the calmness and courage of everyone' (25 August). In Anthony Heap's block of flats south of the Euston Road there was a cellar shelter entered from the courtyard, equipped with benches: 'The alarms go off three times a day with so much regularity that they hardly seem worth mentioning. They have become part of our daily lives' (5 September). Heap noticed how theatre audiences generally stayed in their seats when a warning was announced, but after the all clear 'You could "feel" the tension relax.' Olivia Cockett's family in Brockley were able to shelter in their strengthened cellar, but one night when a raid began without warning she lay 'quaking in bed … Felt really frightened, shivers, dry throat, swollen tongue, cold feet … Hope to goodness my nerve doesn't break.' Viola Bawtree, fifty-six, living on private means in Carshalton, on the edge of south-west London, with two sisters and a brother, also had a cellar but not as well fitted out as Cockett's: 'There are mosquitoes there, black beetles, Elaine had a large spider run down her face … something started falling from my hair … it was a large spider, all legs!' Nellie Carver, in West Norwood, with her elderly mother and aunt, spent raids in the kitchen: 'It's strange to hear all the neighbours getting up & going into their shelters – I rather wish we had one after all.'[46]

By 6 September everyone had grown accustomed to air raids to some degree. For those who worked during the day, ARP in offices, shops and factories had also had the opportunity to improve its practice and adjust (and minimise where possible) the disruption to working life presented by daylight raids. Those out during the day had grown used to finding and using public shelters in or close to shopping streets and parks. Besides the nervousness understandably caused by raids, the worst problem was tiredness, with several nights a week disrupted by sirens and the traipse to wherever was used for shelter. Some adapted to this by ignoring the all-clear signal: 'People are now quite reluctant to leave the shelter having settled down for the night,' noted Anthony Heap of his block of flats. Others adapted by bringing beds down to ground-floor rooms where people felt safer than on upper floors. All who stayed in London found some way of living with the changed circumstances which slowly built up momentum through July and August and the first week of September.[47]

These raids also gave Londoners their first taste of death and injury from enemy bombing. There were just those two deaths in July but in August 226 were killed and 393 detained in hospital; between 1 and 6 September a further 257 died and 441 were admitted to hospital. These were significant figures, ghastly for those involved. But set against an anticipated 30,000 casualties in London *per day* they were a grain of sand. The fear of bombing, which people had lived with for so long, had now been shown to be worse than the realities of bombing itself. It was not as terrible as people had imagined or been led to expect, the casualties not so enormous, the damage not so immense, the disruption not so insuperable. Things would get worse, certainly, but they would never be as bad as people had once feared they would be. Even so, there were many long trials ahead.[48]

4

FIGHTING LIKE A WILD CAT:
7 SEPTEMBER–28 DECEMBER 1940

SATURDAY 7 September was just another beautiful day in what had been an exceptional summer. Londoners, now unfazed by daylight raids, were out in force in cinemas and cafes and shops before getting home in advance of the expected night bombing. When the siren sounded at 4.55 p.m. it seemed likely that another daylight attack would be a nuisance to be easily avoided. But today was different. Some 320 German bombers, protected by 600 fighters, approached London from the Thames estuary. Thomas Pointer, thirty-six and a clerk at the Royal Victoria Docks, who had cycled to work that day from Ilford, heard the siren, went to the door of the canteen where he was having tea and looked up. He saw 'over fifty aircraft at a rather low altitude with gunfire bursting in front and around them. They continued straight on travelling almost due West so as to pass over the docks at an angle.' This first flight began bombing as he reached the nearest concrete dugout. Between then and the all clear at 6.36 p.m. he watched flight after flight of fifteen planes in tight diamond formation, so close he could see them 'rock from back to front ... as they released their bombs'. Within minutes all around him was in chaos. Ships and barges in the docks were sinking or alight, the Rank Flour mills 'blazing from top to bottom', quays and railway lines smashed.[1]

Pointer didn't yet know it but all along the Thames, from Wapping in Stepney to Beckton in East Ham, the river and its banks on both sides were ablaze. The Surrey Docks at Rotherhithe, their 250 acres 'containing thousands of standards of timber, including a lot of pitch pine and other resinous woods stored in sheds and in open ground, burst into flames'; the heat blistered paint on a fire boat 300 yards away. Fires at Woolwich Arsenal, West Ham power station, Beckton gas works, rum warehouses at the West India Docks, sugar refineries, oil stores, paint and varnish works and chemical factories met in conflagrations of unexampled complexity. By 7 on the Saturday evening, every available appliance in London was fighting fires along the riverside, with minor blazes from the City to Kensington. Reinforcements were speeding by road from as far afield as Birmingham and Bristol. At 8.30 p.m. the sirens blew again, when 'some 250 bombers resumed the attack'. They were still attacking until just before dawn, the all clear sounding at 4.47 on the Sunday morning. The bombing left nine conflagrations (one needing 300 pumps and another 130), fifty-nine large fires needing over thirty pumps each and nearly a thousand 'lesser fires'. Many were still blazing when the Luftwaffe returned at 7.56 on the Sunday evening.[2]

In West Ham 'An area of 1½ miles between North Woolwich Road and the Thames was almost destroyed', and next-door Silvertown 'was surrounded by fire', some of the people living there having to be rescued by boat, itself a dangerous task with burning barges, cut or broken loose from their moorings, to be avoided. The Metropolitan Police recorded 438 fatalities and 1,424 people seriously injured; there were 139 deaths in Stepney, Bethnal Green and Poplar, and fifty in West and East Ham; south of the river Bermondsey, Rotherhithe and north Southwark were worst hit, with sixty deaths between them. The fatalities included one from the Isle of Dogs, Poplar, recovered by Bill Regan, thirty-two, a bricklayer by trade but now working for ARP rescue and demolition; he was brought up on 'The Island' and lived there still. 'He was an elderly man, fully dressed, still sitting in his armchair, but totally embedded in fine plaster and brick rubble ... packed almost solid around him. We rescued the armchair undamaged.' The night also brought London's first civil defence tragedy: West Ham's Abbey Road council depot, taken over by ARP and the AFS, took a direct hit which killed thirteen men, including the rescue squad leader, Alf Bridgman.[3]

'Black Saturday', as the first day of the 'Big Blitz' became known, brought chaos and panic to the East End. Both were short-lived but they rippled on through the first week of London's ordeal by fire. The gigantic raid in two halves caused the dislocation of civilised life for a time at least: no gas (Beckton gas works), no telephones and no electricity (West Ham power station) for large parts of east London. A direct hit on the Abbey Mills pumping station at West Ham forced north London's sewage to be discharged raw into the Thames. At Woolwich the Southern Outfall sewer was 'blown out', causing similar problems south of the river. Destruction of bakeries, dairies and other provisions suppliers, combined with blocked roads and the difficulties of organising transportation, threatened to cut off food supplies in the East End.[4]

The first response of many was to flee. The 'trek away from Stepney and other Dockside areas' was observed early on by the Home Office: it began before nightfall on the 7th and the expected return of bombing on the Sunday. East Enders headed north-east to Epping Forest, where the scout camp at Fairmead, High Beech, was accommodating at least 5,000 by Tuesday 10 September, while some were roughing it in the open air. Others trekked west through the City and West End, seeking shelter in the basements of big stores and the tubes, many making for Paddington and taking pot luck in trains to the West Country. South of the river people made for the hop fields in Kent, carrying as much of their homes as they could. Observers noted a sullen discontent: 'Class feeling growing because of worse destruction in working-class areas; anti-semitism growing' among Cockneys in the East End because Jews were thought in some way responsible as the intended target and the rich were thought to have been immune. A Mass Observation report, probably written on Monday 9 September, noted that in some streets untouched by bombing 60 per cent had left:

> People were completely unprepared intellectually for the <u>extent</u> of the raid damage ... The whole story of the last weekend has been one of unplanned hysteria. Though there has only been a small amount of open hysterics and violent weeping, the general trend has been strictly hysterical never-theless ... Often those who are on the move express a sort of surprise at finding they were going. Plenty went without any plan at all, without anywhere to go to, and sometimes without any money or prospects.[5]

Many of these difficulties crystallised in Silvertown, where the results of HE bombs in an area of jerry-built Victorian terraces had been espe-cially devastating, causing homelessness on an extensive scale. Evacuation from the area continued on the Sunday afternoon: buses evacuated 1,000 people to Walthamstow at 3 p.m. and a further 1,000 were taken to join them a couple of hours later, but many residents were left, not all desiring to move. There would be a ghastly tragedy in Silvertown on 10/11 September when a crowded reception centre at South Hallsville School received a direct hit, killing seventy-three. It should have been evacuated that afternoon before the nightly raid but the buses failed to arrive due to a disastrous mix-up somewhere. The incident became the first blitz scandal, making sensational copy for the Scottish Labour journalist Ritchie Calder in the *Daily Herald*: he had met some of those in the centre earlier that day, when the transport was thought to be coming shortly. Calder's articles added to the prevailing view in Whitehall and elsewhere that part of the East End's problems, perhaps all, were due to the failures of leadership and organisation in local councils, especially West Ham and Stepney.[6]

There were undoubtedly problems in both. Comparisons with Poplar, which lay between them and which, under its dynamic ARP controller Alderman Charlie Key, had become a model of civil defence, standing up well to Black Saturday and the aftermath, underlined local inadequacies. Stepney had a fraught history, its Labour council antipathetic to government ARP policies and slow to adapt to changing circumstances since the declaration of war. Its ARP controller, Councillor Morrie Davis, was bombastic and bullying and thought to be corrupt – he would eventually be jailed for fare-dodging on the railways. But everything in Stepney was complicated by the strength in numbers and the vigour in action of the local Communist Party (CP). Every criticism of the council was thought to be, perhaps was, communist-inspired; every local organisation not established by the council was thought to be, often was, a CP front. Mutual loathing and town hall paranoia paralysed communications and cooperation between the council and local communities. And a desire for ideological purism could see it operate in opposition to the needs of its stricken ratepayers: 'The Council objected, for instance, to the employment of contractors, and for some time attempted to repair only its own house-property', boycotting homes owned by private landlords. Local clergymen were sometimes able to provide the leadership that the council and councillors, so preoccupied with their own power battles, often failed to do. Some things, though, did improve in the town hall: a dynamic young mayor, Frank Lewey, was able to mobilise resources around him; and Councillor Davis would be removed as ARP controller by Herbert Morrison, the new Home Secretary and Minister of Home Security, in October 1940. Morrison installed a council official in his place, not without objection from Stepney CP, who claimed this to be an affront to local democracy.[7]

West Ham's problems were somewhat different. It had been a Labour Party fiefdom for almost time out of mind and as the party's grip on power had aged so had those councillors clutching the reins. Again, the ARP controllers had been councillors reluctant to see authority pass into officers' hands, and there had been 'a very unfortunate attitude towards voluntary bodies not already established in the borough' who now offered assistance to the people of West Ham. The government for a time contemplated removing all the council's powers and carrying them out from Whitehall, but that would have been politically contentious and administratively challenging, and the idea was dropped. Nevertheless, West Ham remained a dinosaur among London's local authorities until the end of the Big Blitz and beyond.[8]

There were, then, local shortcomings. But just think of what these authorities had to deal with on the weekend of 7/8 September and in the days after: the fires still burning, the roads still blocked, the infrastructure still fractured, the bombs still falling nightly, a population in large part seized with anxiety and ready to flee or actually in flight, and those fleeing and those lying injured in the casualty words searching for someone to blame for their miseries. In High Barnet hospital a nurse, young and no doubt hasty in judgement, saw the unlovely side of the East Enders in her care, 'their moaning, full of class hatred and nearly all out of their wits with fear'. It is surely not a surprise that Stepney and West Ham, both authorities and people, came to breaking point in these first few days. The real surprise is threefold: that Poplar, with a similar political history but better led, stood fast so staunchly despite the Isle of Dogs being nearly as battered as Wapping in Stepney and Silvertown in West Ham; that Bermondsey, where Rotherhithe suffered as badly as anywhere and with its own politics compromised by pacifism, fared similarly well; and that the people of east London north and south of the Thames, at least those who resolved to stay, so quickly recovered their nerve and dug in for the long haul.[9]

NERVES were, though, shaken – and not just in the East End. George Orwell, chatting to a working-class youth from south London on the Thursday following Black Saturday, thought him 'Very embittered and defeatist about the war', cynical about Churchill, convinced Hitler would win, thought all wars were fought for the rich. He 'eagerly took up my point when I said the empty houses in the West End should be requisitioned' for the homeless. Class feeling stoked defeatism in these early days of the blitz. It was encouraged, even organised, by the left and by those pacifist groups stifled but not extinguished by the summer crisis of 1940. In mid-September, East End communists and pacifist clergymen presented a peace petition to the government, the petition hawked round public shelters for signatures. And in West Ham, at the beginning of October, a deputation led by a Plaistow clergyman sought to press the government to approach the Soviet Union to broker a peace with Hitler, 'in view of the increasing horror and devastation of the present air warfare'.[10]

In the end these were hairline cracks that required little or no papering over. Indeed, a rising fury against the Germans to the point of hatred was noted in London during the first days of heavy bombing; and those proud tokens of resistance, Union Jacks stuck in the ruins of tiny houses brought to their knees by bombing, had already begun a tradition that was maintained in London throughout the war. But bitterness and division were also fostered by the suspicion that London was not adequately defended against everything the Luftwaffe was now throwing at it. Suspicion was well founded. The military authorities had planned that London and the Medway should be defended by 480 heavy anti-aircraft (AA) guns. This number had never been provided, and some of those that had been were withdrawn to defend airfields and other targets in the Battle of Britain. On 7 September there were 264 in place, but the majority of these were in the Kent and Essex marshes or on the western outskirts; just ninety-two were in the 'inner city zone' of London's enormous built-up area. Within twenty-four hours of the terrible battering of Black Saturday every available AA gun was rushed to London 'from all over the country'. Soon the number of heavy guns had more than doubled to 199, but they had to be properly sited, a complex business: 'Telephone lines have to be laid, gun positions levelled, the warning system co-ordinated, and so on.' Rather than bring each gun into use when ready, it was decided that all would be deployed in a show of force on the night of Wednesday 11 September. Precise aiming was abandoned. 'Guns were to go to the approximate bearing and elevation and fire. Every gun was to fire every possible round. Fire was not to be withheld on any account.'[11]

The result was the loudest sustained noise in London's history – to that point anyway:

It came as a complete surprise to us all. We had settled down to the usual routine of waiting, when without warning the whole cannonade went up. The noise was beyond description. There were guns that spat sharp and shrilly; guns that made a knocking sound as of a fist on the windows; guns that coughed apologetically or wuffed like great dogs, or shook the house with a clatter of thunder. I have always disliked loud noises, for even when I know them to be harmless, they make me feel slightly sick; but this night I enjoyed them.[12]

Those reactions of Nesca Robb, a schoolteacher from Northern Ireland now living in Chiswick, were typical. 'What a wonderful night last night!' Matilda Draper, another teacher, living in Hornsey, wrote in her diary next morning: 'I hate war, I hate any kind of waste or destruction or hurt and yet I could not help a feeling of exhilaration.' Dorothy Wells, in Ealing, thought it had also made a difference to the Luftwaffe: 'We were all delighted. It seemed so maddening to hear the planes droning overhead all night with hardly a shell fired against them. This is a new plan, and was effective in warning the Nazis. It should have been the biggest raid, but it did not amount to as much as the previous ones.' 'Well done, London. Well done, We, Us & Co. Unlimited,' the chronicler of Paddington ARP exulted in his diary on 12 September. 'Londoners were already standing firm although apparently unable to hit back with any reality. But truly this "go" at the Huns was both comforting and encouraging.'[13]

In truth, AA fire was notoriously ineffective at bringing down bombers, though the new barrage was thought to have forced the attack much higher than intended. But the Luftwaffe would not be deterred, by London's barrage or anything else, for weeks to come. From 7 September to 2 November London was bombed every night by an average of 160 bombers, a total of fifty-seven consecutive nights when undisturbed sleep became only a distant memory for most. Bad weather meant that attacks were weakened on nine nights when fewer than a hundred bombers were used, and it prevented raiding altogether on 3 November; but attacks were resumed the next night and, though on a lighter scale, for the next three weeks. The night of 25/6 November was the first since 7 September without a warning siren.[14]

German records subsequently showed that 7,160 tons of HE and 4,735 incendiaries were dropped on London in October 1940, compared to 220 tons and 369 incendiaries on Liverpool and Manchester combined, the next biggest targets. The unrelenting pressure told heavily on all concerned. Fire services in particular were always at full stretch.

On four nights over a thousand fires were being fought in London. The LFB, supplemented by its AFS colleagues, alone had to deal with 13,000 in September and October. Assistance from brigades outside London Region was sought on 381 occasions. Only eleven of London's sixty-seven brigades were able to cope alone.[15]

There were some notable nights. On 17 September the Luftwaffe dropped by parachute the first of many naval mines on London. It failed to explode and was defused by the Admiralty's disposal squad: 'Now you can play football with it if you like,' the naval lieutenant told the householder in whose back garden it fell. On 18/19 September 350 tons of HE were dropped on London, more than the total used against the United Kingdom in the whole of the First World War. On 15/16 October a 400-bomber raid dropped 540 tons, causing massive damage to London's rail network: all traffic at St Pancras, Marylebone, Broad Street, Waterloo and Victoria stations was stopped, and at Euston, Cannon Street, Charing Cross and London Bridge it was cut by two thirds; District Line tube tracks were severed in three places, and Baker Street and Moorgate stations put out of action. The Fleet sewer was burst and sewage flooded the tube tunnel between King's Cross and Farringdon; Oxford Street was closed and London Bridge was open only southwards; three huge water mains were broken, a delayed-action bomb exploded in Broadcasting House while the 9 p.m. news was being read, and over 900 fires were started, fifteen of them serious. That night over 400 Londoners were killed, with nearly 900 seriously injured.[16]

Among all of this there were also some terrible tragedies caused, like that at South Hallsville School, by a single bomb. Two might be left to stand for many. They happened on consecutive nights at opposite ends of the city. On October 13/14, at Coronation Mansions, Stoke Newington, a public shelter in the basement of a block of five-storey tenements occupied by mainly Jewish families received a direct hit that penetrated the sewer and water mains and brought down the flats above; despite heroic rescue efforts in pitch darkness 154 shelterers died, many from drowning. It was one of the very worst disasters of London's, indeed Britain's, war. Next night a bomb broke through the roadway of Balham High Street and exploded in the tube station beneath. Again, severed sewers and water mains flooded the tunnels, hampering rescuers and drowning many shelterers; havoc was made worse when a bus, fortunately empty apart from the driver, careered into the crater in the road above. Deaths here totalled sixty-eight.[17]

WHEN Alderman Hurley of Wandsworth Council visited the Balham tube disaster scene next morning he found 'The stench was almost unendurable but the rescue parties never flinched.' How did ARP stand up to these appalling events, night after night?[18]

London's frontline 'soldier-civilians' were the warden service, stretcher parties and first aid posts, all staffed, trained and managed by local councils, with workers a mix of full-time paid and unpaid part-time volunteers. The warden service was dominated by men (82 per cent) and part-timers (88 per cent); in the casualty services some 73 per cent were women and 78 per cent part-time. These were national figures, with much local variation. Also in the front line were rescue and demolition squads, the fire services and the ambulance drivers and staff. These were generally county council services, though they often shared ARP depots with local council staff to ease communications. In West Ham, East Ham and Croydon all these services were run by a single authority, each responsible for wardens, first aid, stretcher and rescue parties, ambulances and first aid posts, with its own fire brigade supplemented by the AFS. Metropolitan Police and war reserve constables played important roles in support of wardens and rescue parties; and so to a lesser extent did the Home Guard, who helped in major rescues and occasionally protected bomb sites from scavengers.[19]

All contemporary evidence concurs that these frontline services coped astonishingly well with everything thrown at them. There were individual wardens, stretcher-bearers, rescue workers and so on who failed to turn up for duty or who hid themselves during fierce bombing but, given that these were people whose job it was to stay in the open during raids, the service as a whole hardly faltered and seems never to have broken down anywhere. 'The Civil Defence people have been praised everywhere,' the local newspaper for Stepney and Poplar reported at the end of the first week of major raids, 'for the A.F.S. men and the Fire Brigade have displayed great heroism, and the A.R.P. and Rescue and Demolition Squads have played their part with equal vigour.' Public praise in West Ham was unstinting: the fire services 'worked heroically', 'Praise for the A.R.P. workers ... is general'. The local paper noted in particular the 'Heroic rescue efforts' at South Hallsville School, dealing with 'a mass of twisted girders and debris'. No citizenry in the history of modern Britain had come under stress like this before. That same first week, Herbert Morrison, at this point still Minister of Supply, announced on a visit to Hackney, where he had been mayor twenty years before, that the government would establish honours for ARP workers and other civilians showing selfless bravery under fire: many London civil defence staff would be among recipients of the George Cross and George Medal when instituted at the end of September.[20]

What surprised many was the speed of ARP response. When Nellie Carver was bombed out of her home in Idmiston Road, Lambeth, on 18 September – her forty-ninth birthday – 'Wardens & Rescue Parties had sprung from nowhere & were running along, banging on each door shouting "Is everyone all right in there?"' Nellie and her mother were able to shelter with a neighbour further along the street until the all clear. Those endless months of training in the Phoney War seemed to have paid off here and in the other arms of ARP. Inez Holden, a freelance writer and first aid post volunteer, probably for St Marylebone Borough Council, noted how rescue parties 'got into their cars' with 'pick-axes, spades, shovels, first-aid supplies and so on and drove out up the ramp' of the ARP depot: 'it was so perfectly timed that it seemed to have become only one movement.' A journalist watched a squad of some ten men summoned to an incident in October 1940. They found the 'Incident Officer' from the town hall, who had 'set up his light on a tripod' in the street. It was a big job at a block of council flats and more squads were sent for. A warden arrived with a plan of the block. 'Under cover of tarpaulins, by the light of glow-lamps, hurricane lamps, whatever can be devised, the topman cautiously climbs up in the darkness, a human chain is formed, the wreckage is passed, hand to hand, till the surface rubble is off. Then the attack on the building starts in earnest,' tunnelling towards the basement where people were trapped, shoring as they went. When someone was found alive a doctor equipped with morphine crawled in.[21]

The shifts of these rescue workers lasted twelve hours but were longer in an emergency; pay, recently increased, was £3 13s 6d a week and their work was frequently dangerous, often ghastly. Bill Regan, on the Isle of Dogs in Poplar, had to search an incident site for body parts after it had been ascertained there were no more survivors: 'We gathered three bushel baskets of remains, I picked up two left feet. One of the men saw a body perched on the rooftop. Nobby Clarke climbed up and recovered it. It was badly mutilated, it was some time before we were able to identify it as female.' A couple of nights later, 18 September, a landmine fell on nearby Saunders Ness Road School, now an AFS and ARP depot where about forty men and women civil defence workers were stationed: 'Within minutes we had located the spot they were likely to be, and got two people out, but I don't think they were alive as we were working without lights and they were at best unconscious.' Two days later, 'We keep finding bodies, and we are told that there were at least 42 to be accounted for, and from what we gather, there are nearly 2 dozen still there.'[22]

All these services were intensely local. Barbara Nixon, a warden in Finsbury, recorded how, at Post 13, 'All the wardens had been to the same local school, though at different times, and they knew the family history of nearly everyone in the neighbourhood.' This local knowledge could be vital. Bill Regan had worked on the building of Saunders Ness Road school and near Christmas, when the search for bodies resumed, he knew where to look in what had now, with 'no big stuff to be moved [become] one big heap of small rubble and concrete, which has settled into a tight mass, and requires hand-work'. He found what at first, to another demolition squad worker, appeared to be a doormat: 'I told him it was a bloke, and I knew who it was, Warden Herbie Martin.' All these finds would be processed in council mortuaries, where attendants had one of the toughest jobs of the blitz. These men 'impressed me greatly,' a St Pancras councillor recalled, 'by the kindness and sympathy they showed the sorrowing relatives, who were obliged to identify the bodies of their loved ones'.[23]

Many other workers played heroic roles in these days: water engineers and gas fitters (often wearing asbestos suits) called out to repair mains, frequently with gas burning in the craters where they worked; electricians fixing power lines in wet trenches with a deadly mix of electrics and water; and, of all arms of the ARP front line, few faced more dangers than the firemen, most of them trained amateurs appointed in the last year or so. An anonymous London AFS man recalled a fire in a blitzed riverside warehouse somewhere in the East End. It was his turn to climb an extendable ladder and direct water from above the fire:

When I got to the top (which was about one hundred feet above the street) I hooked myself on and looked down. I felt a little giddy. In the fire I could see the bales and bales of hides burning amongst the debris of the fallen roof. Just at that moment the roof right under me began to go, and as it went, I felt them tip me back and grasped the top rung of the ladder to steady myself. The very slightest movement at the bottom of the ladder means a tremendous arc at the top. I was swung out widely away from the building. Then the roof went in with a roar and a shower of sparks sailed into the evening sky, already darkened by the pall of smoke which hung over everything.

Over the telephone connecting him with the LFB officer below he heard:

'Sorry to move you back like that, but we thought you might get roasted when the roof went in. Now we'll drop you over it a bit. Then put the water where you think best.' ... I called down the phone for more water, and a few seconds later I felt the ladder heave backwards as the extra pressure was put on. I swayed in slowly over the fire again and felt most uncomfortable.

'You all right up there?' shouted the ladder operator.

'I'm O.K.,' I said, 'but I don't seem to be doing any good.'

'Any nonsense from you and we'll cook you, you bastard,' came back the reply.[24]

In a report to the government of early October 1940, Political and Economic Planning, a pre-war 'think-tank' before such things were given a name, concluded that 'London's "first line" civil defences – the wardens' organisation, the fire services, rescue and demolition work, the ambulance and casualty clearing service etc. – were remarkably well-prepared to meet the tremendous strain which intensive bombing attacks have placed upon them.' Even Mass Observation, always ready to criticise the public authorities, remarked at the end of September that in the East End 'the ARP, AFS and first aid services have been working admirably and according to plan'.[25]

All this good work – utterly invaluable in saving lives – has been overshadowed since, and was substantially overshadowed at the time, by two great failures: the condition of shelters and the treatment of the homeless.

THE shelter scandal had been a long time brewing. There were doubtless many instances where local authorities had not reacted with sufficient vigour to civil defence requirements, through either lack of political will or bureaucratic inertia. But local initiative had everywhere been held back by the dead hand of Whitehall, cuffed and pinioned as it was by the Treasury. We might recall damp-proof shelters (West Ham), chemical closets in shelters (Poplar), seats and lighting in shelters (Camberwell), and other cases subsequently emerged (medical attendance in large shelters in Lambeth) where money was at first withheld from London authorities and then provided when the consequences of austerity became clear. We might also remember the unsatisfactory results of ministry guidance appearing to advocate cement-free mortar in street shelters. And when the rebel council of Finsbury, convinced that deep shelters were the only really safe refuge from the Luftwaffe, designed an underground car park that could in the interim provide a deep shelter, the council leader and town clerk were surcharged by the district auditor and required to pay personally the cost of expenditure deemed unlawful. Their creative accountancy was no doubt deplorable, though the cause was honourable. But the failure of civil defence planning adequately to meet the needs of Londoners had dire consequences and they were everywhere to be seen.[26]

The great unforeseen problem, of course, was that raids often lasted from dawn to dusk, so Londoners were having to spend all night in shelters where there was nowhere for them to sleep but on the floor. In Stepney, the Tilbury shelter, railway arches beneath the Commercial Road goods depot, to which many had fled in the First World War and so flocked to again, became one of the horrors of the home front. The arches were owned by the London, Midland and Scottish Railway and the Port of London Authority and when Stepney borough council proposed using part of the depot under both ownerships as a shelter negotiations broke down in the spring of 1940. When bombing began, Tilbury had not been designated by the council as a public shelter but once people gathered there in force something had to be done to improve things; yet conditions at the arches, where some 14,000 sheltered each night, remained deplorable for many weeks. Nina Hibbin, a young communist Mass Observer from the Jewish East End, reported on it in September:

> The structure is colossal, mainly of platforms and arches. The brick is so old, the place so filthy and decrepit, that it would be difficult for the best of artists to convey its ugliness on paper. First impression is of a dense block of people, nothing else. By 7.30 p.m. each evening, every available bit of floor space is taken up. Deck-chairs, blankets, stools,

seats, pillows – people lying on everything, everywhere. When you get over the shock of seeing so many sprawling people, you are overcome with the smell of humanity and dirt. Dirt abounds everywhere. The floors are never swept and are filthy. People are sleeping on piles of rubbish. The passages are loaded with dirt. There is no escaping it.[27]

Tilbury was close to the multiracial district around Cable Street and so sheltered a very mixed population of cockneys, Jews, Indians and other people of colour. Jews generally clustered in the right-hand arches, cockneys in the middle and 'Indians' on the left. 'Race feeling was very marked,' Hibbin thought, with cockney and Jew drawn untypically together 'in unity against the Indian'. But the unhealthy conditions took an immediate toll, she believed, on the shelterers. When Hibbin wrote of 'dirt' she meant human excrement, for the few buckets behind make-shift screens of blanket were inadequate and inaccessible; and the crowding brought a nightly epidemic of coughing. Hibbin herself 'developed a cough and sore throat, in the early stages of the evening'. Official fears of shelter epidemics provoked an inquiry into shelter health and hygiene that reported with great urgency as early as 18 September 1940. It recommended the installation of bunks, chemical closets (Elsans), the appointment of shelter wardens, medical inspection, first aid posts in large shelters, improved ventilation by air conditioning where possible and spraying with disinfectant where not. These recommendations were accepted and implementation put in hand. But the problem was vast and materials in short supply and little improved quickly. Tilbury at the end of October had just one tap and merely a 'handful of lavatory buckets in the dark, behind a common screen'.[28]

Tilbury remained probably the worst large shelter in London throughout the main blitz. But at the beginning almost everywhere was filthy, stinking, uncomfortable and overcrowded. Euan Wallace, formerly Minister of Transport but now the Senior Commissioner for London Region, visited Southwark tunnel, an official shelter in use since August, on 23 September, the day after conditions there had been exposed in the Sunday Pictorial – 'Shelter Scandal: Stop This Now! These kiddies are our country's future.' 'It was a perfectly horrible sight,' he thought, 'packed with people sleeping in every uncomfortable attitude on the stairs and the bare concrete floor.'[29]

The Southwark tunnel had one key advantage. It was a disused deep tube tunnel and so guaranteed safety. And it became clear almost immediately after 7 September that Londoners were fleeing to the tubes, just as they had done in September 1917. Within a week tube sheltering was widespread. In September some 177,000 were bedding down in the tubes nightly, the highest numbers of the whole war, despite official disapproval and nothing being done for their health or comfort. None of that mattered in the aftershock of Black Saturday, for the tubes were generally very safe and immune from the noise of guns and the tremble of bombs. Conditions at first were chaotic and remained so through September and well into October. They were also unhygienic, most tunnels below the London sewerage system, with buckets and Elsans only grudgingly provided to what the London Passenger Transport Board considered its unwelcome guests. Around 21 September the authorities were forced to bow to what Londoners had now made a fait accompli, reversible only at the cost of mass public disorder. By 22 September it was decided to decommission the Aldwych tube spur from Holborn on the Piccadilly Line, converting track and platforms into a shelter for 2,000 or so people, mostly East Enders, and opening by 7 October. Beyond that, the tube remained an uncomfortable option until organisational and other improvements got under way. Things weren't helped by infestations of bedbugs imported on people's bedding and a plague of mosquitoes, not disease-carrying but with a wicked bite, breeding in stagnant water in the older tunnels. Even so, the tubes were considered a godsend to London. Godfrey and Laurie Clarke in North Kensington, exhausted by sleepless nights spent in the shop basement, decided to try the tube at Notting Hill Gate in late September. Laurie spent a night there on 21 September and they both went on the 24th, but could only get a space on the stairs 'about 80 odd steps "down". Made ourselves as comfortable as possible – but oh the "up & down" all night! What an experience in the 20th Century to think that one has to "go to earth" like rabbits or foxes!' Even so they went again next night, but found it besieged by 'crowds waiting at 7.30pm & were unable to get in'.[30]

Although tube sheltering provided a defining image of Londoners at war, in fact most never used the tube at all and others, like the Clarkes, only very rarely. Hilda Neal, for instance, who had sheltered in the tunnel connecting South Kensington tube station to the Exhibition Road museums in a bad raid on 9 September, had decided by the 17th that loneliness even in a big empty house at 'home' was preferable to the tube. She was one of a large majority. The first London shelter survey, in November 1940, revealed 9 per cent in public shelters (like

Tilbury, street shelters and basements allocated to public use), 4 per cent in the tubes and 27 per cent in shelters at home, mainly Andersons and strengthened basements, like Olivia Cockett's; in Pimlico, Westminster, some 8,000 coal cellars under the pavements were fitted out as shelters, many provided with electricity. The proportions in public shelters and the tube would have been greater in September and October but not hugely so. In November, that left 60 per cent making do somehow at home – under the stairs (Arthur Buddell), on the stairs or in a ground-floor room (Hilda Neal, Nellie Carver), in the basement or cellar (the Clarkes, Viola Bawtree) or another room which felt the safest available. This proportion would also have included people whose Andersons had flooded. Bill Regan and his wife, Vi, on the Isle of Dogs had 'a good night's sleep' in their Anderson on 11 September, but two mornings later 'I climbed out of the bottom bunk, straight into knee-deep water; must arrange for other accommodation.' That was Bill's joke, but of course they had to. He was on duty most nights so the worry was Vi; earlier, when an unexploded bomb (UXB) had meant she should have left the house, Warden Herbie Martin had suggested she shelter in Saunders Ness Road School, but she didn't fancy the idea and now, fortunately, still preferred to make her own arrange-ments. 'Vi has decided to sleep, no, <u>shelter</u> in the front room, with the table pushed beside the fireplace, mattress and blankets under the table. The window is now heavily boarded, and Vi is confident that she will be safe.'[31]

THE London shelter was in the public eye from the outset. But what worried the authorities behind the scenes was London's second-line ARP defences – the rest centres and the treatment of Londoners made homeless by bombing. The South Hallsville School disaster in Silvertown had shone a fleeting searchlight on this issue, but below the surface the numbers were deeply worrying.

The homelessness crisis in London resulted from a failure in Whitehall planning, for which the Minister of Health later handsomely admitted departmental responsibility in the House of Commons. Everyone had focused on casualties – the dead without number to be interred in cardboard coffins and mass graves; the wounded in their scores of thousands every week. These never materialised. But what had not been foreseen was the vast numbers of Londoners made homeless by HE blast or burned out by incendiaries. Many could find refuge with neighbours or friends for a time, move to relatives in or out of London, rent new homes locally or, if comfortably off, find rooms in hotels and country retreats. But all of these solutions might well need time to negotiate. And many others had nowhere to go even temporarily, depending on the council to find them somewhere to live. Often people were shattered by the experience of losing their home and loved ones and were ill-equipped, psychologically and practically, to cope. These were the people who in their thousands ended up in county council rest centres and found themselves having to stay there night after night after night.[32]

Homelessness before the war had been a poor law problem and although the poor law had been in theory ended in 1929 old attitudes and bureaucratic red tape had survived in Whitehall and town hall alike. The victims of bombing – often with no cash, no food, no furniture, just the clothes they stood up in – found themselves for the first time as recipients of public welfare, often grudgingly given. The main objective of officials at the rest centres was to move people on as quickly as possible. But that required the third line of raid services to respond effectively. This was the billeting of homeless people in new homes, a task of the borough councils. But where in an area like badly bombed Stepney or West Ham, with empty properties often blitzed or with keyholders who were unknown or who might have fled the borough, were new homes to be found? The result was a backing up in huge numbers of people who had no option but to stay where they were, in the rest centres.

The centres themselves were ill-equipped for a stay of any more than a few hours. They had minimal cooking facilities, usually sufficient only for making hot drinks and vulnerable to stoppages of power and water. Government penny-pinching was said to have capped LCC rest centre expenditure before 7 September at £2,000 for equipping all their first-line centres in the whole of inner London. Accordingly, 'Blankets were few and far between. A diet such as was normally provided in poor law casual wards [to tramps and vagrants, heavily dependent on bread and margarine] was offered at the centres, mobile feeding canteens having been dismissed [by the Ministry of Health] as an unnecessary refinement in wartime. There was no first aid equipment' and information about how or where to get additional help was hard to find. Small sums of money were available 'but only for the poor'. Many were bombed out in their night clothes, but the need for large stores of reserve clothing 'had not been foreseen'. In the early days of the Big Blitz conditions in rest centres under the greatest stress might be appalling. In one Stepney school, 200–300 slept nightly on 'blankets, mattresses and bundles of clothing' on the floor, using ten buckets and even coal scuttles as lavatories, which overflowed as the night wore on, with seven basins to wash in, without soap or towels, with drinking water kept in zinc baths.[33]

The numbers coming into the centres dwarfed those going out. Councils had been urged by the government to requisition houses only as a last resort. Those worst bombed found their billeting options massively reduced by bomb damage and so needed the assistance of neighbouring boroughs. That was generally forthcoming but there was no mechanism to organise mutual aid across London as a whole. To provide one, a special commissioner for the homeless was appointed for London Region on 27 September, Henry Willink, Conservative MP for Croydon North.

But just where people should go remained a major problem. There was often a great reluctance among East Enders to move to empty properties in Westminster or Marylebone, where accommodation was available for them, sometimes preferring to move out of London altogether. Even so, some 20,000–25,000 from Stepney, West Ham and Bermondsey were moved to other parts of London and neighbouring parts of Essex in the early days of mass bombing. Often these moves provided only a temporary solution. By mid-September some Essex authorities were feeling the strain and West Ham people in rest centres there had to be bussed again, this time to Finchley in north London. Some West Ham residents billeted in St John's Wood found themselves bombed out there too; when they were moved to Marylebone, they were bombed out again. It must all have seemed rather personal. Taken to Marylebone rest centres, they understandably refused to budge unless they were removed from London to the country. They were taken eventually by authorities in outer west London at Feltham, Hayes and Sunbury. In Stepney, 'Someone seems to be spreading a rumour … that people who want to go to the country should assemble at the People's Palace', a cultural and education centre in Mile End Road and now the temporary town hall, the real thing damaged by bombing. Within a day 500 had assembled there ready-packed. Some were carried to railway stations in council dustcarts, no other transport available in the rush to move them before the sirens sounded again. The officer in charge of a rest centre in Hammersmith where West Ham residents had been moved feared a riot if they weren't taken out of London; on the other hand, homeless from Bermondsey taken to Chelsea refused to get off the buses and demanded to be taken back to their home borough, where council resources were badly stretched because the town hall had been destroyed by bombing. This was the sort of chaos that faced Henry Willink and his regional staff as they took up post at the end of September.[34]

The numbers of London's bombed-out homeless effectively living in rest centres peaked on 25 September at 25,590; 14,000 of them were in the LCC's rest centres in inner London. The number never dropped below 10,000 a night until the end of November and there was another peak on 23 October of 24,000 after the severe raids in the middle of the month. But it was not just raids that caused the problem. From August it had become clear that unexploded bombs (UXBs) were requiring the evacuation of thousands of Londoners who had to move out of their homes until the bomb was dealt with or it exploded. These were either bombs that were 'duds' or 'time-bombs' whose fuses deliberately delayed explosions to cause major damage to rescue and other services. This was another problem not fully anticipated by the authorities. The large numbers of UXBs caused great consternation. They accounted for about a third of the rest centre population, people who would not be moved on until 'their' bomb could be made safe, one way or another. On 30 September some 1,200 UXBs were awaiting disposal in London and bomb disposal sections of the Royal Engineers had to be increased from twelve teams in August to eighty in October. By the end of the year the number of UXBs in disposal queues had fallen to 200 and the numbers of homeless in the rest centres to 6,000.[35]

In the interim, one UXB had etched a famous name for itself. On 12 September a one-ton HE bomb narrowly missed the south-west tower of St Paul's Cathedral and buried itself into London clay. Once there it proceeded to sink slowly deeper into the ground. It fractured a gas main, which caught fire and had to be extinguished and repaired before the bomb disposal squad under Lieutenant Robert Davies could get to it. By that time it lay twenty-seven and a half feet below ground. It could not be defused and had to be drawn out by steel hawsers attached to two lorries. On 15 September it was recovered from the ground, loaded onto one of the lorries and driven 'at high speed', Davies at the wheel, through streets cleared of people; it was detonated on

Hackney Marshes. Davies and Sapper George Wylie were later awarded the George Cross for their bravery.[36]

THE 20,000 or more moved out of the three worst-hit boroughs in the first month of the main blitz were not the only Londoners on the move. In Poplar too, especially from the vulnerable Isle of Dogs, people clamoured to be evacuated, it was reported by the Home Office on 11 September. Next day Bill Regan thought that 'Fortunately, few people to get hurt now'; those left were generally working men with jobs on 'the island', their wives taken off to other billets. Another evacuation scheme for unaccompanied schoolchildren was got under way – the third since September 1939 – and some 20,500 were removed from London in September; but numbers fell to below 10,000 in October, 4,000 in November and just 760 in December. Some mothers with young children were part of this official exodus, a number moving from Chelsea to the West Country in October, for instance.[37]

But in and around these organised evacuations were countless private moves of a voluntary nature, families or individuals taking shelter with relatives in the outer suburbs or beyond, others taking pot luck. Arthur Buddell moved Mary and May to Southport, where he'd been billeted as a civil servant before Christmas 1939. Anthony Weymouth sent his family from Marylebone to Beaconsfield, renting a house there and going down himself at weekends. Godfrey and Laurie Clarke rented billets in Chalfont St Giles, Buckinghamshire, and travelled to shop and office by Green Line coach or sometimes got lifts from people driving in. John Colville, a civil servant at 10 Downing Street, moved his elderly parents from Pimlico to a friend's house in Staffordshire. Hilda Neal's friend Follie went to stay with an acquaintance in Devon, and so on. There was no accurate tally of such movements at this stage in the war but they must have been legion – all these moves but one took place in September, nervous Follie fleeing on the 8th. All were middle-class people, but it's clear from the inner East End that many working people were among them too. Mrs Caroline Wright of Ocean Street, Stepney, 'nicked off' on 9 September to the hop fields in Kent – she returned on 24 September but then had to move out because of a UXB. And 'South London families who have evacuated themselves to safe areas' were complaining in September of a 'rent ramp', having to pay 50s a week for a single room. It was thought to have been started by 'wealthy people' moving into the same areas who were able to pay over the odds and outprice working-class refugees.[38]

Indeed, the Big Blitz widened old wounds of class hostility. They crystallised around the old trope of a suffering East End and an indifferent West End, the 'rich swine' (Orwell's term) bolting to the country while leaving their mansions locked and barred behind them. At first it was thought that the West End had not been bombed at all and then, when it was clear that it had, a political point could be made of that too: Hilda Neal recorded an 'Aggressive Labour bus driver' proclaiming that the great AA barrage of 11 September opened up solely because the West End had been hit. CP leaflets circulating in the East End spread the word that better shelters had been provided in the West End – true enough in respect of private accommodation in hotels and so on, but not true for public provision. Class loathing worked both ways of course. Barbara Nixon, the Finsbury warden, middle-class and left-wing, thought 'attempts were made' to exclude East Enders from West End shelters in the first few days:

On a 38 bus in Piccadilly a wretched-looking woman with two children got in and sat down next to me; they still had blast dust in their hair and their tattered clothing; they were utterly miserable, and the lady opposite moved her seat and said, loudly, that people like that should not be allowed on buses. Fortunately, the conductor announced with promptitude that some ladies could take taxis.[39]

Whether attitudes like this, or fear of something similar, lay behind East End discomfort over accepting West End billets seems likely, together with practical reasons such as the costliness of shopping in west London and the relative dearth of street markets. But in areas like Soho and the theatre districts, where Jewish and cockney East Enders felt comfortable, there were fewer reservations. Klara Modern, her lover, Otto, now holding a senior position in Westminster ARP, used from October the basement public shelter under Stagg and Russell, drapers, on the north side of Leicester Square: 'about 150–300 East End people come here every night with their bedding and sleep here either on the floor or on the benches which have been provided'. By this time some amenities were being installed – 'a water-tap, a canteen, a first-aid room and some bucket-lavatories behind curtains'.[40]

The West End, and west London generally, got a fair share of bombing from pretty much the outset, though the inequality of sacrifice, especially in the first week of the Big Blitz, would never entirely be rectified. Perhaps it was the bombing of Buckingham Palace, where the royal family were in residence, on 11, 13 and 15 September, which seemed to demonstrate that every Londoner really was in it together. It was a symbolic moment, made much of by the press: 'The bomb does not discriminate. Rich and poor alike, king and commoner,' as the Labour *Daily Herald* put it. And very soon the bomb damage in the West End and around, in streets and places familiar to almost every Londoner, became all too apparent. Madame Tussaud's in Marylebone Road was badly damaged over the first weekend and Anthony Heap, an inveterate blitz tourist, as were many others – understandable when newspapers were so vague about where bombs fell and the BBC worse than useless – went to take a look: 'It was one of the sights of London today.' By the end of September he took in the badly blitzed Holborn (Covent Garden, Bloomsbury, High Holborn into Finsbury), the extensive damage in Oxford Street and Oxford Circus (where Bourne and Hollingsworth, D. H. Evans, John Lewis, Selfridge's and Peter Robinson's, where Heap had worked, were all badly blasted), the bombed University College, the blitzed City in Cheapside and around, a bomb-scarred Charing Cross and the Strand, really everywhere in central London had its wounds from early on. Nowhere was immune – even the London of the 'rich swine' seemed fast disappearing when the Carlton Club was reduced to rubble in early October. 'As we drove to No. 10,' wrote John Colville on 22 September, 'I noticed how many houses, in Berkeley Square and Bruton Street, are crumbled to dust.'[41]

Even so, there were many consolations for the wealthiest among those of the West End's private citizens who chose to slog it out as Londoners rather than 'nicking off' to the country as they might easily have done. The upmarket restaurant trade adjusted quickly to difficult circumstances. The Hungarian, 16 Lower Regent Street, moved underground, offering tables, a dance floor and a 'Tzigane band', and beds for the night in the event of a bad raid; the waiters were trained in ARP, but if customers didn't fancy staying then 'A team of private cars, driven by tin-hatted chauffeurs, is ready to escort you ...' It was the big London hotels, steel-framed monsters dating from the turn of the century, as resistant to the Luftwaffe's battering as any buildings in the land, that became the epicentre of London wealth. They all played their part but the Dorchester in Park Lane was considered for the really well-off 'the focal point of London after dark'. The Coopers, Lady Diana and Duff, had a suite there and so did Lord Halifax, then still Foreign Secretary. Chips Channon had dinner there on Guy Fawkes Night, all bangs and whizzes courtesy of Herr Goering: 'London lives well: I've never seen more lavishness, more money spent, or more food consumed than tonight, and the dance floor was packed. There must have been a thousand people.' When he left there was a raid on so he wore his tin hat – a club servant told him he had 'a screw loose' and fastened it for him: 'The contrast between the light and gaiety within, and the blackout and the roaring guns outside was terrific: but I was more than a little drunk.'[42]

Naturally enough, such contrasts provoked resentment in the battered East End. It was nurtured by the CP, keen to point up the shortfalls of Tilbury, say, with deep-shelter luxury in the West End hotels. The message was driven home by a demonstration at the Savoy Hotel in the Strand on the evening of Saturday 14 September. A seventy-strong party from the East End, women prominent among them, demanded shelter and refreshment. It was an ill-tempered affair but it made a strong point. That night or the next the windows of the May Fair Hotel south of Berkeley Square were broken in what was thought to be an organised demonstration. The authorities were worried for a moment, but this was a manufactured outrage that failed to catch fire – perhaps, as a CP provocation too far, was never intended to.[43]

ON the same day that Henry Willink was appointed commissioner for London's homeless, Sir Warren Fisher, an experienced senior civil servant, was made commissioner for an equally worrying consequence of mass bombing: the clearance of rubble and the restoration of London's road network. Some 20,000 Army Pioneer Corps and a further 20,000 council highways staff were drafted in to assist the LCC architects' and engineers' departments, hitherto overwhelmed by the problem. Work began in early October. Anthony Weymouth, for one, was impressed by the results within a week. Certainly the effort was badly needed. The combined menace of UXBs and roads blocked by debris made London a city of dead ends and tortuous diversions. That, combined with damage to railway tracks and – worst of all – railway bridges had made Londoners' journey to work a nightmare from the very first Monday of the blitz, 9 September. Unless you lived within walking distance of your job, a rare luxury for Londoners, every morning and every evening were puzzles to test the firmest resolve. Getting to your destination was a daily victory. Vivienne Hall battled from Putney to the City through 'pavements and roads ... thronged with people' but 'there's absolutely no panic or grumbling anywhere. We picked up odd people on the way and two to four hours to get to work seems quite the usual time, but still we get to work, Mr. Hitler!' 'Our railway is in action again, but no Piccadilly trains available,' recorded Dorothy Wells. 'I travelled District, got out at Charing Cross and went by emergency bus service to Temple, and arrived [at Aldwych] at 9.30a.m. "Buy a season ticket and see the world."' Some journeys were more exciting than others. It was 'An adventurous journey to Town' for a breathless Arthur Buddell on 13 September:

E. Croydon to Balham. Light delivery van at Balham on way to Stockwell[.] Alighted at Clapham Common at 9.40 because of alarm. Took shelter in public shelter but atmosphere so bad after 40 mins that I decided to quit. Raining heavily. Managed to Board a GPO charabanc going to Town[.] Halted on Mall when a Molotov breadbasket [of incendiaries] was dropped [by a plane that 'zoomed over me']. One incendiary landed 4 feet from bonnet of charabanc – we all fell on floor. Put it out many others also fell within small radius Walked to Piccadilly[.] Took Tube to Holborn. Private car from Holborn to London Bridge – walked to office. Arrived 1pm. All clear 2pm.[44]

Inevitably, every form of public transport was stuffed to the gunwales – holes in London's bus fleet had to be repaired by importing 472 multicoloured vehicles from provincial companies in late October, to Londoners' bemusement – and car, van, lorry drivers, even the carters of horse-drawn wagons and drays gave lifts where they could. In all of this it was the young women of London working in West End stores and Whitehall and City offices who most impressed – well, impressed the men at least. In the West End 'the London girl has never been more inspiring than she is to-day,' wrote 'A Warden' at the time. 'It makes one feel proud to belong to such a race.' 'No need to doubt our morale with such witnesses as these,' wrote a Fleet Street man in praise of 'our fine young London women ... hastening briskly and bravely afoot to their shops and offices in the morning ...' He thought it 'the most reassuring and certainly the pleasantest sight in London to-day'. Perhaps they were favoured, observers noting how good looks were an easy passport to an obliging lift.[45]

Against all the odds, the London taxi – those left intact from AFS tendering duties – managed to provide a service for those who could afford it, even when bombs were falling. 'Just not taking any notice?' a character in Nigel Balchin's 1942 novel *Darkness Falls from the Air* asks a cabbie: '"Naow," said the driver. "Goin' to get you it will. Business as usual. Where do you want?"' Apparently, though, there were cabbies and cabbies. The journalist Charles Graves, living in Marylebone, an inveterate taxi user and needing one in a light raid, found that 'Baker Street cab-rank has again turned it up, but Welbeck 1721 (the cab-rank by Great Portland Street) produced a taxi as usual. I asked the driver about it. He said there was a bunch of ex-Servicemen like himself who were determined to carry on during the blitz.' Another newspaper man noticed that some drivers had a suitcase beside the driving seat filled with clothes in case they should find their home blitzed at the end of a shift. 'I hope that future historians,' wrote Vera Brittain at the time, 'will chronicle the part played in the Battle of Britain by London's taxi-drivers, who have constantly braved death by day and by night, and do not even demand an extra tip for the rides they take.'[46]

With roads deadlocked and railways cut, the river seemed to have the chance to come into its own once more. On those stretches of the riverside most bombed the difficulties of getting around London became almost insuperable for a time. Many people worked in docks and factories on the Isle of Dogs but lived south of the river; in the first days the only way across, the Blackwall and Greenwich foot tunnels out of action, was a river ferry from Greenwich reached over a 'beach in thick mud,' across two barges and onto a 'boat made for about twenty and carrying fifty'. A two-hourly riverboat service was set up from Westminster to Woolwich from 13 September to 2 November, but it wouldn't have helped the islanders much or those who worked there. It failed to catch on, carrying only about a thousand passengers a day.[47]

With all these difficulties getting around, employers with safe shelters frequently allowed staff to bed down at work, and others paid for them to stay in modern hotels considered structurally robust. It was a symptom of a new normality in blitz conditions. For those staying in London, how to get safely through the night became everyone's obsession. For many thousands this included a trek to the tube or public shelter. It involved a routine – safeguarding as best one could a personal or family space, assembling at the same time each night, perhaps packing valuables and documents as well as bedding. For Anthony Heap and his mother, the search for a suitable refuge involved much trial and error. They found the shelter at St Pancras New Church crypt, where Mrs Heap was an air raid warden, a 'dusty filthy hole'; they tried the Royal Hotel in Woburn Place but thought the shelter there none too safe and so went to and from both places for a time, settling at neither. They eventually, in mid-October, heard of a new shelter for fifty people opening under Friends House on Euston Road, not far from their home, and sheltered there for the rest of the blitz. They struck lucky, for many public shelters even in mid-October were still found wanting: the 500 people using the Chant Street shelter in West Ham had to raise umbrellas in heavy rain because the concrete roof leaked. Perhaps for that reason, perhaps from a desire for privacy, most people – as we have seen – preferred staying at home, either in 'the Andy' or other garden shelter or somewhere in the house where they felt safest. It was also often possible to move to another home considered safer than the one they were in: almost everyone rented and at this point in the war could find another place with relative ease. But very many just stayed in their beds, even if moved downstairs, and took pot luck. As the journalist James Langdale Hodson put it in late October, 'Four-fifths of us – and it may be far more – have no security that is worth twopence – except the security of chance, the security that tells you it is 25,000 to 1 each day against being killed.'[48]

Whether at home or in a shelter, most Londoners (outside the small circle of the super-rich in the West End's great hotels) obeyed a self-imposed night-time curfew in the worst weeks of the blitz, through September, October and into November. This attenuation of London's social life was a notable feature of these weeks. 'The blitz disrupted social relationships,' recalled David Low, the renowned political cartoonist of the *Evening Standard*, living then at Golders Green. 'Places of meeting blew up ... people disappeared, "sources" dried up ...' 'I think it's been rather lonely in the Blitz,' a character in Lettice Cooper's *Black Bethlehem* is made to say. 'There used always to be somebody in after supper, but so many people have gone away or given up any kind of social life that often I don't see anyone at home all the week except Piers', her married lover. To escape both the dangers and the isolation of the blitz, many Londoners negotiated weekend breaks away from London with relatives or friends, or booked rooms in hotels. For those who couldn't get away, and couldn't stand too many lonely hours at home, then the immortal pub was the Londoners' mainstay during these hectic first few weeks of heavy bombing, its cellar a handy shelter if things got too warm.[49]

WHEN Alderman Hurley visited the aftermath of the Balham tube station disaster he reported that 'the sum of £500' was found on a woman's body. 'Numbers of people took their valuables down the station with them every night ...' That £500 must have been found and handed in by a civil defence worker of one kind or another and it is some indication that the temptations of ARP were almost as great as the discomforts and dangers. Not everyone could resist; indeed, perhaps few could. Pay was so ungenerous and conditions so onerous that to succumb to the desire to retrieve and keep, even sell on for a few bob, some item of property deemed abandoned or lost must have often appeared a pretty venal sin. The press and magistrates gave theft from bomb sites the lurid title 'looting'. 'The *Daily Mirror* shouts: "Hang a Looter, and Stop this Filthy Crime." Quite right too,' thought Charles Graves, but some of it must have seemed little different from stealing by finding. It wasn't treated like that in the police courts. 'This looting business is getting a bit too hot for some of the boys,' complained an anonymous London AFS diarist in October 1940. '*The important point about it is that everybody loots.* After that's been set down in black and white, they should start deciding what to do about it.' 'Jim has been arrested for looting,' he recorded later. 'Why don't they put us all inside and get done with it?' The light-fingered fireman became a byword among London traders: when the AFS urged a pub landlord to leave his dangerous blitzed premises he refused until he could personally supervise the rescue of his till.[50]

Councils appointed salvage officers to oversee the recovery of blitzed property, but it was like trying to carry water in a colander. Court cases involving ARP and fire service personnel were common from the outset of the Big Blitz – there were some before but the opportunities multiplied from 7 September onwards. Among many cases coming to court in these four months were two LCC rescue squad workers accused of stealing twelve charred £1 notes from a dead man's life savings of £608; they were each given twelve months' imprisonment at the Old Bailey. Six AFS men were given five years' penal servitude for stealing whisky, gin and socks from fire-damaged shops; one was released later on appeal, all were of previous good character. A fifty-year-old member of a Hoxton demolition and rescue squad, described as 'a very brave man who had been highly commended', was given six months' hard labour for stealing lengths of suiting material 'left exposed or unprotected as consequence of war operations', as the official looting charge had it. And an acting suboicer of the LFB was imprisoned for eighteen months for stealing cloth from a blitzed shop in Stoke Newington; he too had a record of bravery at fires and was a Great War veteran.[51]

Of course, much looting was also carried out by opportunistic thieves, like the fifteen-year-old Ilford youth imprisoned for fourteen days for taking seven torches from a damaged radio shop; he had been touring East End streets looking at bomb damage, or so he said. Three young men from Shoreditch and Islington were given three months' for taking clothes and bedding from a bomb-damaged house, and so on. And some was by professional thieves taking advantage of literally heaven-sent opportunities. 'Air-raids, when they didn't drop something right on top of you, were the best ally London's crooks ever had,' wrote Wally Thompson, an Islington thief with a long pre-war criminal record. Presumably the 'gang of young thieves' from Finsbury Park, seven youths aged eighteen and younger, who broke into tobacconists' during raids would have agreed; they sold the stolen cigarettes to tube shelterers. Thompson himself worked in rescue and demolition for ARP in the City, where every night must have seemed like Christmas. He later boasted of his 'little gang' using '"jelly"' (gelignite) to open safes and vaults, one bang being much like another on raid nights. On a smaller scale, Sidney Day from Highgate, an illiterate building worker imprisoned for theft before the war, was taken on by Hornsey ARP for rescue work, becoming a team leader. 'There weren't much honesty in the ARP,' he recalled years later:

> We was supposed to give in anything we found at the bomb sites to the council depot back at our station, but we all helped ourselves rather than let that lot have it. All we thought about when we got to a bomb site was could we get anything for our wives and kids. If we seen food or clothing we picked it up but we didn't take notice of much else. I took tins of this home and packets of that. All I wanted in that war was to know that there was plenty of food for me family.[52]

This dark side, as it were, of ARP was mirrored in other aspects of London at war in these months. There were numerous incidents, for example, of theft in public shelters – Hilda Neal, a voluntary worker in the canteen of St Martin-in-the-Fields crypt, reported the 'shelter-box' for charity donations broken into and petty theft from collections – and rows and other bad behaviour between shelterers were commonplace. Among the most unpleasant of these were racially aggravated incidents and these too were common in the East End and elsewhere. A thirty-five-year-old motor driver, Lot Black, used abusive language at a Hackney shelter, shouting, 'It's a — Jews' war.' When an ARP warden remonstrated, Black assaulted him with the warden's own steel helmet. A row over a street shelter in Dalston between Jewish and Gentile couples led to 'a kind of a dog fight' in the street; Ernest Roberts, sixty-seven, of independent means, was fined 40s for assault. And there was an ugly scene at Turnpike Lane tube in early November when Leah Downs, forty-five, a fur machinist from Stoke Newington, tried to bed down for the night among some 1,300 shelterers. She said, 'there was plenty of room for everyone on the platform, but because she was a Jewess some of the people did not want her there and they started pushing her and kicking her things about.' She was arrested for disturbing the peace and fined 20s with costs. 'Anti-Semitism has increased markedly,' noted a Mass Observer at the outset of the Big Blitz and historians have charted its persistence throughout the air attacks on London.[53]

YET despite these signs of inter-communal strife, and of Londoners getting out of the war what they could and not at all bothering about other people's property in doing so; despite the flight from London of those who couldn't stand the sleepless nights without end; despite the ongoing fears of those who chose to stay or had no option but to do so and couldn't hide their fright from loved ones or the diaries they confided in; despite the loss of home and the loss of family members, friends or acquaintances, through bombing; despite the eternal smell and taste of brick and plaster dust and the cacophony of bombs and guns and the nerve-scratching sound of broken glass being swept up morning after morning; despite all this and more, Londoners in general stood firm, kept working and even nourished a sense of humour through it all. 'The Londoners, as the Americans are saying, can take it, and London itself – this grey sea of a city – can take it,' J. B. Priestley told the nation in his Sunday night broadcast on the second weekend of the Big Blitz, and by then it was a conclusion that many in London had reached themselves. Colin Perry, living in Tooting and working in an office in Lothbury in the City, was making his way to Bank tube when the siren sounded: 'But no fear, panic, alarm, entered their being; they, we, were Londoners! We were the soldiers of the very front line, and no ties of uniform need bind us.' 'Everyone,' thought Godfrey Clarke in North Kensington, was 'behaving in a wonderfully cool, collected way. It will take a lot of senseless & indiscriminate bombing to really "shake up" us Londoners!' 'London Pride', celebrated early in the following year in a hit song by Noël Coward, himself a native of Teddington in the south-western suburbs, was felt by many to be a badge of honour in that autumn of 1940. The so-called 'myth of the blitz', an obsession of historians for more than sixty years, crystallised early on and took shape first among Londoners themselves.[54]

Pride in their own resilience was reinforced by what outsiders were saying about them. The behaviour of Londoners surprised many who had been accustomed to think them pampered and effete. The *Daily Express* journalist Hilde Marchant confessed she had never liked London or its people, preferring the 'straight-speaking, open-hearted folk' of her native North Country. But now:

> London was no longer the bejewelled dowager, wealthy, secure, full of sham graces. She was a magnificent slut, with her raiment torn, her hair wild, her face bleeding and grimy, fighting like a wild cat, crying Liberty, Equality, Freedom ... That fine, robust, active spirit of Elizabeth's time, that had been deadened and choked by a hypocrisy of wealth, is in London's streets again.[55]

London and Londoners in the blitz, standing tall against the worst bombardment of a civilian population in history to that point, became an inspiration to the rest of the nation and to the free world. When the City of London's Lord Mayor opened a London Air Raid Distress Fund on 11 September donations flooded in from Britain, the Empire and worldwide, reaching £1 million by 6 October. Help from America was especially generous, stimulated by clever propaganda, including *London Can Take It*, a documentary film narrated by the nicotine-voiced correspondent for *Collier's Weekly*, Quentin Reynolds. It opened in New York before the end of October. There were regular radio broadcasts and newspaper articles from London by a clutch of brilliant hardbitten American correspondents, Ed Murrow the star among them. Murrow, Reynolds, Ben Robertson and others became the voice of

London at war not just for American listeners but for Londoners too. American and Commonwealth aid rolled in to the British Red Cross and other relief agencies. It was often smartly targeted: the Mayor of Eastham, Massachusetts, and his 606 townsfolk collected clothes and food for their somewhat larger near-namesake in east London; the American Relief Fund sent 'many thousands of dollars' for the use of Stepney Citizens' Advice Bureau; and shattered West Ham received countless gifts from the American 'Bundles for Britain' scheme and elsewhere:

> The American Red Cross Society, the town of Philadelphia, the Knights of the Round Table of New York, the American Air-raid Relief Fund, the citizens of Boston ... the Canadian Ayrshire cattle farmers, the non-British staff of the Buenos Aires Great Southern, Western, and Midland Railways in the Argentine – have all given mobile [canteen] units of various sorts, expressly for West Ham.[56]

As the blitz developed, instances of charitable giving and collective self-help multiplied. The Lord Mayor's Fund was distributed through local town halls and helped those who had lost clothing and furniture. In numerous suburban districts mutual aid was forthcoming in a variety of good neighbour schemes, like MAGNA in East Ham. By the time the Big Blitz opened there was something similar but on a smaller scale in Edgware, Mill Hill, Southall, Marylebone and no doubt elsewhere. These collective ventures, or the self-help urge that brought them about, underpinned the haphazard development of street night-time fire-watching patrols, raising the alarm to neighbours when incendiaries fell. Arthur Buddell in Croydon 'Joined the local private vigilance patrol' on 22 September, his first duty between 1 and 2.30 a.m. A similar 'Vigilance Squad' was set up in Clissold Crescent, Stoke Newington, that same month, and there were many more.[57]

The WVS proved a great boon to this collective mutual aid. Their Housewives Service was developed even before the war, the first it seems in Barnes, south-west London, and by the summer of 1940 was established in many boroughs. They helped staff mobile canteens for ARP and fire service workers at bomb incidents and received training to assist with first aid and other civil defence tasks. In Shoreditch, where a Housewives' Service was formed in early November 1940, they provided wardens with a nightly census of who was living in their own and neighbouring houses, essential knowledge should it come to a rescue. The novelist Noel Streatfeild was a WVS trainer in Deptford, where it 'became unusual to see a window which had not got a [Housewives' Service] card in it'.[58]

These initiatives might be assisted by important bodies like the WVS or Red Cross but they were truly local in inspiration. Just as before the blitz it was local councils which had pushed the government into making shelter improvements, they continued to show the way ahead once bombing began in earnest. So, for instance, Stoke Newington Borough Council seems to have been the first to install bunks in shelters, from the second week of mass bombing, some weeks before the government began a London-wide programme for the tubes and public shelters. Most, but not all, tubes and public shelters had bunks by the end of the year, with first aid posts and medical attendance in the largest. But it's worth stressing that much of this was achieved only by pushing back against resistance in government: Charlotte Haldane, the ARP scientist's wife (though increasingly distanced from his communist allegiance), was a Labour councillor in St Pancras, active on the ARP Committee: 'Gradually, we were able to introduce many amenities into our shelters; heating, lighting, and canteen services. But each of them had to be fought for, against organisational red tape, less locally than in the Ministry of Health.'[59]

Similarly, Walthamstow Borough Council established London's first civic restaurant as early as August 1940, when bombing began to interrupt gas and other supplies. A privately established model had already, in June 1939, been started for residents of the Peabody Trust's Dalgarno Estate in North Kensington: as the blitz opened it was catering for 3,000 people a week. The Ministry of Food picked up the idea and suggested to the LCC a few days before 7 September that it should provide hot food for blitz victims who were not homeless but had no cooking facilities. The council quickly began a vigorous programme of communal feeding centres which later became the Londoners' Meal Service, prototype for the national British Restaurants scheme that developed later. The first meals centre opened on the Isle of Dogs on 15 September, but Lambeth Council stole a march with a restaurant in The Cut offering, from the 10th, lunch (meat and two veg plus a pudding) for 8d. Once begun, the LCC moved with commendable speed. It had 49 centres open by 2 October, 76 by the 24th and 192 by the 29th, often located at first in those multipurpose school buildings which had been such a communal resource for London. By November they were serving some 42,000 hot meals a week to households without cooking facilities and to men living alone; as in Lambeth, meals were 8d but customers were asked to provide their own cutlery, the LCC's no doubt quickly evaporating. By this time too the LCC's public assistance staff had organised kitchens catering directly for homeless persons in the rest centres.[60]

These also had improved greatly, at least in the LCC area, the council having at last been given a 'free hand' by the government to spend what was necessary on staff and facilities. By the end of the year they were properly heated and had adequate blankets, beds and first aid or medical services; they were generally equipped with shelters or used public shelters nearby. The same was not true everywhere in outer London – West Ham rest centre service continued to struggle – but the improved situation for the homeless was marked. Attitudes changed too, at least in the LCC area, where the poor law, it was said by an authoritative voice, was thrown out of the rest centres altogether. And progress was made with that other great difficulty, providing information and assistance to the homeless without the need to traipse all over a borough for help piecemeal. Hilde Marchant had accompanied a woman and her two children bombed out in early September. 'They had to go to six different departments in six different parts of the enormous borough. They walked from one to the other – the billeting office for tickets, another building for clothes, another for identity cards, another for relief, another for food. They walked miles and there were queues of hundreds wherever they went.' An answer for this problem was again initiated locally. Hackney Borough Council had commandeered the huge Salvation Army Central Hall across the road from the council offices and brought together there all the services needed by the borough's homeless. These were not just provided by the borough but involved staff from Whitehall (the Assistance Board) and the LCC's County Hall dealing with public assistance. There were similar early developments at Wembley and Fulham, and the idea of this early 'one-stop shop' was encouraged by Commissioner Willink to operate across London Region. East Ham was another of the earliest boroughs bringing its post-raid services together, in sad contrast to West Ham. There, ten departmental offices, some of them three quarters of a mile apart, provided services to the homeless, several of which would be needed by anyone bombed out.[61]

There were, then, solid achievements by December, visible almost everywhere. But the role of London's local authorities in bringing them about was largely discounted by the press. Ritchie Calder, with his reports from South Hallsville School, had set the tone from the start. There was a telling moment in a lengthy *Picture Post* feature in November, extolling the efforts of vicars in the East End who had worked hard to support their communities, especially their elderly folk, under great stress from the bombing and its effects. One of them was the Reverend Frank Ferraro of St Matthew's, the parish church of Bethnal Green, who reportedly told someone trying to get help replacing blitzed furniture that '"the Council are doing their best ..." He turned to me [the journalist]. "Aren't they?" he said. The parson is sometimes confronted with the painful necessity of lying to comfort his people.' A week later Ferraro wrote in 'to correct an unfortunate misunderstanding':

> I remember your contributor visiting my parish, and her evident interest and sympathy in all she saw. But why she should conceive I was not sincere when I told 'the bombed old man' the Local Council was doing its best for him, I cannot understand. I speak only for Bethnal Green, but I do believe all in authority are doing and have done their best. Delays and confusion there were bound to be at first (not always due to local administration) but from our young Mayor [Councillor Jimmy Edwards] downwards, all are striving to grapple with an ever-present problem.[62]

Many of these developments were making life easier for the generality of Londoners through November and December 1940. They were aided by a slackening of the Luftwaffe's attacks. The number of raids by day and night had totalled fifty-one in September and sixty in October; it dropped to forty-two in November (Coventry had its disastrous raid on the 14th) and in December twenty-five. After the first siren-free night of 25/6 November light raids resumed for three succeeding nights. There was then a heavy raid on 29/30 November causing considerable damage, followed by a couple of nights of light bombing. This game of cat and mouse continued into December, when some nights and even the best part of a weekend were clear of raids with just the odd siren.

The last raid before Christmas ended at 1.19 a.m. on Christmas Eve. There was then what many Londoners interpreted as a 'Christmas truce', reminiscent of Christmas 1914 on the Western Front. It was brought to an end by a heavy raid on the evening of Saturday 28 December. Even so, this December had given Londoners more quiet nights than at any time since the middle of August.[63]

It all offered the chance for people to draw breath, even for London to get back on its feet, if only shakily. Take the port, so badly damaged on the first weekend of the Big Blitz that many must have thought it was out of commission for the rest of the war. Yet some 1,200 vessels each month were still able to enter and leave it, not disastrously down from the 1,800 of July 1940, before serious bombing began. Take education, seriously disrupted once more by bombing in September and October, so much so that the whole notion of compulsory education in London was quietly dropped. Despite evacuation being vigorously canvassed by the authorities, the numbers leaving were relatively small and in Greater London there remained some 279,000 schoolchildren (125,000 in the LCC area). On 3 December the LCC reinstated compulsory education and other areas quickly followed suit, though in some places parents protested there was no school to send their children to. Even so it was some sort of return to normality, if understandably incomplete. In addition, London's evening classes for adults kept going throughout the blitz; when the evenings proved too risky they met on Saturdays and Sundays. 'Nothing could stop them,' wrote an educationalist at the time.[64]

Take the West End, which had also suffered a terrible knock in the early days from 7 September, with theatres damaged and closed and shows abandoned mid-run. By Christmas things were still pretty bleak, the West End 'woefully short' of new theatrical offerings. *Aladdin* at the Coliseum was the main pantomime draw; Lupino Lane was back in *Mother Goose*, but only in the suburbs at Streatham Hill Theatre. There were fewer than a handful of other West End theatres running plays, though Donald Wolfit was almost single-handedly keeping Shakespeare alive at the Strand Theatre with *The Merry Wives of Windsor*. Even the Windmill's famously naked 'Non-Stop Revue' was closing early because of the raids (7.30 p.m.) but was open daily for the eager from mid-morning. Music lovers too had only depleted fair, the National Gallery concerts taking a Christmas break, though there was a performance of *Messiah* at Queen's Hall as usual. Cinema, however, was more than holding its own, this season's must-see film, Charlie Chaplin's *The Great Dictator*, opening simultaneously that December at the Gaumont (Haymarket), the Marble Arch Pavilion and the Prince of Wales Theatre (Coventry Street); there was a host of other new offerings too, 'up West'.[65]

There were also entertainments for the 'sheltered life' that Londoners quipped they were now having to lead. From the first week of the Big Blitz a striking development of collective life in public shelters was witnessed across London. It was home-grown, if only because there were too many shelters to claim the attention of local authorities starved of manpower and cash. In the frequent absence of council help, shelterers got on with it themselves, though the single most important development – the appointment of shelter wardens or 'marshals' – was overseen by councils, who formally accepted them into the ARP services. Marshals were often supported, sometimes no doubt annoyed, by committees whose members were elected among the shelterers. All of this was helped if shelterers were more or less like-minded, and people who were out of step – we might remember Leah Downs – were encouraged to go elsewhere, sometimes excluded. The character of each shelter marshal seemed to be crucial in defining how the shelter was run. Some, like Mickey 'The Midget' Davis, an optician in Spitalfields, became literally world-famous for their good humour under fire and for the respect they won from shelterers and authorities alike. Mrs Sedgwick, voluntary marshal at 'The Warren', a trench shelter used by 300 in Lewisham, was said to 'have transformed a jumble of shelters into an ordered, busy community in which one forgets self in working for the others'. And in Finsbury, Barbara Nixon thought:

> After the first few nights, people began to select the company they preferred, and very quickly each of our shelters developed a distinct character of its own, which was dependent to a large extent on the shelter marshal. Mrs. Barker, in charge of No. 2, brought down her gramophone, and her shelter was noisy and gay. With a lusty voice she led the singing, and kept it up till three or four in the morning if it was a noisy night ... The next shelter was in the charge of a retired post office worker with silver white hair, and they were all very nervous and quiet ... Male and female marshals would go back to their houses several times during the night, while the raids were on, and make great jugs of tea to be handed round.[66]

Whatever the character of the marshal or committee, though, there was now a clear line of command for keeping the shelter clean and equipped with sanitary and other facilities; for running some sort of canteen or arranging for the WVS to have a mobile facility called in; for negotiating a supply of bunks, electricity and so on from the council or from shelter owners like railway companies or wharfingers. Shelter marshals were often grouped by councils into district organisations to communicate with the authorities and help determine priorities: Mickey Davis became Chief Shelter Marshal for Stepney, for instance. Some tube shelters, where around 105,000 were bedding down on average each night in December, used the same or similar methods, even publishing shelter newspapers to keep people informed and to canvass opinion – like *The Station Searchlight* at the Oval in Lambeth, *The Swiss Cottager* in Hampstead and many others north and south of the river. Canteen facilities were also vastly improved, some installed in larger stations (the first at Holland Park station in October 1940) or provided by mobile canteens in tube carriages travelling the network. And at the Chislehurst Caves in outer south-east London, a complex of privately owned tunnels in the chalk dating back to Saxon times if not before, a sophisticated underground township slowly honed its facilities under the superintendence of twenty-four marshals, a system of 'captains' for each fifty families and precise regulations for the management of 14,000 people at the peak.[67]

The need for more than tea and disinfectant to keep shelterers' chins up had been spotted from the outset, but not by the authorities. Nat Travers, a cockney music-hall comedian specialising in coster songs, whose career stretched back to the 1890s, organised a Friday night entertainment in big public shelters around the Mile End Road, Stepney, from the first week or so of mass bombing; he was still going strong two months later. Travers was a big star to the East Enders, but most had to make do with what they could get, like local talent and the concert parties that ARP organisations had thrown up from the beginning; usually they had nothing at all. But shelter culture took off once the basics of some sort of nightly order and comfort had been achieved. In November a London-wide coordinating group, deadeningly titled the Central Advisory Committee on Entertainment and Instruction, was set up. Formed of representatives of local councils and government departments, it encouraged local authorities to hire in entertainers and adult education courses. Bermondsey and perhaps others were ahead of the game, establishing its own Council for Social Activities in October and planning to run 'theatreshows' on makeshift stages in shelters.[68]

Christmas gave everything a boost. The West End's theatreland may have been sadly muted but the rich determinedly enjoyed themselves in their hotels, even organising a Blitz Ball in a Park Lane venue, the Grosvenor House hotel's underground ballroom, on 14 December: 600 attended in aid of maternity care for servicemen's wives at Queen Charlotte's Hospital. But good cheer showed most in the ranks of London's ARP services. Admiral Evans, the dapper Regional Commissioner for London's civil defence, who was always to be seen at major incidents in impeccable naval uniform, wrote shortly after the war that the ARP's 'Wardens Service' was 'the greatest community movement we have ever seen'. So it surely was. It proved itself not only among the rubble and bomb victims but at every Christmas and New Year throughout the war. The Christmas of 1940, in the midst of mass bombing, was no exception. Children's parties organised and collected for by ARP staff were universal across London: at the Warwick Road Shelter, Ealing, by the wardens of Post C5; by the wardens of Post K4, Hounslow, for local children, with Master Gerald White, eleven, delighting all with his accordion and drums; for adults and children using the shelter at Anerley Hill, Upper Norwood, by the volunteer wardens of Penge Post No. 2; for children at air raid shelters in Mitcham with Father Christmas (Shelter Marshal Harvey) appearing through the escape hatch in lieu of a chimney; at Balham, with 'the wardens' own "crazy-gang"' causing 'screams of laughter'; indeed, in every borough, at all points of the London compass.[69]

These were fun moments in what was generally a quiet Christmas in London. Dorothy Wells, a clerk in a firm in Aldwych, spent it at home in Ealing with her elderly mother and Ken, her brother, whose unpromising allotment was beginning to bear fruit. 'Clear morning, not too cold – the best London Christmas Day weather for four years,' she thought. After morning service with Ken at their Methodist church:

Home to a very nice dinner – just roast beef, Yorkshire, potatoes, Ken's sprouts, Christmas Pudding and cider, but we were very thankful to have so much. We all dozed in front of the parlour fire most of the afternoon, but have now had tea – 7.45 p.m. and mean to have a few games before bedtime. Jerry has not as yet been over. It seems like a Christmas truce, though the idea of one has been mooted and scoffed at in the papers.[70]

The truce, if that's what it was, would soon end with a bang.

5

WHEN WILL IT ALL END?
29 DECEMBER 1940–21 JUNE 1941

WHETHER by accident or design, 29 December 1940 was a lucky night for the Luftwaffe. It was a Sunday and so the City was largely empty of night-workers, with only haphazard arrangements in place for care-taking unoccupied buildings; it was an exceptionally low tide in the Thames, the river confined as the evening wore on to a shallow channel midstream; and there was a strong breeze from the south-west. This was the perfect night for the largest fire-raising raid so far attempted on London or any other city.

The warning sounded at 6.01 p.m. and bombing began quarter of an hour later. Some 136 bombers dropped HE and 22,000 incendiaries on central London – mainly the City but in adjoining parts of Westminster, Southwark and Holborn – and there was bombing too in Poplar, Camberwell and Lewisham. The raid was brief compared to many that had gone before, with the all clear given at 11.39 p.m. By then, 1,460 fires had been started, all but twenty-eight in central London and most of them in the City; they included six conflagrations, twenty-eight major fires and fifty-two classed as serious. All available pumps in London Region, some 2,680, were in action and a further 300 were summoned from brigades outside the capital. Firefighters were badly hampered by shortage of water, the low level of the Thames rendering use of fire-boats difficult or impossible. Hoses were run over streets half a mile or more from the river in a maze of connected fifty-foot lengths, but results were meagre. Water mains were exhausted or shattered and the large number of static canvas or steel emergency water tanks available in the City were sucked dry and couldn't be replenished. The many water-carrying units brought in from outside London were a help, but soon pumps ran empty and often the firemen could do little more than stand and watch as the fires took hold. 'As I walked along the streets,' a BBC correspondent recalled a few days later, 'it was impossible to believe that these fires could ever be subdued. I was walking between solid walls of fire.' 'I have just spent three days helping to put out the City of London,' wrote a London AFS man on 1 January, when the last fires were finally extinguished. 'More accurately we didn't put it out. It burnt out.'[1]

This 'Second Great Fire of London' was much more destructive than its predecessor of 1666. The helpless firemen were confronted by banks of flame a dozen storeys high. As each warehouse burned, its contents released what became a medley of 'a thousand smells' – coffee, cinnamon, bad eggs, burning hay and gramophone records, cocoa, tobacco, tea and paper, for this was 'a holocaust of books', some five million said to have been destroyed in the publishers' repositories long-clustered in Paternoster Row and St Paul's Churchyard. The cathedral itself was the very centre of the drama. It was protected by dedicated teams of fire-watchers, in place since the outbreak of war to defend the best-loved building in London as well as they could. Twenty-eight incendiaries fell on St Paul's and its precinct. The water mains failed here too and 'the Watch' had to rely on buckets, stirrup pumps and sandbags. Disaster looked likely when a messenger from Cannon Street fire station reported that the cathedral's dome was alight, but luckily the incendiary that had lodged under its outer skin burned through timbers and fell to the Stone Gallery, where it was smothered by cathedral staff. Subsequently Herbert Mason's famous photograph, taken from the roof of the *Daily Mail* building, of St Paul's triumphantly rising above the inferno of smoke and flame below, came to symbolise for Britain and the world an apparently indestructible London.[2]

Much else, though, had been destroyed. The fifteenth-century Guildhall, itself partly restored after the first Great Fire, was gutted despite brave efforts by its 'fire squad'. Eight City churches, all designed by Wren, were burned out, with their priceless artefacts, including carvings by Grinling Gibbons, lost for ever. The old City halls of the Girdlers', Coopers' and Saddlers' companies were destroyed and others badly damaged. Sappers of the Royal Engineers would demolish with explosives the remains of dangerous buildings for a couple of weeks to come. In all about a third of the Square Mile was lost in a single night. There were losses too among the Londoners. Some 163 were killed, mostly outside the City itself, and 509 badly injured. They included sixteen fire personnel killed and 250 treated in hospital, many with faces and hands blistered by fires fought from a distance; eye injuries, red-hot sparks caught under the eyelids, caused temporary blindness in many. 'It was the firemen's night,' as Robin Duff put it for the BBC.[3]

Some firemen, however, were critical of their officers for mismanaging the water shortage and for a lack of coordination of resources on the ground. Worse, it seemed that the City had burned due to a lack of foresight by business owners, by the City Corporation and by the government itself. Some buildings, St Paul's most famously, had been saved by prompt action from trained staff in place to safeguard important places at night. Why not make such precautions general and compulsory? After such a disaster, even though it seemed the horse had already bolted, the government had little scope but to agree. Two nights later, on New Year's Eve, Herbert Morrison, Home Secretary and Minister of Home Security, broadcast to the nation: 'I am here to call upon you – some millions of you – for urgent duty.' Recalling Anthony Eden's Home Guard broadcast of June, Morrison announced the creation of a 'Civil Defence Home Guard' among householders and business owners to watch over homes and enterprises by night and prevent a repeat of another destructive fire-raid. The responsibility of organising neighbourhoods was given to council air raid wardens; businesses had the duty to set up a fire watch among their staff or to combine with other firms in a rota. This duty to join a fire watch was to be compulsory, with penalties for non-compliance, but regulations would take time to put in place and in the interim people should organise among themselves as volunteers: 'Now then! The latest answer to the latest attack. See your warden at once. Fall in, the fire-bomb fighters!'[4]

The fire guard proved to be a massive extension of civil defence in London. At first the fire-watching duty fell on men, who had to spend forty-eight hours on duty in any month in their workplaces or street (though workplaces took precedence). But both men and women under sixty had to register with their local councils for duty should they be called upon and many women volunteered: 'It seems mean to leave it to the men just because women are not yet to be compelled,' thought Doreen Bates at her City tax office in Seething Lane, untouched on 29 December. Women would not be compelled to join a fire watch until May 1942, but in small concerns their participation was unavoidable – and sometimes onerous: 'we're so short of men,' wrote Phyllis Warner of the small private school where she taught, 'that we shall have to volunteer to make the thing work. So it's going to mean spending one whole night a week and one whole weekend a month on the job. What a ruddy nuisance. It's funny how a mere irritation like this brings war home much more effectively than anything you read in the papers, or even the air raids.'[5]

It was in London's homes and streets that the new responsibilities told most heavily. Every house was affected. In suburban Carshalton, Viola Bawtree listed the new requirements:

> Hatchet, or some such implement to be left outside, so that rescuers can burst the door in if necessary. Rake, long handled fire shovel, bag of sand, pail of water, all in kitchen, bag of sand in as many rooms as possible, pails of soil & pails of water. It was the warden asked us to leave the hatchet outside.[6]

Although, as we have seen, fire-watching patrols had not been uncommon in London – in a Gallup poll in January, some 40 per cent of those in fire parties claimed to have joined before Morrison's appeal – the new duties were a massive extension not just of ARP but of neighbourhood collective life. Dorothy Wells, forty, living in Ealing and working in Holborn, found things changed by the fire guard more than by anything else in the war so far. She and her brother Ken volunteered for fire-watching at their church and in their street, Ken also watching at his place of work, a warehouse in the West End:

> Ken and I went to the meeting held for the folk in our road in the Scout Hall at the bottom of Rosebank Road. Dim light, about fifty people there, all standing up, Mr. Peck – warden – set the ball rolling. Mr. Carter was made leader and Mr. Pearce, secretary, seven were elected to the committee and eight people to collect 1/- per household for equipment. A rota of duties is to be posted in Eke's shop.[7]

A local laundry loaned its 'strengthened basement' as a post for the fire party and paid for heating and lighting – self-interested benevolence perhaps – and those on the rota worked in pairs for two-hour shifts. Equipment would have included stirrup pumps, buckets, ladders and 'tin hats', shared between watchers. The attachment to their home street was strong among the London fire guard and there would be trouble

Wednesday 28 September 1938. London newspaper sellers announce a last-ditch effort to avert war with Germany over Hitler's threatened invasion of Czechoslovakia. Chamberlain flew to Munich next day to meet Hitler and Mussolini, and Daladier of France. The agreement, signed on 30 September, allowed Chamberlain to proclaim 'Peace for our time'. Six months later, Hitler invaded anyway.

By 'ARP Sunday', 25 September 1938, the imminent threat of war – and fear of a furious German bombing onslaught – prompted the government to require trench shelters to be dug in London's parks. Here the citizens of Westminster, led by council engineers, dig shelters in St James's Park for anyone caught in the open when bombing began.

On 1–2 September 1939, the LCC evacuated around 700,000 people from Greater London. They included 394,000 'unaccompanied' schoolchildren travelling under the supervision of council staff, mainly teachers. Here, children from Myrdle Street School in Stepney make their way to a London railway station to start their journey.

Between September 1939 and June 1940 an additional 700,000 people left London as private evacuees. Families and single persons reluctant to face the risks of bombing in London took themselves off to provincial relatives or arranged stays in hotels and cottages in rural Britain. Middle-class areas emptied dramatically, as here in a single Hampstead street in early 1940.

The submarine war quickly hit British food imports. To ensure fair shares for consumers, sugar, butter and bacon were rationed from 8 January 1940 and butchers' meat and other foods were added by the summer. The ration card now became one of life's essentials, this queue for the first issue in Westminster photographed on 10 January.

Protecting residents in London's countless working-class streets, with shared houses and cramped backyards, posed a massive problem. In spring 1940 a huge programme of street shelters got underway, with each few houses allocated one to share. At first they were vulnerable to near misses but once strengthened they proved their worth against everything but a direct hit.

With Hitler's invasion of Belgium on 10 May 1940, refugees began arriving in London just three days later. The party pictured here, leaving a London station, were met by Women's Voluntary Services helpers (like the two women in the left foreground) and were billeted in homes and empty houses throughout London by local councils.

In June 1940, invasion fears prompted the authorities to seize around 27,000 people born in Germany, Austria and Italy, most of them men living in London. They included a large number of Jewish refugees, self-evidently anti-fascist. Here male 'enemy aliens' enter a London railway station for internment without trial, probably in the Isle of Man.

Around 5 p.m. on 7 September 1940, London's docklands were attacked by a force of 320 German bombers, the first major onslaught of the blitz. Huge fires were started north and south of the river. These helped guide a second attack from 8.30 p.m. as night fell. Some 438 Londoners were killed that Saturday and early Sunday morning.

The first response of many East Enders from Sunday 8 September was to flee. Evacuations from Stepney and West Ham were organised by the authorities but were often haphazard. Some made their own way out of the East End. Here people in a blitzed street scramble onto a lorry, probably to camps quickly set up in Epping Forest.

Casualties from bombing never reached the levels feared but homelessness far exceeded the help at first available to those bombed out. Here scores of East End families gather their belongings and await council help in the challenging first days of the blitz. By late September, 26,000 homeless Londoners were making do in ill-equipped rest centres.

The East End was bombed first but it quickly became clear that nowhere in London would be safe. This scene at Harrington Square, just east of Regent's Park, on the first Monday morning of the blitz shows the destructive and random impact of HE bombing. The bus was fortunately empty but eleven people died in the houses.

London's front line was its local council ARP and other civil defence services. First on the scene were the wardens and then the stretcher and rescue parties, as here in Willesden, rescuing a child from a bomb-damaged house, probably in September 1940. Pictures like this remind us that the Battle of London was won from the bottom up.

Within a week or two of 7 September, 177,000 Londoners were sheltering in the underground, despite the government wanting to keep it solely for transport. Platforms were badly crowded, as here at Holborn. By the end of 1940 order was established and bunks were generally provided, though just 4 per cent of Londoners regularly used the tubes for shelter.

With disruption to gas and power supplies, mobile canteens were an essential support for bomb victims and rescue workers. Some were gifts to London from sympathisers in the USA, like the one photographed here in October 1940. Generally staffed by WVS workers, canteen vans were a notable feature of bomb incidents throughout the war.

On Sunday night, 29 December 1940, the Luftwaffe staged a spectacular fire raid on the City and nearby. Some 1,460 fires were started, many uniting in conflagrations of unstoppable ferocity. Firefighters, like this man on top of a 100ft ladder, were hampered by strong winds and by poor water supplies caused by a low tide in the Thames.

in March when the authorities sought to make them sign up to watching others' streets instead of their own. In general, though, street fire-watching was keenly embraced: by early March there were over 700,000 street fire-watchers enrolled in London Region. It all brought an entirely new camaraderie to London's streets, including among Dorothy's suburban neighbours in Osterley Park View Road: 'We went across to the Davis's basement, and had a very interesting two hours. Mr. Carter, Mr. Hufford and Mr. Wilson (my friend of last week) and we had a good chat. The Yellow Warning was up but there was no warning while we were there.'[8]

THERE were, indeed, quite a few breathing spaces in these first weeks of 1941. Eighteen raids struck London in January, six of them by day only, so nineteen nights were clear of bombing and some were free from warnings too. Most raids were moderate or light in nature, though the sharp 'hit and run' daylight attacks were alarming to experience. The worst of all the raids that month were on the nights of 11/12 and 12/13 January, which killed 105 and 106 respectively. Bad weather – ice and snow making Londoners shiver for the second consecutive harsh winter of the war, with January to May unseasonably cold – was thought to have deterred more vigorous efforts by the Luftwaffe. In February there were two daylight raids and fourteen by night, leaving fourteen free from bombing; and for the next two weeks, till the middle of March, there were nine raids, one a major attack on the night of 8/9 March, the remainder classed as light.

By January, Londoners had endured over four months of bombing. Everyone had adjusted to some extent. The experience of Phyllis Warner, a resident of Mary Ward Settlement, Tavistock Place, in battered Bloomsbury, might no doubt have been echoed by many:

I'm distinctly pleased with the fact that I haven't slept in the shelter for a month, in spite of warnings, planes, guns, and a few bombs around. Last night an odd incident showed me that my nerve has improved. There was no warning on and I was sleeping peacefully in my bed when I was suddenly jerked awake by a terrific high-pitched whistle. It shrieked over my head, then came an explosion so near that the bed gave an enormous heave, and in the same moment I heard the heavy buzz of a German plane dying away ... I heard footsteps hurrying down to the basement, and after a minute the warning going, but I turned over and went off to sleep again. It bucks me up to know that I couldn't have done this a few weeks ago.[9]

It was an adjustment shared by workers in civil defence and the regional and local authorities across London. Quiet nights and light raids left scope for improving ARP in many directions. In early 1941 London's ARP was everywhere still work in progress, nowhere the finished article. It continued to be hampered by government penny-pinching. Finchley was told that it couldn't install heating in shelters, Leyton was ordered to sack thirty wardens because it was overstaffed, and similar pressures were experienced in Chelsea and no doubt else-where. Despite the obstacles from above, however, improvements were built on strengths and initiatives developed from below. In early January Alderman Charlie Key, Poplar's ARP chief, became yet another special regional commissioner London-wide, this time overseeing shelter provision. It was recognition of his and Poplar's solid work through those first cataclysmic months of the blitz and he urged London to follow his borough's example, making street shelters safer and more comfortable. Still viewed with suspicion in many neighbourhoods, street shelters had generally proved safer than expected, despite the discovery of a design fault in government specifications which failed to anchor the roof to the walls. Now they would be improved by a programme of damp-proofing, their walls and roof would be strengthened with a new concrete outer skin, and they would have 'bunking' and electric heaters and safe 'slow-combustion stoves' installed. By the end of January some 462,000 bunks had been installed in shelters, 142,000 in that month alone. In addition, the government and London Passenger Transport Board were ramping up the programme to equip the tubes with steel bunks, with 1,200 installed from January and many more planned for eighty stations.[10]

Communal feeding too was improving everywhere. In the tubes there were 127 canteens 'serving hot soup, sausages, sausage rolls and meat pies, also cake, chocolate, buns, biscuits, tea and coffee at low charges'; mothers could get a sterilised bottle of warm milk for 1½d. Outside the tubes, by early February, canteens had been provided for 1,980 public shelters, serving 200,000 shelterers, and mobile canteens were seen everywhere, many of them funded by well-wishers abroad: 'Argentine employees' of a Buenos Aires meat-packing firm provided two for Finsbury by April, for instance. For shelters of 500 persons or more, 154 of them in London excluding the tubes, almost all had a medical aid post, and the remaining handful were to get them soon; smaller shelters were to be provided with medical posts on a group basis. In all, 250 trained nurses and over 200 visiting doctors were already in post. Some borough libraries had begun lending books to shelters, an initiative now embraced by the London Civil Defence Region; St Pancras established the first mobile library in London in February. And the entertainments that had begun to flourish before Christmas sustained Londoners' enthusiasm into the new year: LCC teachers offered drawing, art and handicraft classes; shelter committees organised sewing bees; Morley College music students gave concerts in the arches under Waterloo Station, where 6,500 might find shelter, including some 500 homeless who were living there semi-permanently, refusing billets elsewhere. A bright new development in many places was 'discussion groups'. 'In the Bermondsey shelter I go to,' wrote Millicent Rose, the future historian of the modern East End, 'we have discussed all kinds of topics, from travel talks to town-planning, from unemployment to "Should women have equal pay for equal work".'[11]

There were developments elsewhere too. Rescue and demolition teams were being trained in tunnelling through rubble, thought to 'offer a much more rapid means of rescue, in certain circumstances, than ordinary methods of removal of debris' from the top; pay for skilled men had been raised to £4 2s for an eighty-four-hour week; and a 'tic-tac language', pinched from racecourse bookies, enabled signalling for special items when the noise of the blitz drowned out even a navvy's shout, the signs illustrated in the LCC's new training guide in June. Billeting of the homeless was assisted in two ways. An Emergency Repairs Committee was established in February to assist local councils to patch up houses after a bad raid; skilled men released from the army were organised in teams and drafted into blitzed districts. And hostels were established for men, youths and young women whose homes had been broken up by evacuation or enemy action; the first was opened by Mrs Churchill in Hoxton in January. Finally came a new initiative on the domestic shelter front. The Andersons, properly installed, had proved almost indestructible in raids. But many households had no garden and were 'sheltering' at home, like Vi Regan under the dining-room table, in varying degrees of safety. To improve shelter indoors, which is where most people wanted to be, 'Morrison' table shelters went into production in January and began to be delivered at the end of March. They were steel rectangular boxes with hinged wire sides, sheltering two adults and two small children, given free to families with incomes below £7 a week and on sale eventually at £7 to those who could afford to pay; Boy Scouts in west London were helping house-holders assemble the 200–300 separate parts involved in building a Morrison that June.[12]

There continued to be shortcomings. West Ham's dysfunctional ARP system was plagued by public infighting between officers and council-lors and by rapidly changing controllers. Officials of the government's Assistance Board continued to get a bad press for their unsympathetic attitudes to the homeless. Bad behaviour continued in some shelters, notably the Tilbury in Stepney, where tempers between cockneys and 'foreigners' were often frayed and where communist anti-war agitation still festered, both landing numbers in the courts. Looting continued by ARP wardens, rescue workers and those light-fingered men in blue: poor Vi and Bill Regan had their Isle of Dogs home blitzed with much fire damage but what hurt most was a theft from their living room – 'We had spent months paying off this chimney clock, and now a bloody fireman had swiped it.'[13]

The help given to the homeless provided new opportunities for cheating by the unscrupulous and might have accounted for some offi-cial defensiveness: Sarah Bannister, thirty-six, still-room maid of Kennington Road, Lambeth, was given six months' hard labour in March 1941 for defrauding Assistance Board officials in Tottenham, Stoke Newington and Camden Town, claiming air raid losses for homes she'd never lived in: 'Getting Money in this Way for Some Time' was the headline in a local paper. As Bannister shows, taking advantage of the war's opportunities was not a monopoly of ARP. Far from it. Every day, it seemed, shopkeepers were fined for overcharging, for selling food without ration coupons, for imposing an unlawful condition on sale ('no oranges without apples' in Bethnal Green in January) and more. Looting and shop-breaking by petty thieves remained extremely common, their ranks swelled by a growing number of army deserters who depended on theft for their livelihood. And a Marylebone magis-trate pronounced a public warning from the bench in January about a new opening for depredations in London: 'Railways at the present time are being robbed to an appalling extent: men in the company's service for years are taking advantage of the difficulties of observation during the black-out; goods are disappearing wholesale; and I cannot describe it as anything but extremely serious.' As the writer William Sansom, himself a London AFS man, wryly commented a few years later: 'Londoners were celebrated for "taking it", and in fact quite a number took as much they could immediately lay their hands on.'[14]

THE ten weeks between the start of 1941 and the middle of March may have been a time of relative recuperation for London's civil defenders, but they included two major challenges, dreadful tragedies both. In the heavy seven-hour raid that started on Saturday 11 January and continued into Sunday, a bomb struck crowded bus stops close to Liverpool Street station. One bus was blown over, one covered in building debris and two others 'disintegrated'. 'Over forty corpses were splayed all over the road and pavement. Severed arms and legs could be dimly discerned by the light of the flickering flames.' A quarter of a mile away worse was to happen. An HE bomb burst through the roadway outside the Bank of England and exploded in the booking hall of Bank tube station. The blast travelled through the top subways and escalators and swept shelterers and passengers off the platforms into the path of trains pulling in. Fifty-two died, bodies and remains taken to the City's mortuary and others nearby:

> They varied from wax-like forms, looking for all the world as if they had been brought from Madame Tussaud's chamber of horrors, to mere handfuls of grubby offal hardly identifiable as human. One woman was completely naked, every shred of clothing torn from her by blast: at first sight she appeared to be a negress, until one noticed that she was covered from head to foot in a thick film of black train-oil. Another headless trunk wore only a pair of corsets, and had not the slightest evidence leading to identification; yet when the corsets were removed, they were found to be completely lined with 950 £1 notes.[15]

The bomb left a deep crater in the middle of an interchange of seven major City streets, blocking all traffic above ground and three tube lines below. The City's highway engineers, supplemented by army sappers, set to work clearing the chaos of concrete and steel on Sunday morning. In two weeks the 'largest crater in London' was free from rubble and on 1 February a temporary iron and steel road bridge began to inch out from Cornhill to Poultry. It was completed, and opened by the Lord Mayor, on Monday 3 February. The station was in use again by 17 March and by May the bridge had been removed and the seven-road interchange was flowing once more.[16]

The heavy death toll at Bank station and the remarkable efforts to make good the damage were overshadowed by the second tragedy of these 'quiet' weeks. A four-hour raid by around ninety bombers hit central London hard on the night of 8/9 March, 'a date which became known everywhere as the Café de Paris night'. The Café de Paris, a two-tiered oval basement with balcony in Coventry Street, Leicester Square, was an especially popular venue for rich young West Enders. It had been made fashionable when Prince Edward frequented it in the mid-1930s and customers continued to be drawn there by its famous dance band of black musicians led by Ken 'Snakehips' Johnson, from British Guiana. Its restaurant and dance floor were fairly deep underground and 'advertised as "the safest place to dance in Town"'. At 9.50 p.m. two bombs fell on the building overhead but did not explode. Both penetrated the basement; one failed to detonate and spilled its contents over the floor. The other burst in the restaurant's confined space, bringing down the balcony and creating a bloody shambles. Bystanders outside heard the bombs' whistle but no explosion and even two days later 'The Café de Paris still looks absurdly untouched.'[17]

The lack of damage above ground confused observers and there was a delay in getting a clear message about the scale of the disaster to the Westminster control room; the nearest warden's post, as luck would have it, was also short-handed that night. This confusion led to some ambulances not getting there till an hour later. Below ground, in deadly chaos, Johnson and many of the band were killed instantly: 'the best swing band in London gone,' lamented Joan Wyndham in Chelsea. Killed too was the Café's owner, Martin Poulsen, a former Danish Olympic athlete, Poulsen's head waiter and many staff and customers. It might have been even worse: the cabaret was between shows and the chorus girls remained unharmed in their dressing rooms. As news reached the street civil defence staff and first aiders rushed to help, the staircase became a confusion of injured clambering up and rescuers struggling down. Among them were two nurses from Charing Cross Hospital on duty at a nearby air raid shelter:

> They had to grope about in the darkness by the light of their torches. 'There was dust everywhere,' says one Sister. 'Moving away the dead and injured in the debris, with only the dim light of our torches to guide us,

was a ghastly, and really ghostly, experience. It was difficult to sort out the dead from the living. With help from a number of wardens, we carried the victims as fast as we could to the ambulances, which instantly rushed off to the Hospital. Many of those taken away were already dead, and it was the living really who needed our help. There was no water at all. But with great presence of mind a Sister, also from Charing Cross, said "Use every soda syphon you can find" and with that we made our soda-bicarbonate compresses to apply to the burns.

'In the confusion we noticed that a number of looters had come in from the street and were stealing whatever they could lay their hands on. Sister Lavis dashed off to the shelter in St Martin's crypt, where she remembered seeing some soldiers of the Scots Guards having a cup of tea, and brought them back with her. The soldiers formed a ring round the Café de Paris and so kept out the looters.'[18]

The haphazard effects of blast were illuminated that night by the experience of the sister of the well-known BBC broadcaster Macdonald Hastings. Sitting at a table, she discovered that people either side were killed instantly while she and her friend were not 'as much as blasted off their chairs'. Her bottle of wine was unbroken. But when she fumbled in the rubble for her handbag she picked up something strange and examined it 'in the flame of a cigarette lighter. It was the broken half of a thick gold wedding ring.' Years later, a surgeon found the memories of that night 'seared into my brain. I shall never be able to forget it.' He and his colleagues were operating on casualties for forty-eight hours after, 'removing shrapnel, fragments of wood, glass and crockery' from those brought out alive. Thirty-four died at the Café de Paris or soon after and eighty wounded were taken to hospital. The looters – 'Soho thugs', the Café's historian called them – were after jewellery, gold cigarette cases and watches; the cuff links were stolen from Poulsen's corpse.[19]

The 'Café de Paris night' was very much a West End tragedy, though people died in smaller numbers in many other London districts too. Ten days later, 19/20 March, a 350-bomber raid lasting six hours hit the East End even harder. This was London's worst raid for five months and, in terms of casualties, the worst of the war so far, killing 751. It started 1,881 fires, three classed as conflagrations. Stepney, Poplar and West Ham suffered badly and the worst incident of the night struck Poplar, where a direct hit on a public shelter killed forty-four and injured fifty-two more. This night, which failed to capture the world's attention in the way the Café de Paris bombing had, lodged in East End memories as 'The Wednesday'.[20]

THERE was just one more raid in March and that, for London, was light, on the night following the East End's 'Wednesday': 'Wretched night again,' complained Nellie Carver in the Central Telegraph Office. '"Red" from 8pm to 2.30am – planes constantly overhead apparently going past us this time. Do hope they are not starting another "Blitz" on London – we have had enough.' Carver's hopes seemed to be answered, for there now followed a period of eerie quiet. A National Day of Prayer on 23 March, one of a number throughout the war, probably also sustained believers for there were no more raids for the rest of the month or the first week in April. 'No raids last night,' Hilda Neal wrote on the 7th; '17 quiet nights in succession. What is it the prelude to? Gas? We wonder, and carry our masks.'[21]

In fact, bombing would begin again that night and the following two; it was troublesome but light and was followed by another pause. The game of cat and mouse pursued before Christmas seemed to have been revived. There were just six raids in April and three in May. But they would include the three heaviest hammer blows that London experienced during the whole of the war.

The night of 16/17 April would become 'The Wednesday' for the West End and suburban London, recalled as such years later. 'We were quite unprepared for the awful attack we had at 9pm until 4.30am,' wrote Nellie Carver in West Norwood, close to the very eye of the storm. Some 685 bombers, including those who bombed twice after rearming in France, launched London's deadliest attack of the war so far. 'More bombs and more parachute mines were dropped, more fires were started, more civilian damage done, and more casualties caused than in any previous raid,' LCDR recorded a few days later. Some sixty-six local authority areas in London were bombed, though the greatest weight fell outside the East End. The West End, central London north and south of the river, and south-east London suffered worst. Three nights later, 'The Saturday', was nearly as frightful and might even have turned out worse: bad weather interrupted the Luftwaffe's plans, dividing the raid into two phases. The second was more destructive and once more the East End and the port received most attention. The worst incident was in Nuttall Street, Hoxton, where three blocks of LCC flats and an underground shelter were all destroyed, killing nearly fifty: rescue efforts involved 'fifty volunteer soldiers', a mobile crane operated by firefighters and a score of rescue parties drawn from Shoreditch and nearby boroughs.[22]

Some 2,600 Londoners died as a result of these two raids and over 3,300 were taken to hospital. The damage was immense, including in the City, where St Paul's received a direct (but not disastrous) hit and two more churches were destroyed. The toll of public buildings damaged elsewhere included the Houses of Parliament and the Law Courts. Eighteen hospitals were damaged and civil defence posts were blitzed in many boroughs. The numbers of homeless people in rest centres reached their highest since October 1940, nearly 17,000 on the night of 19 April. Over 5,000 water mains and a dozen major sewers were broken, and in Lambeth over half the population were without gas. There was massive dislocation to railway and underground lines, and services at Waterloo, Charing Cross, Cannon Street and London Bridge were still disrupted on 23 April, with no trains at all at Holborn Viaduct.[23]

These two terrible nights, damage from the first raid still being made safe when the second struck, were followed by seventeen days and nights virtually raid-free. Once more, Londoners held their breath and were left to survey their tattered city. 'Chelsea seems haunted, and the streets full of unhappy ghosts,' thought Hilda Neal, the borough's Old Church, in part a survival from the fourteenth century, now a pile of rubble.[24]

More was yet to come, and that the worst of all. On Saturday 10 May, with clear skies and a full ('Bomber's') moon, a five-hour attack by around 320 bombers, some making 'double and even triple sorties', began at 11.10 p.m., the all clear not sounding until 5.51 a.m. In many ways it was a lighter attack than on 16/17 April, but it had even more disastrous consequences notwithstanding. Over 1,450 people died, mostly on the night though with some 200 dying in hospital over the succeeding days; 2,154 fires were started in London Region, 1,863 of them in the LCC area; 2,500 pumps were supplemented by seventy to a hundred brought in from outside London. The main areas of damage were central London north and south of the river, with a conflagration destroying much of the Elephant and Castle area of Southwark, and yet more damage in the City. Though there were fewer fires than on 16/17 April they proved more destructive, some burning for two days after the Sunday morning: again, a low tide on the Thames hampered the firefighters. Westminster Abbey, Westminster Hall, the British Museum, the Mansion House and more City churches were all hit; a further five City livery companies had their halls demolished; Queen's Hall in Langham Place, London's premier classical concert venue, was burned out and never used again. The chamber of the House of Commons was 'destroyed': as Winston Churchill put it, 'One single bomb created ruin for years.'[25]

The night had a disastrous impact on civil defence personnel. The mayors of Westminster and Bermondsey were both killed while on duty, fire and ambulance stations and wardens' posts were burned out, destroyed or damaged in a dozen boroughs, Battersea lost all or most of its mobile canteens, put out of action by a landmine. In Finsbury's Post 2, three wardens were killed, one dying next day; 'a piece of railing had blown into his stomach.' There or elsewhere in Finsbury, warden Henry Finch was also killed: he had been awarded the George Medal for bravery earlier that day. This was also the worst night for London's transport. At the end of it every mainline rail terminus in London apart from Marylebone was wholly or partly closed; all the City's major roads were blocked, so that not a single bus could run in the Square Mile. Seven Thames bridges were shut. The underground system was hit in twenty places and ten sections of line put out of action. Homelessness spiked in the rest centres again, to over 13,400 on the Sunday evening. In all, this was London's worst night of the whole war.[26]

Nellie Carver had spent it at work, 'pretty well scared' in the telegraph office's underground bunker, the building above them badly damaged by HE. She and Ada, a colleague, left at 8 a.m. to make their way home:

> Holborn was hardly recognisable for smoke & dirt. A large crater was in Giltspur Street (just missed our main gates) so we couldn't pass that way. A big slice of the Old Bailey had been cut clean away ... after six attempts we managed to crawl down the Viaduct steps into Farringdon Rd [in fact, Street]. On both sides of the way buildings were blazing fiercely & to get along at all we had to walk in the centre of the road, plunging through pools of water & gingerly stepping over hoses. At any other time the Firemen would never have let us get anywhere near such fires but today they didn't even see us – they had too much to do & we didn't have time to be nervous – altho the roar of the flames was awful. It was a beautiful morning but we couldn't see the sky for clouds of

smoke coloured red & thick black flakes were showering down all around. Coming to Blackfriars Bridge we breathed a little easier but it was a terrible sight to look back & see the whole riverside buildings either burning or blotted out by smoke ... Waterloo was closed – crowds outside waiting patiently with their luggage. I tried to walk to the Elephant but both sides of Waterloo Road were burning so I turned back & found Ada again. We then wearily trudged towards Westminster hoping to see a bus or something on wheels to help us along [and] when we arrived at Lambeth Baths (a very sorry spectacle – burning & half destroyed) I was thrilled to see a nr 3 coming along so in I jumped & was I thankful to get out of that ghastly mess! Arrived home about 10.30am which wasn't at all bad.[27]

Barbara Nixon, in Finsbury, thought that after the raid of 10/11 May, 'Depression settled over London, all the more serious in that it was not particularly vocal.' Quentin Reynolds described something similar. In a long wire to New York reporting on the raid and its immediate aftermath, he noted how 'The streets were filled with grim-faced sullen-looking men and women' staring 'at the debris of treasured landmarks'. He 'sensed a new intensified hatred of Germany in the people of London'. After what had seemed like a merciless bombardment over nine miserable months, this furious battering brought with it an exhaustion and resignation never quite felt before. Sister Gwyneth Thomas, thirty-three, ordinarily working a day shift at Highgate Hospital, was called in to treat casualties arriving that night. As the raid eased off so did the flow of wounded and at 4.30 a.m. she went back to the nurses' home. 'I am beyond sleep, besides, I have told the night sister to call me again if they have more casualties. It is very quiet now, perhaps very soon the raid will be over, and the all clear will go. When will it all end?'[28]

Everyone wanted to know the answer. Two nights of light raids followed and then – nothing for the rest of May. There were five half-hearted raids in June, killing not a single Londoner, the last on the night of 22/23 June when a parachute mine was dropped by a lone raider on Barkingside: it caused some damage to a hospital but no casualties. But who could reasonably think that London's ordeal was over, even if only for a time?[29]

*

In fact, the great raid of 10/11 May marks the classic end of the Big Blitz, which had begun with the huge raid of Saturday 7 September. There would be bombing aplenty to come, some of it uniquely terrifying, but repeated attacks over many months by large numbers of enemy aircraft were at an end.

From 3 September 1940 to the end of May 1941, London suffered ninety-five air raids by day and 166 by night, a total of 261. In those nine months 19,788 Londoners were killed by bombing; the worst months were September and October, with some 5,500 and 4,900 deaths respectively. Around 25,500 had been injured and detained in hospital and a further 45,672 slightly injured and treated at first aid posts and other facilities. A measure of London's overwhelming precedence in the punishment handed out by the Luftwaffe to Britain in these months is figures showing the tonnage of HE bombs dropped in major night raids: London endured eighty-five raids, comprising 23,949 tons; the nearest comparator was Liverpool–Birkenhead with eight raids and 1,957 tons.

Inevitably, casualties were not evenly distributed across London. The worst-bombed boroughs, measured by bombs per square mile, were Holborn (568), Stepney (442), the City (392), Bermondsey (373) and Southwark (342); West Ham, a large borough, was the worst-bombed area in outer London on this measure (207). Elsewhere in the East End, Poplar (208), Bethnal Green (242), Shoreditch (285) and Deptford (302), together with Stepney and West Ham, indicated the priority given to the river and the port in the Luftwaffe's main campaign against the capital, the Thames with its characteristic bends a bomb-aimer's dream. Indeed, the largest number of bombs of all calibres to fall on any London district was 1,525 on West Ham, notoriously London's worst-performing civil defence authority: no doubt the unique weight of bombing itself had an impact on how the defenders were able, or unable, to cope.

The five worst-bombed districts as measured by fatalities were Lambeth (a very large borough bordering the river opposite Westminster and stretching miles to the south, with 1,300), West Ham (823), Westminster (800), St Pancras (another large borough, 724) and Southwark (695). In the East End north of the Thames (Stepney, Shoreditch, Bethnal Green, Poplar and West Ham) 2,756 residents were killed; the eastern districts south of the river (Southwark, Bermondsey, Deptford) 1,587; the West End and inner west London (Holborn, Westminster, St Marylebone, Kensington and Paddington) 1,940. Inner east London north and south of the river and West Ham thus accounted for 30 per cent of all London's fatalities and inner west London some 10 per cent, so the case for inequality of sacrifice between working-class and middle-class areas was plainly made. But 70 per cent of fatal casualties lived outside those eight east London districts, and almost no London authority's area had escaped unscathed (just Barnet Rural District and Waltham Holy Cross Urban District on London's outermost northern edge recorded no fatality).[30]

In general, civil defence in London Region acquitted itself well in dire and unparalleled circumstances. No other city anywhere in the world had yet withstood such a battering. Much of the impact of mass bombing had been unanticipated and the planning and resourcing by central government for shelters, rest centres and communal feeding had sold millions of Londoners short. Lessons had to be learned in the teeth of the firestorm and some learning had been hesitant and painfully slow. But by the end of the blitz London's civil defence had been tempered in the fire and was robust and efficient almost everywhere. And for those frontline local authority services – wardens, first aid, fire, ambulance and rescue – the energy and endurance of countless brave men and women, whose jobs required them to stay in the open under a terrifying and deadly bombardment, were beyond all praise. They won recognition in the awards for bravery, in the tributes printed in local newspapers, in the crowds silently lining the streets for civil defenders' funerals: 'nothing said could be an exaggeration of the wonderful behaviour of our Civil Defence Units,' wrote Nellie Carver that April. Reflecting some years later on 'all the workers in the civil defence, fire, police and ambulance services', Sir Harold Scott, the chief administrator of London Region, summed up their achievements: 'They were indeed magnificent.'[31]

The judgement of posterity has tended to be less generous. Angus Calder, the greatest historian of the British home front, roundly concluded that 'London local government emerged discreditably from the blitz'. And Tom Harrisson, the leader of Mass Observation in these years, looking back from the mid-1970s, found similar grounds for disappointment: 'Democracy with good government,' he thought, 'has to start from the assumption that chaos is not acceptable and is avoidable.' In fact, the evidence shows a much more nuanced picture of achievement and failure under titanic pressure. Historians have been led astray by a few contemporary journalists who had to shoulder responsibility for nothing and for whom there was no story without someone to blame. And Harrisson's test was a counsel of perfection unattainable by any human society known to history.[32]

IN the late 1930s, London's detractors had made much of the capital's size as the greatest bombing target in the world – unmissable, and thus ripe for slaughter from the air. In fact, as people quickly came to realise, its sheer size was its greatest asset. Winston Churchill, who had memorably described London as a 'tremendous fat cow' before the war, found cause to change the zoological metaphor after the blitz. In a little-reported speech at the LCC's County Hall in July 1941 he turned that peacetime weakness into a wartime virtue: 'London is so vast and so strong that she is like a prehistoric monster into whose armoured hide showers of arrows can be shot in vain.' It was true. London could not be destroyed by the weapons then available and the undamaged parts of the city would always leap to the succour of the blitzed districts. It could reconstitute and replenish itself. 'In London,' wrote Barbara Nixon, 'if one borough was getting more than it could cope with, there was always another one fairly close, and fully prepared, to help it out.' It was the smaller cities like Coventry and Plymouth that were vulnerable to the knockout blow but never the metropolis and its much-despised 'urban sprawl'.[33]

But if London couldn't be slaughtered it could be wounded. By June 1941 the scars were everywhere. The City, in particular, had been changed almost beyond recognition and many Londoners felt the pain of loss as sharply as if they mourned a friend. The Square Mile had never stood still, of course, and redevelopment in the thirty years before the blitz had removed some treasured buildings and characterful nooks and corners, but the Luftwaffe seemed now to have added 'the finishing touch'. The writer F. Tennyson Jesse thought the destruction of the Temple and its church, the Guildhall and the Wren churches 'beyond computing' and the desolation around St Paul's reminded many of 'Ypres in the heart of London'. Phyllis Warner explored the damage during the February lull in raids:

I visited the City ... today for the first time since the great fire raid of December 30th. I took a bus there, and got my first shock as I was balancing on the step waiting to get off. The bus swung onto a temporary bridge over a crater, and I suddenly found myself gazing down into the bowels of the earth – straight into a deep tunnel ... I went on to look at the inconceivable ruins of the Guildhall, St. Lawrence Jewry, Friday Street, Bread Street, St. Bride's, Newgate Street, Paternoster Row, Amen Lane. This last part is the worst of all. Such a fascinating quarter of London, and the devastation now so utterly complete ... The escape of St. Paul's is amazing: completely encircled by ruins, it stands superbly and dauntlessly the same – Thank God.[34]

In the end, though, it was the passing of the old familiar London that plucked loudest at the heartstrings. Inner London had lost 36,164 houses demolished or beyond repair from bombing; another 46,514 needed major repairs to make them habitable. But these too were unevenly distributed and some neighbourhoods had been laid flat. Grace Williamson, forty-four, an LCC infant school teacher living with her husband in Eynella Road, East Dulwich, Camberwell, corresponded frequently with her son Austin, who had moved to Edinburgh to take on a teaching job at Fettes College; poor eyesight had disqualified him for military service. All day long, Grace told Austin on Sunday 11 May, there had been 'a pall of smoke all over London – We could not see the sun at times for it.' A day or so later she wrote to tell him of damage to the Elephant and Castle, the shopping district Austin and the family had known so well:

Do you know the railway bridge in Walworth Rd? Well from there on to the Elephant all the shops are completely down except perhaps the last two – Burton's the Tailors on the corner – The hotel in the middle of the road is still standing but beyond that, Isaac Walton's & all those shops up to that bridge in Newington Causeway are just a heap of rubble – The Jerries did their work well and truly – In Peckham Bournemouth Rd has had another big affair, Brayards & Caulfield also Pemmells Place – Several streets round about our school [Woods Road LCC school, later John Donne School] were roped off yesterday owing to D.A.s [delayed-action bombs]. A surface shelter was hit in that narrow road that runs by the side of the Co-op Chemists – When I got to the Heaton Arms yesterday morning, the remains of plate glass windows were being swept into the gutter by the people who work in the Co-op & Humphries – It did look a mess.

Austin's father, Arthur, added a postscript from the City, where he worked: 'Am afraid Bow Bells has gone up in smoke after very narrowly escaping the December fires.'[35]

In the East End too the loss was personal. On the Isle of Dogs, Bill Regan

decided to walk round the Island to see what damage has been done. From our house [271 Manchester Road] to the Pier Tavern is looking sick, number 263 is still occupied by Bob Collier, 259 by Ted Chastell, and 257 the estate agents by Lew Smith, so I carried on round the bend to Seyssel Street, where the houses backing on to the Saundersness school are looking sick. The first four or five houses, although they took as much blast as the school, still have their party walls standing. One house has a row of china tea-cups, unbroken, still hanging on their hooks, the rest of the dresser has joined the wreckage below. The garden wall of the first house is still in place, but the close-boarded fence that topped it, is lying on the pavement. I remember that fence very well. During the first World war, about early 1916, Fred Smith who was then about thirteen years old and the leader of our gang of boys, had carved the initials of five of the girls who lived in this row of houses, very neatly on the last panel. I heaved at the fence until it was free of debris, turned it over, and there was the neat line of letters.

ER. NC. EG. DL. BL.

Edie Rogers, Nellie Cox, Eileen Greenaway, Daisy Lavender, and Bessie Lavender. I wonder where they are now.

This became a depressing journey ... I wandered along as far as the Magnet and Dewdrop, but the poor old Island was so wounded I could not carry on, so I went to the Depot and cadged a free dinner from Mrs Warren.[36]

Some people, outsiders almost all, felt elements of this loss to be no loss at all. As early as July 1939 some hackles had been raised by a newspaper columnist claiming that 'if nine-tenths of the City of London were blown off the face of the earth, the world would not have lost a single building of any architectural value whatever, or any house that could not be rebuilt with advantage'. Now an attempt had been made to do just that and a few benefits were apparent to some. Anthony Heap thought the destruction 'a blessing in disguise. The City so badly needed re-planning.' William Kent, a dedicated London-lover, noted with approval the unearthing of a bastion in London's Roman City wall, exposed by a bomb crater near St Giles Cripplegate; and F. Tennyson Jesse thought that 'one good thing the Germans have done … is to open up St. Paul's cathedral, which stands in a desolation comparable to Ypres'. The loss of working-class streets, 'slums' in most eyes apart (generally) from those of the people whose homes they were, could be looked at coolly by outsiders taking a long view, who thought they saw that 'a better London, more worthy of our times, will eventually arise from the ashes of the old'. It was a position that would gather a host of adherents in the three or four years to come.[37]

THESE esoteric gains may have provided solace for a few but in general the damage of those nine months of intensive bombing was felt by almost everyone. The loss of life, the loss of treasured buildings and favourite neighbourhoods, the disruption of day-to-day existence – these were the common experience of all who had stuck it out. Many did not, either following their own inclinations to get out of London or responding to the call of duty away from home. These moves out continued throughout the blitz and could be provoked at any time by a near miss, by homelessness, family tragedy or other disturbing event. The resident civilian population of inner London in mid-1939 had been marginally more than 4 million; at the end of May 1941, according to the tally of ration books, it was 2,241,309, a fall of 44 per cent. In outer London the comparable figures were 4,730,000 and 3,809,062, 19 per cent lower. For the capital as a whole there were 2,690,000 (30 per cent) fewer Londoners in 1941 than before the war.

That was the picture London-wide. The movements in individual boroughs could be dramatic. West Ham's population fell by 65 per cent, Stepney's by 64 per cent, Poplar's by 63 per cent, Bermondsey's by 56 per cent. These were the worst-bombed east London districts and huge numbers chose to flee the Luftwaffe or were billeted away from their home districts by the end of the main blitz. Others chose to get away from the bombing in other ways than leaving altogether. The murderous raids of April and May led to a new spike of 87,500 people hunkering down in the tubes, up from 65,000 in March. The impact of migration and underground living was apparent everywhere. Even in little-damaged streets in the East End, the novelist Willy Goldman noticed how deserted they all were, even by day: 'The silence does not suit them as it does the widely terraced and richly foliaged suburb. It is the gossiping, the street cries, the children, the dogs that give a slum the "life" it has. Without these manifestations it might well be a desert.'[38]

There were other losses too. The education of London's schoolchildren was also blitzed and scarred. In May 1941 there were estimated to be 104,400 school-age children in the LCC area, of whom over 93,000 were listed on a school roll; more than 11,000, then, were attached to no school at all and of those on the rolls no attendance figures were collected. Things would improve in the months to come, but some would never make good the schooling they had lost. Teachers noted 'indiscipline and lack of attention, that children were more restless and noisier' than before the blitz, and for those staying much time in shelters there was a noticeable lack of personal cleanliness. Even two years later, with time to have made good some of the deficit at least, London school inspectors concluded that the average setback among thirteen-year-olds was six to twelve months. There was not, however, any special rise in juvenile delinquency noted by the police over the period 1940–41. For preschool children and infants, psychiatrists thought that the experience of bombing was less disturbing than evacuation had been, as long as the children were with their families. Even when small children were bombed out of their homes 'there were no signs of traumatic shock' provided they were with their 'own mothers' or 'a familiar mother-substitute'.[39]

For adults, the psychological trauma was hard to measure. Psychiatric casualties – like men suffering shell shock in the First World War – had been expected in droves but failed to materialise. Trauma – 'air raid strain' – was often present but apparently quickly faded. In the early days especially, the raids caused 'widespread lethargy and lack of energy, even after lost sleep had been made up, and pessimistic feelings about the future'. Psychiatrists noted cases of exhaustion and 'anxiety symptoms ... mental inhibition, depression or irritation. Some persons were seen in the East End districts of London who, upon viewing the destruction of their homes, became speechless for a time; they were unable to eat and wandered about in an aimless and apathetic way'. But these effects were generally transient, in part because people adjusted to the new norms imposed by recurrent bombing, and in part because those most affected left London, unwilling to take more punishment. As time went on, psychiatrists noted, '*there was a definite decline in overt fear reactions as the air blitz continued, even though the raids became heavier and more destructive*'. Even so, the individual trauma deriving from bombing shouldn't be underestimated. Henry Painter, a printer's ware-houseman of Stratford, who had been ill and depressed since losing his home in September 1940, went back to 'the roofless building' in August 1941 and hanged himself from a gas bracket.[40]

AFTER 10/11 May, as the bombing eased once more, Londoners continued to wonder what might now be coming their way. Even more gigantic raids? Gas? A rumoured secret weapon? Nothing seemed impossible, including invasion. With the approach of kinder weather and calmer seas, it seemed eminently feasible that Hitler was mustering his forces for the fatal blow against his impudent enemy across the Channel. 'Do you think the Germans will try an invasion of this country during this year?' Gallup had asked in January and 62 per cent thought they would. There was a scare in the quiet days of March, when Dorothy Wells reported 'instructions on the wireless today as to what to do when invasion comes. The authorities seem to have no doubt of it.' In early May, just before the last great raid, Charles Graves recorded 'a real flap about a German plan to land 40,000 parachutists in Central London in these next few nights, coming by glider'. Graves was in the Home Guard and 'It looks as though I shan't sleep at home for some weeks after tomorrow.' And pondering the 'long and puzzling lull in heavy air attacks' in mid-June, the journalist Mollie Panter-Downes thought 'that something big and especially unpleasant must be cooking. When and if the invasion starts' she hoped the home defences, particularly fire-watching and firefighting, might be better organised than they were at present.[41]

But everyone was looking the wrong way.

6

LIFE IS DULL NOW:
22 JUNE 1941–30 NOVEMBER 1942

'BIG news today is that Germany has declared war on Russia,' Dorothy Wells noted in her war diary on 22 June 1941. At 3 a.m., Hitler launched an attack with 3.6 million ground troops, 3,600 tanks and 2,700 aeroplanes, 'the largest force in European military history', across the Russian border from the Baltic to the Black Sea. The British had tried to warn Stalin that an invasion was brewing but he thought the intelligence black propaganda and Russia remained wilfully unprepared. Churchill, broadcasting to the world that night, claimed the Soviets as an ally and promised 'all aid to the Communist scum,' as Anthony Heap, for whom Stalin was a far more malevolent foe than Hitler, put it. But Phyllis Warner, writing from the Mary Ward Settlement in Bloomsbury, expressed the thoughts of many who grappled with the war's bigger picture: 'Well we've got a powerful new ally. One thing is certain, the Russians won't give up like the French, because they've got something they believe in to fight for.'[1]

The implications for London and Londoners were immense and immediate. Fears of invasion, stoked by the Luftwaffe's recent restraint seemingly mustering reserves for an all-out attack, receded and remained improbable for some time to come. 'Do you believe that the Germans will try to invade this country this year?' Gallup asked in August 1942, and only 8 per cent thought they would. The probability of a resumed blitz, with enemy planes now fully committed on the Eastern Front, also seemed vanishingly remote. For the rest of 1941 there would be just one raid on London, on Monday 28 July, when a sharp attack for two hours in the early morning killed some 110 people, mainly in the inner East End, although two street fire-watchers were also killed in a

'South London suburb'. For the rest of the year there were no raids at all; even warnings were few and far between, just sixteen in the remaining five months. In 1942, there were a handful of light raids, almost trivial for those not on the receiving end, perhaps by one or two raiders: one in June, three in July and one on 13 August, the worst, killing seven at New Barnet on London's northern boundary. The chronicler of Paddington ARP summed up London's quietest full year of the war, recording twenty-six alerts in 1942 lasting twelve hours in total.[2]

The other impact on London was political. Since September 1939 the most vociferous and effective opponents of Britain's war effort had been the Communist Party, with an influence in working-class London, especially the East End, out of all proportion to its card-carrying numbers. The Party's mischievous campaign for deep shelters, and its justified agitation for shelter improvements once bombing began, had vexed authorities locally in the East End, elsewhere in London region and, indeed, nationally. Its support for a People's Convention, which had its first meeting in London early in 1941, sought to exploit any evidence of 'war-weariness' among the blitzed Londoners to further the communist campaign for a negotiated peace. In January 1941, goaded beyond endurance, the government had suppressed the CP's *Daily Worker* and *The Week* for undermining the country's war effort against Nazi Germany and her allies. But on the streets of London the morale-sapping drip of communist propaganda had never let up for a moment. In March, to cite one case among many, a twenty-four-year-old Jewish pastry cook and communist agitator was fined for 'spouting' in Mare Street, Hackney: he told his audience that the rich were getting all the food while the poor would soon be starving – '"What a country to fight for!"' Now, overnight from 22 June, the Party's axis shifted 180 degrees. For the rest of the war the nation's efforts would have no more militant supporters than the communists. They took leading positions in the immense efforts to send aid of one kind or another to Soviet Russia, and their objectives in the munitions and aircraft factories changed from near obstruction to Stakhanovite enthusiasm at the blast of a factory hooter. The popularity of Russia also did wonders for the CP's membership, which increased greatly in London and elsewhere.[3]

ENTHUSIASM was needed in the workplace, despite the vigour with which Churchill's national government had addressed the war effort since May 1940. J. T. Murphy, a skilled engineer, worked as a turner in a 'railway engineering shop' in London from July 1940 till about April 1941: 'there was no Dunkirk atmosphere here. The fact is, I had struck a "cushy" job. Here were no piece-work system, no overtime, no nightwork and no [progress] "chasers"; just plain time-work, with everyone going more or less at his own pace, although everyone received a bonus.' It was effectively run as a closed shop with all its workers in one trade union or other, most in the National Union of Railwaymen (NUR). Some, at least, of the roots of ARP collectivism in London were visible here, the NUR conducting 'an amazing amount of social insurance work. It ran schemes for raising money for its orphanages, the Labour Hospital, the injured and the sick among its members, and the bereft families of members who had died.' But in terms of the job at hand, 'The question of speeding up production in any way simply did not arise.'[4]

Murphy's experience shows that, despite progress having been made by the spring of 1941 in bringing people into the workforce, it was not always easy to get much work out of them when they arrived there. Even so, the numbers at work were impressive. In June 1941 the national workforce had increased by 1.58 million from June 1939 and unemployment in insured trades had fallen from 1.27 million to just 198,000. The picture in London was somewhat different. It had long been the most economically active region in the country, but all the new munitions and aircraft factories planned during national rearmament from 1935 were built outside the capital and some workers were encouraged to leave London as part of decentralisation. Bombing and the evacuation of jobs and families added to this decline in London's workforce, but 'on a far smaller scale than the fall in population'.

The decline in the insured labour force through conscription and the transfer of workers to other areas has been largely made good by the increased employment of workers not previously insured, particularly women. There has been a great expansion of industries such as engineering, vehicle and aircraft manufacturing, and electrical cables and apparatus, and in 1942 total employment in the larger factories of Greater London was still at about the level of the years immediately before the war.[5]

London was denied in this war the industrial primacy it had enjoyed in the First World War and the years after, but it continued to play an important part in war production. The versatile industrial base of the capital, founded largely on small but flexible workshops, could switch to war work with relative ease. This was especially so for the garment industry, where the inexhaustible demands for uniforms drove workers at a high pitch from the beginning of the war, but it was also true of London's engineering and electrical industries. Here the switch-over from producing for civilian consumption to war work was widespread by the summer of 1941. Addressograph, for instance, a Cricklewood (Willesden) firm making rapid printing machines before the war, now also turned out breach mechanisms for field guns and tanks, range-finding instruments and other munitions components, 22 million items by the end of the war. Metal Box had long made boxes and cans for food products and these were in unprecedented demand during the war, but now it also made gas mask containers, anti-tank mines and projectiles, smoke generators, grenades, Sten gun magazines and much more, all in huge numbers. A Wembley factory making aluminium foil before the war turned over to making energy cells for night-vision devices until the 'Windows' radar distraction system produced a need for aluminium strips in unheard-of quantities. Vehicle part makers before the war now made shock absorbers and engines for tanks. Ford at Dagenham, which the government was at first reluctant to use for war manufacture because of its likely vulnerability to bombing, had produced 347,371 army lorries, RAF tractors and troop carriers by the time war was out. And London's enormous Gas Light and Coke Company, whose workforce engaged heroically with burning gas mains during the blitz, turned out by-products for explosives and tar for landing strips.[6]

Although growth in new munitions and aeroplane plant took place largely outside London, firms like Napiers of Acton could expand at nearby Park Royal, producing engines there for the new Hawker Tempest fighter and Typhoon fighter-bomber from 1942. Similarly, the Royal Ordnance Factories (ROFs) at Woolwich, despite their risky location and the siting of new ROFs outside London, still employed some 20,000 workers on munitions, and the gun and carriage factories worked at full pelt throughout the war, especially in developing new weapons; the Royal Small Arms Factory at Enfield also continued to play a large part in rifle production for the duration.[7]

Similarly, London remained important to aircraft manufacture. Nearly one in four workers employed by the Ministry of Aircraft Production (MAP) in December 1941 worked in London and the South East.

Especially important was Handley Page, a Cricklewood firm since before the First World War, later expanding at Radlett in Hertfordshire, which made the prolific Halifax, the RAF's first four-engined heavy bomber. Production of the Halifax was assisted by a consortium of five contractors, all vehicle builders in west London, including the London Passenger Transport Board's bus body and engine works at Chiswick. This London Aircraft Production (LAP) group made various parts – tail units, flaps, fuselages, undercarriages and so on – which were then assembled outside London: LAP's first Halifax was flown in December 1941 and by the end of the war it had made 710, the last named *London Pride*. A host of other London engineering firms made parts for the Mosquito (developed by De Havilland at Stag Lane, Colindale, and their main Hatfield works, north of London), Spitfires (developed by Vickers Armstrong at Weybridge in Surrey) and many more. And 8,000 workers were employed underground on aircraft components in a five-mile stretch of the unopened Central Line between Leytonstone and Gants Hill. All these firms and subcontractors expanded their workforces to meet the needs of Britain's air war: LAP employed 9,000, for instance, on the Halifax. And there was no end to the outsourcing of component manufacture when the pressures were too great to be handled by the large factories alone: from April 1941 J. T. Murphy moved to an aircraft factory working on heavy bombers, probably for LAP, which in turn put out work to around 130 subcontractors 'in cellars and sheds, improvised outhouses, in buildings never intended to become workshops, in back streets and villages'.[8]

Mark Benney, a writer who had a memorable early career as a London burglar before the war, had received some early training as an engineer at a government factory in the Cotswolds in 1940. In the summer of 1941 he got a job as a semi-skilled engineer at the Chrysler plant at Chiswick and Kew, a partner in LAP. He worked on Halifax tail units and witnessed the uprooting of the vehicle assembly line to work on the new structures. The commitment of management and technical staff was impressive but it was still a task that took six months before war production could begin. Benney felt 'the entry of the Soviet Union into the war' produced a 'new responsiveness among the men and women' on the factory floor. Stimulated by communists in the workforce, trade union membership grew by hundreds, and though there was an uneasy relationship between trade union organisers and CP members, there was now no doubt of the commitment of everyone to war aims and to maximising the contribution the factory could make. Perhaps the CP was also behind a move by shop stewards at a Camberwell munitions factory who publicly invited management to discuss ways of speeding up production, detecting a complacent 'Leave it to Russia' attitude in the boardroom.[9]

For men, full employment, increased trade union membership (the Amalgamated Engineering Union, AEU, more than doubled its number of members between 1938 and 1943 to 909,000), overtime and the frequent recourse to night work on enhanced pay all led to an unparalleled hike in wage rates and earnings. This was especially so in London, where most wages of all grades of labour had historically been higher than in the rest of the country. In the aircraft industry, for instance, at the end of 1940, Napiers were paying their skilled London men £5 0s 10d for a forty-seven-hour week but just £4 2s 6d to similar men in the north-west of England. Time rates for ship repairers in the Port of London in March 1941 were £4 14s 6d for a forty-four-hour week but £4 3s 6d for forty-seven hours elsewhere. Weekly earnings, given the high demand for labour in London and the ready availability of overtime there, would have been higher still. In general, family incomes in London had never been higher than in the years of full employment from June 1941. There was, though, a downside, in addition to long hours. Industrial conscription for men might require them to go where directed to work, by a series of controls that tightened progressively from January 1941; but, in all, it was a small price to pay.[10]

Steps were also taken to assist others to share in the general rise in household incomes. Old age pensioners saw their weekly payments rise and, from late 1940, supplementary allowances were made to the poorest among them. There were some steps too to bring disabled people into the workforce: blitz victims – men and women – who had lost limbs were being helped into industry by the spring of 1942, room found at the bench in aircraft and munitions factories.[11]

There was still residual poverty, though, among those soldiers' wives with young children who were without childcare enabling them to take up paid work. Their situation would eventually be eased a little by 'wartime nurseries' and, from 1944, improved allowances, but until then a woman with three children would have to live on just £1 13s a week, literally a pittance compared to most contemporary family incomes. So the majority of women who could work did, and from the summer of 1941 unmarried women were made to work through conscription, beginning with young women aged from twenty to twenty-one and, through progressive steps, to women aged from fifty to fifty-one in November 1943. Through 1941 and 1942 women shouldered an increased share of work outside the armed forces and auxiliary services. In 1939 4.84 million women worked in civil employment (27 per cent of the civil workforce); in 1940 the figure was 5.31 million (30 per cent), in 1941 5.91 million (33 per cent) and in 1942 6.58 million (37 per cent). These were national figures and it's likely that the traditional availability of women's work in London manufacturing would have made these proportions higher in the capital than in many other parts of the country.[12]

Much women's employment filled the gaps in the workforce left by men conscripted into the armed forces. The LPTB lost 22,580 men to armed services or full-time ARP and filled part of the vacuum with 16,500 women, including 11,250 (out of 18,800) bus and tram conductors, 950 (out of 1,150) station porters, 400 booking clerks and 3,000 in engineering workshops. Dorothy Wells saw her first woman porter on Barons Court underground station in the summer of 1940, 'dressed in a white coat, very dolled up – probably did it to give herself confidence'. Similarly, Southern Railway had recruited 5,000 women by 1942 and doubled the number by 1944; and the LMS by the end of the war employed 39,000 women in '250 different railway grades, including such diverse jobs as concrete workers, sailmakers, assistant architects, fitters, electricians, boiler cleaners, weighbridge men, painters, lock-keepers, stablemen and even blacksmiths!' Ford at Dagenham had not employed women on the factory floor before the war but labour short-ages meant they had to be taken on from the end of March 1941: by September there were 1,100, with 3,500 by the end of the war. The Granada cinema chain recruited over 200 women film operators, including some mothers with young children for whom the hours were childcare-friendly if they had partners at home. Dolly Scannell's husband was a collector for the Prudential Assurance Company on the LCC estate at Dagenham, where they lived; when he was called up the Pru trained her to take over. Women, indeed, were everywhere – Britain's first woman crane-driver, her cab 120 feet off the ground, was Violet Wenborn, a Lambeth housewife with a baby son, in May 1942. Even so, some industries had still to overcome institutional barriers before women were accepted: the AEU only lifted the ban on women members on 1 January 1943.[13]

This recruitment to take the place of men was accompanied by three expanding industries where women were a mainstay of wartime production: aircraft and munitions manufacture, and the civil service. In June 1940 73,000 women were employed nationally in making motors, cycles and aircraft; by March 1941 this had more than doubled to 153,000 and by December 1942 it had more than doubled again to 377,000, some 35 per cent of the industries' workforce. These figures are for full-time equivalents, two part-time women workers counting as one, so the real numbers of women would have been significantly higher. Women working in explosives (bomb and shell filling), chemicals and related industries outnumbered men (from March 1942), as they did in electric cable manufacture (from June 1941); in scientific instrument manufacture they made up nearly half the workforce by the end of 1942. These again are national figures, but some London women were volunteering for munitions work not only in their home districts but also in the West Midlands, for instance, where labour shortages were acute in early 1942.[14]

By 1942 the munitions and aircraft factories were great melting pots of class and age, and gender too because most (though not all) supervisors, trainers, progress chasers and inspectors were men. At Morrisons Engineering Works in Purley Way, Croydon, the workforce more than tripled to some 500 as the factory turned over to making aircraft components for Vickers at Weybridge. Morrisons made parts for Lancaster and Wellington bombers, Hurricanes and Spitfires – war work of real significance for all Londoners who had endured the blitz. Responding to the nationwide call for women to take up war work, two middle-class London women who, since 1935, had run a tea shop in rural Surrey threw it in and ended up working at Morrisons. Kathleen Church-Bliss and Elsie Whiteman, forty-one and forty-six respectively when they first worked at the bench, kept a lively diary together, consumed by the daily dramas that beset them and their comrades in the factory. Class distinction could never quite be eliminated but it expressed itself more in wry amusement than in snobbery. Their training had been extensive and complex under experienced engineers, not all able teachers, at a government training centre at Waddon, Croydon, lasting from February to June 1942. When they arrived at Morrisons they found niggling discontents – endless queues to clock off work if everyone finished at the same time, persecuting foremen, stingy helpings at the canteen – but it was all endlessly fascinating. And fun:

> There is an odd assortment of women at Morrisons. A bunch of nice middle-aged grannies with kindly worn faces and amiable manners. Then there is a horde of ghastly looking wantons with long golden locks and buffon erections on top and enamelled faces. Sometimes they bulge out of trousers, at others they sprout out of skintight jumpers. Always they are conscious of one thing only – their exceeding beauty, charm and glamour. Quite a bit of their time is spent hidden away in the Women's Cloaks making up their faces at Morrisons' expense.[15]

Wages in war industries were generally high, but then so was the cost of living. The writer Inez Holden worked for a time in a scientific instrument factory in north London that had once made cinema projectors but was now making camera parts for bombers and reconnaissance planes. The pressure of work meant that the factory operated round the clock, introducing a night shift for the first time. A married woman worked out how far her wages would go:

> If the war bonus came in and the piece-work bonus and the Sunday overtime as well as the overtime which we were already getting for war work, it would be possible on the sixty-hour week to reach a wage of just over £4. 'Then as you've got to take off fares and food, that brings it down to £3 5s. you're actually getting. Me rent's 19s. 6d., a week, that leaves £2 5s. 6d., which at the present cost of living is worth about 25s. I've got to pay for all me clothes, heating, lighting and cigarettes – it don't leave much for going to the pictures of a Saturday afternoon, do it?'[16]

Away from the bench, in the burgeoning ranks and departments of the wartime civil service, middle-class women were drafted in droves. Office dramas were no less intense than in the workshops. The novelist Lettice Cooper joined the public relations department of the Ministry of Food. It was a vital section in a war of exhortation to avoid waste, dig for victory and keep on the right side of the ever-shifting regulations. The new staff were a motley crew who found it hard to settle into civil service ways:

> the clash was acute, for we who came in with the war are an ill-regulated lot – writers, broadcasters, advertising people, journalists. We have all

fought our way up to a certain point in our own professions, and most of us belong to professions where you can have a good deal of your own way and are not hidebound. So when we came under this impartial and sometimes cumbrous discipline we were sulky, subversive and impatient. At times we still are ...[17]

In very many ways, despite the long hours and niggling oppressions of life at a bench or a desk, despite having to juggle work with being a housewife and mother, as many had to, and despite helping out in YMCA canteens on evenings and weekends, as many chose to, these were hugely stimulating times for working women. 'For many women the war became a liberating thing,' recalled a Greenwich woman who had worked on market research before the war and at the Ministry of Supply during it. 'It took them out from under the eyes of their neighbours and all the conventions and social pressures they had been under. I thought it was tremendously important for them to find out what they could do. I knew, and always felt, women could do most of the things that anybody else did.' 'You got friendship out of working. We'd got our independence during the war,' thought Lisa Haddon, working on munitions for £4 a week while her husband earned £1 10s in the army.[18]

Independence showed itself in many ways. The London Women's Parliament (LWP) was born out of a 'Housewives' Club' in Ruislip, Hillingdon, in early 1941. The club invited various trade unions and women's organisations, including the WVS and the Women's Co-operative Guild, to join in a campaign for nurseries for mothers of young children who wished to work in war production. In July representatives of 345 organisations met at Conway Hall, Red Lion Square, in the LWP's first session. Some communist infiltration was detectable from the outset – the plight of Russia was always prominent in resolutions – but the nursery issue was the front-runner. It was an agitation that had found its moment and a voice, the LWP's campaign powerfully supported by the *Daily Mirror*. The agitation caught fire, with 'nursery committees' active in 1942 in many localities, including Bermondsey, Hackney, Hendon, Chingford, and Hayes and Southall. By the summer of that year nurseries were opening everywhere – Leyton (two), East Ham, West Ham, Lambeth, Hackney (two), Stoke Newington (two) and many more. Lewisham housewives, hard done by with no local nursery established, staged 'Perambulator Parades' outside the town hall, securing promises from the council to act; and mothers in Hampstead held a 'Baby Riot', mums waving placards demanding 'Nurseries for Kids! War Work for Mothers!'[19]

Nurseries would continue to open across London throughout 1942 up until 1944, all staffed and run by local councils, who also channelled government funding to charity-run nurseries. Klara Modern worked in a St Pancras Borough Council nursery in a poor area off the Hampstead Road, west of Euston Station: 'We look after children of mothers engaged upon war work. The children I have to look after are between nine months and about two years, but there is a larger proportion of smaller children. They are very sweet, incredibly dirty, in every sense of the word and the work is really hard.' The hours were 7 a.m. to 7 p.m., and Klara had two hours off in the day, taking meals on the premises. But the war nursery programme could never fully meet the demands of war-working mothers, who continued to have to rely on friends, neighbours and grandmothers for childcare.[20]

Another campaign taken up by the LWP and others was equal pay. Everywhere women were paid less than men for the same jobs, although determining whether one job was 'the same' as another could be difficult. But in ARP, for instance, precisely similar jobs brought a distinctly higher wage packet for male rest centre managers compared with female, £6 a week against £5, despite the women being 'much more successful than men'; and ARP women wardens earned £1 4s 6d a week less than men. Lambeth councillor Elsie Boltz led a campaign for equal pay in ARP but to no avail. Average weekly earnings in manufacturing and some other industries, collected nationally, showed men aged twenty-one and over earning £4 19s 5d in July 1941 and £5 11s 5d in July 1942, while women earned £2 3s 11d and £2 14s 2d, or less than half; and while this reflected men's superior skills in many trades the injustice was apparent to most. 'Do you think that women should or should not be paid the same wages as men if they are doing the same work?' Gallup asked in October 1941; 68 per cent thought they should, 26 per cent thought not.[21]

The new self-confidence of women who found their labour in huge demand if the war were to be won expressed itself too in a desire for an equal share in fighting the enemy should he dare to invade. From the spring of 1942, in South Tottenham, Streatham, Lambeth, Chelsea, Hammersmith and elsewhere, Women's Home Defence (WHD) forces began to develop as a female equivalent of the Home Guard, from which women were barred. The idea originated in the summer of 1940 with Mrs Venetia Foster, wife of a naval officer living in Bloomsbury, and it had started as a women's rifle club and 'Amazon Defence Corps'. It failed to take off and suffered some ridicule in the press, but by 1942 its time had come, aided by the powerful advocacy of Dr Edith Summerskill, Labour MP for West Fulham. The WHD had considerable purchase among lower-middle-class 'housewives, shop assistants, typists and clerks,' as one local paper put it, and trained women in 'musketry', bayonet practice and sharp-shooting. They had to buy or borrow their weapons – the organisation not recognised, even deterred, by government – but West Norwood WHD were sufficiently proficient to challenge all comers to a six-a-side shooting competition in October; they had been taught to shoot by the local Home Guard until the men were instructed not to assist their women neighbours. Eventually, though, in September 1943, WHD corps were officially recognised as Home Guard women auxiliaries.[22]

This enlarging world for women emerged as some aspects of life on London's home front became ever more difficult to manage. The tasks of managing fell heaviest on women. The bombing may have stopped, or largely so, but obstacles to daily living cropped up at every turn. The biggest problem was food. To those staples rationed from early 1940 were added preserves in March 1941 and cheese in April. In December people were allocated 'points' which had to be used to buy a range of tinned foods, biscuits, rice, cereals, condensed milk, dried fruits and pulses; consumers could choose on which of these restricted foods to 'spend' their points. And chocolates and sweets were rationed from July 1942. Rations could go up and they could go down – the sugar and fat rations were raised for Christmas in November 1941 and cut in January 1942 – and foods could be added to the list for which points had to be used in a purchase. This was a system that, all agreed, sustained (even improved) nutritional health and provided more food than had been available for most Londoners in the worst months of the First World War.[23]

But food was often unappetising and unvaryingly dull; and there were many shortages that, depending on preference, caused inconvenience, even privation. The early months of 1941 saw an almost complete absence of onions – 'I think we shall go in for onion binges when the war is over,' wrote Vere Hodgson, a social worker living in Kensington, in February – and of fruit. Anthony Heap, worried about his bowels, ate his first orange of the year on 28 April and Phyllis Warner had hers more than a month later on 31 May: 'Did it taste good!' Oranges would disappear again before staging a comeback in August, but some things seemed permanently out of stock. 'Eggs to be rationed,' noted Hilda Neal in early June, and although they were not they were so scarce that grocers could only supply regular customers with one a week, if they had them. 'None are to be had in most places,' Hilda complained. A couple of weeks later and 'No fish or potatoes procurable at market today; but got a fine mackerel at [Civil Service] Stores for 7d, and rather maggoty potatoes at 1d a lb; felt lucky.' In August, when Anthony Heap went to a West End cafe with his fiancée and her brother, they found 'No jam, no cakes', no fish for fish and chips and 'shocking service', and there was a beer drought in the summer of 1941 and periodically thereafter. 'Tins of meat and fish have been unobtainable for a long time,' complained Dorothy Wells in Ealing at the end of October. By then, according to Gallup, 'shortages and restricted supplies' were as big a worry as air raids and four out of ten were finding difficulties getting unrationed items, with the problems worst in London.[24]

Food was now an obsession for Londoners. 'We all think and talk about food eternally,' wrote Phyllis Warner that summer, 'not because we are hungry but because our meals are boring and expensive and difficult to come by ... In London I haven't seen an egg for months.' In this climate of periodic dearth, wasting food was nosed out and punished by the authorities: poor Ethel Sparks was reported by a Stoke Newington food inspector who had rooted around in her dustbin after a tip-off and discovered 'five rounds of bread and one small slice which were found to be in good condition'; she was fined 10s – '"It is a shame – a hard-working woman like me,"' she told the inspector. And it wasn't just the shortages and the unforgiving authorities. Rationing made life so complicated, as Sheila and David, living in sin in west London, found in Monica Dickens's novel *The Fancy*:

The owners of the flats held a check-up every few months and it was silly to call herself Mrs. Fielding when her identity card said Sheila Blake, single. They might get suspicious and think she was an alien. The rations were an awful nuisance. David was registered at Earl's Court, and she had to leave the train there on Saturdays and get his rations before going home to get her own. His landlady had registered him with all her friends, who kept rickety little shops in Warwick Road and never had anything but tinned plum jam and cheese in silver paper. She was going to be very efficient and re-register him when the next period started, if she could find out how it was done. She had enough trouble with the milkman, who was as obstructionist as a whole Government Department, and they had to share her ration of milk for weeks while his landlady was getting all his.[25]

It was now that Londoners' gardens and allotments came into their own. The suburbs were especially favoured. Kathleen Tipper, just twenty-two at the end of the blitz, lived with her parents, a sister and brother on Woolwich Borough Council's Page Estate. Kathleen was a clerk at a shipping company's office in the Strand. The family were not well off but by late 1942 had learned to make the most of what they had:

> As we were having tea today my Father remarked that the table did not look like the table of a country in the fourth year of war, so I noted down what we were having. Spam, cheese, tomatoes, celery, beetroot, pickled onions and two sorts of home-made chutney, Swiss roll and apples. Really we ought never to grumble about the food we get, although everything on our table except the Spam and cheese and Swiss roll came from the garden and in this we are fortunate.[26]

Even the Wells family's unpromising allotment in suburban Ealing was providing rich pickings through 1942, though it needed long hours of hefty labour to cultivate and gather in onions, potatoes, French beans, lettuces, beetroots, cabbages, leeks, marrows, radishes, enough to furnish a Mayfair greengrocer's stall. There was one problem. Ken, forty-four, whose idea it had been, had found a girlfriend and hoeing, digging, raking, fertilising and harvesting were now all left to Dorothy and their seventy-eight-year-old mother, Florence.[27]

The allotment was also inner London's saviour. There were thousands in the LCC parks (Victoria Park had at least 400 in the summer of 1941), and in borough council parks and gardens; bomb sites were cultivated in Bethnal Green in the following year and a 'Victory Garden' flourished on a Battersea bomb site. Everywhere seemed to be sprouting vegetables: the topsoil covering Anderson shelters proved especially fruitful for marrows. Competitions and allotment shows sprouted with equal vigour: Lewisham Heavy Rescue Service B Shift staged a vegetable and flower show, with prizes for 'long carrots', 'short carrots', 'long beet', 'globe beet', cut flowers, sweet peas and more, in September 1942, for instance. And so did societies and competitions devoted to breeding animals, now treasured as much for food as for good looks. In Lewisham,

'Utility Poultry Societies' were established in Downham, Bellingham, Ladywell, Catford and Forest Hill, each meeting weekly in the spring of 1942 – 'All poultry keepers are welcome.' Lewisham might have been exceptional – PC Holness, a local man, won 'best allotment in London' for his ten-rod plot – but it was far from unique. Mrs Kathleen Neal of Loughborough Road, Brixton, had a miniature farm in her back garden, with hens, ducks, two twenty-week pigs (Sally and Susie) and a goat for milk – 'I regularly take her shopping, often without a lead.' ARP and fire service outfits were famous for their pig clubs. Rabbit shows and clubs ('the fancy') were legion, rabbit breeders like poultry keepers favoured with a special food ration. The Bethnal Green Men's Institute's rabbit show of 1941 had 200 entries from men and women breeders; next year, its twenty-first annual show could boast of the club's 7,000 'fur-bearing' rabbits raised for pelts. 'Many of the wives and daughters of members,' the Institute's head announced, 'wear fur coats, capes and scarves made from skins, which are the product of this backyard industry.'[28]

Besides all this domestic endeavour, which eased the food plight of hundreds of thousands of Londoners, there were other legitimate sources of supply. Country friends and relatives were a ready lifeline: Hilda Neal's great friend 'Mac', living in Crowhurst, Sussex, 'sent me a large box of onions, apples, parsley and shallots; all so welcome now'; Edward Fisher, running a guesthouse in Battersea for theatrical folk, brought back from relatives in Bude, Cornwall, two rabbits, a plucked chicken, ten eggs, apples, potatoes and a jar of cream in two heavy suitcases – 'Didn't Mum smile when she saw them,' he wrote to his daughter, away at school in Hampshire – and Charles Graves's former housemaid Eleanor, whom he'd begrudgingly seen drafted into the Land Army, brought her ex-employers in Marylebone a gift of spring onions and strawberries, 'the first strawberries we've been able to eat at home'. Some received food parcels from further afield, just like the British Red Cross but more personally directed: 'Everybody was thrilled to see the butter and the other lovely things,' Klara Modern told her family in New York, who had sent her a parcel. Loyal Klara was quick to reassure them that rations were more than adequate, supplemented in her case by the local British Restaurant, 'very cheap and good at the same time'.[29]

*

FROM Sunday 1 June 1941, however, food was not the only worry. 'Quite a shock for us all this morning,' wrote Nellie Carver next day, Bank Holiday Monday. 'We are to have clothes rationing now! Very clever of the Govt to announce this over the weekend.' Anthony Heap, a natty dresser, was at first relaxed about the new system. His sixty-six coupons a year could be used in any way he wished but each article purchased ate into his balance: twenty-six coupons for a suit, sixteen for an overcoat, seven for shoes, five for a shirt and three for socks: 'Hats and a few other items like shoe laces and braces are exempt. No price limit, nothing very drastic – albeit a complete surprise.' The screw would only begin to tighten in the following spring, when it was announced that from June 1942 sixty-six coupons would be cut to sixty and over fourteen months not twelve. Inez Holden thought that clothes rationing would have 'a toning-down effect, although probably not much at first. The rich people will still be able to have better quality clothes,' and they had bigger wardrobes already to choose from. But she was right that rationing would prove a class leveller, George Orwell noting how 'it seems rather "the thing" for people not in uniform to look shabby' by the summer of 1942. To economise on coupon use, women especially were encouraged to 'Make Do and Mend', occupying many a spring evening in 1942 in preparation for the coming summer months: 'Bought some [artificial] flowers at Civil Service [Stores],' wrote Dorothy Wells, 'and trimmed my 6/11d flat cream straw hat with them and some black velvet I had in stock. I trimmed a big straw that I had discarded years ago on Wednesday. It took me a long time, but was quite successful in the end.'[30]

For spinster needlewomen like Dorothy, there was much fun to be had from these quiet pursuits which could be timed to run alongside a favourite wireless programme, and much satisfaction from stretching skills and inventiveness. For housewives with families it was just one more burden, with the added frustration that many women had more money in their purses than ever before and could easily have bought things which were now unobtainable. The list of these, though, extended far beyond the sides of the wardrobe. Incidental shortages of domestic commodities were as common as disappearing foodstuffs. In early 1941 there was a shortage of matches and in June a sudden shortage of cigarettes, with tobacconists putting notices in windows stating 'No Cigarettes' and even 'No Tobacco'; it lasted on and off till the spring of 1942. 'Think "favourites" get them surreptitiously now and then,'

Hilda Neal suspected, though what evidence there is indicates that favourites were few and far between. The City's fire-raid resulted in a shortage of office stationery in London, diarists often making do with second best. There were shortages of wrapping paper (shoppers having to do without that Christmas), razor blades and shaving cream, cosmetics, china, glassware, pots and pans for the kitchen, playing cards (snapped up for the services), any new furniture and torch batteries (indispensable for the blackout – 'is it another ramp?' wondered a correspondent in *Picture Post*), and soap was rationed in February 1942.[31]

Alongside these frustrations, often involving tedious visits to innumerable shops to find what you wanted, or joining long queues in sometimes bitter weather, was the added grievance caused by uppity shopworkers. For once, people felt, shop assistants and shopkeepers now had the whip hand and were wreaking revenge for years of snootiness and botheration from their customers. It was the shopper's turn now to be treated with rudeness and off-hand behaviour from 'the food shop assistant [who] often seems to take a delight in ignoring my presence, while she chats with another assistant, sips a cup of tea, or indulges in some other mild pre-occupation'. 'I am not asking any favours,' this Lewisham shopper wrote. 'Nor, to secure priority, will I slip a packet of cigarettes or other gift into an assistant's hand.' 'We poor shoppers can only mutter to ourselves "there will be an after the war",' grumbled Kathleen Tipper darkly in nearby Woolwich.[32]

A suspicion of 'favourites' and under the counter sleight of hand was encouraged by much talk in these months of a 'black market' in rationed goods that undermined a policy of fair shares for all. Shopkeepers were prosecuted everywhere for selling above controlled prices or without coupons, and housewives in Stepney, and no doubt elsewhere, agitated locally against 'food racketeering'; there was also the odd prosecution for selling horsemeat disguised as something more respectable. Stealing was another way of beating the system, including the fruits of your neighbours' hard-won efforts: some East Ham allotment holders organised a special watch to deter 'persistent' thefts in the autumn of 1942 – a seventy-two-year-old bricklayer was caught green-handed with six cabbages and fined 20s.[33]

Bigger money was to be had by stealing those household commodities in periodic short supply. Razor blades were popular swag in mid-1941 – two men from Poplar and one from Dagenham were charged with stealing 3,888 of them in July. Pilfering from Cossor's radio factory at Highbury Grove, Islington, became an epidemic in late 1942, losses valued at £500 a week; thirteen employees were fined or imprisoned for stealing radios and parts like valves – 'practically unobtainable in the open market,' police explained. And eleven workers at Lewis Berger's paint factory in Homerton, Hackney, were fined for stealing paint and varnish around the same time: the main receiver was a leading fireman in south-east London. Some of this perhaps might have been siphoned off to the lucrative trade in black-market cosmetics, some of them 'substandard to the point of being dangerous', according to the women's-page editor of *Picture Post* in September 1941.[34]

But the biggest money of all was in schmutter, gear, togs, clobber, a very different kind of cabbage – in a word, clothing. Thefts of cloth from Polikoff's of Hackney 'had been very prevalent since the rationing order came into force', the court was told in July 1941 as Abraham Levy, a cutter, was fined £15 for stealing pieces of cloth worth 50s. A few days later and a Shoreditch ARP warden was given six months' hard labour for looting 'silk material' from bombed premises in Curtain Road. The slippery traders of Petticoat Lane on the eastern edge of the City came under the watchful eye of the Board of Trade, nine of them fined for selling shoes, socks and ties without coupons in August. And fifty-seven mainly women employees of Siemens in Charlton, Greenwich, were prosecuted for buying and selling stockings and underwear without coupons in another Board of Trade case that same month. A well-publicised case of handling stolen clothing material, in this case rolls of silk, resulted in the imprisonment of Isaac 'Flash Izzy' Bernfield, of Golders Green, for five years in March 1942; four other men were jailed for the robbery. The Bernfield case fuelled a popular prejudice that Jewish shopkeepers were especially prone to trading under the counter or other black market offences, though in fact it merely reflected the extensive Jewish presence in retail and wholesale, especially in the East End. In Hoxton, the clothing black market fell into the hands of a very different class, ruthless professional thieves who before the war had waged a bloody struggle with rivals offering 'protection' to racecourse bookies. The most lucrative trade of all was in stolen or forged clothing coupons, easier to handle than any bundle of cloth. A former Hackney Council food officer was given five years' penal servitude at the Old Bailey in April 1942 for stealing 130,000 of them. By then too, much London crime was perpetrated by army deserters. In July 1942 Michael Fogarty, twenty-four, AWOL from the Royal Ulster Rifles, was given three years' penal servitude for forging post office savings books and defrauding the post office of various sums of money. Fogarty was said to have run 'a school for forgers' in furnished rooms at Walthamstow, 'attended largely by Army and Navy deserters. Classes were held almost daily.'[35]

FEW things could have given more affront than Fogarty's crime because by now savings were a cornerstone of the British war effort, almost as fundamental as the manufacture of bombers. Before the war just 3 per cent of personal income had been saved compared to 9 per cent taken by direct taxation, while 88 per cent was absorbed by consumer spending of all kinds; by 1944 consumer spending had fallen to 69 per cent of income, tax had risen to 16 per cent and savings were close behind at 15 per cent. Much of the fall in spending was explained by the shops having so little for sale, so to that extent saving was made easy. But even so, not everyone could save. Bill Regan, bombed out of the Isle of Dogs in 1941 and now living in Beckenham, was struggling to make ends meet in early 1942, as the building industry laid off workers through harsh weather: 'Don't know how to pay the rent next week, we already owe one week, 28/-. I lose 17/- today, and 12/- for this month for H.P. on 3 Piece Suite, is due. A war, no work, and exhortations to "save, lend, and economise spending", plastered on walls and windows, or pushed through the letterbox. (Save – what).' A month later and he was told he owed Poplar Borough Council (collecting for the LCC) the whacking bill of £44 6s for his two children's evacuation costs – he was allowed to pay it off at 12s a week.[36]

No doubt there were many more like Regan. But for the lower middle classes and above – and for very many working-class communities and workplaces where people could put aside a shilling or two a week – gorging the savings bug was a significant part of home life. It became inescapable from the spring of April 1941 when some increases in income tax were set aside as 'post-war credits', deferred pay to be released after hostilities had ceased. Apart from this compulsory element there were three main voluntary savings streams, all prompted by government since the beginning of 1940, where the purchase of savings certificates entitled the buyer to a dividend payable when the war was over. One was at work, where offices and factories opened savings schemes for staff, sometimes competing with other local enterprises: 'Gave Mr. Cole my week's money for the Spitfire Fund,' wrote Dorothy

Wells in early 1941, her generous employers offering to pay her income tax bill for a time; she received so many bonuses out of the firm's rocketing profits from 'Sisalkraft' building paper that she became embarrassed at her 'unearned' income. In larger firms the sums put aside for government use could be immense, Ford workers at Dagenham, for instance, raising £2.65 million before the war was out.[37]

Second were the annual government-sponsored campaigns, with War Weapons Week in May 1941 setting a target of £100 million for Londoners. Nellie Carver bought ten savings certificates at Norwood on the opening Saturday morning: 'Quite a lot of excitement. Processions & Bands & flags also scores of selling booths all over the place, so cheerful after months of bombs!' These arrangements were organised by the local borough councils, which adopted, or were given, targets to contribute to the London total: Lewisham's, for instance, was £500,000 collected through 430 'War Savings Groups' in the borough, mainly workplace-based. Its week opened with a march a half-mile long including three bands, vans and tableaux, walking groups of wardens, stretcher parties, Red Cross nurses and so on. In the end, Lewisham's savings reached £688,046 – 'Triumph!' boasted the local paper. 'Great Enthusiasm All Over the Borough.' There were other campaigns in 1941, some stimulated by the announcement of 'V Day' on 20 July, the V nightly marked by the muffled tympani beat in Morse code before the BBC's nightly news. A few weeks later fifty couples stamped out Deptford's new 'Victory Dance' at the town hall: 'It is really a medium between the Lambeth Walk and the Palais Glide. There are three short stamps and one long step,' explained Deptford Savings Campaign's secretary.[38]

The main campaign for 1942 was Warship Week, with London seeking to raise £125 million. Again, there were local celebrations. In St Pancras Anthony Heap thought it 'A tawdry shoddy affair. No colour, no music, no showmanship. Wasn't worth walking across the road to see,' but elsewhere a great deal of effort went in, with local civil defence much to the fore. In Lewisham there were exhibitions and sports competitions, with the Croydon National Fire Service Dramatic Society performing *Aladdin* out of season for the children of Sandhurst Road School, Catford. Bethnal Green's Warship Week procession was led by the band of the Queen's Own Cameron Highlanders of Canada, with civil defence workers, the St Simon Zelotes Church Lads' Brigade bugle band, a twenty-foot model on wheels of HMS *Portland* made by the Portland

Place rescue squad, the town hall shelter department's float displaying one of the nurses as 'a beautiful "Britannia"', eloquently set off by the salvage department's 'two live pigs eating kitchen waste, on a lorry'. Working-class Bethnal Green and Shoreditch easily exceeded their targets, Bethnal Green raising £315,000 against a target of £250,000 and Shoreditch £662,000 against £500,000. Such high sums enabled boroughs to 'adopt' and pay for the construction of new warships: Stepney's, for instance, was HMS *Rocket*, Lewisham's HMS *Meteor*.[39]

The third main savings strand was the organisation of street savings groups, prompted by government in the autumn of 1941 but really getting under way in London in the spring and summer of 1942. There was a competitive edge between the various boroughs here too. Lewisham, its citizens having already saved £4.3 million since the start of the war by early 1942, had 280 street groups in May and were seeking 730 more; only Wandsworth had more groups, though Fulham was 'running them close'; a month or so later and Lewisham could claim 500. The National Savings Committee complained in July that London was lagging behind other big cities: 'Londoners showed they could "take it". *Let them now show they can "give it"* – or more properly speaking, lend it!' Among so much exhortation – national salvage campaigns were being trumpeted that same summer – it must have been difficult to sustain the energy of appointing street collectors, balancing the books every week, buying and distributing the certificates, especially in streets badly bomb-damaged and partly emptied of people. Nevertheless, battered Stepney proved outstanding. Its national target was 405 street savings groups; in mid-September it had 512.[40]

Another way of saving – both family pockets and national resources – was to 'holiday at home', as recreational use of the railways was discouraged and many coastal spots in any event were out of bounds. The summer of 1941 saw extensive programmes of events in parks (the LCC and local borough councils sharing the burden of organisation) and the following year saw this enlarged to a higher level of sophistication. Holidays at home also helped knock some of the stuffiness out of local administration in London, the LCC (long straitened by a puritan streak) removing its old ban on fairs in its parks from June 1942, and some outer boroughs abandoning their objections to opening parks for sports on Sundays. Music was brought into the heart of London with military band concerts, very popular at the time, up to three times a week at lunchtimes in Trafalgar Square, St Paul's Cathedral steps and

St James's Park, with weekly performances on evenings and lunchtimes elsewhere. Dance bands offered 'dancing round the bandstand' on summer evenings, concert parties organised variety shows in the parks, and there were children's entertainers, sports days and swimming galas in the open-air lidos. Programmes were sometimes supported by the government's Committee for the Encouragement of Music and the Arts (CEMA), founded in January 1940. Outside the LCC area, local initiative flourished. In Leyton, a three-week Shakespeare season was given at Coronation Gardens by the Regent's Park Open Air Theatre Group. In East Ham the park programmes had the full range of dancing and band music (including from the local ARP orchestra and the fire service military band), concerts by Galle Lambert's 'Radio Personalities', whist drives and a knockout cricket tournament.[41]

Indeed, sport was experiencing something of a revival, despite a puritan backlash against any pleasure that seemed to take the worker's mind off the war effort. Greyhound racing was restricted, at the urging of the water-drinking Lord Privy Seal, Sir Stafford Cripps, to eighteen London meetings on Saturday afternoons from March 1942, and other forms of gambling long illicit (off-course betting, street gambling with dice and coins and back-room gaming) continued to receive police attention. First-class cricket had been abandoned from the outset of the war, although scratch teams of professionals and senior school cricket continued to draw big crowds at Lord's and the Oval, including, for the first time in history, on a Sunday. Football proved more robust, the twelve London clubs (including Reading) joining a breakaway London league in 1941, refashioned as an officially approved Football League South in 1942–3, with Arsenal, under George Allison, league champions in both years; and cup finals continued to be played at Wembley. There was also a flourishing of local sport encouraged by competitiveness within the new culture of London ARP: Lewisham Civil Defence Sports Association, for instance, had league and cup competitions for billiards, snooker, chess, table tennis and football, and Lewisham Home Guard put on a boxing championship.[42]

Entertainment generally was able to flourish once the invasion of Russia signalled a likely hiatus on London's air war front. The cinema prospered especially. London's Granada cinema chain recorded a 'boom' in 1942 when 'many house records were broken. War workers earning bigger salaries', undeterred by ticket prices now inflated by a tax levy, attended several times a week: 'it was quite usual for children barely as high as the pay-box to present pound notes for 2s 3d tickets'. Bill and Vi Regan in Beckenham went to the cinema about twice a week, and for Dorothy Wells any cause for celebration at home, like a birthday, could not be marked without a visit to the 'pictures'. Favourites in these months included *Mrs Miniver* ('relieved to discover I had not lost my power of feeling!' recorded an overwhelmed Nellie Carver), *Young Mr Pitt* ('every word was appropriate to our times'), *How Green Was My Valley* ('Cheapest seat for 2/6d,' noted Vere Hodgson. 'Enormous price for a film ... But it was worth it') and Greta Garbo in *The Two-Faced Woman* ('Good, but rather too seductive' for Dorothy Wells's taste).[43]

Dorothy Wells, like other Londoners who lived in the suburbs but worked in town, had the best of both worlds. She was a frequent attender at West End early-evening shows and a special fan of Donald Wolfit's Shakespeare productions at the Strand Theatre, attending alone or with church or work friends. She would have applauded the parliamentarians who stamped on a campaign to open theatres on Sundays, defeating in April 1941 an enabling Bill that most thought likely to pass into law. 'What a triumph for the mealy mouthed puritans,' complained Anthony Heap, a first-nighter for more than a decade. Despite this setback, the London theatres experienced their own 'boom' after the invasion of Russia. 'The Theatres are all packed out because everybody is having an orgy of playgoing whilst the black-out still permits,' Phyllis Warner reported in July: not many shows 'but the acting super'. In contrast to the blitz months, Warner now counted twenty-two theatres playing in London, a number she thought in September 1941 likely to increase.[44]

The art galleries too shared in London's cultural revival from the summer of 1941. The National Gallery began cautiously to expose some of its hidden treasures brought up to the light from Wales – literally because they were buried in a mountainside – in a 'picture of the month' scheme, beginning with a Titian in March 1942. It proved immensely popular, supplemented by a programme of temporary exhibitions, including an annual display of the work of official war artists. Some boroughs also put on their own exhibitions of work by local professionals and amateurs: opening Islington's in September 1942, Sir Kenneth Clark, director of the National Gallery, praised the show as containing 'even better work than I had expected. Your standard is very high ...'[45]

The National Gallery, of course, was still home to the lunchtime concerts begun by Myra Hess and music of all kinds continued to be in great favour. Military bands and dance music – the latter having a new venue in Covent Garden theatre, where opera had given way to 'crooners' and swing by the spring of 1942 – were London's staples, but serious music continued to get an airing. In London, 'people were avid for music,' recalled Ursula Lock, then the lover of the composer Ralph Vaughan Williams, 'and music which had never been considered "popular" before drew packed and attentive audiences'. Opera and ballet were kept alive at Sadler's Wells, in Finsbury. With the Queen's Hall, Langham Place, destroyed by the 10 May raid, the Royal Albert Hall stepped in to rescue the Promenade Concerts in the summer of 1941; BBC broadcasts of the Proms would resume in 1942, after a two-year gap, the corporation withdrawing funding for broadcasts in 1940 of its own accord. A highlight of this 1942 season was the first UK performance to a live audience of Shostakovich's Symphony No. 7, the 'Leningrad'.[46]

Domestically, the wireless was the great entertainment lifeline of the age. Almost everyone had one, though Nellie Carver was a late convert, buying her first – 'a portable G.E.C. Radio rather a nice little chap – green covered and worked from a Battery' – in early December 1941. Nellie bought it for the *Nine o'clock News*, the fulcrum around which much family life turned, but for many the radio's pleasure value was priceless. The jewel in that crown was *ITMA* ('It's That Man Again'), with Tommy Handley and a host of favourites. First produced in 1939 and revived each year, it achieved mass popularity in 1942. For young Kathleen Tipper it was 'a programme I try never to miss. I think it is the best variety programme we get from our studios.' London itself was also a star, the Saturday evening *In Town Tonight* having run for almost nine consecutive years by September 1942, broadcasting ordinary Londoners and others talking about their lives and showcasing local variety talent.[47]

Alongside the wireless, reading also remained a staple of domestic life. New books were very hard to get, economies in binding, paper and printing forcing publishers into short books and small print runs, wartime tastes favouring slim volumes as more in tune with busy lives. 'Everybody is reading,' remarked Macdonald Hastings on the BBC in early 1941, and a year later the critic Jack Marlowe thought 'there was a greater demand for books than ever before'. In West Ham the borough library service was excelling itself, opening branches in abandoned shops, remitting fines and, of course, sending books to shelters. In firms too many staff book clubs were started up. Dorothy Wells's office library at the builders' merchants in Aldwych ran to eighty-one volumes by February 1941; a year later Dorothy herself was one of the buyers after members of the firm had voted for their favourite choices – Gerald Kersh's *They Die with Their Boots Clean* was a surprising early selection for 1942.[48]

Conviviality outside the home remained subject to restrictions despite the end of the Big Blitz. The pub retained its attractions for London workers and the London louche of Soho, Fitzrovia and Chelsea – where, according to almost every memoirist of the times, a sloshed Dylan Thomas propped up every bar – although the beer shortage of late summer 1941 and the winter of 1941–2 caused consternation among customers who couldn't stretch to spirits. Dining out proved more problematic. The British Restaurant attracted all classes of customer, self-service or 'help yourself' a wartime innovation there and in some Lyons restaurants. But for the gourmet things were becoming a bit of a trial. From the spring of 1942 restricted supplies meant that diners needed to be prompt, even early: at the Reform Club in April, 'You have to be on the dot at 1 p.m. to lunch in comfort,' J. L. Hodson discovered. 'Already the jacket potatoes were "off"; likewise the chicken.' To hope for a West End meal after a show was unrealistic and even a famous restaurant in the Strand was reduced to selling roast mutton instead of its traditional roast beef: 'only four small legs of mutton for the whole of Simpson's,' wondered Charles Graves, 'and we got the last two helpings at 6.50 p.m.' Nor did people always know what was appearing on their plate. 'I do not think many of our wartime customers,' wrote Simone Prunier, proprietor of a famous French restaurant in St James's Street, 'suspected that the pigeon *pâté* they praised so highly at Prunier's was really made of rooks.' In June restaurant prices were capped so that no one, on the face of things, could spend more than 5s per person on a meal kept to three courses, only one a 'main'. But ways round the 'five bob meal' were quickly found, the key loophole allowing smart places to make a 'house charge' of up to 7s 6d per cover, negotiated with the local food office. The Dorchester's normal charge was '12s. 6d. for supper. From June 15th onwards they charge 5s. for supper, 7s. 6d. cover charge, and an extra half-crown for dancing. So once again the public has to pay.'[49]

These sumptuary laws seem to have had little deterrent impact on London's nightlife after pub and cinema closing times (10.30 p.m.). Nightclubs were ostensibly open to 'members only', many with famous dance bands, throat-clutching drink prices, a bohemian clientele and eccentric management:

> It was their total lack of charm, elegance and even the most common-place amenities that gave these war-time night-clubs their attraction. They were invariably crowded and hot; and the atmosphere was dim and dense – so dense that, towards the end of the night, one felt that it was becoming semi-solid; and the entertainments they offered were strikingly monotonous. At the *Nut-House*, for example, the proprietor and a macabre young negro waiter each stood up to sing a song; and the fact that their repertoire never varied, and that the proprietor's ditty had a weird and meaningless chorus –
>
> You push the damper in, and you pull the damper out
> And the smoke goes up the chimney all the same!
>
> in which his audience loudly joined, gave one the impression that one was attending some barbaric tribal ceremony or primitive religious rite.[50]

NELLIE Carver's GEC portable had arrived just in time. Next morning, Monday 8 December, she heard news of the attack on Pearl Harbor, and the US declaration of war on Japan – but not on Nazi Germany. That day 'in London, events seemed to be moving so rapidly that one couldn't keep pace with them,' recorded the writer Margaret Crompton in her journal. 'Everywhere people were buying newspapers, anxiously reading placards and screaming headlines. One heard elderly men discussing in loud voices the rival merits of the American and Japanese navies. American servicemen in London blossomed forth abruptly into uniform.' On 11 December Hitler himself ended the uncertainty by declaring war on the USA and at last Britain had secured the ally she had sought for so long. From June 1940 to June 1941 Britain and her Commonwealth had stood alone against the Axis; now, within six months, she had secured through no action of her own the two most powerful countries in the world as her allies. Even the disastrous news of the sinking by the Japanese of HMS *Prince of Wales* and HMS *Repulse* on the day that Germany declared war could not disturb the feeling that now hostilities had taken a decisive turn and that Hitler must in the end be defeated.[51]

Spirits were mostly high that Christmas. The West End was thriving. There was pantomime with *Babes in the Wood*, at the Stoll Theatre,

Aldwych, full of topical jokes about 'the shortage of onions, oranges, and bananas' and the panto giraffe called 'roof-spotter'. London's suburban music halls were booming, with the Bedford (Camden Town), the Met (Edgware Road), Collins's at Islington Green, the Finsbury Park Empire, the Chelsea Palace and more all playing to full houses. At Covent Garden market 'there were fir-trees in plenty, a good deal of holly, and a fair supply of mistletoe'. In most homes food shortages were not sorely felt, but the poorest – large families on low incomes, the elderly, the disabled – even now needed help. Hoxton Market Mission in Shoreditch distributed 1,000 food parcels, 500 fewer than the year before, containing a 1lb Christmas pudding, a loaf, cocoa, a cake, rice, meat paste, custard powder, cornflakes, Oxo, tea and one tin of either baked beans, fish, carrots, soup or mixed vegetables; usually parcels would have included a joint of meat and half a hundredweight of coal, 'but these were unobtainable this year'. Anthony Heap was now a clerk in the finance department of St Pancras Borough Council. To his delight, he had failed his army medical on Armistice Day 1941 and was newly married to Marjorie (a West Country girl working at Highgate Hospital's first aid post); their first home was in a block of flats south of Euston Road, not too far from Anthony's mother. They were able to do better than the Hoxton charity fare. He signed on at the town hall, where he was now doing ARP control-room night duty, and after a brisk walk alone on Hampstead Heath got back

> at 1.0 in time to hear *Brains Trust* programme on radio. Mother came over to dinner at 2.0 and stayed for the rest of the day. Our dinner consisted of roast chicken (M's Mum had sent us one from Somerset) in lieu of turkey, with sausages, roast potatoes and swedes, followed by home-made Christmas pudding. Washed down with a bottle of port which Mother brought over, accompanied by a bottle of whisky. We did very well as things are at present.

He slept at the town hall for an uneventful night on duty.[52]

THE New Year's weather heralded another savage winter. January and February were even colder than 1941, January even colder than 1940, and although things cheered up in April, May was again unseasonably chilly. The absence of coal from the Hoxton relief parcels proved an ominous sign. London suffered once more from short measures for the third winter running. 'Bitterly cold again and now a coal shortage,' complained Anthony Heap; 'the coalmen have become very surly and independent and refuse to carry coal up to such a dizzy height as the third floor. It's all very tiresome and trying.' The Heaps' coal crisis was solved by Anthony's well-connected and energetic mother, who magically secured a regular supply for the newly-weds. Others weren't so lucky. The 'Coal Famine' in south London hit poorer families once more in Camberwell, Lambeth and elsewhere because 'coal merchants prefer to dispatch their fuel in the ton and half tons ordered by better-off customers to hawking it around flats'. In March coal merchants in London Region were ordered to restrict deliveries to larger residential premises, hotels and clubs in favour of 'poorer consumers', but some councils were having to buy in stocks for needy ratepayers even in mid-April. In Poplar, and no doubt elsewhere, ARP was drafted in to carry coal to householders living in buildings too high for the 'lazy' coalmen to carry upstairs. Bill Regan, now again working in heavy rescue, found not everyone a deserving case:

One old lady, crawled from the top floor to ask for some, and I sympathetically carry 1 cwt to her flat, and I'm nearly beat when I get there. Entering, I find a robust fellow, and bigger than I, sprawled on a sofa … Another person, had a cupboard full of coal, and wants more, while neighbours are without, 'If you can't get it in mate, put it on the floor.' I do, all over it.[53]

There were now few people for Bill to rescue and with hands no longer full this winter ARP turned their collective energies to organising charitable events, especially for children. Parties and treats were given by the Shoreditch Medical ARP Social and Welfare Club; the Shoreditch Civil Defence Musical and Dramatic Society 'achieved its biggest success' yet with a panto of *Red Riding Hood* given to several audiences, one comprising 400 servicemen's children who 'almost yelled themselves hoarse' joining in the chorus; Lewisham ARP treated 1,600 children to parties; Bermondsey ARP, aided by Drexel Biddell, US Ambassador to the Allied Countries, and his wife, gave parties to all the children in the borough; and the Marcia Road and District Street Fire Party, also in Bermondsey, 'held its first tea-party for children, and a social for adults at the "Dun Cow"', Old Kent Road: 'As they left each child was given sweets, an apple, a toy and a shilling.'[54]

Fire-watching, we might recall, was a relatively new branch of London civil defence, its first birthday coinciding with New Year's Day 1942. There were other innovations too. Organisationally, the most important was the creation of a National Fire Service (NFS) in July 1941, when all brigades and AFS units in the country were nationalised and merged in one centrally managed service. Instead of the patchwork of sixty-seven brigades in Greater London with the LFB in the inner area, Greater London was now divided into four quadrants radiating from the centre, each with a unified management. The takeover was master-minded by Herbert Morrison, former leader of the LCC, now Home Secretary and Minister of Home Security, who had been contemplating the change even before the last great raid of 10 May. Although London firemen had assisted other brigades, notably Liverpool, before the main blitz ended, Morrison invited them to think of themselves as a resource not just for London but for the country as a whole. He promised that the brigades would be returned to local government after the war, and the NFS remained in place for the duration.[55]

Morrison perhaps was tempted to nationalise further, announcing in May 1941 a new standard uniform for civil defence staff countrywide, but organisation was sensibly left in local hands. The shelter programme continued in London, mostly focusing on strengthening and improving accommodation in street shelters, and a stalled schedule of a few deep shelters was given new life. Tardiness here was caused not by bureau-cratic short-sightedness in Whitehall but by genuine shortages of mater-ials and, above all, labour and finance: the cost of tunnelling beneath existing tube lines proved significantly greater than original estimates. In the end, eight deep shelters were finished during 1942, though not opened for public use. They were connected to tube stations at Belsize Park, Camden Town, Goodge Street, Chancery Lane, Stockwell, Clapham North, Clapham Common and Clapham South. Finsbury, long ambi-tious for deep shelters, got a surrogate: the disused City Road tube station was converted into a shelter for around 500 people and made available for use in 1942.[56]

Shelter use during these eighteen months from the petering out of the Big Blitz naturally dropped off, though some shelterers were wary of abandoning their security. In the tubes, where around 87,500 were sheltering in the peak nights of May 1941, there were still nearly 40,000 in July, some 27,500 in October and nearly 15,000 in December. In 1942 the tubes were generally sheltering 5,000 or fewer each night.

Barbara Nixon in Finsbury thought shelter users in the lull tended to be families with young children and the 'very old', along with some adolescents, there for the canteens where these were still running. It is clear too that some single homeless people preferred the safety and company of shelter life to seeking a more permanent (and costly) billet through the council. The downside of continuing shelter life in this period was a growing epidemic of scabies, 'the itch', caused by a mite burrowing under the skin and causing an irritating inflammation. Scabies was made notifiable in London by the Scabies Order, November 1941, parents and doctors having to report cases to the local council's public health department, which organised treatment and disinfestation of clothes and bedding. And a plague of rats in London, drains broken by bombing allowing them to surface from the sewers, was causing consternation to all shelterers in cellars and Andersons; rats remained a chronic problem in the capital for much of the rest of the war.[57]

Indeed, the dangers of post-blitz London were everywhere apparent. The psychic toll on ARP personnel was evident in the suicides of Harry Gostling, fifty-five, a Hackney stretcher-bearer who had become so nervous and depressed after dealing 'with some very bad cases' that he had to be discharged from civil defence and gassed himself in his kitchen before Christmas 1941; and John Stone, thirty-five, an East Dulwich dentist and part-time warden who gassed himself in January 1942, having become 'obsessed with the idea that he was a coward', telling his mother 'that if there was another air-raid he would not be able to pick up bits and pieces of bodies again'. Less than a month later, by a disastrous stroke of ill luck, on the night of 10 February, a Wellington bomber crashed on the Harrow Green ARP depot in Trinity Street, Leytonstone. Five ARP men and the aircrew of six died, the wardens apparently burning to death as the plane's fuel tanks exploded; a disaster fund raised £600 for the men's families within a month.[58]

There were particular dangers for children. By 1942 they were returning to London in increasing numbers – that October there were 214,300 children in LCC schools compared to just 125,000 still in the country. The fascination of shattered abandoned houses, each filled with mystery, was inexhaustible but potentially deadly. A bombed house in Spencer Road, Walthamstow, collapsed and killed two boys in April 1942; there were eleven or twelve boys and girls building dens in that and neighbouring houses at the time. The static cisterns of London's emergency water supply proved an even greater menace. They had grown in number since the great fire-raid of 29 December 1940 and were often situated in the basements of demolished buildings. There were scores of fatalities from children drowning in them across London till the end of the war, each case a family tragedy and a lasting trauma for those attempting a rescue or recovering the bodies. One must stand for many. Peter Knibbs, five and a half, of Alabaster Buildings, Appold Street, Shoreditch, had been allowed out to play with his younger brother, Gordon. Their father was in the NFS and their mother usually took them out or kept them in the flat to play. This one time she let them play in a bombed and cleared area a little away from the water tanks in Vandy Street, just north of Broad Street Station. 'Gordon came in, and when she asked him, "Where is Peter?" he replied "Peter's in the water."'[59]

The biggest danger of all proved to be from UXBs. London's civil defence was given a terrible jolt at 9.30 p.m. on Saturday 6 June 1942 when an undetected mine exploded at Gurney Street, Southwark, near the Elephant and Castle. The device was enormous, probably weighing 1,000 kilograms, and the devastation in this street of four-storey tenement houses, a family to a floor, was immense: photographs show that it looked like an earthquake had struck. At least nineteen people died, including many children, and some thirty-five were injured and detained in hospital. Not everyone was crushed by rubble. Walter Wells saw his father killed in front of him: 'Mother was brushing father's coat. He was just going out when a piece of railing came through the window and killed him before our eyes.' Recovery attempts on the night were heroic: 'Rescue workers toiled all Saturday night by floodlight, and in 18 houses they got 28 people out alive.' Next morning they were reinforced by scores more men with heavy cranes, some on caterpillar tracks, searching for the three final persons not ticked off the ARP's street lists as being recovered. One couple lost all four children, identified by scraps of clothing, a silver ring, a scar. Around a thousand were made homeless and the Lord Mayor's relief fund quickly donated £1,000 to an immediate appeal for assistance for the victims: it was needed, for looters had descended like magpies on the chaos, even as the rescuers were searching for survivors.[60]

London was, of course, no stranger to UXBs, and undetected bombs were being uncovered as demolition and clearance revealed unexplained pits and craters. In May the licensee of Foresters Hotel, Whitwell Road, Plaistow, in West Ham, discovered that he and his wife had been living over a six-foot heavy-calibre bomb since 10 November 1940. The pub had been badly damaged and repaired since with a new concrete floor to the cellar but the local air raid warden had nagging doubts, and after seeing a new instructional film revisited the scene and alerted the bomb squad.

The Gurney Street mine, apparently a new type in a low-magnetic casing and detached from any parachute, fell on 10 May 1941, the busiest night of the blitz; it destroyed a house before burying itself in the ground. The destruction looked like it had been caused by a small bomb and the wardens had no reason to question whether a far bigger device lay deep under the ruins. The tragedy caused heart-searching and some recriminations in Southwark, but a London Civil Defence Region inquiry concluded that no blame attached to ARP workers; given the dreadful battering the Elephant and Castle took that night, it was an understandable conclusion. But Gurney Street was an unforgettable alarm call and from that date Southwark and other boroughs began revisiting every incident record from 1940 and 1941, questioning whether any report of a bomb falling had not been properly followed up: by mid-July several more UXBs had been discovered in Southwark and made safe, and there were similar finds elsewhere. Eighty years on and UXBs from the Big Blitz were still being recovered from central London.[61]

In April 1942 James Lansdale Hodson visited a fellow journalist friend who had worked in civil defence through the blitz and was now in an 'A.R.P. sick bay with a swollen leg'. 'Speaking of the spirit of England, he said that London folk are bored and critical because life is dull now. Not long ago London had a daylight air warning. He said: "I was in bed but I hopped out feeling fine. I opened the window. The policeman started wisecracking with me; everybody was smiling."' But a few warnings, in the absence of raids, were insufficient to keep the massed ranks of civil defence in London gainfully employed. Everyone felt the pressure was slowly coming off. From July 1942 it was no longer necessary to carry gas masks in public, and anyway most people had no longer bothered to do so for some time. Public shelters were more likely to be vandalised – electric fittings broken or stolen the commonest complaint – than valued as something that might save lives again. Londoners were already speaking of the period since Hitler's invasion of Russia as 'the "lull"', recognising that mass bombing or something equivalent was likely to recur, but in the interim the country's manpower was stretched to snapping point and the armed and auxiliary fighting services, war industries and essential services were all clamouring for men and women to work in them. The problem was recognised within the ranks of civil defence, where all, or most, wanted to make themselves as useful as possible. NFS fire stations turned their hands to war production in their spare time. Plessey's put out some radio assembly to depots in Stepney, in Fulham they made ammunition boxes, elsewhere 'the shaping of paddles for aircraft dinghies'; by 1943 munitions like Sten gun springs, gun slings, armour plate, 'tank covers' and more were being produced from 280 London fire stations and many were also making toys for nursery children and for children's Christmas presents.[62]

Despite this extramural usefulness, cuts in civil defence staffing seemed inevitable. From September 1941 men under forty were culled from gas decontamination squads and from October men under thirty from stretcher parties. The amalgamation of stretcher and rescue teams, which progressed through the winter of 1941–2, released some 10,000 civil defence personnel in London; in addition, 9,000 workers were to be transferred from casualty services, half each from first aid posts and ambulances. From May 1942 whole-time warden posts were cut by a third and part-timers in report and control centres by a half, releasing some 7,000–8,000 men and women for work in industry. As a result some services – first aid posts in large shelters, for instance – were mothballed. Some boroughs protested but on a balance of national priorities, in the light of the very different direction of the war from June 1941, it was difficult to object to these painful cuts. One consequence was to involve more part-time volunteers in civil defence (who all had to be trained by local authorities of course) and, therefore, more women. The London AFS recruited some 1,300 additional women as telephonists, watch-room and canteen workers from May 1941, for instance. In Stoke Newington, and no doubt elsewhere, public meetings in September 1941 called for women to take the place of ARP men called up for other services. Klara Modern, before she became a full-time nursery worker, became a part-time warden in Finchley Road, Hampstead, for four hours, 8 p.m. to midnight every fourth night: 'If I get the time I'll try and collect badges of various kinds, First Aid, Artificial Respiration etc.' She put up a 'picture of Mr. Churchill with the Austrian colours around it' in her room. Women in the auxiliary services were also more visible in London, especially Women's Auxiliary

Air Force (WAAF) balloon operators and Auxiliary Territorial Service (ATS) anti-aircraft range-finders working with Home Guard and regular gunners.[63]

IN this 'dull' time, bodies were still being recovered from blitzed buildings. In November 1941, for instance, the remains of three firemen were recovered during excavations in Bunhill Street, Finsbury. 'They were last seen on the top floor' of the building on 14 October 1940, the LFB district officer told the coroner. 'He went up to where they were working and found the hose burnt off and that they had simply disappeared.'[64]

Other bodies presented more of a mystery. On 17 July 1942 builders repairing a bomb- and fire-damaged chapel in Kennington Lane, Lambeth, unearthed an incomplete and partially burnt skeleton under the vestry floor. At first the remains appeared to be those of some unnamed victim of the blitz, but no one had been reported missing from any incident nearby and it appeared that the corpse had been deliberately mutilated with a view to preventing identification. Police records showed that an unexplained fire had been discovered there and extinguished on the night of 14/15 April 1941, Easter Monday and Tuesday. There had been no raid that night. A small fire was not much for the authorities to worry about, except that two days before, Mrs Rachel Dobkin, of Brady Street, Whitechapel, had been reported missing by her sister; and Harry Dobkin, her estranged husband, had been fire-watcher for a firm of solicitors who had a document store in the chapel yard at Kennington Lane. Dobkin had been on duty that night of the fire and had given the alarm. Suspicions were aroused sufficient for police to make a cursory search of the chapel crypt in April 1941. Nothing was found and enquiries into Rachel's disappearance finally came to nothing. Now, though, a body had been found and, with some brilliant forensic medical reconstruction, Rachel Dobkin's remains were identified and the cause of death proved to be manual strangulation. Harry Dobkin, a Jewish street trader living with his elderly parents in Navarino Road, Dalston, was convicted of her murder. He was hanged at Wandsworth Prison; Dobkin appealed against conviction but finally confessed to the crime.[65]

Wartime London seemed to present the perfect scenario for murder. There were not just bomb damage and the destruction of corpses; the confusion of the times meant that people might go missing, apparently without trace, and perpetrators too might have good reason to be always on the move. There were many London murders in these years and many London murderers. But those which stand out as the most brutal and sadistic, and where it proved most difficult to bring the killer to justice, were the murders of women.

The true numbers will never be known, but of those cases which came to light at the time we might mark three in London in the autumn of 1941. In the case of Theodora Greenhill, a sixty-five-year-old Kensington widow battered to death for her money, her murderer was discovered and hanged. The murderer of Eleanor Humphries, about forty years old, an AFS cook living in Gloucester Crescent, Regent's Park, who had been savagely attacked in her bed, was never found. And nor was the murderer of Mabel Church, nineteen, a clerk at Hackney Council's electricity department, who was strangled on her way home from the cinema. She lived in Tufnell Park but her body, 'practically naked', was found in a bombed house two or three miles away in Hampstead Road.[66]

That was October 1941. Four months later, a few journalists were linking the Humphries and Church murders with some gruesome finds being investigated by police in central London. In the space of three or four days in February 1942 four women were found strangled and horribly mutilated before or after death. Evelyn Hamilton, forty, was killed in an air raid shelter behind the British Museum; the second, killed next morning in her room in Wardour Street, Soho, was Evelyn Oatley, aka Nita Ward, thirty-four; within a day or two Margaret Lowe, forty-three, was killed in her room at Gosfield Street, Marylebone; and Doris Jouannet, thirty-two, was killed in her two-room flat in Sussex Gardens, Paddington. The press quickly nicknamed the killer 'the Blackout Ripper'. Then, on Friday 13 February, another woman was attacked in a Haymarket air raid shelter but she fought the man off and screamed for help; her assailant ran out, leaving his service gas mask behind. Gordon Cummins, twenty-eight, a married man born in Yorkshire, was training as a pilot in the RAF. He had tried to attack other women in the West End besides the one who proved fatal to him. Tried and convicted for the murder of Evelyn Oatley, Cummins was executed at Wandsworth Prison on 25 June 1942.[67]

Evelyn Oatley and Margaret Lowe were prostitutes and so were no doubt some of the women Cummins attacked but, for whatever reason, didn't succeed in killing. Cummins was considered a handsome man and presumably charmed or offered money to Hamilton and Jouannet, the latter married to a seventy-two-year-old hotelier and considered 'flighty' by police. Cummins's victims would not have been hard to find. Street prostitution had been endemic in London for generations without number but the Second World War offered prostitutes excellent opportunities for rich pickings. It was a risky profession and murders of London prostitutes did not stop when Cummins was hanged; a number of these too were unsolved. But the risks were never enough to keep women off the streets for long.

It was the West End where prostitution seemed most flagrant and where, of course, it was most visible to Londoners. From the first blackout of 1939 Gladys Langford, out in the West End with a man friend, thought prostitutes had increased in number, darkness favouring 'the older and uglier ones', she felt. Certainly, artistic use of the hand torch in the blackout, uplighting faces, showing legs and more, was noticed by many. The West End streets from Leicester Square through Piccadilly Circus, and along Piccadilly to Bond Street and the streets off, were well known for prostitution – even sedate Jermyn Street, catering to the sartorial needs of the gentleman about town, had a reputation as 'a great street for tarts'. The most notorious quarter of this part of the West End, long favoured by smart French women, was the area of Mayfair north of Piccadilly and south of Curzon Street, between Stratton Street and Hamilton Place and most certainly including Shepherd Market. The American war correspondent A. J. Liebling, in London in the summer of 1941, put up in Fleming's Hotel in Clarges Street:

Outside the window drapes that veiled this inner nodule of British propriety there resounded pretty continually the cheerful click of the Piccadilly tarts' high heels. Half Moon and Clarges Streets, which are traverses between Piccadilly and Curzon Street, are important trade routes of summer evenings. The Piccadilly packets, having picked up cargoes, convey them back to their Curzon Street and Shepherd Market home ports. They come back up Clarges Street light, chattering happily. The police, except for enforcing certain trade agreements, deal with the girls in the same spirit of comradely venality as cops in any other country. The fine aroma of larceny in the air makes a New Yorker feel at home ...[68]

Among their number was Marthe Watts, a Frenchwoman who had married an English alcoholic and moved to London in 1937. Between then and 1940 she claimed to have made over 400 appearances at Bow Street police court, costing £2 a time but easily recouped. In 1940 she was living with her maid in New Burlington Street, north of Piccadilly, but the blitz drove Marthe and two other French prostitutes living nearby to seek peace and quiet in Ilfracombe, which must have livened up the natives. Back in London by Christmas, she set up in a block of flats in Jermyn Street, frequenting the Palm Beach Club in Wardour Street. It was there, in April 1941, that Marthe met and eventually teamed up with the Messina brothers, Sicilian migrants to Malta and then to London, schooled in the brothel trade by their father, in Alexandria and elsewhere. Marthe and Eugenio (Gino) Messina hooked up for the duration, eventually moving to the Shepherd Market area.[69]

Outside the West End, prostitution was widely spread almost everywhere, with notable clusters in the East End (Cable Street and nearby), in the north (Finsbury Park) and around all the mainline railway stations north and south of the river. Of these, the epicentre of west London prostitution, especially the brothel trade, was Paddington. From Edgware Road west, from Bayswater in the south to Maida Vale in the north, through Sussex Gardens where poor Doris Jouannet was murdered, brothels and prostitutes abounded in countless numbers. Not for the first time, the Ecclesiastical Commissioners, who owned the freeholds of this once-grand property now seedy beyond description, won embarrassing notoriety as the wealthiest and most respectable whoremongers in the country.

> Who strolls so late, for mugs a bait,
> In the mists of Maida Vale,
> Sauntering past a stucco gate
> Fallen, but hardly frail?
> You can safely bet that it's French Lisette,
> The Pearl of Portsdown Square,
> On the game she has made her name
> And rather more than her share.[70]

From the middle of 1942, increasing official anxiety about venereal disease and the risk that 'loose women' posed to Britain's fighting mettle began to have something about it of the great moral panic of 1917, though without that period's hysteria. But just as worrying was the number of dead and abandoned babies found in London's streets and backyards, and the great number of abortions that ended in the deaths of women. The new worlds opening up for women at work, with husbands away in the services or working outside London, combined to make the opportunities and the desire for sexual experimentation blossom. Many women got 'caught' as a consequence and strove to avoid their embarrassment in one way or another. In the bitterly cold March of 1942, twin boys, some four to six weeks old, were found abandoned on the steps of a building in Cambridge Heath Road, Bethnal Green; one subsequently died in hospital of pneumonia. The mother soon gave herself up to police. Phoebe Burking from Boston, Lincolnshire, was the wife of a soldier on active service but the twins were not his; she said she came to London to get them adopted and when she ran out of coal couldn't care for them any longer. In April, the body of a newborn baby was found on the roof of an outbuilding in Hoxton; it had survived a few minutes, doctors thought, before its skull was fractured, possibly by being dashed against a floor or wall. In May, also in Hoxton, the body of a newborn baby girl was found in a brown-paper carrier bag left in a bombed house: she may have been stillborn. And so on.[71]

Abortion cases were almost as common. Beatrice Cox, forty-nine, was given six years' penal servitude in January 1942 for the manslaughter of Hilda Goldstein, thirty, of Shore Place, Hoxton, who died from 'blood poisoning, following an injection of scalding fluid'. The body of Phyllis Newberry, thirty-five, lodging in Shepherd Market, Mayfair, was found by a policeman in an alley off Stockwell Road, Lambeth. She had died in an attempt to procure a miscarriage by two south London women, aided by a local pharmacist; all three were given two years' imprisonment at the Old Bailey in September. And in December Betty May Power, thirty-six, from Leytonstone, was accused of murdering Emmie Rix, thirty-seven, an Ilford woman three months pregnant, who died from shock when 'a quantity of strong soap fluid' was introduced. There were many more in these months, in every London district.[72]

EVERY one of London's neighbourhoods had, by late 1942, been greatly changed by three years of war. Post-blitz demolition and clearance had tidied up many areas of devastation – 'How admirably does London hide its scars!' thought Robert Henrey, revisiting Leicester Square at the end of 1941 – but some were too deep to hide. James Lees-Milne, the architectural historian, had gone to look at the City in March:

> I walked through the devastated area to the north of the cathedral. It was like wandering in Pompeii. The sun was shining warm and bright. There was not a breath stirring, only the seagulls wheeling and skirling over the ruins. Not a sound of traffic when I was in the midst of the isolation. From one spot there is waste land visible as far as the eye can roam. It was most moving.[73]

'In one's own immediate neighbourhood,' noted Anthony Weymouth in Marylebone, 'one gets accustomed to the holes in the ground where houses used to be and a year later, one takes them for granted.' But in other parts of London now revisited 'you're pretty sure to get a nasty shock,' as in Smith Square, Westminster, where he found Thomas Archer's gigantic early eighteenth-century church now just 'four walls standing stark and roofless'. Lees-Milne hoped that at least the spires of the gutted Wren churches in the City might be preserved after the war, but in the ruined Temple Phyllis Warner felt 'this island of learning should remain as an island of desolation, a perpetual monument to the bestiality of war, and an object lesson to future years'. The whole question of how – even whether – London should be rebuilt would become a momentous issue in the year and more to come, though one triumphant victory for a future London was notched up in the opening to two lanes of traffic of Sir Giles Gilbert Scott's new Waterloo Bridge, in August 1942; the number of women steel erectors and other builders working on the project led some to christen it 'The Ladies' Bridge'.[74]

London's appearance was hardly improved by the removal of area and garden railings for recycling as war weapons, a programme that began in the summer of 1941 and lasted into the spring of 1942: 'Your Railings Will Keep Hitler Out' ran the Islington Gazette's hopeful headline. Everywhere in London suffered, leaving scarred and damaged walls behind, but it did have the advantage of opening up parks and the gardens of squares that might otherwise have been inaccessible to the public. In Green Park, however, the view and access were abruptly spoiled by soldiers laying 'massive coils of barbed wire between the grass mounds and the pavement of Piccadilly'. There was worse nearby. From the blitz months of 1941, 'an immense dump of old bricks, wood and scrap iron' was made in Hyde Park to receive bomb debris capable of reuse. 'It was a cemetery of iron bedsteads, burned-out motor cars, lorries, baths, gas cookers, electric stoves, geysers, water tanks,' all next door to dozens of family allotments. In Kensington Gardens nearby, 'an immense pile of pink rubble', consisting of thousands of tons of bricks brought from all over London, 'grew to tremendous proportions, rising high against the trees like a palace of oriental coral, undulated its beauty over several acres'; it was added to daily by lorries climbing on ramps and tipping their loads. Most of this rubble would eventually be shipped by rail to help build 150 airfields and their runways in East Anglia.[75]

Among all these reminders of the blitz, moving around London was proving not much easier than it had during the worst months. There was less road traffic so cycling was safer and road deaths were down – 436 in London Region between 1 September 1941 and 28 February 1942 compared to 771 in the same period the year before. With so few private car drivers able to get petrol, and taxis now even scarcer than before, the horse was making a surprising comeback to London's streets. High prices were obtained at the Monday horse sales at Elephant and Castle, where 'the demand is exceeding supply'. George Orwell noted 'two women driving in an old-fashioned governess cart' and 'two men in a carriage and pair' in the spring of 1942, for instance. The horse notwithstanding, it all put tremendous pressure on public transport. Overcrowding led to frayed tempers among Londoners. In the spring of 1942, queueing at London bus stops became compulsory where six or more people were waiting. Even before, the LPTB had by-laws in place to enforce queueing at very busy stops – an unreasonable AFS man was fined 40s for queue jumping and causing a ruckus at a crowded trolley-bus stop at Dalston Junction in February, for instance.[76]

One reason for the crowds was that during 1942 London found itself filling up again. At the end of the year inner London had a civilian population of 2,477,700, some 236,000 more than at the end of May 1941, a rise of over 10 per cent. The numerical gains in outer London were even larger, its population now 4,204,200 as against 3,809,100, an increase of 395,100 (also 10 per cent). It was a modest gain, sure enough, but the houses lost through bomb damage in badly blitzed areas could not be made good and it all meant increased pressure on the surviving houses of Greater London. In suburban areas like Harrow, Hayes and Wembley semi-detached houses were being divided into two or even four flats to accommodate war workers in west London's aircraft and munitions factories. Problems were reported from everywhere. In Stepney children and families were returning to a borough badly knocked about and where housing, even in the peace years, was generally poor; yet they would not accept billets outside the borough, exacerbating overcrowding there. In Leyton there was an acute housing shortage and the council had asked the Ministry of Health for requisitioning powers; in Lewisham the demand for family houses could not be met; in Kensington 'flatlets' were not to be had for love nor bribery and Westminster Council began an inquiry into inflated rents. 'The demand for London flats is unprecedented,' reported an estate agent in Mayfair, 'and as so many of the larger buildings have been requisitioned [for offices] by the Government it has become extremely difficult to satisfy ...'77

THE heroic resistance to Nazi Germany shown by the Russian people added a new dimension to London's war as the blitz receded into recent history. Sympathy showed itself in many ways. Membership of the CPGB more than doubled to 60,000 in the country as a whole, with some 24,000 in London, overwhelmingly the CP's stronghold despite its decline in population. 'Everything "Russian" is in vogue today,' wrote Ambassador Maisky in October 1941, 'Russian songs, Russian music, Russian films, and books about the USSR.' Many London boroughs sponsored 'Anglo-Russian' friendship organisations that encouraged Aid to Russia collections of one kind or another: Conservative Lewisham's Anglo-Soviet Committee pledged to raise £1,500 for a mobile X-ray unit for the Red Army, for instance, presenting a cheque to Maisky in October 1942; it held cross-party celebrations, like an Anglo-Soviet Week in June and a great rally at the Plaza Cinema, Catford, with Maisky in attendance, in November. Similar events happened everywhere in inner London, but Labour Finsbury claimed a special place in Anglo-Russian endeavours. Lenin had lived in the borough for a time and in March 1942 a plaque was unveiled on his temporary home, 30 Holford Square, by the ubiquitous Maisky. A celebratory procession toured the borough in which 1,200 took part, led by the Middlesex Regiment band, the mayor, councillors and other local dignitaries, with civil defence, home guard and other organisations on the march; it ended with a demonstration at Clerkenwell Green, where Lenin had edited his journal *Iskra* from No. 37a. Next month, Maisky unveiled a bust of Lenin commissioned by the council and made, uniquely it was thought, of reinforced concrete: both the Lenin memorial and the bust would be vandalised by fascists a few months later.[78]

In early April some 30,000 Londoners demonstrated in Trafalgar Square in favour of a Second Front in 1942 to force the Germans to withdraw troops from Russia and fight an Allied force in Western Europe; throughout the year communists organised a chalking and leafleting campaign for this more warlike message than the one they had peddled before 22 June 1941. It too would prove a barren endeavour, at least for 1942.

EVEN SO, 'Russian news,' as Mollie Panter-Downes wrote in February 1942, 'has been London's one solid comfort in the daily accumulation of disappointments.' It was true enough. The fall of Singapore that month 'has depressed everyone,' thought Nellie Carver. 'You cannot see the end of all these disasters but can only keep plodding on as usual.' 'We are not talking much about it,' Dorothy Wells confided to her diary, 'but everybody feels pretty grim.' There was other bad news too as enemy warships unaccountably gave the Royal Navy the slip in home waters, and the Conservative MP Chips Channon, close to the heart of things in Westminster, sensed real 'ANGER. The country is more upset about the escape of the German battleships than over Singapore ... The capital seethes with indignation and were Londoners Latins there would be rioting.'[79]

In April and May the Germans, who seemed dauntless on every front, mustered sufficient Luftwaffe resources to bomb a handful of treasured English towns. These attacks were lamented by most Londoners, but in working-class areas a rather different feeling was detectable, harking back perhaps to the psychic bruising of evacuation before and during the blitz. Level-headed Bill Regan in Poplar noted, 'Bath raided again last night. Hear they are asking for volunteers to help them. I can feel no sympathy for Bath. They did not rush to us, in our time of need, neither did they show any feeling. I have spoken with several people, who all express the same opinion.'[80]

Tempers weren't helped by a revived invasion scare in October, seeming to originate in LCDR, perhaps worried about complacency seeping into the capital's civil defence. Wardens went door to door asking what householders could offer by way of aid to the civil power should German paratroopers land in Hyde Park, and a City of London Civic Guard recruited volunteers among commuters willing to stay on and defend the Square Mile by day or by night. Even the enlarging presence of uniformed Americans on the streets of London seemed at this stage to offer not much by way of reassurance.[81]

Then almost out of the blue came relief, even salvation. At 11 p.m. on Wednesday 4 November the BBC announced news of the Axis retreat from El Alamein. 'Joyful and sobering news,' wrote Hilda Neal in South Kensington. 'All feel much heartened today. My cleaner, who doesn't know Libya from Chelsea opened round saucer eyes when I told her and said, "It's wonderful what they can do," hoping that was a propos.' There had been so much bad news that everyone feared this too might prove an illusion: 'People say little about it,' thought Dorothy Wells, at work in Aldwych, 'our policy being to avoid too much elation over victories, but it really seems to be one.' It really was. Soon everyone felt free to enjoy it. 'London was a city of smiling people,' wrote Mollie Panter-Downes on Sunday 15 November, the day that church bells were allowed to peal again; they had been silenced from May 1940, only to be rung should the expected invasion begin. The British and Commonwealth victory in North Africa was consolidated for Londoners by the crushing defeat of the Germans by the Russians at Stalingrad. These heady events pretty much coincided with the publication of the government's official history of the blitz, *Front Line 1940–41*, a vividly illustrated pamphlet selling for 2s. 'What a rush there is to buy *Front Line*,' noted Kathleen Tipper. 'I have been buying copies for different friends, and quite regularly they are sold out.' She could understand the appeal:

> many people here [at her office in the Strand] like nothing better than to talk about the Blitz and what happened on this and that night. Somehow the wonderful spirit which seemed everywhere at that time seems to have left us to a great extent, and I feel that many people would like it to return. I don't think it will unless we have another period of communal suffering, as we did then.[82]

Thoughts of the past, though, seemed overwhelmed by expectations of the future. Already, during this difficult but finally uplifting year, people were beginning to wonder what sort of London, and what sort of Britain, might be built after the war was finally won, as nine out of ten Britons now thought it surely would be. London authorities, like Hackney, for instance, were establishing 'Post-War Reconstruction' committees or something similar. The needs of youth were being addressed with increasing vigour, with clubs and 'youth centres', organised sports and discussion groups. Women at the LWP and elsewhere were beginning to voice what help they expected after the war for working life, family support and modern housing. And a couple of days after *Front Line* was published, Kathleen Tipper recorded that hundreds of Londoners were queueing patiently outside the government stationery office to buy another official report. Instead of looking backwards, this seemed to open a window on what a post-war Britain might ideally look like.[83]

7

AFTER THE WAR:
1 DECEMBER 1942–31 DECEMBER 1943

'THERE are two sets of people in this country to-day,' wrote J. B. Priestley in the summer of 1942, and they were defined by what they thought would happen after the war. One set thought the country would return to the 'settled society' of 1939. The other felt the changes brought about by war were long overdue and that it would be impossible to go back. Now, Priestley believed, 'many of the worst features of our pre-war life have vanished or are rapidly dwindling'. Who could contemplate a return to 'our fantastically gross and really sinful inequalities' or the 'vast army of unemployed, ill-nourished and hopeless masses'?[1]

This apprehension of a possible return to the pre-war settlement of mass unemployment, of endless acres of slums and the petty tyrannies of the means test was widely shared in London. Evacuation had exposed the poverty and squalor of much working-class life, and the blitz had laid bare the mean living conditions and exiguous domestic resources of a large proportion of London workers. Rationing had done something to bridge the equality gap and bring the living standards of the well-off closer to those of the wage earner. Rising wages and household earnings favoured those who worked with their hands in factories and workshops and were doing much to level up family incomes across classes. And the social mixing of people from widely different backgrounds in a common cause, in civil defence especially, had done something to mitigate class hostility. These were perceptible gains, felt as such at the time, and many Londoners thought it would be tantamount to a crime to relinquish them once the war was over. '[W]hen I think what the people of the East End have been put through with this lot,' remarked the anonymous 'AFS man' at the end of the blitz, 'if they don't do something about putting things right afterwards, I'll become an anarchist and go round shooting everybody ... The truth of the matter is that the East End will probably do all that on its own account – without my help.' Bill Regan, a real East Ender, felt something similar, struggling to feed his family as bitter weather in early 1942 threw him off the building job where he'd been working: 'What an existence. Will we ever have State Control. The end of this war must be the beginning of better conditions for the backbone of the country. Enough of this, it makes me want to kick somebody hard.'[2]

It is not difficult to see why so many Londoners queued outside the government stationery office in Kingsway, Holborn, to secure an early copy of *Social Insurance and Allied Services*, a densely printed 300-page report by Sir William Beveridge, a nationally famous authority on unemployment and its cures. Beveridge seemed to offer a blueprint to prevent a return to the pre-war Britain that so many feared. The publication of the Beveridge Report – often written about at the time as the 'Beveridge Plan' – on 1 December 1942 was 'one of the key dates in the wartime history of Britain':

> Beveridge set out in detail a comprehensive scheme for social insurance for all citizens against sickness, poverty and unemployment together with proposals for a national health service, family allowances and the maintenance of full employment. No official report has ever aroused greater popular interest or enthusiasm. Beveridge's proposals, presented with the passion of a reformer as well as the authority of an expert, crystallised the ill-defined but widely felt desire to make a radical break with the past and create a society freed from its social evils and inequalities. Here at last was a programme, more than that, a manifesto, on which people could fasten. For or against 'Beveridge' became the test of allegiance to the future or the past, and those who were 'for' were in no mood to listen to qualifications or doubts.[3]

The Beveridge Report provoked huge interest in London. The report's recommendations were widely circulated in daily and local newspapers and from the earliest moment it was the subject of widespread debate. Even on 1 December, a meeting of the Hammersmith Branch of the Old Age Pensioners' Association at Shepherd's Bush received a 'forecast' of the report: 'The Secretary stated that he had ordered a copy for the use of the members. It was felt that everyone should be on the alert to study the report.' Beveridge was the subject of discussion at Labour and Co-operative Party branch meetings, Conservative and Unionist associations and local Liberal branches, receiving general support almost everywhere. Its virtues were extolled from January in a local advertising campaign by the newly formed Common Wealth Party ('Socialism minus the class war,' George Orwell thought), which announced 'The Beveridge Plan must go through NOW!' Resolutions from wartime London's myriad local associations, urging that the report be adopted by Parliament, were sent to MPs of all persuasions, like one to the Conservative MP for Spelthorne from eighteen members of the Feltham Unit of the 21st Column (4th GPO) Battalion of the Home Guard, in February. Public lectures were available everywhere by speakers advocating full, or almost full, acceptance of the report's recommendations. The letters columns of local papers across London were filled with comment from December to April, so much so that it sometimes appeared there was little else to talk about. The Beveridge Report refocused the imagination of Londoners, whether they lived in the inner areas or the suburbs: indeed, because disagreement (from insurance company employees and shareholders and from medical men, for instance) was more vocal in suburban districts, the debate there raised passions often not present in solidly working-class areas. But everywhere a new preoccupation had been added to the daily concerns of Londoners. It was the lead-up to this Christmas of 1942, the writer Mollie Panter-Downes felt, that 'brought the phrase "after the war" back into active circulation'.[4]

The whole direction of the war from November had shifted the temper of everyone to an optimistic expectation that it would be won, that this might happen quite soon and that the kind of settlement proposed for everyone by Beveridge could indeed be brought about. Optimism pervaded the weeks leading to Christmas, making even the most enervating frustrations of daily life somehow easier to bear. 'Cheered by the persistently brighter news from the battle-fronts, and in spite of the increasing call on the country's man power, people generally are facing the fourth Christmas of the war in good heart,' reported the *Lewisham Borough News*. Despite tighter rations, a 'scarcity of turkeys and poultry' and a dearth of 'seasonable gifts', 'it is doubtful whether stores and shops, particularly in the afternoons, have ever been more crowded'. Mrs W. Brand of Gordon Road, Camberwell, read a *Picture Post* feature on the privations of the Soviet people just after she had brought home her 'Christmas grocery order for my family of four – a pound of sultanas, half of dates, two tins of milk, one of syrup, one of meat, one of fish, also the usual butter, tea, jam, dried eggs, sugar, etc., cigarettes, two pounds of chocolate and one of boiled sweets'; she realised how lucky 'We in Britain, despite the blitz,' really were. Everyone seemed to have ample and to have special reason to be grateful for it. 'This has been the most cheerful Christmas since Hitler's aggressions began,' concluded Anthony Weymouth in Marylebone. 'We are cheerful, we are optimistic.' On Christmas Eve he and his wife had a dozen guests round to share 'a bottle or two', 'a large turkey pie and some lobster patties', though he had no idea where his resourceful wife, busy with her nursing duties, found them. Even the Wells family in Ealing had a goose, though the Christmas pudding lacked 'the necessary fruit, eggs and peel'.[5]

Everywhere, except among the very poorest and those afflicted by loss or sickness, Londoners had reason to be cheerful. There were many opportunities to join in the fun. At Kathleen Tipper's YMCA canteen in Woolwich the celebrations 'were quite like a pre-war party', with 'Christmas cake iced and marzipaned, jellies, trifles, pastries of all kinds, and lovely sandwiches'. And, as always, the talented ranks of civil defenders played their part: the Shoreditch Medical ARP Social and Welfare Club gave a concert for children in a school in New North Road; Holloway's civil defence and fire-watchers gave a party for 800 children at New Court Church Hall, Tollington Park; TS1 Ambulance Station at East Dulwich gave a celebration tea for children and also provided the toys – 'The C.D. men made tanks and tommy-guns for the children; and the women made stuffed toys, dolls and animals of all descriptions.' Besides these treasures, the children took home sweets and slices of cake.[6]

That New Year's Eve, Nellie Carver, living with her elderly mother in West Norwood, not too far away from those happy children, reflected on this end to a climactic year: 'A quiet uneventful end to 1942 – rather different to 1940! So thankful for the turn of events which is much more favourable to us than we dared hope. Weather mild with slight frost this week – so hope we may not have another winter like last. Sat up to welcome 1943 with sober confidence.'[7]

NELLIE'S hopes for the weather would – literally – bear fruit: 1943 would be the warmest year of the war to date by far, the early winter months, spring and summer especially favoured. It was a huge relief given the bitter openings to the previous three years. German air raids too would – in the run of things since September 1940 – be mild, though not as inconsequential as in the previous twenty months or so. RAF attacks on Berlin and other German cities provoked retaliation in a pattern that would become all too clear for Londoners. 'Is it worth it?' wondered Anthony Heap in St Pancras. 'Why the hell can't they leave Berlin alone and let sleeping dogs lie ...' The heaviest raid of 1943 as measured by the numbers of attacking bombers (118) struck London on the night of Sunday 17/18 January: it was the worst since May 1941. Southern and eastern districts of the capital suffered the most damage, though casualties were relatively light. The night was notable for the ferocity of the anti-aircraft barrage. Throughout the year, deaths from AA shells exploding as they hit the ground, and from shrapnel, added significantly to the casualty toll. Deaths would occur even when no bombing took place, AA gunners perhaps with nervous trigger fingers or misled by false sightings. Three people were killed that Sunday night by an AA shell falling near the Admiral Vernon public house in Broad Street, Dagenham. 'London Hears the Sirens Again,' reported an East End paper. 'The almost forgotten sound came as a surprise after such a long period, and it was immediately recognised as a reprisal for the pounding of Berlin.'[8]

Three days later would come the first serious tragedy of the year. Twenty-eight fighter-bombers with a numerous fighter escort attacked London from the south-east around midday on Wednesday 20 January. The raid was fast and low and took the defences completely by surprise. The balloon barrage had been grounded and couldn't be raised in time, and sirens were sounded only after bombing began. The low trajectory of the HE released by the planes caused bombs to ricochet, hitting buildings amidships and collapsing them rather than blowing them apart, causing special problems for the rescue teams. An unlucky strike by a 500-kilogram bomb hit Sandhurst Road LCC Central School, Catford, whose pupils had been entertained by Croydon ARP the previous spring. The school dining hall was crowded as children and staff queued for lunch. Thirty-eight children and six teachers died at the scene or later in Lewisham Hospital, where over seventy more were treated for injuries. Frantic attempts were made by rescue squads and passers-by to free trapped survivors. 'A police officer, digging in the debris, found the body of his 13-year-old son', and an off-duty gunner lost two daughters, discovering one himself: '"Her forehead and cheek were cut badly. Her little arm lay over her face as if she had tried to protect herself. I am glad it was me who found her."' A 'communal funeral' and burial for thirty-three of the victims took place the following week at Hither Green cemetery, with 7,000 mourners in attendance.[9]

The unready defences and the tragic consequences provoked parliamentary questions and ripples of unease, stirred up locally by the Communist Party. One Bermondsey councillor even blamed a 'Fifth Column' for not sounding the siren until it was too late: the school's shelter was said to be untouched and the children could have been got there in minutes. But recrimination soon constructively gave way to helping parents and surviving children recover from their great loss. The Sandhurst Road School tragedy touched the nation, even the world. A Lewisham Bombed School Children's Fund was established by the borough's mayor and within a week or so gifts of money raised countrywide quickly reached £1,000 and grew rapidly. The needs of injured children were a priority. The Queen visited victims in hospital, passing on a gift of bananas from the Princesses that had been sent them by Lord Mountbatten, then in Casablanca. Injured children were given holidays in the Midlands. Clothes and sweets, gifts to London from the people of Southern Rhodesia, were sent by Rhodesia House in the Strand. And in August a memorial plaque was unveiled at the communal grave by the head of the 'Mexican Colony in London'. It was a gift from

The children of the Schools of Mexico
To the children and teachers of the Sandhurst-road School,
Lewisham,
Cruelly sacrificed in an air raid on the 20th January, 1943.[10]

For a time, unsurprisingly, the Catford tragedy made parents reluctant to send children to school, fearful of a repeat from scattered daylight raids in February and again in April. The LCC responded by tightening school attendance enforcement, with 'street raids' to flush out children by checking all addresses on school rolls in chosen districts. Summonses were brought wholesale against parents for their children's non-attendance across London in the early months of the year. Besides truancy, the difficulties in the way of teachers were legion: 'there is a terrible shortage of things like nibs and pencils' and schools were dirty because caretakers had been called up for more essential duties; 'the children are losing interest in school' and all teachers 'can do is to keep order and dispel basic ignorance'. London's slum children, it was said, 'in behaviour resembled the "wild children" who were a by-product of the Russian civil war ... not only dirty, ragged, undernourished and unbelievably obscene in language and corrupt in outlook, but they were all thieves, and as intractable as wild animals': that, according to George Orwell, was the picture in 'Branch Street', Paddington, probably the Clarendon Crescent area, Westbourne Green. An LCC survey of older children's attainment in 1943 concluded for children across London that there had been 'an average retardation of up to a year' compared to a similar survey in 1924. If the comparison had been with 1938 the loss 'would have been more marked'. This blow to the education of London's children would be a stain on the future that even Beveridge couldn't erase.[11]

In the weeks that followed the raids of mid-January Luftwaffe activity faded out once more, with just one further light daylight raid (9 February) and an intended heavy bombardment on 3/4 March that misfired, just twelve tons of HE falling on London out of the hundred intended. Even so, the evening of Wednesday 3 March would see the greatest civilian disaster to befall Britain in the whole of the Second World War.[12]

The news of heavy British bombing raids on Berlin, receiving extensive coverage in the London press, met with mixed feelings in the East End. Satisfaction at the German capital getting its just deserts was tempered by fear of reprisals from the Luftwaffe. Many East Enders took once more to the shelters and the tubes in readiness for a resumption of bombing that since the mid-January raids seemed all too likely. An especially heavy raid on Berlin on 1 March, revealed in jaunty headlines in the London papers next evening, produced jitters in the East End that night, though many took the view that any reprisals were more likely on the following day. So it was that by eight o'clock on the evening of Wednesday 3 March 1943 some 500 to 600 people had already entered the shelter at the unfinished tube station and tunnels at the junction of Roman Road and Cambridge Heath Road, Bethnal Green. Above ground more were making their way there when at 8.17 p.m. the air raid sirens sounded the alert, bringing hundreds of local people from their homes to the shelter; their numbers were swollen as passing buses stopped to let passengers join the crowds at the shelter entrance, formed of a wide funnel leading to a narrower staircase with a right-angled turn near the bottom. Some 1,500 had made their way down the dimly lit staircase when at 8.27 an AA rocket salvo was discharged from a battery a few hundred yards from the tube shelter. This was a new weapon, previously unheard locally. The noise was terrifyingly loud and unexpected and was interpreted by many as the sound of falling bombs. The crowd at the head of the staircase surged forward, propelled by those pushing behind. On the third step from the bottom of the flight of nineteen leading to the booking hall a woman, thought to have been carrying or leading a child, tripped and fell. Within seconds, ten or fifteen at the most, the staircase became 'a charnel house': 173 people, including eighty-four women and sixty-two children, were crushed and suffocated in 'an immovable and interlaced mass of bodies' that it would take rescue workers hours to untangle.[13]

The incident was followed by a strict news blackout as to the where-abouts of the tragedy or the numbers of casualties. In the absence of information rumours flourished. Most prominent among them, dressed as fact, travelling as fast and far as any telegraph so that it was heard and believed 'so far afield as Bristol' by 4 March, was a belief that the accident had been caused by 'a Jewish panic'. As the Ministry of Information reported shortly after, that 'the trouble was occasioned by the Jews is reported from all parts of London, with the exception of Bethnal Green where there is full knowledge that any such statement is untrue'. For the Bethnal Green tube shelter did not serve a Jewish area, had in fact been avoided by Jewish shelterers because the Salmon and Ball public house across the road was a notorious haunt of the British Union of Fascists, and only five of the victims were thought to have been Jewish.[14]

An inquiry into the causes of the disaster was quickly established. It took evidence in private and when it reported to the Home Office the chairman, a senior London stipendiary magistrate, Laurence Rivers Dunne, roundly dismissed any suggestion that the disaster was caused by 'a Jewish panic. This canard had a much wider circulation [than other rumours] and was, I understand, endorsed by the broadcast utter-ances of a renegade traitor from Germany [William Joyce, 'Lord Haw-Haw']. Not only is it without foundation, it is demonstrably false. The Jewish attendance at this shelter was, and is, so small as to consti-tute a hardly calculable percentage.'[15]

A relieved Herbert Morrison duly made a statement to the House of Commons on 8 April 1943, scotching the 'Jewish panic' rumour, while declining to publish the inquiry report, allowing numerous conspiracy theories to continue to flourish.[16]

Once more, the disaster was followed by recriminations. Bethnal Green Borough Council had urged the London Passenger Transport Board since 1941 to erect a better barrier at the entrance to the shelter, but the board said the cost, at £89, would be too high. The police were criticised for not having a constable at the entrance once crowds began to form. Mrs Annie Baker, who lost her husband and daughter in the crush, sued the council for not itself erecting the barrier it knew was necessary and won substantial damages. The council appealed and lost, then contemplated an appeal to the House of Lords but thought better of it and withdrew. The government eventually underwrote the council's liabilities from the claims that inevitably followed. One improvement that might have helped, quick and cheap to install, was a handrail in the middle of the ten-foot wide staircase; temporary handrails were put in place within days of the disaster.[17]

The dreadful accident at Bethnal Green, like the UXB explosion at Gurney Street, caused soul-searching and safety reviews across civil defence and in London's tube shelters. Training of civil defenders had never stopped but now it intensified. The Home Guard conducted invasion exercises across the capital and wardens and others made meticulous preparations should mass bombing begin once more. George Beardmore, a billeting officer in Stanmore, north-west London, attended one 'operating from the Honeypot Lane Rest Centre', Harrow, in March:

> I watched the WVS take charge of the 'rendered homeless' as they appeared, one with pretend-measles, one only in her nightgown and rendered helpless by a fit of the giggles, and another with pneumonia who 'died' in the night. In the morning (Sunday) I reported at 8.30 a.m. and made 27 calls at addresses given to me by the WVS, secured 40 billets, and filled 13 of them with Unaccompanied Children. Pearswood Gardens I found to be Out of Bounds due to an unexploded bomb and that after I had placed three families in it. When I asked a Warden about the disposal of the supposed UXB he replied: 'It's no use asking me, old cock, I've been killed.'[18]

The continuing small number of raids – just the one in March, three in April and five in May, all of them light – raised the question as to whether the civil defence workforce in London, even after the reductions of 1942, was really required by the task in hand. Further cuts were made in July 1943, and everywhere in London was affected. Control centre staff were reduced generally; Shoreditch lost twenty-two full-time wardens and thirty from light rescue and stretcher-bearer squads; Lewisham lost eighty-three wardens, roughly one in four of full-time staff and seventy in light rescue, seven from each team. Volunteer part-timers, many women among them, helped plug the gaps in the wardens' service. As some compensation, welfare arrangements for those who remained improved through 'group activities', including 'P.T.' (physical training), lectures and study classes, sports and games, art and handicrafts, music and drama. Men and women in civil defence also continued to make their own welfare arrangements, the NFS at station C.27 in the East India Docks 'adopting' Joan Marriott, 'a little girl whose fireman father was killed in the Blitz, and whose mother died shortly afterwards of a broken heart'; they raised £70 to pay her an allowance. Next-door West Ham, however, continued to struggle. Its new ARP controller, Reverend Paton, a former councillor, was sacked in April amid much municipal acrimony.[19]

West Ham's performance in other areas was far more encouraging. The year's big savings drive that March was 'Wings for Victory', with London set to raise a total of £150 million. The object was an attractive one to Londoners, who had suffered much from the Luftwaffe, and to start savers' money flowing a Stirling bomber was set up on the giant bomb site around St Paul's and a Lancaster was put on display at Trafalgar Square. Hilda Neal in South Kensington withdrew £300 from her post office account and bought War Savings Certificates; they would be worth £410 in 1953, she was told, though sadly for Hilda that would be substantially below the post-war inflation rate, with £300 in 1943 equivalent to £490 ten years later. Bermondsey, its savings slogan 'A bomb for a bomb', pledged to purchase twenty Flying Fortresses for the USAAF. Most London boroughs overachieved their targets, including Bermondsey, though the money contributed to only three planes, one named 'Rotherhithe Revenge'; West Ham clocked up savings of over £819,000 against a target of £750,000.[20]

Savings were mirrored by a salvage drive in the spring and early summer. This year the campaign focused on books, recycled to help meet the nation's paper shortage, stocks driven drastically down by import difficulties. London was set a target of salvaging five million books and again most boroughs met their objectives. Hackney set itself 350,000 volumes and recovered 362,000; of these 3,000 were earmarked for the forces, with just 2,200 for the borough's blitzed libraries. The rest were pulped. Collections were enthusiastically driven by school 'book commandos', hundreds of children drafted in to collect door to door with handcarts and barrows; twenty books brought to school made a sergeant, 250 a field marshal. 'Only the urgency of war,' lamented Watcher, the perspicacious columnist of the *South London Press*, 'could make us do the present foolish things. Only the national paper-shortage could inspire men to glamourise the destruction of books.'[21]

A different sort of book was exercising many Londoners in these same months. The new food ration books were issued by councils in June and millions had to be collected by householders. Whatever system was adopted (asking people to turn up on days specified for surnames in alphabetical order was a favourite), long queues taking ages to move forward were the order of every day. At the Chelsea food office a friend of Klara Modern, Annie Ellerman, who wrote novels under the pseudonym Bryher, joined the queue early one morning:

> We lined up along a street just off the King's Road in front of the Food Office and those of us who were lucky enough to get a place towards the entrance faced a large sign that said *Prams*. There we stuck, a lump of ammonites halfway up a cliff but holding in the process ... There was a rattle of bolts. The doors slowly opened. We moved into a dignified scrum to push into a parlor and face a large poster begging us to 'Dig for Victory' ... A clerk chewed the top of her Utility pencil, looked at her face carefully in a pocket mirror, replaced the glass in her handbag and put this into a drawer. Then, and only then, she deigned to glance at us. 'First, please,' she snapped.
>
> By the time I got out, clasping the two books for Hilda and myself, the queue stretched far down the King's Road.[22]

The ration and the huge bureaucracy underpinning it could do little to eliminate the unpredictable shortages and inexplicable gluts that continued to plague Londoners' lives. Hilda Neal saw a mass of fish roe 'heaped up on ice on the slab', supposedly brought in by Spanish trawlers who had put in to Penzance in bad weather and had to unload their catch there, but then 'No tomatoes or fruit to be seen in the shops, though I see them coming into [Covent Garden] Market.' English canned fruit was suddenly taken off points in May, perhaps because of defects in the canning: 'I called in at various shops,' recorded Vere Hodgson in North Kensington, 'and collected four tins. Ten minutes later there was nothing!' 'Liquor is not officially rationed, but it often seems as if it might as well be,' complained Mollie Panter-Downes; some shops could only dole out a bottle of gin every four months or so, and that reserved for regular customers.[23]

Few could make good the liquor shortage but the allotment remained the backbone of many Londoners' food supplies. Nationally, personal expenditure on food in 1943 was down by almost a sixth on 1938, but a lot of that shortfall was made good by vegetables (and some meat and eggs) grown at home. The vigorous communal activity of growers and breeders was apparent across London, attaining probably its peak level of productivity this year. The Victoria Park and District Allotment Association had trebled its membership since 1941 and was holding an allotment competition in June, a summer show of vegetables in July and an autumn show in September; that month, the Poplar Borough Allotment Society was showcasing 'Parsnips a Yard Long'. The Queen visited Bethnal Green's bomb-site vegetable gardens in June, all begun by local children. Islington Poultry Club was founded in the run-down Caledonian Road area in March and could mount its first egg show in May. Shoreditch Borough Allotment Association was only formed in 1943 but had a hundred members by July; seed was sent to them from the USA and two American ladies were shown over the plots, one the celebrated anthropologist Margaret Mead, no doubt intrigued by this very different sort of islander from those she had previously studied.[24]

The NFS pig clubs, swelling since the 'Bore War', continued to thrive, bringing new life to bomb sites in Lincoln's Inn Fields in Holborn, in Clerkenwell and even 'off Oxford Street'. 'Already,' thought *Picture Post*, 'there's more livestock in the heart of London than there has been for about three hundred years.' Pig club members were entitled to share half the meat produced, the rest going to the government: Bethnal Green and Victoria Park Pig Club, set up in April 1942, had sent 1,274 pounds to the Ministry of Food by early 1943. Bethnal Green's Rabbit and Cavy Club continued to breed with its customary vitality. Indeed, Bethnal Green, astonishingly, even had a Young Farmers' Club. All this communal self-help, distinctively locally based, mushroomed London-wide. And those allotment holders who were not particularly joiners in collective enterprise still gathered in the fruits of their labours. Dorothy Wells and her mother (Ken still largely AWOL) could boast 'spinach, broad beans, dwarf and runner beans, peas, potatoes, beetroot, lettuce, radishes, ridge cucumbers, marrow, rhubarb, carrots, brussel sprouts, shallots, parsnips, onions and heaps of cabbages'.[25]

When Dorothy ate out – she lunched frequently near her Aldwych office – she was often disappointed. 'Lunched at Stoll – very poor grub for 1/9d'; 'Lunched at A.B.C. Cafeteria just opposite Aldwych – roast pork, lots of it but uneatable', perhaps from those Lincoln's Inn bomb sites nearby. Hers was a common experience. Few things marked the levelling of classes in London so much as the dreadful restaurant fare available even to those with well-lined pockets. 'Luncheon cost 17/- for two, without drinks,' complained James Lees-Milne of the Berkeley Hotel, Piccadilly. 'It consisted of indifferent soup made of God knows what, minced chicken hash and no pudding. Really scandalous.' At the Athenaeum Club in Waterloo Place, Anthony Weymouth was treated to 'a very "austerity" meal – soup, a tiny omlette [sic], and buttered egg with half a tomato. Wine of course has now disappeared from clubs and restaurants ...'[26]

It all put the Londoners' Meal Service, now absorbed into the nation-wide brand of British Restaurants, into perspective. They were providing over 600,000 meals a day in 2,000 establishments by 1943. Some 281 were in the LCC area, forty-six of them run by voluntary organisations, the rest run by the council. Each one fed an average of around 300 'diners' a day, more than half of them men, and just about divided half and half between working and middle class. Most were happy with what they received. Dorothy Wells lunched with work colleagues at the British Restaurant in a former school in Shelton Street, Seven Dials, in a seedy part of the West End: 'A jolly good lunch, well served, for 1/3.' Even hard-to-please Anthony Heap was impressed by a self-service British Restaurant in the Euston Road, perhaps also benefiting from the pig-club craze: 'I had roast pork and two vegetables for 10d and Christmas pudding and custard for 3d. And even if the portion of pork was infinitesimal and the pudding hardly a "blow out," it was still quite good value.' He approved of the buffet arrangement too: 'Nor does it involve the accursed tipping system.'[27]

IN this universal nexus of irksome restriction, most people played the game. But not everyone. Defaulters and sidesteppers were brought in large numbers before the courts by the police or borough councils or the Ministry of Labour. The first cases at North London Police Court of women fire-watchers failing to turn up for duty were brought by Islington Council and fined in January 1943. Fire-watchers were punished for taking to air raid shelters during raids and for stealing from the premises they guarded. Two young Leyton sisters were prosecuted for refusing to accept war work in Coventry, more than a hundred miles away; they wanted to work locally but there were no vacancies. They now promised the court they would go where directed and the charges were held in abeyance. The odd case of civil defence cheats of one kind or another still came to light, among them a Brixton senior air raid warden given eighteen months in prison for stealing a radiogram from a bomb-damaged house. Thefts of light bulbs from public air raid shelters continued wholesale, Camberwell council losing 6,000 a year. There were numerous cases of selling clothes without coupons, generally stolen or black-market gear or some made from 'cabbage' (excess cloth) liberated by cutters and tailors from their workshops. There were instances too of petty trickery and theft that left an unpleasant taste. When a scared young East Ham woman carrying her baby ran out of her house during the January raid, she was told by two men in the street to take cover. They watched her go to a neighbour's house and broke into her home; luckily, they were held by the fire guard as they came out. Set beside the general compliance, accepting or grudging as it might have been, and the readiness of so many to volunteer for extra duties even when not conscripted, such instances were relatively trivial. Even so, people did have to watch their backs. '"Whatever you do, dear",' Bryher was told by a 'pleasant girl porter' at Paddington Station that autumn, '"don't leave your bag for an instant."' She also noticed many people taking their rabbits on holiday with them – not, presumably, for the change of scenery.[28]

Among all these petty depredations, the London underworld continued to prosper, its ranks swollen by an unstoppable trickle of forces deserters. Frankie Fraser, from north Lambeth, just twenty in 1943, had been a thief for as long as he could remember. Released from youth detention in January, he was promptly called up for the army but didn't report for duty, going 'under the radar' with others like him in Notting Hill:

The War organized criminals. Before the war thieving was safes, jewellery, furs. Now a whole new world was opened up. There was so much money and stuff about – cigarettes, sugar, clothes, petrol coupons, clothing coupons, anything. It was a thieves' paradise. I was a thief, everyone was a thief. People who I'd known before the War at the races who were villains but who weren't thieves – now they were. They'd been called up and didn't fancy the Army so they were on the run. They couldn't make money at the races because that was the first place people would look for them, and so they'd turned to thieving. And some of them turned out to be very good thieves and all. So it was a whole new world.[29]

There were many absconders like Fraser, all badly needing papers (identity cards, ration books, army exemption certificates), forged, stolen or traded. Ruby Sparks, another south London thief of an older generation, made a name for himself as the most notorious prison-breaker of his generation; rearrested in May 1943 he was given another term, this time for receiving a stolen identity card and Army Services book. The big money, though, was still to be made from under-the-counter clothing, especially coupons. Five million were stolen from an army depot at Earlsfield in Wandsworth, south-west London, in September 1943. Three men laid a railway sleeper over the barbed-wire fence and calmly walked in. The ringleader was Lieutenant Ernest George Savage of the Royal Army Service Corps, imprisoned for five years; another was a deserter from the Royal Marines who had bought his 'discharge papers', real or fake, for £10.[30]

MOST Londoners were barely touched by this dark side of the capital's war, and in the summer and autumn of 1943 there was much to feel hopeful about. The war news was consistently good. 'Wonderful news of 8th Army,' recorded an overoptimistic Nellie Carver in May. 'Tunis and Bizerta captured – lots of excitement – should not be long now.' This news was followed by the Allied invasion of Sicily and its rapid evacuation by Axis forces in July and August. 'What a lot of geography we're learning in following the course of the war,' was Anthony Heap's wry comment, but he became more excited when Italy surrendered in early September: 'even I feel quite bucked about it'. The Luftwaffe's desultory summer offensive against London (five raids in the second half of May, eight in June, two more in July but none in August) was generally light with localised impact. It involved one great spectacle, the gutting by fire of Mount Pleasant central parcel sorting office by a single incendiary or HE on the evening of 18 June, the largest blaze in the capital since May 1941.[31]

Summer holidays at home were again the order of the day, although this year travel restrictions were less onerous than previously and the prospect of less crowded railway journeys tempted many away: Nellie Carver and her mother had a fortnight in Ilfracombe, 'the first we've spent for years'; Anthony and Marjorie Heap went to the in-laws in Somerset; and Dorothy Wells had a week at a Methodist holiday home in Bangor in September. Nor were just the better-off favoured. 'Double wages' in the hop fields of Kent and Sussex attracted some 100,000 pickers from the East End and south London, travelling as usual with families and belongings in special trains from London Bridge and New Cross stations in early August.[32]

In general, though, people stayed home in this, the best summer since 1940. Those Londoners who remained in the capital were never more rooted to their local neighbourhoods than in these years of total war. Collectivism was woven into the fabric of every neighbourhood, despite the destruction: the street fire-watchers and savings groups, the neighbourhood wardens, the district fire and rescue teams, all neighbours who now knew one another's names and family circumstances as never before. Now too amusements were locally based and quite often provided by local people. Victoria Park was east London's great centre of communal fun, hosting a London Civil Defence Region Group 3 sports meeting where teams from eight central London boroughs competed against each other, but where also band concerts and dancing, Sanger's circus (for the first time), Sadler's Wells ballet, opera, concert parties and a pep talk from J. B. Priestley filled the bill. Islington's Highbury Fields showcased variety (*Islington Takes the Air*), with bands and more dancing, and open-air theatre, including a play by Arthur Wing Pinero, who had been a local man. Many of the dance bands too were local, like south London's Fred Hedley's Dance Band, though others were definitely not – the USA Army Band was a popular feature in Horniman Gardens, Forest Hill.[33]

For home birds, the radio remained indispensable and, ironically in this year of mass book-drowning, reading took off. These were frustrating times for the book buyer: 'new books go out of print often before you know they exist,' lamented Anthony Weymouth. They were equally frustrating for the humble library subscriber. Anthony Heap, a keen reader, bought on New Year's Day a premium subscription at

Boots Lending Library (£2 5s against the normal 19s 6d a year, so more than twice as much) to get new books '"On Demand"': 'I'm tired of having to wait several months, sometimes a year or more, for desired books and, as often as not, being unable to get anything on my list at all.' It proved a waste of money. At the end of the year the 'On Demand' service was suspended for the duration, but it was no loss: 'I've had almost as much difficulty in getting the books I want' as before. Every book collection was under stress. The luxuriously stocked Reform Club had to write to members complaining of 'the serious loss of books from the Library'. No doubt London's public libraries were similarly vulnerable but these were flourishing, despite the depletion of Londoners. Remarkably, Finsbury public libraries loaned nearly 246,000 books in 1942–3, a thousand more than the previous peak year of 1937–8; yet Finsbury's population had shrunk by 30,000 or 52 per cent. Similar results were reported elsewhere. Two authors were apparently in special demand. One was Anthony Trollope – 'can't get "The Last Chronicles of Barset",' reported Hilda Neal, in search of a copy for a friend; her bookseller reported 'hundreds of customers' waiting for a new Trollope edition reportedly in the press. A few days later she tracked down an expensive edition in Cecil Court, having to pay 22s 6d for it. Indeed, Victoriana was greatly in vogue at this time, not just among readers but in the cinema and on the stage. The other in-demand author was a near contemporary of Trollope but from further afield: 'a tremendous Tolstoy boom here,' reported Mollie Panter-Downes in January, with a radio serialisation of War and Peace and a 30,000-copy reprint selling out in less than a month.[34]

Indeed, everything Russian remained in vogue. Local Aid to Russia weeks were organised by one or other London borough throughout the year. Poplar, for instance, sent out 350 collecting boxes to schools and pubs, civil defenders and NFS firefighters made collections door to door, and there were fund-raising dances, auctions of donated treasures and factory contributions collected from the workforce. There were some celebrity events, like the twenty-fifth anniversary of the Red Army, staged at the Albert Hall in February. Most remarkable of all was the Stalingrad Sword made in honour of the 'steel-hearted citizens of Stalingrad' who had successfully resisted the encircling German forces for six months. Something similar had been done for the senior Red Army officer Marshal Timoshenko, who had been presented with a fine saddle paid for by public subscription in July 1942, but the sword was altogether more spectacular. Four feet long, made to a design chosen by the King, the handle was solid silver with gold twine and a pommel of rock crystal. It was on public display at Goldsmiths' Hall, at the Victoria and Albert Museum and at Westminster Abbey; thousands queued to see it in October. And it was not just the courage of the Russian people and the success of their fighting forces that were celebrated by Londoners this year. Russian triumphs seemed to be living proof of the effectiveness of a planned economy and of planning more generally. When the Association of Scientific Workers held a conference at Caxton Hall, Westminster, in February to press for a 'Central Planning Body to Coordinate Scientific Work', a message in support from the Soviet Academy of Science 'won more applause than any of the speakers'.[35]

CERTAINLY, planning of every kind was under the spotlight in 1943. The Beveridge Plan for social and health security for all had monopolised public discourse at the start of the year. For its supporters there had been disappointment in February when the government clumsily shelved further consideration of Beveridge's recommendations, provoking a major (if temporary) rebellion in the Parliamentary Labour Party. But in the summer a different kind of plan provided a new talking point for Londoners.

For some years before the war, the mounting dislike among opinion formers of London's growth in population and economic power, seen by many as being at the expense of the nation as a whole, had frequently resulted in calls for a plan for London that would cut it down to size. That had long been the case among garden city enthusiasts and town planners and those politicians and policymakers who had been fellow travellers of the planning movement for more than twenty years. These included not only the then Prime Minister, Neville Chamberlain, the most vigorous champion of a London plan, but a broad spectrum of centre and centre-left opinion. Significant members of the Labour Party's ruling group on the LCC were vocal among those calling for satellite towns and garden cities to relieve pressure on London's growth. Herbert Morrison had been the prime mover behind the Green Belt or Green Girdle strategy, intended to lock London into the boundaries of its present built-up area, the LCC and other local authorities from 1935 funding acquisitions of undeveloped countryside to withhold it from the speculative builder; purchases of Green Belt land continued even into the first weeks of the blitz. But by the end of the 1930s, the urgent need not just to restrain but to diminish London became the fashionable opinion among novelists and poets and journalists and academics and armchair military strategists and politicians of every complexion. As war appeared to inch ever closer, opinion became increasingly strident. During 1937 and the opening months of 1938 it seemed as though almost every public figure was lining up to say that something must be done to move people and jobs out of London: Sir William Beveridge, Clement Attlee, David Lloyd George, Hugh Dalton and numerous planning and architectural experts throughout the land. By the end of 1938, stopping the growth of London became official Labour Party policy as part of its ARP manifesto issued that December.[36]

By that time Chamberlain had announced the terms of reference of a Royal Commission on the Distribution of the Industrial Population under the chairmanship of Sir Montague Barlow, a barrister and former Conservative MP. Among the commissioners was Patrick Abercrombie, the most celebrated architect-planner of the age. The commission's deliberations concluded before the outbreak of war but the publication of the Barlow Report, recommending that the 'continued drift of the industrial population to London and the Home Counties' receive 'immediate attention', was delayed until January 1940. By then, winning the war was the only government priority demanding 'immediate' anything. There things stuck.[37]

But the need for a plan for London was an idea that had taken root. The destruction caused by bombing, and the questions raised over how London was to be rebuilt, put it unavoidably on the agenda. From the autumn of 1940 there were calls from the professional press, from London government and from local newspapers, all urging that it was time to capitalise on the Luftwaffe's 'ill wind blowing us some good'. After the Big Blitz many councils set up reconstruction committees to consider questions of planning, open space, roads and – most important of all – housing, once the war was over: West Ham's Post-War Reconstruction Committee was set up in September 1941, for instance. During 1941 and 1942 a number of competing plans saw the light of day. Some were dreamed up by local enthusiasts, like John Battley, a printer and Labour Party activist, who produced a plan for Clapham in April 1942. Most were devised by professional organisations like the Royal Society of Arts (March 1941), the Royal Institute of British Architects (May 1941), the Modern Architectural Research Group (June

1942), and the Royal Academy (October 1942), whose proposal for an airport at the Elephant and Castle upset the locals.[38]

But what everyone awaited was the official plan for inner London devised for consideration by the LCC. The LCC had recognised the need for a reconstruction document within a month or so of the main London blitz beginning, but the key event was a meeting in January 1941 at the Ministry of Health with officials from several ministries and chief officers of the LCC and the City Corporation, where it was agreed that plans for both the County and the City would now be prepared. It is likely that Abercrombie's name was suggested or discussed at that time, and it was Patrick Abercrombie whom the LCC instructed as their planning consultant to help prepare a plan for the post-war reconstruction of the County of London, excluding the City, in April 1941. The *County of London Plan*, under the joint authorship of J. H. Forshaw, architect to the LCC, and Patrick Abercrombie, was published in July 1943.[39]

London had never been comprehensively planned, had indeed grown in defiance of constraints and notional views of order. What planning there had been had taken place estate by estate, as opportunity favoured. Generations of Londoners had adapted and moulded the results to suit their needs, largely untroubled by those with tidy minds who wished for 'improvements'; when implemented, which was not often, these too had been piecemeal, even bitty. Now Londoners were offered the first attempt ever to impose a rational order of sorts on almost the whole of inner London north and south of the river.

The County of London Plan (CLP) was an impressive document, imaginatively – in its way, beautifully – presented. The plan rejected the unregulated rebuilding of post-war London at one extreme, or its breaking up with its population scattered over the south-east at the other, for a pragmatic modernisation working with what was already on the ground, while deploring its 'lack of coherent architectural development'. This lack would be made as good as was possible by stamping order and tidiness on post-war London. 'Communities' of 6,000–10,000 persons would be designated around local elementary schools, so that no child should have to cross a main road to get there, and organised around 'nodal points' of prominent buildings. London's historic functional areas would be defined in 'major use zones' – theatres in the West End, government offices around Whitehall and the Houses of Parliament, commercial and industrial areas around the City and port.

Zonal planning would define a neighbourhood's function and discourage offending uses from locating there, gradually separating out industrial and residential areas. The 'maldistribution' of open space in London called for more parks, with houses and businesses removed to provide them on a ratio of four acres to every thousand people, including parkland along stretches of the river in central London. Roads were to be radically recast and enlarged 'in the form of a ring-radial-cross system', with three ring roads: an 'A' road around Westminster, the City, north Lambeth and Southwark; a 'B' road cutting through the Victorian suburbs, running north of Regent's Park, across the river at Battersea and the Blackwall Tunnel and as far south as Clapham Common North Side; and a 'C' road completing the north and south circular roads, much of it outside the County boundary, so beyond the plan's statutory area. Housing would be subject to 'comprehensive redevelopment', especially areas of nineteenth-century housing, with the East End receiving priority attention; rebuilding would be at notional 'densities' of 100 or 136 persons per acre, depending on proximity to the centre, with 200 at the centre itself. The plan's preference almost everywhere was for 100 persons per acre to accommodate as much open space as possible. There were numerous other points of detail. But the main aim of the plan was 'decentralisation': the post-war County of London should accommodate between 500,000 and 600,000 fewer people than in 1939; a similar number of jobs should also be relocated from the County, to elsewhere in London or beyond.[40]

This plan to remove people and industry from London had long been a dream of Abercrombie, who had refused to sign the Barlow Report because it had not gone far enough in that direction. Now he had made a first step in making his dream real. He would take a second step within the next eighteen months. The Minister of Town and Country Planning had appointed him the consultant to prepare a Greater London Plan (GLP). It was published in December 1944. The GLP would again make decentralisation a top priority. In response to criticism from the Town and Country Planning Association that Abercrombie had not been brave enough in the CLP (they argued that the County needed to shed 1.5 million people), with similar concerns from the new Ministry of Town and Country Planning, he now enlarged the numbers to be removed from the County to 618,000 and rolled up the emigration target to a planned decentralisation of 1,033,000 from Greater London. Only 125,000 of these displaced persons would relocate in Greater

London, with the rest in the plan's 'outer country ring', in satellite towns outside the Green Belt, or outside the plan area entirely. A further component of voluntary emigration would bring the total to be moved out of London's built-up area to some 1.25 million. The press was in no doubt that the 'main aim' of the plan was to stop London growing and remove a large slice of its population. It all added up to what the *Daily Herald* called the 'biggest mass-migration in our history', the brainchild of 'Professor Patrick Abercrombie, the monocled leader of planning'. Again, industry would be decentralised too, to ensure that London's population did not rise again as people continued to come there to work.[41]

FEW voices were raised against the dispersal policy of the plans, at least in principle. The City Corporation's first 'preliminary draft' reconstruction plan was one of them, arguing for retention of at least some of the City's old neighbourhood and street patterns and arguing, utterly against the spirit of these post-Barlow times, that office, warehousing and factory space should be rebuilt to provide for a possible 800,000 jobs in the Square Mile, substantially more than the half a million jobs accommodated there before the war; the plan was swiftly abandoned, in some embarrassment, for a more Abercrombian approach. There was a little more dissent, though, in the metropolitan boroughs. Many councils wished to reduce the impact of Abercrombie's density rules on population loss and argued that they should retain more people and jobs than the plans prescribed, at the expense of open space if necessary. The plan for Stepney, for instance, envisaged a post-war population of 94,000, but Stepney Borough Council wished to build for 130,000; both Fulham and Chelsea argued for a density of 136 persons per acre rather than the 100 proposed; others worried about jobs declining faster than people and so on. There was even caution in the LCC: Lord Latham, the council's Labour chairman, objected to the Town and Country Planning Association's draconian proposal to remove 1.5 million from the County as advocating 'the dismemberment of London'.[42]

It was an irony of the times that, among all this talk of London losing people through planning, the capital itself seemed to be filling up again. The resident civilian population increased by some 62,000 between December 1942 and December 1943 to over 6.69 million. Now too there were many more servicemen and women in London, Americans especially notable among them. All these people had to squeeze into a smaller portion of usable space. War damage had left some areas pretty much deserted even two years after the blitz, and not just in the East End. When Verily Anderson moved to St John's Wood, Marylebone, sometime this year, she found that 'Only one other house in the road was inhabited. Behind us a long crescent of over a hundred huge empty villas was slowly disintegrating, with the aid of the weather and former bombing.' The population rise put ever more pressure on the housing that was left. Estate agents found the London housing market in 1943 for furnished and unfurnished lets, and freehold and leasehold sales, brighter than at any time since the declaration of war. 'London is packed with people,' thought Hilda Neal in February; 'everywhere full, they say; no flat or hotel accommodation to be secured.' A city full of flat-hunters brought a concomitant rise in the prices of second-hand furniture, with a scarcity in particular of 'Good beds', carpets and rugs. The shortage created its own black market: the manager of Islington Council's store for preserving furniture collected from bombed premises was given four months' imprisonment in September 1943 for helping himself to the stock.[43]

All these pressures seem to have helped stoke the interest with which people approached the question of what London would be like to live in after the war. A huge amount of attention was paid in London's localities to the County of London Plan. The detail was pored over by borough reconstruction committees and set out for readers of the local press, where correspondence columns were alive with comment. 'Public Town's Meetings' were held in Poplar and no doubt elsewhere to widen discussion among ordinary folk. Local exhibitions were held in borough libraries and a monster display for inner London was staged at the LCC's County Hall in July and August, moving to the Royal Academy in November 1943; in all, some 77,000 went to see it – visitors to County Hall included the King and Queen. The first edition of the *County of London Plan*, selling at 12s 6d, quickly sold out its 7,000 copies and a further 8,000 were printed later in the year; in 1945 a popular edition of the plan was produced for the LCC by Penguin, with an introduction by the modernist architect Ernö Goldfinger. The most vehement local discussions of all concerned the housing question and that revolved mainly around the relative merits of flats versus houses. The latter won everywhere in the popularity stakes. Flats, despite nearly half a century of LCC and borough council flatted estates, had never quite shaken off the taint of Victorian semi-charitable 'barrack' buildings of the Peabody variety in the minds of working-class Londoners. Almost everyone craved a house with a garden. Poplar Council, for instance, wanted the post-war borough to have one third flats against two thirds houses; if the matter had been put to a local vote the proportion of houses would have been far higher.[44]

The prospects for life in London after the war stimulated conversations well beyond the council chamber. In the services, the Army Bureau of Current Affairs (ABCA) promoted discussion groups among fighting men, with Beveridge a frequent though controversial item for debate; an ABCA pamphlet on Beveridge had to be hurriedly withdrawn in January 1943 when it was considered too radical in aligning Britain's fighting aims with acceptance of the report. ABCA was a movement begun from above, but in the NFS, 'Discussion Groups were … a movement which grew up amongst the men [and women] themselves.' There were over a hundred in London in 1943, each with a group leader to organise meeting places and help select the topics. A similar urge was at work in civil defence more generally. In March the Finsbury Park Fireguard formed a 'local parliament' or Finsbury Park Forum among the watchers in a district that crossed the borders of Islington, Hackney and Hornsey. In Lewisham, and no doubt elsewhere, the 'wardens of "C" District have recently been holding discussion groups' to help build 'a sense of civic duty in preparation for the days of peace'. A 'brains trust' among anti-aircraft personnel, men and women, debated London's housing problems at the Housing Centre in June; feeding into the debate were the views of AA batteries across London, where housing had been discussed for some weeks, informed by talks from 'experts'. Indeed, 'The Brains Trust, like the crossword puzzle, seems to have come to stay,' it was said in October, this format of question and debate pinched from the popular radio programme; it cropped up everywhere in London to debate an inexhaustible range of topics from home and abroad, mostly about the future. The London Women's Parliament continued to campaign, this year against industrial slacking, for trade union membership and war nurseries, for improved health at work and home, and for better housing: 'Down with the Speculator!' And 'Youth Parliaments' were established across London to discuss the topics of the day: 'We, the youth of Islington, while welcoming the Beveridge Report as a beginning,' one reported in April, 'believe that great changes must be made to equalise the distribution of the means of life.'[45]

This epidemic of brains trusts, discussion groups and youth and other 'parliaments' fostered the kind of radical consensus that Bill Regan would have supported in Poplar. While Rotary Clubs and some other middle-class gatherings might have treated Beveridge with circumspection (though rarely outright opposition), the general tone everywhere was radical: *for* town planning and better living conditions, and *for* Beveridge along the lines of Barbara Wootton's Social Security League at 51 Tothill Street, Westminster, founded 'to prevent the Beveridge Plan from becoming one of those noble, lost causes whose ghosts haunt the vaults of British history'. Almost everyone seemed to be swept up in this desire for a better and fairer world. Sister Gwyneth Thomas at Lewisham Hospital, worried about her brother fighting in the 8th Army, wondered

> where all this fighting and loss of life will bring us this time, back to the old England[?] I, like many other ordinary people, hope not; not the England where only the rich lived, while the rest of us just existed, but let us hope that ordinary man will have the courage to stamp out all that we knew of England before this war.
>
> We see relics of it even now. A lad of 18 years is sick with T.B.; strong and healthy before he did 'his bit' in this war. He has only a mild attack and he will be sent to a ward where each patient has virulent T.B. – he is poor. Now if he had an officer for a brother, instead of a porter, he would have every chance of a side ward, and would be in a sanatorium in no time, but he has no position in this life, so no one who could do anything for him does. This class distinction must be wiped out.[46]

A burning question for London's many brains trusts from November 1943 was whether Sir Oswald and Lady Mosley should have been released from detention under Defence Regulation 18B. Herbert Morrison had sanctioned the Mosleys' release on health grounds. It provoked a storm of protest across London, especially in the East End. There was a violent clash outside Parliament between protesters, including many communists, and police. But prison releases of a different kind bucked up Londoners no end that same month. Prisoners of war (POWs) repatriated in an exchange with Germany were welcomed home across London. Local fund-raising for prisoners' parcels through the Red Cross Penny-a-Week Fund had been a feature of borough activity since Dunkirk and now came the chance to applaud some of the men's homecoming two or three years on. Streets in east London were decked with bunting, parties were given and mayoral receptions held in town halls. Many men had hard stories to tell. Rifleman Frank Crisp, from Stratford, was taken prisoner at Calais in 1940: 'He was interned in Germany, and worked in iron mines and saw mills,' where he lost some of his fingers in an accident.[47]

Despite the prisoner exchange, Londoners were given cause to know that their war wasn't over yet. This autumn saw a resumption of bombing on a more persistent scale than anything seen since May 1941. There were eleven raids in October and seven in November, though just two in December, the last of the year on the 21st. Most bombing was light, with south and east London particularly under attack. These short raids were known as 'Tip and Run' or 'Bomb and Run' and AA shells at times seemed almost to inflict as much damage as the bombs themselves. The worst incident of the autumn, however, resulted from a brief raid between 8.37 and 9.23 p.m. on Sunday 7 November. A 500-kilogram bomb hit the crowded Cinderella Dancing Club at 343 Putney High Street. The Club was over a Rego clothing factory but there was also a milk bar on the ground floor, packed with people. 'The building collapsed from the upper floors and the floors pancaked on top of each other burying many casualties.' Some seventy-seven died and 128 were injured. Rescuers included servicemen, passers-by, RAF men and women from a nearby balloon site and the Home Guard, 'But the heroines of the scene were the women wardens and ambulance workers. With quiet efficiency they worked for hours at their task. *Many were slim girls who worked in the heart of the damage, ignoring the danger of walls collapsing on them.*'[48]

Tube shelter numbers, which had risen through March and April to peak in May at just under 30,000 a night but then rapidly tailed off as the threat of retaliatory raids faded, rose again and plateaued at around 19,000 through September to November. Some of this anxiety was no doubt also promoted by the heavy RAF raids on Germany that Londoners could see building overhead as the planes made their way to the Continent every night. Most welcomed the sight, perhaps reflecting how they had helped pay for some at least of those same 'Wings for Victory'. 'Night after night,' recorded a wary Anthony Heap early in September, 'huge forces of bombers bound for Germany and North Italy incessantly soar their way over London for an hour or two after sunset. Strangely enough most people seem to get quite thrilled by the sight and sound ... Some even stand out in the street cheering.'[49]

That autumn too rumours spread of a German secret weapon soon to be used against London. The government had been increasingly apprised of the threat through intelligence reports from Europe from April on, and by July fresh evacuation plans for London were being worked up in the Home Office. From November, rumours were widespread and public, though most people were sceptical. 'The Germans say that they are preparing a new secret weapon to use against this country,' a Gallup survey stated that month. 'Do you think they are bluffing or telling the truth?' Only 21 per cent thought they were telling the truth, while 59 per cent thought they were bluffing; but 20 per cent confessed they didn't know one way or the other. A few weeks later, on Christmas Day, in raids kept secret from the public, the RAF would bomb launch sites nearing completion for pilotless planes in northern France. Every runway was pointed at London.[50]

It is doubtful whether rumours of secret weapons disturbed the plans of many Londoners that fifth Christmas of the war. They were far more likely to be worried by a flu epidemic, the worst for six years. It laid up the King at Buckingham Palace for a time and caused many deaths, mainly among the elderly. Recovered victims were left 'with a vicious cough, so at the moment every movie theater, restaurant, and public vehicle is in a continuous and explosive uproar,' reported Mollie Panter-Downes. Florence Wells in Ealing, born the month before Garibaldi's visit to London in early 1864, was ill enough to worry Dorothy and Ken from 10 December almost to Christmas Day. Dorothy had to do her mother's daily chores – 'I have got the fire and the breakfast each early morning this week, and managed quite well.' Florence was up and about, though, by the big day itself to receive Ken's thoughtful presents: a scarf, a soap dish, 'and a hoe like a three-pronged fork' to encourage his seventy-nine-year-old mother's efforts on that valuable allotment. 'Mrs. Benson sent us up a lovely duck from her little farm – Mother collected it at Hanwell Station on Wednesday – and it was really plump and good. There were also 6 big red and yellow apples. Our Christmas Pudding (just prunes, sultanas and margarine) was a success too.' It was some duck. 'Duck and Plum Pudding' provided dinner on Boxing Day and the day after too. Anthony and Marjorie Heap also had help from the country, with 'a plump chicken', half a dozen 'new laid eggs, some homemade butter and a few pieces of holly'. Without a country benefactor, Londoners struggled to celebrate in the old-fashioned way. Vere Hodgson thought, 'We are pretty well on our beam ends as far as Christmas Fare is concerned, though we all have enough to eat ... No chance of turkey, chicken or goose – not even the despised rabbit. If we can get a little mutton that is the best we can hope for.' Hilda Neal put in a shift at the canteen in St Martin-in-the-Fields crypt on Christmas Day: 'Had lunch of stew! And very grateful for it.'[51]

Outside the home things were a little more expansive. The West End had thirty-one theatres playing at full pelt, plus a revue each at the Whitehall and Windmill. There was a fuller programme of concerts than at any time since war was declared. And across London the cinema continued to attract large audiences, this year's highlights being *For Whom the Bell Tolls* (with Gary Cooper and Ingrid Bergman), *Girl Crazy* (starring Judy Garland), Samuel Goldwyn's *North Star* and more. Nor did Londoners have to travel very far for the pictures. Lewisham's numerous village centres, for instance, each had one or more cinemas, so there were at least ten of them running full programmes offering West End fare.[52]

In general, though, New Year's celebrations were muted, indoors and out. Nellie Carver, on duty that night at the telegraph office, with time to write up her diary for the past few days, found some reason to be 'cheerful & happy'. She was especially pleased at the Prime Minister's recovery from a nasty bout of pneumonia after attending an Allied conference in the Middle East. 'Such good news of the rapid progress of Winston towards recovery in Africa. The news of his illness cast a shadow over our Pre-Christmas shopping & we are all the more thankful now. So ends this year – hopeful & forward-looking.' Perhaps she might have felt differently had she heard the Deputy Prime Minister's New Year's Eve broadcast to the nation: '1944 will be hardest year yet, Attlee warns,' was the *Daily Mirror*'s headline next morning.[53]

8

OCCUPIED TERRITORY:
1 JANUARY–12 JUNE 1944

'WELL here we go again to another year – and each one we hope will be the last of war, blackout, death and misery – maybe I'll live to write otherwise maybe not and anyway what does it matter?' Vivienne Hall, the City shorthand typist living in Putney, was not quite her irrepressible self at the opening of 1944, now keeping a diary again after her mother had ordered the destruction of some earlier volumes, not caring for what Vivienne had written about her. Spirits revived, though, with a visit to a friend's 'A.R.P. show – very good indeed'. Casting a professional eye over the actors, Vivienne thought: 'I wish I could get myself amongst them, I'd make a fine set of performers out of 'em – there's talent a'plenty but they want producing.'[1]

There were ARP shows of one kind or another everywhere that New Year. They were very welcome to the children who had been brought back in droves to London from evacuation over the Christmas period. Five hundred children were given a party by civil defence depot staff in Hilda Road, West Ham – or perhaps East Ham, for there was a Hilda Road in both – that included clowns, comedy turns, a Punch and Judy show and community singing, with each child 'given a paper hat, a bag of sweets, an apple and a sixpence from Father Christmas'. But it would have been difficult to top the efforts of ARP Post 24 in Kenton Road, South Hackney, on 8 January. With music from Post 26 dance band, 210 local children

> joined in singing popular choruses, beating time on the table with their spoons. For the meal there were meat and other sandwiches, sausages, jellies, blancmanges, small cakes and cut cake. The wardens had given

up their points rations to provide ingredients for the cakes, ham etc., as well as for sweets that were distributed later. Most of the cooking had been done by Warden Mrs. Law ... The wardens had made 300 really beautiful toys in their spare time. There were dolls, Teddy bears, elephants, dogs and other animals, tanks, trucks, and magnificent engines. Every child received a toy, and the larger ones, as well as half-crown savings stamps, were awarded as spot prizes during a dancing interlude.[2]

There were other reasons to be cheerful that January. 'Great news!' rejoiced Anthony Heap, the council finance clerk in St Pancras, when he read that the utility clothing restrictions imposed in May 1942 on menswear had been lifted. He could once more have his 'turn-ups, a double-breasted jacket and full complements of pockets, pleats and buttons'. 'My heart leapt up ... In fact I could hardly have been more overjoyed if peace had broken out.' Heap's priorities weren't everyone's, but all could share in the relief of another mild January. There was flu around, though, which laid low Vivienne Hall, and a coal shortage in the East End caused worry and discomfort for some. With extensive miners' strikes in South Wales in particular that spring, coal supplies would continue to be a problem in London. Vere Hodgson was without coal or coke in North Kensington right through an untypically warm April, but managed to put a brave face on things: 'Five weeks with no hot water! A small inconvenience, but I record it.' Another inconvenience that month was a bus strike, broken by the London Passenger Transport Board bringing in soldiers from the Royal Army Service Corps to act as drivers and conductors.[3]

But the worst trouble of the early months of 1944 was far more deadly. From early January through to mid-April the Luftwaffe renewed their night-time air war against London. The Baby Blitz or Little Blitz – or, because of their brief but hectic nature, the Scalded Cat Raids – used the full range of bombing weaponry against the capital. HE was now more powerful than ever before, with some 1,000-kilogram bombs dropped by parachute to maximise blast; great numbers of incendiaries were concentrated together, often in 'bread-baskets'; and there were even anti-personnel weapons that exploded when disturbed by rescue teams. In all, 1,244 Londoners were killed and 2,540 seriously injured. There were twenty-six raids from 3 January to 18 April, thirteen of them moderately heavy or worse. This was nothing like the relentless intensity of the opening weeks of the Big Blitz of 1940, but the Baby

Blitz delivered an unpleasant shock to Londoners that reminded them the war was far from over and their old foe far from defeated.[4]

This bombing campaign was also notable for the ferocity of London's AA defences. On 21 January, the first of the big raids, when more 2,500-kilogram bombs were dropped than during the whole war till then, they were all brought to bear. Bill Regan, who had experienced everything so far in the Isle of Dogs heavy rescue team, was astonished: 'Most terrific barrage I've ever heard, lasted for half an hour continuously at one period.' 'Gee, aren't we giving Jerry something now,' wrote Edward Fisher, a Battersea boarding-house keeper, to his daughter, safely at school in Hampshire. Daisy, his wife, reiterated the point a couple of days later: 'my goodness what a barrage we are putting up now'. A month on and Nellie Carver and her elderly mother 'Got up in the perishing cold & put our heads under the stairs. This was the most concentrated so far – guns nearly tearing the roof off – Rocket Guns (like Express trains) roaring overhead. How long the doors & windows will stand this – I don't know – or ourselves for that matter! ... London is hitting back with a vengeance!'[5]

Spare a thought for those in the midst of it. Betty Holbrook (as she became), originally from Lancaster, was an ATS plotter and range-finder for rocket batteries in Victoria Park Ack-Ack, where some 200 men and twenty women worked at red-hot speed in the raids:

> Crack, crack crack! That wretched mobile gun is firing now. The mobile gun rushes round the roads in the park and fires wildly in all directions. We hope that it will not shoot off our aerials. Shrapnel is coming down like hailstones, bouncing and rattling on our roof. We hope that none of it comes through. SWIISSH! Another lot of our rockets are off! The cabin is shaking with the vibration of the gunfire and when the big naval guns five-two-fives from Hackney Marshes let go we are literally bounced around inside. The barrages now being put up nightly are quite the heaviest ever.[6]

Despite the robustness of London's defences, Londoners generally met this new blitz with dismay. Vivienne Hall was not the only one to ask herself, 'how much longer is this going on, I wonder? I know we are amongst the lucky ones to be at home and not being killed or maimed deliberately, only when we are unfortunate enough to be bombed – but God, how tired we all are!' There was an intense outbreak of irritability apparent to many by the end of January. 'Londoners, normally as good tempered a crowd of people as you could hope to find anywhere, are beginning to show the strain,' thought Mollie Panter-Downes. 'Tired bus conductresses ... bawl out passengers ... Shop assistants snap at customers ... everybody's nerves are frayed.' The writer James Lees-Milne unwisely stepped into a row at Paddington Station between a woman ticket collector and a woman passenger who 'punched and scratched and finally became interlocked, each grasping the other's hair which came away in handfuls'. When he intervened 'they both hit me. I roared for help'; he had to be rescued by two policemen. Looking back on these months some three years later, William Sansom, in the London NFS during the war, reflected on Londoners' reactions to the Baby Blitz. 'People suffered from the old illusion,' he thought, 'that having once been hit they had "taken it" and were not eligible for a further dose. And here was the same experience to be faced all over again. It was depressing.' 'Many optimists', *Picture Post* readers were told, 'believed the days of air attack on London were over and have been disillusioned ...'[7]

The raids settled into something of an irregular pattern through February and March. The 'Bomber's Moon' which had encouraged raiding in the Big Blitz was avoided in this briefer rerun because of more effective night fighters. Now it was the dark nights to be feared. Most Londoners acclimatised, but the old ebullience of those who stuck out 1940–41 with stoicism had gone, to be replaced by something more resentful, sullen and vengeful. Many found comfort by keeping in mind that Berliners and others in Germany were getting far worse in return. Some, though, couldn't adjust a second time. Ellen Brightley of Peabody Buildings, Walworth, died with her head in her gas oven in early April; her sister told the inquest that Ellen was very frightened of the raids.[8]

The crushing HE now available to the Luftwaffe, the gaily coloured flares dropped to assist bomb aiming and the concentrations of every kind of incendiary all made the Baby Blitz a tumultuous experience on the ground. Some 343 fires were started by the raid of 28/9 January, with the Surrey Commercial Docks in Rotherhithe fired destructively for the third time since September 1940. Four raids between 18 and 24 February were the worst of the whole Baby Blitz and the heaviest since May 1941. South-west London north and south of the river was especially badly hit. Fulham on 20 February suffered its worst night of the war, 'worse than anything during the old Blitz; at one time there were a hundred incidents on the board'. Across the river in Battersea, in a small district of some twenty acres, 3,000 houses 'were destroyed or made uninhabitable', probably by a new phenomenon of these months, sticks of four 500-kilogram bombs landing close together, 'sometimes in line, sometimes in diamond pattern – Less frequently 3 bombs have fallen in an L pattern. The damage caused by the bombs has frequently merged and an area of devastation has been caused.' The worst single incident of the campaign was on 23 February at Guinness Trust Buildings in King's Road, Chelsea, when a direct hit killed fifty-seven people, with forty-seven badly injured. They were flats for working people: 'Many killed; won't be got out for several days, they say,' recorded Hilda Neal in South Kensington next day. That night too the London Library in St James's Square, Westminster, was blitzed, with much destruction to the book stacks and over 16,600 volumes destroyed or damaged. It was one more addition to the toll of books the war had inflicted on London, not all of it from enemy action.[9]

On Putney Hill, Wandsworth, Vivienne Hall had some lively times between 19 and 21 February:

What a night! The sirens about 11.30 and plenty of gunfire, then the hideous well-remembered swaying of the house as one after another came the thumps of near bombs – the frightful roar of the plane as it dived to deliver its messages and then the crump and tinkle of broken glass. How I hate myself for being sick with fear, but there it is ... It ended of course and then out to see just what had happened – next door but one had most of its drive hurled into the roadway with a nasty hole in its middle – our garden wall was mostly down with another behind it, the garage opposite just wasn't any more, a delayed action bomb was sitting in the road behind us while two old ladies had been killed just beyond as they tried to get downstairs – and over all this curled the pink smoke of many fires ...

And Sunday night!! About 9.20 the sirens wailed again and then we had to listen to the horrid thumps as more bombs came down – looking towards my living room was horrified to see smoke and flame and on investigation found something had forced a mass of soot on the fire. This had caught alight and was making a pretty flame – tipped half a bucket of sand over it and it went out. More bombs, more glass smashing, the front-door had its lock torn out and most of the cupboard doors opened as though pulled by strings – hell couldn't be much worse than this awful feeling of waiting ... How many times will this go on I wonder? It's nothing of course to the endless bombing we are giving Berlin and the other German cities, so we must expect it and put up with it.[10]

Dorothy Wells was a fire-watcher in her Ealing street but on the evening of 23 February was off duty and at home with her mother; Ken was fire-watching at his workplace in Wardour Street, Soho, and it was just the two women at home:

> At 9.40 p.m. the Alert, and an exciting time! A good deal of gunfire and we heard at least three bombs come down, shaking the shelter. Then there was a rustle, and a basket of incendiaries fell, all around the top of our road. I went out with buckets of water and sand, and helped where I could. Several of the houses between Grant's and Palmer's had fires in the upper storeys. Davis' laundry, the Red Lion, Wells's old shop, a pile of timber in the derelict yard at the top of the road, and Coachcraft's first shop were on fire. There was also a big fire just outside the Anglian wall, across the canal. Fire engines came and our local fires were put out, but poor Elsie's living room was badly damaged ... There is a time-bomb behind the Belmont Laundry in our road, and two in the Elthorne Park area – possibly on our allotment![11]

As things turned out, the cabbages were safe.

At the end of February Vivienne Hall had to evacuate her home because of two UXBs nearby and was taken in by friends a few streets away. On 14 March the house where she rented a flat with her mother was hit: 'I have a horrible feeling that Putney Hill is a definite target now' – a popular delusion being that the Luftwaffe could single out one's street for special attention. The house was badly knocked about by incendiaries and Vivienne helped shepherd her elderly neighbours to safety downstairs: 'By this time wardens and fireguards seemed to be all over the place and two accompanied me upstairs to see if the place was ablaze or not.' It wasn't but it could well have been: a phosphorus bomb had burst through an upstairs wall, wrecking the shared bathrooms on the way, and was safely burning in the garden, where what she thought were 200 more were lying in a crater. 'Wardens, police and fireguards bravely tackled the lot ...'[12]

ARP everywhere acquitted itself generally very well, wardens and fire guards in particular. Clearly the cuts of 1941–3 had dented neither morale nor efficiency. Intensive training had continued, the conscription of many women into the fire guard who were often now in senior positions had reportedly improved efficiency and great strides had been made to increase the availability of water for firefighting, with more static tanks, mobile teams of engineers to fix broken mains and 'deep-lift pumps' to take water from the Thames and other London rivers.[13] But when the bombs fell it was the courage and endurance of men and women from humble backgrounds that mattered most. Fred Bodley and his wife, Kathleen, were both wardens at Worcester Park, a south-western suburb in Sutton. Fred was a warehouseman for a vacuum-cleaner company when war broke out, and Kathleen was working at home on 'unpaid domestic duties'; both were forty-four or thereabouts. They too had a lively time on the night of 23/4 February. The warning sounded at 9.39 p.m. (so Fred recorded), although the ack-ack barrage had already begun:

It was not long before wardens arrived from a lecture that had been taking place. I logged thirteen wardens, the Deputy Senior Fire Guard and two messengers. The now familiar heavy barrage was being put up. At 10.4 p.m., those that had been standing outside the post, suddenly made one dive inside as something heavy was coming down. There was an almighty explosion which really shook everything and everyone. It seemed to come from the direction of Worcester Park Station. At 10.21 p.m., a phone message was received from W.4 post ... to the effect that they needed reinforcements as the seat of damage was too large for them to tackle single-handed ... The Post Warden informed W.4 that he would send assistance as soon as the 'raiders passed' had gone, as he did not wish to leave his own area uncovered. When this eventually sounded (10.50 p.m.), all wardens ... proceeded to the seat of damage. What I saw on arrival was utter destruction. Five houses on one side of the road and six on the other were practically flat. It is now believed that a parachute mine of a large calibre was the cause of this terrible scene. The corner house was alight.

A Canadian soldier came staggering over the debris in my direction; he was capless and obviously suffering from shock. Another warden and I assisted him out of the smoke a short way up Donnington Road ... I returned to Kath [off duty, at home] and told her the situation and almost immediately we set out to give a hand. At the scene of operations, W.6. wardens [Fred and Kath's post] were feverishly working to release four trapped people; one of whom we knew to be dead. An elderly gentleman was sitting in an armchair which was partly on its side. A beam had fallen across his back. The other three were not visible until we had tunnelled towards them.

I remember holding my torch to enable the doctor to fill his hyperdermic [sic] before administering morphia to the victims. Later, the headlamps of the Heavy Rescue lorries provided the illumination for operations. Brick chains were formed and later, debris bins were produced, which were passed along full by one line of wardens and back empty via another. When it was required that debris should be removed to alleviate pressure, we turned to with a will. I had no idea that Kath could lift such heavy loads. She worked like a Trojan. It fell to my lot to act as stretcher bearer to one of the women victims that had just been released … If one wanted any tool, say a saw, all you had to do was to shout for it and within seconds, one would be produced from somewhere …

At 4 a.m., Kath and I came home and made a large enamel jug of tea for those who could not leave their job.

The Bodleys finally left at 5 a.m., when it was clear they could be of no more help: six people had been killed and thirteen injured, 'a miracle, when one sees the damage caused'.[14]

Unsurprisingly, the Baby Blitz drove people back in large numbers to the tubes and public shelters – some street shelters were still being given their concrete overcoats that January. Over the worst nights of late February around 150,000 'took shelter for short periods varying from 1–3 hours' in the tubes, numbers not seen since October 1940, with 20,000 cramming into Piccadilly Circus alone. The number of permanent shelterers spending every night there rose from 3,000 to about 50,000. In south London, 'thousands of Tube station shelterers' petitioned Herbert Morrison to open the deep shelters built after the main blitz but never used: one petitioner complained that 'naturally we don't feel satisfied when we know that first-rate deep shelters – like young towns they're supposed to be – are still closed'. That was late February, and a couple of weeks later the Communist Party hopped on this old bandwagon to petition afresh, but with no effect on Whitehall. Hilda Neal was pressed by a nervous fellow lodger in their South Kensington house to go to the tube with her, against Hilda's better instincts – 'Felt very humiliated at having to go underground for Hitler!' Vivienne Hall, caught in a raid on 8 March, found herself sheltering for the first time in a tube, at Gloucester Road station: 'No, I shouldn't choose it, despite the fact you can hear nothing of the noises going on above. The long rows of people, young and incredibly old, huddled in all manner of rug, blanket or coat on the bunks and on the platform itself ... Oh no, give me the raids above ground thank you ...'[15]

It was unsurprising too that people once more sought a way out of London altogether. This was not through homelessness, because those bombed out and thrown on public resources in the rest centres seem now at last to have been well looked after, especially where WVS volunteers played a large role: like civil defence generally, 'post raid services maintained a very high standard of performance,' as the London Civil Defence Region put it. The importance of information or 'Enquiry Posts' at incidents, often staffed by the WVS, made all the difference here as the helpful linkage between bomb victims and the town hall one-stop shops and billeting officers. Rather, it was the people whose nerves were racked as they waited for 'their' bomb to bring chaos and injury or worse, and who had resources sufficient to remove themselves from danger, who took themselves out of London. Verily Anderson, after a terrifying night in St John's Wood, took shelter first with her parents in Sussex and then with friends in Moreton-in-Marsh, Gloucestershire. Vivienne Hall's mother, 'in a fine state of nerves', left with a neighbour for Westmorland a couple of weeks before their home was badly damaged and stayed away for the rest of the year, good news at least for Vivienne's diary. Bill and Vi Regan, whose two daughters had returned from evacuation in 1943, now sent them back to their former foster parents at Lidstone in rural Oxfordshire. After the 23 February incendiary raid in Ealing, Dorothy Wells reported that her neighbour 'has gone down to her sister in Maidenhead'. 'There seems to have been an exodus on a quite considerable scale from this town,' Anthony Weymouth, the Harley Street physician, concluded in early March. 'People are finding the air-raids much more difficult to face up to than they did in 1940/41. From every side comes the same tale – people jittery and trying to find sleeping accommodation outside London.'[16]

THE final cluster of Baby Blitz raids took place at the end of March, with two more light attacks in the middle of April. Then nothing. The slow but steady rise in the civilian population in 1943, and the noticeable build-up of Allied troops in London – on leave or, for some Americans, lodging there more permanently – may have been dented by the Baby Blitz but it was far from stifled. 'Raids or no raids, people keep on moving back into town,' thought Mollie Panter-Downes. 'More and more Londoners who left during the blitz are opening up their homes again or trying to find new ones ...' That was at the end of January, before the big raids of February and March, but certainly once that shock was over London began to fill again. Between New Year and July 1944 some 45,000 more civilians were added to London's population, a small number but all contributing to the pressures. Robert Hutton, working for a firm of West End estate agents around this time, was employed in 'the letting or selling of properties furnished or unfurnished' and as 'the demand greatly exceeded the supply ... it was as easy as falling off a log'.[17]

The trouble was that London's supply of liveable lodgings was shrinking and the Baby Blitz made everything worse. London's housing was now approaching a crisis. From late 1943 an epidemic of dry rot was widely reported to be affecting even the smart parts of west London. In January 1944 government guidance explained it was due to bomb damage laying houses open to the weather, aggravated by burst pipes in severe winters and the prevailing shortage of building materials and labour. Some dry rot could now be treated as war damage and so was eligible for financial aid to eliminate it. But carrying out war damage repairs was far from easy. At the end of March Stepney Borough Council was refused government permission to repair bomb-blasted flats in its ownership, officials presumably worried that further damage would mean throwing good money after bad. Perhaps they were thinking of the 13,426 Islington houses where new windows had been installed after bomb damage by early January, just in time for the Baby Blitz to blow many of them out again. War damage claims were, though, processed and repairs duly carried out: one of them was for Dorothy Wells's roof, repaired 'free of charge under the War Damage Insurance' in April.[18]

To help increase the housing supply, empty properties continued to be requisitioned by councils for homeless or overcrowded families – Hackney Council requisitioned forty-seven in June, for instance. Some authorities worked on other solutions to the supply problem, though at this stage they were envisaged coming into play only once the war was ended. Poplar planned to erect prefabricated houses on bomb sites, the borough's 'electricity chief' designing a prefabricated '"Poplar" Kitchen Unit' to local, even national, acclaim. The Ministry of Works exhibited its experimental 'Portal' house in June outside the Tate at Millbank: 'most carefully thought out,' recorded an impressed Anthony Weymouth, noting that improved versions were likely to follow. Though these initiatives offered some hope for the future, it seemed likely they would be deferred until air attacks ceased altogether. In the interim, everything was getting worse. Londoners could notionally spend up to £100 on repairing their homes without a Ministry of Works building licence, but labour and materials were both extremely hard to come by, so few could exercise these new freedoms. Absentee landlords were unwilling to spend on their tenants' homes when their investments could be wasted by the next bomb. Almost nowhere in London had been given a lick of paint for four years and there had been virtually no new building, no slum clearance – indeed, long-condemned houses were now having to be used again as people's homes – and few repairs. This simmering crisis in London housing would boil over in the months to come.[19]

Some of the money not spent on housing no doubt ended up in the ever-deepening pockets of National Savings. The campaign for 1944, cannily timed to precede the Second Front, was 'Salute the Soldier Week'. London was expected to raise £165 million. All these campaigns proved popular in London but this was the most enthusiastically supported of all. Everywhere targets were set to help contribute to the London total and almost everywhere were exceeded by the time sums were totted up in early April. Factories and offices set targets: Vere Hodgson's social work charity in North Kensington aimed to raise £20 but had collected double by the end of the week; Nellie Carver's Central Telegraph Office's grand total exceeded their target with £6,714 17s 5d; in factories across south London, workers had been forming 'Bob in the Pound' groups, contributing a shilling for each pound earned since January, 'supplementary to ordinary street and club group savings'; Southwark Council offered a trophy for the borough's highest saving firm. Streets set targets too: Comyn Road, Battersea, aimed for £125, Horniman Drive in Lewisham raised no less then £1,105 10s. Clubs and organisations (Rotary, Conservative and Labour Party branches) set targets; so did civil defence (NFS area 37 in south-east London raised £28,000 and Lambeth's Wardens' Post 34 £13,209), and even schools, with St Saviour's and St Olave's schools in Southwark raising £644 between them. Across London, borough targets were exceeded, often greatly. West Ham set itself £800,000 and reached £881,000, and pretty much everywhere else did as well; 'Largest Borough Smashes

"Salute" Target with £1,900,000 Total' was the headline reporting that Wandsworth raised £400,000 more than anticipated. In all, London reached £166,629,273. 'Good work London,' wrote Nellie Carver, '– after such horrible nights.'[20]

Enthusiasm for the cause had been stoked in central London by a display in Trafalgar Square of anti-aircraft and field guns, camouflage netting, an amphibious vehicle, a mechanical repair shop and, on the opening day (Saturday 25 March), Allied soldiers of every nation who mingled with the crowd. On the Monday there was a huge march from Finsbury Circus through the City and Westminster for which the King took the salute from a dais outside Buckingham Palace; there were many marching bands and it was all watched by cheering crowds. But it was the local celebrations that reached most Londoners and probably meant more to them. In Hackney, for instance, there were marches of military bands, NFS, ARP, the Home Guard and others, a tank and ack-ack gun outside the town hall, speeches, a 'Town Hall dance', band concerts and more. Similar events took place in every borough. Some, perhaps, had more fun than others. The American film star Bebe Daniels visited the army exhibition at, bizarrely, Spurgeon's Tabernacle, Elephant and Castle. She invested £500 in Southwark's Salute the Soldier Week and sold savings certificates to the locals. To anyone buying more than two she gave an orange and an egg; other purchasers merely received a signed photo, rich testimony to the value of an egg and an orange at the Elephant in March 1944.[21]

Perhaps there were other reasons for Londoners' enthusiasm over Salute the Soldier. Everyone knew, of course, that the Second Front, so much clamoured for in the first half of 1942 and then shelved after the bloody Dieppe Raid that August, was now likely to happen, and by all understanding sometime soon. The great burden would be borne by the soldiers being celebrated this spring. But London had also been greatly moved by the returning POWs in late 1943. Many of them had been injured or sick, with some now recovering, and others dying, in London hospitals. Local efforts to look after London's POWs still in German or Japanese camps redoubled from early 1944. A West Ham Local Joint Committee of Prisoners of War Organizations put on a party for the 140 children of the borough's POWs in the New Year, and the WVS workers at a 'Third Line Rest Centre' in Lee, Lewisham, together with 'the Housewives of "A" District, held a "Make Do & Mend" Sale' for Lewisham's POW fund, raising nearly £150.[22]

The POW cause was helped in May by an exhibition of prison camp conditions put on in the grounds of Clarence House, adjoining St James's Palace, next to the park. Hilda Neal visited, paying 1s entrance and 6d for the programme, and was most impressed:

> Barbed wire encirclements with two high lookouts for guards, with a wooden ladder to reach them and 'Eingang verboten' on them (for the uninitiated – 'Entrance forbidden'). We went through about seven or eight huts showing how the prisoners sleep in bunks, decorated with shelves ... photos of their loved ones, and so on. Then a display of the arts and crafts with which they have been occupying their spare time and trying to kill their boredom. Many of them were excellent, especially the portraits and models of trains ... tins, cups and all sorts of useful articles. There were rugs made from the wool of socks, tapestry from sackcloth; bags and slippers from string, plaited or crocheted and then sewn together, and even decorated with colours. Most ingenious.[23]

The Red Cross, who had helped organise the exhibition, used the publicity to help regularise street collections across London. There were 750 POWs from Islington, where industrial and house-to-house collections were well supported: a Penny-a-Week Fund concert was put on at the Central Library to coincide with the Clarence House event. And in Lewisham, where 700 POWs held by the enemy had their homes, Red Cross volunteers for each council ward enrolled street collectors for the fund: a map was produced giving the name and address of each ward organiser so that volunteers could contact them.[24]

ANOTHER kind of soldier was much on Londoners' minds that spring. London felt so full in part, at least, because it seemed invaded by Americans. 'Traffic on the streets seems thicker than usual,' noted Mollie Panter-Downes in early May, 'most of its liveliness being contributed by American jeeps and glossy staff cars,' and it was true that there had never been so many Americans in London – or so many visible and audible – as in the first five months of 1944.[25]

Americans had of course been in London since the declaration of war. Many had visited or made temporary homes there for generations. There had been an exodus after 3 September 1939, sure enough, but some of the vacuum had been filled by Anglophiles arriving to show their support and by Americans fleeing other parts of Europe as nation

after nation was overrun by Germany. The many American correspondents, for whom London was a safe haven, best served with transatlantic
communications, helped fill West End hotels, especially from the fall of
France. Their significance can hardly be exaggerated. They fixed, as no
other journalists did, the world's view of London as the city hunkered
down under the blitz. As we have seen, they even helped define the
Londoners' view of themselves.

But journalists, diplomats, even military attachés, though legion, were
largely anonymous and invisible to the general run of Londoners
throughout 1940 and almost all of 1941. That would change with
Germany's declaration of war on the USA in December 1941, and
President Roosevelt's quick resolution that the defeat of Hitler was his
country's prime objective. So, from the spring of 1942, Americans in
uniform began to be an increasingly palpable presence in the streets of
London. They first made an impact in Mayfair, close to the US Embassy,
which was then at 1 Grosvenor Square in the south-east corner. 'The
Americans came to our village in the chilly fogs of March,' recorded
Robert Henrey, a journalist living close to seedy Shepherd Market,
north of Piccadilly. 'The Americans passed silently through our narrow
alleys. These transatlantic soldiers were models of cleanliness, and made
our own Tommies look rather shabby in contrast. The cloth of their
uniforms, their smart collars and ties, their bright leather belts, their
carefully shaven faces were as impressive as their thoughtful expres-
sions.' There were other differences too: 'The N.C.O.s carry revolvers,'
noted Charles Graves that same month.[26]

By June there seemed to be Americans everywhere. They notoriously
monopolised the remaining taxicabs but injected much-needed cash into
retail and entertainment: 'London at the moment is a boom-town,'
reported Mollie Panter-Downes at the height of the summer, 'owing
mostly to the money of the American troops on leave.' In August 1942
the real invasion began as every GI in the country seemed to descend
on London on a leave pass – 15,000 or so of the 1st Infantry Division
were given passes to London on their first weekend in Britain that
month, for instance. These temporary but constantly rotating influxes
of troops were accompanied by the consolidation of Mayfair as a semi-
permanent extraterritorial US dependency. In 1942 there were more
than 3,000 staff working for the US government in London, not all of
them Americans but most were. The numbers would grow greatly over
the next two years. The streets north of Piccadilly were known as

'Eisenhower-Platz', South Audley Street was 'a miniature Fifth Avenue', baseball was played in Hyde Park and, in a parody of the famous song of a nightingale in Berkeley Square, it became a joke to say, 'I heard an Englishman Speak in Grosvenor Square.' It was there, at No. 20 on the north-west corner, that General Eisenhower set up his European Theater of Operations HQ in June 1942. And it was nearby that a cluster of giant American Red Cross clubs were established for GIs on leave or London-based, the most famous of them Rainbow Corner, 23 Shaftesbury Avenue, close to Piccadilly Circus, which first opened its doors on 11 November 1942 and would not finally close them till January 1946.[27]

In September 1942 Nellie Carver and a friend left the office 'to see the American soldiers march to Guildhall via St Paul's to a Lunch given by the Lord Mayor. They looked fine coming up Ludgate Hill with Bands playing & flags flying. As they passed St Paul's they all looked up at the Cathedral. I wondered what they thought of our poor Blitzed old City?' Doubtless their thoughts were various, but the reaction of one US soldier, Sergeant Arbib, who first visited London around this time might have surprised Nellie:

> I always thought of London as the hub of the world in those days. Here was not only the throbbing heart of the British Empire, but here too was the capital-in-exile of half a dozen other nations. Here the strategy and plans were being conceived, from here the vast armed forces were being marshalled and directed, and on London were the eyes of the world. Battered and dirty, worn and scarred, it swarmed with scores of different uniforms, and it spoke in a hundred different tongues. No matter where you were going in the United Kingdom, you had to go through London, and no matter how long you stayed you never saw it all. London was the babel, the Metropolis, the Mecca. London was It.[28]

The number of Americans in the UK in 1942 peaked at 220,000 in October and then fell away by almost half as men left for operations in North Africa. But from the summer of 1943, with the Second Front in Europe now being planned for an invasion of France in the following spring, numbers rose again. By Christmas there were some 650,000 in the country, all of whom we can confidently assume spent some time in London. By May 1944 the number had risen to 1.5 million and, again, all but the very newest arrivals would have received a weekend pass or more to spend time in the city that 'was It'. By then the West End had much of the appearance and soundscape of an American city, a view not weakened by the very visible presence of 'Snowdrops', US military police, fresh in their new uniforms issued by Eisenhower that February:

> Their glaring white helmets, belts, gloves and spats continually attract the passer by and can even be seen in the black-out quite a good distance away. A pair of these tough looking stalwarts are now posted at regular intervals all the way along the main thoroughfares. About time too, the Yanks have been allowed to run wild around the West End long enough.[29]

For many Londoners, these large numbers proved uncomfortable: 'it is difficult to go anywhere in London,' George Orwell concluded about the American presence in December 1943, 'without having the feeling that Britain is now Occupied Territory'. A couple of weeks later he related that 'I can hear few good words for the Americans anywhere.' Certainly, the response of many Londoners was ambivalent at best. Kathleen Tipper met many Americans at the YMCA club in Lewisham where she was a volunteer helper:

> and in the process of drawing them out I discovered that most of them think (or know) that they are disliked here and are resentful of the fact. Several of them told me that they think it is because they are paid much more than our troops, but I don't think this is the real cause, because some of our Dominion troops are paid as well as the Americans. I put down the fact that they are disliked by many people here, because they are so aggressive.

'If only they didn't boast so much about their wonderful U.S.A.,' thought the writer Margaret Crompton's son, who had lately met many in London, 'they would be all right. It seems they consider themselves a few steps above everybody else and they don't mind people knowing it.'[30]

The Americans were indeed well favoured in London. They stood out in their smart uniforms (nattily cut jacket, smart collar and tie, trousers immaculately pressed); and they were remarkable for their impeccable dentistry, despite their apparently inexhaustible stores of gum and candy and cigarettes. 'I met a few Americans,' Anthony Weymouth recorded at Christmas 1943, 'and they told me what supplies they had. This made my mouth water. After all, it *is* some time now since we saw, far less tasted, real cream, chocolate creams (of pre-war standard), dates, almonds and raisins, to say nothing of the lashings of butter and meat which they seem to have in plenty.' It was notorious too that Rainbow Corner and the other American Red Cross clubs, with their dance bands, juke boxes, pin-tables and pool, far outstripped the rest provision for British soldiers in London.[31]

But there was another and far sharper source of envy in play. It wasn't only the taxicabs that Americans monopolised in the West End of London. Kathleen Tipper and a girlfriend were waiting in a West End cinema queue in the autumn of 1944 when 'a taxi drew up beside us and two girls aged about 15 got out ... one said to the other, "We'll wait here, then we can pick up two Yank officers" – and they did!!' C. L. McDermott, then in US Army air crew, who wrote a novel based on his wartime experiences in London, described in the introduction how the West End seemed to him at just that time: 'Piccadilly Circus in wartime was the only place I had ever known which exemplified such complete, universal lack of restraint, in which so many people so openly and frankly pursued the same libertine objectives.' It was a pursuit in which the Yanks handled all the heavy weaponry. One reason for their unpopularity among the Londoners was their unrivalled supremacy when it came to obtaining sex just when and where they wanted: paid for in sterling, traded in nylons and cigarettes and booze, or just for the love of it. 'I watch them from my office window some-times,' wrote Hilda Neal from her vantage point in the Strand, 'coming out of the Tivoli [Cinema] and signalling for taxis. The girls seem chiefly of the factory or working-class type, hatless and stockingless.' The 'amorous Yanks' were 'much more demonstrative than English boys ... Openly holding girls' hands, or cuddling them brazenly on escalators, station platforms, trains, in the streets – everywhere they can'. Hilda noticed it was having an effect on how London girls now chose to look. 'The Americans just openly pick up any girl they fancy – synthetic blondes for preference; so many brunettes do their best with peroxide to improve on Nature.'[32]

How much this 'wave of sexual mania', as Anthony Heap charac-terised it in this same autumn of 1944, was commercial, how much the promise of a good night out, expenses paid and services rendered, and how much genuine affection is a moot point. All three no doubt played a part from night to night. But it was the commercial trade in sex that was most visible to Londoners. There was a great deal of prostitution that plainly relied on the enormous American presence in the West End, and that had increased to meet the bottomless demand. The smart trade around Shepherd Market flourished as never before. There 'the more elegantly clad of them would stand quietly and wait – expensive and aloof. No privates or corporals for these haughty demoiselles. They had furs and silks to pay for.' Many of these superior women were French, like Marthe Watts, now in the Messina stable, where Gino was at first chary of letting her entertain Americans, perhaps worried about her succumbing to a rival's charms. There was no great risk because she was allowed only ten minutes per client and was ordered not to take her clothes off – as she said, 'we never had time!!' But eventually the money proved too great a temptation and from her room in fashionable St James's Place she was allowed 'to take Americans, and this improved our financial returns considerably, for these Americans were very generous'.[33]

By the autumn of 1944, Anthony Heap thought that in the West End 'prostitutes post themselves every two or three yards along the main thoroughfares. Some, of course, are genuine professionals, but the vast majority are obviously amateurs – girls in their 'teens for whom the thousands of overpaid and over-sexed American soldiers roaming around are easy prey.' Girls were 'everywhere,' remembered Sergeant Arbib: 'At the Underground entrance they were thickest, and as the evening grew dark they shone torches on their ankles as they walked, and bumped into the soldiers, murmuring, "Hello, Yank" "Hello, soldier." "Hello, dearie!"' To Airman McDermott, these were 'Piccadilly Commandos'. Similar young women, 'who preferred the relatively easy life of prostitution, or semi-prostitution, to that of work in the British war plants', were to be found as 'hostesses' in nightclubs – like the 'Court Club', as McDermott christened it, behind the Cumberland Hotel at Marble Arch, 'a typical London bottle club, supported by American soldiers'. Membership cost 10s plus a 10s entrance fee, and drinks were only affordable on GI pay rates: 'a fifth of Scotch' for £4 10s and soda water and a bowl of ice for 5s more.[34]

All the Americans' physical and financial virtues that made them so attractive to young women in London exerted strong appeal too among men looking for sex with other men. 'This brand new army of (no) occupation flowed through the streets of London like cream on strawberries, like melted butter over green peas,' remembered the irrepressible Quentin Crisp, at this time an artist's model.

> Labelled 'with love from Uncle Sam' and packaged in uniforms so tight that in them their owners could fight for nothing but their honour, these 'bundles for Britain' leaned against the lamp-posts of Shaftesbury Avenue or lolled on the steps of thin-lipped statues of dead English statesmen. As they sat in the cafés or stood in the pubs, their bodies bulged through every straining khaki fibre towards our feverish hands ... Never in the history of sex was so much offered to so many by so few.[35]

No doubt some of this sex was commercial too, though not it seems in Crisp's case, for whom the fun was both easy and free: 'While the G.I.s were still around, I lived almost every moment that I spent out of doors in a state of exhilaration.' But Anthony Heap's description of the American soldiers as 'prey' had much of truth in it, and not just in the ceaseless propositioning and the whisky at a pound a shot. Americans complained of being plagued by 'children who follow them night and day, cadging sweets', for instance. But there was worse. Some women preferred to court Americans for plunder while offering nothing in return. Ida Marshall, no occupation and living in Stepney, was given three months' hard labour for stealing five £1 notes from a GI in a pub in Brick Lane: she'd called him over and he bought her a drink. A year later, almost to the day, she got another three months' for stealing a watch from a black GI: 'She floats around and gets her living somehow by taking furnished rooms,' police told the court. Marie Bennett, thirty-nine, of Pentonville Road was given four months' for being 'concerned with a man not in custody' in stealing a gold watch and bracelet worth £12 from a US Army corporal: she told police 'that it was "common in this district" for women to take American soldiers into dark alley-ways so that they could be robbed in co-operation with men'. Two women, also from the King's Cross area, were in trouble for stealing by means of a trick from an American soldier who gave them money to find him a room but ran off. 'The Yank and His Watch' was the headline in another case when a woman living in Holloway Road was given two months' for this by now common form of theft. The King's Cross locals seem to have been especially voracious in this regard: six youths pleaded guilty to a series of robberies of GIs between October

1944 and January 1945 in Jimmy Cagney-style stick-ups. Their 'revolvers' were made of wood and painted black. It was a part-time occupation only: all six were in work and earning from £3 to £4 14s a week.[36]

The boom-town created by the US occupation of London flourished especially in the entertainments industry and most of all in dancing. The jitterbug had been first introduced to London by Hollywood in 1939 but from 1942 Londoners could see it done and London's young women could do it themselves with American servicemen. 'War-Time's Most Popular Recreation is Dancing,' a Knightsbridge dance school proclaimed in February 1944, and it undoubtedly was, at least for the younger and fitter among the Londoners. 'The Dance halls are booming everywhere,' *Picture Post* announced in a feature that April. 'Mecca Dancing at the Royal Opera House, Covent Garden,' was crowding in 1,500 dancers twice daily, many American soldiers among them, though jitterbugging was sadly outlawed, that hyper-energetic dance perhaps needing too much room. The Americans had been especially welcome to dance-hall proprietors because their lighter shoes were kinder to dance floors than British and Canadian army boots, though those soldiers too could now wear shoes when off duty. By the spring of 1944, London's local newspapers were full of adverts for dancing schools – 'Better days are coming. Are you ready for your Victory Ball?' – and for dance band musicians. Stan Graham and His Rhythm Boys of Shepherd's Bush wanted urgently 'Dance musicians for comb. re-forming, piano, drums, alto or tenor sax, trumpet etc.', in February, for instance. And there were dances everywhere: in the parks during holiday time, in London's town halls, in municipal swimming baths, where dance floors were laid over the drained pools (Lime Grove Baths a popular venue, also in Shepherd's Bush), and in famous dance halls like the Hammersmith Palais de Danse, the West End Ballroom at Stratford Place, or Holborn Hall, where the Carlton Dance Band were regular performers. In all of this, American jazz, swing and the jitterbug suffused everything, the very rhythms an irresistible seduction. A Mr D. S. Newman, recruiting jitterbuggers – not his word – for the Home Guard in 'Happy Hammersmith', used their frequent dances open to 'W.A.A.F. and A.T.S. sisters' as a draw: 'this is 1944, and the scene has changed. Tastes have undergone a complete overhaul. Comes swing and Bing. The Jitterbug takes the floor and the orchestra almost stands on its ear when it gets really hot.' Even more, 'It won't cost you a plugged-nickel.'[37]

Not everyone, though, was welcome at every dance or every entertainment venue; neither was the hospitality afforded by pubs or hotels open to all comers. The reason was plain: not all Americans were created equal. But which Americans were thought to be more favoured in the eyes of the Londoners and others in the UK would have come as a surprise to many in the US forces. 'The general consensus of opinion,' reported George Orwell in December 1943, 'seems to be that the only American soldiers with decent manners are the Negroes.'[38]

The issue of colour and race took on a new significance with the American occupation of London from 1942. London had not been immune from 'the colour bar', either before the war or during its first years. The then notoriously racist British Boxing Board of Control was still limiting the competitions in which black boxers could fight, based solely on their colour, even in 1941. Certain London venues, the Royal Albert Hall and the National Sporting Club among them, barred black boxers entirely. It was said that some London hotels would not accommodate black or Indian visitors to the 1937 Coronation. The Blue Lagoon Swimming Pool in Orpington, south-east London, one of the largest pools in the country, openly operated a colour bar in the mid-1930s: 'Our experience is that women bathers, in particular, do not like to be in the pool at the same time as coloured men.' There were allegations in 1939 that some London hospitals would not take 'coloured girls' as nurses or 'coloured medical students'. Early recruitment into the wartime navy and air force also allegedly kept out black volunteers. Similarly, Amelia King, a twenty-six-year-old black woman from Stepney, her father in the merchant navy, was barred from the Women's Land Army in September 1943; she was eventually offered a place on a Hampshire farm where none of the other Land Army women 'objected to working with a coloured girl'. There were sufficient instances of either official or informal operation of a colour bar in London entertainments and the tourism industry, in employment and in the London housing market – where some leases excluded 'persons of colour' in 1944 – to indicate that this practice was no alien American import and that any welcome extended by Londoners to black GIs may often have been no more than superficial, skin deep we might say, at best.[39]

Even so, the viciousness that many white American GIs showed to their black comrades shocked those Londoners who encountered it. Cecil King, the *Daily Mirror* chairman, was on a London train in October 1942, with two drunk GIs in his carriage who were complaining about many aspects of army life: 'but the only subject on which they got very animated was negroes. If they could have a chance of shooting their own American negroes over here, then their journey indeed would have been worth while.' There were many cases of racial abuse and violence between white and black US soldiers instigated mostly, according to all reports, by the former. As the American build-up peaked in the spring of 1944, the numbers of black GIs in the UK reached around 100,000. Many of these, like their white compatriots, had passes to London. In the capital and outside the US military authorities kept their army segregated as far as possible – a policy notoriously pursued in pubs and halls in the countryside around American bases. Even in London it meant that some pubs were in practice 'whites only'. Inevitably there was a reaction. In Fitzrovia, for instance, there was a pub 'where only Negro GIs went, as the other publicans had put up the colour bar: now in consequence the negroes had established their own bridgehead which none of us might pass,' recalled the writer Julian MacLaren-Ross, out on a pub crawl with some tipsy cronies. 'A huge one standing in the open door, tunic unbuttoned, pint glass in hand, ready to repel invaders, shouted "No white folks allowed in here," in a Southern accent as we straggled by.'[40]

A celebrated instance of the pernicious effect the US forces were having on race relations in London played out at the Imperial Hotel, Russell Square, in September 1943. Learie Constantine was a 'famous West Indies cricketer', well known and liked in the UK, where he'd lived for fifteen years. He was in London as part of his role as a welfare officer, helping West Indian migrants settle into their work in the munitions industries of north-west England. He arrived at the hotel with reservations for himself, his wife and daughter, two friends and a secretary. Constantine's party were told, '"We won't have niggers in this hotel."' When a senior official turned up to explain that Constantine was a civil servant engaged on government work, and a British subject, the hotel manageress retorted '"He is a nigger."' Constantine sued the Imperial Hotel for breach of contract and won nominal damages in the High Court in June 1944. The Imperial's unsuccessful defence tried to put the blame elsewhere. There were said to be between 200 and 300 American officers and other ranks staying at the hotel who, the manager said, 'objected to the Negro race'.[41]

Constantine's case was received sympathetically by the British public, who deplored – publicly at least – such blatant and universal American segregation methods as an unwelcome and un-British intrusion. There were other sites of resistance to American methods too. The long-standing popularity among white audiences of black musicians in Britain, whether American or Caribbean, had been largely untarnished by racism. Black bandleaders like 'Snakehips' Johnson, for instance, were radio stars at the height of their careers, and Paul Robeson, the great American bass and film star, was universally revered across the nation. This wide-spread acceptance of black musical culture encouraged the USAAF to establish a 'negro chorus' that performed widely in the UK, opening with two concerts filling the Royal Albert Hall in September 1943. Rudolph Dunbar, a classical clarinettist and conductor from British Guiana, became a noted celebrity in these years too, conducting the London Symphony Orchestra among others at the Albert Hall in 1942 and 1943. And music underpinned the network of 'London's Coloured Clubs', which increased in number as black GIs swelled the clientele. Clustered around Soho, the Bouillabaisse International Club, Frisco's, The Nest, Smoky Joe's, the Shim-Sham, Tig's and more served London's small permanent black population, now greatly enlarged from America and elsewhere.[42]

These clubs also attracted many white women to dance and drink, and where US attitudes did have some sympathetic resonance among the British was over the issue of mixed-race relationships – in these years the 'problem' of black men and white women. 'Would you like your sister to marry a black man?' was asked in a debate on 'The Colour Question' at the Brentford and Chiswick Discussion Group in November 1942. Most would have answered 'no'. This issue was the primary motivation behind the colour bar being extended, with little local adverse reaction, to dances near US Army and Air Force bases. That seems not to have been practised in London, probably because of the difficulty of enforcing any colour bar in its crowded dance halls, where local resentment might have caused a riot. But there were diffi-culties notwithstanding: to give one instance, there was a nasty brawl, with glass tabletops smashed and used as weapons, at the George Hotel in Hammersmith Broadway in September 1943, when an American soldier in the Canadian Army insulted two West Indian soldiers who'd brought in a white woman for a drink.[43]

As the number of troops in the UK – British, US, Canadian and others – massed in huge numbers in the early months of 1944, so did the problem of deserters on the run. Many sought out London as a hiding place, its vast population always offering the promise of succour to the fugitive. Throughout the war it remained also the best place to get papers, the deserter's greatest need: a senior Finsbury council official, a local police constable and a deserter AWOL since 1941 were each given twelve months' imprisonment at the Old Bailey in January 1944 for conspiring to provide forged and stolen identity cards and other papers to army deserters, and there must have been many similar plots that went undetected. Of all the lawbreakers that the Metropolitan Police dealt with in 1944, 'Deserters were the most difficult – and dangerous,' according to Fred Narborough, in charge of the CID in L Division (Lambeth, Battersea and Camberwell). 'They had no identity documents, or forged papers at best. Their worry was the next meal, drop of drink, or bed for the night. They seldom cared how these were obtained.' Those who had undertaken commando or other special forces training were especially difficult for the police to handle.[44]

Whatever a deserter's background, London was full of them. Three army deserters were fined and sent back to their units in January for breaking into a Poplar shop and stealing 20,000 cigarettes: they sold them to a cafe proprietor in the East India Dock Road who was given three months' imprisonment for receiving. In March a Canadian deserter, AWOL for five months, was given four months' hard labour for stealing clothes and a radiogram from an East End house; his accomplice was a Stepney seaman. In the same month a deserter from the Belgian army, living with a twenty-year-old Stepney woman, was given six months' hard labour for stealing furniture. These were East End cases but deserters were a London-wide problem. There were notorious clusters in Soho, Fitzrovia and Notting Hill, all places where generations had long lived on their wits. In May 1944, with the Allied armies keen to reclaim as many men as possible for the forces, US and British military police, aided by the civilian police, conducted sweep searches of Soho nightclubs and West End cinemas, dance halls and hotels. Expecting trouble, the military police fixed bayonets to their rifles.[45]

The Metropolitan Police recorded a big jump in indictable offences reported to them in 1944. These had numbered 95,280 in 1938 and 93,869 in 1940, but rose to 99,533 in 1941; then they fell away to 91,205 in 1943; now, in 1944, they were 103,804 and there would be an even bigger rise next year too. Crime committed by deserters clearly added to these numbers but much petty thieving of the traditional London variety was experienced this year as well. John Harris, the magistrate presiding at Thames Police Court on the riverside, confronted by an unstoppable wave of pilfering from the docks, announced that he had given up fining offenders and promptly sentenced a dock labourer to one month's hard labour for stealing a tin of evaporated milk worth 8½d. Light-fingered fire-watchers stealing factory stock continued to be sent to prison by the courts. There was an 'epidemic' of bicycle thefts reported from Lewisham in January. Hilda Neal's YMCA canteen in the crypt of St Martin-in-the-Fields that April 'started 1s deposit for knife, fork and spoon; thousands get stolen, and we are so short'. Vere Hodgson noted that same month that there were 'No daffodils in the Park – all stolen the minute they come out. Very mean.' And Anthony and Marjorie Heap had their flat south of Euston Road broken into one afternoon in February. His best suit was taken – with turn-ups, presumably – and other clothing, packed in one of their suitcases, but cash, a post office savings book, clothing coupons and more were all fortunately overlooked. The Heaps had to install a new mortise lock on the front door – 'exorbitant cost of 30/-'.[46]

A couple of months later, in the third week of April, Anthony Heap began to notice that there were 'very few soldiers, American or otherwise,' to be seen in the London streets. 'Which naturally leads me to surmise that they are being massed on the coast in readiness for the invasion. Yes, it looks as though that long-threatened event is really about to materialise at last. Anyway if it doesn't take place within the next week or two I doubt if it ever will.'[47]

Londoners had been anxiously anticipating the Allied invasion of the Continent since the early spring began to promise better weather. 'I expected this to be the date of the European invasion,' Dorothy Wells noted in her diary as early as 1 March, 'but nothing yet.' 'Everyone seems to expect the European invasion to start this week,' she thought a fortnight later, 'possibly on March 15th', and six weeks on, in late April, 'The Second Front is imminent.' The delay stoked 'a state of irritable tension' in the nation, but it had a peculiarly threatening dimension in London, where many expected they would suffer immediate and deadly retaliation by the Luftwaffe. '"You'll see London will be bombed day and night when it starts,"' Vivienne Hall heard people say. '"We shall just live in our shelters when it starts" and so it goes on …' By early May she was feeling the tension herself, her nights disturbed by apparently ceaseless formations of Allied bombers heading for France, and the artillery bombardment of the Pas de Calais from Kent, now audible in London:

> I must admit and this is the only place I'll admit it – that my nerves are in a horrid state – each night I determine not to be frightened and doze off uneasily. I wake about 12 to the sound of endless planes and the gunfire and, try as hard as I can, I go through the same stupid shaking. My tummy hates itself and I have to rush upstairs to lose everything in it – the shaking and pain go off after about 10 mins –, but the whole thing's so ridiculous – why should I behave like that?[48]

Unbeknown to Vivienne, and most other Londoners, the capital had played a large but silent part in the invasion preparations, apart from offering respite to hundreds of thousands of American, British and Dominion troops between the summer of 1943 and the spring of 1944. Thames-side boatyards as far upriver as Teddington built various types of landing craft. They included LCTs (landing craft tanks) made on the west side of Barking Reach, on the Isle of Dogs, where the East India Company had once built great wooden ships. Some 1,200 Thames barges, oar-powered, were converted to 'power barge ramps', with 1,000hp engines fitted by Thornycroft of Chiswick and steel ramps added in the bows to deliver military supplies to the beachheads. Between Barking and Erith, components of the Mulberry floating harbours were built. These were 135 'Phoenix units', giant hollow blocks of concrete sixty feet high, which were sunk in the river to hide them from the enemy, then raised again when ready to be towed to France from Tilbury. The great drums or reels for PLUTO, the 'pipeline under the ocean' that brought fuel direct from the Thames estuary refineries to Normandy, were made on the riverside. And at Wanstead Flats, some four miles north of the Thames, huge POW cages were built to receive German prisoners who, if things went well, would be brought into London by river. All these preparations, some of which were put in hand from

1942, were strictly secret. But according to A. P. Herbert, the MP and Royal Navy non-commissioned officer who was helping to defend the Thames, 'The odour of D-Day hung over every reach. We knew nothing, we asked no questions; but we could smell it.' From mid-May dock workers and the port's NFS contingent were 'impounded', having to live in the docks to prevent details of last-minute preparations from leaking out.[49]

In London proper the tension mounted as May wore on. The deceptive withdrawal of troops that Anthony Heap noted in April was followed by a last dash for leave in the final two weeks of May. Maps of Europe were displayed in the ground-floor windows of Fleet Street newspaper offices, with 'the biggest crowd … outside the "Daily Telegraph"'. Then, towards the end of the month, like a cistern emptying, the soldiers withdrew from London again. Bank Holiday trains for the Whit weekend were cut and reserved for soldiers travelling to their disembarkation points or to camps to be held in reserve. BBC newsreaders were ordered to sleep in Broadcasting House from 31 May to be ready for bulletins day or night. News of the fall of Rome reached Londoners' ears on 4 June, but even a few days before, in suburban Harrow, George Beardmore felt that 'A grim kind of exultation is in full flood'. Not for everyone, perhaps, for the tension got to people in different ways. 'Felt rather poorly today,' recorded Dorothy Wells on 5 June, 'heart a bit "dicky" and a touch of rheumatism in the left shoulder'. That night the RAF activity overhead seemed especially relentless. Dorothy 'took it to be an exercise'.[50]

Next morning, 6 June, was D-Day. At first there was no official bulletin. The 8 a.m. BBC news was silent on the matter, though some listeners picked up warnings to the French at that time and German radio was said to have reported landings, so rumour abounded in London. News of the invasion was finally announced on the wireless at 9.45 and heard at home in Lambeth by Nellie Carver. She was on duty at the Central Telegraph Office in the City an hour or so later. 'I went into St Paul's for a few minutes before 11 am. I don't think anyone in there had heard – all was quiet until I reached the office which was seething with excitement.' Anthony Heap had been 'kept awake half the night' by Allied planes so wasn't surprised by the 'vague rumours' heard in St Pancras Town Hall of an invasion. 'But even they didn't detract from the thrill of hearing the official announcement on the radio at lunchtime … So it's happened at last!' In the East End, 'At one o'clock people gathered in the doorways of shops where wireless sets were audible.' There was, though, no public exultation. Rather, people seem to have let the news sink slowly in. Mollie Panter-Downes, writing about Londoners' reactions for an American audience, thought 'Everybody seemed to be existing wholly in a preoccupied silence of his own, a silence which had something almost frantic about it ...' She noted long queues at the newspaper stands later in the day and a 'queer hush' over London. Arthur Williamson, a City solicitor's managing clerk, thought much the same. He wrote to his son Austin, teaching in Edinburgh, on the night of 6 June:

> The City looked deserted to-day no soldiers & no army trucks to be seen. The river too was very quiet and peaceful. It was hard to believe there was a war on ... No balloons up at all to-day & we have had some low flying fighters scorching across at times. All very quiet as I write (11 p.m.) Hope it remains so.[51]

Others hoped so too. 'Well here it is, the long waited dreaded expected looked for second front,' Vivienne Hall noted that day. 'Yet here we are at office having travelled up with no discomfort – how long this will last is of course a different matter.' Everyone knew what was on each other's minds. 'I wonder whether we shall have any heavy raids now?' asked Nellie Carver. 'Some people seem to fear so.'[52]

Yet the days ticked by, with reassuring news from Normandy; the nights too, untroubled but for the Allied flyers overhead continuing to pound German defensive positions and road and rail communications. So passed the 7th, 8th, 9th and 10th. On 11 June, Margery Cossins, a 'paying guest' at a genteel boarding house in Chepstow Villas, Bayswater, made an entry in her journal. Margery was about sixty, a widow, and living in one room in a house shared by others of independent means. 'Everyone is asking "where is the Luftwaffe?" One expected to be visited the first night. Now one thinks they are saving up for something very enormous. We shall see.'[53]

9

IT'S OURS!
13 JUNE–31 DECEMBER 1944

THE first air raid warnings that Londoners had heard for two months sounded in the early morning of Tuesday 13 June 1944. Three brief alerts at 3.45 a.m. for eighteen minutes, 4.12 for twenty-four minutes and 5.03 for forty-four were accompanied by gunfire and one loud explosion. This was at 4.25 a.m. at Grove Road, Bethnal Green. Six people were killed and around thirty more seriously injured. Some twenty houses were demolished or shattered and 200 people were made homeless. The badly damaged railway bridge crossing Grove Road blocked the LNER mainline, disrupting traffic into Liverpool Street Station. Next morning the chaos was reported to have been caused by a German plane brought down by anti-aircraft fire, and indeed a Messerschmitt fighter, probably on a reconnaissance mission, did crash at Barking Marshes around the same time. But the police war diary for 13 June gave the first true inkling that what had hit Bethnal Green that early morning was 'a suspected P.A.C. (pilotless aircraft)'.[1]

This first V-1 announced the beginning of the final phase of the air war against London. For many it was the worst. The *Vergeltungswaffe Eins*, 'revenge' or 'vengeance weapon one', was a jet-engined flying bomb or ballistic missile that looked like a small monoplane, around twenty-five feet long and with a wingspan of seventeen and a half feet. Made of steel and plywood, it carried 850 kilograms (just less than a ton) of HE packed into its nose. Most, though not all, were aimed at central London, the target Tower Bridge; luckily not one found it, though one was said to have passed through the towers, falling in the river nearby. The engine was timed to cut out when a small propeller on the nose had completed a pre-set number of revolutions. It flew at around 350mph at an altitude of some 3,000 feet, though speed and altitude could vary. Once the engine cut out the V-1 would fall to earth, in either a steep dive or a shallower glide; it exploded on contact with the ground, sometimes before in mid-air but at low level. Observers some distance away reported a distinctive white flash, followed by a red flash and a terrific explosion; in built-up areas it raised a huge dust plume hundreds of feet high. Because it didn't bury itself deeply in the ground the V-1 caused little damage to water mains, gas mains or sewers. But its blast capacity was enormous, causing destruction to buildings over a wide radius. The blast caused havoc with people unlucky enough to be caught in it, scattering body parts over a wide area and rendering identification difficult; some people were destroyed without trace. In general, however, fatal casualties were light, although some incidents would prove greatly destructive of life; but the V-1 tended to cause a greater number of injuries compared to normal HE, mainly through flying glass. The proportion of fatalities to injuries in the Big Blitz in London was thought to be 1 to 3.6, but 1 to 7 in the V-weapon attacks.[2]

The first salvo of V-1s that early morning of 13 June totalled ten flying bombs; four reached southern England, three falling harmlessly in the countryside, with only the Grove Road bomb striking the target. The next attack was launched on 15 June, a much more serious affair, with 244 V-1s sent from fifty-five hidden sites in northern France; of these fifty were aimed at Southampton, embarking point of the D-Day invasion force, the rest at London. Of 144 crossing the Channel, seventy-three reached London, two thirds falling short of the central districts and hitting south of the Thames. The V-1s would prove pre-eminently a war on London's southern suburbs, though everywhere was vulnerable and every Londoner would become only too well acquainted with the flying bomb's distinctive growl – 'like a Model-T Ford going up a hill', as it was described at the time.[3]

Between 13 June and 5 September, 2,340 V-1s hit London, on average around twenty-eight a day, and at all hours, day or night. This spread caused difficulties for civil defence, which was better resourced at night, many volunteers at work during the day. The worst weeks were from mid-June through to early August, with 3 August the worst day of all when ninety-seven V-1 incidents were recorded in London. V-1s in this period killed 5,475 Londoners, a little more than two per bomb, and seriously injured nearly 16,000 more. London remained overwhelmingly the main target, though some were aimed at and fell on Southampton, Norwich and a few other cities; many others fell short, causing casualties and damage in a south-east corridor or 'bomb-alley', especially in Kent. The nature of the attack from pilotless planes was briefly announced in a House of Commons statement by Herbert Morrison on 16 June; but London was not given as the main target, the government merely speaking of 'Southern England' when referring to any damage caused.[4]

That night the BBC substituted a recording for Big Ben's chimes to open the main 9 p.m. news, in case the live sound hitherto used picked up a passing V-1 and provided clues for the Germans. Also on 16 June London's barrage balloons – a feature of the wartime cityscape since September 1939 – and the city's mobile AA guns were moved to Kent and the North Downs. Although the first V-1s had been met with ack-ack fire in London this was soon stopped because it couldn't prevent the weapon from causing damage; in any event, AA shells added to the danger. In mid-July 441 static guns in and around London were moved to the coast. Fighter squadrons equipped with planes capable of outstripping the V-1s were boosted in number to shoot down the 'robot' planes over the Channel and open country. These defences proved of great value to Londoners, bringing down 3,463 V-1s in these same hectic twelve weeks, so considerably more than those that got through.[5]

It would be difficult to exaggerate the fear and disruption caused by the V-1, especially in the opening weeks of the campaign. This was the second great hammer blow aimed at London in 1944. The first, the Baby Blitz, had been bad enough. But the peculiar malevolence of this new ordeal, its random mindlessness and its trappings of terror, made it even more difficult to endure. Vivienne Hall lived in Wandsworth, which was hit by 124 V-1s during the whole campaign, a number exceeded only by Croydon's 140. She felt caught up in

a colossal and hideous game of spite; just to send these things over haphazard to make life a chancy unpleasant thing for we miserable and long-suffering Londoners. Ah well, we've had to face up to horrible things for nearly five years, I suppose we shall continue to do so – but, God, how tired we are of it!! ... I thought the blitzes frightening enough but this horrible machine is worse, you are always listening, always waiting for the drone of the machinery which drives the pilotless plane nearer and nearer – oh hell, it's a hateful business.[6]

Nellie Carver's June in West Norwood, Lambeth, a borough that took sixty-nine V-1 hits, might stand for many. On the night of 15 June, in an alert that lasted, she thought, from 11.35 p.m. to 9.35 a.m., 'we were very scared,' the 'planes ... sounded different & much quicker than usual & when our gunners fired at them, it was after they had passed'. Next evening, she read in the newspapers of the 'pilotless planes'. 'This is a horrible development, what can we do with them? ... Up most of the night, such a noise – these things go about 350 miles an hour & roar like express trains.' A day on and she felt, 'This is just like the worst times in 1940 – snatching a few minutes sleep in between the guns thundering & planes roaring.' This day, the 17th, she caught her first glimpse of them in the early evening, 'like small planes, but with fire coming from their tails'. That night 'was noisier & more alarming than Friday: we were dazed with the row & had no sleep again. We certainly cannot stand too much of this.' That was the last use of ack-ack, and from now on 'it was rather alarming to hear sudden crashes in the dark but much easier to bear without gunfire. Once they have crashed you know you are safe ...' Nellie at first found sleep very difficult, 'as unable to get used to this kind of raid', but soon she could 'sleep at intervals'. She and her mother took what precautions they could in their 'shelter' under the stairs: 'We lie down dressed at night & go into cupboard during crashes. In the early hours was an awful one,' and she went to see what had happened: 'Such an awful scene of wreckage, worse than all I'd seen in Blitz ...' On Friday 24 June they were due to spend the coming weekend at a friend's house in rural Gloucestershire but Nellie asked if they could come a day earlier: 'She said "Yes come now" so we hurriedly packed clothes & caught 8.35 pm. Such a lovely calm night.' Back in Lambeth on the Monday she chatted with Mrs Smith, her neighbour, who was an air raid warden and now on almost constant duty. It was Mrs Smith who told Nellie of the new American name for the flying bomb, 'buzz-bomb' or 'bumble-bomb': '"Doodle-bugs" – quite a good name!'[7]

Nellie didn't know it, because the news was kept out of the papers for three weeks, the authorities cautious about revealing locations and no doubt reluctant to give Hitler satisfaction, but the worst incident this June – indeed, the worst of the whole V-1 campaign and one of the worst of the war – was a direct hit on Sunday morning the 18th at the Guards Chapel at Wellington Barracks, Birdcage Walk, on the south side of St James's Park. A special service was in progress and so at 11.20, when the V-1 struck, the chapel was packed. The death toll reached 121, sixty-three of them servicemen and women, with sixty-eight seriously injured. Elisabeth Sheppard-Jones, an ATS subaltern, was in the congregation and heard 'a noise so loud ... as if all the waters and winds in the world had come together in mighty conflict'. She was buried under stone and plaster next to a lifeless soldier. She slowly became aware of rescuers above her: '"Please, please, I'm here," I said, and I went on saying it until my voice was hoarse and my throat ached with the dust that poured down it ...' Eventually someone reached her:

I think I must have been given a morphine injection for I still felt no pain, but I did begin to have an inkling that I was badly injured. I turned my freed head towards a Guardsman who was helping with the rescue work, and hysterically I cried out: 'How do I look? Tell me how I look!' ... 'Madam,' he said, 'you look wonderful to me!'

But her back was broken and she was paralysed from the waist down. She never walked again, though she would go on to write much-loved children's books.[8]

Another serious incident struck central London on the last day of June. Forty-seven V-1s hit the capital that day. Dorothy Wells, who like most Londoners had also endured by this time two weeks of sleepless nights while holding down a full-time job during the day, was in her builders' merchants' in Aldwych, Holborn:

Alert and Danger Signals all the morning. Sandwiches in for lunch. At just after 2p.m. Mr. Shearman came in and we were teasing him about being scared at "Imminent Danger" – when suddenly everything blew in – glass, files, beams etc. A bomb dropped in front of Bush House, and the blast badly affected Aldwych House. The opposite buildings are terribly battered – the post office has disappeared and at least one bus. [Just four members of staff needed treatment for minor cuts.] Wonderful that it was no worse. Dow. [Dowling, her boss] was blown down outside our door, and one of the swing doors fell on him – unhurt but terribly shaken. Most of us got on with the clearing up – a terrible mess – even the partition walls bent and shifted.[9]

Margery Cossins had just finished lunch with a friend in the City – 'atrocious food' – and was on a bus on her way home to Paddington. Along Holborn:

> I suddenly saw some roof watchers running for shelter to a doorway and then peering upwards to the sky, and felt alarmed, but the people in the streets seemed calm till suddenly there was a tremendous bang ... A pillar of smoke went up on my left, and, crossing Kingsway immediately afterwards a great cloud of black smoke seemed to rise in the middle of it from the road.

Cecil King heard what happened from two *Daily Mirror* reporters who had been on the top deck of a City-bound bus that had just entered the Strand. The V-1, which perhaps fell in a long glide because no one mentioned the engine's roar, apparently hit 'the roof of the Air Ministry', Adastral House, on the corner of Kingsway, 'then came into the road, where it went off, completely wrecking two buses' and killing and maiming people in the busy streets around. King ran round to see for himself and 'by the time I arrived the fire brigade and ambulances were there, bleeding girls in ragged clothes were being got down from the first floor of Bush House, a trouserless man was taking refuge in the Air Ministry', a WAAF on a stretcher 'was being pushed into her ambulance, and others with slight cuts were being helped away'. The Aldwych V-1 killed forty-six, with 152 seriously injured; many more were cut by flying glass. Charing Cross Hospital nearby received 220 casualties: 'We were kept busy operating all that Friday afternoon and all through the night, all Saturday and even part of Sunday until all the victims had been dealt with. It was a terrible, a ghastly experience. Many of the patients were very badly mutilated.'[10]

'I think the edge of our fear has worn off,' recorded an uncertain Vivienne Hall around 30 June; 'we sleep now during the nights in our shelters or on our beds, ready to take cover when we hear the engine of the bomb coming toward us – and we all go about our business as usual ... damn, there goes another beauty –'. But adaptation could only be piecemeal. People might speak familiarly of the 'doodles' or discharge their fear with a joke – 'Hitler'll get hisself disliked if he goes on like this!' a woman greengrocer was heard to say in Aldwych just after the V-1 exploded – but much of this just put a brave face on things. That was important, though, as Virginia Graham wittily put it in 'Losing Face' that year:

> This is my doodle-bug face. Do you like it?
> It's supposed to look dreadfully brave.
> Not jolly of course – that would hardly be tactful,
> But ... well, sort of loving and grave.
>
> This is my doodle-bug voice. Can you hear it?
> It's thrillingly vibrant, yet calm.
> If we weren't in the office, which *isn't* the place,
> I'd read you a suitable psalm.
>
> This is my doodle-bug place. Can you see me?
> It's really amazingly snug
> Lying under my desk with my doodle-bug face
> And my doodle-bug voice in the rug.[11]

Londoners, then, bore with things as best they could and counted themselves very lucky if they avoided a close encounter. Many could not. George Orwell and Eileen Blair were blitzed from their flat at Mortimer Crescent, St John's Wood, on 14 July. After squatting in the writer Inez Holden's empty house in George Street, Mayfair, they moved to Canonbury Square, Islington, in early October; Orwell took a barrow back and forth to their uninhabitable flat to retrieve his books. Arthur and Grace Williamson were bombed out of Eynella Road in East Dulwich the day before by a V-1 that landed 'about the length of our garden away from us'. Things had been 'very grim this last month,' she told her son in Edinburgh. 'We have been losing windows regularly almost every day and we have been held together with string.' They moved out to stay with relatives in Hayes, Bromley, 'much quieter than Dulwich', despite being in 'bomb-alley'. Vivienne Hall had to leave 21 Putney Hill when a V-1 landed in the road: 'the house shook all its glass to bits, doors flew in in pieces, ceilings and walls cracked and in some cases broke and all hell seemed to be loose.' She helped some elderly fellow tenants from the wreckage and in a couple of weeks everyone had fled, leaving the house empty. With her mother still in Westmorland, Vivienne took a room in a 'boarding house' in Sudbury, Wembley, not immune from V-1s but less vulnerable than blasted south London.[12]

Government guidance for those likely to be caught at home in a V-1 raid was all about avoiding flying glass – keep windows open, take down mirrors and pictures – but in an emergency people just had to 'take the best available cover: duck under a table, go into an inner passage or under the stairs or behind a thick wall ...' It was all very sensible. But sometimes there was no time. A note in pencil on an 'armaments requisition form', perhaps Home Guard issue, tells of 'The Events Which Took Place during the first Minutes after the V.1. on June 21st 1944'. Neither the writer's name nor his address has come down to us; nor can we pinpoint the incident, because this was just one of thirty-nine 'fly' recorded by police to have hit London that day. He wrote that he and his wife were woken by the noise of the approaching V-1: he was so frightened and his throat so dry he could barely whisper to confirm that it 'was one'. His wife 'jumped from the bed' and prepared to go downstairs to their three young children in the Morrison shelter. He got out of bed too, and 'the hum which had gradually increased suddenly started to become a roar of such increasing volume everything seemed to vibrate. I shouted (for by this time I had found my voice) "It's ours!"' He flung himself on the bed just as his wife opened the bedroom door to go out:

In doing so I turned my face towards the window ... A flame shot across the window obliterating everything else, the houses, the trees, even daylight [and] simultaneously came the explosion. I can only describe this as if all the thunder, bombs and guns I have heard could be made into one tremendous crash, that was it – everything was moving in a most erratic way. I saw the window frames bulge right into the room and the glass fly in every direction ... The window board, in one piece, was coming straight at me, but fell short, the ceiling itself crashed on my head. Mid all this turmoil I could hear the tiles on the roof sliding as an avalanche and crashing on the cement path below. Broken glass was tinkling down everywhere, while the rumble of falling masonry seemed as if it would never cease. [He got to his feet.] The dust was so thick, I could not see more than a yard in front of me, picking my way down the stairs, inches deep in plaster. At the bottom I had to step with caution over a heap of wood that had once been our front door, hall table and hat rack. My wife by this time was in the shelter room where the whole glass door had been sucked in the room, in a thousand pieces, smashing the door into the hall.

The children were safe. Two had heard nothing till woken by the explosion. Their two pet birds, hanging in cages either side of the bay window and still swinging from the blast, 'were singing for all they were worth ...' When he went into the road, all around was devastation, their house and many of their neighbours', largely demolished over their heads.[13]

The V-1s would remain unrelenting through most of July. On the 6th Winston Churchill gave further details to the House of Commons about the flying bomb onslaught. He made plain to the country for the first time that London was the target and that the V-1 was causing immense damage there. At last everyone knew of the Londoners' predicament: 'poor old London has had the largest share,' Nellie Carver noted; 'we in London feel very depressed. We've had so much to put up with & Winston sees no end to the attack until the Troops take the bases ... Well – we must be patient, I suppose.' The V-1s were received rather differently by some on Wanstead Flats. Cyril Demarne of the NFS attended an incident nearby on 13 July: 'As we toiled, several V1s roared across the sky and there came a chorus of "Sieg Heil, Sieg Heil," from hundreds of German throats in the P.O.W. camp, a few hundred yards along the road.'[14]

Among some notable incidents this month one stands out. Towards the end of July there occurred one of those ghastly catastrophes of London's air war that had punctuated the months since September 1940. Like many others, it involved large numbers of civilians caught in the wrong place at the wrong time. Lewisham was the third-worst-hit borough, receiving 117 V-1s in the whole campaign. On the 26th Lewisham LCC Hospital had been badly damaged by a V-1 which set some wards ablaze; there were around seventy casualties, mainly among the patients, three of whom subsequently died. The consequences would have been far worse but for the heroism of staff, 'rescue squads, soldiers, firemen, police, priests and ministers, W.V.S... .' and others. 'Above all,' wrote Sister Gwyneth Thomas, who had been in the thick of it, 'I take my hat off to the firemen.' Two days later, Friday 28 July, an exhausted Sister Thomas was ordered to take the day off by Matron. She decided to get away to some friends out of London but, as an afterthought, turned back to her quarters to pick up some things to take with her for safe keeping at her friends' house:

Just that little act saved me from either being killed or injured; when I did get out by the bus stop, a bus was just leaving so I missed it. There was no warning, but a bomb passed over, and dropped on the market place, about 2 minutes ride in the bus in the direction I was going. I got on the second bus, not knowing then that the bomb had blocked the road, so when we reached Lewisham shopping centre, it was to be met with such a sight I shall never forget, or wish to see again. Marks & Spencer was ablaze, people trapped, screaming, dead, lying in the roadway, girls with hair and clothes alight, could be seen running wildly in the blazing building, a girl with half her scalp off, an old lady lying naked in the roadway, people running everywhere, shouting, screaming, dying, burning. This was hell with all its fury let loose, no battlefield could be worse, or more bloody. Suddenly, as if out of the air, ambulances, vans of all description, fire services, rescue squads, all working like fury. I just felt sick, but got out of the bus. (The one before it was caught and all its occupants injured.) ... Eventually I reached the station; never have I had a bigger fight to keep from screaming, so at last I reached my friends, and there I broke down. I suppose I knew there was no need to fight any more – I collapsed and screamed and Hilda gave me brandy.[15]

With no alert there had been little time to seek shelter. Some fifty-one were killed and 216 injured. Because of the damage previously caused to Lewisham Hospital some of the wounded were taken to hospitals in Maidstone and even Cardiff.[16]

The swift response of civil defence was a prominent feature of the V-weapons campaign. A V-1 did not pose the same challenges as did heavily blitzed areas in 1940–41, or the Baby Blitz, where incidents merged to form large areas of devastation. The V-1 was immensely destructive but each event was readily circumscribed. 'Surprising how *localised* these explosions are,' George Beardmore, working for Harrow civil defence, wrote at the time. When fires were started, as they were in 38 per cent of incidents, they never coalesced in a conflagration and could usually be rapidly dealt with. The isolated nature of each V-1 explosion lent itself to some civil defence refinements. Lookouts with good local knowledge were posted on NFS training towers or on the roofs of control centre buildings to identify 'the fall of "fly"' and imme-diately dispatch town hall incident officers, marked out by blue covers over their civil defence helmets, and an 'Express Light Rescue Service' to the spot; the incident officer would then call in heavy rescue, fire crews and ambulances as necessary. When incident officers decided they were needed, the WVS greatly assisted the civil defence response by running 'Incident Inquiry Points' to help identify casualties and missing persons, information pieced together from wardens' and fire guards' local censuses of who lived where and who might be away from home. A council information officer would then contact next of kin. The terrible impact of blast on bodies was distressing to survivors but daylight incidents attracted sightseers, dubbed 'Raid Gogglers' or 'Raid Ghouls', who obstructed the effective deployment of civil defence and medical help; a number cycled to any incident near at hand to get a ringside view. Many householders whose homes were uninhabitable but not destroyed would not go to rest centres for fear of looting and waited till council staff had docketed and removed their belongings for safe keeping. The WVS mobile canteens helped enormously here by providing hot drinks and sandwiches while people huddled near their blitzed homes. The WVS helped too in the rest centres where the homeless who had nowhere else to go were taken for respite and then helped to find a new place to live, though in some badly hit boroughs that was not easily done.[17]

At the incidents themselves the heavy lifting fell, literally, to the wardens and the rescue squads, supplemented in these months by Home Guard, soldiers on leave and even American GIs: 'One giant U.S. truck bore the words "Crazy Yank" across the bonnet; it was right in the thick of the damage where the soldiers were co-operating with local services.' But it was the local services themselves that bore the brunt, often with great camaraderie, as in Streatham, SW16 – mainly Wandsworth but taking in small parts of Lambeth and Croydon – where civil defence efforts on Streatham's forty-one V-1s were celebrated in a collective memoir published in 1945. There were many instances of heroism by ordinary Londoners acting with extraordinary fortitude and daring. One might stand for many. In July a V-1 fell in Commercial Road, Stepney. Among people trapped was Harry Sullivan, a docker, buried under tons of 'live debris' in a cellar, pinioned by his feet, which were badly crushed. Unable to reach him from above, the heavy rescue team leader, Reg Freeman, and his driver, George Bracci, went next door, pulled the fireplace from the adjoining cellar, broke through a wall two and a quarter feet thick and crawled through, working debris backwards as they went. They propped up joists to protect Sullivan, who was in great pain, from falling debris. Their tunnelling took two hours and it took a further five to free Sullivan and pull him clear. They, or a doctor – doctors would sometimes hand a syringe to a rescue worker instead of crawling in themselves – injected Sullivan with two 'quarters' of morphine, the maximum dose: '"Mr. Sullivan was one of the most wonderful men I have ever met,"' Freeman said later. '"He was in terrible agony and suffering all the time. He was a marvellous man and certainly went through something."' Freeman and Bracci who, as driver, was not expected to help with the rescue, were awarded the British Empire Medal; Harry Sullivan survived his ordeal. 'All reports show,' concluded a Home Office report, 'that the work of the [Civil Defence] Services has never been better. They have been helped by the fact that incidents are single ones, but it is only through long and intensive training that an almost clock-work precision has been reached. Many incidents have been cleared up within an hour.'[18]

IN many ways this was London's most unnerving time of the whole war. Even steady hands began to shake. On 27 June, Herbert Morrison had been so dismayed by the V-1 attack that he asked the War Cabinet to consider using poison gas against Germany. And on 6 July, the day of his statement to the Commons, Churchill recommended that all means of retaliation, including gas and biological attack, be considered as a means of getting Germany to stop the onslaught. The idea never went anywhere but that it was contemplated at all is an indication of an unwonted moment of panic at the pinnacle of the home front.[19]

Most Londoners, their memories perhaps dulled by three preceding years of tumultuous events, thought the V-1s even worse than the Big Blitz. Bill Regan, in Poplar heavy rescue, found his colleagues all of one mind: 'Peculiarly, everyone is unanimous in their dislike of these things … There is not one man I know, who is getting used to it; if anything, it is getting everyone down. The sound of a motor far or near, brings everyone to their feet, with no exceptions.' That was early in the campaign, 27 June, but there is no indication of a change of heart before he discontinued his diary in mid-August. More than a normal share of courage offered no immunity. Evelyn Waugh, a former Royal Marine commando and almost recklessly brave, had withstood what he'd experienced of the Big Blitz with equanimity; but he confessed to his wife he found the V-1 'very unnerving'. 'One gets into the habit of listening to motor-cars & wondering if they are bombs, which distracts one from rational pleasure during the day & keeps one awake at night. I did not at all enjoy my few days in London …' Albert Turpin had fought through the blitz in the AFS and London Fire Brigade in Bethnal

Green but now 'most people, including myself, confessed that for the first time since the horrible business began they were good and frightened'. Cyril Demarne, who had a senior position in the West Ham fire brigade in 1940–41, found the V-1 'terrifying'. 'It is impossible to describe the nervous tension' of hearing the bomb approach with its 'shattering roar, like that of a dozen motor cycles with open exhausts,' and then waiting for it to fall. 'Anyhow there are fierce fights between people who would rather have the Blitz and people who would rather have the bugs,' the novelist Bryher wrote to a friend living outside London. 'I think the bugs are worse myself but it is a moot point.' Many others, it seems, shared her preference. 'Do you find that the flying bombs are more or less trying than the blitz of 1940–41?' Gallup asked in August; 44 per cent thought they were more trying and 27 per cent thought less.[20]

The context, of course, contributed to people's difficulties here. The peculiarly wearing circumstances accompanying the V-1 onslaught got everyone down. Londoners felt they had done more than 'their bit' in 1940–41. The Baby Blitz was a reminder that the war still had a terrible sting in the tail for them. Then D-Day seemed to promise the rapid bonus for Londoners that airfields in northern France and Belgium might be quickly overrun. Now this terrible robot weapon, both indiscriminate and inhuman, disrupting every hour of day and night, was causing horrible deaths and bottomless destruction, and though there might be an end in sight no one could tell just when that would be. As a working-class London woman recorded by a Mass Observer in late June remarked, 'If they don't do something to stop them soon we shall go mad, that's all I've got to say.' But it didn't stop. No wonder that some just couldn't stand any more. By the end of August there was a rash of suicides where inquests were told the victims were 'Worried over Air Raids'.[21]

THE V-1s drove Londoners to their shelters once more. In the tubes some 75,000–80,000 a night were sheltering in June and July. They included Hilda Neal, driven by fear of the V-1s to use the Albert Hall tunnel at South Kensington tube: she nearly fell victim to a sneak thief there, but wideawake Hilda scared him off. The numbers in the tubes now were around 15,000 more than had regularly used them in the Baby Blitz. At that time there had been something of a campaign to open the deep shelters, never yet used after their completion in 1941–2, but it had been resisted by government. There was now, by the end of June, a fragmentary agitation to open them against this new terror weapon, and Clement Attlee was reported to have visited women from 'Southern England' who had petitioned Downing Street. On 6 July a question in the Commons after the Prime Minister's statement elicited the promise from Churchill that now the deep shelters would be available for Londoners. Over the next three weeks, starting on 9 July, five of the eight deep shelters were opened, three south of the river (Stockwell, the first, Clapham North and Clapham South) and two north (Camden Town and Belsize Park, the last to be opened, on 23 July). They had the combined capacity to shelter 40,000; tickets for bunks were allocated to local councils and distributed on application, with families and elderly people prioritised. In fact, they were underused; the highest number of shelterers in all of them together on any one night was 12,297 on 29 July. Even so, they were highly appreciated. '"This is a thousand times better than the tubes,"' reported one Stockwell shelterer. '"It's all clean and new, there are canteens, not to mention washing facilities. They even send your laundry away for you if you like."' Opening hours were 6 p.m. to 8 a.m., canteen prices were low – supper and breakfast could be had for 1s – and lights were out by 11 p.m. to encourage regular habits.[22]

Public shelter accommodation everywhere in London had greatly improved from the under-resourced improvisation of 1940–41, with bunks, lighting and heating now pretty much standard. Many took advantage of the better conditions. Elsie Whiteman and Kathleen Church-Bliss, the workers at Morrisons Engineering in Croydon, were driven into the public shelters on Duppas Hill after some scary nights from V-1s spent in a downstairs room at home. After a couple of near misses Anthony and Marjorie Heap spent their nights in the cellar of an industrial firm now designated a public shelter just south of Euston Station: 'This is definitely September '40 all over again,' Anthony thought. But the surprise of the V-1 campaign was the excellence of the strengthened street shelters, which stood up 'wonderfully' to blast. London Civil Defence Region reported them to be 'universally and deservedly popular', perhaps especially so in the poorer streets where accommodation was cramped and a place of safety hard to find. Generally, though, people stayed at home, some people in the suburbs feeling the need to provide strengthened cellars or make other provision now for the first time during the war. The Anderson too continued to do its job and the Morrison 'table shelter' became increasingly popular and respected.

Arthur Buddell, whose civil service duties had shifted from Cardiff, where he'd been since November 1940, back to London a few days before D-Day, slept with his wife, May, in a Morrison in their Croydon dining room (their daughter, Mary, had been shipped out to relatives in the country) and many middle-class families bought their own Morrisons and did the same. Buddell's niece, Lily, had been killed by a V-1 in Forest Hill, Lewisham, in June and no one in outer south London could afford to take chances any more. As some indication of the balance of shelter choices at this time we might consider the results of a Paddington census on the night of 3 July, when some 21,400 shelterers were surveyed: 3,470 were in the borough's tube stations, 4,219 in public shelters in basements, 5,383 in street surface shelters, 4,658 in Andersons and 3,624 were sheltering at home in other ways.[23]

It was only to be expected, though, that the peculiar terrors of the V-1 – and the fact that it was a weapon overwhelmingly used against Londoners alone – would drive many from London altogether. Official evacuation plans were dusted off once the V-1 campaign got fully under way and on 1 July the LCC was asked by government to organise and operate a scheme not just for London Region but for those south-eastern districts in bomb-alley. The first parties of schoolchildren accompanied by teachers, and homeless mothers with children under five, left on 5 July and groups were added throughout that month – other mothers with young children, children in the London hospitals, the old and infirm and so on. In this way over 307,000 were evacuated to officially arranged billets, mostly in the North, North-West, the West Country and Wales: anywhere other than London was generally very safe. In addition, over 550,000 were given travel warrants and 'billeting-certificates' to arrange their own accommodation. Expectant mothers and the evacuation of residential nurseries brought the total of those getting government help to leave London to 'not far short' of a million people; that was more in a month than had left in the eight months of the Big Blitz. In the third quarter, July–September 1944, 1.1 million removals from London were registered in official counts, though the net loss was 752,000 because there were still new arrivals and some who left had moved back by the end of September. Many of the leavers were middle-class people with no need for official assistance. London had been a city of 8.75 million in mid-1939. At the end of September 1944 its civilian population had fallen to 5,887,000; the figure for the end of July would certainly have been lower. This period of the V-1 campaign was London's wartime population low point, in many ways the capital's wartime nadir. For those left behind there was one compensation: 'the shopkeepers were suddenly very cordial.'[24]

In general, the evacuation went far more smoothly than in September 1939, though the railways, now with military demands on them, were not what they might have been. Given the state of the war in France, everyone could see that this would be a short-term arrangement. That, and the seemingly endless punishment taken by the Londoners, prompted a spirit of generosity in the reception areas that some had found lacking five years before. No doubt too, Londoners had learned from that first bruising encounter and were able to equip their children better; anyway, this was high summer when wellington boots and warm clothing were inessentials. A Mass Observation survey recorded hosts in the reception areas being pleasantly surprised by the low numbers of those they considered 'slum dwellers' sent to them. Though the children seemed easier to handle, adults were more shaken than in previous evacuations. WVS helpers in the reception areas noted many adult evacuees describing themselves as 'nervy'. One from Ashburton in Devon thought the evacuees were in a far worse mental state than in the main blitz. They needed more counselling to talk them through their individual traumas than had been necessary in 1940–41, perhaps because each V-1 seemed such a personal assault on those on the receiving end.[25]

Londoners were grateful for the help they received in the reception areas. Well, usually. Unaccompanied children seem to have been made more at home than those mothers who had brought their babies and toddlers with them. Bath was singled out by the *South London Press* for its 'smug' residents who made Londoners feel unwelcome and similar criticism was doled out to the people of Blackpool and Leeds. It led to a bit of a spat, provincial municipal honour stoutly defended, but it showed that Londoners' wounds of 1939–40 were still tender. And only they knew what they were going through in the summer of 1944.[26]

THE last two weeks of June and the four weeks of July were the worst, though there was a very brief lull around 11–12 July. From 7 August, Bank Holiday Monday, the numbers of V-1s reaching London were noticeably reduced, though they continued to arrive daily, sometimes causing numerous deaths and injuries. From about 15 August, as V-1 launching sites were moved back from the advancing Allied front line, the numbers reaching London declined still further, though every day and most nights were marked by several V-1 explosions and some days dozens died, again mostly south of the river. On the 26th no V-1 was recorded in the capital, though they resumed for the next five days. Then, on 1 September, no bomb reached London, the ground-launching units having all moved to Holland, Belgium and Germany and reoriented to attack targets on the Continent. A salvo of nine aimed at the capital was launched by air in the early morning of 5 September but none was recorded falling in Greater London.[27]

A full programme of holidays at home had been planned for London's parks and town halls since April, but London was not the place to be in the summer of 1944. 'Such lovely summer weather,' as Nellie Carver said at the end of July, 'if we could enjoy same.' If people could get away for their holidays they did. In August, Nellie took her mother to stay with friends out of London for ten days or so, Nellie sleeping there too but coming up to Waterloo Station each day to work in the City. 'Waterloo was a sight! I've never seen anything like the crowds & the heat,' with 'heaps of people going away for the Hols. good luck to them'. The Heaps themselves got away to Marjorie's parents for a week in Somerset, 'the complete antidote to London at the moment – and never was an antidote more acceptable'. That was late June, but they had another week there in August too. Vere Hodgson, the social worker in North Kensington, had a week in the Cotswolds with her mother. At the end of July she recorded that the 'Crowds at Paddington today were the largest in living memory. They had to close it for two hours, and admit people in batches. Ban is lifted from Devon and Cornwall, and people are going there. I don't blame them.'[28]

When no flying bombs reached London in early September, the relief of Londoners was heartfelt. 'Great days for poor old London,' Nellie Carver noted in her diary for 1–3 September: 'no "Alerts" day or night. We cannot believe it after all these weeks from June 15th. Have had long peaceful nights of sleep – undressing properly for the first time since they started,' eleven weeks before. On 5 September it seemed that the reason for the lull was made plain: 'A strong rumour swept London this afternoon that Germany had capitulated,' reaching Dorothy Wells in her bomb-scarred office in Aldwych, but sadly it was 'Denied in the final evening editions' of the London papers. There was some genuine good news a couple of days later, though, when it was announced that the blackout was at last to be lifted a little, with curtains to be sufficient in residential dwellings before the end of the month. But the best news of all came on 7 September at a press conference given by Duncan Sandys, the Prime Minister's son-in-law, who had been coordinating Britain's response to the anticipated secret-weapon threat since April 1943. 'Except possibly for a few last shots,' he promised, 'the Battle of London is over.' Sandys confirmed that 92 per cent of V-1 casualties were in London Region, but he also revealed that without effective defences things could have been much worse: on 28 August, when 101 V-1s aimed at London approached the coast, ninety-seven were shot down and just four got through.[29]

Sandys's statement had, Vivienne Hall thought, a worrying effect. She had been on holiday in Norfolk from the beginning of September and returned on the 11th:

> Home all too soon in a crowded train. The Government announcement that the flying bombs were over and that dim-out not blackout will be the order of the winter had made people rush back to London – I feel that they are too soon and that there is still a possibility of another smack for us, but there they were, all crowded on to the train with dogs, flowers, all stages of children and aged relatives, returning to London.[30]

In fact, the return of evacuees who had fled London wholesale in June and July had begun in August, while the V-1s were fewer though still deadly. Part of this early movement back was probably due to mothers willing to take their chance in London with a diminished bombardment in preference to staying in reception areas where they felt out of place. Whatever the reason, the return spelt problems. When the coast seemed clear in early September and the return became a rush, 'serious' food shortages were reported in south London: 'Women are trying to buy all the things they could not get during evacuation, when many were billeted in country villages with only one store which could hardly meet the needs of the local inhabitants.' There was also a bureaucratic headache, with mothers having to queue for long periods to change food cards registered at their reception area addresses and then queue again for the food they wanted. And billeting officers found themselves asked to do the impossible: 'Even when their homes are still uninhabitable some are coming back ... We have to send them to [poor law] institutions until houses can become available.'[31]

*

Duncan Sandys's statement that 'the Battle of London is over' would haunt him for some time to come. Next day, Friday 8 September, at 6.43 p.m., Nellie Carver was dozing after getting home from work. She was 'Awakened by a bang like a gun in the distance, but no alert or anything further'. The first V-2 to hit the UK fell at Staveley Road, Chiswick, just north of the Thames at a bend in the river. A few seconds later another fell harmlessly in open farmland at Epping, outside London Region. Police recorded the Chiswick explosion as killing three people and injuring twenty, light casualties given that it demolished ten houses and caused 'extensive damage to many others'; 'the cause is at present unknown'.[32]

The V-2 was a formidable weapon, of world-beating technological ingenuity. A rocket as tall as a four-storey building and five feet across at its widest point, its warhead was packed with 1,000 kilograms of HE, so not much more than the V-1. Flying at a speed of up to 3,600mph, reaching a height of fifty or sixty miles, it was undetectable and unstoppable. Its supersonic flight in the earth's atmosphere was signalled with a sonic boom and moments later by the explosion as it struck at 2,200mph, leading to a double 'thunderclap' heard frequently by everyone in London over the next six months. Because it gave no warning at all of its approach, no alert could be sounded or evasive action taken. The damage it caused was very different from the V-1. The V-2 buried itself in the ground, its crater some fifteen feet deep. It caused great wreckage to subterranean services like sewers, water and gas mains, and it demolished nearby buildings. But its blast was curtailed by the depth at which it exploded and so proved less damaging to wide areas and generally was less destructive of human life – unless there was an unlucky strike in a crowded place.[33]

The V-2 launch sites in Holland were hard to detect from the air and so at first were impossible to attack. The government was keen to prevent any knowledge of the whereabouts of V-2 landings reaching German ears, so there was an intelligence blackout that lasted until November before the use of such a weapon was officially disclosed. At first the Chiswick explosion and a few that followed were ascribed to faulty gas mains – 'flying gas mains', some Londoners dubbed them. In fact, people worked out what was going on very quickly. Nellie Carver recorded the subsequent V-2 attacks in her diary, for wherever they fell pretty much all Londoners heard, and sometimes felt, them. None was launched on 9 September, but then three landed on the night of 10/11

September, one near Dartford in Kent and the others further away still, yet audible in parts of London. 'Heard a few more loud bangs – not very near,' Nellie noted. 'They seem to think they are rockets fired from guns. I thought we've been too quiet. Went to Church in evening – very draughty – all the windows out.' By the 12th, when four V-2s struck Kew, Dagenham, Bromley and Rochford in Essex, the dots were being joined together. 'Another bang at 6.30 pm – generally supposed now to be V2 (Rockets). Its nasty having no warning, but so far they are only a few.' Sixteen reached London between 8 and 17 September, when Allied advances in Europe caused a hiatus of a week or more.[34]

Unfortunately, Duncan Sandys's 'few last shots' for the V-1 proved an understatement. Overrunning the French launch sites had seemed to knock that menace on the head. But from 16 September the V-1 offensive resumed, with the flying bombs now launched (as a few had been before) in darkness from planes based in Germany. That night at least nine were released; five were shot down, two fell in open countryside and two hit London, at Woolwich and Barking. Thirteen Londoners were killed. Between then and 14 January 1,200 V-1s would be fired; many failed, were aimed at other targets in Europe or were destroyed by AA fire and fighters, but sixty-six landed on London. From 3 October the V-2 assault resumed from launch sites near The Hague, and for the rest of the year London was under attack from both V-weapons. In October thirty-two V-2s hit London, increasing to eighty-two in November and falling back to forty-seven during December. On 10 November the Prime Minister finally informed the House of Commons that Britain was under attack from V-2 rockets, something Londoners had worked out for themselves two months before. He did not, however, state that London was the target.[35]

The worst event of the whole V-2 campaign against London happened on Saturday 25 November. At 12.20 p.m. a V-2 landed behind shops in New Cross Road, Deptford, opposite the town hall and close to the station. Woolworth's and a Co-operative store, both crowded with shoppers, were totally destroyed, with passers-by and road traffic caught in the mayhem. One man on the spot recalled six months later, 'Old women and children were being brought out of the wreckage, all dead, one after another.' The death toll reached 168, the highest through enemy action of any single incident in London's war, only eclipsed by the catastrophic accident at Bethnal Green tube twenty months earlier.[36]

This was dreadful ill fortune, while testifying to the destructive power of this new form of warfare. Despite that, most Londoners were far less worried by the V-2 than by the V-1. The arrival of the rockets did little to deter the return to London – the population at the end of December had picked up to 6.3 million, 422,000 more than three months before. The V-2 had nothing of the spooky terror of the V-1, heard from a distance, getting closer and closer before the engine cut or passed on. They were something to worry about. But with the V-2, 'What I says is if your name's on it you'll get it. No good worrying 'cos you can't do anything about it.' Most would have agreed with that labouring-class sixty-year-old man from south-east London whose opinion was jotted down by Mass Observation. Or the young working-class woman who said, 'I don't mind them as much as the others. We haven't had any damage from them', reflecting the widespread destruction caused by the V-1 and the circumscribed impact and relatively small numbers, in comparison, of the V-2. Not everyone would have agreed with A. P. Herbert that the V-1 'was surely by far the worst thing [Hitler] did to London', but most would. Both weapons, however, revealed Hitler's insatiable malevolence, even as it became plain to the world that his days were numbered and his time fast running out. This was plainly understood by Londoners at the time and it bred a consequent steeliness in their hearts. Anthony Weymouth, the Harley Street physician living in Marylebone, felt in November 'that public opinion here is hardening towards the enemy. The German people are now held to be responsible for the war itself and its conduct. Their guilt is increasing as they remain passive to these various brutal acts' – he meant the V-weapons – 'acts which they admit can do nothing to help them to victory.' Some weeks before, at the outset of the V-2 campaign, Kathleen Tipper, in Woolwich, not normally vindictive, put it more pithily: 'How the RAF and American Air Force are pounding Germany. I think all Londoners are enjoying it at last.'[37]

THE public statements of July from the Prime Minister and of September from Sandys, together with news coming out of the capital, had all clarified that London was the special target of the V-weapons and that Londoners were overwhelmingly the victims. In many areas of the country there was a great deal of sympathy for Londoners, now taking it again as they had in 1940–41. During the Big Blitz, eventually, many other cities would come to take it too, and others had suffered since.

This time, though, Londoners were facing up to these new and vicious terrors pretty much alone, and other parts knew little or nothing about the dreadful ordeal they were living through. Sympathy prompted generous action, first in the reception areas taking evacuees in July, though there were – inevitably perhaps – criticisms. But the Londoners' plight found a wholehearted response in two other directions in particular. First, during July and August, provincial volunteers enrolled to help out stretched London services: the GPO asked for volunteers to come to London to help run telephone exchanges and young women arrived from all over the country in July. Even more impressively, air raid wardens across England volunteered to come to London to assist their metropolitan colleagues deal with the V-1 menace. Given the risks involved, this was a remarkable gesture of solidarity. Just over a thousand provincial wardens came to London and were distributed to the forty-three local authorities (out of ninety-five) who had asked for this extra aid. Most gave up their annual holidays to help London out. The whole scheme worked well and the London regional commissioners felt it had 'done much to draw London and the provinces more closely together'. It was true enough, and not just the provinces. Messages of support for London flew in from cities at home and abroad, including from Mayor La Guardia in New York. Closer to home, the help could be more concrete. Nottingham wardens and the city council 'adopted' Lewisham for special aid, offering that blitzed borough's wardens respite weekends and holidays in the Midlands; some gave even more, because a Nottingham warden, James Gray, was killed by a V-1 in Lewisham during the campaign. Other Midlands towns clubbed together to pay for a treat for Southwark civil defence – 200 were taken downriver from Hampton Court to Windsor and given a free lunch at the Castle.[38]

A similarly generous movement took place among the WVS. This was the year that they really came into their own, developing a niche for themselves in civil defence operations as well as building on their evacuation experience once more in the reception areas. In July and August some 1,971 women came to London for a week or more to work in post-raid services at information points, in rest centres and in mobile canteens at incidents. Even more important was the 'good neighbour' or 're-homing' scheme from late 1944 onwards. This also capitalised on provincial sympathy for London's renewed plight by collecting surplus furniture and domestic appliances from householders in the shires and towns. With a touch of brilliance, counties and cities were invited to 'adopt' individual boroughs in London, practical sympathy encouraged by posting photos of blitzed neighbourhoods and families from the chosen areas in church halls and elsewhere. Once the furniture arrived in London, the boroughs' WVS volunteers arranged for secure storage and then distribution of the furniture on a points system borrowed from rationing. Councils identified families whom they had rehoused as homeless; those whose houses had been completely destroyed were given priority in fixing up a new one from the WVS stores. There were some internal transfers within London too – Holborn residents were asked to help Bethnal Greeners in October 1944, for instance – but it was help from outside that proved so useful. The results were very impressive. Warwickshire adopted Shoreditch (Solihull alone sent sixteen and a half tons of furniture and gadgets, '7,500 articles, large and small', from mid-January 1945), Lincolnshire was twinned with Leyton, Derbyshire with Stoke Newington, Shropshire adopted Hackney (where early loads included 'sideboards, tables, chairs, mattresses, eiderdowns, pillows, blankets, sheets, crockery and other kitchen equipment'), Hampshire adopted Deptford and so on. Gifts of children's toys from Belgium and Australia and no doubt elsewhere were distributed through the same WVS system. Not everywhere in the provinces was so open-handed. The Lord Mayor of Birmingham declared himself 'ashamed of his city' in its lack of generosity to Islington, its adopted borough: its target was twenty vanloads of goods but 'Up to now [early February 1945] we have only collected one vanload, and at the present rate I don't think we shall ever see ten.'[39]

THE society photographer Cecil Beaton returned to London in late September 1944 after a trip to America that had lasted almost a year. He was in for a shock. 'The flying bombs and those beastly V2s, exploding from out of nowhere, have created new havoc,' he thought:

I was stunned to see such wreckage to poor inoffensive streets which contain no more important a target than a pub at the crossroads. Miles of pathetic little dwellings have become nothing but black windowless façades. Old, torn posters hang from scabrous walls, the leaves on trees have changed to yellow under a thick coating of cement powder. Nothing has been given a wash or a lick of paint. Everything's so shabby and sordid.[40]

The 'havoc' in London was indeed immense. Up to the end of May 1944, after nearly four years of intermittent, sometimes ferocious and sustained, bombing 1.4 million houses in London had been damaged by enemy action. Of these 84,611 were completely destroyed or damaged beyond repair, and a further 155,258 had been seriously damaged, some not habitable. Many of these were destroyed or damaged in 1940-41, since when great strides had been made to make habitable those houses not past saving. The Baby Blitz had undone much good work and left a backlog of repairs that was still being made good when the first V-1 struck six weeks later. Now, in the 107 days from 15 June to 30 September 1944, over a million more houses had been damaged in London; 25,511 had been completely destroyed and 129,307 seriously damaged, some no longer habitable. In the sustained attack of July some 21,000 houses a day were being damaged or destroyed in London. These were huge figures in a short period of time, and from early September through the rest of the year the toll of the V-2s and a continuing tally of V-1s was adding to the totals every day. By the end of the war, 88 per cent of houses in Streatham would be damaged; in Croydon 56,968 would be struck and 1,032 completely destroyed.[41]

The London housing crisis brewing in early 1944 with the Baby Blitz became a full-scale catastrophe in the autumn. Fairly or not, the failure to keep up with the pace of damage inflicted by the V-1 came to be seen as a national scandal. On 7 October *Picture Post*'s main feature highlighted 'London's Bombed Houses: A Defeat on the Home Front'. In contrast to 'the story of an organisational triumph for giving immediate help to bombed-out people' in the rest centres and town hall one-stop shops, this was 'another aspect of the Battle of London – the tragic failure to speed the repair of damaged houses'. The article cited the case of Elmfield Road, Balham, in Wandsworth, where over a hundred houses had been damaged. Many residents had gone away but some of those who stayed had been waiting eleven weeks and more for repairs; some roofs stripped of their tiles didn't even have a tarpaulin to cover them. Discontent was bubbling over into collective action, with associations formed, petitions collected, protest meetings held. *Picture Post* called for more builders and materials and for 'an *ad hoc* Central Repair Organisation' to get a grip.[42]

Repairing London's housing now became an emergency for the nation as a whole. Before the V-1s, 28,000 men were working on London housing repairs. Once the V-1s began to fall, the armed services released building workers from the ranks and assigned 2,000 from the Pioneer Corps to London, despite the needs of the British Army in Normandy; the Royal Marines, RAF and other army units provided an additional 2,700 men. By August 60,000 were employed on London repairs, in September 100,000 including 45,000 from the provinces, even from as far away as Scotland. By November there were 112,000, in December 132,000. By the New Year 40 per cent of the nation's building workers were humping bricks and nailing slates in London. By then, a new organisation had indeed been set up to run the show under the Ministry of Works, where the hapless Duncan Sandys was the incoming minister; the London Repairs Executive was in action before its first official meeting on 1 December, with Sir Malcom Trustram Eve, a distinguished barrister, Great War veteran and chairman of the War Damage Commission, as its highly effective head.[43]

How could all these provincial building workers find somewhere to live in this battered city when even Londoners were desperate for housing? There was no easy solution. Some 3,000 were put up in huts and houses in Onslow Square, South Kensington, in places originally intended for French refugees. A second hutted camp was quickly assembled at Wembley Stadium and hostels formerly used for refugees from Gibraltar, now returned, were passed on to building workers. In Croydon some 1,250 men were housed in 'schools and other buildings', and in West Norwood, Lambeth, builders publicly thanked residents for all the offers of billets they had received. But there were problems too. Forty builders were put up in a boarding house on Duppas Hill, Croydon; they complained of filthy living conditions, poor food and no shelter during raids. There was reportedly nowhere for building workers in Hackney Wick to get a hot meal on Sundays, when British Restaurants were closed. Provincial building workers struck for a day in Lewisham in early December over inadequate billets and there was trouble later that month among men who found themselves working in verminous houses at Porthcawe Road, Sydenham, Lewisham.[44]

However many men were at work, though, the continuing damage and the pent-up demand meant there was always an enormous backlog of repairs. Complaints poured in to local town halls, responsible for organising the work, and councils lobbied government for more help. Although protests were most vociferous in October, before builders arrived in great numbers and so when performance was at its slowest, the problems persisted throughout the year. The LRE reported in mid-December that 719,300 houses in Greater London were scheduled for repairs that winter and, although more than a third had been repaired, over 460,000 were still waiting their turn. Nor would the standard of repairs allowed have satisfied the house-proud. No 'inessential' rooms were to be worked on, only minimal painting to keep the property weatherproof was permitted, and the cheapest available substitutes were to be used where possible (the poorest-quality slates, concrete tiles not clay, unskimmed plasterboard for ceilings and so on). Wartime boarded ceilings, with crossed laths pinning the boards to the joists, would be a familiar sight in Victorian houses across London for the next thirty years and more.[45]

The large numbers of houses destroyed or otherwise rendered unusable, and the return to London of people willing to take their chances once the V-1 menace diminished, produced another great crisis, this time of overcrowding. It could only be mitigated, not met, by councils requisitioning empty houses. So the programmes of building prefabricated 'hutments', planned for implementation once the war in Europe had ended, were now brought forward. 'Prefabs' were ordered wholesale and were soon being erected in many boroughs before Christmas. Some of the first to be built in London were in Glengall Grove, Millwall, on the Isle of Dogs. The first occupiers were Mr and Mrs John Green and their three children, Margaret (eleven), John (seven) and Christine (two), who moved into their new home in October. Before that happy event all five had been living in one basement room ten feet by six. At night Mrs Green had slept with her head under their table, while the children and Mr Green had shared an Anderson with five other grownups. The waters were muddied a little by a *News Chronicle* journalist who visited the prefab while the Greens were out and reported a list of imperfections, but in general Poplar's Portals proved popular. Just like repairs, however, the great demand far exceeded supply. Stepney Borough Council wanted 500 but was told it could only have 200; Shoreditch needed 400, asked for 200 and was allocated 115; Lewisham sought 3,250, the largest number in London, but was promised only 1,250 by March 1945 and so on. There was some good news, though. In Lambeth 300 skilled US Army builders put together a little township of thirty-eight prefabs at the junction of Minet Road and Loughborough Road, Brixton, before Christmas, a welcome present for some families at least. The LCC estimated in December that 20,000 prefabs were needed in the County of London alone; the land, it thought, did not exist to build them all in the County, so some would be built in outer London and allocated to families prepared to move out. 'If you could get it,' Gallup asked, 'would you prefer one of these [temporary prefabricated] houses, or would you rather wait longer for a permanent house?' The results were equivocal, with 27 per cent saying they would take a prefab if they were offered it, 31 per cent saying they'd wait and 36 per cent saying they wouldn't move anyway. But that was in June, and by September Londoners were in a very different position from before the V-1 attacks began. By August the housing problem was at the top of most people's priorities. 'If you had to say which question should be tackled the very first by the government returned at the general election, what should it be?' Thirty-nine per cent chose housing, 29 per cent employment, 7 per cent social security and pensions; nothing else registered more than 3 per cent.[46]

THE other thing on Londoners' minds this autumn would have been disorder of one kind or another. Wholesale destruction of homes had brought the looting problem once more to public attention. Stories of looting were so prevalent that Herbert Morrison made a statement to the House of Commons denying that the problem, at least till the end of July, was as severe as it had been in the blitz of 1940–41. In fact, though, thefts known to the police from bombed property in 1944 were higher at 6,007 than in each of the blitz years (4,584 and 5,483 respectively), but then all crime was higher in 1944 than at any year in the war so far. Half the people arrested were under eighteen, almost all male. A Home Guard acquaintance of Kathleen Tipper broke his leg in three places chasing looters like these from a bomb site in Plumstead, Woolwich: 'Here is this man, in hospital and out of action for months, all because other so-called citizens of London are behaving like vultures …' But the usual suspects were also brought to court: air raid wardens, demolition men, a driver for the 'LCC Debris Survey' and the NFS; three firemen were given three months' hard labour for taking two carpets and a stair-runner from a bomb-blasted house in Hither Green, Lewisham, in December, for instance. The culprits included a fifty-four-year-old volunteer warden from Worcester imprisoned for fifteen months for stealing a gold watch and foreign stamps from a house in Stoke Newington, where he was aiding the local civil defence; and two young Welsh builders, fined £3 each, for stealing bed linen and blankets from their billet in a Barking school.

It wouldn't have made a difference to their sentences, but 'police courts' were renamed magistrates' courts this autumn to stress their independence from the prosecuting authorities.[47]

No doubt deserters also swelled the ranks of looters, as much by receiving stolen property as by taking the risk of getting caught red-handed themselves: a Pioneer Corps deserter living in a public air raid shelter at Whipps Cross, Leytonstone, was imprisoned for twelve months in September for receiving swag from other deserters and youths living in the same shelter, for instance. The most notorious crime of 1944 also involved a deserter, this time from the US Army. Private Karl Hulten, twenty-two, a GI who had deserted and donned the stolen uniform of an officer in his US parachute regiment, had taken up with a young Welsh striptease dancer, Elizabeth Marina Jones, eighteen. They had been living together for a few days at Jones's room in Hammersmith and had indulged in a series of assaults and robberies, facilitated by Hulten's access to a US Army truck. On 9 October they murdered George Heath, a private hire-car owner from Kennington. Hulten shot Heath in the back and the pair robbed him. They then drove to Staines, where they dumped the body on the common. Heath had a distinctive cleft chin, and 'The "Cleft Chin" Murder', as the case was quickly dubbed, gripped many Londoners, including Anthony Heap. Among all the war news, 'I find it quite a change to read of an individual case. It brings a welcome touch of colour and variety.' It was a question of taste. While conceding this was 'the most talked-of English murder of recent years', George Orwell famously thought it symbolised the 'Decline of the English Murder'. Hulten was hanged at Pentonville on 8 March 1945; Jones, also sentenced to death, was reprieved.[48]

A little more 'colour and variety' were added to most Londoners' lives that autumn and winter of 1944 with a welcome improvement to street lighting as the likelihood of bombing raids by manned aircraft receded further. In September some boroughs installed 'star lighting', which offered merely a cautious glimmer. It still antagonised some nervous residents: in Wandsworth, people smashed the star lights 'when the "doodle-bugs" came over', somehow thinking the robot had eyes and a brain, causing damage costing £7,000 to make good. In November the government said that full street lighting could be restored, though it must be turned off if there was an alert, but the response was all a bit hit and miss. Shoreditch had no master switch so couldn't turn the lights off during an alert but was happy to leave them on if the government would permit. Other boroughs wanted a cast-iron assurance from government that their residents would be safe. While a cross-borough liaison committee was seeking a meeting with the Ministry of Home Security to discuss the matter, a few boroughs – St Pancras and Bethnal Green among them – jumped the gun and switched the lights back on. They were promptly labelled 'blacklegs' by their neighbouring councils, while residents of unlit boroughs clamoured for their lights to be brought back too. But by the end of November most of London was noticing something like a return to a pre-war night-time, and street lighting continued to improve till the New Year. There were other signs too that the capital was getting back to normal and beginning to put the war behind it: street fire-watching parties were disbanded as no longer needed at the end of October, and on 3 December the Home Guard was stood down, an event marked with local ceremonies across London.[49]

Despite these hopeful signs, as the run-up to Christmas began in late November Anthony Weymouth detected the return of one of those occasional 'periods of depression not accounted for by the news ... People you meet are saying they're sick of the war, and asking you when it is going to end. As if one knew!' The weather didn't help, the days cold and sunless from October through December, with occasional dense fogs bringing public transport to a near standstill: 'Eight days of fog and ice' would conclude the year. From mid-December too the war news got suddenly and anxiously worse, as the Wehrmacht broke out from the Ardennes and forced back the American front line. The worsening depression that made this, for George Beardmore and many others, the 'grimmest Christmas to date' found no relief in the shops. 'The poverty displayed in shop windows – those that still have glass in them – reminded' Cecil Beaton 'of Moscow in 1935 and is just as depressing'. That was in September but very little cheer was evident three months later. Toys were shoddy – mainly made of wood, metal so short – and very expensive: 'Father Christmas is ashamed of this rubbish – AND THE PRICES' ran one local headline. Shops were crowded enough but shoppers were frustrated and frequently disappointed. 'Even books, the customary happy solution, aren't very easy to find,' reported Mollie Panter-Downes, though oranges and nuts were for once plentiful. A full slate of pantomimes offered children and parents some compensation for the absence of stocking fillers, though the fog and ice got in the way here too, deterring many from venturing out at night. In the cinema, Olivier's timely *Henry V* was the blockbuster of Christmas 1944.[50]

Even food was problematic this Christmas, though Marjorie Heap's family in Somerset sent the customary – and very welcome – relief parcel of 'chicken, eggs, apples, nuts, holly'. Anthony's mother brought round 'port and vermouth to supplement our half bottle of gin and half a dozen bottles of beer' and they all shared roast chicken and Christmas pudding, with Christmas cake for tea. Dorothy Wells, Ken and their mother had a 'beautiful' chicken, no doubt garnished with some of the five pounds of Brussels sprouts, a couple of cabbages and some carrots picked from their fruitful allotment two days before. Both families fared better than Nellie Carver and her mother, at home in south Lambeth, who had an 'Early dinner – cold Roast Beef & Xmas Pudding' before Nellie caught the 1.08 p.m. train to work in the City. She was met by a strike on the underground. Anthony Weymouth and his wife braved a fiercely cold and foggy Boxing Day to have 'Lunch at a West-End hotel. Watery soup, omelette à la dried egg, and cold apple-tart. Waiting very off-hand and, on our part, a good deal of waiting.' It seemed fitting that *Bleak House* was the Christmas serial on the wireless that year.[51]

The run-up to New Year's Eve was equally spartan and just as depressing as the holidays. Robert Henrey took a short walk from his home to see what was happening as midnight neared:

I had expected to see a great crowd in Piccadilly, and a still greater one at the Circus, but this was not at all the case. There were sounds of mild revelry from the restaurant of the 'Berkeley' and a few chinks of light through the joins in the curtains, but most of the people wending their way towards the Eros pedestal were American soldiers anxious to make the best use of their short leave.

Anthony Heap, on ARP control room duty at the town hall, popped home to see the New Year in with Marjorie 'over a glass of port': 'Not that sitting listening to the special New Year's Eve radio made a very festive ending to the year, but it was at least an ending.' Nellie Carver tuned in too: 'Sat up to hear 11–12 Broadcast Hour – ending in St Pauls service – it was very suitable and fitting end to a memorable year – good from a military point of view but one of the worst for us Londoners. Several bangs during the night. Hitler's welcome to 1945.'[52]

10

SO THIS IS V-DAY:
1 JANUARY–15 AUGUST 1945

VIVIENNE Hall sat down in her Wembley boarding house on Friday 5 January to write up her opening weekly diary entry of the New Year. She was not in an optimistic mood:

> this first week has been a wonderful foretaste of what is before us – it has been intensely cold, again London was the coldest place over Christmas – fog and ice have been the rule and now a biting wind has added its joy! The rockets are falling much faster and the horrible rolling explosions are now becoming as frequent as our other familiars. One wonders sometimes just how much longer we can stand this? We shall, of course, we always do, but we middle-aged women [she was thirty-seven] are very weary.[1]

There were good reasons for being apprehensive. Over the next eighty-seven days, from 1 January to 28 March, Londoners were under almost constant attack from long-range rockets or flying bombs, sometimes by both. Only eight days would be free from bombing. The V-2s were now falling at a faster rate than before, averaging some four a day, with as many as eleven on some; 340 fell on London Region during this period, with 114 each in January and February and 112 in March, though March would be the deadliest month of the three. V-1s were launched by air in the first half of January, with eleven hitting London; after a seven-week lull, thirteen more struck London from 3 March, launched from ground bases deep in Holland. Defences against the V-1s continued to be robust, bringing down seven times more than got through, but there would never be a defence against the V-2. Whereas the V-1 had ravaged suburban south London in particular, the V-2 favoured London's eastern areas, with the suburbs again badly hit; Essex now took the place of Kent as the V-2's 'bomb alley'. But when a V-2 hit central London or any crowded space the consequences would be disastrous. The heavy weight of a V-2 strike produced additional demands on civil defence, with eight ambulances and extra parties from light and heavy rescue teams now sent to each incident as a matter of course.[2]

This was a dreadful game of chance but the V-2, even in these greater numbers, was not the terror weapon that the V-1 had been and, even in these smaller numbers, remained. Shelter figures in the tubes around this time stabilised at some 12,000 and in the five deep shelters – or New Deep Tubes, as they were officially dubbed – at around 4,000 between them. People knew they would be very unlucky indeed to have a deadly encounter with a V-2, given the size of London and the relative infrequency of attack. But the impact of V-2 strikes could be heard nearly every day and night and their effects could be seen all over London.

On 20 January 1945, R. S. Simmons (his first name has not come down to us) was on his way home from his grammar school in High Barnet. There were lessons that morning, even though this was a Saturday, and he would have to get his own lunch because his mother was at work in the Air Ministry; his father, who had been a commercial traveller before the war, was with the army in Belgium. Simmons was fifteen and a half but, like many other schoolboys, had a civil defence responsibility – he was a messenger for the NFS. At 1.20 p.m., the fifth of eight V-2s to strike London that day hit New Barnet during a heavy snowstorm. Out of nowhere, he recalled some years later, came 'an electric blue flash, a second later an enormous roar and the ground shook'. He was a couple of hundred yards from home and the closer he got he could see that things were not as they should have been. The front door was off its hinges, curtains were blowing through the smashed windows and the front path and garden were full of broken tiles. Inside, rooms were covered in soot and fallen ceiling plaster, and shards of broken glass were buried deep in the walls. After he had finished putting up blackout shutters to keep out the snow a school friend called round. The rocket had landed in Calton Road, two streets from his home. Grabbing his steel helmet Simmons went to see if he could help:

The destruction was quite complete. The V2 had fallen in the middle of the road, creating a large crater, big enough for two houses, and from the sides of the crater the broken gas mains were lazily burning, creating colour to the white background. Miraculously, a brick built street bomb shelter alongside the crater still stood, but the houses had collapsed like packs of cards – roof timbers sticking out like broken fingers from piles of masonry and bricks which a few moments before were people's homes.

Several people were trapped and calling for help.

One person was caught up in the roof timbers and several of us already on the scene tried to get up to him, and while we were trying to do our pathetic best, the first A.R.P. wardens arrived. They were better organised with tools, saws and ropes and soon started to tackle the obvious visible casualties. Looking round the scene not one house in Calton Road was unaffected, and ... as far as the eye could see roofs were stripped off all the houses, windows blown in, doors hanging off, trees denuded of branches and garden fences down.

As soon as all the main rescue forces had arrived, as well as troops stationed nearby, the rescue became well organised. Each house that had been demolished was allotted a gang of people, and silences were called for to listen for trapped victims under the rubble, whistles being used for that purpose. Alsatian dogs also were quickly on site and they and others crawled under the wreckage seeking the injured or dead. Being reasonably small, I was asked to crawl into one pile of wreckage as a rescued neighbour said there was a little girl in the house. As I crawled into the wreckage, the first thing I noticed was the smell or smells. A mixture of masonry, sewage and fire. The house had collapsed in such a way that the roof frame was laying more or less intact at ground floor level and the bedroom furniture was mixed up with the ground floor contents. A small fire was smouldering against the wall, no doubt this was from the grate but there was no flame. Every now and then rubble shifted and you froze fearing the timbers above you would come crashing down. I called out several times 'Is anyone there?' but each time there was no response. I searched every accessible space but found nothing so crawled out into the cold afternoon air. About this time, the rescue authorities decided to level the rubble of the demolished houses by throwing all the debris into the crater, and so making sure that no-one was left unaccounted for. I noticed at this stage several bodies being removed by stretcher bearers picking their way over the rubble to waiting ambulances. The afternoon was growing dark, and searchlights were being set up and directed to those houses where the occupants were still untraced. It was at about this time that I heard that a woman had only just been found after several hours, at the bottom of the gardens where she had been blown by the blast and no-one had seen her until her moans were heard.

As I previously mentioned the particular house I was working on, had a little girl missing, and her cries could now be heard. But from the direction of her cries, a fire was starting to build up, and the smoke beginning to thicken. It was then a chain of rescuers really began to level off the rubble, while firemen played their hoses on the smoke. A policeman was at the head of the chain and he worked feverishly sending back bricks, bits of furniture, wood, anything down the human chain of hands and finally into the crater. Eventually she was found, covered in blood and in shock, but I understand that when they cleaned off the blood she was only slightly cut and bruised.

Twenty-three people died in the Calton Road V-2 incident, he thought. At the Air Ministry in central London his mother had distinctly heard the boom at 1.20 but had no idea where it had landed.[3]

As Germany's plight grew ever more hopeless in March 1945, it seemed that Hitler's thirst for vengeance against London was unquenchable. With the Rhine threatened at many points, the V-weapons reached their final deadly climax. Every day of that month until 24 March, V-1s or V-2s struck London. There was an especially deadly period between the 5th and the 8th, when thirty V-2s killed around 275 people and injured 860, the bloodiest few days of the whole V-weapon campaign. It saw one especially awful incident at Smithfield at the northern edge of the City. A V-2 struck the Central Markets Building at 11.10 a.m. on Thursday 8 March. The markets were crowded with salesmen and with customers queueing for meat, fish and poultry – a consignment of rabbits had come in and had attracted many purchasers. The rocket drilled through roof and floors and exploded in the underground service railway. It blasted a huge crater into which rubble and victims fell in a monstrous chaos of shattered brick, stone, timber and iron. Some 115 people were killed and 129 seriously injured.[4]

By late March, with Allied forces across the Rhine and closing in on the mobile launch sites near The Hague, well hidden from the air and frustratingly impervious to bombing, there came a twenty-four-hour lull on 25 March. But any hope Londoners might have treasured that this was the end of the deadly air war against them was shattered over the next two days. Eleven V-2s struck London in one final flailing by an implacable and malevolent foe, killing around 162 and injuring 212. The last V-2s to strike London Region all fell on Tuesday 27 March at 12.23 a.m. at Edmonton, 3.05 a.m. at Cheshunt and 3.40 a.m. at Ilford. At 7.20 a.m. a V-2 fell on Stepney. It was the worst incident of 1945 and it struck an area of London that had already suffered so much, a Jewish district that it seemed to some had been marked out as a target by Hitler's special animus. Indeed, most of the victims at Hughes Mansions, a modern block of workers' dwellings just fifteen years old in Vallance Road, were Jewish, though many were not. For any V-weapon strike, the dead were only second in number to the Deptford disaster of November 1944. In all, 134 were killed at Hughes Mansions and forty-nine seriously injured. They included seven members of Ernest Beckett's family; he and his son Donald, on leave from the army in Burma, could only watch as rescuers toiled to recover the injured and the dead. The WVS information point at Deal Street rest centre dealt with a queue of anxious enquirers that never seemed to diminish through the day, some returning again and again to see whether any news had come through. At the London Hospital nearby, the mortuary quickly filled and bodies were laid outside in the courtyard: soon 'a crowd was queueing in Mount Street to identify dead relatives'. In doing so, a mistake was made. Mrs Annie Freedman was killed in the explosion and her daughter saw her body at the scene. But she was unable to bury her mother because she had been claimed as a relative by someone else. The coroner officially presumed Mrs Freedman dead some weeks later. 'It has happened,' he told the inquest, 'that bodies have been buried under wrong names in this way.'[5]

The last V-2 to hit London fell on Orpington at 4.57 p.m. It killed one person, Mrs Ivy Millichamp, the last fatal victim of the air war against London. The last V-1s fell next morning, Wednesday 28 March, at 7.45 a.m. (Chislehurst) and 7.56 a.m. (Waltham Abbey); three people were injured in the blasts.[6]

So ended the air war against London that had begun fifty-six months before in August 1940. Of the 146,777 casualties in the UK from all forms of bombing, 80,397 (55 per cent) occurred in London. In all, the official figures for those killed in the capital over that period totalled 29,890, slightly less than half the national figure of 60,595. Of those

London deaths, over 20,000 had been killed in the eight months of the Big Blitz; 1940 was the most destructive year of all with 13,596 deaths. In 1944, which was the worst year for injuries, 7,533 Londoners had died, mainly in V-1 incidents, and in 1945 1,705, almost entirely from V-2s. In all, 518 rockets landed on London, killing 2,511 and seriously injuring some 5,900 more. Of total V-2 casualties in the UK, 89 per cent were in London.[7]

This final German attack seemed to many Londoners needlessly vindictive. Plainly, from the Allied point of view, it could not stave off the Reich's defeat and so it had no defensive or strategic purpose. It hardened some Londoners' hearts against a nation now undergoing pitiless bombardment from the air. Kathleen Tipper, living in Woolwich and hearing in February of a six-year-old whose legs were blown off in a V-2 explosion, thought people in London 'will be getting much satisfaction from the sufferings of the Germans at the present time'. But that wasn't everyone's view. That same month Anthony Weymouth, in Marylebone, confessed, 'I know it shouldn't – but my heart bleeds for those poor souls' who were 'now undergoing, as Churchill promised they should, more than they ever made us suffer'. When reconnaissance photos and newsreel were shown in March of the devastation wreaked in Berlin and elsewhere, Albert Turpin, who had worked as a fireman through the East End blitz, listened to young people in cinemas laughing at the newsreels of German cities and felt 'sick at the stomach' at their reaction. 'Londoners,' thought Mollie Panter-Downes, 'who have had plenty of experience in calculating piles of rubble in terms of human misery, are apt to whistle incredulously at the shots of Cologne street scenes.' She thought it made Germany's last throw of the V-weapons' vengeful dice somehow easier to understand.[8]

From the afternoon of 28 March Londoners could only wait and wonder. The end of the air war against London had to come at some time but could this really be it? There had been so many past disappointments that it seemed foolhardy to hope and reckless to believe that this might mean that the attack was truly over. On 29 March Vivienne Hall drew a tentative conclusion from the continuing silence: 'we are hopeful – once more – that the end of these beastly things is near. It seems the war is going so amazingly well that perhaps we shall have a rest from them soon. – And my God I really do think that we Londoners deserve it – four long weary years of continuous bombing – no other city can beat that!' On Easter Sunday, 1 April, Nellie Carver in West Norwood, south Lambeth, dared to 'Think Rockets must have been interrupted as no bangs since Friday' – in fact Thursday – and three days later, 'Monty's men are cutting off the Rocket sites. Wouldn't it be marvellous if we had no more or Doodles? Our poor old road <u>does</u> look a wreck.' On 5 April news of 'carefully camouflaged' V-2 sites being overrun in Holland by the Allies gave firmer cause for optimism. '[W]e are told we may hope they had stopped altogether,' Vivienne Hall recorded next day, 'wouldn't this be wonderful?! A whole week has now passed without 'em and we in London feel we've all been given a bonus and 500 coupons to buy clothes!!' It still took time to sink in and for a cautious confidence to build that this really was the end. Hilda Neal, in South Kensington, who had been spending her nights at home rather than in the tube since the V-1 menace had receded, noted of the rockets on 10 April, 'We have had none for about 10–11 days, so we trust they <u>have</u> finished. It's a huge relief to be able to undress at night properly and feel one need not <u>listen</u> ...' The definitive announcement would have to wait another fortnight. On 26 April, when the Prime Minister was asked in the House of Commons if he was now able to make a statement on the rockets, he replied, 'Yes, Sir. They have ceased. (Loud laughter and cheers.)'[9]

It was a relief to others too. The last four months were the swansong of civil defence. It had been a long time coming, but the spring of 1945 would see the final demise of a citizen army building in large numbers from September 1938, blooded in 1940–41 and honed to something approaching perfection by 1944.

This final civil defence year began like all the others – with a beano. The shocking memories of March 1943 were set aside for a time when 400 children using Bethnal Green's public shelters were given a New Year's party by ARP wardens 'in the Tube Shelter, Roman-road', where the disaster took place. Wardens, NFS, fire guards (even though officially disbanded) and WVS gave parties in Norwood, Hounslow, Brentford and Chiswick, Kenton, Pinner, Heston and Isleworth and probably everywhere else, with toys, plenty of 'eats', Punch and Judy, Father Christmas, film shows, talent competitions with prizes for elocution, dancing, singing and much else, and games and entertainments. There were also parties this year given for wardens and others in appreciation of their work holding together London's front line. Hammersmith wardens for the White City area were treated to a day out at a Queen's Park Rangers match, guests of the club's directors; local wardens invited some provincial wardens who had helped out in the summer of 1944 – they saw Rangers beat Arsenal 3–2. And many west London businesses combined to give a grand New Year's party for 1,500 civil defence workers from Westminster and neighbouring boroughs at the Seymour Hall, Marylebone.[10]

The official dismantling of the various arms of civil defence began even while rockets were still falling on London. Neither the V-1s nor the V-2s had caused a serious risk from fire and it was the part-time ranks of the NFS who were stood down first, on 18 March. The event was marked by a concert at the Royal Albert Hall and a march in Hyde Park with Herbert Morrison, the service's founder, taking the salute. It was a lovely afternoon and Margery Cossins travelled from her Bayswater guest house to see her friend John on his final parade:

> Very much struck by their war-worn faces, thin & pinched, many very anaemic-looking. One in John's company fainted, was laid on the grass & attended to by ambulance men. Was very much struck too, by what a decent set of men they appeared to be. Over-worked, honest-looking, unobtrusive creatures. Felt very proud of them ... Thought John looked dreadfully tired, & found that they all did with hardly any exceptions. Never had the effect of the War [been] so brought home to me.

The full-time NFS, of course, remained and so did those static water tanks which continued to cast a fatal spell over London children: two boys, thirteen and eleven, drowned trying to cross a tank in Canton Street, Poplar, in April – they had used a door as a raft – and a five-year-old drowned in the same borough just a week or so later.[11]

On the last day of March the River Emergency Service was stood down and on 23 April, St George's Day, the blackout was officially lifted. A week later, on the last day of the month, the end of the V-weapons now officially accounted for, Herbert Morrison announced that civil defence general services (wardens, rescue teams, first aid posts, but not auxiliary police or ambulance services in London) would be stood down on a date to be fixed. Admiral Sir Edward Evans and Alderman Charlie Key of Poplar resigned their posts as London regional commissioners that same day, though Sir Ernest Gowers, the senior commissioner, stayed on to oversee demobilisation. The 'appointed day' came in a rush, just two days later on 2 May, with civil defence

The Second Great Fire consumed much more of the City than the original of 1666. It finally burnt out on New Year's Day 1941. From then, a system of fire watchers, at first voluntary but eventually compulsory, required Londoners to watch businesses and streets through the night. The City, especially round St Paul's, remained devastated into the 1950s.

As the blitz settled into an almost nightly routine through the autumn and winter of 1940–1, shelter life became more sophisticated. Facilities were installed by the council, and shelter wardens and committees kept order and arranged entertainments. Mickey Davis, a Spitalfields optician less than four feet tall, was perhaps the most famous – and photographed – shelter warden of all.

Shelter entertainments were often organised as talent shows among shelterers themselves, though professionals performed gratis or for a small collection, presumably as here with a black pianist in the YMCA headquarters shelter in Great Russell Street, Bloomsbury, in 1940. Lectures, evening classes and 'brains trust' discussions would all become part of the fun.

On Saturday night, 8–9 March 1941, a HE bomb exploded in the Café de Paris, a basement nightclub in Coventry Street, Leicester Square. The place was crowded with well-off Londoners dancing to 'Snakehips' Johnson's swing band of black musicians. Johnson and other band members were among the thirty-four dead. Corpses were looted as first aiders fought to save the injured.

Civil defenders, community groups and householders throughout London were keen harvesters of livestock. Rabbits, chickens, ducks, geese and pigs were all bred to ease food shortages. Here National Fire Service men based in Holborn tend their pigs, fed from kitchen waste brought by club members. Some meat was distributed within the club but most was sold to the government.

Despite the blitz, most schoolchildren stayed in London, with 125,000 in just the LCC area at Christmas 1940. Children found the city's ruins an irresistible lure, though one with obvious dangers. Deaths and injuries were common from unexploded AA-shells and collapsing buildings; many were drowned in flooded basements, kept by the fire service to help fight fires.

Low-flying fighter-bombers added to London's perils in 1943. On Wednesday 20 January, a 500kg bomb was dropped without warning on Sandhurst Road School, Catford, as pupils were queueing for lunch; thirty-eight children and six teachers died. The tragedy resonated across the world. A mass funeral was held, wardens prominent at the graveside in their white helmets.

Sir Oswald and Lady Mosley were interned as prominent anti-war fascists in May 1940. They were released on 20 November 1943, doctors reporting Sir Oswald to be in poor health. Protests against their release were prominent in London, as here in Battersea, often led by communists who had been as anti-war as Mosley at the time of his internment.

Black GIs were generally welcomed in London, though there were numerous instances of racial prejudice against black Londoners before and during the war. However, the formal segregation of US forces in Britain was mostly unwelcome and took everyone by surprise. Here a segregated audience of black GIs appreciate a USAAF 'negro chorus' at the Albert Hall.

Some of the few London-wide celebrations during the war revolved round annual national savings campaigns, borough competing with borough over the number of savings certificates bought by its citizens. Parades were essential and any spectacle was worth turning out for, as here in Fleet Street for Salute the Soldier Week, Spring 1944.

The V-1 was a terrifying weapon, first deployed in June 1944. A jet-propelled pilotless plane carrying a warhead of 850kg of HE, its approach could be heard as a vibrating growl for many miles which, as it got close, swelled to a roar like an oncoming train. Once the engine cut it would drop from the sky and create devastation where it fell. Here is a V-1 about to fall on London.

At the Aldwych on 30 June 1944, a V-1 fell in the street killing 46 and seriously injuring 152 others. Among them were many young women returning to their offices after lunch. This photo, censored for publication, must have been taken moments after the V-1 exploded; a young woman's body is not yet covered and a stretcher bearer is waiting for help to remove her.

Suburban south London suffered especially badly from the V-1 onslaught, as here in a crowded incident scene in Clapham. V-1s caused few fires, but NFS crews attended to help wardens, police and light and heavy rescue teams. Here an injured young woman is stretchered to safety over the heads of civil defence workers and others keen to help.

The V-2, Hitler's ultimate weapon, carried a warhead filled with one ton of HE. An unlucky hit could cause mass casualties, as here at a crowded Smithfield Market on 8 March 1945, when 115 were killed. The photo was taken just as firemen, police and wardens were arriving and while market workers were rescuing colleagues. Censored at the time, it was not published until October 1948.

Crowds in Piccadilly Circus on the evening of 7 May 1945 celebrate the announcement of the German surrender earlier in the day, with a two-day public holiday granted for 8 and 9 May. Victory in Europe had been eagerly anticipated for weeks. These joyful Londoners stealing a march on the official celebrations were captured by a *Daily Herald* photographer.

The General Election of July 1945 was an ill-tempered affair in London. Voting took place before the war was eventually won in the East. To the surprise of almost everyone, Churchill and the Conservatives were defeated and the Labour Party, led by Clement Attlee, won by a landslide. Here Attlee campaigns before a predominantly young audience in his East End constituency.

disbanded, air raid sirens discontinued and public shelters closed; they were soon to be demolished, labour permitting. 'Local authorities may arrange at their discretion for final local parades,' they were told, so there would be no national send-off as had been afforded the NFS irregulars. The 'scant ceremony' marking the final wind-down of civil defence did not go unnoticed and left some with a sense of grievance. But perhaps it was fitting after all. These were such very local services, neighbour looking out for neighbour, that they could best be celebrated borough by borough.[12]

The haste with which the appointed day followed the government announcement of disbandment did mean, however, that local celebrations were not coordinated and no special day could be set aside London-wide. Parades, marches and church services dribbled out across the spring and summer and were sometimes mixed in with the victory celebrations of early May. Some 1,800 of Westminster's civil defence staff were treated to a farewell celebration hosted by the city council at the Odeon Cinema, Leicester Square, on 6 May, probably pipping everyone else to the post. Harrow hosted a parade, a march past and church service a week later and so did Hammersmith, and other boroughs followed suit. Everywhere seems to have done something, even if civil defenders had to wait till July (like Hackney and Stoke Newington) for their special moment. All Londoners knew the debt they owed to their local civil defence. Some owed their lives to it. And everyone knew of wardens and rescuers who had given their own lives in the service of others. What should be uppermost in Londoners' minds as the end of the war in Europe neared, one local paper thought, was 'a feeling of unbounded and unqualified gratitude to the whole of the personnel of Civil Defence ...' No one could forget how they 'toiled to succour the bereaved and the wounded, to care for the homeless and the distressed, and to solve the thousand and one problems and difficulties arising from enemy bombing'.[13]

THIS greatest difficulty of the Londoners' war, the risk of sudden death from the air, slowly eased away in the early months of 1945, but there were other problems too, some of which proved even harder to shift. That snowstorm in which R. S. Simmons met the V-2 was an indication of a frostbitten January, not in fact as bad as 1940 but feeling worse to many. 'This sixth winter of war is just about as much as we are going to be able to manage we middle-aged weary ones!' complained

Vivienne Hall in Sudbury. 'Did you have any burst pipes at home during the recent cold spell?' Gallup asked in February, and 29 per cent said they had. Misery was multiplied by another London coal shortage. Cold and coal combined as one of the war's great class levellers. Everyone suffered and perhaps those less used to it suffered more. James Lees-Milne, from a prosperous background, now living in one room with shared facilities in bomb-battered Cheyne Walk, Chelsea, felt the pinch sharply. 'The cold persists,' he wrote on 11 January. 'It is appalling, and I have run out of anthracite. I only have two bucketfuls of coal left. I ordered 10 cwt. of anthracite, my first order since March of last year, in November. It has not been delivered yet.' It still hadn't arrived over a week later when, 'snowing again and freezing', he fled to his club, Brooks's in St James's Street, and huddled in front of the fire. When a thaw came his pipes burst and he had no water: 'Which predicament is the worse? At any rate we are warmer now, thank God.'[14]

Lees-Milne's anthracite was top-drawer fuel but even a bucket of 'nutty slack' was hard to lay a shovel on in working-class London in early 1945. There were problems everywhere in the country but the shortage in London was considered a 'crisis'. There were multiple causes: the need to supply the invasion forces in France, output problems in the coalfields, distribution difficulties on the railways, a shortage of labour among coal merchants, their manpower down by a quarter on pre-war figures and the exceptionally bitter weather. The authorities tried to blame Londoners for being insufficiently 'Fuel Conscious', while Londoners themselves thought they were merely short of coal. Some mitigating measures were, though, put in place by government. A scheme was adopted to ease the purchase from nominated shops of coal in small quantities from fourteen to twenty-eight pounds; households in London were limited to a maximum of four hundredweight of 'kitchen coal' in February; those with five hundredweight in stock could get no more 'for the time being'. Occasionally frustration boiled over. Police were called when a hundred people, mostly women, rushed a 'coal dump' in Lambeth; they'd been queueing a long time when staff tried to lock the gates so they could take their lunch hour. Coal supplies in Southwark were running low at the end of January and, worryingly, there were no plans to top them up if they ran out. Paraffin was also in short supply, with most shops unable to buy stocks: 'when I see a queue of people with cans outside an ironmonger's,' George Beardmore reported from Harrow, 'I make it my business to hurry home and fetch our cans and join 'em'. Luckily the weather relented in February and though the queues continued for a time people were at least assured of a reward for their patience.[15]

There were other vexing shortages too. 'For the first time since the war began, there is a shortage of potatoes,' complained Anthony Heap, living in St Pancras, in January and the cry of 'no spuds' persisted till the end of April at least. The shortage was no doubt taken into account by the LCC when it announced early in the New Year that allotments in its parks and elsewhere could continue in cultivation for the rest of 1945, 'whatever the military situation'. But bread was a little whiter, or at least less grey, in these months as refined flour became more available, improved milk supplies were reported in the spring ('This helps a lot,' thought Vere Hodgson in North Kensington) and there were more eggs. In general, though, much was still in short supply. 'Food is scarce,' George Beardmore noted in June. 'Most days I go to the British Restaurant for a mid-day meal,' and there does seem to have been a general improvement in catering supplies in other restaurants too compared to the low point of 1944. Even so, 'I suffer from stretches of lassitude, mostly in the evening when I usually like to go gardening. I put it down to deficiencies in this or that protein or vitamin,' but perhaps helping his wife to cope with a small baby had something to do with it. Certainly there was no shortage of energy on the Wells family's allotment in Ealing, where forty-four-year-old Dorothy and her mother, Florence, eighty-one in March, were out in all weathers to harvest those eternal cabbages, sprouts and leeks, and preparing the ground for shallots, onions, lettuces, parsnips, yet more cabbages, marrows and potatoes for later in the year. Ken, forty-seven, was usually otherwise engaged, busy courting; he went on to marry his girlfriend, Connie, in the summer.[16]

When she was not on the allotment Dorothy, who held down a senior administrative job in central London through the week, often spent evenings at home in front of the wireless repairing and adjusting her wardrobe. Despite daily travel to work, a full task list of duties at her local church at weekends which included running the Sunday school, some competitive tennis when the weather allowed, and that back-breaking allotment, she had somehow contrived to put on weight throughout the war. She didn't like it, but she'd learned to live with it. 'Home tonight and started enlarging my blue cherry skirt. Have about finished my Air Force blue coat,' and a couple of days later 'got to work on my tennis frock in the afternoon ...' Shortages of material improved somewhat in 1945 over the lows of 1944, but most things were harder to get than in 1942, when restrictions started, and the ration was cut again in 1945, making twenty-four coupons last seven months instead of six. Making and mending, for those with the skills to do so, were essential if appearances were to be maintained. Nellie Carver, for instance, made her own 'undies' from '2½ yards of Celanese' that she exchanged for a D. H. Evans voucher she'd received for Christmas: 'Am in sore need of new ones.'[17]

Shortages meant queues, and it was in these first six months of 1945 that queues seemed to be everywhere and for everything. 'Went out early to do W/End shopping, such long queues,' reported a 'leg weary' Nellie Carver at the end of March. Vere Hodgson, in Kensington High Street in mid-February, 'saw all round Pontings queues of women. I was told it was sheets. The Government had released some, and so short is everyone that women were outside the shop at 5 a.m. Not hundreds, but thousands. Police were controlling the queues. Some of the happy buyers got in my bus ... loaded.' It was all getting beyond a joke. That spring, the novelist Bryher later recalled, 'The gaiety of the formerly patient queues was replaced by an ugly discontent.'[18]

In April, Anthony Heap notched up one more cause to grouse: 'Another cigarette shortage – almost comparable with the famous fag famine of '41'. But even smokers had other things to think about that month. 'Terribly shocked to hear this morning of the death of President Roosevelt,' Nellie Carver noted in her diary on the 14th, though the news had reached London the evening before. 'Everyone is very grieved.' 'We, the very ordinary British working class feel his loss deeply,' thought Sister Gwyneth Thomas at Lewisham Hospital, perhaps remembering his New Deal as much as his equivocal support for Britain before December 1941. But there was no doubt of his popularity in London, where his death 'came as a stupefying shock,' according to Mollie Panter-Downes. On the 17th a memorial service for Roosevelt was held at St Paul's. Nellie Carver went 'but was too late to get near front ... Hundreds of people. We had so hoped to see him in London. Everyone wanted to show what we thought of him.'[19]

There was more grim news in April, this time from Europe. On the evening of the 15th, a broadcast by Ed Murrow revealed for the first time the horrors of Buchenwald discovered by US troops. 'It doesn't seem possible – even for Germany,' thought Nellie Carver, though for

Vivienne Hall it was 'hideous evidence of the bestial mentality of the Nazi mind'. Soon Londoners could see for themselves. Many newspapers printed photographs of camp conditions and by the end of the month, 'There are long queues of people waiting silently wherever the photos are on exhibition. The shock to the public has been enormous.' It certainly registered with Kathleen Tipper: 'I feel that many people here at last realise how vile the Nazis are ...' On 2 May Hilda Neal went with a friend to a 'news theatre' and watched newsreel from Buchenwald and Belsen: 'It was far worse than the imagination could have conjured up from description.' She held roundly anti-Semitic views, and though the reports and the films may have given her pause for thought, there was no mention of Jews in the film she watched or in her diary entry. Indeed, the significance of Jews as victims was understated in all reports, fears of stoking sympathy for Jewish migration to Palestine uppermost in the official mind. Anthony Heap, another anti-Semite and an early supporter of Hitler – though that had worn thin of late – made no reference to the camp exposures at all.[20]

DESPITE the bitter January, with its coal and other shortages, and with two more months to come of attack from the air, London continued to fill with people. Even in January, it was thought that 10,000 a week were returning or moving there afresh. The return of evacuees became something of a rush in April, once the V-weapons were thought definitely to have ended. A reverse evacuation scheme was formally announced on 2 May to coincide with the standing down of civil defence. At first people continued to make their own way back to London with the help of government travel warrants, with the first special trains being put on a month later. It was organised once more by the LCC for the whole of Greater London and reportedly 'It went like clockwork.' Among the children were some so young that they must have been born in the country, getting their first sight and taste of London on the receiving station platforms. By the end of June a net 405,000 had moved back to London during the first six months of 1945.[21]

They returned to a housing crisis that had continued to deepen and widen since the New Year. The problem of repairs persisted. Between the spring of 1944 and the end of March 1945, 'more than a million houses in Greater London and South-East England had been destroyed or damaged'. The London Repairs Executive (LRE) had been set the task of making 'tolerably comfortable' some 719,000 houses damaged

by enemy action up to 22 September 1944. By January just over half
had been dealt with and by the end of March all had been fixed to
that minimum standard of something less than comfort; houses were
being repaired at the rate of some 32,000 each week. It was all good
progress. But after 22 September London suffered six more months of
rocket attack, with some V-1s thrown into the mix. It undid some of
the LRE's good work and added more damaged houses to the problem.
Each V-1 damaged or destroyed on average 400 houses (in built-up
areas the figure was 2,000) and each V-2 around 650. In all, between
8 September and 28 March around 353,000 further houses were blitzed
in London Region in addition to the historic backlog; some were
destroyed or damaged beyond repair, the rest needing work of some
kind. By the end of March about 80,000 had been brought to the
minimum standard, leaving a shortfall of 290,000.[22]

This was not quite running to stand still, because great strides were
made, but the resulting problems were felt everywhere in London and
even 'repaired houses' left a very great deal to be desired. Residents
blamed their councils: H. E. Burgess, roofless and speechless, wrote to
the local paper in February 'to express ... my indignation at, and
contempt for, the paltry methods of the Bomb Damage Repair Committee
of Leyton Corporation', and there were similar outbursts across the
capital. Councils, in turn, and some London MPs, blamed government
in the shape of 'an incompetent war cabinet' and the LRE. Wandsworth,
badly hit since June 1944, received so many complaints of inadequate
repairs from its residents that in May 1945 it launched a public relations campaign to explain the difficulties and remind people just what
had been achieved – 7,500 building workers had already repaired 50,000
dwellings. In Islington nearly 79,000 houses damaged by all types of
enemy action had been repaired, but some had been 'damaged and
repaired two, three, and even four times'. In February 1945, in this one
borough, there were still 19,000 houses awaiting repairs to the
'maximum permitted standard'; many would have received 'field dress-
ings' to make them wind- and weatherproof; but this only provided a
single dry room and no plastering, and even these urgent necessities
had to wait their turn. London-wide, these were nightmarish problems.[23]

Everything was made worse, of course, by the shortage of labour
and materials that could be devoted to this single task when so much
else needed to be done. Even so, the nation threw vast resources at the
London housing problem. Building firms brought their own men and

equipment to London from all parts of the UK, other building opera-
tives made their own way from the provinces, skilled men from the
army, navy and air force were drafted in and the US forces chipped in
generously too, with about 3,000 GIs helping with repairs and building
prefabs. By the end of March 143,000 men were repairing houses in
London, around 50,000 of them from outside the capital. While the
bombing continued, these strangers to London were also caught up in
the ongoing drama of the V-weapons. A Mr Dilks from Ilkeston,
Derbyshire, was knocked off his feet by a V-1 blast in Hackney in the
New Year but then turned to help in the rescue: 'I crawled beneath the
second floor of a house and found a woman with her arm hanging off.
I managed to bandage it up without her seeing it, and told her "It's all
right, Ma. Your head's just a little bit cut."' Not all acted so creditably.
At that same incident two provincial repair workers stole 'tobacco from
a bomb-damaged shop while the woman shopkeeper lay trapped beneath
the wreckage'; they were given fourteen and twenty-one days' by the
magistrate. Billeting was still a problem, though eased a little by hostels
organised by local councils and the Ministry of Works. And local discontents cropped up from time to time: 600 out of 4,425 repair workers
in Camberwell had failed to return from their Christmas break at the
New Year, and in early May a mass meeting of men in Lewisham voted
to strike if their wages weren't increased to a minimum of 3s per hour.[24]

Everywhere in London had been shaken by bombing and everywhere
shared in the generic neglect of the capital's housing that set in from
September 1939. When, in the summer of 1945, Verily Anderson was
looking for a house to buy in smart South Kensington she found just
the thing at 43 Pembroke Square. It had been vacant since late 1940.
Her husband popped round to take a look and found 'dry rot in more
than one place, the roof is damaged, one of the walls is out of true at
the top and will have to be taken down and rebuilt, and there's a
jasmine plant growing through the scullery floor'. They bought it nonetheless, anticipating a war damage grant. Nowhere was 'smart' in the
London of 1945.[25]

Even worse than the condition of property was the housing shortage
for those already living in London, for those returning and for those
wishing or needing to move there. Overcrowding in London was
desperate and so was homelessness, with thousands in temporary billets
and some living in shelters because they had nowhere else to go. A
Daily Mirror article in February exposed the plight of two Shoreditch

couples, one with a child, living in a street shelter: one family was rehoused by the borough, but Mr and Mrs Pollington stayed put, demanding rehousing in Southend, where their application was rejected. West End councils, including Westminster and Kensington, established a joint scheme to convert a hundred grand houses into flats and to divide some luxury flats into smaller dwellings, all for needy families in other districts; it was thought they could accommodate 10,000 people. From the summer there were some early instances of what would become an extensive post-war squatting movement, frustrated at continuing homelessness, inadequate requisitioning of empty houses by councils and the all too apparent numbers of properties left empty for one reason or another. This 'Vigilante' agitation was said to have begun in Brighton and by July there was organised squatting in Camberwell and Deptford, targeting vacant flats over shops. Squatters installed Mrs Dorothy Shuttle and her overcrowded family in Friendly Street, Deptford: '"I didn't know the men who moved me in but I believe they came from the Brighton Vigilantes. Not only did they find the place and move the furniture in on handcarts, but they came in and cleared up the place as well."' When the police came and told her she shouldn't be there, '"they didn't say any more when I told them I had nowhere to go"'. Mrs Shuttle's husband was serving with the army in Germany.[26]

Local agitations on behalf of the homeless were sometimes condemned as communist stunts but that the cause was not fabricated was plain for all to see. Nor did the housing shortage affect only the poor. Vivienne Hall's boarding house in Wembley was sold and all the paying guests told to leave. She desperately sought a place for her and her mother, still in Westmorland, and visited 'endless estate agents', but 'there's nothing to be had in the way of a home unless you know someone who can pull some strings'. She reluctantly had to accept an offer of a temporary room from an eccentric lady in Richmond and was there when her diary came to its final entry in May. Anthony and Marjorie Heap were also keen to move but in the local paper for the last two weeks under 'unfurnished flats to let' were the same six advertisements: 'Four of them offered houses for sale, one a single roomed "flatlet" for one person and the other one an actual flat – at £4 a week!' It was around this time that London councils began to devise rationing schemes for their own housing, allocating families points for numbers of children, degree of overcrowding, length of local residence and so on, as a way of prioritising rehousing applications.[27]

The only way that councils could increase their housing supply was by requisitioning empty houses, done in quite large numbers, perhaps 25,000–30,000 in London County alone, or by building prefabs. The numbers of prefabs were tiny given the size of the problem: just 6,569 planned for thirty-four London local authorities of which 2,378 had been built by May. Prefabs were not without their problems. Most were built of 'curved asbestos', the risks of which for manufacturers, builders and tenants would only become clear some years later. Lambeth's 'Curved-Asbestos Nissens' in Brixton, built by US troops, were prone to condensation and lacked cupboard space, and tenants had difficulty putting fixings in walls for shelves and pictures. Prefabs also seemed to be greedy of space. Bomb sites in Wandsworth selected for Portals had once accommodated houses providing for 1,846 families; the Portals built in their place could house only 834. It was this 'housing loss' which probably weighed most heavily with the LRE, who urged that labour and cash would be better used on repairs than on building new 'huts'.[28]

To add to these frustrations of disrepair and the housing shortage, Londoners were treated to a revival early this year of homes exhibitions of one kind or another. In February Nellie Carver and a friend 'went to Dorland Hall', in Regent Street, 'to see Kitchen Exhibition – very cheery – like the Ideal Home of Pre-War days'. In June the *Daily Herald*, a Labour paper, went on to stage a 'Post-War Homes Exhibition' at the same venue: one of the attractions, 'No Burst Pipes'.[29]

BY the end of April it was becoming clear to everyone that the war in Europe could not last much longer. The collapse of Germany was happening at breakneck speed. 'We are waiting breathlessly for the end,' wrote Nellie Carver on the 27th: 'All sorts of rumours.' On the 28th the government stated that the German forces had offered to surrender to the British and US forces, but this had been rejected because they would have to surrender to the Soviets too. Kathleen Tipper, who had become increasingly virulent in her loathing of Germany since the V-weapons and the concentration camp revelations, didn't mind the delay: 'I hope the country is really battered before they give in.' On the 29th came news of Mussolini's grisly death at the hands of Italian partisans and, on the evening of 1 May, a report that the German armies in Italy had unconditionally surrendered. Then, next day, 2 May, Kathleen Tipper wearily noted, 'Hitler is dead. Words we longed to hear five years ago are almost unimportant now and people don't seem really interested.' She was more concerned with a bus and tram strike: 'it took me ages to get to work' at her shipping company office, bombed out from the Strand and now in Kingsway. 'This is a dreadful time for these men and women to come out on strike – so near the end of the war …' Others were more upbeat. 'This is a <u>Star Day</u> indeed,' Nellie Carver thought, cheered too that there would be '<u>NO MORE SIRENS</u> from today! … Home by 7.43 seething with excitement and hope.' Overnight, Kathleen Tipper seems to have caught the same feeling, for on 3 May, after a late-night announcement on the BBC which she picked up that morning, she could celebrate something at last: 'The Russians have captured Berlin – surely the most thrilling news of this wonderful week.' But the workers at home still gave her grief. She got soaked on her long way home from work, that transport strike forcing her to walk long distances, 'and causing a great deal of inconvenience to people in our part of the world who depend almost entirely on trams, buses and trolleys to get to work'. On 4 May came the news of the surrender of the German armies in Denmark, Holland and north-west Germany to British armies – 'My-oh-my can we stand any further excitement?' wondered Nellie Carver – and two days later, 6 May, the armies fighting US forces laid down their arms.[30]

Through the weekend of 5–6 May Londoners waited expectantly for news that the war was finally over. That Sunday, in Lowndes Square, Chelsea, Bryher 'spent the morning on a round of "Happy Peace" visits. There were only two topics of conversation, "When will the news break?" or "If they close the shops as they say for three days, will they let us get our rations in advance?"' All day she and her friends waited. 'Then we listened solemnly to the 9 o'clock news but the announcer sounded as baffled as we were. It was rapidly turning into a nightmare.'[31]

By Monday 7 May it seemed surely to be all over. 'Back to work,' Kathleen Tipper wrote that morning after a grim weekend, invited to stay with a friend at her miserly aunt's in Southend:

although everyone is certain the war will be over today, and we didn't do much work, nor did anyone else in the buildings around us. The Air Ministry windows opposite were full of people all afternoon, and when the news of the surrender of all U-boats was announced we really thought it over. First people said Mr. Churchill was speaking at 11 a.m., then 2 o'clock, then 3 o'clock, then 4, then 6 o'clock.[32]

All this faltering at the final fence had international causes. Stalin had objected at the last moment to any announcement that the war was over until he was ready to say so, demanding the surrender document be signed in Russian-held Berlin. It sorely wrong-footed Churchill and his widely flagged desire to announce the war in Germany to be over at last, but Harry Truman, the new US president, agreed to the delay, causing general consternation in Whitehall.[33]

Finally:

At 9'oclock we heard the news 'Mr. Churchill will speak at 3 o'clock tomorrow and announce V-E Day, and the following day will be a holiday'. I think this whole thing has been badly managed, and all the spontaneity has gone from us. A few of us wandered around Trafalgar Square on the way home, and certainly the flags and bunting are coming out in a big way now. Flags do look attractive, especially the lovely things they hang on some of the more important buildings. We are still undecided as to what to do tomorrow, but I think I will ring D. [her friend Dorothy] in the morning around 8 a.m. How strange to think that the war will soon be over. It will need a lot of getting used to I think. As we went to bed, many bonfires had been lit all around – a little early celebrating. The roads all around look colourful, and no doubt by tomorrow it will all be gay.[34]

In fact there was much gaiety that night too, in the West End and elsewhere. Across London bonfires were lit in many streets and on the river foghorns blared into the early hours. 'There was a great glow over London when we went to bed,' wrote Dorothy Wells in Ealing. 'It seemed like a proper fire but it proved to be bonfires in the streets.' It was all brought to a stop around 1.30 a.m. when a terrific thunderstorm had everyone running for cover.[35]

'So this is V-Day,' wrote Kathleen Tipper next morning, 8 May. It was a fine day and many were up early at the bakers', queueing for bread in response to a news item saying they'd be open for an hour. Then the 6.5 million Londoners settled down to enjoy the moment – spread over two days of public rejoicing, 8 and 9 May – in their own way. Dorothy Wells and Florence spent the 8th in front of the wireless, listening first to the Prime Minister's broadcast at 3 p.m. and then the King's at 9 p.m., with other famous voices in between. They ventured out to the bonfire in the middle of their road at 'the bottom end' and then to another one a couple of streets away, but found the 'half-drunk mob' there distasteful. Dorothy felt distant from the celebrations: 'I don't seem to feel much of anything. If Victory had been declared in the middle of the Flying Bombs or Rocket Period, we should all have felt tremendous relief, but we have had about six weeks quiet, and to folk like me with no near relative in the Forces, the relief is much less.'[36]

In the evening of the 8th Kathleen Tipper went with 'Pop' (her father) and sister Joyce – her mum had sadly died of cancer in November 1943 – 'up West', 'with Pop saying the whole time "My this is nothing like Armistice night, 1918," the while trying to get through the vast mob of people.' She was there again with friends next evening too, the 9th, joining the crowds to see the King and Queen and the Princesses on the balcony of Buckingham Palace. She saw Mr Churchill 'sitting on the top of a car ... I wondered if he was thinking "How long will they think of me this way?"'[37]

Anthony and Marjorie Heap, Anthony a keen recorder of any moment that might seem 'historic' to posterity, started out for the West End early on the morning of the 8th, listened to Churchill's broadcast with thousands of others as it was relayed over loudspeakers in Trafalgar Square, went home for a wash and tea, 'for it was a sweltering hot day', and then came back in the evening. They too saw the royal family and then watched the Prime Minister give an impromptu speech from the balcony of the Ministry of Health in Whitehall. Anthony, an early opponent of the war who had loathed the 'warmonger' Churchill, at last found himself won over: 'It was a great moment – even more thrilling than the scene at Buckingham Palace ...' They stayed till late, taking it all in, and got home at 1 a.m.: 'it had been a grand day'. They were out after lunch next day too, doing pretty much the same trek over again. 'And so we came to the end of two perfect days. They couldn't have furnished a happier set of memories to look back on in my old age.'[38]

Nellie Carver was working till 6.30 p.m. on 8 May, but put up her flags – some saved from the 1937 coronation – before she went in. She and her mother spent the evening walking round their part of battered West Norwood and 'saw all decorations' before returning home for the King's and other broadcasts. They went out again to enjoy the bonfires and fireworks and the music and singing before going to bed 'absolutely happy'. Next day she was off work and she and her mother had more of the same, with even bigger bonfires and a children's tea party in a nearby street: 'Where they got all the fancy cakes from I can't think!' That night, 'The searchlight display over London was a sight in itself. I stayed until nearly 12 ock [sic] watching it all & marvelling anew at our people …'[39]

As with Armistice Day in 1918, many absentee Londoners wanted to return to the city that had borne the brunt of hostilities on the home front. Verily Anderson was in Sussex, staying with her mother; she hopped on a train, winkled her husband out of his club and joined the crowds outside the Palace. Naomi Mitchison had left her London home for the safety of the Scottish Highlands in 1939, though venturing back for occasional visits. She took the train overnight from Glasgow, arriving at Euston on the morning of the 8th, camped out in her Hammersmith home and saw out the celebrations. Even for non-Londoners, the capital was the place to be if you could possibly wangle it. The poet Henry Treece was in the RAF and a Midlander by background, but he got leave from his base to come up to London with some comrades, arriving at King's Cross at 1.15 p.m. on the 9th: 'As we walk along the platform, the Tannoy announces a fanfare in honour of all Service men. It's a very inspiriting fanfare, and makes a lump come into my throat.'[40]

When they got to the West End they found the celebrations generally decorous. There was some drunkenness among servicemen and no doubt among servicewomen, and many of both sexes were out for a good time, but everyone of Pop Tipper's age and experience contrasted this sober VE day with the riotous abandon of 11 November 1918. For one thing drink was in very short supply. Henry Treece and his party had to make do with lemonades in the first pub they entered, though drink was to be had if you knew where to get it. The jazz musician Humphrey Lyttelton, an Old Etonian guardsman, had come up from his barracks at Caterham and brought his trumpet with him. After a 'picnic champagne supper in the Park' he gathered round him an impromptu band that processed playing round and round the Victoria Memorial outside Buckingham Palace. Ronald Delderfield, an Air Ministry clerk and later a well-known novelist, found it hard to discover anything 'untoward' among the VE day crowds, though not for want of trying. At last he found it, at Piccadilly Circus:

> Three G.I.s had climbed on to a piece of scaffolding enclosing the Regent Street entrance to the Underground and with them was a pretty girl. They were all slightly drunk, or perhaps they were pretending to be, for

in the beam of a spotlight operated by someone on one of the tall buildings across the Circus you could see them staggering and gesticulating. They seemed to move in calculated jerks, like amateur actors simulating tipsiness. The space around them was packed with sightseers and it was impossible to move in any direction. Every face was raised hopefully towards the four young people on the crash barrier and at least they did not disappoint us. Amid encouraging cheers the girl began to undress and the Americans, standing round like attentive and conscientious grooms of the bedchamber, took her garments one by one and tossed them into the crowd. It was all done rather solemnly, like a long, complicated conjuring trick and when the young lady was naked the audience responded with a sustained and rather breathless giggle of mass embarrassment. Then some constables moved forward, shouldering their way through the crowd and began to reason with the Americans, so that presently one of them draped the strip-tease artist in his greatcoat and they all climbed down. We were all left wondering not what happened to them but where they got their liquor. There was none on sale for us anywhere.[41]

The West End attracted Londoners and newcomers in hundreds of thousands but it was the local celebrations, like those witnessed by Dorothy Wells in Ealing and Nellie Carver in West Norwood, that brought out Londoners in their millions. In the Jewish East End the 'dancing and singing crowds' at Aldgate 'on the evening of VE Day', aided by pub pianos wheeled onto the pavements, had much to celebrate and it seemed that all East Enders were on their feet and out of doors from before midnight on the 7th to midnight on the 9th. Floodlit dancing on the 8th at King Edward Memorial Park, Shadwell, on the riverside, drew 'record crowds':

> Nowhere in East London were the decorations more thickly together than in such places as The Highway, Juniper Street, King David's Lane, and a hundred nearby turnings. Parties in fancy dress, and followed by crowds of children, went dancing along Cable-street, where in every side turning red and golden flames were dancing from the fires in the middle of the roads.[42]

The children's party that Nellie Carver and her mother had fun watching in Rosendale Road, West Norwood, on 8 May was quick off the mark. Just one was noted in the East End local press for that day, at Manchester Road, in the Isle of Dogs, where Bill Regan had lived through the blitz. Bill was now living in Lewisham and it says much for the bashing taken by the island since September 1940 that there were only thirty children in this long road able to take advantage of the 'feast of good things to eat, including ham, beetroot and salid [sic], spam sandwiches, jellies, ices and cold custard'. But after, with the dust settled on the VE days themselves, celebrations continued across London for days to come. 'Stepney's big VE procession' on Sunday 13 May assembled at Tower Hill and marched through the borough's blitzed streets to the People's Palace in Mile End Road, where the 'Victory Mayor', Councillor W. J. Edwards, took the salute. The march was led by men from the Royal Navy and the merchant service, in which Edwards had sailed on the Russia convoys; there were Wrens, the band of the Middlesex Regiment, representatives of the 'blue clad men and women of Stepney's own warden's service', the NFS, WVS, Red Cross, St John Ambulance service and youth groups including the Scouts. Every borough in London put on something similar. There were children's street parties everywhere, now that there had been adequate time to arrange things. Adults had parties too, in their favourite boozers, and there were more floodlit dances in the parks and outside cinemas in the main streets. Children's parties continued in the East End and else-where for the rest of May and well into June.[43]

The mood of joy, and especially relief, felt in London was universal. It was at its sharpest on those astonishing two days, 8 and 9 May 1945. Nellie Carver summed it all up next morning:

This was the end of VE Hols – the real end for us Londoners – of 5 years of strain & struggle – of nights & days crouching under the stairs while all Hell was let loose above us, of inky-black nights crawling through the Yard of K.E.B. [King Edward Building, Newgate Street, in which was her part of the Central Telegraph Office] fearing to hear the howling of the Alert before reaching home. The end of Bombs, Doodlebugs, Rockets and Blackout. How can we ever be thankful enough?[44]

Some Londoners had more cause to be thankful than others. Klara Modern, the Austrian Jewish refugee who had worked in a children's nursery at Euston, was now Clare Deveson, living in Dulwich. She had married Charles, a schoolteacher and German speaker who was an officer in the Army Intelligence Corps, interrogating high-ranking German prisoners of war held at Trent Park, Enfield. Klara, as she still signed herself in letters to her family in America, was expecting a baby in July. On 16 May she wrote to her sister to describe how 'London celebrated royally' and how 'Everybody was immensely relieved'. She felt 'immense gratitude that all my friends and relations and I myself are still alive':

> But my dear, what deep, wonderful, everlasting satisfaction to think that at last these bloody, beastly, cursed, devilish Nazis, the Party and a large, large part of the German (and also the Austrian) people, all those swine, who used to parade in the [Vienna] University, whom one hated so much and wanted to see crushed, that they really have been defeated, smashed, broken up and humiliated in every way.[45]

RELIEF, even exultation, did not linger long. Nor did any lively hope for the immediate future. After all, so little could change. Men were still in the services, trying to sort out the catastrophic mess in Europe, or preparing to join the fight against the Japanese in the Far East. Relations with Soviet Russia, complicated by its brutal handling of the Polish question on which Britain had gone to war in the first place, gave solid grounds for long-term anxiety. The economic woes of a shattered UK economy snuffed out any hopes 'of pretty clothes, of ample meals'. Everyone knew that there could be no miracle cure for a blitzed London and its ill-housed population. And after all, the government was the same one that had been established to fight the war five years before. A report from Mass Observation, an organisation consti-tutionally disposed to look on the gloomy side of life, thought with probably only a little exaggeration that the joy of VE day 'gave way in a matter of days, perhaps even a matter of hours, to one of doubt, distrust and bewilderment, steadily growing as the weeks passed'. There was, it thought, an overall sense of 'disappointment'. Certainly, Kathleen Tipper picked it up on her journey to work on 10 May: 'as I looked around in the tram I realised that we all looked as grim as ever.'[46]

One other factor was picked up by Mass Observation: 'Some people mention with bitter regret the disappearance of the camaraderie of wartime life, and the ill-will and backbiting among all classes of people which they feel has succeeded it.' It was a feeling exemplified within days by the fractious political situation in Westminster. There had not been a general election since 1935 and the Labour Party in particular had chafed at the inability to pursue post-war policy while its leaders were yoked to Churchill's coalition government. Attlee and Churchill both wanted the coalition to keep together until the war in Japan had been won, an event that seemed in May 1945 to be potentially twelve months away, even more. But an agitation within the Labour Party to leave the coalition now that Hitler was defeated, an agitation in which Herbert Morrison played a key role, proved unstoppable. Attlee told Churchill that Labour would have to leave the coalition but wanted the break-up to wait till July or August, for international affairs to pass an important stage at the planned Potsdam Conference with Russia and America, for time to organise campaigns among service voters stationed abroad, and for the stale electoral register to be refreshed by local returning officers conducting a house-to-house canvass. Churchill refused. If Labour wanted to leave, then it should go now. He dissolved the coalition on 23 May and replaced it with a National Conservative 'Caretaker' Government under his leadership. The general election would be held on 5 July. Just who had been responsible for a rushed general election in which many might be disenfranchised would embitter the opening weeks of the campaign. It also caused huge uncertainty about what the results might be: in south London boroughs within the County of London, the 1935 electoral roll had registered 800,000 parliamentary voters; now, through migration to the suburbs, the chaos of war and an unreliable register, just 550,000 could have a vote.[47]

That uncertainty did not seem reflected in the opinion polls, however. Throughout the war, Churchill had polled extraordinarily high satisfaction numbers over his conduct of the war, with Gallup generally recording figures around 80 per cent. There had been occasional wavering but nothing like a trend showing a decline in his popularity over time. On the other hand, when Gallup asked, at any time after May 1940, which party people would vote for in an election 'tomorrow', Labour was always ahead and usually substantially so. Nothing had changed when polling began in earnest. In February 1945 42 per cent said they would vote Labour and 24 per cent Conservative; asked what they thought the result would be the numbers dropped to 33 per cent forecasting Labour would win and 22 per cent Conservative, with 16 per cent thinking 'Some sort of coalition' was likely. In March 90 per cent of people said they were likely to vote, though this didn't include service personnel abroad, who were given postal votes, and those who didn't know that they weren't on the register and so disbarred from voting anyway. In April the gap between Labour and Conservative had narrowed a little, 40 per cent against 24 per cent, with the Liberals moving up a point from 11 to 12 per cent. In June the gap narrowed significantly when a different question was asked to exclude the 'Don't Knows'. When those who said they would definitely vote were asked for which party, Labour polled 47 per cent, Conservatives 41 per cent and the Liberals dropped back to 10 per cent. Even so, these figures were still clear cut in Labour's favour. Almost no one seems to have believed them. George Orwell wrote in early June that 'I have predicted all along that the Conservatives will win by a small majority, and I will stick to this, though not quite so confidently as before, because the tide is obviously running very strongly in the other direction.' Anthony Heap didn't know what to think and on the day the election was called put the conundrum in a nutshell: ''Twill be interesting to see whether Churchill's personal popularity is still going strong enough to counter the swing to the left that has been going on for some time.' He thought, 'It looks like being a very close contest anyway.'[48]

'On the surface, the electorate seemed to display but little interest in the coming decision,' Mass Observation reported:

Wearing of party colours was almost non-existent; street brawling and rowdyism on election issues were conspicuous by their absence. Yet under this cloak of apathy the country was doing some hard thinking. From all the pre-Polling Day material one gets the same impression – of a practical, unemotional weighing-up of pros and cons – in marked contrast to the emotional, almost hysterical nature of much of the propaganda from both sides.[49]

Most of Mass Observation's material on which this conclusion was based came from close contact with just one election campaign – in London, at East Fulham, a mainly working-class community 'with a smaller middle-class area around Baron's Court'. In fact, Mass Observation's own work in East Fulham shows any 'cloak of apathy' to be far from the case when it came to the Labour Party's campaign and the interest in it shown by potential Labour voters. The numbers of Labour Party posters, for instance, far outweighed those for rival parties – a count in two working-class streets found one Liberal, eighteen Conservative and fifty-one for Labour. Organised heckling of opponents' speakers at indoor venues and on street corners was aggressive and disruptive from the Labour side, just scattered and random among the other parties. The Conservative candidate, the sitting member because East Fulham, despite its class make-up, was a Tory seat with a slim majority in 1935, was the patrician W. Waldorf Astor, additionally a serving naval officer. Up against him was Michael Stewart, a captain in the Royal Army Educational Corps and a university lecturer in economics, untried politically and with a dry and unemotional speaking style compared to the stylish and experienced Conservative. Astor's meetings were ill-attended by his supporters, though audiences were swollen by noisy Labour hecklers who frequently shouted down voices from the platform. But Stewart's meetings were jammed to overflowing, with town hall rooms seating 600 spilling over into galleries, the doors left open so that people queueing up the stairs could hear what was said. Stewart brought in big Labour guns to bolster his appeal, notably Ernest Bevin, Dr Edith Summerskill (MP for West Fulham), the well-known *Daily Herald* columnist Hannen Swaffer and the prominent left-wing controversialist Harold Laski, also an alderman on Fulham Borough Council. On the eve of poll Laski turned up at 10 p.m., the meeting having begun at 7 p.m., stand-in speakers having kept the audience content to wait. Despite the long delay he received an enthusiastic reception, his listeners laughing dutifully at his anti-Churchill jibes; it was his sixth meeting of the night. In London, at least, if there was any 'apathy' in this election it was not on the Labour side. And there is nothing to suggest from the local newspapers that anything much different was happening elsewhere in the capital.[50]

The campaign nationally was set alight by Churchill's radio broadcast of 4 June in which, among other things, he claimed that Labour would need a 'Gestapo' to police the totalitarian society it was planning. It seems to have been universally condemned, causing 'real distress and concern that a figure so admired, even by his opponents, should so lower his prestige'. Despite this, Churchill remained a charismatic and popular figure, in London at least – his very own battleground – and especially among women: 'if Churchill was returned to power,' a forty-five-year-old man of the artisan class told Mass Observation in East Fulham, 'it would be as a result of the women's vote – they were solidly behind him ... their attitude was one of immense gratitude and admiration'. A poll of voting intentions, almost certainly again in East Fulham – Mass Observation shy of confessing the shallow evidence on which its authoritative judgements were based – did indeed reveal a gender split, but by no means as clear as this widely shared view of Churchill's support would suggest. Some 62 per cent of men intended to vote Labour, just 30 per cent Conservative; for women the figures were 47 per cent and 43 per cent, with still a significant majority for Labour.[51]

Policy differences between the parties did not rank highly with the electorate in the campaign. Every manifesto emphasised the difficulties of the war and international relations, and the country's difficult economic position. The Liberal Party's strongest platform was 'a radical programme of practical reform' based on the Beveridge Report; Sir William Beveridge, the party's greatest asset, was now a Liberal MP and fighting to retain his seat in this election. The Conservative Party put the whole weight of its appeal on Winston Churchill and stressed Britain's role in a changing world, pledging to revive the economy through vibrant public enterprise. *Let Us Face the Future*, the Labour Party's manifesto, promised to finish the war and build the peace through a limited programme of public ownership and 'a new National Health Service', 'free for all'.[52]

But the only one of the many policy issues on offer that fired electoral interest in any way was housing. This had been the case for some time but was overwhelmingly so in 1945. 'What do you think is the most urgent home-front problem that the government must solve during the next few months?' Gallup asked in February, and 54 per cent thought housing, 13 per cent employment and nothing else registered more than 4 per cent. In May, with the campaign just under way, Gallup asked voters which issues they thought would be most discussed in the campaign: 41 per cent thought housing, 15 per cent full employment, 7 per cent social security, 6 per cent nationalisation of industry, 5 per cent international security and the rest 3 per cent or less. Asked in June who should get government assistance to build houses, 44 per cent thought it should be local authorities, 19 per cent private builders and 29 per cent thought both equally. The most significant response of all was this: asked which party would handle the housing problem better, 42 per cent thought Labour and 25 per cent Conservative. This was despite the only firm manifesto pledge on numbers to be built by an incoming government being made in the Conservative manifesto: 220,000 house completions in the first two years with a further 80,000 starts. The other parties had stressed the importance of housing, of course, but did not put a number on what they would be able to build.[53]

In the campaign in London it was the housing issue that galvanised voters. A report of Bevin's speech to a Labour Party public meeting in East Fulham in June gives a flavour. He'd begun with international relations and the Conservatives' pre-war record on appeasement, winning some laughter from the audience with one burst of clapping for four seconds when he praised Labour's contribution to the wartime coalition. He then moved on. 'The real issue of domestic policy: HOUSING. We should have a policy for housing, like the policy for producing shells, tanks and aeroplanes' ('Applause, 6 sec.'). 'Instead of dealing with the job through local authorities, it should become a State job taken over by the Government, just as it undertakes the defence in war' ('Hearty clapping, 8 sec.'). 'If Labour is returned we'll begin to finance the housing of this country as we financed the war. It should be a national emergency' ('Deep & heartfelt hear-hears from different parts ... Clapping. 10 secs.'). 'People's passions are more easily roused over the sticky problem of housing than on any other,' Mass Observation concluded, and it was a truth recognised by the Conservative candidate, Waldorf Astor, too: '"Whatever party gets into power will have to show results on housing. The mood of the masses isn't to be trifled with. Housing will be the test case."'[54]

East Fulham was in inner London, where the metropolitan housing problem was at its worst, but 'people's passions' were roused about housing in the suburbs too. They had been ravaged much by the Baby Blitz and most by the V-weapons of 1944 and 1945. 'Housing was the most acute problem now facing Harrow,' a meeting of Harrow and Pinner Townswomen's Guild was told by a local, probably Conservative, councillor in March. A letter in the *Norwood News* in June, noting that 'a considerable portion of your paper is devoted to the acute housing situation', called for 'an extensive national plan' to build 'homes for the people' free from interference by 'vested interests'. Ken V. Smith, the writer, was a 'Serviceman', his wife and he 'both from the Streatham area', who had 'no home as yet'. Another local resident, Nellie Carver, a Conservative supporter in West Norwood, a suburban constituency where Duncan Sandys was the sitting MP, wrote in her diary a few days later that 'Some folks think Labour will get in on Housing, but in the meantime it's all very hectic.'[55]

WINSTON Churchill made an open-air speaking tour of many London constituencies in early July, the last 'very hectic' days of polling. Wherever he went he was received with great enthusiasm – not unalloyed, it's true, because boos mingled with the cheers. But many people cheered him for his personal part in the nation's – and London's – victory while not intending to vote for his government now that the real war was over. He visited East Fulham on 2 July: 'CHURCHILL HERE AT 5 p.m.', the placards announced on Walham Green. The green itself was 'packed with people' and the roads were lined five deep. Traffic was diverted to accommodate the crowds. Astor spoke at 5 'and his speech was quite well received'. As Churchill's car passed – '"There he goes! There's his little 'at!"' – some people ran after it to get closer to where he was to speak. There was 'a confusion of boos and cheers, with cheers predominating', the noise so great that the observer could hear nothing of what he said though just twenty yards away. 'The cheers and support of Churchill came more from women than men.' 'All the comments agreed that he looked old and very tired, in spite of later newspaper reports that he looked fit and well.'[56]

Amid the scores of open-air stump speeches on Churchill's London tour, next day at 9 p.m. he was in Clapton, Hackney, a mixed working- and lower-middle-class area, like so much of inner London. According to the local paper, 'he was given a reception which, if possible, was even more enthusiastic than that of the great cities of the Midlands and the North of England. Only a very small section of the waiting crowd manifested hostility, and its booing and barracking were drowned by overwhelming counter cheers.' 'In response to the call "Are we downhearted?"' – a favourite of Churchill's visits to Londoners during the blitz – 'there were loud shouts of "No!" and more outbursts of cheering, and the police slowly forced a way through the dense crowd as the Prime Minister proceeded to Bethnal Green, the next stage in his homeward journey'. If 'homeward' meant back to 10 Downing Street, then most readers would have agreed that it would probably prove to be so.[57]

One of Churchill's last steps on the eve of poll was to beard the Labour lion in his den. Herbert Morrison, Home Secretary and Minister of Home Security in Churchill's War Cabinet and a close colleague of the Prime Minister, had decided in January to abandon his ultra-safe Labour seat at South Hackney and challenge the Tory incumbent at East Lewisham, Sir Assheton Pownall, who had held the seat since 1918. Morrison proclaimed his faith in 'the reasoned appeal the Labour Party can make to all sections of the community – manual workers and "blackcoats" alike ... [T]he soundest Labour Party appeal is that which is most universal in its scope.' If Labour could win East Lewisham, with its Tory majority of some 6,500, it could win almost anywhere in London. In the circumstances of this very uncertain election it was a brave switch. Brave but not foolhardy. Under the then Conservative LCC from the 1920s on, West and East Lewisham had been sown with council cottage estates, overspill housing for inner London workers in housing need. The LCC had turned Labour in 1934 and the new council had planted one more estate, Whitefoot Lane, in Morrison's new constituency, homes for over a thousand families and all built after the last general election had been held.[58]

On this evening of 4 July in Lewisham, Churchill was at his most pugnacious, perhaps his most out of control. Again, immense crowds came out to see and hear him speak with the aid of a microphone from his open-topped car. Again he was met by cheers and boos, though the cheers seemed once more to 'have it'. Again came '"Are we down-hearted?"' and the traditional response. But Churchill had a special message for the people of Lewisham. He was speaking in Lewis Grove, close to where so many had been killed by a V-1 in July 1944, and used the occasion to make a personal attack on Morrison – '"Of all the colleagues I have lost, he is the one I am least sorry to see the last of"' – who, Churchill said, had publicly held him responsible for the disaster that day. '"Don't you think it rather a cowardly and un-British thing for a Cabinet Minister, sitting with his colleagues and taking part in the proceedings to try to throw the blame of a particular incident on someone else? But it is thoroughly characteristic of Mr. Morrison himself."' Morrison would subsequently clarify that he had said that, in answer to a question during an election meeting, Churchill had instructed, 'without consultation with his colleagues', that no warning should be given in respect of single V-1s. It was an instruction that, after Lewisham, Morrison said he reversed. Churchill made a final plea to the crowd: '"I hope that Lewisham will throw this intruder out. He only came here because he ran away from a Communist in Hackney."' It was unseemly, undignified and unlikely to change anyone's mind. Churchill ended the campaign as he had begun it, in ill-tempered mudslinging.[59]

ON polling day, 5 July, in East Fulham and no doubt nearly everywhere else in London, motorcars touring with loudspeakers and numerous

open-air meetings endeavoured to whip out the vote. Anthony Heap
was a clerk at the polling station in working-class Sandwich Street,
south of Euston Road. There were 870 on the register with a supplementary armed forces roll of over ninety. Through the day there was
a 'slow steady stream' of voters, around thirty to forty an hour. 'But
in the evening the average rose to about 70 an hour and, by the time
we closed at 9.0, 587 civilian and 92 service voters (the latter mainly
by proxy) had been recorded, roughly two-thirds of the register.' In a
quiet moment Anthony had nipped out to vote Conservative in another
polling station in the same school building. That was the poll, but the
votes would not be counted for three weeks to give time for all the
service votes to arrive from abroad.[60]

There then, according to Mass Observation, followed 'a strange
calm – one would have called it apathy' – that misleading word again –
'had not this been belied by the intense interest when the results actually did appear'. It was said that the canny top-hatted gents at the
London Stock Exchange were voting 6 to 4 on a Labour victory and
by the day of the count it seemed they might know a thing or two.
Anthony Heap was a clerk at his local town hall helping sort the votes,
postal votes kept in a separate pile from the rest: 'from what I saw of
them this morning I should be very surprised if the Reds don't romp
home in St. Pancras. If they fail to, it won't be for any lack of support
from the forces who have obviously been badly bitten by the bolshevist
bug. At least about 95 per cent of them.'[61]

The results were announced next day, Thursday 26 July. The Labour
victory was as crushing as it was astonishing. The party fortunes had
been reversed compared to ten years before. Nationwide there had been
164 Labour MPs in 1935; there were now 393. There had been 358
Conservative MPs in 1935; there were now 198. The Liberals performed
disastrously: even William Beveridge had lost his seat in Berwick-upon-
Tweed.

Londoners played a large part in Labour's victory. They switched
their allegiance to the Labour Party in greater proportions than voters
in any other part of the country. There were sixty-one constituencies
in the County of London. In 1935 Labour had held twenty-eight of
them; the party now had control in forty-nine – it would have been
fifty had not Mile End (Stepney) been lost to Phil Piratin, the Communist
Party candidate. The Labour gains included East Fulham, where Michael
Stewart won comfortably with a majority of over 5,000, and all three

St Pancras seats. Even more surprising were the Labour gains in suburban areas of Greater London outside the County: 'If Labour had won fewer seats in this area, it would have had a much smaller majority in 1945,' was the subsequent judgement of one election historian.[62]

There had been a redistribution of seats in 1944 to create twenty-five new constituencies, reflecting geographical shifts in the British population between the wars. Seventeen of these new seats were in Greater London. Twelve were won by Labour, seven in Middlesex (out of eight new seats in the County), four out of five in metropolitan Essex (the fifth, Woodford, was won comfortably by Winston Churchill with a majority of over 17,000) and one out of two in metropolitan Kent. Labour gains in suburban London, in and out of the County, included Brentford and Chiswick, Chislehurst, Dulwich, Enfield, Hendon North, Ilford North, East Lewisham (where Herbert Morrison romped home with a 15,219 majority), West Lewisham, Mitcham, Norwood (where Duncan Sandys's majority of some 6,500 in 1935 was now a Labour seat with one of over 2,000), Uxbridge and Wimbledon. The largest movement to Labour in the whole country was in north-west Kent (areas like Chislehurst and Bexley, a new constituency) with a swing of 22 per cent. Middlesex and the residential areas of London were not far behind with 18.5 per cent; the national average was 12 per cent. Turnout nationally was a respectable 72.8 per cent, higher than 1935 (71.1) but lower than the huge turnout on a refreshed voting register in 1950 of 83.9 per cent, the highest ever in a British general election.[63]

Among Labour voters the results were received as much with amazement as with delight. Mass Observation detected 'a feeling of awe, almost alarm, at what they had themselves done'. Nor was there much public rejoicing: 'Wild celebrations would have been quite out of keeping with the sober, serious mood of the country throughout the election, and we find that Labour supporters took the result with quiet satisfaction rather than jubilation.' Kathleen Tipper voted Labour and was delighted with the result: 'One of the most astonishing days of my life.' Others reacted with 'horror and dismay'. Anthony Heap thought it 'a terrible calamity for the country … To think that England should sink to this!' For Hilda Neal the result 'fulfils our gloomiest forebodings'. Dorothy Wells deplored the Labour victory and so did Nellie Carver: 'poor Duncan Sandys is out! It's a very strange affair as I've seen such a few Labour posters about in our windows.' She thought 'it must be the Forces Vote, as cannot hear all around, who <u>has</u> voted Labour! Very depressing, anyway. Fancy Mr Attlee as Prime Minister – am simply furious at the unthinking ingratitude of the public.'[64]

WHY *did* so many Londoners vote Labour in 1945? Mass Observation, whose observers were busiest in London during the election and who drew most on this experience when considering the result, helpfully divided Labour's supporters into three broad (though overlapping) constituencies. One important section was working-class voters, who believed the party sympathised with them and essentially represented their interests. Second were anti-Conservative voters, who associated the Conservative Party with the failures of economic depression, austerity, appeasement and the culmination of all these in the crisis of May 1940. Third were 'intellectuals', generally though not exclusively educated and middle-class, who thought that 'socialism will raise the standard of living for the masses and increase the general happiness and security of the nation as a whole'. We might usefully consider how these three constituencies played out in the London electorate in 1945.[65]

The link between Labour and the London working class indeed had strong roots. From 1919 on, in some places like Poplar, West Ham and Woolwich for a generation before that, working-class districts generally voted Labour in local and parliamentary elections. As middle-class migration, or 'flight', to the suburbs increased with the great expansion of suburban house building and owner occupation there in the 1920s and 1930s, working-class tenants occupied the housing deserted by the middle class, usually renting by the floor or even room; and as workers moved in and 'lowered the tone', then the middle-class exodus gathered pace. We can chart, ward by ward in many inner London boroughs, the consolidation of Labour majorities moving from the centre outwards from one local election to another, precisely in line with this working-class migration. There were anomalies: south St Pancras should have been Labour on this count but wasn't and South-West Bethnal Green was Liberal, while all around was Labour, because of a much-loved local MP, Percy Harris, who was duly turned out in 1945. But, generally, this had been true for a quarter-century before 1945. Demographic change alone, then, would have accounted for many constituencies changing from blue to red in this election. Probably ten or a dozen Labour victories (including the two southerly constituencies in St Pancras, and East Fulham) would have been expected because of internal migration taking place after 1935, even leaving aside the impact of war. Working-class migration to some suburbs, through LCC and other council estates, and a small amount of working-class owner occupation, would also have enlarged Labour's natural voting base in the outer reaches of London County and even beyond, though it clearly didn't account on its own for victories of the size of Morrison's in East Lewisham.

This working-class identification with Labour in London was strengthened, not weakened, by war. Intensification of class feeling had two main wartime strands. Evacuation caused a deep-seated psychic bruising for families exposed in their poverty and despised for it. And the blitz of 1940–41 produced resentment that working-class areas had suffered worse than middle-class, and that East Enders had not been offered the same protection as people in the West End and elsewhere. Communist propaganda at the time no doubt inflamed some of this class feeling, rewarded by Phil Piratin's victory in Mile End, but it was merely scratching at an angry rash. Those first eighteen months of war left a grievance among many working-class Londoners that subsequent events – the suburban sufferings of the Little Blitz and the V-weapons – could not expunge. They wanted a party to right their wrongs and they found it in Labour.

Additionally, the rise of trade unionism in wartime London, in the engineering, munitions and aircraft manufacturing industries in particular, had endowed men and very many women with a sense of their own worth as workers contributing to winning the war. The burly figure of Ernest Bevin, a former trade union leader and member of Churchill's War Cabinet, more powerful than anyone but the Prime Minister himself, was important here as a hero and symbol of workers' power. So too was the model of a 'workers' state' that many saw in Soviet Russia. This was not just communist manipulation. London's workers were often inspired by Russia's sacrifices and its apparently classless equality of exertion and sacrifice. Closer to home, workers could see what workplace solidarity might achieve in increased wages, better working conditions and improved productivity for the war effort. They wanted a party that could take these wartime achievements into a post-war Britain that would work for all classes, especially for those neglected by the pre-war political settlement.

The war also had a seismic influence on middle-class London that weakened, not strengthened, its attachment to the Conservative

Party – the Liberals had lost their London purchase more than a generation before and never regained it. The London middle classes were particularly heterogeneous, making generalisations impossible. This was a socially fluid capital city where the great growth between the wars of office work, retail and wholesale trading and public services was far greater than in other parts of the country. These white-collar workers included large numbers of young men and women whose parents were working-class, who themselves aspired to the dress, manners and pleasures of the lower middle class at least, who didn't lack sympathy for working people but who might look to marry someone like themselves and buy a house in the suburbs. Education had opened new doors for many, like Dorothy Wells, a policeman's daughter, who could write several languages and had an important position in a Holborn builders' merchants' office; or Kathleen Tipper, a well-educated shipping clerk whose parents had met as munitions workers in the First World War. These were often people with equivocal class allegiance, not fixed in their views, who might well find themselves among the 'don't knows' when it came to answering an opinion poll on voting intentions.

Even London's established professional and middle classes were especially difficult to pin down in their political views. Some, like Hilda Neal, were fixed by origin and temperament in the Conservative politics they were brought up with. Those politics characterised parts of London like South Kensington and Mayfair, as dyed-in-the-wool politically as West Ham and Poplar were Labour. But many had found a natural home in the fertile radical milieu that had long been a part of London's political life – socialism of one complexion or another, feminism, free-thinking, conscientious objection to war, an infinity of nonconforming religious sects, Fabianism, the Labour and Communist parties. The war had stimulated radicalising tendencies by opening out the opportunities for public discourse in new organisations or movements (the London Women's Parliament or Common Wealth, for instance); and by providing an object lesson in how greater equality of sacrifice and consumption was necessary to win the war, and perhaps to win the peace too. Fairer shares in coal, food, clothing, domestic commodities of all kinds, even housing, where rents were fixed and everyone had to wait in line for war damage repairs, had been overwhelmingly accepted as both necessary and just. There may have been avoidance at the margins, with technical infringements of regulations so vast and complex that no one could claim to know them all, but large-scale and sustained use of a black market in food or other commodities was relatively rare. Londoners with friends in the country fared better than others through food parcels, but they were of all classes, as were the allotment diggers and animal breeders.

The cross-class experience of civil defence, both the official elements in local government and their voluntary sector aids like the WVS and Red Cross, strengthened this feeling of united effort and solidarity. All classes were involved daily in keeping Londoners safe from the most extensive and long-lasting bombardment aimed at any city in the world. The civil defence bond in London was especially strong, if only because it was on its toes from August 1940 to March 1945. It spanned every working-class district and suburb in the capital. Its charitable work in all those children's parties and toy making; its collective enthusiasms in theatricals, dance bands, choirs, orchestras, concert parties, sporting teams and art shows; its long practice in working together to free bomb victims and to care for the injured and the homeless; the shared dangers of men and women under fire, sometimes as fierce as many soldiers might experience under arms: all this predisposed people to a view that mutual aid and a caring all-encompassing state was something that had been essential in wartime and would be invaluable in building the peace. It did not make them all Labour voters, but it at least made understandable the Labour point of view.

One more collective experience is worth mentioning here. The war in London spawned in uncountable numbers discussion groups, brains trusts, local forums for women and youth and so on. Some were based in civil defence, Home Guard and AA batteries and others were more broadly based in local communities. All built on existing foundations in trade union branches, local trades councils, political party organisations, pensioners' clubs and semi-charitable bodies like the Rotarians, Freemasons and others. The Beveridge Report of December 1942, with its enticing view of a caring state that would nurture health and welfare and eliminate poverty, gave these grass-roots initiatives a huge push – here really was something to talk about. So had the London plans of 1943 and 1944 that focused on just what the capital might be when peace finally came. Collective discussion brought many people in London closer to politics, to what might be made of a future 'after the war', and to what their own contribution might be.

These elements of collectivism underpinned the leftward shift that so many in London had noted taking place since the great crisis of May 1940. The Chamberlain government and its heritage were loathed from that point on – not by all but certainly by most, even by most active Conservatives. The association of the Conservative Party with past failure became unbreakable in many people's minds. Building a new future would have to abandon class inequality, unemployment and the means test and replace them with fairer shares, social security, economic and land-use planning in the national interest, and the public ownership of essential industries. These also seemed to be the best features of Stalin's Russia, which had fought Nazi Germany with such determination, courage and sacrifice, and which remained for many in 1945 a convincing argument why Britain should travel some way down the communist road.

Finally, housing. When people in East Fulham were asked during the campaign 'what they thought were the most important things being discussed at the election … housing was mentioned so often that everything else became by comparison unimportant. Yet,' thought Mass Observation, 'it could scarcely be said that housing was an election issue in any real sense,' presumably because the manifestoes had been largely platitudinous – all parties agreed that vast numbers of houses would be needed after the war – and because there was little active disagreement on policy. But it was housing that most Londoners had on their minds in the summer of 1945. That was so whether they lived in slum or suburb. And they voted most of all for the party they trusted to get the job done. That was Labour – because it cared and because it saw this as a task for the state and not private enterprise. 'There can be little doubt that one of the reasons for the defeat of Mr. Churchill's Government at the General Election was widespread dissatisfaction with their attitude to the housing question,' a leader in the *Municipal Journal* concluded a few days after the result. 'They made the grave mistake of thinking that this priority number one problem could be tackled by old threadbare methods, whereas a new outlook and a deeper realisation of the fundamentals were required.' When people were asked who should do the building, it was local councils that they trusted most of all, in part at least because it had been local councils and their civil defence services – greatly helped by the WVS, Red Cross, St John Ambulance and others – who had done so much to keep them safe during the war. And Labour was clear that the state would have to do most of the building, which meant in practice local councils too.[66]

THE election result still left a lot of business undone. For a time things continued pretty much as before. Dealing with the repairs crisis made some progress, even if only to the modest wartime standards. The LRE was finally disbanded in August. Since June 1944 over a million dwellings had been repaired to the 'emergency standard'. It had all been done on a fair-shares-for-all basis. 'The degree of comfort which has been provided is low. But any other policy would have meant prolonging still further the misery of countless families living in roofless and windowless homes.' It might have been left to individual householders to call in their own builders, 'but this would have delayed the general rate of progress, and would inevitably have created a sense of injustice in those whose homes were left out. The only fair and efficient way,' the *Estates Gazette* thought, 'was to allow local authorities to plan the programme as a whole, and to tackle it methodically street by street. That is what has been done.'[67]

That August, with precipitate suddenness, the war in the Far East came to a climax. The atomic bombs on Hiroshima on 6 August and on Nagasaki on the 9th caused a crisis in the Japanese state, where militarists had long held sway but where a 'peace party' had recently pushed an opposing view. The matter was decided in favour of surrender at an Imperial Conference on 14 August. Next day Emperor Hirohito announced to his people that Japan had accepted defeat. The war was over.

Prime Minister Attlee broadcast the news to the nation at midnight on 14/15 August. Then, or later on the morning of Wednesday the 15th, a breathless Nellie Carver heard that:

This day has been declared VJ – at last – the real end of the War – got up to be on at 8 – but heard on Radio that today was a Hol! Rushed round to get some bread – 9am were long queues. It was raining but felt I must go up to Town as the King was opening Parliament, (by a lucky chance). Put on old clothes & thick shoes & buzzed off. Met Hilda Brading at Tulse Hill & together we climbed on top of 33 Tram bound for Westminster. There was 'some' crowd when we alighted, but we edged our way nearer to the front. It was a damp, but such a jolly & excited crowd. We couldn't see much of the Procession but the tops of heads, but we joined in the cheers, however, & after it was over got out on the Embankment & along Whitehall to Trafalgar Square. [There] was another large concourse here but we stood in the Mall & had the luck to see the King & Queen very well on their way back to the Palace. More rain came on but we lingered about, watching a Guards Regiment being dismissed & enjoying the fun. When we arrived in front of the Palace hundreds of thousands of people were waiting, hoping that the Royal Family would come out on the Balcony. I went towards Victoria eventually, but just as I passed the Gates they did come out, so I ran back to the front again. It was grand – they looked so fine & the cheers were deafening. It was now 1pm so I hurried off hoping to catch a number 2, which I was lucky enough to do & got home by 1.45. Had dinner & a quiet afternoon. Put out all the flags again. Took a walk in the evening, there was fireworks & Bonfires as before, but this was not so exciting to us as May 8th.[68]

Some boroughs, notably Lewisham, were 'caught very much "on the hop"' by the speed of Japan's surrender. It could only arrange for the mayor to give a short speech on the balcony of Catford Town Hall at 8.55 p.m., just five minutes before the King's speech was relayed to the crowd by loudspeaker; it was followed by 'dancing in the forecourt'. East Enders, always ready for a knees-up, were far quicker off the mark. Bonfires had been piled in expectation in 'every street' all through 14 August, blitzed houses raided once more for all they could yield. Some piles were fifteen feet high. At midnight, as Attlee broadcast, ships' sirens on the river brought everyone from their beds. The bonfires soon lit up Wapping and Shadwell. Celebrations were hampered later in the day by shortages of cigarettes and beer, but some pubs had shut their doors for a couple of days to conserve supplies for the big moment and were now opening. The first street parties were held that day: Lowell Street, Limehouse, had been planning its party for some eight weeks and gave a 'first-class tea' to its twenty-six 'boys and girls'. At a bomb site in Turin Street, Bethnal Green, a forty-foot bonfire composed of thirty-five tons of waste timber was ceremoniously lit by the mayor; it had been prepared by the deputy borough surveyor, who no doubt had his fingers crossed. Effigies of Hitler, Mussolini and Hirohito were burned on another huge fire at Cambridge Heath. And in Lambeth on that same Wednesday, Field Marshal Montgomery, a local lad, received the freedom of the borough in front of 'cheering laughing crowds';

police had to clear a way so that his open horse-drawn landau – a quaintly Victorian touch for this master of mechanised warfare – could make progress. Bonfires and street parties continued across London for the week to come. There were flags everywhere, though they were few and far between, some noticed, in Oxford Street: perhaps it too had been caught on the hop.[69]

London's war had finally come to an end. It had been six years of terror and boredom, of dislocated lives and material deprivation, of endless frustration and rare moments of boundless joy. But what would it all mean for London and the Londoners when the bonfires eventually burned themselves out and the flags were taken down?

11

LET US FACE THE FUTURE

THE Second World War was a triumph for Londoners. They had acquitted themselves with extraordinary resilience against the most sustained attack on a civilian population ever experienced. Their spirit had been dented at times but never broken. The very fact that they failed to break in 1940 was one reason why Britain was able to carry on alone against Nazi Germany, laying foundations for an alliance that eventually succeeded in winning the most destructive war in human history. The reputation of the capital and its citizens in 1945 could hardly have been higher. And it was Londoners too who were instrumental in moulding the future of peacetime Britain by helping put into power a reforming government that had the welfare of all the country's citizens high on its policy agenda. For ordinary Londoners, this – the Battle of London, 1939–45 – could truly be said to have been 'their finest hour'.

But when the dust had settled on the summer of 1945, the aftermath of war began to tell a different story. What can we make of the legacy of war on the nation's capital and its citizens? In general, there can be only one answer. The Second World War was in many ways a disaster for London. And it was a disaster that had consequences for forty years to come.

WE might begin with the toll of war on Londoners' bodies. Almost 30,000 lost their lives to enemy action between 1940 and 1945. A further 139,349 were injured, 50,507 of them seriously enough to be admitted to hospital rather than being sent home after first aid treatment. Many of those 50,000 would have had lives changed or shortened by the injuries they received, and carried their hurt with them into the post-war world. Amputation, motor disability, brain and lung damage, this was the legacy for thousands of Londoners who could have looked forward to the years of peace only with bruised hopes and stunted expectations.[1]

The lives of many others had been compromised by the impact of war and the adjustment of health services that the fear – later the realisation – of bombing had brought about. The evacuation of London hospitals in 1939 discharged to their homes many who could ill afford to be without the treatment they were getting. They included many tuberculosis patients in a 'highly infective state'. In England and Wales some 8,000 TB patients were sent home in this way, many in London. There quickly followed a spike in notifications: the TB death rate in the County of London rose by 72 per cent between 1938 and 1941, when 2,895 died from all forms of this pernicious disease. It was thought that shelter life had done much to shorten the lives of patients with advanced pulmonary TB and helped spread the disease among shelterers. By the end of the war things had returned to somewhere close to the pre-war mortality levels, but the increased rate of infection left an excess of patients having to live with TB into the post-war years. Deaths from heart disease showed a similar pattern, with a rise from around 3.3 per 1,000 living in 1938 to over 4.4 in 1940–41, falling away to 3.6 in 1945. Influenza deaths during the war had spiked in 1940 and especially 1943 (with 726 deaths), but seasonal flu, despite the severe winters, had not been particularly deadly in this war, as it notoriously had been in 1918–19.[2]

There were, though, some gains. Infant mortality, babies dying before their first birthday, was considered the 'most sensitive index of a nation's health'. The higher the number the worse a community's health was thought to be. The infant mortality rate reflected the extent of material deprivation (poverty and overcrowding in particular) impacting on maternal diet and the ability to care for infants in the home. Despite the worsening in housing conditions, the trend in infant mortality in inner London (generally higher than the out-County districts around it) was downward, though the number fluctuated annually. In 1938 the figure had been 56.5 per 1,000 live births but it fell in 1939 to 47, the lowest ever recorded in inner London till that time; it rose to 57 in 1941 but fell away to 50 in 1942, 51 in 1943 and 1944, and to 44 in 1945, a substantial improvement on the previous best. For much of the war inner London's figures were better than those for England and Wales as a whole. Almost every metropolitan borough saw an improvement. Shoreditch, 'one of the poorest and most overcrowded of London boroughs,' its medical officer of health reported, 'with old housing, badly damaged through enemy action,' ended the war with better figures than inner London as a whole (36 in 1944 and 39 in 1945). While praising his own staff's achievements in the infant welfare centres, and the work of council midwives and health visitors in mothers' homes, he rightly sought the causes in the broader context of war: 'evacuation, better wages, better food due to rationing, fairer distribution of food, and the benign influence of an enlightened Ministry of Food policy on nutrition'. Outside inner London even the poorest districts, like West Ham, shared in this good fortune too.[3]

Better family incomes, with mothers usually earning before their babies were born and, with the help of wartime nurseries, when they were young, were fundamental here, but so was the wartime diet. More vegetables, lower fat and sugar intake, the use of more unrefined flour in 'wheatmeal' bread, however unpalatable it seemed to many, all improved nutritional standards. Improvements arose less from scientific food policy than the unavoidable adjustments demanded by submarine warfare and the consequential agricultural shift to improve the nation's self-sufficiency. But food policy did become important when it came to the diets of mothers and young children. Free or cheap milk was made generally available to mothers and preschool children under the National Milk Scheme from July 1940, reaching 93 per cent of mothers nationally by 1943. Free or cheap 'vitamin foods' were offered to expectant mothers and young children, with vitamin supplements added to feed for babies over six months old. Concentrated orange juice from the USA and cod liver oil were free for children under five and pregnant women from December 1942. Despite occasional shortages and many frustrations with the food supply, the wartime diet was a big improvement on what had gone before, at least for working-class Londoners. On the other hand, some of these benefits to health during the war were offset by the rise in smoking: by 1948, 82 per cent of men in the UK were smokers of one kind or another, and 41 per cent of women.[4]

In all, then, the health legacy of the war was equivocal: for the uninjured, for those not bearing long-lasting scars from bereavement and for young children, their health status was a reasonably solid foundation for the future, whatever it might bring.

*

Londoners' personal relationships bore a similarly mixed legacy. The marriage rate in the County of London rose sharply at the outbreak of war. In 1938 the rate was 22.1 per 1,000 unmarried people but in 1939 it was 27.1. Marriages were concentrated in the second half of that year in the months before and after the declaration of war. In 1940 the rate was 32.9 and it remained above the 1938 level until 1943. There was an increase in 1945 to 24.1 compared to 19.1 in 1944. Mainly because of London's population imbalance, skewed to young adults and especially people aged between twenty-five and thirty-four, the London marriage rate was in normal years some 25 per cent in excess of the national rate, so marriages were more frequent in London than elsewhere. All these extra young married couples seemed to betoken well for London's post-war future.

On the other hand, wartime marriages, certainly those taking place after September 1939, were often under great strain. A psychological study of 200 London working-class marriages, undertaken between October 1943 and January 1946, included about a quarter (forty-four) who had married after war was declared with the husband 'already in uniform'. For them, marriage changed their status but generally 'left living habits largely unaltered'. Making a home was often impossible. Separation 'for months or years' meant that no normal relationship could be established. Instead there were 'occasional brief meetings of ten to fourteen days, which were more like honeymoons than normal married life'. Most newly-wed wives 'remained at work and continued to live in their parents' home', a compromise that was 'an outstanding feature of war marriages'. They were deprived of much companionship with people of their own age, having to rely on letter writing for communication. When husbands were demobbed after the war these couples came together as virtual strangers. But for all marriages, not just these new ones, the war brought dislocation. Separation might impact on older couples with partners called up for the services or drafted out of London on war work. Many had been bombed out of their homes, sometimes more than once. 'A quarter of our families were living as semi-permanent guests with relatives, or sharing a home with them. Half of the remainder occupied part of a house or had rooms,' with 125 of the 200 surveyed having nothing like a stable home.[5]

Separation threw up a myriad anxieties, most notably over infidelity. 'Some men admitted they had had extra-marital experiences of a transient kind' while in the services: there was a distinct spike in venereal disease cases in inner London from 5,481 in 1945 to 10,243 in 1946, especially among servicemen returning home. The study revealed that 'most' of the men who admitted to flings while away had apparently told their wives. 'These women were not deeply concerned,' forgiving passing infidelities, at least if they'd taken place overseas. Some wives confessed to having similar flings themselves, in two cases with builders carrying out war damage repairs, and among husbands mistrust of Allied servicemen in London, particularly Americans, Canadians and Poles, was rife. Fear and suspicion of infidelity must have been as corrosive of relationships as the real thing. But the study only included couples who were remaining together, with those intending to separate or divorce refusing to take part, so we know little about why marriages ended. Although there were no annual statistics of divorces, the 1951 census revealed that the County of London divorce rate was twice as high as the rate for England and Wales, 1,260 per 100,000 persons over twenty years old, against 626.[6]

One consequence of unfaithfulness could be unwanted pregnancies. It is impossible to know the true extent of the problem here. Both the numbers of criminal abortions and newborn babies destroyed or abandoned were probably far greater than the police statistics suggest. Nor were there figures for informal and formal adoptions of children given up to grandparents or friends or religious agencies, one more way of dealing with a tragic difficulty. But these were no doubt marginal consequences of wartime London's complications in marital relationships. The biggest effect of the increase in marriages during these years was an immediate rise in the number of children being born in the capital. The birth rate in London had tended to lag behind the England and Wales average, which had itself been in overall decline since the 1870s; generally, as families became better off, they chose to have fewer children. In the County of London in 1939 the birth rate was 13 per 1,000 total population compared to 14.8 in England and Wales.

Things changed during the war. Births in London rose in 1940 compared with a downturn in the country as a whole and in 1942–5 followed the upward movement nationally; the nationwide peak of 17.7 in 1944 was suppressed in London, probably by evacuation following the V-1 onslaught, to 16.2. But in the first three post-war years the inner London birth rate significantly exceeded the national figures, and from 1949 there was rough parity between the two. It all caused immense problems for London's overstretched maternity services. Many mothers had to be evacuated from London to have their babies in the country. In London the ratio of midwives to mothers was cut and the lying-in period reduced; general hospital beds were emptied to deal with the influx. It was a crisis that lasted till the end of 1947. On the bright side, the wartime London baby boom seems to have been widely welcomed by young families, despite the difficulties of finding anywhere decent to live. That London sample of 200 couples had 278 children, some of whom would have been born before the war: a third of these pregnancies were planned and a further 53 per cent were 'unplanned but welcome'. Just thirty-two children were considered 'unwanted', for whatever reason.[7]

Some of the children in the survey might well have included a number conceived outside marriage though born 'legitimately', in the language of the time. But it is a further mark of the disruption caused by war that the proportion of children born to unmarried mothers increased, especially in London. There is a distortion in the figures here because many mothers seeking to hide an illegitimate birth came to London to have the baby while living permanently elsewhere; and because some babies would have been born legitimately had not separation through war service prevented parents from marrying. But the figures themselves show a steady rise from 5.9 per cent of live births to unmarried mothers in the County of London in 1939 (against 4.2 in England and Wales) to 9.3 in 1944 (7.2 in England and Wales). There was then a steep increase in 1945 to 11.4 per cent (9.4 in England and Wales) which fell back to 8 per cent in 1946 (6.7 in England and Wales).[8]

The 1945 blip probably had much to do with the massive troop movements out of the country from mid-1944 which prevented many couples from regularising conceptions before marriage. One element in the wartime rise, however, was a shift in attitudes among 'a "new type"' of unmarried mother whose 'spirit of independence was considerable' and who had 'little of the sinner and penitent about them'. These women gratefully accepted their babies and were determined to make a home for them without any assistance from 'moral welfare' organisations. Among this new wartime breed was Doreen Bates, whom we have met before. She was a tax inspector living in Croydon with her mother and sister, and she had a lover, a married man also working for the Revenue. Doreen desperately wanted children. She persuaded her lover to get her pregnant and she bore twins, a boy and a girl, in October 1941. She had her babies at a nursing home in Stanmore and set up home for her new family close to where she was brought up in Croydon. With the help of a nanny she continued working. The twins' father was eventually able to spend alternative weekends with Doreen and the children but didn't leave his wife. Doreen never married.[9]

Though comfortably circumstanced, Doreen, like everyone else in these years, found somewhere to live a tricky prospect. In Greater London as a whole some 116,000 houses had been destroyed by bombing or damaged beyond repair, but in 1945 that was offset by the population falling by almost 2 million compared to 1939 (6,850,000 against 8,746,000). Even so, overcrowding continued to be rife, particularly in multi-occupied houses, where more than one household shared amenities in common with others. In the County of London, the demand for housing at the end of the war was considered 'unprecedented'. Even though housing had been London's most pressing disability for generations, this was no exaggeration. Some 37 per cent of the London married couples in the 1943–6 study were living in rooms in multi-occupied houses and their living conditions were dire indeed:

> Some of these so-called 'flats' lacked any proper kitchen or larder, had no bathroom, or lacked adequate sanitation, heating or lighting. Many of the families were short of both bedrooms and beds. Not one of them but had to live under serious disadvantages. We found attics, top floors and basements; rooms over shops, pubs and off-licences; bomb-damaged houses still unrepaired or partly repaired; unpainted cracking walls and ceilings; damp, draughts, and black-out arrangements permanently in position. The families who lived in these homes had inadequate storage (e.g., for prams and cycles), inadequate washing facilities, and had the usual troubles with children, noise and wirelesses. Many had no furniture of their own, or had lost everything in a raid. Others had to make do with bare half-furnished rooms, decked out with the few pathetic bits and pieces they had been able to collect. Small rooms were cumbered with Morrison shelters. Stairs were often dark and rickety. There was no possibility of isolation from others in the house, and relations with the landladies were usually strained.[10]

For these married couples, facing the future in places like this was a nerve-shredding prospect. There would be no easy solution.

*

IF London at the end of the war was not much of a place to bring up a family, it was especially difficult if there were school-age children. Out of 1,200 schools in inner London 1,150 were bomb-damaged, some 290 so badly that they had to be rebuilt. Much of the stock of buildings was in any event old, many dating back to the School Board for London's building programme from 1870 to 1903. Most had obsolete sanitary conveniences, generally in outbuildings. In 1946 some 326 schools were still lit by gas. Book stocks in school libraries had to be replenished and classroom furniture had to be recovered from evacuation reception areas as far apart as Norfolk and Cornwall.[11]

Nor were schools fit for purpose in other ways too. The wartime and post-war baby boom increased pressures on London's already overstretched education system from the mid-1940s on. The raising of the school leaving age, due to take place in 1939, was delayed until 1947; even so, there was a shortage of secondary schools to cope with the new numbers. From the end of the war, education authorities were required to provide nursery education for children aged two to five – a welcome support for working mothers. The government set a maximum size of thirty for nursery classes, but in inner London this was impossible and the LCC negotiated a maximum of forty. In 1945 class sizes were set nationally at forty in primary schools and thirty in secondaries. Although the average class sizes in inner London were marginally below these limits, many thousands of classes were larger: as late as 1954, 3,518 classes in primary schools (47 per cent of the total) and 2,391 (55 per cent) in secondary schools were over the limits. Some of this might have been eased by new school buildings in London; but the shortage of labour and materials for construction, and competing national priorities, meant that not a single new school had been built in London by 1948.

The limitations of out-of-date school buildings in the capital were not the only problem. There was a chronic shortage of teachers in London after the war: it had long been difficult to recruit teachers to the capital and to retain them once there. At the same time the whole of inner London secondary education was being turned upside down. The LCC decided in 1944 to move to a system of comprehensive schools for older pupils to educate 'a complete cross-section of the surrounding population of secondary school age', rather than teaching pupils streamed by notional ability in separate schools. The transition process took many years: 'the distinctions between the different kinds of county secondary schools' were reported as only 'beginning to disappear' in 1954. In sum, the disruption of war and its aftermath left the education of a whole generation of working-class and lower-middle-class London children, born between about 1926 and 1945, permanently blighted.[12]

Some contemporaries saw in this the roots of a much-discussed wartime and post-war rise in juvenile delinquency, though it is impossible to distinguish inadequate schooling from the consequences, among other things, of many fathers being away from home, many mothers now out at work and the increased opportunities for plunder from wartime's empty and bomb-damaged shops and houses. Certainly, the numbers of children aged eight to thirteen arrested by police in London climbed by 29 per cent between 1938 and 1946; persons aged under twenty accounted for 38 per cent of all property crime arrests in 1946, including nearly half the arrests for burglary and housebreaking and two thirds for shopbreaking. The police thought too that there was a growing tendency to form 'juvenile gangs'. Whatever the causes, the consequences of a police record and perhaps a spell in borstal added one more incubus to the toll of war on the peacetime prospects for London youth.[13]

WHAT of the grass-roots collectivism and comradeship that had shown such vigorous growth in London life during the war years? Structure, organisation, civic endorsement and mutual protection against the common enemy had all been vital here, so with stand-down in the spring and summer of 1945 much of this fellow feeling ebbed away. But Londoners recognised how important all this had been for their social well-being and there were many local attempts to sustain it after the war. Civil defence associations of one kind or another continued to commemorate the service and its spirit of collective self-help, much as the British Legion had long brought together ex-servicemen and women. In Uxbridge, Cowley Post War Civil Defence Association was formed as the war ended 'with a view to keeping alive the spirit of comradeship and the ideal of voluntary social service so marked in the Civil Defence services during the war'. At Penge in south London, a similar association was formed in early 1946, organising social events, concert parties, children's beanos, talent and sporting (well, snooker) competitions, with 'community singing' and dancing figuring large on every bill. Others, like Hammersmith's, focused charitable efforts on helping former civil defence workers now on their uppers, whether association members or not. In post-war Chelsea there were three associations – for former wardens, fire guard and light rescue. Meeting in rooms at the town hall, they wanted to form 'a "Civvy Legion"' with their own 'general assembly place', but the times, or more precisely labour and materials shortages and the famine of usable accommodation of any kind, were against them. These networks were extensive across London. When, in 1948, civil defence revived again as the Cold War heated up, it was these 'old soldiers of the past Civil Defence army' who proved keenest to answer the call, but membership fell away as time took its toll and as nostalgia for the busy war years of public service evaporated.[14]

That collective urge in wartime London had been one element in Labour's historic parliamentary victory in 1945. Labour's fortunes in London remained strong in the first year or so of peace. The party performed exceptionally well in the county council elections of 1946. Labour's LCC manifesto unsurprisingly put housing as its 'priority No. 1 for the coming years', making much of its £45 million plan for rebuilding Stepney and Poplar, though the timescale of thirty years for completion would have disappointed many. Labour doubled its majority in County Hall from twenty-eight at the last elections, way back in 1937, to fifty-six, winning eighteen seats from the Conservatives, often in suburban areas, but losing two each to the Liberals (including Percy Harris in Bethnal Green South-West) and the Communists (both in Stepney Mile End). Middlesex followed a similar pattern, where the strong showing in the suburbs during the general election now translated into local power. Labour won control of the County for the first time in history, with forty-two seats out of eighty; in 1937, Conservatives (Municipal Reform) had had fifty councillors to Labour's twenty-two.[15]

If these elections showed something of wartime idealism persisting into the early post-war period, it didn't last long. Growing frustration with the Labour government, deepened by an austerity budget just before the county council elections of March 1949, played out disastrously for the party in those suburbs that had contributed so much to the victory of 1945. This time it was the London Conservatives who could make much of the running on housing, citing the 160,000 families queueing for better homes on the LCC's housing waiting list and making 'only this one promise. When returned to power we will give Londoners more new homes than the Labour Party has ever done.' In a shocking reversal, Labour lost overall control of the LCC for the first time since 1934, tying with the Conservatives at sixty-four seats each. The Liberals retained one seat, that of the seventy-three-year-old Percy Harris, who found himself holding the balance of power. He allied with Labour, keeping them in power, much to the disgust of Henry Brooke, the Tory group leader, who complained of 'backstairs methods' and a 'plot' to keep Municipal Reform out of power despite Londoners voting for change. Labour's reversal in Middlesex was clearer-cut. There were now ninety seats on an enlarged council: Conservatives won sixty-three and Labour twenty-three. These same Middlesex boroughs, and other suburban seats in Greater London, turned against Labour also in the general election of 1950: the average swing nationally to the Conservatives was 2.9 per cent but in Middlesex it was 7.1 per cent. London's suburban seats stayed with the Conservatives in 1951, when they narrowly won power at Westminster. The suburbs of London were important in determining the main political parties' national fortunes throughout the early post-war period.[16]

LONDON remained a devastated city after 1945 for years to come. Some areas had been wiped off the map, most notably the City east of St Paul's; in places it was possible to walk for half a mile 'without passing a single standing structure', and so it would remain until about 1960. Empty sites around St Paul's Churchyard and the Barbican had to wait until 1973 to be finally filled. In the East End the thirty-year plan for rebuilding Stepney and Poplar was never realised. The Lansbury Estate, in Poplar, was an early success, begun to coincide with the Live Architecture exhibit at the 1951 Festival of Britain, but the rest of the battered East End had to wait years longer for housing investment, most of it coming only in the 1960s and 1970s. The same was true of south London. There further destruction was added to bomb damage around the Elephant and Castle with the clearance of the remaining old houses and their replacement over the next thirty years by a 'comprehensive redevelopment area' comprising new estates, a shopping centre, offices, raised walkways and a huge road system; it all involved much concrete. There was one incidental benefit from the blitz. The clearance of rubble from London's wastelands was an enormous task: a million tons of bomb debris were dumped on Hackney Marshes, raising the height of the land by several feet and protecting it from flooding by the River Lea, to which it had long been prone.[17]

There was one exception made to the areas of London that had to wait in the queue for post-war investment. Money was quickly found to bring the Port of London up to full operating capacity so that it could play its part in Britain's world export trade, a vital component of national economic recovery. The Luftwaffe gave the port a terrific battering in 1940–41, the Surrey Docks on the south side of the river repeatedly burned to the ground in the Big Blitz and after. Bombing, submarine warfare and air attacks on shipping reduced tonnage passing through the port from over 62 million in 1938–9 to 14.75 million in 1942, so by more than three quarters. Yet by 1954 the port's trade exceeded the pre-war figure with 68.55 million tons, London taking year on year a slight increase in its share of the national trade. Of all London's blasted areas and amenities, the port was the quickest to recover. It was for London a post-war success story, though it didn't last long: the Upper Port was obsolete within a couple of decades of 1954, undermined by another wartime development, the roll-on-roll-off ferry, adapting for the years of peace lessons learned in the Normandy invasion and elsewhere.[18]

WHY, in general, was London's recovery so prolonged? The answer lies in the gravest hurt that the war did to London. This was the adoption by central and local government of key elements of the wartime plans of 1943–4: in particular, the decision to run down London's industry and population and to diminish its place in the national economy. It had adverse consequences that lasted for a generation and more.

The London plans' principal argument, that people and jobs should be moved out of the capital, had become both a planning and a political orthodoxy some years before the plans were even published. By 1940 the proposition that London was too big and powerful united political parties, with a committed advocate in Neville Chamberlain on the right and the whole of the Labour leadership with any view on the matter on the left. Patrick Abercrombie had long been a proponent of that view too. His authorship of the County and Greater London Plans gave him the authority at last to put a number on the Londoners to be displaced and to recommend to the LCC and the coalition government that steps be put in place to make it happen.

Abercrombie had looked on the evacuations from London in 1939 and 1940 as a Luftwaffe-sent opportunity to reduce the London population to the planning densities – a figure meaning much to town planners but little to anyone else – that he sought: 'it is interesting to note that, if none of those still evacuated from London in January, 1942, were to return, an automatic reduction to the density of 136, which we recommend, would have occurred without the necessity of any "decanting" ...' Interesting or not, in the real world Londoners wanted to return and did so, eventually in droves. In mid-1945 the population of Greater London was over half a million more than in mid-1941, by 1946 1.5 million more, 1947 1.8 million, in 1948 over 2 million more. By then even inner London had a million more living there than in the middle of 1941, a couple of months after the main blitz had ended. This urge to return or settle in London was just as strong among industrialists and business owners. At the end of 1945 it was reported:

> One of the most striking features of the past year has been the desire of large organisations to return to Central London after having suffered all the inconvenience of dispersal during the war ... The shortage of office, showroom and factory accommodation in London is acute and rents and prices have been forced up by the overwhelming demand.[19]

Left to its own devices, then, it is clear that London would have recovered to something like its pre-war vigour with remarkable rapidity, despite the hammering it had taken from the Luftwaffe and the V-weapons. If Londoners wouldn't leave of their own accord there would need to be some push for the 'bold reduction' in population and jobs envisaged by the plans to be achieved.

There had been an attempt to put something in place even before the war ended. Hugh Dalton, a key member of Labour's wartime leadership, had been since the late 1930s a confirmed advocate of restricting industry in London as a means of diverting investment to the depressed areas. A Cambridge-educated clergyman's son born in Glamorgan, Dalton had been an academic economist before he was elected Labour MP for Camberwell in 1924. He found Camberwell politics fissiparous and uncongenial, and switched for the 1929 election to a seat in the North-East, in one of the distressed areas that was meant somehow to benefit from stopping industry moving to London. As President of the Board of Trade in the wartime coalition he steered through Parliament in June 1945 a Distribution of Industry Act firmly along Barlow and Abercrombie lines. He had wanted the power to declare Greater London a prohibited area for further industrial development but dropped the clause in the face of opposition from London Conservative Members, and from Prime Minister Churchill. Everything would have to depend on the thrust of peacetime government policy after the forthcoming general election.[20]

Clarity was not long in coming. With Labour in power, Dalton's policy objective was secured by other means. On 5 March 1946 Lewis Silkin, Minister of Town and Country Planning and a long-term sympathiser with the desire to slim London down, finally adopted the Barlow Report of 1940 and the Abercrombie plans of 1943–4 as the basis for the Labour government's policy on 'the planning of London'. Silkin had had a very different upbringing from that of Dalton but his convictions on decentralisation were equally unshakeable. He had been born in Poplar in 1889, the seventh child of a recent Jewish immigrant family from Lithuania. A boy of some brilliance, he won a scholarship to Oxford, but his parents couldn't afford to send him and he went to work as a clerk at the East India Docks. From there he moved to a solicitor's office, ending up with his own law firm and living in Dulwich. He was elected a Labour councillor on the LCC in 1925 for South-East Southwark and was briefly leader of the Labour group before handing over amicably to Herbert Morrison; he had been a keen rambler in his youth, loved the countryside and was an active proponent of the Green Belt. He was elected to Parliament for Peckham in a by-election in 1936.[21]

Silkin's policy announcement faithfully followed the Barlow–Abercrombie proposals for decentralising London's people and industry. First, the growth of London would be restrained to achieve for the nation 'a better balance of the distribution of industry', especially in what now were called 'the Development Areas'. Second, 'a planned programme of decentralisation to the outer areas of Greater London should replace the uncontrolled sprawl of the inter-war period'. This would involve the removal of about a million people and 'a related quota of industrial firms to be accommodated further out – mainly in a few new towns and in selected existing towns within 20 to 50 miles of London's centre'. Third, the pattern of decentralisation would 'broadly conform' to Abercrombie's proposal in the Greater London Plan. The displaced people were to come from the County of London and from the inner urban ring; the suburban ring of outer London would be 'static'; the Green Belt would be 'carefully safeguarded' to 'act as a barrier to further suburban growth'; and the Outer Country Ring should serve as the main 'reception area' – adopting the term familiar from the planned evacuations of September 1939 – for people and industry moving to 'compact settlements surrounded by open country'. Thus far Abercrombie's plans became government policy, but no further. His highway proposals and the location and number of new towns would be considered later; and the details of his plans for low housing density, more parks and neighbourhood units would be left to local planning authorities to determine. No voice was raised in opposition to Silkin's statement in the House of Commons. The decentralisation of London had become a policy truism endorsed by all political parties.[22]

Just how decentralisation was to be brought about was not yet clear, but civil servants quickly began to use what tools they had in furtherance of a planning objective they – like almost every other expression of public opinion – had long favoured. They realised what they were up against if the government's new policy were not to be frustrated:

> The majority of the blitzed firms wish to rebuild in London and will, no doubt, eventually be permitted to do so [because of their rights under War Damage legislation]. At the same time, all available information suggests that the plan for building new factories and extensions by firms already established in Greater London or by new firms would, if unchecked, greatly exceed the volume of industrial premises likely to go out of use through the decline or demise of firms with establishments in Greater London.

Officials concluded that 'the entry of firms new to the area must be rigorously opposed', expansions must be 'strictly controlled' and as many firms as possible 'persuaded' to move out – especially (but surely unrealistically) to the Development Areas. In officials' discussions with industrialists, stress would be laid on the great difficulty of getting building permitted in Greater London except for blitz replacement and then only the most important; on the shortage of labour in Greater London; and on the strategic dangers of industry in London from enemy attack. This was 1946, but even so the chiefs of staff had advised at the end of the war that 'vital installations' should not be put in London. So the old strategic arguments against locating industry in the capital had a life beyond victory, even though, in the post-atomic world, everywhere was vulnerable and nowhere safe.[23]

In opposing the location of jobs in London, officials had an armoury of controls in their briefcases to frustrate that 'overwhelming demand' for business accommodation from being realised. Even while the new policy was in gestation every possible obstacle was being placed in the way of jobs returning to London. 'So far,' a central London estate agent reported in January 1946, 'there are few signs of encouragement being given to owners willing to develop commercial sites, but, on the contrary, deadlock is created by the lack of prompt decisions upon building applications and the postponement of interim development consents by town planning authorities.' Early that year, a new order restricting conversions from residential to commercial use held up office and showroom development in Mayfair, where such changes had become common since the First World War. Manufacturing was stymied too. Panel A, the Ministry of Town and Country Planning's official mechanism for approving industrial developments in Great Britain, could restrict them in Greater London by refusing building licences. No licence, no factory. In the two years between January 1945 and January 1947, Panel A permitted just 262 industrial projects in Greater London out of 2,736 in Great Britain as a whole; permissions in the Development Areas were three times as many. The picture revealed in the Barlow Report had now in just a few years been turned on its head. London was being made into a new 'depressed area', not through any lack of demand for land or investment but as a direct result of government policy.[24]

THAT lack of investment might best be seen in the state of London's homes. The London housing problem proved intractable for years after 1945. For the first four post-war years the emphasis was on continuing the wartime policies of repairing bomb-damaged houses and erecting prefabs. By 1949 around 40,000 empty dwellings in inner London, some in shared houses and tenement blocks, had been repaired and brought back into occupation; a further 24,000 dwellings were provided by converting houses into flats. By 1955, including 'huts' built during the war, the net total of 'temporary prefabricated bungalows' in inner London had reached 14,700. But it was all a thimble-drop in the Thames. The 1951 census revealed that more than two thirds of inner London households – some 2 million people and more – lacked exclusive access to the five basic amenities of piped cold water (hot running water not yet a standard amenity), a stove, a sink, a water closet and a fitted bath. In Islington, for instance, there were 82,000 households: 48,500 had access to no fitted bath at all, and 16,500 had to share one; just one in five, 16,841, had their own. The quantity of housing available was as bad as the quality: 67,629 three-person households or larger lived in just one or two rooms in the County of London in 1951, some 233,000 people.[25]

The government's answer to the London housing problem was not to build more houses in the capital but to move Londoners out. The dam on commercial investment and new jobs would have eventually taken a toll on the numbers of people wanting to live in London, but something else was needed if decentralisation was to begin now. The answer lay in directing public housing investment away from London. Very little private housebuilding obtained building licences until the 1950s, just 750 houses a year built by developers in inner London from 1945 to 1954, so only public housing could make a difference. It made no sense to build much new housing in inner London, and in the adjacent parts of Greater London, when it was desired that a million Londoners should move away. New housing did get built, because the need was so great and the empty bomb sites so egregious; in the ten years after the war some 66,600 dwellings were built by public authorities in inner London, including war-destroyed properties rebuilt. Despite this, the LCC's housing waiting list alone – the boroughs kept their own lists too – had 165,571 families queueing for housing in 1955, over 52,000 of them 'in serious need'.[26]

Most LCC building, in accordance with the principles of the London plans, took place far away from the County itself. In general, if Londoners wanted new housing after the war they were most likely to get it if they moved out of London altogether. So by 1950 the LCC was developing estates in over a dozen locations, mainly outside Greater London or on its edge, like Oxhey (Watford), Debden (Loughton), Slough, Woking, Merstham (Surrey) and Borehamwood (Hertfordshire). Some estates made provision for factories to be built nearby so that tenants with the right skills could find work close to their new homes instead of having to commute to London. This programme was closed down by the Conservative Housing and Local Government Minister, Harold Macmillan, in 1955 as not moving people far enough away from London and so not in accord with planning policy for the capital. On the other hand, the desire to move Londoners further out continued to get hefty government investment. The New Towns programme, which Macmillan vigorously supported when the Conservatives gained power in 1951, and which had achieved thirteen designations between 1946 and 1949, dedicated eight New Towns for London, with plans to take

460,000 newcomers, mainly from the capital. Development was slow in the early years and had to be supplemented, with LCC support, by the Conservative government's expanded towns programme under the Town Development Act of 1952 – there were eleven in all, with Letchworth, Harpenden, Hertford and St Albans in the north, Slough, Camberley and Woking in the west and south, and Chelmsford, Brentwood, Billericay and Thurrock in the east. Here London's 'over-spill', as it was called, was facilitated by existing town centres whose infrastructure could more easily accommodate house and factory building than the New Towns, some of which were planted around a village nucleus and pretty much in open country.[27]

The government policy enunciated by Lewis Silkin in 1946 remained (in precisely the same terms) as LCC policy into the 1960s. When opportunities came to relocate factories away from London they were taken. When employment in central London rose phoenix-like through the huge expansion of office jobs in financial services, commercial and public-sector employment in particular, the LCC agitated for means of restricting more incursions: in 1963 government established the Location of Offices Bureau to move offices out of the centre and, if possible, out of Greater London altogether.[28]

The mirror image of all this, the continuing and deliberate neglect of inner London, began eventually to raise serious concerns. The dire condition of London's housing was exposed in great detail by Sir Milner Holland's official inquiry report, commissioned by government and published in 1965; by then London's housing problems had become complicated by 'New Commonwealth' immigration, especially in inner London but also in the boroughs around it. This newly discovered 'inner-city' crisis of the 1960s was in fact a continuation of the unprecedented problems brought about by war and the twenty years of policy-driven neglect that followed it. It made of the Abercrombie plans a self-fulfilling prophecy. Voices were raised, by intellectuals and others, against the depopulation of inner London and there is evidence that many working-class Londoners would have preferred to stay put rather than move. But the die had been cast. The County's population lost 20,000 a year between 1951 and 1961, falling from 3.7 to 3.5 million. Thereafter, as talk about the 'twilight areas' between London's commercial centre and the suburbs grew ever noisier, the population went into free fall for twenty years – down to 3 million in 1971, to 2.5 million in 1981, 2.3 million in 1991. Similar, though less extreme, trends were

apparent in Greater London as a whole, where the population fell to
6.7 million in 1981, a census figure that took the wider capital back
nearly to its 1901 population.[29] London would not recover its 1939
population until the second decade of the twenty-first century.

THE searing impact of the war on London was felt, then, for forty years
after 1945. London's fortunes began to revive from the late 1980s;
through the 1990s and the first two decades of the twenty-first century
they made a spectacular recovery. But nothing is permanent. The history
of London's Second World War and its direful aftermath is a warning
that success is fragile and, for a 'world city' like London, depends most
of all on international events and national policies.

At the end of it all, the 6 million or so Londoners who stuck out
the war in the capital with stoicism, even heroism, might justifiably
have felt that they had fought and won the Battle of London. Looking
back a generation later, they could have been forgiven for wondering
whether London's war had in fact been lost.

ACKNOWLEDGEMENTS

I would like gratefully to acknowledge the help of staff at a number of libraries and archives: the National Archives at Kew; the British Library, especially the staff in the Newsroom; the London Library; Stefan Dickers and staff at the Bishopsgate Institute; Simon Blundell, librarian and archivist at the Reform Club; and the enormously helpful Simon Offord and the lady archivists at the Imperial War Museum search room. I have found the online archives of Mass Observation and the Wellcome Library immensely helpful and those of *The Times* and the British Newspaper Archive have proved indispensable; in accordance with the wishes of the Mass Observation Trustees I have anonymised diarists' names that are not already in the public domain. I have had huge assistance from Dr Robin Woolven, who has read every chapter in draft and from whose valuable insights and inexhaustible knowledge I've learned a great deal; and I've learned much from supervising the thesis of Dr Darren Bryant, who worked on the local aspects of the air war on London. I am also grateful, as ever, to my editor at the Bodley Head, Jörg Hensgen, and to my copy-editor, Lesley Levene, who have endeavoured to keep me on the straight and narrow. I'm conscious too that there are many excellent books about London during the Second World War: they have not tended to figure largely in my footnotes for the simple reason that, for good or ill, I've preferred to make my own way in the primary sources, most of all those written at the time.

I would also like to acknowledge the following copyright holders, who have allowed me to reprint or publish for the first time material in their ownership: the Imperial War Museum for permission to quote from the private papers of A. E. Buddell, OBE, and Miss N. V. Carver; Richard Deveson for permission to cite from his mother's letters, privately published in Klara Modern, *My Dearest Family: An Austrian Refugee's Letters from London to America, 1938–1945*, 2017; Islington Local History Library and the London Record Society for permission to quote excerpts from the diary of Gladys Langford; the Taylor and Francis Group for permission to quote an excerpt from M. J. Fogarty, *Prospects of the Industrial Areas of Great Britain*, 1945; Courtesy of the Schaffner family, on behalf of the Bryher literary estate, for permission to quote from *The Days of Mars: A Memoir, 1940–1946*, 1972; permission to quote an excerpt from *The Happy Years: Diaries 1944–48*, Weidenfeld & Nicolson, 1972, has been granted by the Literary Executor of the late Sir Cecil Beaton, reproduced by kind permission of Rupert Crew Ltd; Yale Representation Ltd for extracts from *The Maisky Diaries*, 2015, Reproduced with permission of The Licensor through PLSclear; the Bishopsgate Institute for permission to quote from the diaries of Godfrey Clark and Rhona Little; excerpts from my article 'The "Dismemberment of London": Chamberlain, Abercrombie and the London Plans of 1943–44', *London Journal*, Vol. 44, No. 3, December 2019, © The London Journal Trust, is reprinted by permission of the Taylor and Francis Group, http://www.tandfonline.com on behalf of the London Journal Trust; the extract from *Black Bethlehem*, 1947, by Lettice Cooper reprinted by permission of Peters Fraser & Dunlop (www.petersfraserdunlop.com) on behalf of the Estate of Lettice Cooper; Ariane Bankes for permission to quote an extract from *Night Shift*, 1941, by Inez Holden; the London Metropolitan Archive and the London Record Society for permission to quote from the diaries of Anthony Heap; the London Record Society for permission to quote from the diaries of Kathleen Tipper; Duff Hart-Davis for his generous permission to quote from the verses of William Plomer; James Morton for permission to cite an extract from Frankie Fraser's *Mad Frank: Memoirs of a Life of Crime*, 1994; Dick Warner for permission to reproduce extracts from the private papers of his aunt, Phyllis Warner; David Higham Literary, Film and TV Agents for permission to quote from John Lehmann's *I Am My Brother: Autobiography II*, 1960, and R. F. Delderfield, *For My Own Amusement*, 1968; the Council of Hanwell Methodist Church, custodians of the diaries of Dorothy Wells, for permission to quote from them; The History Press for permission to quote from Sue Bruley (ed.), *Working for Victory: A Diary of Life in a Second World War Factory*, 2001; Persephone Books to quote from three important texts that they have republished: Vere Hodgson, *Few*

Eggs and No Oranges: A Diary Showing How Unimportant People in London and Birmingham Lived Through the War Years 1940–45 Written in the Notting Hill Area of London, 1976, Mollie Panter-Downes, *London War Notes 1939–1945*, edited by William Shawn, 1971, and Virginia Graham, *Consider the Years 1938–1946*, 1944. The quotation from *The Life and Times of Ernest Bevin*, Vol. II, *Minister of Labour 1940–1945*, is reproduced with permission of Curtis Brown Group Ltd on behalf of the Beneficiaries of the Estate of Alan Bullock © Alan Bullock 1967; for quotes reproduced from the speeches, works and writings of Winston S. Churchill: Reproduced with permission of Curtis Brown, London on behalf of The Estate of Winston S. Churchill © The Estate of Winston S. Churchill; for quotes reproduced from the archive of Mass Observation: Reproduced with permission of Curtis Brown, London on behalf of The Trustees of the Mass Observation Archive.

I have been unable to contact the rights holders in a number of texts from which I've cited quotations. In respect of papers held by the Imperial War Museum this applies to the 'Account of a V1 Attack on London, June 1944' and the private papers of Mrs M. Crompton, R. S. Simmons, Miss G. Thomas and A. F. Williamson. I will gratefully acknowledge in future editions any permissions to quote from this or any other unacknowledged material received after the date of first publication.

LIST OF ILLUSTRATIONS

Anxious Londoners, September 1938 (Getty Images)

Digging trench shelters in St James's Park, September 1938 (Getty Images)

Evacuation of children from London, 1 September 1939 (Popperfoto/ Getty Images)

Voluntary evacuation, early 1940 (Getty Images)

Queuing for ration cards, January 1940 (Getty Images)

Street shelters under construction, early 1940 (Getty Images)

Belgian refugees arrive in London, May 1940 (J. A. Hampton/Getty Images)

'Enemy aliens' on their way to internment, June 1940 (Getty Images)

The Blitz begins in earnest, 7 September 1940 (Getty Images)

East Londoners getting away, September 1940 (Bert Handy/Getty Images)

Bombed out (Getty Images)

Near Mornington Crescent, 9 September 1940 (H. F. Davis/Getty Images)

Blitz rescue, Willesden, September 1940 (Getty Images)

Taking over the Underground (Getty Images)

Mobile canteen helping bombing victims, October 1940 (Getty Images)

Fighting the great fire of London, 29 December 1940 (Bert Handy/ Getty Images)

St Paul's and the devastated City, January 1941 (Getty Images)

A meeting at Mickey Davis's shelter, Brushfield Street, Spitalfields (Getty Images)

Shelter entertainments, YMCA HQ, Central London, September 1940 (A. J. O'Brien/Getty Images)

The Café de Paris disaster, 8–9 March 1941 (Reg Speller/Getty Images)

NOTES

Abbreviations

CLP   County of London Plan
HC   House of Commons
MO   Mass Observation
TNA   The National Archive

Preface

1   John Lehmann, *I Am My Brother: Autobiography II*, 1960, p. vii.

The Greatest Target in the World:
11 November 1918–31 August 1939

1   Patricia and Robert Malcolmson (eds.), *A Free-Spirited Woman: The London Diaries of Gladys Langford, 1936–1940*, 2014, p. 64 (29 August 1938) and p. 67 (12 September 1938). Mass Observation Day Survey Respondent 097, 14 September 1938.

2   The 'factory girls' were in Hammersmith; *West London Observer*, 30 September 1938. For Westminster see Robin Woolven, 'Civil Defence in London 1935–1945: The Formation and Implementation of Policy for, and the Performance of, Air Raid Precautions (later Civil Defence) Services in the London Region', University of London PhD thesis, 2002, Ch. 2. For Wandsworth see Alfred James Hurley, *Days That Are Gone: Milestones I Have Passed in South-West London*, 1947, pp. 198ff. For Croydon see W. C. Berwick Sayers (ed.), *Croydon and the Second World War: The Official History of the War Work of the Borough and Its Citizens from 1939 to 1945 Together with the Croydon Roll of Honour*, 1949, pp. 10–11. For Bethnal Green see George F. Vale, *Bethnal Green's Ordeal 1939–45*, 1945, p. 3. For Brentford and

Chiswick see *West London Observer*, 30 September 1938. MO Respondent 097, 25 September 1938.

3 John G. O'Leary, *Danger Over Dagenham*, 1947, p. 12. The headlights are in *Daily Herald*, 27 September 1938. For Wandsworth see Hurley, *Days That Are Gone*, pp. 198ff. For St Pancras see Woolven, 'Civil Defence in London', Ch. 2. The observer was Diana Cooper, *The Light of Common Day*, 1959, p. 241.

4 MO Respondent 097, 24 September 1938. Vincent Brome, *J. B. Priestley*, 1988, p. 233. Domestic shelters and gas-proof rooms had been encouraged since 1935.

5 Hurley, *Days That Are Gone*, p. 198ff. Woolven, 'Civil Defence in London', Ch. 2, Table 3.

6 Cooper, *The Light of Common Day*, p. 243. Malcolmson (eds.), *A Free-Spirited Woman*, p. 70, 21 September 1938.

7 Naomi Mitchison, Mass Observation Day Survey Respondent 123, 28 September 1938. *The Times*, 30 September 1938.

8 Mass-Observation, *Britain*, 1939, pp. 100–101.

9 V. S. Pritchett, *Midnight Oil*, 1971, pp. 220–21. Arthur Ernest Newens, *The Memoirs of an Old East-Ender*, Harlow, 2006, p. 36.

10 For the Munich crisis and ARP see Mass-Observation, *Britain*, Ch. 2; Terence H. O'Brien, *Civil Defence*, 1955, pp. 153–65; Susan R. Grayzell, *At Home and Under Fire: Air Raids and Culture in Britain from the Great War to the Blitz*, Cambridge, 2012, p. 251ff.

11 *West London Observer*, 30 September 1938.

12 Jerry White, *London in the Twentieth Century: A City and Its People*, 2001, pp. 26–7.

13 William A. Robson, *The Government and Misgovernment of London*, 1939, passim.

14 Jerry White, 'The "Dismemberment of London": Chamberlain, Abercrombie and the London Plans of 1943–44', *London Journal*, Vol. 44, No. 3, December 2019, pp. 206–26.

15 For the autumn and winter of 1917–18 in London see Jerry White, *Zeppelin Nights: London in the First World War*, 2014, pp. 215–9, 249–53.

16 See Michele Haapamaki, *The Coming of the Aerial War: Culture and the Fear of Airborne Attack in Inter-War Britain*, 2014, Chs 1 and 5.

17 O'Brien, *Civil Defence*, pp. 16, 96.

18 Cited in Alan Allport, *Browned Off and Bloody-Minded: The British Soldier Goes to War*, 2015, p. 15 (Liddell Hart, 1924) and Haapamaki, *The Coming of the Aerial War*, p. 24.

19 HC Debates, Vol. 285, Col. 1197, 7 February 1934; Vol. 292, Col. 2368, 30 July 1934.

20 O'Brien, *Civil Defence*, pp. 117, 178–80.

21 Ibid., pp. 78–9; Woolven, 'Civil Defence in London', Ch. 2.

22 See Bernard Donoghue and G. W. Jones, *Herbert Morrison: Portrait of a Politician*, 1973, Ch. 19.

23 For population comparisons nationwide see *The Registrar-General's Statistical Review of England and Wales for the Year 1937, Tables Pt II, Civil*. See also Harold Scott, *Your Obedient Servant*, 1959, p. 109; Scott was chief administrative officer for the London Civil Defence Region from 1938 to 1943. The functional responsibilities of Greater London's local authorities were extremely complex, some lower-tier authorities having more responsibilities than others: see

Robson, *The Government and Misgovernment of London*, passim; LCC, *London Statistics 1936–38*, Vol. XLI, 1939, pp. 7–11.

24   John W. Wheeler-Bennett, *John Anderson: Viscount Waverley*, 1962, pp. 205–6, 213ff. Ann Scott, *Ernest Gowers: Plain Words and Forgotten Deeds*, Basingstoke, 2009, pp. 91, 94–103; Admiral Lord Mountevans, *Adventurous Life*, 1946.

25   *Report of the Commissioner of Police of the Metropolis for the Year 1939*, 1940, Cmd 6201, p. 6. F. Tennyson Jesse (ed.), *Trials of Timothy John Evans and John Reginald Halliday Christie*, 1957, p. xliii.

26   Frederick H. Radford, 'Fetch the Engine ...': *The Official History of the Fire Brigades Union*, 1951, p. 108ff.; Anon., *The Bells Go Down: The Diary of a London A.F.S. Man*, 1942, passim. For the group arrangements in Greater London see Neil Wallington, *Firemen at War: The Work of London's Fire-Fighters in the Second World War*, Newton Abbot, c. 1981, p. 34.

27   Charles Graves, *The Story of St Thomas's 1106–1947*, 1947, p. 59; for the arrangements generally see C. L. Dunn, *The Emergency Medical Services*, Vol. I, *England and Wales*, 1952, pp. 44–9. For critical comments collected by the LCC at the end of the war see LCC/PH/WAR/1/1.

28   *Daily Herald*, 22 April 1940 (H. V. Morton, 'Tin Hats for the Thames'); A. P. Herbert, *Independent Member*, 1950, p. 113; Anthony Powell, *To Keep the Ball Rolling*, Vol. III, *Faces in My Time*, 1980, p. 91.

29   On the fourth arm see O'Brien, *Civil Defence*, p. 166.

30   Wheeler-Bennett, *Anderson*, pp. 221–3; Paterson is sometimes given as Patterson. See also Grayzell, *At Home and Under Fire*, who gives a different explanation, though Wheeler-Bennett's seems to be generally accepted.

31   For Barking see *Municipal Journal*, Vol. 48, 30 June 1939, p. 1498; new town halls were also opened at Acton and Greenwich in the last six months of 1939.

32   On the deep shelter controversy see O'Brien, *Civil Defence*, pp. 190–3; J. B. S. Haldane, *A.R.P.*, 1938, p. 212ff.

33   The list of evacuation and neutral areas in Greater London are in HLG 7/608; O'Leary, *Danger Over Dagenham*, p. 13.

34   For evacuation planning see R. M. Titmuss, *Problems of Social Policy*, 1950, Ch. III; P. H. J. H. Gosden, *Education in the Second World War: A Study in Policy and Administration*, 1976, pp. 10–12. The evacuation scare was reported in *The Times*, 6 January 1939. Malcolmson (eds.), *A Free–Spirited Woman*, p. 87, 3 April 1939.

35   *Estates Gazette*, Vol. CXXXIV, 30 December 1939, p. 951. For Standard Telephones see *Municipal Journal*, Vol. 48, 14 July 1939, p. 1620. Charles Wilson and William Reader, *Men and Machines: A History of D. Napier & Son, Engineers, Ltd. 1858–1958*, 1958, p. 152. David Rogers, *Shadow Factories: Britain's Production Facilities during the Second World War*, Solihull, 2016, pp. 287–91.

36   *Boroughs of Poplar and Stepney and East London Advertiser*, 16 September 1939 (Poplar); Woolven, 'Civil Defence in London', Ch. 3, Table 4.

37   For types of wardens' posts see *Municipal Journal*, Vol. 48, 21 July 1939, p. 1647, and 4 August 1939, p. i. Vale, *Bethnal Green's Ordeal*, p. 15. W. E. Holl, 'Civil Defence Goes Through It: Paddington, 1937–1945', typescript, British Library, 1946, p. 19. For Fulham see Mass-Observation, *War Begins at Home*, 1940, p. 119. *Lewisham Borough News*, 19 September 1939. George H. Gallup, *The Gallup International Public Opinion Polls: Great Britain 1937–1975*, Vol. One, 1937–1964, New York, 1976, pp. 18–19.

38 Reginald Bell, *The Bull's-Eye*, 1943, pp. 12–14.

39 MO, *War Begins at Home*, pp. 102–4; Joan Wyndham, *Love Lessons: A Wartime Diary*, 1985, p. 17, 14 October 1939.

40 Aylmer Firebrace, *Fire Service Memories*, 1949, pp. 154–7.

41 *The Times*, 5 June 1939, 'Fire-Fighting Efficiency'; 3 July 1939, 'Citizen Army of Defence'. On the blackout trial see Titmuss, *Problems of Social Policy*, p. 90. Frances Faviell [Olivia Faviell Lucas], *A Chelsea Concerto*, 1959, pp. 5–8. Stuart Maclure, *One Hundred Years of London Education 1870–1970*, 1970, pp. 132–3.

42 Diaries of Rhona Mary Linton Little, Bishopsgate Institute, GDP/178, 22–28 August 1939. For the BBC see Stuart Hibberd, *'This – Is London'*, 1950, pp. 173–4. For the Elgin Marbles see *The Times*, 6 April 1946. Suzanne Bosman, *The National Gallery in Wartime*, 2008, p. 17ff. For the candles see Noel Streatfeild, *Saplings*, 1945 (Persephone, 2000), p. 60. Anne Oliver Bell (ed.), *The Diary of Virginia Woolf*, Vol. V, *1936–1941*, 1984, pp. 230–31, 25 August 1939. See also O'Brien, *Civil Defence*, p. 286ff.

43 For the practice see *Middlesex Chronicle*, 2 September 1939. Malcolmson (eds.), *A Free-Spirited Woman*, p. 116, 25 August 1939. For the confusion see the manuscript Diary of David Euan Wallace, Minister of Transport, at Bodleian Library, GB 161 MSS Eng. Hist. c.495–8, 30 August 1939. I am grateful to Dr Robin Woolven for access to his edited transcription of the Wallace diary.

2. Oh! What a Lovely War:
1 September 1939–9 April 1940

1   See generally R. M. Titmuss, *Problems of Social Policy*, 1950, pp. 103–8; Bernard Darwin, *War on the Line: The Story of the Southern Railway in War-Time*, 1946, pp. 32–6; Stuart Maclure, *One Hundred Years of London Education 1870–1970*, 1970, pp. 132–4; P. H. J. H. Gosden, *Education in the Second World War: A Study in Policy and Administration*, 1976, pp. 12–18; John Macnicol, 'The Evacuation of Schoolchildren', in Harold L. Smith (ed.), *War and Social Change: British Society in the Second World War*, Manchester, 1986, pp. 3–31; John G. O'Leary, *Danger Over Dagenham*, 1947, pp. 42–4.

2   Diary of David Euan Wallace, Bodleian Library, GB 161 MSS Eng. Hist. c.495–8, 1 September 1939; O'Leary, *Danger Over Dagenham*, pp. 42–4.

3   Chaim Lewis, *Of No Fixed Address*, 2009, pp. 59–61; Maurice Goymer, *Bombs, Stinging Nettles and Doodlebugs*, 2006, pp. 26–7; Dorothy Scannell, *Dolly's War*, 1975 (1977 edition), p. 78; Bryan Magee, *Growing up in a War*, 2007, pp. 8–9, 28.

4   Charles Graves, *The Story of St Thomas's 1106–1947*, 1947, pp. 59–60; A. E. Clark-Kennedy, *The London: A Study in the Voluntary Hospital System*, Vol. 2, *The Second Hundred Years 1840–1948*, 1963, pp. 234–9; H. Willoughby Lyle, *An Addendum to King's and Some King's Men (London) Being an Added Record of King's College Hospital and of King's College Hospital Medical School to 5 July 1948*, 1950, p. 104; Hilary St George Saunders, *The Middlesex Hospital 1745–1948*, 1949, pp. 79–91; Hujohn A. Ripman (ed.), *Guy's Hospital 1725–1948*, 1951, pp. 47–8; Frank W. Law, *The History and Traditions of the*

Moorfields Eye Hospital: Volume II Being a Continuation of Treacher Collins'
History of the First Hundred Years, 1975, pp. 117–18. See also London County
Council, *The LCC Hospitals: A Retrospect*, 1949, pp. 61–8. For the maternity
services problem see Sheila Ferguson and Hilde Marchant, *Studies in the Social
Services*, 1954, pp. 42–52.

5   For Mobilisation Friday see Michael Wassey, *Ordeal by Fire: The Story and
Lesson of Fire over Britain and the Battle of the Flames*, 1941, p. 43. Albert
Turpin, *The East End: My Birthright*, 2017 (but written 1945–6), p. 90. Henry
Green, *Caught*, 1943, pp. 35–6. Verily Anderson, *Spam Tomorrow*, 1956, pp.
48–9. A. P. Herbert, *Independent Member*, 1950, pp. 143–6.

6   For an assessment of the impact of the blackout see Terence H. O'Brien, *Civil
Defence*, 1955, pp. 319–23; for September 1914 see Jerry White, *Zeppelin
Nights: London in the First World War*, 2014, pp. 39–41; the tin-hatted
policeman is in John Lehmann, *I Am My Brother: Autobiography II*, 1960, p.
23. *East London Advertiser*, 16 September 1939.

7   Olivia Cockett, *Love & War in London*, edited by Robert Malcolmson, 2008,
p. 24. Private Papers of Miss N. V. Carver, Imperial War Museum, Docs. 379,
4 September 1939.

8   For the car driver see police instructions in *An ABC for Special Constables and
Police War Reserves*, 1939, p. 110; the mask is advertised in *The Times*, 27
September 1939. Patricia and Robert Malcolmson (eds.), *A Free-Spirited
Woman: The London Diaries of Gladys Langford, 1936–1940*, 2014, p. 125,
15 September 1939. John Postgate, 'Glimpses of the Blitz', *History Today*, Vol.
43, 1 June 1993, pp. 21–2. Michael Sheridan, *Rowton Houses 1892–1954*,
1956, p. 68. *East London Advertiser*, 16 September 1939.

9   Chiang Yee, *The Silent Traveller in Wartime*, 1939, p. 21. Turpin, *The East End*,
p. 92. On the missing crowds see F. Tennyson Jesse and H. M. Harwood, *London
Front: Letters Written to America (August 1939–July 1940)*, 1940, pp. 5–6.

10   For a shaken Chamberlain see Robert Rhodes James (ed.), *Chips: The Diaries
of Sir Henry Channon*, 1967, p. 215, 3 September 1939. George Beardmore,
Civilians at War: Journals 1938–1946, 1984, p. 34, 3 September 1939. Diaries
of Rhona Mary Linton Little, Bishopsgate Institute, GDP/178, 3 September
1939. Private Papers of A. E. Buddell, OBE, Imperial War Museum, Docs. 26502,
3 September 1939. Private Papers of Miss Vivienne Hall, Imperial War Museum,
Docs. 3989a, 3 September 1939. 'The Second World War Diaries of Hilda Neal',
Imperial War Museum, PP/MCR/59, 3 September 1939. Robert Barltrop, *Bright
Summer – Dark Autumn: Part III Growing up in North East London between
the Wars*, 1986, p. 35. W. C. Berwick Sayers (ed.), *Croydon and the Second
World War: The Official History of the War Work of the Borough and Its
Citizens from 1939 to 1945 Together with the Croydon Roll of Honour*, 1949,
p. 20. Tom Harrisson, *Living Through the Blitz*, 1976, pp. 44–50, while noting
many incidents of panic in response to this first siren, acknowledged the mixture
of reactions, defying generalisation.

11   *Lewisham Borough News*, 5 September 1939. Asa Briggs, *The War of Words:
The History of Broadcasting in the United Kingdom*, Vol. III, 1970, pp. 29–30,
107, 111, 114–15. For the City see David Kynaston, *The City of London*, Vol.
III, *Illusions of Gold 1914–1945*, 1999, p. 463; Elizabeth Hennessy, *A Domestic
History of the Bank of England, 1930–1960*, Cambridge, 1992, pp. 6–11. For
Hulton's see Tom Hopkinson, *Of This Our Time: A Journalist's Story, 1905–50*,
1982, p. 169. O. S. Nock, *Britain's Railways at War 1939–1945*, 1971, pp. 16–17.

12 For many of the civil service moves see National Council of Social Service, *Dispersal: An Inquiry into the Advantages and Feasibility of the Permanent Settlement out of London and Other Great Cities of Office and Clerical and Administrative Staffs*, 1944, p. 12. Negley Harte, *The University of London 1836–1986: An Illustrated History*, 1986, pp. 235–7; E. H. Warmington, *A History of Birkbeck College University of London during the Second World War 1939–1945*, 1954, pp. 18–29.

13 Charles Ritchie, *The Siren Years: Undiplomatic Diaries 1937–1945*, 1974, p. 44, 3 September 1939. Vera Brittain, *England's Hour*, 1941, p. 21. Anthony Weymouth, *Journals of the War Years (1939–1945) and One Year Later*, 2 vols., 1948, Vol. 1, p. 43, 11 September 1939. Beardmore, *Civilians at War*, pp. 44–5, 2 November 1939. Titmuss, *Problems of Social Policy*, p. 543.

14 Hilda Kean, *The Great Cat and Dog Massacre: The Real Story of World War Two's Unknown Tragedy*, 2017, pp. 48–9, 63; there had been a similar event at the time of the Munich crisis. *Lewisham Borough News*, 26 September 1939. *Stratford Express*, 1 August 1941; the vet remembered that the killing began from 1 September.

15 Anthony Heap remarked on the uniforms in Robin Woolven (ed.), *The London Diaries of Anthony Heap 1931–1945*, Woodbridge, 2017, p. 285, 6 April 1940. Carver Papers, 4 September 1939. For the pillar boxes see Mollie Panter-Downes, *London War Notes 1939–1945*, edited by William Shawn, New York, 1971, pp. 3–4, 3 September 1939.

16 Woolven (ed.), *The London Diaries of Anthony Heap*, p. 262, 21 September 1939.

17 Ibid., p. 256, 4 September 1939; they don't seem to have got a replacement until April 1940. For the criticism see Briggs, *The War of Words*, pp. 77–9, 96–7, 102.

18 For the tubes see Nock, *Britain's Railways at War*, p. 29; T. C. Barker and Michael Robbins, *A History of London Transport: Passenger Travel and the Development of the Metropolis*, Vol. II, *The Twentieth Century to 1970*, 1974 (1976 edition), pp. 305–7. Panter-Downes, *London War Notes*, p. 20 (bicycles). For the housing changes see *Estates Gazette*, Vol. CXXXIV, 16 September 1939, pp. 455–6; *Municipal Journal*, Vol. 48, 15 September 1939, p. 2059.

19 Harold Scott, *Your Obedient Servant*, 1959, pp. 112–20. O'Brien, *Civil Defence*, p. 344; for the ambulance staff etc. numbers see LCC, *Interim Report of the County Medical Officer of Health and School Medical Officer for the Year 1945*, 1946, pp. 47–8.

20 John Strachey, *Post D: Some Experiences of an Air Raid Warden*, 1941, pp. 17–18.

21 Mass Observation Diarist, MO/D/5285, January 1940. Private Papers of F. R. Bodley, Imperial War Museum, Box No. 09/37/1, ff.1–3, n.d. [after 30 October 1939].

22 Hall Papers [apostrophe silently added].

23 Hall Papers, 18 October and 21 November 1939.

24 Hall Papers, 13 September 1939; Woolven (ed.), *The London Diaries of Anthony Heap*, p. 262, 19 September 1939; *Picture Post*, Vol. 5, 23 September 1939, p. 33 for Prince Monolulu, who was in fact not from Africa but from the Caribbean. Mass-Observation, *War Begins at Home*, 1940, pp. 42–3, 128–9.

25 See *Estates Gazette*, Vol. CXXXIV, 21 October 1939, p. 625 (Bolton House), 14 October 1939, p. 579 (landlords' obligations).

26 *Lewisham Borough News*, 17 October, 7, 14 and 28 November 1939 and 7
    May 1940 (Andersons); 24 October (provision for 30,000) and 30 January
    1940 (Forest Hill). *Stratford Express*, 27 October and 10 November 1939
    (Leyton and Barking); for West Ham see Doreen Idle, *War Over West Ham: A
    Study of Community Adjustment*, 1943, pp. 108–9. *Municipal Journal*, Vol. 49,
    19 January 1940, p. 79 (Westminster); *East London Advertiser*, 13 January
    1940 (Stepney).

27 Mass Observation Archive, File Report 291, 'Brick Shelters', July 1940, passim.
    East London Advertiser, 11 April 1940.

28 MO File Report 291, p. 5.

29 C. M. Kohan, *Works and Buildings*, 1952, pp. 357–60; O'Brien, *Civil Defence*,
    p. 369. Idle, *War Over West Ham*, pp. 108–9; there were similar problems in
    Southwark – see *South London Press*, 14 February 1941, 'Who Is to Blame?'.

30 The Bethnal Green children are in National Federation of Women's Institutes,
    Town Children Through Country Eyes: A Survey on Evacuation 1940, Dorking,
    1940, p. 19; the WVS worker is in Patricia and Robert Malcolmson, *Women
    at the Ready: The Remarkable Story of the Women's Voluntary Services on the
    Home Front*, 2013, p. 32. There is a large literature on the evacuation 'scandal'
    but for some contemporary views see also Richard Padley and Margaret Cole,
    Evacuation Survey: A Report to the Fabian Society, 1940; Celia St Loe Strachey,
    *Borrowed Children: A Popular Account of Some Evacuation Problems and Their
    Remedies*, 1940; Susan Isaacs (ed.), *The Cambridge Evacuation Survey: A
    Wartime Study in Social Welfare and Education*, 1941; *Our Towns: A Close-Up.
    A Study Made in 1939–42 with Certain Recommendations by the Hygiene
    Committee of the Women's Group on Public Welfare (in Association with the
    National Council of Social Service)*, 1943; H. C. Dent, *Education in Transition:
    A Sociological Study of the Impact of War on English Education 1939–1943*,
    1944; Titmuss, *Problems of Social Policy*, Chs. VII–IX.

31 National Federation of Women's Institutes, *Town Children Through Country
    Eyes*, passim.

32 Gosden, *Education in the Second World War*, pp. 14–18.

33 On the financial contribution see Titmuss, *Problems of Social Policy*, pp. 156–7.

34 For the LCC's strictures on returning children see *The Times*, 10 November
    1939, 2 January 1940. For Wood Green see *Municipal Journal*, Vol. 48, 3
    November 1939, p. 2289. Malcolmson (eds.), *A Free-Spirited Woman*, p. 131.
    For returning mothers see Maclure, *One Hundred Years of London Education*,
    p. 135; for the children see Padley and Cole, *Evacuation Survey*, pp. 46–7,
    200–201, Titmuss, *Problems of Social Policy*, pp. 171–3. Accurate figures are
    elusive because an unknown number of privately evacuated working-class chil-
    dren stayed out of London and were in education elsewhere.

35 For Plaistow see *Stratford Express*, 13 October 1939. Padley and Cole,
    Evacuation Survey, pp. 200–202; Maclure, *One Hundred Years of London
    Education*, pp. 135–6; Gosden, *Education in the Second World War*, pp. 28–30.

36 The magazines are in Robert Hewison, *Under Siege: Literary Life in London
    1939–1945*, 1977, pp. 10–11. Beardmore, *Civilians at War*, pp. 36–7, 7
    September 1939; p. 42, 15 October 1939. Dorothy G. Wells, 'Diary of the War',
    Imperial War Museum, Docs. 26780, Vol. 1, p. 19, 10 September 1939. For
    building see H. M. D. Parker, *Manpower: A Study of War-Time Policy and
    Administration*, 1957, pp. 22–3. For motors see Weymouth, *Journals*, Vol. 1,

p. 219, 7 April 1940. *Picture Post*, Vol. 5, 7 October 1939, p. 47. *East London Advertiser*, 9 September 1939.

37 Spender the poet is in Stefan Schimanski and Henry Treece (eds.), *Leaves in the Storm: A Book of Diaries*, 1947, pp. 15–16, 12 September 1939; Beardmore, *Civilians at War*, p. 42, 7 October 1939. George H. Gallup, *The Gallup International Public Opinion Polls: Great Britain 1937–1975*, Vol. One, 1937–1964, New York, 1976, p. 26. O'Brien, *Civil Defence*, pp. 322–3.

38 *Report of the Commissioner of Police of the Metropolis for the Year 1939*, 1940, Cmd 6201, Ch. 6; *Report of the Commissioner of Police of the Metropolis for the Year 1940*, 1941, pp. 36–9. Wells, 'Diary of the War', p. 156, 29 November 1939. Hall Papers, 11 December 1939. 'Second World War Diaries of Hilda Neal', 7 January 1940. Arthur Christiansen, *Headlines All My Life*, 1961, pp. 187–8.

39 For the IRA in 1939 see *Report of the Commissioner of Police 1939*, pp. 27–8. Diary of Godfrey W. Clarke, Bishopsgate Institute, GDP/258, 22 February 1940. W. E. Holl, 'Civil Defence Goes Through It: Paddington, 1937–1945', typescript, British Library, 1946, p. 27, 17 March 1940.

40 For south London crime see *South London Press*, 12 January and 8 March 1940, and *Lewisham Borough News*, 23 January and 9 April 1940; for the West End see Peter Beveridge, *Inside the C.I.D.*, 1957, pp. 73–7. For the reduction in recorded crime see *Report of the Commissioner of Police 1940*, p. 12. For wartime crime generally see Edward Smithies, *Crime in Wartime: A Social History of Crime in World War II*, 1982; Donald Thomas, *An Underworld at War: Spivs, Deserters, Racketeers & Civilians in the Second World War*, 2003; Simon Read, *Dark City: Crime in Wartime London*, Hersham, 2010.

41 For the libraries see *Hackney Gazette*, 17 January 1940. Hall Papers, 12 October 1939. For Sadler's Wells see *Penguin New Writing*, No. 18, February 1944, p. 127.

42 Mass Observation File Report 33, 'Music Halls', February 1940, passim. Private Papers of Miss P. Warner, Imperial War Museum, Docs. 3208, MS of 'The London Theater', a version of which was published in the *Washington Post*, 15 February 1940.

43 Eric Maschwitz, *No Chip on My Shoulder*, 1957, pp. 130–33. Edward R. Murrow, *This is London*, New York, 1941, pp. 41–3, 26 November 1939. For the bottle parties see *Picture Post*, Vol. 5, 28 October 1939, pp. 36–8.

44 Suzanne Bosman, *The National Gallery in Wartime*, 2008, p. 35ff; *Picture Post*, Vol. 5, 11 November 1939, pp. 22–3.

45 Art McCullough (ed.), *The War and Uncle Walter: The Diary of an Eccentric*, 2004, p. 89, 11 November 1939.

46 Hall Papers, 20 and 25 December 1939. Gabriel Gorodetsky (ed.), *The Maisky Diaries: Red Ambassador to the Court of St James's 1932–1943*, 2015, p. 246, 31 December 1939. Woolven (ed.), *The London Diaries of Anthony Heap*, pp. 269–70, 25 and 31 December 1939. Joan Wyndham, *Love Lessons: A Wartime Diary*, 1985, p. 34, New Year's Eve.

47 For Pankhurst, then still just fifty-eight, see *Picture Post*, Vol. 6, 30 March 1940, pp. 28–9. *Stratford Express*, 2 February 1940. *East London Advertiser*, 4 May 1940.

48 R. J. Hammond, *Food*, Vol. II, *Studies in Administration and Control*, 1956, Ch. XXXII; Lizzie Collingham, *The Taste of War: World War Two and the Battle for Food*, 2011, pp. 366–7.

49   For the start of Dig for Victory see Margaret Willes, *The Gardens of the British Working Class*, 2014, p. 280. For Leyton see *Stratford Express*, 13 October 1939. *Lewisham Borough News*, 21 November 1939. Wells, 'Diary of the War', 9 March 1940. The pig club is in *Picture Post*, Vol. 6, 3 February 1940, pp. 41–3.

50   W. A. L. Marshall, *A Century of London Weather*, 1952, p. 94 and Plate III.

51   Clarke, Diary, January–February 1940.

52   Clarke, Diary, 1 March 1940. Buddell Papers, 15 February to 27 March 1940.

53   W. H. B. Court, *Coal*, 1951, pp. 62–6. Jesse and Harwood, *London Front*, pp. 194–5, 9 February 1940. Carver Papers, 6–9 March 1940.

54   *South London Press*, 9 and 16 February 1940.

55   Weymouth, *Journals*, Vol. 1, p. 145, 7 January 1940. *Estates Gazette*, Vol. CXXXV, 10 February 1940, p. 178. Anne Oliver Bell (ed.), *The Diary of Virginia Woolf*, Vol. V, *1936–1941*, 1984, pp. 267–9, 16 February 1940.

56   Malcolmson (eds.), *A Free-Spirited Woman*, p. 169, 3 January 1940.

57   Hall, Papers, 21 October and 10 December 1939. *East London Advertiser*, 6 January 1940 (Whitechapel); *Stratford Express*, 12 January 1940 (Barking); *Hackney Gazette*, 8, 15 and 19 January 1940.

58   *Stratford Express*, 6 and 13 October 1939. For the jibes see Neil Wallington, *Out of the Flames: The Story of the Fire Services National Benevolent Fund 1943–2003*, 2003, pp. 20–21. For the boys see Green, *Caught*, p. 136. See also Titmuss, *Problems of Social Policy*, p. 140.

59   *Hackney Gazette*, 1 January 1940. *South London Press*, 2 January 1940.

60   Holl, 'Civil Defence', 28 March 1940. *Lewisham Borough News*, 16 January 1940. *East London Advertiser*, 27 January 1940. *Stratford Express*, 5 January 1940 (London AFS). Scott, *Your Obedient Servant*, pp. 120–21.

61   On the City parade see *The Times*, 23–4 February 1940. Hall, Papers, 10 April 1940. Woolven (ed.), *Diaries of Anthony Heap*, p. 286, 9 April 1940.

3. The Last Barricades of Europe:
10 April–6 September 1940

1   Olivia Cockett, *Love & War in London*, edited by Robert Malcolmson, 2008, pp. 82–3, 9 April 1940.

2   Robin Woolven (ed.), *The London Diaries of Anthony Heap 1931–1945*, Woodbridge, 2017, p. 287, 23 April 1940.

3   For the Steerses and van den Bergs see *Lewisham Borough News*, 28 May 1940.

4   For Tottenham see *Hackney Gazette*, 27 May 1940. For the spy scares see MO File Report 143, 'North London Refugees', p. 2, from Cricklewood, Willesden, 27 May 1940. For Wandsworth see Alfred James Hurley, *Days That Are Gone: Milestones I Have Passed in South-West London*, 1947, pp. 209–11. For Chelsea see Frances Faviell [Olivia Faviell Lucas], *A Chelsea Concerto*, 1959, pp. 44–7.

5   For the Belgians in London in the First World War see Jerry White, *Zeppelin Nights: London in the First World War*, 2014, pp. 73–5. Private Papers of A. E. Buddell, OBE, Imperial War Museum, Docs. 26502, 14 May 1940. For the US announcement see *The Times*, 18 May 1940. Diaries of Rhona Mary Linton Little, Bishopsgate Institute, GDP/178, 27 May 1940.

6   'The Second World War Diaries of Hilda Neal', Imperial War Museum, PP/
    MCR/59, 28 May 1940.

7   Paul Addison and Jeremy A. Crang (eds.), *Listening to Britain: Home Intelligence
    Reports on Britain's Finest Hour, May to September 1940*, 2010, pp. 16, 52,
    71, 714, 21 and 29 May, 3 June 1940. See also Wendy Webster, *Mixing It:
    Diversity in World War Two Britain*, Oxford, 2018, pp. 48–50.

8   Diary of Godfrey W. Clarke, Bishopsgate Institute, GDP/258, 29 May 1940.
    Private Papers of Miss N. V. Carver, Imperial War Museum, Docs. 379, 30 May
    1940.

9   O. S. Nock, *Britain's Railways at War 1939–1945*, 1971, pp. 84–6. Mary Morris,
    A Very Private Diary: A Nurse in Wartime, 2014, pp. 3–4, 31 May–1 June 1940.
    Private Papers of Mrs G. Rennie, Imperial War Museum, Docs. 5090, pp. 1–2.
    Private Papers of Miss G. Thomas, Imperial War Museum, Box No. 90/30/1, 3
    June 1940.

10 Aylmer Firebrace, *Fire Service Memories*, 1949, pp. 163–4; *Municipal Journal*,
    Vol. 49, 14 June 1940, p. 777; Faviell, *Chelsea Concerto*, pp. 53–4; *The Times*,
    10 June 1940.

11 Peter Davidson (ed.), *The Complete Works of George Orwell*, Vol. 12, *A Patriot
    After All 1940–1941*, 1998, p. 174, 'War-time Diary', 1 June 1940. For the new
    evacuation see R. M. Titmuss, *Problems of Social Policy*, 1950, pp. 243, 249.
    For the reservations see Addison and Crang (eds.), *Listening to Britain*, pp.
    16–17, 52, 54, 21, 29 and 30 May 1940.

12 Ben Robertson, *I Saw England*, 1941, pp. 44–5. For the reception scheme see
    Sir Geoffrey Shakespeare, *Let Candles be Brought In*, 1949, pp. 243–72. Robert
    Rhodes James (ed.), *Chips: The Diaries of Sir Henry Channon*, 1967, p. 259,
    24 June 1940.

13 Neal, Diaries, 14 June (Mabel) and 4 July (Mayfair) 1940. F. Tennyson Jesse
    and H. M. Harwood, *London Front: Letters Written to America (August 1939–
    July 1940)*, 1940, p. 410, 8 June 1940. James Leutze (ed.), *The London
    Observer: The Journal of Raymond E. Lee*, 1972, p. 6, 22 June 1940. Anthony
    Weymouth, *Journals of the War Years (1939–1945) and One Year Later*, 2 vols.,
    1948, Vol. 1, pp. 291–2, 19 July, and p. 278, 8 June 1940 (Savoy). Theodora
    Fitzgibbon, *With Love*, 1982, p. 53. Robert Henrey, *A Village in Piccadilly*,
    1942, p. 13.

14 For population estimates see C. L. Dunn, *The Emergency Medical Services*, Vol.
    II, *Scotland, Northern Ireland and the Principal Air Raids on Industrial Centres
    in Great Britain*, 1953, p. 196. T. C. Barker and Michael Robbins, *A History
    of London Transport: Passenger Travel and the Development of the Metropolis*,
    Vol. II, *The Twentieth Century to 1970*, 1974 (1976 edition), p. 307 (LPTB),
    George Beardmore, *Civilians at War: Journals 1938–1946*, 1984, pp. 60–61
    (BBC). Robert Colls, *George Orwell: English Rebel*, Oxford, 2013, p. 145. For
    the LDV generally see Charles Graves, *The Home Guard of Britain*, 1943.
    Winston S. Churchill, *The Second World War*, Vol. II, *Their Finest Hour*, 1949,
    p. 235, 5 July 1949.

15 Neal, Diaries, 17 June 1940.

16 Carver, Papers, 17 June 1940.

17 Clarke Diary, 17 June 1940. On the railways see Terence H. O'Brien, *Civil
    Defence*, 1955, p. 370. *Hackney Gazette*, 10 April 1940. *East London Advertiser*,
    3 August 1940. *Picture Post*, Vol. 8, 17 August 1940, pp. 18–19. For Camberwell

see *South London Press*, 19 July 1940. For West Ham's reputation see Diary of David Euan Wallace, Bodleian Library, GB 161 MSS Eng. Hist. c.495–8, 4 July 1940, Wallace at this point Senior Regional Commissioner for LCDR; for its progress see *Stratford Express*, 6 August 1940.

18 For the Southwark Tunnel see *News Chronicle*, 24 June and 4 September 1940. On the shortfall see Wallace, Diary, 7 August 1940: the shortfall in public shelters was 250,000, in domestic shelters 900,000.

19 On Anderson's announcement see *Estates Gazette*, Vol. CXXXVI, 27 July 1940, p. 101. Cockett, *Love & War in London*, p. 114, 27 June 1940. Doreen Bates, *Diary of a Wartime Affair: The True Story of a Surprisingly Modern Romance*, 2016, p. 219, 6 August 1940. Dorothy G. Wells, 'Diary of the War', Imperial War Museum, Docs. 26780, Vol. 3, 2 July 1940. For the handymen see *Picture Post*, Vol. 8, 14 September 1940, p. 33, letter from Stuart Murray offering a specification for home-made bunks in Andersons.

20 For the messengers see *Municipal Journal*, Vol. 49, 12 July 1940, p. 919. *South London Press*, 30 July 1940 (Camberwell and Deptford). *Stratford Express*, 1 March 1940 (West Ham). *East London Advertiser*, 29 June 1940. For the WVS generally see Patricia and Robert Malcolmson, *Women at the Ready: The Remarkable Story of the Women's Voluntary Services on the Home Front*, 2013.

21 *Stratford Express*, 19 July and 2 August 1940.

22 Addison and Crang (eds.), *Listening to Britain*, p. 239, 17 July 1940 for the invasion scare. Neal, Diaries, 15 May 1940.

23 The importance of Britain's potential fifth column was spelled out in *The Times*, 16 and 23 April 1940. The number of refugees is uncertain: see Charmian Brinson and Richard Dove, *Politics by Other Means: The Free German League of Culture in London 1939–1945*, 2010, p. 7.

24 John W. Wheeler-Bennett, *John Anderson: Viscount Waverley*, 1962, pp. 239–40.

25 For Churchill's fears see Peter Fleming, *Invasion 1940: An Account of the German Preparations and the British Counter-Measures*, 1957, p. 53. For the numbers see Miriam Kochan, 'Women's Experience of Internment', in David Cesarani and Tony Kushner (eds.), *The Internment of Aliens in Twentieth Century Britain*, 1993, p. 147; Tony Kushner, *The Persistence of Prejudice: Antisemitism in British Society during the Second World War*, Manchester, 1989, pp. 142–5.

26 Eugen Spier, *The Protecting Power*, 1951, Chs. 1 and 2 and passim. Livia Laurent [Eva Maierhof], *A Tale of Internment*, 1942, pp. 11–44.

27 Klara Modern, *My Dearest Family: An Austrian Refugee's Letters from London to America, 1938–1945*, Milton Keynes [privately published], 2017, Preface (by Richard Deveson) and pp. 69–71, 83–5, 86–8, Letters to her Family in New York, 25 January, 8 and 21 July 1940. See also Marietta Bearman et al., *Out of Austria: The Austrian Centre in London in World War II*, 2008.

28 *Marylebone Mercury*, 27 April and 8 June 1940.

29 Lucio Sponza, 'The Anti-Italian Riots, June 1940', in Panikos Panayi (ed.), *Racial Violence in Britain in the Nineteenth and Twentieth Centuries*, 1996 (revised edition), pp. 131–49; MO File Report 184, 'Anti-Italian Riots in Soho', 11 June 1940; *Stratford Express*, 14 June 1940; *East London Advertiser*, 15 and 22 June 1940. Elena Salvoni with Sandy Fawkes, *Elena: A Life in Soho*, 1990, p. 45.

30 *Daily Herald*, 9 July 1940.

31 *Hackney Gazette*, 14 February 1940; Young was given a month's imprisonment but appealed and was eventually bound over in the sum of £20 (ibid., 24 April 1940). Mosley is in the *Stratford Express*, 23 February 1940. For East London fascism see Thomas P. Linehan, *East London for Mosley: The British Union of Fascists in East London and South-West Essex, 1933–40*, 1996, Ch. 5.

32 Woolven (ed.), *The London Diaries of Anthony Heap*, p. 290, 24 May 1940; Neal, Diaries, 23 May 1940. For the Freemans see *Hackney Gazette*, 12 June 1940 and *Yorkshire Post*, 6 July 1940; for the Whetstone case see *Hendon and Finchley Times*, 2 August 1940. For the New British Broadcasting Station see Fleming, *Invasion 1940*, pp. 118–23.

33 Pollitt is cited in *Stratford Express*, 16 February 1940. *Lewisham Borough News*, 16 July 1940.

34 *South London Press*, 5 and 30 January, 2, 6, 9 and 13 February 1940.

35 Fenner Brockway, *Bermondsey Story: The Life of Alfred Salter*, 1949, pp. 225–6 and passim. *South London Press*, 24 May (Bermondsey depot workers) and 28 June 1940; for north of the river see *Hackney Gazette*, 21 and 28 June 1940, and *West London Observer*, 7 June 1940. *South London Press*, 7 June 1940, for the strategic withdrawal and *West London Observer*, 7 June 1940, for Paddington.

36 Cockett, *Love & War in London*, p. 117, 1 July 1940. Verily Anderson, *Spam Tomorrow*, 1956, p. 74.

37 Addison and Crang (eds.), *Listening to Britain*, p. 125, 17 June 1940. Clarke Diary, 17 June 1940: it was Fairbrother (1873–1941). Little, Diaries, 1 June 1940. Woolven (ed.), *The London Diaries of Anthony Heap*, pp. 293–4, 27 June, and pp. 299–300, 5 August 1940. Wells, 'Diary of the War', Vol. 3, 18 and 20 June, 4 July and 3 August 1940. *East London Advertiser*, 3 and 17 August 1940.

38 Hilde Marchant, *Women and Children Last: A Woman Reporter's Account of the Battle of Britain*, 1941, p. 45. For Norway see Dik Lehmkul, *Journey to London: The Story of the Norwegian Government at War*, 1945, pp. 110–11. For Poland see Count Edward Raczynski, *In Allied London*, 1962, pp. 52–3. For de Gaulle see David Drake, *Paris at War 1939–1944*, 2015, pp. 69–70; Churchill, *Their Finest Hour*, pp. 191–2. For the national movements see A. J. Liebling, *The Road Back to Paris*, 1944, p. 130.

39 The eagle is in Diana Cooper, *Trumpets from the Steep*, 1960, p. 47. On the French Jewish refugees see MO File Report 238, 'Refugees', 30 June 1940. For Gibraltarians in a Fulham (West Kensington) mansion block see *Estates Gazette*, Vol. CXXXVII, 28 June 1941, p. 668; for the number see Sir Arthur Salusbury MacNalty (ed.), *The Civilian Health and Medical Services*, Vol. I, *The Ministry of Health Services; Other Civilian Health and Medical Services*, 1953, pp. 219–20.

40 Raczynski, *Allied London*, pp. 52–3; Keith Sword et al., *The Formation of the Polish Community in Great Britain 1939–1950*, 1989, pp. 31–2. Lehmkul, *Journey to London*, pp. 112–3, 116–7, 120–21. Erik Hazelhoff, *In Pursuit of Life*, Stroud, 2003, pp. 95–6. Debra Kelly, 'Mapping Free French London: Places, Spaces, Traces', in Debra Kelly and Martyn Cornick (eds.), *A History of the French in London: Liberty, Equality, Opportunity*, 2013, pp. 300–301. For the Belgians see *The Times*, 20 November 1940.

41 John Lehmann, *I Am My Brother: Autobiography II*, 1960, p. 70, probably 6 July 1940. Colin Perry, *Boy in the Blitz: The 1940 Diary of Colin Perry*, Stroud, 2000, p. 28, 28 July 1940.

42   For the first bombs see TNA, MEPO 4/126 Pt 2, 19 June 1940; MH 101/58,
      19 June 1940. Buddell Papers, 25 June 1940. For the fatalities see Winston G.
      Ramsey, *The Blitz: Then and Now*, 3 vols., 1987–9, Vol. I, p. 230. For the pattern
      of bombing in July see MEPO 4/126 Pt 2.

43   MEPO 4/126 Pt 2, 3 and 9 August (for the leaflets) and succeeding days for
      August 1940. W. C. Berwick Sayers (ed.), *Croydon and the Second World War:
      The Official History of the War Work of the Borough and Its Citizens from
      1939 to 1945 Together with the Croydon Roll of Honour*, 1949, pp. 35–9; some
      other sources give sixty-three dead, casualty figures often imprecise. Perry, *Boy
      in the Blitz*, pp. 66–7, 17 August 1940.

44   For the accidental bombing see O'Brien, *Civil Defence*, p. 385n.; Ramsey, *The
      Blitz*, Vol. I, p. 232. *South London Press*, 30 August 1940; the address was given
      in the issue of 15 March 1940.

45   For the tubes see Michael H. C. Baker, *London Transport in the Blitz*, Hersham,
      2010, pp. 50–51. The warnings are in MEPO 4/126 Pt 2, 23 July 1940. Hilary
      St George Saunders, *Ford at War*, 1946, p. 23; for roof-spotters generally see
      Helen Jones, *British Civilians in the Front Line: Air Raids, Productivity and
      Wartime Culture, 1939–45*, Manchester, 2006, pp. 100–102.

46   Beardmore, *Civilians at War*, p. 68, 30 June 1940. Neal, Papers, 29 August 1940.
      Clarke Diary, 7 September 1940. Wells, 'Diary of the War', Vol. 3, 25 August
      1940. Woolven (ed.), *The London Diaries of Anthony Heap*, pp. 308–9, 302,
      15 August 1940. Cockett, *Love & War in London*, pp. 154–5, 26 August 1940.
      Imperial War Museum, Private Papers of Miss V. Bawtree, Docs. 1807a–b, n.d.
      [2 September 1940]. Carver, Papers, 25 August 1940.

47   Woolven (ed.), *The London Diaries of Anthony Heap*, pp. 307–8, 31 August
      1940. The significance of this period has been acknowledged by many historians:
      see, for instance, Tom Harrisson, *Living Through the Blitz*, 1976, pp. 55–7;
      Angus Calder, *The Myth of the Blitz*, 1991, pp. 124–5.

48   Casualty figures for August are in Dunn, *Emergency Medical Services*, Vol. II,
      p. 210; see also p. 199 for the anticipated casualties; for September 1–6 in
      O'Brien, *Civil Defence*, p. 677.

4. Fighting Like a Wild Cat:
7 September–28 December 1940

1   Private Papers of T. H. Pointer, Imperial War Museum, Docs. 3957, 7 September
     1940.

2   Aylmer Firebrace, *Fire Service Memories*, 1949, pp. 165–9.

3   Terence H. O'Brien, *Civil Defence*, 1955, pp. 388, 454–5; for warning times see
     MEPO 4/126 Pt 2, 7/8 September 1940. Private Papers of W. B. Regan, Imperial
     War Museum, Docs. 781, 'Document 1: Approximately early September 1940',
     pp. 1–2. For Abbey Road see Winston G. Ramsey (ed.), *The Blitz: Then and
     Now*, 3 vols., 1987–9, Vol. 2, pp. 56–61. Sources disagree about some details
     (numbers of casualties, numbers of bombers, times of warnings etc.); I've gener-
     ally followed official histories and the contemporary Metropolitan Police War
     Diary. See also Peter Stansky, *The First Day of the Blitz: September 7, 1940*,
     2007, passim; and generally, the excellent Juliet Gardiner, *The Blitz: The British
     Under Attack*, 2010.

4   TNA, MH 101/58, incidents 7–8 September.

5   Mass Observation Archive, MO File Report 392, 'Evacuation and Other East End Problems', 10 September 1940, pp. 3–4. See also Paul Addison and Jeremy A. Crang (eds.), *Listening to Britain: Home Intelligence Reports on Britain's Finest Hour, May to September 1940*, 2010, pp. 407–11, 9–11 September 1940.

6   *Daily Herald*, 11 and 12 September 1940; *New Statesman and Nation*, 21 September 1940, pp. 276–8; Ritchie Calder, *The Lesson of London*, 1941, Ch. 1. Calder put the 'true figure of deaths at the centre at around' 450, a figure that has survived in mythology ever since. The suspicion of far larger casualties appears to have arisen in an early news blackout and the reputed entombment of body parts in deep concrete soon after the incident. But there is no evidence at all to shake the authorities' figure of seventy-three, itself a very high figure for the main blitz; see Ramsey (ed.), *The Blitz*, Vol. 2, p. 77.

7   See Stephanie Bird, *Stepney: Profile of a London Borough from the Outbreak of the First World War to the Festival of Britain, 1914–1951*, Newcastle upon Tyne, 2011, Chs. 7 and 8; Henry Felix Srebrnik, *London Jews and British Communism, 1935–1945*, Ilford, 1995, Ch. 3. For Stepney and contractors see R. M. Titmuss, *Problems of Social Policy*, 1950, p. 295. For the communists see *East London Observer*, 19 October 1940. Davis was replaced in October by the council's town clerk, who was in turn replaced by the town clerk of Islington in December, also by Morrison. For further detail see also Robin Woolven, 'Civil Defence in London 1935–1945: The Formation and Implementation of Policy for, and the Performance of, Air Raid Precautions (later Civil Defence) Services in the London Region', University of London PhD thesis, 2002, Ch. 5. For the mayor see Frank R. Lewey, *Cockney Campaign*, 1944.

8   See Doreen Idle, *War Over West Ham: A Study of Community Adjustment*, 1943, pp. 31, 63–4, 71.

9   Private Papers of Mrs G. Rennie, Imperial War Museum, Docs. 5090, pp. 2–3.

10 Peter Davidson (ed.), *The Complete Works of George Orwell*, Vol. 12, *A Patriot After All 1940–1941*, 1998, p. 255, 'War-Diary', 12 September 1940. Addison and Crang (eds.), *Listening to Britain*, p. 434, 19 September 1940 for the communist petition; see also Bird, *Stepney*, pp. 160–61, and Harold Nicolson, *Diaries and Letters 1939–1945*, 1967, pp. 115–16. For Plaistow see *Stratford Express*, 4 October 1940.

11 Basil Collier, *The Defence of the United Kingdom*, 1957, pp. 238, 479. General Sir Frederick Pile, *Ack-Ack: Britain's Defence against Air Attack during the Second World War*, 1949, pp. 150–52; I've transposed sentences in a more logical order. See also Anon., *Roof Over Britain: The Official Story of the A.A. Defences, 1939–1942*, 1943, pp. 48–51.

12 Nesca A. Robb, *An Ulsterwoman in England 1924–1941*, Cambridge, 1942, p. 129.

13 Mass Observation, MO/D/5438, 12 September 1940. Dorothy G. Wells, 'Diary of the War', Imperial War Museum, Docs. 26780, Vol. 3, 12 September 1940. W. E. Holl, 'Civil Defence Goes Through It: Paddington, 1937–1945', typescript, British Library, 1946, p. 39; this period of Holl's chronicles was 'transcribed from personal diaries' etc. (p. xi).

14 Anon., *Roof Over Britain*, pp. 49–50. Collier, *The Defence of the United Kingdom*, pp. 251–2.

15 O'Brien, *Civil Defence*, pp. 454–6.

16   For the naval mine see *Hackney Gazette*, 20 September 1940. Collier, *The Defence of the United Kingdom*, pp. 256–7; O'Brien, *Civil Defence*, pp. 387–90.

17   Ramsey (ed.), *The Blitz*, Vol. 2, pp. 178–83. See also Camilla Loewe, *Just Like the End of the World: Stories of the Coronation Mansions Disaster*, 2012.

18   Alfred James Hurley, *Days That Are Gone: Milestones I Have Passed in South-West London*, 1947, pp. 219–20.

19   For the proportions of whole- and part-timers etc. see O'Brien, *Civil Defence*, p. 690.

20   *East London Advertiser*, 14 September 1940; *Stratford Express*, 13 September 1940. *Hackney Gazette*, 13 September 1940. For the honours see *The Times*, 4 January 1941, when ARP staff from four London boroughs were honoured.

21   Private Papers of Miss N. V. Carver, Imperial War Museum, Docs. 379, 18 September 1940. Inez Holden, *It Was Different at the Time*, 1943, p. 68. *Picture Post*, Vol. 9, 2 November 1940, pp. 14–17.

22   Regan Papers, Doc. 1, pp. 10, 12; 'Document 2', p. 14; n.d. [16, 18 and 20 September 1940].

23   Barbara Nixon, *Raiders Overhead*, 1943, p. 79. Regan Papers, 'Document 3', p. 30, n.d. [Christmas 1940]. Charlotte Haldane, *Truth Will Out*, 1949, p. 189.

24   Anon., *The Bells Go Down: The Diary of a London A.F.S. Man*, 1942, pp. 51–3. See also H. S. Ingham, *Fire and Water: An Anthology by Members of the NFS*, 1942, passim.

25   TNA, AST 11/32, Note by PEP, 'The Welfare of Air Raid Victims', 3 October 1940. Mass Observation File Report 431, 'Survey of the Activities of Official and Voluntary Bodies in the East End, during the Intensive Bombing September 7–27, 1940', p. 5.

26   For Lambeth see *South London Press*, 13 December 1940; for Finsbury see *Islington Gazette*, 10 March 1944.

27   *New Statesman and Nation*, 28 September 1940, pp. 300–301.

28   See *Recommendations of Lord Horder's Committee Regarding the Conditions in Air-Raid Shelters with Special Reference to Health; and a Brief Statement of Action Taken by the Government Thereon*, Cmd. 6234, November 1940. On Tilbury after Hibbin see *Picture Post*, Vol. 9, 9 November 1940, pp. 14–15; Ritchie Calder, *Carry on London*, 1941, pp. 39–42.

29   *Sunday Pictorial*, 22 September 1940; Diary of David Euan Wallace, Bodleian Library, GB 161 MSS Eng. Hist. c.495–8, 23 September 1940.

30   For East Enders in the Aldwych tube see William Sansom, *Westminster in War*, 1947, p. 135. For the mosquitoes and other problems see Sir Arthur Salusbury MacNalty (ed.), *The Civilian Health and Medical Services*, Vol. I, *The Ministry of Health Services; Other Civilian Health and Medical Services*, 1953, pp. 204–10. Diary of Godfrey W. Clarke, Bishopsgate Institute, GDP/258, 21–25 September 1940 [punctuation silently corrected].

31   'The Second World War Diaries of Hilda Neal', Imperial War Museum, PP/MCR/59, 9 and 17 September 1940. For the survey see O'Brien, *Civil Defence*, p. 508. For Pimlico see Sansom, *Westminster*, p. 133. Regan Papers, Doc. 1, pp. 7–9, n.d. [11–15 September 1940].

32   HC Debates, 9 October 1940, cols. 400–412.

33   Titmuss, *Problems of Social Policy*, pp. 255–6, 261.

34   Details of moves and problems, all before the end of September 1940, from TNA, MH 101/58. The dustcarts are in Lewey, *Cockney Campaign*, pp. 21–2.

35 For the numbers in rest centres see Woolven, 'Civil Defence', Ch. 5, Table 6. For the bomb disposal teams see TNA, HO 186/952, LCDR, Intelligence Branch Report No. 1, 1 January 1941, p. 6.

36 W. R. Matthews, *Saint Paul's Cathedral in War-Time 1939–1945*, 1946, pp. 36–7; *The Times*, 10 October 1940.

37 For Poplar see Addison and Crang (eds.), *Listening to Britain*, pp. 416–17, 11 September 1940; Regan Papers, Doc. 1, pp. 8 and 12. For the official evacuation see Titmuss, *Problems of Social Policy*, p. 285. For Chelsea see Frances Faviell [Olivia Faviell Lucas], *A Chelsea Concerto*, 1959, p. 127.

38 Private Papers of A. E. Buddell, OBE, Imperial War Museum, Docs. 26502, 20 September 1940. Anthony Weymouth, *Journals of the War Years (1939–1945) and One Year Later*, 2 vols., 1948, Vol. 1, p. 325, 16 September 1940. Clarke Diary, 27 September 1940. John Colville, *The Fringes of Power: Downing Street Diaries 1939–1955*, 2004, p. 217, 7 October 1940. Neal Diaries, 8 September 1940. *Picture Post*, Vol. 9, 12 October 1940, pp. 9–11. *South London Press*, 4 October 1940.

39 Davidson (ed.), *The Complete Works of George Orwell*, Vol. 12, p. 263, 'War-time diary', 17 September 1940. Neal Diaries, 16 September 1940. The CP leaflets are in Wallace Diary, 18 September 1940. Nixon, *Raiders Overhead*, p. 19.

40 Klara Modern, *My Dearest Family: An Austrian Refugee's Letters from London to America, 1938–1945*, Milton Keynes [privately published], 2017, pp. 100–102, letter to her family in New York, 23 October 1940.

41 Robin Woolven (ed.), *The London Diaries of Anthony Heap 1931–1945*, Woodbridge, 2017, pp. 310–11, 9 September 1940 et seq. Colville, *Fringes of Power*, p. 209.

42 For the Hungarian see *Picture Post*, Vol. 9, 2 November 1940, pp. 18–19. The Dorchester as focal point is in Charles Graves, *Off the Record*, 1942, pp. 10–11, 19 November 1940. Robert Rhodes James (ed.), *Chips: The Diaries of Sir Henry Channon*, 1967, p. 272, 5 November 1940. See also Diana Cooper, *Trumpets from the Steep*, 1960, pp. 63–8; and Matthew Sweet, *The West End Front: The Wartime Secret of London's Grand Hotels*, 2011, passim.

43 For the Savoy see Phil Piratin, *Our Flag Stays Red*, 1948, pp. 73–5; Stanley Jackson, *The Savoy: The Romance of a Great Hotel*, 1964, pp. 106–7; Sweet, *The West End Front*, p. 50ff. for the May Fair (as it then was) see Wallace Diary, 16 September 1940.

44 Private Papers of Miss Vivienne Hall, Imperial War Museum, Docs. 3989a, n.d. [probably 16 September 1940]. Wells Diary, Vol. 3, 14 October 1940. Buddell Papers, 13 September, interpolation from 14 September 1940.

45 For the buses see T. C. Barker and Michael Robbins, *A History of London Transport: Passenger Travel and the Development of the Metropolis*, Vol. II, *The Twentieth Century to 1970*, 1974 (1976 edition), p. 306. A Warden [Adrian Bury], *Dusk to Dawn: Letters by a Warden*, 1941, p. 49. J. A. Hammerton, *As the Days Go By … Leaves from My War-Time Diary 1939–1940*, 1941, p. 220, 14 September 1940. I'm afraid I've lost the reference to good looks, though I've certainly read it.

46 Nigel Balchin, *Darkness Falls from the Air*, 1942, pp. 16–17. Graves, *Off the Record*, 1942, p. 67, 23 December 1940. The suitcase is in Hammerton, *As the Days Go By*, p. 282, 31 December 1940. Vera Brittain, *England's Hour*, 1941.

47 Mass Observation File Report 403, 'The Effect of Air Raids on the Isle of Dogs', 15 September 1940, p. 4. The river service is in Barker and Robbins, *A History of London Transport*, p. 333.

48 Woolven (ed.), *Diaries of Anthony Heap*, pp. 318, 23 September; 323-4, 9 October; 326, 18 October 1940. *Stratford Express*, 18 October 1940; the report gave Chantry Street but that was in Islington. James Lansdale Hodson, *Through the Dark Night: Being Some Account of a War Correspondent's Journeys, Meetings and What Was Said to Him, in France, Britain and Flanders during 1939-1940*, 1941, 20 October 1940.

49 David Low, *Low's Autobiography*, 1956, p. 346. Lettice Cooper, *Black Bethlehem*, 1947, p. 159. For the famous wartime pubs of Soho and Fitzrovia during the war see Ruthven Todd, *Fitzrovia & the Road to the York Minster*, 1973; for sheltering in a pub cellar see Bryan Magee, *Growing up in a War*, 2007, p. 106.

50 Hurley, *Days That Are Gone*, p. 220. Graves, *Off the Record*, 1942, p. 23, 26 November 1940. Anon., *The Bells Go Down*, p. 103, October 1940, and p. 165, April 1941; p. 121, November 1940.

51 *Hackney Gazette*, 11 October, 20 November and 9 December 1940; *Daily Herald*, 19 October and 21 November 1940; 26 February 1941.

52 *East London Advertiser*, 21 September 1940 (Ilford youth); *Hackney Gazette*, 11 October 1940 (Finsbury Park). Wally Thompson, *Time Off My Life*, 1956, Ch. 19. Sidney Day, *London Born*, Beaminster, Dorset, 2004, pp. 149-50.

53 Neal Diaries, 16 September 1940. *Hackney Gazette*, 18 and 20 September, 8 November 1940. MO File Report 392, p. 3. See Tony Kushner, *The Persistence of Prejudice: Antisemitism in British Society during the Second World War*, Manchester, 1989, pp. 53-8; Jerry White, 'Jews and Bombs: The Making of a Metropolitan Myth', in Colin Holmes and Anne J. Kershen (eds.), *An East End Legacy: Essays in Memory of William J. Fishman*, 2017, pp. 117-33.

54 J. B. Priestley, *All England Listened: The Wartime Broadcasts of J. B. Priestley*, New York, 1967, pp. 104-5, 15 September 1940. Colin Perry, *Boy in the Blitz: The 1940 Diary of Colin Perry*, Stroud, 2000, pp. 129-30, 11 September 1940. Clarke Diary, 20 September 1940.

55 Hilde Marchant, *Women and Children Last: A Woman Reporter's Account of the Battle of Britain*, 1941, pp. 185-6.

56 *Stratford Express*, 25 October 1940 (East Ham). Quentin Reynolds, *A London Diary*, 1941 (Popular Library edition, New York, 1962), pp. 26 (6 October) and 68 (24 October 1940). Lewey, *Cockney Campaign*, p. 41 (Stepney). Idle, *War Over West Ham*, pp. 73-4.

57 *Hendon and Finchley Times*, 16 February, 12 April and 14 June 1940 (Edgware and Mill Hill); *Middlesex Gazette*, 14 September 1940 (Southall); *Marylebone Mercury*, 17 August 1940. Buddell Papers, 22 September 1940. *Hackney Gazette*, 8 January 1941.

58 Mass Observation File Report 292, 'Note on the Hampstead Housewives Service', 20 July 1940, p. 1, for the Barnes original. *Hackney Gazette*, 4 November 1940. Noel Streatfeild, *Beyond the Vicarage*, 1971, p. 137.

59 *Hackney Gazette*, 20 September and 14 October 1940; *Municipal Journal*, Vol. 49, 18 October 1940, p. 1322. Haldane, *Truth Will Out*, p. 186.

60 For Walthamstow see *Municipal Journal*, Vol. 51, 22 January 1943, p. 93. For Kensington see *Picture Post*, Vol. 9, 5 October 1940, pp. 22-5. For Lambeth see *South London Press*, 13 September 1940. For the LCC's programme see LMA, LCC/RC/GEN/01/001, 'History of the Londoners' Meal Service';

R. J. Hammond, *Food*, Vol. II, *Studies in Administration and Control*, 1956, pp. 320 and n.; 369n. For the cutlery, in Poplar at least, see *East London Advertiser*, 16 November 1940. See also Titmuss, *Problems of Social Policy*, pp. 266–7; his figures of LMS centres show 170 open in May 1941 – probably some had been merged and some destroyed by bombing.

61   On rest centre improvements see Titmuss, *Problems of Social Policy*, pp. 262–6, 269. Marchant, *Women and Children Last*, p. 71. For Hackney and other initiatives see TNA, AST 11/32. *Stratford Express*, 8 November 1940 (East Ham). Idle, *War Over West Ham*, pp. 66–7.

62   *Picture Post*, Vol. 9, 23 November, pp. 9–13; 30 November 1940, p. 35.

63   The numbers of raids are in C. L. Dunn, *The Emergency Medical Services*, Vol. II, *Scotland, Northern Ireland and the Principal Air Raids on Industrial Centres in Great Britain*, 1953, p. 209. For raids by night see MEPO 4/126 Pt 2.

64   For the Port see HO 186/952, LCDR, Intelligence Branch Report No. 2, 15 January 1941, p. 7. H. C. Dent, *Education in Transition: A Sociological Study of the Impact of War on English Education 1939–1943*, 1944, pp. 70–75; P. H. J. H. Gosden, *Education in the Second World War: A Study in Policy and Administration*, 1976, pp. 41–5.

65   See the entertainments pages of *The Times*, 16 and 23 December 1940.

66   For Mickey the Midget see Calder, *Carry on London*, Ch. 3; Lewey, *Cockney Campaign*, Ch. XVIII; Drew Middleton, *The Sky Suspended: The Battle of Britain*, 1960: Middleton was a US journalist covering London for the *New York Times*. For Mrs Sedgwick see *Lewisham Borough News*, 17 December 1940. Nixon, *Raiders Overhead*, p. 51.

67   For the work of one shelter committee see *The Hermitage Shelter Minutes December 1940*, 1990, published by the History of Wapping Trust. For the Oval see *South London Press*, 22 November 1940. For the caves see Lewis Blake, *Red Alert: The Story of South East London at War, 1939–1945*, 'New Enlarged Edition', 1992, pp. 77–80. See generally MacNalty (ed.), *Civilian Health and Medical Services*, Vol. I, pp. 195–9.

68   For Travers see *East London Advertiser*, 21 September and 9 November 1940; Lewey, *Cockney Campaign*, pp. 118–19. For Bermondsey see *South London Press*, 29 October 1940.

69   *The Times*, 16 December 1940 (Blitz Ball). Admiral Lord Mountevans, *Adventurous Life*, 1946, p. 225. *Middlesex County Times*, 28 December 1940 (Ealing); *Middlesex Chronicle*, 4 January 1941 (Hounslow); *Norwood News*, 27 December 1940 (Penge and Balham).

70   Wells Diary, Vol. 4, 25 December 1940.

5. When Will It All End? 29 December 1940–21 June 1941

1   *London Calling*, No. 70, 2–8 February 1941, pp. 3–4 (Robin Duff); Anon., *The Bells Go Down: The Diary of a London A.F.S. Man*, 1942, p. 139. See also Terence H. O'Brien, *Civil Defence*, 1955, p. 457; Basil Collier, *The Defence of the United Kingdom*, 1957, pp. 272–3; Winston G. Ramsey (ed.), *The Blitz: Then and Now*, 3 vols., 1987–9, Vol. 2, pp. 366–72; Cyril Demarne, *The London Blitz: A Fireman's Tale*, 1980 (revised and enlarged edition, 1990), Ch. 4. See also Margaret Gaskin, *Blitz: The Story of 29th December, 1940*, 2005.

2 Anon., *Bells Go Down*, p. 144 (smells); William Kent, *The Lost Treasures of London*, 1947, p. 1 (books). W. R. Matthews, *Saint Paul's Cathedral in Wartime 1939–1945*, 1946, pp. 44–7. For Herbert Mason see Ramsey (ed.), *Blitz*, Vol. 2, p. 359.

3 Ibid., p. 370 (casualties); Aylmer Firebrace, *Fire Service Memories*, 1949, p. 187 (firefighter casualties). *London Calling*, No. 70, 2–8 February 1941, pp. 3–4.

4 *The Times*, 1 January 1941.

5 Doreen Bates, *Diary of a Wartime Affair: The True Story of a Surprisingly Modern Romance*, 2016, p. 245, 19 January, 1941. O'Brien, *Civil Defence*, p. 599 (women's compulsion). Private Papers of Miss P. Warner, Imperial War Museum, Docs. 3208, 'Journal Under the Terror', 29 January 1941.

6 Imperial War Museum, Private Papers of Miss V. Bawtree, Docs. 1807a–b, 24 January 1941 (spelling silently corrected).

7 George H. Gallup, *The Gallup International Public Opinion Polls: Great Britain 1937–1975*, Vol. One, 1937–1964, New York, 1976, p. 39. Dorothy G. Wells, 'Diary of the War', Imperial War Museum, Docs. 26780, Vol. 4, 28 January 1941.

8 For the trouble in March see *Municipal Journal*, Vol. XLIX, 28 March 1941, p. 373. For the numbers see Morrison's statement in HC Debates, Vol. 369, cols. 996–7, 6 March 1941. Wells, 'Diary', 4, 12 February 1941.

9 Warner Papers, 18 January 1941 [punctuation silently adjusted].

10 *Municipal Journal*, Vol. XLIX, 17 January 1941, p. 82 (Finchley); *Stratford Express*, 14 March 1941 (Leyton); Frances Faviell [Olivia Faviell Lucas], *A Chelsea Concerto*, 1959, p. 200. For street shelters see C. M. Kohan, *Works and Buildings*, 1952, pp. 361–2 and n. For Key and the improvements see *East London Advertiser*, 11 and 25 January 1941; *Municipal Journal*, Vol. XLIX, 14 February 1941, p. 187.

11 For the tube canteens see *Picture Post*, Vol. 10, 11 January 1941, pp. 22–3. For other improvements see *Municipal Journal*, Vol. XLIX, 14 February 1941, pp. 187, 203. For Finsbury see *Hackney Gazette*, 9 April 1941. The Waterloo arches are in Bernard Darwin, *War on the Line: The Story of the Southern Railway in War-Time*, 1946, pp. 67–8. Rose is in *Picture Post*, Vol. 10, 29 March 1941, pp. 16–17.

12 On tunnelling see TNA, HO 199/394A, 'Further Lessons of Raiding. Working of A.R.P. Services', February 1941, p. 1. For pay and conditions see *Municipal Journal*, Vol. XLIX, 2 May 1941, pp. 527–8. On tic-tac see *Picture Post*, Vol. 11, 21 June 1941, pp. 18–19. On the repairs see Kohan, *Works and Buildings*, pp. 210–14; for hostels see *Municipal Journal*, Vol. XLIX, 31 January 1941, p. 142. For Morrisons see O'Brien, *Civil Defence*, p. 528; *West London Observer*, 20 June 1941.

13 For West Ham see *Stratford Express*, 31 January, 7 and 14 February and 4 April 1941. For criticism of the Assistance Board see letters in *Picture Post*, Vol. 11, 17 May, p. 5, and 24 May 1941, p. 5. For Tilbury see *East London Advertiser*, 11 January, 22 February and 8 March 1941. Private Papers of W. B. Regan, Imperial War Museum, Docs. 781, 10 May 1941.

14 *Hackney Gazette*, 21 March (for Bannister) and 27 January 1941 (Bethnal Green). For Marylebone see (oddly) *Stratford Express*, 24 January 1941. William Sansom, *Westminster in War*, 1947, p. 126.

15 Charles Graves, *London Transport Carried On: An Account of London at War 1939–1945*, 1947, p. 71 (Liverpool Street). Reginald Bell, *The Bull's-Eye*, 1943, p. 70 (Bank). For casualty numbers see TNA, HO 186/952, LCDR, Intelligence Branch Report No. 2, 15 January 1941, p. 2.

16 Ramsey (ed.), *Blitz*, Vol. 2, pp. 397–9.

17 Café de Paris night is in Faviell, *Chelsea Concerto*, pp. 208–9. Safest place in Robert Henrey, *A Village in Piccadilly*, 1942, p. 33. Two days later is in Charles Graves, *Off the Record*, 1942, p. 110, 10 March 1941.

18 Joan Wyndham, *Love Lessons: A Wartime Diary*, 1985, p. 178, 9 March 1941. R. J. Minney, *The Two Pillars of Charing Cross: The Story of a Famous Hospital*, 1967, pp. 197–8.

19 *London Calling*, No. 80, 13–19 April 1941, p. 6 (Macdonald Hastings). Minney, *The Two Pillars of Charing Cross*, p. 198. See Charles Graves, *Champagne and Chandeliers: The Story of the Café de Paris*, 1958, pp. 115–25; Ramsey (ed.), *Blitz*, Vol. 2, pp. 460–61. In Anthony Powell, *The Soldier's Art*, 1966, the Café de Paris figures largely, as 'the Madrid'.

20 HO 186/952, Report No. 7, 26 March 1941, p. 2. Ramsey (ed.), *Blitz*, Vol. 2, pp. 488–91.

21 Private Papers of Miss N. V. Carver, Imperial War Museum, Docs. 379, 19 March 1941; the raid was on Plymouth-Devonport. 'The Second World War Diaries of Hilda Neal', Imperial War Museum, PP/MCR/59, 7 April 1941.

22 For this raid also remembered as 'The Wednesday' see Lewis Blake, *Red Alert: The Story of South East London at War, 1939–1945*, 'New Enlarged Edition', 1992, pp. 86–98. Carver Papers, 16 April 1941.

23 Details for both nights from HO 186/952, Report No. 9, 23 April 1941, passim.

24 Neal Diaries, 26 April 1941.

25 Firebrace, *Fire Service Memories*, p. 193. For the numbers of sorties see Collier, *The Defence of the United Kingdom*, p. 278. Winston S. Churchill, *The Second World War*, Vol. III, *The Grand Alliance*, 1950, pp. 41–2.

26 Details from HO 186/952, Report No. 11, 21 May 1941, passim. For Finsbury see Barbara Nixon, *Raiders Overhead*, 1943, pp. 138–9; *Hackney Gazette*, 3 September 1941. The raid of 10/11 has a good book to itself – Richard Collier, *The City That Wouldn't Die*, 1959.

27 Carver Papers, 10 May 1941.

28 Nixon, *Raiders Overhead*, p. 149. Quentin Reynolds, *Only the Stars Are Neutral*, 1942, pp. 32–5. Imperial War Museum, Private Papers of Miss G. Thomas, Box No. 90/30/1, 10 May 1941.

29 Raid details are from TNA, MEPO 4/127 Pt 1 (Metropolitan Police War Diary for 1941).

30 Statistics and calculations from the invaluable C. L. Dunn, *The Emergency Medical Services*, Vol. II, *Scotland, Northern Ireland and the Principal Air Raids on Industrial Centres in Great Britain*, 1953, pp. 209–16; figures for raids and tons of HE are in Collier, *The Defence of the United Kingdom*, p. 506. There was a margin of error in all these figures, records made under great stress never completely reliable.

31 For reports of ARP wardens' funerals see, for instance, *Stratford Express*, 28 March 1941. Carver Papers, 19 and 21–30 April 1941. Harold Scott, *Your Obedient Servant*, 1959, pp. 143–4.

32 Angus Calder, *The People's War: Britain 1939–45*, 1969, pp. 192–3. Tom Harrisson, *Living Through the Blitz*, 1976, p. 298.

33 *Yorkshire Post and Leeds Mercury*, 15 July 1941; see also Winston S. Churchill, *The Second World War*, Vol. II, *Their Finest Hour*, 1949, p. 328, where he borrows from his speech. Nixon, *Raiders Overhead*, p. 120.

34 J. A. Hammerton, *As the Days Go By ... Leaves from My War-Time Diary 1939–1940*, 1941, p. 284, for the finishing touch. F. Tennyson Jesse and H. M. Harwood, *While London Burns: Letters written to America (July 1940–June 1941)*, 1942, p. 201. For Ypres see Cecil Beaton, *The Years Between Diaries 1939–44*, 1965, pp. 58–9, 30 December 1940. Warner Papers, 17 February 1941. See also James Pope-Hennessy and Cecil Beaton, *History Under Fire*, 1941; J. M. Richards (ed.), *The Bombed Buildings of Britain: A Record of Architectural Casualties*, 1942; Joseph Bató, *Defiant City*, 1942; A. S. G. Butler, *Recording Ruin*, 1942; Wanda Ostrowska and Viola G. Garvin, *London's Glory*, 1945.

35 For the houses see HO 186/952, Report No. 12, 4 June 1941, p. 3. Private Papers of A. F. Williamson, Imperial War Museum, Docs. 3106, letters to Austin from his parents, 11 and 13 May 1941.

36 Regan, Papers, Doc. 2, pp. 27–8 [late 1940].

37 For the City see *Estates Gazette*, Vol. CXXXIV, 29 July 1939, p. 191; Robin Woolven (ed.), *The London Diaries of Anthony Heap 1931–1945*, Woodbridge, 2017, pp. 341–2, 5 January 1941; Kent, *The Lost Treasures of London*, pp. 78–9; Jesse and Harwood, *While London Burns*, p. 261. Art McCullough (ed.), *The War and Uncle Walter: The Diary of an Eccentric*, 2004, p. 188, 14 May 1941.

38 Figures and calculations from HO 186/952, Report No. 13, 18 June 1941; the tube figures are in Sir Arthur Salusbury MacNalty (ed.), *The Civilian Health and Medical Services*, Vol. I, *The Ministry of Health Services; Other Civilian Health and Medical Services*, 1953, p. 196. Willy Goldman, 'The Way We Live Now – II', *Penguin New Writing*, No. 3, 7 February 1941, pp. 9–15.

39 P. H. J. H. Gosden, *Education in the Second World War: A Study in Policy and Administration*, 1976, p. 45. For the setback see Stuart Maclure, *One Hundred Years of London Education 1870–1970*, 1970, p. 138. *Report of the Commissioner of Police of the Metropolis for the Year 1943*, 1944, Cmd 6536, pp. 7–8. Dorothy Burlingham and Anna Freud, *Young Children in War-Time: A Year's Work in a Residential War Nursery*, 1942, p. 29.

40 Irving L. Janis, *Air War and Emotional Stress: Psychological Studies of Bombing and Civilian Defense*, New York, 1951, pp. 73–4, 88, 111, collating evidence collected at the time by psychiatrists in London (italics in original). *Stratford Express*, 29 August 1941.

41 Gallup, *The Gallup International Public Opinion Polls*, p. 40. Wells, 'Diary', 4, 16 March 1941. Graves, *Off the Record*, p. 151, 6 May 1941. Mollie Panter-Downes, *London War Notes 1939–1945*, edited by William Shawn, New York, 1971, p. 154, 15 June 1941.

6. Life Is Dull Now: 22 June 1941–30 November 1942

1 Dorothy G. Wells, 'Diary of the War', Imperial War Museum, Docs. 26780, Vol. 5, 22 June 1941. I. C. B. Dear and M. R. D. Foot (eds.), *The Oxford Companion*

to the Second World War, Oxford, 1995, p. 109. Robin Woolven (ed.), *The London Diaries of Anthony Heap 1931–1945*, Woodbridge, 2017, pp. 363–4, 23 June 1941. Private Papers of Miss P. Warner, Imperial War Museum, Docs. 3208, 'Journal Under the Terror', 22 June 1941.

2 George H. Gallup, *The Gallup International Public Opinion Polls: Great Britain 1937–1975*, Vol. One, 1937–1964, New York, 1976, p. 63. For raids in 1941 see MEPO 4/127 Pt I, for 1942 MEPO 4/128. For the south London fire watchers see *South London Press*, 29 July 1942. W. E. Holl, 'Civil Defence Goes Through It: Paddington, 1937–1945', typescript, British Library, 1946, p. 117.

3 On the People's Convention see Douglas Hyde, *I Believed: The Autobiography of a Former British Communist*, 1951, pp. 94–5. *Hackney Gazette*, 12 March 1941; street orators were 'spouters' in London.

4 J. T. Murphy, *Victory Production!*, 1942, pp. 12–18.

5 Employment figures from Peter Howlett (text), *Fighting with Figures: A Statistical Digest of the Second World War*, 1995, p. 38. M. P. Fogarty, *Prospects of the Industrial Areas of Great Britain*, 1945, p. 430.

6 William Freeman (compiler), *War-Time Memories: A Brief Record of the Activities of Addressograph-Multigraph Ltd. in the Years 1939–1945*, 1946, p. 54. W. J. Reader, *Metal Box: A History*, 1976, pp. 120–22. Robert Hutton, *Agent Jack: The True Story of MI5's Secret Nazi Hunter*, 2018, p. 173ff, 188 (aluminium); James Lansdale Hodson, *Home Front: Being Some Account of Journeys, Meetings and What Was Said to Me in and about England during 1942–1943*, 1944, pp. 72–7, 11 June 1942 (shock absorbers). Hilary St George Saunders, *Ford at War*, 1946, p. 19. Stirling Everard, *The History of the Gas Light and Coke Company 1812–1949*, 1949, p. 356.

7 Charles Wilson and William Reader, *Men and Machines: A History of D. Napier & Son, Engineers, Ltd. 1858–1958*, 1958, pp. 152–5. William Hornby, *Factories and Plant*, 1958, Ch. IV.

8 MAP workforce figures are in P. Inman, *Labour in the Munitions Industries*, 1957, p. 216. For LAP see Charles Graves, *London Transport Carried On: An Account of London at War 1939–1945*, 1947, pp. 81–7; Michael H. C. Baker, *London Transport in the Blitz*, Hersham, 2010, p. 33; T. C. Barker and Michael Robbins, *A History of London Transport: Passenger Travel and the Development of the Metropolis*, Vol. II, *The Twentieth Century to 1970*, 1974 (1976 edition), p. 306; *The Times*, 7 December 1944; a list of subcontractors working in London on the Halifax from January 1940 is in TNA, AVIA 10/267. For manufacturing of aircraft parts see Sue Bruley (ed.), *Working for Victory: A Diary of Life in a Second World War Factory*, Stroud, 2001, pp. xx–xxi. Murphy, *Victory Production!*, pp. 53–9.

9 Mark Benney, *Over to Bombers*, 1943, p. 145 and passim; Mark Benney, *Almost a Gentleman*, 1966, pp. 141–8. *South London Press*, 2 September 1941.

10 For the growth of trade unions see Angus Calder, *The People's War: Britain 1939–45*, 1969, pp. 394–5. M. M. Postan, *British War Production*, 1952, pp. 150–51 (Napiers), Inman, *Labour in the Munitions Industries*, p. 109 (ship repairers). For the controls see H. M. D. Parker, *Manpower: A Study of War-Time Policy and Administration*, 1957, Ch. VII.

11 For pensioners see R. M. Titmuss, *Problems of Social Policy*, 1950, p. 516. For blitz amputees see *Lewisham Borough News*, 8 April 1942.

12   Robert Mackay, *Half the Battle: Civilian Morale in Britain during the Second World War*, Manchester, 2002, pp. 104–5 (soldiers' wives). For women's conscription see Parker, *Manpower*, p. 491; W. K. Hancock and M. M. Gowing, *British War Economy*, 1949, pp. 306–9. For numbers see Howlett, *Fighting with Figures*, p. 38, figures for June in each year. See generally Penny Summerfield, *Women Workers in the Second World War: Production and Patriarchy in Conflict*, 1984, and *Reconstructing Women's Wartime Lives: Discourse and Subjectivity in Oral Histories of the Second World War*, Manchester, 1998.

13   Barker and Robbins, *A History of London Transport*, p. 307. Wells, Diary, Vol. 3, 19 June 1940. Bernard Darwin, *War on the Line: The Story of the Southern Railway in War-Time*, 1946, p. 173. George C. Nash, *The LMS at War*, 1946, p. 80. Saunders, *Ford at War*, p. 21. Guy Morgan, *Red Roses Every Night: An Account of London Cinemas under Fire*, 1948, p. 61. Dorothy Scannell, *Dolly's War*, 1975 (1977 edition), pp. 93–4. *South London Press*, 15 May 1942 (Mrs Wenborn).

14   Howlett, *Fighting with Figures*, pp. 48–52. For the Midlands volunteers see *Stratford Express*, 6 and 13 March 1942.

15   Bruley (ed.), *Working for Victory*, p. 56, 25 July 1942.

16   Inez Holden, *Night Shift*, 1941, p. 100.

17   Lettice Cooper, *Black Bethlehem*, 1947, p. 175.

18   Pam Schweitzer et al. (eds.), *What Did You Do in the War, Mum? Women RecallTtheir Wartime Work*, 1985, pp. 28–30 ('Tess'), p. 52 (Lisa Haddon).

19   LWP, *You Can Get a War-time Nursery in Your District*, 1942, passim. There had been a LWP at the height of the suffragette agitation, meeting at Caxton Hall, Westminster, in 1908, for instance, but this forerunner seems to have been an unconscious inspiration for the Second World War iteration. For the first meeting see *Middlesex Chronicle*, 26 July 1941. See, for instance, *Daily Mirror*, 19 January 1942. *Lewisham Borough News*, 9 and 30 June 1942; *Picture Post*, 6 June 1942, p. 15 (Hampstead).

20   Klara Modern, *My Dearest Family: An Austrian Refugee's Letters from London to America, 1938–1945*, Milton Keynes, 2017, pp. 157–8, letter to her family in New York, 12 December 1942. See also, generally, Sheila Ferguson and Hilde Marchant, *Studies in the Social Services*, 1954, Ch. VI.

21   Doreen Idle, *War Over West Ham: A Study of Community Adjustment*, 1943, p. 117 (rest centres); *South London Press*, 8 July 1941. For national statistics see Howlett, *Fighting with Figures*, p. 236. Gallup, *The Gallup International Public Opinion Polls*, Vol. 1, p. 47; in December 1942 the figures were very similar, 68 per cent and 27 per cent.

22   For the ridicule see *Sunday Pictorial*, 1 September 1940. *Fulham Chronicle*, 12 December 1941. *Hackney Gazette*, 13 May 1942 (housewives). *South London Press*, 7 August and 20 October 1942.

23   For the rationing measures see Ina Zweiniger-Bargielowska, *Austerity in Britain: Rationing, Controls and Consumption, 1939–1955*, Oxford, 2000, pp. 34–5. For the comparison with the First World War see Peter Davidson (ed.), *The Complete Works of George Orwell*, Vol. 13, *All Propaganda is Lies 1941–1942*, 1998, pp. 134–6, 'British Rationing and the Submarine Warfare', BBC broadcast, 22 January 1942.

24   Vere Hodgson, *Few Eggs and No Oranges: A Diary Showing How Unimportant People in London and Birmingham Lived Through the War Years 1940–45*

Written in the Notting Hill Area of London, 1976 (2010 edition), p. 126, 16 February 1941. Woolven (ed.), *The London Diaries of Anthony Heap*, p. 357, 28 April and 26 August 1941; Warner, Journal, 31 May 1941. 'The Second World War Diaries of Hilda Neal', Imperial War Museum, PP/MCR/59, 11 and 30 June 1941; for eggs see also R. J. Hammond, *Food*, Vol. II, *Studies in Administration and Control*, 1956, pp. 74–6. Wells, Diary, Vol. 5, 1 November 1942. Gallup, *The Gallup International Public Opinion Polls*, Vol. 1, p. 48, October and November 1941.

25 Warner, Journal, 4 August 1941. *Hackney Gazette*, 15 August 1941. Monica Dickens, *The Fancy*, 1943, p. 116.

26 Patricia and Robert Malcolmson (eds.), *A Woman in Wartime London: The Diary of Kathleen Tipper 1941–1945*, 2006, p. 62, 17 November 1942.

27 Wells, Diary, Vol. 7, passim.

28 *East London Advertiser*, 23 August 1941, 11 July 1942 (Victoria Park and Bethnal Green); *South London Press*, 17 July 1942 (Battersea). *Lewisham Borough News*, 28 April, 15 September, 10 November 1942. *South London Press*, 27 May 1942 (Mrs Neal). *Hackney Gazette*, 20 August 1941; 22 July 1942 (Bethnal Green).

29 Neal, Diaries, 12 September 1942. Imperial War Museum, Private Papers of Miss D. I. Fisher, Docs. 2324, letter 24 January 1942, Edward Fisher to Delia Fisher. Charles Graves, *Londoner's Life*, 1942, pp. 166–7, 4 July 1942. Modern, *My Dearest Family*, pp. 135–6, letter to her family in New York, 10 January 1942.

30 Private Papers of Miss N. V. Carver, Imperial War Museum, Docs. 379, 2 June 1941. Woolven (ed.), *The London Diaries of Anthony Heap*, p. 362, 1 June 1941. Inez Holden, *It Was Different at the Time*, 1943, p. 93. Davidson (ed.), *The Complete Works of George Orwell*, Vol. 13, p. 520, 'London Letter, 29 August 1942'. Wells, Diary, Vol. 6, 21 May 1942; there were several Civil Service Stores in London, this probably the Strand shop, close to Dorothy's work in the Aldwych.

31 Neal, Diaries, 20 July 1941. *Picture Post*, Vol. 17, 19 December 1942, p. 3.

32 *Lewisham Borough News*, 14 July 1942. Malcolmson (eds.), *A Woman in Wartime London*, p. 11, 1 October 1941.

33 *East London Advertiser*, 5 and 12 July 1941 (Stepney). *Hackney Gazette*, 24 April 1942 (horse flesh). *Stratford Express*, 16 October 1942 (East Ham).

34 *East London Advertiser*, 26 July 1941; *Hackney Gazette*, 18 January 1943 (Cossor's), 29 January 1943 (Berger's). *Picture Post*, Vol. 12, 27 September 1941, pp. 22–3.

35 *Hackney Gazette*, 4 and 7 July and 11 August 1941; 29 April 1942. *Lewisham Borough News*, 25 August 1942 (Siemens). For Bernfield see John Capstick, *Given in Evidence*, 1960, pp. 59–67; *Daily Mirror*, 31 March 1942. Bryan Magee, *Growing up in a War*, 2007, pp. 138–40 (Hoxton, where Magee's father was a gents' outfitters). *Stratford Express*, 17 July 1942; for deserters and clothing coupon thefts see Peter Beveridge, *Inside the C.I.D.*, 1957, pp. 101–7.

36 W. K. Hancock and M. M. Gowing, *British War Economy*, 1949, p. 76 (savings). Private Papers of W. B. Regan, Imperial War Museum, Docs. 781, journal, pp. 52–3, 61, 12 January and 27 February 1942.

37 Hancock and Gowing, *British War Economy*, p. 328 (post-war credits). Wells, Diary, Vol. 4, 3 January 1941; Vol. 6, 20 May 1942. Saunders, *Ford at War*, p. 79.

38   Carver, Papers, 17 May 1941. *Lewisham Borough News*, 13, 20 and 27 May 1941. *South London Press*, 12 September 1941.

39   Woolven (ed.), *The London Diaries of Anthony Heap*, p. 392, 21 March 1942. *Lewisham Borough News*, 17 and 31 March 1942. *Hackney Gazette*, 23 and 30 March, 18 September 1942.

40   *Lewisham Borough News*, 19 May and 30 June 1942. The Savings Committee is cited in *Hackney Gazette*, 10 July 1942; 18 September 1942 (Stepney).

41   For Leyton and East Ham see *Stratford Express*, 26 June and 24 July 1942.

42   George F. Allison, *Allison Calling: A Galaxy of Football and Other Memories*, 1948, pp. 203–4, 221. *Lewisham Borough News*, 14 October 1941 and 17 March 1942.

43   Morgan, *Red Roses*, p. 46. Carver, Papers, 13 August and 30 September 1942. Hodgson, *Few Eggs and No Oranges*, p. 293, 21 June 1942. Wells, Diary, Vol. 6, 12 March 1942.

44   Woolven (ed.), *The London Diaries of Anthony Heap*, p. 351, 2 April 1941. For the boom see Basil Dean, *The Theatre at War*, 1956, pp. 294–302. Warner, Journal, 30 July and 13 September 1941. See also *Penguin New Writing*, No. 15, February 1943, pp. 122–6, 'English Theatre in War-Time' by 'Theatre Critic'.

45   Suzanne Bosman, *The National Gallery in Wartime*, 2008, pp. 95, 126. *Islington Gazette*, 25 September 1942.

46   Ursula Vaughan Williams, *R.V.W.: A Biography of Ralph Vaughan Williams*, Oxford, 1964, pp. 246–51. Asa Briggs, *The War of Words: The History of Broadcasting in the United Kingdom*, Vol. III, 1970, p.582n. *BBC Year Book 1943*, p. 43.

47   Carver, Papers, 7 December 1941. For ITMA see *BBC Year Book 1943*, p. 49. Malcolmson (ed.), *A Woman in Wartime London*, p. 65, 27 November 1942. For 'In Town Tonight' see *Radio Times*, Vol. 76, No. 988, 6–12 September 1942, p. 1.

48   *London Calling*, No. 74, 2–8 March 1941, p. 9 (Hastings). *Penguin New Writing*, No. 13, 21 July 1942, pp. 145–6 (Marlowe). Idle, *War Over West Ham*, pp. 85–6. Wells, Diary, Vol. 4, 11 February 1941; Vol. 6, 16 January 1942.

49   Hodson, *Home Front*, p. 7, 13 April 1942. Graves, *Londoner's Life*, p. 90, 20 February, and p. 143, 26 May 1942. Madame [Simone B.] Prunier, *La Maison: The History of Prunier's*, 1957, p. 265. See also Mark Roodhouse, *Black Market Britain 1939–1955*, Oxford, 2013, pp. 65–6.

50   Peter Quennell, *The Wanton Chase: An Autobiography from 1939*, 1980, p. 24; see also *Picture Post*, Vol. 13, 1 November 1941, pp. 8–12. The Nut House was at 26 Kingly Street, Soho.

51   Imperial War Museum, Private Papers of Mrs. M. Crompton, Docs. 13803: Journal of the War Years 1939–1945, 9 December 1941.

52   Robert Henrey, *A Village in Piccadilly*, 1942, pp. 67–9 (panto and Covent Garden); *Picture Post*, Vol. 13, 27 December 1941, pp. 17–21 (music hall). Woolven (ed.), *The London Diaries of Anthony Heap*, pp. 384–5, 25 December 1941.

53   W. A. L. Marshall, *A Century of London Weather*, 1952, p. 94 and Plate III. Woolven (ed.), *The London Diaries of Anthony Heap*, p. 390, 26 and 30 January 1942. *South London Press*, 17 February and 14 April 1942. *Hackney Gazette*, 4 March 1942 for the order to coal merchants. Regan, Papers, p. 63, 26 March 1942.

54 *Hackney Gazette*, 24 December 1941, 18 and 25 February 1942; *Lewisham Borough News*, 27 January 1942; *South London Press*, 26 and 30 December 1941.

55 *Municipal Journal*, Vol. XLIX, 18 July 1941, p. 871. The NFS was disbanded and fire services returned to local authorities on 1 April 1948. See also Terence H. O'Brien, *Civil Defence*, 1955, pp. 468–503.

56 Ibid., pp. 539–40; Fred Copeman, *Reason in Revolt*, 1948, pp. 192–5; *Municipal Journal*, Vol. L, 18 September 1942, p. 1161.

57 Sir Arthur Salusbury MacNalty (ed.), *The Civilian Health and Medical Services*, Vol. I, *The Ministry of Health Services; Other Civilian Health and Medical Services*, 1953, p. 196 (tube shelter figures). Barbara Nixon, *Raiders Overhead*, 1943, p. 60. For the homeless see *London Calling*, No. 95, 1–8 August 1941, pp. 7–8. On scabies see, for instance, Royal Borough of Kensington, *Annual (Interim) Report on the Health of the Borough for the Year 1942*, p. 1.

58 *Hackney Gazette*, 12 December 1941; *South London Press*, 20 January 1942; *Stratford Express*, 13 February and 13 March 1942.

59 The numbers of children are in *South London Press*, 23 October 1942. *Stratford Express*, 10 April 1942. *Hackney Gazette*, 26 June 1942.

60 Accurate casualty figures are elusive: I've followed MEPO 4/128, which tallies with some press reports. *Daily Herald*, 8 June 1942; *South London Press*, 9 and 12 June 1942; Winston G. Ramsey (ed.), *The Blitz: Then and Now*, 3 vols., 1987–9, Vol. 3, pp. 142–3.

61 *Stratford Express*, 8 May 1942. *South London Press*, 3, 14 and 17 July 1942; for other UXBs uncovered in this period see *Stratford Express*, 10 July 1942 (West Ham); *Hackney Gazette*, 29 June 1942 (Stoke Newington). In early February 2020 a UXB was discovered by builders underneath a house in Dean Street, Soho. The report on the Gurney Street device is in TNA, HO 207/26; I am grateful to Dr Robin Woolven for this reference.

62 Hodson, *Home Front*, pp. 5–6, 12 April 1942. For gas masks see O'Brien, *Civil Defence*, p. 436. For vandalism see *East London Advertiser*, 17 January 1942 (Poplar). For Stepney see Jack Dash, *Good Morning Brothers!*, 1969, pp. 49–51; for Fulham see Bill Goble, *Life-Long Rebel*, 1984, pp. 26–8; for elsewhere, Aylmer Firebrace, *Fire Service Memories*, 1949, pp. 239–40; for munitions see *Hackney Gazette*, 27 August 1943; for toys see *East London Advertiser*, 1 May 1943; see also *Municipal Journal*, Vol. L, 27 March 1942, p. 381.

63 For the cuts see TNA, HO 186/952, London Region Intelligence Branch reports for the months July 1941 to May 1942. For first aid posts see *Municipal Journal*, Vol. L, 22 May 1942, p. 648. AFS women in May 1941 see *Municipal Journal*, Vol. XLIX, 2 May 1941, p. 541. *Hackney Gazette*, 17 September 1942 (women's meetings). Modern, *My Dearest Family*, pp. 138–40, letter to her family in New York, 31 January 1942.

64 *East London Advertiser*, 22 November 1941.

65 C. E. Bechhofer Roberts (ed.), *The Trial of Harry Dobkin*, 1944, passim; William Rawlings, *A Case for the Yard*, 1961, pp. 178–88.

66 See *Daily Herald*, 14 October 1941. *Hackney Gazette*, 12 December 1941.

67 The link with the earlier murders was made in the *Aberdeen Evening Express*, 10 February 1942. Edward Greeno, *War on the Underworld*, 1960, pp. 116–23; Julia Laite, *Common Prostitutes and Ordinary Citizens: Commercial Sex in London, 1885–1960*, Basingstoke, 2012, pp. 168–9.

68   Patricia and Robert Malcolmson (eds.), *A Free-Spirited Woman: The London Diaries of Gladys Langford, 1936–1940*, 2014, p. 130, 22 September 1939. For torches see Norman Collins, *London Belongs to Me*, 1945, p. 537; Anthony Powell, *The Soldier's Art*, 1966 (1997 Mandarin edition) pp. 399–400. Charles Ritchie, *The Siren Years: Undiplomatic Diaries 1937–1945*, 1974, pp. 66–7, 14 September 1940 (Jermyn Street). A. J. Liebling, *The Road Back to Paris*, 1944, p. 119.

69   Marthe Watts, *The Men in My Life*, 1960, pp. 165–82.

70   For the Ecclesiastical Commissioners see *Estates Gazette*, Vol. CXLI, 23 January 1943, p. 80; for sample brothel cases see *West London Observer*, 8 December 1939, 19 January 1940, 30 May 1941 and 27 March 1942. *Penguin New Writing*, No. 4, 11 March 1941, pp. 53–4, William Plomer, 'French Lisette: A Ballad of Maida Vale'.

71   For the VD scare of 1917 see Jerry White, *Zeppelin Nights: London in the First World War*, 2014, pp. 191–4. *Hackney Gazette*, 4 and 23 March, 17 April, 8 and 15 May 1942.

72   *Hackney Gazette*, 2 January 1942. *South London Press*, 21 August 1942; *Norwood News*, 25 September 1942. *Stratford Express*, 4 and 18 December 1942. For the rise in criminal abortions known to the police in England and Wales in these years see Edward Smithies, *Crime in Wartime: A Social History of Crime in World War II*, 1982, p. 162; the figures represent the tip of the iceberg.

73   Henrey, *A Village in Piccadilly*, p. 80, 30 December 1941. James Lees-Milne, *Ancestral Voices*, 1975, p. 35, 14 March 1942.

74   Anthony Weymouth, *Journals of the War Years (1939–1945) and One Year Later*, 2 vols., 1948, Vol. 2, p. 97, 20 March 1942. Lees-Milne, *Ancestral Voices*, p. 35, 14 March 1942. Warner, Journal, 2 November 1941.

75   *Islington Gazette*, 17 March 1942. Henrey, *A Village in Piccadilly*, p. 139 (Green Park, April 1942), pp. 35–6 (Hyde Park, about April 1941). William Sansom, *Westminster in War*, 1947, pp. 166–7 (Kensington Gardens). O. S. Nock, *Britain's Railways at War 1939–1945*, 1971, pp. 150–51.

76   Casualty figures are in *Lewisham Borough News*, 5 May 1942. For the horse fair see *Picture Post*, Vol. 16, 5 September 1942. *London Chronicle*, No. 73, 23 February–1 March 1941, p. 7, Macdonald Hastings, 'The Horse Returns to London's Streets'. Davidson (ed.), *The Complete Works of George Orwell*, Vol. 13, p. 299, 'War-time Diary', 6 May 1942. For the new queueing law see *Municipal Journal*, Vol. L, 1 May 1942, p. 531. *Hackney Gazette*, 18 February 1942.

77   Population figures from TNA, HLG 7/608, 31 December 1942. For west London see Fogarty, *Prospects of the Industrial Areas of Great Britain*, p. 434. *East London Advertiser*, 13 June 1942 (Stepney); *Hackney Gazette*, 31 July 1942 (Leyton); *Lewisham Borough News*, 1 December 1942; Hodgson, *Few Eggs and No Oranges*, p. 300, 19 July 1942; *Estates Gazette*, Vol. CXL, 12 December 1942, p. 560, and CXLI, 9 January 1943, p. 39 (Westminster).

78   For CPGB membership see Geoffrey G. Field, *Blood, Sweat, and Toil: Remaking the British Working Class, 1939–1945*, Oxford, 2011, pp. 316–17. Gabriel Gorodetsky (ed.), *The Maisky Diaries: Red Ambassador to the Court of St James's 1932–1943*, 2015, p. 394, 12 October 1941. *Lewisham Borough News*, 10 March, 23 June, 6 October and 10 November 1942. *Islington Gazette*, 17 March and 24 April 1942. For vandalism see *Islington Gazette*, 9 February 1943 (Holford Square).

79   Mollie Panter-Downes, *London War Notes 1939–1945*, edited by William
     Shawn, New York, 1971, p. 207, 14 February 1942. Carver, Papers, 16 February
     1942. Wells, Diary, Vol. 6, 16 February 1942. Robert Rhodes James (ed.), *Chips:
     The Diaries of Sir Henry Channon*, 1967, p. 321, 13 February 1942.
80   Regan, Papers, p. 69, 27 April 1942.
81   For the invasion alert see Ann Scott, *Ernest Gowers: Plain Words and Forgotten
     Deeds*, Basingstoke, 2009, pp. 126–7; Philip Ziegler, *London at War 1939–1945*,
     1995, pp. 209–11; Hodgson, *Few Eggs and No Oranges*, p. 322, 11 October
     1942. For the City see *Municipal Journal*, Vol. L, 16 October 1942, p. 1255.
82   Neal, Diaries, 5 November 1942. Wells, Diary, Vol. 7, 5 November 1942. Panter-
     Downes, *London War Notes*, p. 249, 15 November 1942. Malcolmson (eds.),
     A Woman in Wartime London, pp. 66–7, 30 November and 4 December 1942.
83   Gallup, *The Gallup International Public Opinion Polls*, 1, p. 67, November
     1942. *Hackney Gazette*, 29 April 1942. For women see *Picture Post*, Vol. 16, 1
     August 1942, pp. 21–2, Jennie Lee, 'A New Life Opens Out for Women'.
     Malcolmson (eds.), *A Woman in Wartime London*, p. 66, 2 December 1942.

7. After the War: 1 December 1942–31 December 1943

1   *Picture Post*, Vol. 15, 27 June 1942, pp. 21–2.
2   Anon., *The Bells Go Down: The Diary of a London A.F.S. Man*, 1942, p. 134.
    Private Papers of W. B. Regan, Imperial War Museum, Docs. 781, 'Diary', p. 53,
    13 January 1942.
3   Sir William Beveridge, *Social Insurance and Allied Services*, 1942, Cmd. 6404;
    it sold for 2s. For the queues see Mollie Panter-Downes, *London War Notes
    1939–1945*, edited by William Shawn, New York, 1971, pp. 252–3, 13 December
    1942. Alan Bullock, *The Life and Times of Ernest Bevin*, Vol. II, *Minister of
    Labour 1940–1945*, 1967, p. 225.
4   *West London Observer*, 4 December 1942 (pensioners); *Middlesex Chronicle*,
    20 February (Spelthorne) and 30 January 1943 (Common Wealth). Peter
    Davidson (ed.), *The Complete Works of George Orwell*, Vol. 15, *Two Wasted
    Years 1943*, 1998, pp. 108–9, 'London Letter', *Partisan Review*, July–August
    1943. Panter-Downes, *London War Notes*, p. 256, 27 December 1942.
5   *Lewisham Borough News*, 22 December 1942. *Picture Post*, Vol. 17, 26
    December 1942, p. 3. Anthony Weymouth, *Journals of the War Years (1939–
    1945) and One Year Later*, 2 vols., 1948, Vol. 2, pp. 183–4, 25 December 1942.
    Dorothy G. Wells, 'Diary of the War', Imperial War Museum, Docs. 26780, Vol.
    7, 25 December 1942.
6   Patricia and Robert Malcolmson (eds.), *A Woman in Wartime London: The
    Diary of Kathleen Tipper 1941–1945*, 2006, p. 71, 23 December 1942. *Hackney
    Gazette*, 21 December 1942. *Islington Gazette*, 22 December 1942. *South
    London Press*, 12 January 1943.
7   Private Papers of Miss N. V. Carver, Imperial War Museum, Docs. 379, 27–31
    December 1942.
8   For the weather see W. A. L. Marshall, *A Century of London Weather*, 1952,
    pp. 94–5. For raids in 1943 see TNA, MEPO 4/129, and Basil Collier, *The
    Defence of the United Kingdom*, 1957, pp. 313–14, 515–16. Robin Woolven

(ed.), *The London Diaries of Anthony Heap 1931–1945*, Woodbridge, 2017, pp. 416–17, 18 January 1943. *Stratford Express*, 22 January 1943.

9 For the ricochets from low-level daylight raids see TNA, HO 199/394A, 'Lessons Based on Recent London Raids', n.d. [pre-July 1943]. For the policeman see *Lewisham Borough News*, 6 January 1943; subsequent reports gave the boy's age as eight. Winston G. Ramsey (ed.), *The Blitz: Then and Now*, 3 vols., 1987–9, Vol. 3, pp. 204–13. The number of planes, but not the number of casualties, is disputed in the sources. For the funeral see *Lewisham Borough News*, 2 February 1943. See also Lewis Blake, *Red Alert: The Story of South East London at War, 1939–1945*, 'New Enlarged Edition', 1992, pp. 115–20.

10 *South London Press*, 26 and 29 January 1943. *Lewisham Borough News*, 2 and 23 February, 16 March and 31 August 1943.

11 For prosecutions in bulk see, for instance, *Hackney Gazette*, 26 February and 30 April 1943. For the nibs see *Picture Post*, Vol. 18, 16 January 1943, p. 24, letter from an LCC teacher, 'name and address supplied'. For the wild children see Davidson (ed.), *The Complete Works of George Orwell*, Vol. 16, *I Have Tried to Tell the Truth 1943–1944*, 1998, pp. 334–5, a review of Marie Paneth, *Branch Street*, 1944; Orwell's language was typically more lurid and condemnatory than Paneth's own, a Jewish émigré from Austria. P. H. J. H. Gosden, *Education in the Second World War: A Study in Policy and Administration*, 1976, pp. 69–70, 73–4.

12 On the miscarried raid see Collier, *The Defence of the United Kingdom*, p. 314.

13 L. R. Dunne, *Report on an Inquiry into the Accident at Bethnal Green Tube Station Shelter on the 3rd March, 1943*, 1945, Cmd. 6583, pp. 4–7. Ramsey (ed.), *The Blitz*, Vol. 3, pp. 220–29.

14 TNA, HO 205/231, letter of 11 March to L. R. Dunne from Gordon Liverman, chairman of the Jewish Defence Committee of the Board of Deputies of British Jews. TNA, INF 1/292, Pt 3, Home Intelligence Weekly Report, 2–9 March 1943, f. 194. See also TNA, HO 205/379, Dunne Tube Shelter Inquiry, Transcript of Evidence, evidence of Police Superintendent Hill and Divisional Inspector Hunt.

15 Dunne, *Report on an Inquiry into the Accident at Bethnal Green Tube Station Shelter on the 3rd March*, p. 12.

16 *The Times*, 9 April 1943. See also Mass Observation File Report 1648, 'Recent Trends in Anti-Semitism', wrongly dated '10.3.42' but referring to the tube disaster. There is further detail in Jerry White, 'Jews and Bombs: The Making of a Metropolitan Myth', in Colin Holmes and Anne J. Kershen (eds.), *An East End Legacy: Essays in Memory of William J. Fishman*, 2017, pp. 117–33.

17 *Hackney Gazette*, 6 July and 11 December 1944; 8 January and 9 March 1945.

18 George Beardmore, *Civilians at War: Journals 1938–1946*, 1984, p. 141.

19 For the cuts see Bullock, *The Life and Times of Ernest Bevin*, p. 250; *Hackney Gazette*, 23 July 1943; *Lewisham Borough News*, 21 September 1943. For the welfare improvements see *Municipal Journal*, Vol. 51, 24 December 1943, p. 1764. *East London Advertiser*, 24 April 1943 (Joan Marriott), *Stratford Express*, 2 and 30 April 1943 (Paton).

20 'The Second World War Diaries of Hilda Neal', Imperial War Museum, PP/MCR/59, 8 March 1943; the inflation is according to the UK Inflation Calculator. For Bermondsey see *The Times*, 8 March 1943. The results are in *South London Press*, 16 March 1943, and *Stratford Express*, 19 March 1943; for the planes see *South London Press*, 18 February 1944.

21 *Hackney Gazette*, 14 May and 28 June 1943; *South London Press*, 28 May 1943.

22 Bryher, *The Days of Mars: A Memoir, 1940–1946*, 1972, pp. 93–5.

23 Neal, Diaries, 3 March and 19 June 1943. Vere Hodgson, *Few Eggs and No Oranges: A Diary Showing How Unimportant People in London and Birmingham Lived Through the War Years 1940–45 Written in the Notting Hill Area of London*, 1976 (2010 edition), pp. 388–9, 30 May 1943. Panter-Downes, *London War Notes*, pp. 271–2, 1 March 1943.

24 *East London Advertiser*, 23 January (Victoria Park) and 18 September 1943 (Poplar). *Hackney Gazette*, 21 June (Bethnal Green) and 23 July 1943 (Shoreditch). *Islington Gazette*, 19 March and 4 May 1943.

25 *Picture Post*, Vol. 19, 3 April 1943, pp. 18–19. *Hackney Gazette*, 5 February and 28 July 1943. *East London Advertiser*, 3 July 1943 (Young Farmers). Wells, Diary, Vol. 8, 27 May 1943.

26 Wells, Diary, Vol. 8, 15 May and 16 July 1943. James Lees-Milne, *Ancestral Voices*, 1975, p. 141, 1 January 1943. Weymouth, *Journals of the War Years (1939–1945) and One Year Later*, Vol. 2, p. 248, 23 September 1943.

27 For the numbers nationally see Ina Zweiniger-Bargielowska, *Austerity in Britain: Rationing, Controls and Consumption, 1939–1955*, Oxford, 2000, p. 33. London Council of Social Service, *The Communal Restaurant: A Study of the Place of Civic Restaurants in the Life of the Community. Prepared in the Spring and Summer of 1943*, 1943, pp. 12–19. Wells, Diary, Vol. 7, 11 January 1943. Woolven (ed.), *The London Diaries of Anthony Heap*, pp. 411–12, 24 December 1942.

28 *Islington Gazette*, 19 January (fire-watchers), 16 July (cabbage) and 13 August (thefts by fire-watchers). *Hackney Gazette*, 15 January (fire-watcher), 26 February (stockings and underwear sold to Ever-Ready factory workers) and 28 May (theft by fire-watcher). *South London Press*, 8 January 1943 (air raid warden). *Stratford Express*, 29 January 1943 (Leyton girls and East Ham mother). Bryher, *Days of Mars*, pp. 111–12.

29 Frankie Fraser, *Mad Frank: Memoirs of a Life of Crime*, 1994, p. 26.

30 *South London Press*, 21 May 1943; see also Ruby Sparks, *Burglar to the Nobility*, 1961, passim. Edward Greeno, *War on the Underworld*, 1960, pp. 150–56.

31 Carver Papers, 8 May 1943. Woolven (ed.), *The London Diaries of Anthony Heap*, p. 429, 17 August, and p. 431, 8 September 1943. For the raids see MEPO 4/129.

32 Carver Papers, 19 June–4 July 1943. Woolven (ed.), *The London Diaries of Anthony Heap*, p. 428, 24 July 1943. Wells, Diary, Vol. 8, 18 September 1943. *South London Press*, 6 August 1943.

33 *East London Advertiser*, 17 April and 3 July 1943. *Hackney Gazette*, 11 August 1943. *Islington Gazette*, 28 May 1943. *South London Press*, 11 June 1943.

34 Weymouth, *Journals of the War Years (1939–1945) and One Year Later*, Vol. 2, p. 235, 10 August 1943. Woolven (ed.), *The London Diaries of Anthony Heap*, p. 415, 1 January, and p. 437, 31 December 1943. Reform Club Archive, General Committee Minute Book, 30 October 1935–14 June 1945, pp. 221–2, 28 January 1943. *Islington Gazette*, 11 May 1943; population figures for March 1943 (28,020) from TNA, HLG 7608, and for 1937 from LCC, *London Statistics 1936–38*, Vol. XLI, 1939, p. 39 (58,700). Neal, Diaries, 21 and 24 July 1943. Panter-Downes, *London War Notes*, p. 264, 24 January 1943.

35 *East London Advertiser*, 27 February 1943 (Poplar). Gabriel Gorodetsky (ed.), *The Maisky Diaries: Red Ambassador to the Court of St James's 1932–1943*, 2015, p. 487, 21 February 1943. For the saddle see Panter-Downes, *London War Notes*, p. 236, 19 July 1942. For the sword see *The Times*, 25 June and 6 October 1943; it plays a memorable part in the opening pages of Evelyn Waugh, *Unconditional Surrender*, 1961. *Picture Post*, Vol. 18, 13 February 1943, pp. 16–18 (Caxton Hall).

36 For the continuing purchases of Green Belt land see *Estates Gazette*, Vol. CXXXVI, 26 October 1940. For Beveridge see *The Times*, 22 February, 1937. For the rest see *Town and Country Planning*, Vol. VI, No. 22 (1938), pp. 24–31. *The Times*, 20 December 1938 (manifesto). For more detail of this lengthy story, dating back to 1920, see Jerry White, 'The "Dismemberment of London": Chamberlain, Abercrombie and the London Plans of 1943–44', *London Journal*, Vol. 44, No. 3, December 2019, pp. 206–26.

37 *Report of the Royal Commission on the Distribution of the Industrial Population*, 1940, Cmd. 6513.

38 For some early calls for a plan to capitalise on the Luftwaffe's destruction see *Municipal Journal*, Vol. 49, 25 October 1940, p. 1361; *Estates Gazette*, Vol. CXXXVI, 9 November 1940, p. 527; *Hackney Gazette*, 15 November 1940; *East London Advertiser*, 15 March 1941. *Stratford Express*, 26 September 1941 (West Ham). *South London Press*, 16 October and 17 November 1942.

39 LMA, LCC/CL/TP/1/33, file notes January–April 1941. J. H. Forshaw and Patrick Abercrombie, *County of London Plan*, 1943.

40 *CLP*, passim.

41 *Estates Gazette*, Vol. CXLI, 11 September, 1943, p. 249, for the Town and Country Planning Association; LMA, LCC/CL/TP/1/38, County of London Plan, Observations of Government Departments. Ministry of Town and Country Planning, p. 2. *The Times*, 14 December, 1944. R. Gordon Cummings, 'Plan for a Million People to Move Their Homes', *Daily Herald*, 14 December, 1944. Patrick Abercrombie, *Greater London Plan 1944*, 1945, pp. 5, 37–8.

42 *Report ... on the Preliminary Draft Proposals for Post-War Reconstruction in the City of London*, 1944, p. 13; Michael Hebbert, *London: More by Fortune Than Design*, Chichester, 1998, pp. 70–72. *East London Advertiser*, 11 February 1944. See the responses in LMA, LCC/CL/TP/1/39. *Estates Gazette*, 30 October 1943, p. 416.

43 The population figures are calculated from data in TNA, HLG 71/694. Verily Anderson, *Spam Tomorrow*, 1956, pp. 150–51. *Estates Gazette*, Vol. CXLIII, 1 January 1944, p. 16; 8 January 1944, pp. 40–41; 15 January 1944, p. 66. Neal, Diaries, 15 February 1943. *Picture Post*, Vol. 19, 3 April 1943, pp. 22–4. *Islington Gazette*, 27 September 1943 (store manager).

44 For Poplar see *East London Advertiser*, 8 and 22 October 1943; for Islington's library exhibition see *Islington Gazette*, 14 April 1944. Marco Amati and Robert Freestone, 'All of London's a Stage: The 1943 County of London Plan Exhibition', *Urban History*, Vol. 43, No. 4, Cambridge, 2016, pp. 539–56.

45 For ABCA see Jonathan Fennell, *Fighting the People's War: The British and Commonwealth Armies and the Second World War*, Cambridge, 2019, p. 635ff; for the furore over the pamphlet see HC Debates, Vol. 386, 2 February 1943, cols. 848–60. William Sansom, James Gordon and Stephen Spender, *Jim Braidy: The Story of Britain's Firemen*, 1943, p. 60. *Islington Gazette*, 30 March 1943

(Finsbury Park) and 20 April 1943 (youth). *Lewisham Borough News*, 1 January 1944. *Municipal Journal*, Vol. 51, 11 June 1943 (AA batteries). *West London Observer*, 15 October 1943 (Brains Trusts). For the LWP see *International Women's News*, 5 February 1943; LWP, *Health and Housing. Report 4th Session London Women's Parliament*, 1943, passim.

46 For Wootton see *Picture Post*, Vol. 20, 18 September 1943. Private Papers of Miss G. Thomas, Imperial War Museum, Box No. 90/30/1, 28 July 1943.

47 For anti-Mosley protests see, for instance, *East London Advertiser*, 26 November and 10 December 1943. *Stratford Express*, 5 November 1943.

48 For the raids see MEPO 4/129. For the dance hall see HO 199/394A, 'Recent Raids on London', 15 November 1943, pp. 1–2 (which gives seventy-one dead and 113 injured); *Daily Herald*, 8 November 1943 (italics in original); see also Ramsey (ed.), *The Blitz*, Vol. 3, p. 313.

49 The tube figures are in Sir Arthur Salusbury MacNalty (ed.), *The Civilian Health and Medical Services*, Vol. I, *The Ministry of Health Services; Other Civilian Health and Medical Services*, 1953, p. 196. Woolven (ed.), *The London Diaries of Anthony Heap*, p. 431, 7 September 1943.

50 Winston S. Churchill, *The Second World War*, Vol. V, *Closing the Ring*, 1952, p. 201ff. George H. Gallup, *The Gallup International Public Opinion Polls: Great Britain 1937–1975*, Vol. One, 1937–1964, New York, 1976, pp. 83–4. George Martelli, *The Man Who Saved London: The Story of Michel Hollard, D.S., Croix de Guerre*, 1960 (Companion Book Club edition, 1961), pp. 164–6.

51 For the King see *The Times*, 8 December 1943. Panter-Downes, *London War Notes*, pp. 302–3, 19 December 1943. Wells, Diary, Vol. 8, 19 and 25–7 December 1943. Woolven (ed.), *The London Diaries of Anthony Heap*, p. 436, 22 December 1943. Hodgson, *Few Eggs and No Oranges*, p. 436, 19 December 1943. Neal, Diaries, 28 December 1943.

52 See, for instance, *The Times*, 11 December 1943; *Lewisham Borough News*, 21 December 1943.

53 Carver Papers, 28–31 December 1943: Churchill was taken ill in Tunis after attending an Allied conference in Tehran. *Daily Mirror*, 1 January 1944.

8. Occupied Territory: 1 January–12 June 1944

1 Private Papers of Miss Vivienne Hall, Imperial War Museum, Docs. 3989a, 1–7 January 1944.

2 *Stratford Express*, 14 January 1944. *Hackney Gazette*, 10 January 1944.

3 Robin Woolven (ed.), *The London Diaries of Anthony Heap 1931–1945*, Woodbridge, 2017, p. 443, 25 January 1944. *East London Advertiser*, 28 January 1944 (coal shortage). Vere Hodgson, *Few Eggs and No Oranges: A Diary Showing How Unimportant People in London and Birmingham Lived Through the War Years 1940–45 Written in the Notting Hill Area of London*, 1976 (2010 edition), p. 468, 30 April 1944. For the strike see Woolven (ed.), *The London Diaries of Anthony Heap*, p. 449, 22 April 1944.

4 Basil Collier, *The Defence of the United Kingdom*, 1957, pp. 327–8, 520; Terence H. O'Brien, *Civil Defence*, 1955, pp. 439–43. TNA, HO 186/2352, LCDR

Regional Commissioners' Reports for the Periods January to March 1944, p. 1, and April to June, p. 1. MEPO 4/130, Metropolitan Police War Diary 1944.

5 Private Papers of W. B. Regan, Imperial War Museum, Docs. 781, 'Diary', 21 January 1944. Imperial War Museum, Private Papers of Miss D. I. Fisher, Docs. 2324, letter 22 January 1944, Edward Fisher, 39 Comyn Road, Battersea, SW11, to Delia Fisher, Petersfield; letter, ?6 February 1944, Daisy Fisher to Delia. Private Papers of Miss N. V. Carver, Imperial War Museum, Docs. 379, 22 February 1944.

6 Private Papers of Mrs B. M. Holbrook, Imperial War Museum, Docs. 3311, p. 31, February–March 1944 [spelling silently corrected]; the 5-inch/25-calibre naval gun was still in use in the Falklands War.

7 Hall Papers, [30 January]–4 February 1944. Mollie Panter-Downes, *London War Notes 1939–1945*, edited by William Shawn, New York, 1971, p. 310, 30 January 1944. James Lees-Milne, *Prophesying Peace*, 1977, pp. 11–12, 23 January 1944. William Sansom, *Westminster in War*, 1947, p. 178. *Picture Post*, Vol. 22, 11 March 1944, pp. 7–9.

8 *South London Press*, 12 April 1944.

9 HO 186/2352, Report for January to March 1944, p. 1 (Fulham); O'Brien, *Civil Defence*, p. 441 (Battersea). HO 199/394A, 'Further Notes on Recent Raids', 17 March 1944. 'The Second World War Diaries of Hilda Neal', Imperial War Museum, PP/MCR/59, 24 February 1944. *London Library Magazine*, No. 29, Autumn 2015, pp. 32–3.

10 Hall Papers, 19–21 February 1944 [punctuation silently corrected].

11 Dorothy G. Wells, 'Diary of the War', Imperial War Museum, Docs. 26780, Vol. 8, 24 February 1944.

12 Hall Papers, 11–17 March 1944.

13 For the fire guard's improved efficiency under women's management see *Municipal Journal*, Vol. LII, 24 March 1944, p. 486. For firefighting see Sansom, *Westminster in War*, p. 123.

14 Private Papers of F. R. Bodley, Imperial War Museum, Box No. 09/37/1, ff. 97–8, 24 February 1944 [two errors silently corrected].

15 For street shelters see Peter Davidson (ed.), *The Complete Works of George Orwell*, Vol. 16, *I Have Tried to Tell the Truth 1943–1944*, 1998, pp. 56–7, 'As I Please', 6, *Tribune*, 7 January 1944. For the tubes see Sir Arthur Salusbury MacNalty (ed.), *The Civilian Health and Medical Services*, Vol. I, *The Ministry of Health Services; Other Civilian Health and Medical Services*, 1953, pp. 196, 202–3; O'Brien, *Civil Defence*, p. 440. *South London Press*, 29 February and 17 March 1944. Neal, Diaries, 17 March 1944. Hall Papers, 4–10 March 1944.

16 HO 186/2352, Report for January to March 1944, p. 3. For the role of the WVS in Harrow see George Beardmore, *Civilians at War: Journals 1938–1946*, 1984, pp. 154–8. Verily Anderson, *Spam Tomorrow*, 1956, pp. 173–7, 180–81. Hall Papers, 19–21 and 22–3 February 1944. Regan Papers, 27 February and 13 March 1944. Wells, Diary, Vol. 8, 24 February 1944. Anthony Weymouth, *Journals of the War Years (1939–1945) and One Year Later*, 2 vols., 1948, Vol. 2, p. 294, 4 March 1944.

17 Panter-Downes, *London War Notes*, p. 310, 30 January 1944. Population statistics are in TNA, HLG 7/608, from 6.7 million on 1 January to 6.74 million on 1 July 1944. Robert Hutton, *Of Those Alone*, 1958, pp. 207–8.

18 For dry rot see *Estates Gazette*, Vol. CXLIII, 8 and 15 January 1944, pp. 43 and 65. *East London Advertiser*, 31 March 1944. *Islington Gazette*, 25 January 1944. Wells, Diary, Vol. 8, 7 April 1944.

19 *Hackney Gazette*, 23 June 1944. *East London Advertiser*, 7 and 21 April 1944. Weymouth, *Journals of the War Years (1939–1945) and One Year Later*, Vol. 2, pp. 317–8, 1 June 1944. For the 1941 building licence limit see C. M. Kohan, *Works and Buildings*, 1952, p. 140 and n.

20 Hodgson, *Few Eggs and No Oranges*, p. 463, 2 April 1944. Carver Papers, 3–7 April 1944. *South London Press*, 14 January, 8 February, 4 and 7 April 1944. *Lewisham Borough News*, 12 April 1944 (NFS). For Comyn Road see Fisher Papers, letter from Fisher Family to Delia [n.d., March 1944]. *Stratford Express*, 7 and 14 April 1944 (West Ham).

21 For central London see *The Times*, 27 and 28 March 1944. *Hackney Gazette*, 27 March 1944. *South London Press*, 4 April 1944.

22 A repatriated POW, Leading Stoker David Turner of the Royal Navy, died in St John's Hospital, Battersea, in late March, for instance; *South London Press*, 7 April 1944. *Stratford Express*, 14 January 1944. *Lewisham Borough News*, 11 January 1944.

23 Neal, Diaries, 18 May 1944.

24 *Islington Gazette*, 19 May 1944. *Lewisham Borough News*, 2 May 1944.

25 Panter-Downes, *London War Notes*, pp. 320–21, 7 May 1944.

26 Robert Henrey, *A Village in Piccadilly*, 1942, pp. 118, 138. Charles Graves, *Londoner's Life*, 1942, p. 103, 15 March 1942.

27 Panter-Downes, *London War Notes*, p. 242, 30 August 1942. For the 1st Infantry and Eisenhower's HQ see David Reynolds, *Rich Relations: The American Occupation of Britain, 1942–1945*, 1995, pp. 114, 254. For the government staff see Lynne Olson, *Citizens of London: The Americans Who Stood with Britain in Its Darkest, Finest Hour*, New York, 2010, p. 167. For Mayfair see Robert Henrey, *The Incredible City*, 1944, pp. 30, 39. For the Englishman joke see Sansom, *Westminster in War*, p. 168. For Rainbow Corner see *The Times*, 9 January 1946.

28 Carver Papers, 2 September 1942 [apostrophes silently added]. Robert S. Arbib, *Here We Are Together: The Notebook of an American Soldier in Britain*, 1946 (Right Book Club edition, 1947), p. 85.

29 Woolven (ed.), *The London Diaries of Anthony Heap*, p. 445, 20 February 1944. For the term 'Snowdrops' see Robert Henrey, *The Siege of London*, 1946, p. 55. For the numbers see Daniel Todman, *Britain's War: A New World 1942–1947*, 2020, pp. 446, 453.

30 Davidson (ed.), *The Complete Works of George Orwell*, Vol. 16, pp. 12–13, 'As I Please', 1, *Tribune*, 3 December 1943, and pp. 26–7, 'As I Please', 3, *Tribune*, 17 December 1943. Patricia and Robert Malcolmson (eds.), *A Woman in Wartime London: The Diary of Kathleen Tipper 1941–1945*, 2006, p. 45, 2 June 1942. Private Papers of Mrs M. Crompton. Docs. 13803: Journal of the War Years 1939–1945, 21 August 1942.

31 Weymouth, *Journals of the War Years (1939–1945) and One Year Later*, Vol. 2, p. 274, 25 December 1943. For Rainbow Corner and other US clubs see *Picture Post*, Vol. 26, 27 January 1945, pp. 22–4.

32 Malcolmson (eds.), *A Woman in Wartime London*, p. 119, 17 September 1944. C. L. McDermott, *A Yank on Piccadilly*, New York, 1951 (Popular Library edition, 1952), pp. 5–6.

33 Woolven (ed.), *The London Diaries of Anthony Heap*, p. 468, 4 November 1944. Arbib, *Here We Are Together*, p. 86. Marthe Watts, *The Men in My Life*, 1960, pp. 179, 188, 191.

34 Woolven (ed.), *The London Diaries of Anthony Heap*, p. 468, 4 November 1944. Arbib, *Here We Are Together*, p. 86. McDermott, *Yank on Piccadilly*, pp. 105–6. For sex and GIs more generally see Reynolds, *Rich Relations*, pp. 201–6; Olson, *Citizens of London*, pp. 284–5. William Saroyan's autobiographical novel of his war in London from 1942, *The Adventures of Wesley Jackson*, 1947, is also full of interest in this regard.

35 Quentin Crisp, *The Naked Civil Servant*, 1968, pp. 156–7.

36 Ibid., p. 158. For the children see Davidson (ed.), *The Complete Works of George Orwell*, Vol. 16, pp. 12–13, 'As I Please', 1, *Tribune*, 3 December 1943. *East London Advertiser*, 10 April 1943 and 7 April 1944. *Islington Gazette*, 1 April, 25 July and 8 December 1944 and 30 January 1945.

37 *West London Observer*, 4, 11 and 18 February 1944; *Picture Post*, Vol. 23, 22 April 1944, pp. 14–17.

38 Davidson (ed.), *The Complete Works of George Orwell*, Vol. 16, pp. 12–13, 'As I Please', 1, *Tribune*, 3 December 1943.

39 For the instances of discrimination listed here see *Daily Herald*, 17 August 1935, 12 March 1937, 11 March 1939, 11 January 1940, 22 July and 11 September 1943. For Amelia King see also *Daily Mirror*, 27 September 1943. For housing see *Picture Post*, Vol. 25, 9 December 1944, p. 3; for an allegation by an 'African negro' of racial discrimination in the housing market see *Islington Gazette*, 8 January 1943.

40 Cecil H. King, *With Malice Toward None: A War Diary*, edited by William Armstrong, 1970, p. 194, 6 October 1942. For instances of racial violence mainly begun by white Americans see Reynolds, *Rich Relations*, pp. 307–9; Olson, *Citizens of London*, pp. 285–9. Julian Maclaren-Ross, *Memoirs of the Forties*, edited by Alan Ross, 1965 (1984 paperback edition), p. 139.

41 See *Daily Herald*, 3 September 1943 and 22 June 1944; *Daily Mirror*, 3 September 1943 and 20 and 29 June 1944; see also Learie Constantine, *Colour Bar*, 1954; Sonya O. Rose, *Which People's War? National Identity and Citizenship in Wartime Britain 1939–1945*, Oxford, 2003, pp. 248–51.

42 For the chorus see Reynolds, *Rich Relations*, p. 314. For Dunbar see *The Times*, 10 April and 28 November 1942 and 7 August 1943. For the clubs see *Picture Post*, Vol. 20, 17 July 1943, pp. 19–21; see also Mica Nava, *Visceral Cosmopolitanism: Gender, Culture and the Normalisation of Difference*, Oxford, 2007, Ch. 5.

43 *West London Observer*, 13 November 1942 and 10 September 1943. For public attitudes to white women and black GIs see Rose, *Which People's War?*, pp. 75–80.

44 *Islington Gazette*, 28 January 1944. Fred Narborough, *Murder on My Mind*, 1959, pp. 71–6.

45 *East London Advertiser*, 21 January, 3 and 10 March 1944. For the searches see Charles Glass, *The Deserters: A Hidden History of World War II*, New York, 2013, p. 95.

46 *Report of the Commissioner of Police of the Metropolis for the Year 1945*, 1946, Cmd. 7156, p. 28. *East London Advertiser*, 24 March 1944. *Hackney Gazette*, 25 February 1944 (fire-watcher). *Lewisham Borough News*, 25 January 1944. Neal, Diaries, 16 April 1944. Hodgson, *Few Eggs and No Oranges*, p. 468, 23 April 1944. Woolven (ed.), *The London Diaries of Anthony Heap*, p. 445, 22–3 February 1944.

47 Ibid., p. 449, 23 April 1944.

48 Wells, Diary, Vol. 8, 1 and 13 March and 27 April 1944. For the tension see Alan Bullock, *The Life and Times of Ernest Bevin*, Vol. II, *Minister of Labour 1940–1945*, 1967, p. 297. Hall Papers, 15–21 April and 6–12 May 1944.

49 See A. P. Herbert, *Independent Member*, 1950, pp. 221–2, 299–300, 306–11; Cyril Demarne, *The London Blitz: A Fireman's Tale*, 1980 (revised and enlarged edition, 1990), pp. 56–8; L. M. Bates, *The Thames on Fire: The Battle of London River 1939–1945*, Lavenham, 1985, pp. 139–40; Jonathan Schneer, *The Thames*, 2005, pp. 208–16; Gustav Milne and the Thames Discovery Project, *The Thames at War*, Barnsley, 2020, pp. 191–2.

50 For the maps see *Picture Post*, Vol. 23, 27 May 1944, pp. 8–9. Beardmore, *Civilians at War*, p. 159, 29 May 1944. For the BBC see Stuart Hibberd, *'This – Is London'*, 1950, p. 252. Wells, Diary, Vol. 8, 5 and 6 June 1944.

51 For the early rumours from France and Germany see Beardmore, *Civilians at War*, pp. 159–60. Carver Papers, 6 June 1944. Woolven (ed.), *The London Diaries of Anthony Heap*, p. 451, 6 June 1944. *East London Advertiser*, 9 June 1944. Mollie Panter-Downes, *Good Evening Mrs Craven: The Wartime Stories of Mollie Panter-Downes*, 1999, pp. 187–90, 'Letter from London', 11 June 1944. Private Papers of A. F. Williamson, Imperial War Museum, Docs. 3106, letters to Austin from his parents, 5 Eynella Road, East Dulwich, 6 June 1944.

52 Hall Papers, 6 June 1944. Carver Papers, 6 June 1944.

53 Private Papers of Mrs M. Cossins, Imperial War Museum, Docs. 2064, 'Flying Bomb Experiences', 11 June 1944.

9. It's Ours! 13 June–31 December 1944

1 MEPO 4/130, 13 June 1944; see also Winston G. Ramsey (ed.), *The Blitz: Then and Now*, 3 vols., 1987–9, Vol. 3, pp. 384–5.

2 For the flash sequence see Private Papers of W. B. Regan, Imperial War Museum, Docs. 781, 'Diary', 15 June 1944. For the casualties see Terence H. O'Brien, *Civil Defence*, 1955, p. 679. For technical details see Ramsey (ed.), *The Blitz*, Vol. 3, pp. 378–9.

3 Basil Collier, *The Defence of the United Kingdom*, 1957, pp. 370–71.

4 HC Debates, 16 June 1944, Vol. 400, cols. 2301–2.

5 *BBC Year Book 1945*, p. 141. General Sir Frederick Pile, *Ack-Ack: Britain's Defence against Air Attack during the Second World War*, 1949, pp. 328–33; O'Brien, *Civil Defence*, pp. 657–8; Collier, *The Defence of the United Kingdom*, pp. 371ff, 523.

6 For numbers of V-1s per borough see ibid., p. 525; those boroughs south of the river that were very large in area took the brunt. Private Papers of Miss Vivienne Hall, Imperial War Museum, Docs. 3989a, 10–16 and 16–19 June 1944 [apostrophe silently added].

7 Private Papers of Miss N. V Carver, Imperial War Museum, Docs. 379, 15–26 June 1944.

8 Collier, *The Defence of the United Kingdom*, pp. 377–8. Elisabeth Sheppard-Jones, writing in 1985, is cited in Ramsey (ed.), *The Blitz*, Vol. 3, p. 393.

9 Dorothy G. Wells, 'Diary of the War', Imperial War Museum, Docs. 26780, Vol. 8, 30 June 1944; in fact, the V-1 fell at 2.07 p.m.

10 Private Papers of Mrs M. Cossins, Imperial War Museum, Docs. 2064, 'Flying Bomb Experiences', 30 June 1944. Cecil H. King, *With Malice Toward None: A War Diary*, edited by William Armstrong, 1970, pp. 264–5, 30 June 1944. R. J. Minney, *The Two Pillars of Charing Cross: The Story of a Famous Hospital*, 1967, pp. 199–200.

11 Hall Papers, 24–30 June 1944. King, *Malice Toward None*, p. 265, 30 June 1944. Virginia Graham, *Consider the Years 1938–1946*, 1944, p. 81, verses 1, 3 and 4.

12 Peter Davidson (ed.), *The Complete Works of George Orwell*, Vol. 16, *I Have Tried to Tell the Truth 1943–1944*, 1998, p. 238. Private Papers of A. F. Williamson, Imperial War Museum, Docs. 3106, letter to Austin from his parents at 72 Hayes Wood Close, Hayes, Kent, 14 July 1944. Hall Papers, 29 July and 8–11 August 1944.

13 'Account of a V1 Attack on London, June 1944', Imperial War Museum, Docs. 2034.

14 Carver Papers, 6 July 1944. Cyril Demarne, *The London Blitz: A Fireman's Tale*, 1980 (revised and enlarged edition, 1990), pp. 58–9 [spelling silently corrected]; for the date see Ramsey (ed.), *The Blitz*, Vol. 3, p. 417.

15 Private Papers of Miss G. Thomas, Box No. 90/30/1, [27 and] 28 July 1944 [punctuation silently corrected].

16 *Lewisham Borough News*, 12 September 1944.

17 George Beardmore, *Civilians at War: Journals 1938–1946*, 1984, pp. 154–8. Verily Anderson, *Spam Tomorrow*, 1956, p. 165, 25 June 1944. For the proportion with fires see Aylmer Firebrace, *Fire Service Memories*, 1949, pp. 234–5. For the lookouts see HO 199/394A, 'Lessons from Recent Raids – Flying Bombs', 11 August 1944, p. 1. For the role of 'express light rescue' see TNA, HO 186/2352, Report 1 April to 30 June (with flying bomb information till 3 August) 1944, p. 2. For the inquiry points see Noel Streatfeild, *Beyond the Vicarage*, 1971, pp. 155–6; Charles Graves, *Women in Green (The Story of the W.V.S.)*, 1948, pp. 222ff and 219–21 (for canteens). For sightseers see *South London Press*, 18 July 1944; *Stratford Express*, 7 July 1944.

18 For the GIs see *South London Press*, 28 July 1944. *Streatham's 41*, 1945, passim. *East London Advertiser*, 13 October 1944. TNA, HO 199/394A, 'Lessons from Recent Raids – Flying Bombs', 11 August 1944, p. 1; a similar judgement is reached in HO 186/2352, Report 1 April to 30 June (with flying bomb information till 3 August) 1944, p. 2.

19 For Morrison see Daniel Todman, *Britain's War: A New World 1942–1947*, 2020, pp. 583–4. For Churchill see Christy Campbell, *Target London: Under Attack from the V-Weapons*, 2012, pp. 286–9.

20 Private Papers of W. B. Regan, Imperial War Museum, Docs. 781, 'Diary', 27 June 1944. Letter from Waugh, 23 June 1944, cited in Martin Stannard, *Evelyn Waugh: No Abiding City 1939–1966*, 1992, p. 111. Albert Turpin, *The East End: My Birthright*, 2017 (but written 1945–6), p. 150. Demarne, *London Blitz*, p. 118. Cited in Bryher, *The Days of Mars: A Memoir, 1940–1946*, 1972, p. 133. George H. Gallup, *The Gallup International Public Opinion Polls: Great Britain 1937–1975*, Vol. One, 1937–1964, New York, 1976, p. 94.

21 Mass Observation Archive, File Report 2121, 'V1 A Survey on the Pilotless Planes from data collected June 16th to July 3rd [1944] and compiled 18.4.45', p. 9. *Hackney Gazette*, 1 September 1944.

22 Shelter numbers are in Sir Arthur Salusbury MacNalty (ed.), *The Civilian Health and Medical Services*, Vol. I, *The Ministry of Health Services; Other Civilian Health and Medical Services*, 1953, pp. 196 and 198 (for deep shelters). 'The Second World War Diaries of Hilda Neal', Imperial War Museum, PP/MCR/59, 14 July 1944. For Attlee see *Daily Mirror*, 3 July 1944. HC Debates, 6 July 1944, Vol. 401, col. 1334. For the deep shelter numbers see also Robin Woolven, 'Civil Defence in London 1935–1945: The Formation and Implementation of Policy for, and the Performance of, Air Raid Precautions (later Civil Defence) Services in the London Region', University of London PhD thesis, 2002, Ch. 7, Tables 22 and 23. For Stockwell see *South London Press*, 11 and 17 July 1944.

23 Sue Bruley (ed.), *Working for Victory: A Diary of Life in a Second World War Factory*, Stroud, 2001, p. 191, 22 June 1944. HO 186/2352, Report 1 April to 30 June (with flying bomb information till 3 August) 1944, p. 2. Robin Woolven (ed.), *The London Diaries of Anthony Heap 1931–1945*, Woodbridge, 2017, p. 455, 23 June, and p. 457, 5 July 1944. Private Papers of A. E. Buddell, OBE, Imperial War Museum, Docs. 26502, 30 June and 9 July 1944. W. E. Holl, 'Civil Defence Goes Through It: Paddington, 1937–1945', typescript, British Library, 1946, p. 144.

24 For evacuation see R. M. Titmuss, *Problems of Social Policy*, 1950, pp. 426–8, 430n. Population figures are in HLG 7/608. Robert Henrey, *The Siege of London*, 1946, p. 75.

25 Mass Observation Archive, File Report 2199, 'The Flying-Bomb Evacuation', n.d., c. February 1945. Patricia and Robert Malcolmson, *Women at the Ready: The Remarkable Story of the Women's Voluntary Services on the Home Front*, 2013, pp. 228–9.

26 *South London Press*, 11, 18, 25, 29 August and 5 September 1944.

27 Collier, *The Defence of the United Kingdom*, pp. 389–90; MEPO 4/130.

28 Carver Papers, 31 July, 3 and 4 August 1944. Woolven (ed.), *The London Diaries of Anthony Heap*, p. 455, 24 June 1944. Vere Hodgson, *Few Eggs and No Oranges: A Diary Showing How Unimportant People in London and Birmingham Lived Through the War Years 1940–45 Written in the Notting Hill Area of London*, 1976 (2010 edition), p. 484, 18 June–2 July, and p. 504, 29 July 1944.

29 Carver Papers, 1–3 September 1944. Wells, Diary, Vol. 8, 5 September 1944. *The Times*, 8 September 1944. For a thorough-going account of the British struggle against the V-weapons see Campbell, *Target London*, passim.

30 Hall Papers, 1–11 September 1944.

31 For the return see Titmuss, *Problems of Social Policy*, p. 429. For the problems see *South London Press*, 15 September 1944.

32 Carver Papers, 8 September 1944. MEPO 4/130, 8 September 1944. See also Robin Woolven, 'The Middlesex Bomb Damage Maps 1940–1945', *London Topographical Record*, Vol. XXX, 2010, p. 164.

33 Ramsey (ed.), *The Blitz*, Vol. 3, pp. 444–7.

34 Carver Papers, 10 and 12 September 1944.

35 For 16 September see Ramsey (ed.), *The Blitz*, Vol. 3, pp. 458–9. Collier, *The Defence of the United Kingdom*, pp. 523, 527. O'Brien, *Civil Defence*, p. 666. HC Debates, Vol. 404, 10 November 1944, cols. 1653–4.

36 *South London Press*, 1 May 1945. Lewis Blake, *Bolts from the Blue: S.E. London and Kent under V2 Rocket Attack*, 1990, pp. 27–30.

37 HLG 7/608. Gross returns to London in that fourth quarter were 734,000
(Titmuss, *Problems of Social Policy*, p. 430n), although it is impossible to recon-
cile the figures from these two sources precisely. Mass Observation Archive, File
Report 2207, 'V2. A Report on South East London', February 1945, pp. 1, 4.
A. P. Herbert, *Independent Member*, 1950, pp. 311–12. Anthony Weymouth,
Journals of the War Years (1939–1945) and One Year Later, 2 vols., 1948, Vol.
2, p. 360, 13 November 1944. Patricia and Robert Malcolmson (eds.), *A Woman
in Wartime London: The Diary of Kathleen Tipper 1941–1945*, 2006, p. 118,
14 September 1944.

38 Carver Papers, 16 July 1944 (telephone volunteers). For the provincial wardens
see HO 186/2352, Report 1 April to 30 June (with flying bomb information till
3 August) 1944, p. 3; *Municipal Journal*, Vol. LII, 28 July 1944, p. 1206, and
for Mayor La Guardia p. 1282. *Lewisham Borough News*, 12 September 1944
(James Gray). *South London Press*, 15 September 1944 (Southwark).

39 Malcolmson, *Women at the Ready*, pp. 222–3, 276–84. *Hackney Gazette*, 19
January (Shoreditch) and 2 March (Hackney) 1945. *Daily Mirror*, 9 February
1945 (Birmingham).

40 Cecil Beaton, *The Happy Years: Diaries 1944–48*, 1972, p. 1.

41 C. M. Kohan, *Works and Buildings*, 1952, p. 225; H. M. D. Parker, *Manpower:
A Study of War-Time Policy and Administration*, 1957, p. 248. *Streatham's 41*,
p. 47. W. C. Berwick Sayers (ed.), *Croydon and the Second World War: The
Official History of the War Work of the Borough and Its Citizens from 1939
to 1945 Together with the Croydon Roll of Honour*, 1949, p. 104.

42 *Picture Post*, Vol. 25, 7 October 1944, pp. 7–9; see also Nicholas Bullock,
'Re-assessing the Post-War Housing Achievement: The Impact of War-damage
Repairs on the New Housing Programme in London', *Twentieth Century British
History*, Vol. 16, No. 3, 2005, pp. 256–82.

43 Kohan, *Works*, pp. 224–6; Parker, *Manpower*, pp. 248–50; Alan Bullock, *The
Life and Times of Ernest Bevin*, Vol. II, *Minister of Labour 1940–1945*, 1967,
p. 330. *ODNB*, Robin Woolven, 'Arthur Malcolm Trustram Eve, Ist Baron Silsoe
(1894–1976)', accessed 29 July 2020. *The Times*, 21 December 1944.

44 Parker, *Manpower*, pp. 251–2. *Municipal Journal*, Vol. LII, 10 November 1944,
p. 1969 (Croydon). *South London Press*, 10 November 1944 (Lambeth). Bruley
(ed.), *Working for Victory*, p. 200, 25 July 1944 (Duppas Hill). *Hackney Gazette*,
12 December 1944. *Lewisham Borough News*, 12 and 27 December 1944.

45 The repairs figures are in *Estates Gazette*, Vol. CXLIV, 30 December 1944, p.
603. For the standards see Kohan, *Works*, p. 231.

46 For Poplar and Stepney see *East London Advertiser*, 8, 22 September, 13, 20
October and 3, 10 November 1944. *Hackney Gazette*, 15 September and 20
October 1944. The list of requests and LCC estimate are in *Municipal Journal*,
Vol. LII, 27 October 1944, p. 1850, and 8 December 1944, p. 2127. *South
London Press*, 12 December 1944 (Brixton). Gallup, *The Gallup International
Public Opinion Polls*, Vol. 1, pp. 91, 96.

47 HC Debates, 26 July 1944, Vol. 402, cols. 759–60. *Report of the Commissioner
of Police of the Metropolis for the Year 1944*, 1945, Cmd. 6627, p. 5. Malcolmson
(eds.), *A Woman in Wartime London*, p. 99, 8 July 1944. *Hackney Gazette*, 13
September (Hackney council warden), 28 August (LCC driver) and 22 September
1944 (Worcester warden). *Islington Gazette*, 4 August 1944 (demolition men).
Lewisham Borough News, 5 December 1944 (NFS). *Stratford Express*, 8
December 1944 (Welsh builders).

48 *Stratford Express*, 22 September 1944 (Whipps Cross). Woolven (ed.), *The London Diaries of Anthony Heap*, pp. 470–71, 28 November 1944; George Orwell, 'Decline of the English Murder', *Tribune*, 15 February 1946. See also C. E. Bechhofer Roberts (ed.), *The Trial of Jones and Hulten*, 1945.

49 For the street-lighting fracas see *Hackney Gazette*, 17 and 24 November 1944.

50 Weymouth, *Journals of the War Years (1939–1945) and One Year Later*, Vol. 2, p. 363, 27 November 1944. Beardmore, *Civilians at War*, pp. 185–6, 17 and 31 December 1944. Beaton, *Happy Years*, p. 1, September 1944. *South London Press*, 12 December 1944. Mollie Panter-Downes, *London War Notes 1939–1945*, edited by William Shawn, New York, 1971, p. 352, 17 December 1944.

51 Woolven (ed.), *The London Diaries of Anthony Heap*, pp. 472–3, 21 and 25 December 1944. Wells, Diary, Vol. 9, [23 and] 25 December 1944. Carver Papers, 25 December 1944. Weymouth, *Journals of the War Years (1939–1945) and One Year Later*, Vol. 2, p. 370, 26 December 1944.

52 Henrey, *Siege of London*, pp. 157–8. Woolven (ed.), *The London Diaries of Anthony Heap*, p. 473, 31 December 1944. Carver Papers, 31 December 1944.

10. So This Is V-Day: 1 January–15 August 1945

1 Private Papers of Miss Vivienne Hall, Imperial War Museum, Docs. 3989a, 29 December 1944–5 January 1945.

2 TNA, MEPO 4/131, Metropolitan Police War Diary 1945; Basil Collier, *The Defence of the United Kingdom*, 1957, pp. 395–6, 417–9, 527. TNA, HO 186/2352, Report 1 January to 31 March 1945, p. 1.

3 Private Papers of R. S. Simmons, Imperial War Museum, Docs. 3943 [typos silently corrected]. Calton Road was misremembered as Carlton Road. His father's pre-war employment is from the entry in the 1939 Register for 'Burnock', Eversleigh Road, New Barnet; his was the only name registered.

4 HO 186/2352, Report 1 January to 31 March 1945, p. 1; Winston G. Ramsey (ed.), *The Blitz: Then and Now*, 3 vols., 1987–9, Vol. 3, pp. 530–31.

5 For the V-2 timings see MEPO 4/131. For Hughes Mansions see Collier, *The Defence of the United Kingdom*, p. 420; *East London Advertiser*, 4 May and 16 June 1945. A. E. Clark-Kennedy, *The London: A Study in the Voluntary Hospital System*, Vol. 2, *The Second Hundred Years 1840–1948*, 1963, pp. 278–9.

6 Ramsey (ed.), *The Blitz*, Vol. 3, p. 535.

7 R. M. Titmuss, *Problems of Social Policy*, 1950, p. 560; Terence H. O'Brien, *Civil Defence*, 1955, pp. 667–8; Collier, *The Defence of the United Kingdom*, p. 528.

8 Patricia and Robert Malcolmson (eds.), *A Woman in Wartime London: The Diary of Kathleen Tipper 1941–1945*, 2006, p. 150, 9 February 1945. Anthony Weymouth, *Journals of the War Years (1939–1945) and One Year Later*, 2 vols., 1948, Vol. 2, p. 379, 20 February 1945. Albert Turpin, *The East End: My Birthright*, 2017 (but written 1945–6), p. 163. Mollie Panter-Downes, *London War Notes 1939–1945*, edited by William Shawn, New York, 1971, p. 363, 11 March 1945.

9 Hall Papers, 24–29 March and 29 March–6 April 1945. Private Papers of Miss N. V. Carver, Imperial War Museum, Docs. 379, 1 and 4 April 1945. For news from Holland see *The Times*, 5 April 1945. 'The Second World War Diaries of Hilda Neal', Imperial War Museum, PP/MCR/59, 10 April 1945. *The Times*, 27 April 1945.

10 *Hackney Gazette*, 15 January 1945 (Bethnal Green); *Harrow Observer*, 4 January (NFS, north Harrow), 11 January 1945 (wardens, Kenton); *Middlesex Chronicle*, 6 January 1945 (fire guards, Heston and Isleworth, and wardens and the WVS, Hounslow); *Norwood News*, 12 January 1945 (wardens, south Norwood); *Marylebone Mercury*, 13 January 1945 (NFS, Chiswick); *West London Observer*, 12 January 1945 (Rangers); *Kensington Post*, 13 January 1945 (Marylebone).

11 Private Papers of Mrs M. Cossins, Imperial War Museum, Docs. 2064, 'Flying Bomb Experiences', 18 March 1945 [punctuation silently added]. *East London Advertiser*, 20 and 27 April 1945.

12 *The Times*, 30 April and 2 May 1945. The London Auxiliary Ambulance Service was finally disbanded in July 1945. See also Robin Woolven, 'Civil Defence in London 1935–1945: The Formation and Implementation of Policy for, and the Performance of, Air Raid Precautions (later Civil Defence) Services in the London Region', University of London PhD thesis, 2002, Ch. 7.

13 *Chelsea News and General Advertiser*, 11 May 1945 (Westminster). *Kensington Post*, 21 April 1945.

14 For temperatures see W. A. L. Marshall, *A Century of London Weather*, 1952, p. 95. Hall Papers, 7–12 January 1945. George H. Gallup, *The Gallup International Public Opinion Polls: Great Britain 1937–1975*, Vol. One, 1937–1964, New York, 1976, pp. 103–4. James Lees-Milne, *Prophesying Peace*, 1977, pp. 153–9, 11–29 January 1945.

15 W. H. B. Court, *Coal*, 1951, pp. 380–83. *South London Press*, 12, 30 January and 2 February 1945. *Hackney Gazette*, 31 January 1945. George Beardmore, *Civilians at War: Journals 1938–1946*, 1984, pp. 187–8, 28 January 1945.

16 Robin Woolven (ed.), *The London Diaries of Anthony Heap 1931–1945*, Woodbridge, 2017, p. 477, 2 January 1945. Vere Hodgson, *Few Eggs and No Oranges: A Diary Showing How Unimportant People in London and Birmingham Lived Through the War Years 1940–45 Written in the Notting Hill Area of London*, 1976 (2010 edition), p. 584, 27 April 1945. *Municipal Journal*, Vol. 53, 12 January 1945, p. 64 (LCC). Beardmore, *Civilians at War*, p. 195, 3 June 1945. Dorothy G. Wells, 'Diary of the War', Imperial War Museum, Docs. 26780, Vol. 9, 20 January to 24 April 1945, passim.

17 Wells, Diary, Vol. 9, 3 and 5 May 1945. For clothing supply and rationing see E. L. Hargreaves and M. M. Gowing, *Civil Industry and Trade*, 1952, pp. 315, 646. Carver Papers, 8 January and 24 February 1945.

18 Carver Papers, 31 March 1945. Hodgson, *Few Eggs and No Oranges*, p. 566, 18 February 1945. Bryher, *The Days of Mars: A Memoir, 1940–1946*, 1972, pp. 147–8. Neal, Diaries, 2 May 1945.

19 Woolven (ed.), *The London Diaries of Anthony Heap*, p. 485, 21 April 1945. Private Papers of Miss G. Thomas, Box No. 90/30/1, 13 April 1945. Panter-Downes, *London War Notes*, p. 368, 15 April 1945. Carver Papers, 14 and 17 April 1945.

20 Carver Papers, 24 April 1945; Hall Papers, 6–23 April 1945; Panter-Downes, *London War Notes*, p. 379, 21 April 1945; Malcolmson (eds.), *A Woman in Wartime London*, pp. 169–70, 15 April 1945.

21 Collier, *The Defence of the United Kingdom*, p. 417 for the January figures. Bernard Darwin, *War on the Line: The Story of the Southern Railway in War-Time*, 1946, pp. 34–5. Reverse evacuation plans and population figures are in Titmuss, *Problems of Social Policy*, pp. 430–34.

22 The total and averages are in *Summary Report of the Ministry of Health for the year ended 31st March 1945*, 1945, Cmd. 6710, pp. 29, 49–51. Detailed figures for damaged houses and repairs carried out are given in Robin Woolven's introduction to Ann Saunders (ed.), *The London County Council Bomb Damage Maps 1939–1945*, 2005, p. 24; I've added the estimated average damage from the seventeen final V-weapons from 23 March 1945.

23 *Stratford Express*, 16 February 1945 (Leyton). For criticism of the War Cabinet see *South London Press*, 13 February 1945. *Municipal Journal*, Vol. 53, 11 May 1945, p. 956 (Wandsworth). *Islington Gazette*, 20 February 1945.

24 For numbers of building workers and hostels see *Summary Report Ministry of Health year ended 31st March 1945*, p. 49. *Hackney Gazette*, 5 and 8 January 1945. *South London Press*, 5 January 1945 (Camberwell). *Lewisham Borough News*, 8 May 1945.

25 Verily Anderson, *Spam Tomorrow*, 1956, pp. 259–63.

26 *Daily Mirror*, 24 February 1945; TNA, HLG 7/561. For the west London initiative see *The Times*, 17 January, and *Marylebone Mercury*, 27 January 1945. *South London Press*, 24 July 1945, where her name is also given as Stuttle. For the Brighton Vigilantes see also *Picture Post*, Vol. 28, 28 July 1945, pp. 8–9.

27 For an allegedly communist agitation in Hackney Wick see *Hackney Gazette*, 19 and 24 January 1945. Hall Papers, 6–23 April 1945. Woolven (ed.), *The London Diaries of Anthony Heap*, p. 482, 20 March 1945. For points schemes see *Municipal Journal*, Vol. 53, 18 May 1945, p. 992.

28 There were 36,219 requisitioned houses in the County of London in 1949; some of these are likely to have been taken over after the war, but others requisitioned during the war would have passed back to their owners; LCC, *London Statistics, Vol. 1, New Series, 1945–1954*, 1957, p. 109. For numbers of prefabs and the LRE's position see C. M. Kohan, *Works and Buildings*, 1952, p. 234. *South London Press*, 20 March (Lambeth) and 23 May 1945 (Wandsworth).

29 Carver Papers, 7 February 1945; *Daily Herald*, 7 June 1945.

30 Carver Papers, 27 April, 2 and 5 May 1945. Malcolmson (eds.), *A Woman in Wartime London*, p. 173, 28 April, and pp. 175–6, 2–4 May 1945.

31 Bryher, *Days of Mars*, p. 155, 6 May 1945.

32 Malcolmson (eds.), *A Woman in Wartime London*, pp. 177–8, 7 May 1945.

33 Daniel Todman, *Britain's War: A New World 1942–1947*, 2020, pp. 715–16.

34 Malcolmson (eds.), *A Woman in Wartime London*, p. 178, 7 May 1945.

35 Wells, Diary, Vol. 9, 7 May 1945.

36 Wells, Diary, Vol. 9, 8 May 1945.

37 Malcolmson (eds.), *A Woman in Wartime London*, pp. 178–9, 8–9 May 1945.

38 Woolven (ed.), *The London Diaries of Anthony Heap*, pp. 487–90, 8–9 May 1945.

39 Carver Papers, 8 and 9 May 1945.

40 Stefan Schimanski and Henry Treece (eds.), *Leaves in the Storm: A Book of Diaries*, 1947, p. 289.

41 Humphrey Lyttelton, *I Play As I Please: The Memoirs of an Old Etonian Trumpeter*, 1954, pp. 97–8. R. F. Delderfield, *For My Own Amusement*, 1968, pp. 97–8.

42 *East London Advertiser*, 11 May 1945.

43 *East London Advertiser*, 11 and 18 May, 15 June 1945.

44 Carver Papers, 9 [in fact 10] May 1945.

45   Klara Modern, *My Dearest Family: An Austrian Refugee's Letters from London to America, 1938–1945*, Milton Keynes [privately published], 2017, pp. 222–3, letter 16 May 1945 from 74 Overhill Road, Dulwich, SE22.

46   Mass Observation Archive, File Report 2268, 'A Report on the General Election. June–July 1945', October 1945, p. 1. Malcolmson (eds.), *A Woman in Wartime London*, p. 179, 10 May 1945.

47   MO/FR 2268, pp. 2, 4–6. On the political background see Stephen Brooke, *Labour's War: The Labour Party during the Second World War*, Oxford, 1992, pp. 303–18. *South London Press*, 5 June 1945.

48   Gallup, *The Gallup International Public Opinion Polls*, Vol. 1, pp. 104, 106–7, 111. Peter Davidson (ed.), *The Complete Works of George Orwell*, Vol. 17, *I Belong to the Left 1945*, 1998, pp. 163–4, 'London Letter', 5 June 1945, *Partisan Review*, Summer 1945. Woolven (ed.), *The London Diaries of Anthony Heap*, p. 491, 23 May 1945.

49   MO/FR 2268, p. 88.

50   For the East Fulham campaign see Mass Observation Archive, File Report 2267, 'Election Observations', June–July 1945, p. 1; MO/FR 2268, p. 56.

51   MO/FR 2268, p. 13. Mass Observation Archive, File Report 2282, 'Post-Mortem on Voting at the Election', September 1945, p. 2.

52   *Twenty Point Manifesto of the Liberal Party*, 1945, point 4. *Mr. Churchill's Declaration of Policy to the Electors*, 1945. *Let Us Face the Future: A Declaration of Labour Policy for the Consideration of the Nation*, 1945.

53   Gallup, *The Gallup International Public Opinion Polls*, Vol. 1, pp. 105, 109, 111.

54   MO/FR 2268, pp. 59–60, 83.

55   *Harrow Observer*, 8 March 1945. *Norwood News*, 29 June 1945. Carver Papers, 25 June–14 July 1945, probably 4 July.

56   MO/FR 2267, pp. 12–13; MO/FR 2268, pp. 35–7.

57   *Hackney Gazette*, 6 July 1945.

58   *Lewisham Borough News*, 16 January 1945; 'blackcoat' was a traditional term, a little old-fashioned in 1945, for clerks and shopworkers in middle-class stores. LCC, *London Housing*, 1937, p. 150; the Mottingham Estate, its northern part in Lewisham, was also unfinished at the time of the 1935 election.

59   *Lewisham Borough News*, 10 July 1945; see also Bernard Donoghue and G. W. Jones, *Herbert Morrison: Portrait of a Politician*, 1973, p. 338, who wrote that Morrison attacked Churchill 'for allegedly banning warnings for lone flying bombs'.

60   Woolven (ed.), *The London Diaries of Anthony Heap*, pp. 494–5, 5 July 1945.

61   MO/FR 2268, pp. 123, 125. Woolven (ed.), *The London Diaries of Anthony Heap*, pp. 496, 25 July 1945.

62   Michael Kinnear, *The British Voter: An Atlas and Survey since 1885*, 1981, p. 55.

63   For the results see *The Times*, 27 July 1945. For analysis of swing and turnout see Kinnear, *The British Voter*, pp. 55–71; see also Norman Howard, *A New Dawn: The General Election of 1945*, 2005, passim.

64   MO/FR 2268, pp. 126–31 [typo silently corrected]. Malcolmson (eds.), *A Woman in Wartime London*, p. 193. Woolven (ed.), *The London Diaries of Anthony Heap*, pp. 496–7, 26 July 1945. Neal, Diaries, 26 July 1945. Wells, Diary, Vol. 9, 26 July 1945. Carver Papers, 26 and 27 July 1945. The diaries of

Bill Regan, Vivienne Hall, and Gwyneth Thomas, who might have all felt differently, were not kept, or have not survived, for this period.

65 For the three categories I've drawn on MO/FR 2268, p. 87, and Mass Observation Archive, File Report 2415, '"It Isn't There." An Interpretation of Political Trends Based on Mass-Observation Material', 3 August 1946, p. 3.

66 MO/FR 2282, p. 4. *Municipal Journal*, Vol. 53, 3 August 1945, p. 1544.

67 *Estates Gazette*, Vol. CXLVI, 4 August 1945, p. 92.

68 Carver Papers, 15 August 1945.

69 *Lewisham Borough News*, 21 and 28 August 1945; the mayor said other boroughs had been taken by surprise too. *East London Advertiser*, 17 and 24 August. *Hackney Gazette*, 17 August 1945 (Bethnal Green). *South London Press*, 17 August 1945.

11. *Let Us Face the Future*

1 The numbers are in R. M. Titmuss, *Problems of Social Policy*, 1950, pp. 560–61.

2 For TB see Sheila Ferguson and Hilde Marchant, *Studies in the Social Services*, 1954, pp. 254–5; Ministry of Health, *On the State of the Public Health during Six Years of War*, 1946, p. 58ff; LCC, *Interim Report of the County Medical Officer of Health and School Medical Officer for the Year 1943*, 1944, p. 2, and *Interim Report of the County Medical Officer of Health and School Medical Officer for the Year 1945*, 1946, p. 6. For heart disease and flu see LCC, *London Statistics*, Vol. 1, New Series, *1945–1954*, 1957, p. 44, and LCC, *MOH Report 1945*, p. 9.

3 Ferguson and Marchant, *Social Services*, pp. 171–3. LCC, *Interim Report of the County Medical Officer of Health and School Medical Officer for the Year 1940*, 1941, p. 2, and LCC, *MOH Report 1945*, p. 13. Sir Arthur Salusbury MacNalty (ed.), *The Civilian Health and Medical Services*, Vol. I, *The Ministry of Health Services; Other Civilian Health and Medical Services*, 1953, p. 35, for the national comparison. Metropolitan Borough of Shoreditch, *Abridged Report on the Health and Sanitary Condition of the Metropolitan Borough of Shoreditch … for the Year 1945*, 1946, p. 2. The IMR for Greater London in 2017 was 3.3 and in the UK 3.8 per 1,000 live births. County Borough of West Ham, *Annual Report on the Health Services for the Year 1945*, [1946], pp. 3, 5; West Ham's infant mortality rate was 38 in 1945, down from 43.

4 Ferguson and Marchant, *Social Services*, pp. 155–63. See also generally R. J. Hammond, *Food*, Vol. I, *The Growth of Policy*, 1951, pp. 218–27. The smoking statistic is from an Action on Smoking and Health fact sheet, 2016.

5 Eliot Slater and Moya Woodside, *Patterns of Marriage: A Study of Marriage Relationships in the Urban Working Classes*, 1951, pp. 14, 215–6.

6 For the VD rate see LCC, *Report of the County Medical Officer of Health and School Medical Officer for the Year 1946*, 1947, p. 29. The divorce rate is in *London Statistics*, Vol. 1, p. 42. Slater and Woodside, *Patterns of Marriage*, pp. 219–22.

7 *London Statistics*, Vol. 1, pp. 37–40. Ferguson and Marchant, *Social Services*, pp. 50–52. Slater and Woodside, *Patterns of Marriage*, p. 293.

8   *London Statistics*, Vol. 1, pp. 39–40; LCC, *MOH Report 1946*, p. 4.

9   For the 'new type' see Ferguson and Marchant, *Social Services*, pp. 95–6. Doreen Bates, *Diary of a Wartime Affair: The True Story of a Surprisingly Modern Romance*, 2016, pp. 292–305.

10 Houses destroyed in the war are in *Report of the Committee on Housing in Greater London*, 1965, Cmd 2605 [the Milner Holland Report], p. 11. Population figures are in *Census 1951 England and Wales: Report on Greater London and Five Other Conurbations*, 1956, p. xxvi. *London Statistics*, Vol. 1, p. 106. Slater and Woodside, *Patterns of Marriage*, p. 217.

11 Stuart Maclure, *One Hundred Years of London Education 1870–1970*, 1970, pp. 138, 147–8.

12 For nursery schools see LCC, *London School Plan*, 1947. *London Statistics*, Vol. 1, pp. 86–92.

13 *Report of the Commissioner of Police of the Metropolis for the Year 1946*, 1947, pp. 38–43.

14 *Uxbridge & West Drayton Gazette*, 19 December 1947. *Norwood News*, 17 January 1947. *Kensington Post*, 23 January 1948 (Hammersmith). *Fulham Chronicle*, 5 December 1947 (Chelsea).

15 *The Times*, 6 February 1946, for Labour's manifesto.

16 *The Times*, 15 March and 9 April 1949. Michael Kinnear, *The British Voter: An Atlas and Survey since 1885*, 1981, pp. 58–61.

17 Simon Bradley and Nikolaus Pevsner, *London 1: The City of London*, 1997, pp. 125–41, 281–6, 594–9. Bridget Cherry, Charles O'Brien and Nikolaus Pevsner, *London 5: East*, 2005, pp. 651–6. Bridget Cherry and Nikolaus Pevsner, *London 2: South*, 1983, pp. 592–3. W. Eric Jackson, *Achievement. A Short History of the London County Council*, 1965, p. 45.

18 *London Statistics*, Vol. 1, pp. 165–9. John Pudney, *London's Docks*, 1975, pp. 173–5.

19 J. H. Forshaw and Patrick Abercrombie, *County of London Plan*, 1943, p. 33. Population figures are in *Census 1951: Greater London*, p. xxvi. *Estates Gazette*, Vol. CXLVII, 5 January 1946, p. 9; see also Vols. CXLVI, 29 December 1945, p. 559, and CXLVII, 19 January 1946, p. 69.

20 Hugh Dalton, *The Fateful Years: Memoirs 1931–1945*, 1957, Ch. XXIX. See also *ODNB*, Ben Pimlott, 'Dalton, (Edward) Hugh Neal, Baron Dalton (1887–1962)', accessed 30 July 2019.

21 *ODNB*, Richard Weight, 'Silkin, Lewis, first Baron Silkin (1889–1972)', accessed 29 July 2019.

22 HC Debates, Series 5, Vol. 420, 5 March 1946, cols. 189–92.

23 TNA, HLG 71/706, 'Official Committee on the Distribution of Industry. Panel A. Further Industrial Development in Greater London. Principles to be followed' [n.d., c. May 1946].

24 HLG 71/706, 'A Survey of Approvals of Industrial Building Projects in the Greater London Area', 24 January 1947.

25 *London Statistics*, Vol. 1, pp. 103–5, 108.

26 Ibid., pp. 111–12.

27 For the building programme see LCC, *A Survey of the Post-War Housing of the London County Council 1945–1949*, 1949, passim; for Macmillan see Ken Young and Patricia Garside, *Metropolitan London: Politics and Urban Change 1837–1981*, 1982, pp. 263–4, and for housing policy more generally see Ch. 9.

28 LCC, *Administrative County of London Development Plan: Statement*, 1962, p. 3. *The Times*, 26 February 1963.

29 See, for the general picture, Mark Clapson, 'Destruction and Dispersal: The Blitz and the "Break-Up" of Working-Class London', in Mark Clapson and Peter J. Larkham (eds.), *The Blitz and Its Legacy: Wartime Destruction to Post-War Reconstruction*, Farnham, 2013, pp. 99–112. See generally Jerry White, *London in the Twentieth Century: A City and Its People*, 2001, pp 204–8.

BIBLIOGRAPHY

Archival Sources

Bishopsgate Institute

Diary of Godfrey W. Clarke, GDP/258
Diaries of Rhona Mary Linton Little, GDP/178

Bodleian Library

Diary of David Euan Wallace, GB 161 MSS Eng. Hist. c. 495–8

Imperial War Museum

'Account of a V1 Attack on London, June 1944', Imperial War Museum, Docs. 2034
Dorothy G. Wells, 'Diary of the War', Docs. 26780
Private Papers of Miss V. Bawtree, Docs. 1807a–b
Private Papers of F. R. Bodley, Box No. 09/37/1
Private Papers of A. E. Buddell, OBE, Docs. 26502
Private Papers of Miss N. V. Carver, Docs. 379
Private Papers of Mrs M. Cossins, Docs. 2064
Private Papers of Mrs M. Crompton, Docs. 13803: Journal of the War Years 1939–1945
Private Papers of Miss D. I. Fisher, Docs. 2324
Private Papers of Miss Vivienne Hall, Docs. 3989a
Private Papers of Mrs B. M. Holbrook, Docs. 3311
Private Papers of T. H. Pointer, Docs. 3957
Private Papers of W. B. Regan, Docs. 781
Private Papers of Mrs G. Rennie, Docs. 5090

Private Papers of R. S. Simmons, Docs. 3943
Private Papers of Miss G. Thomas, Box No. 90/30/1
Private Papers of Miss P. Warner, Docs. 3208
Private Papers of A. F. Williamson, Docs. 3106
'The Second World War Diaries of Hilda Neal', PP/MCR/59

London Metropolitan Archive

LCC/CL/TP/1/33
LCC/CL/TP/1/38
LCC/CL/TP/1/39
LCC/PH/WAR/1/1
LCC/RC/GEN/01/001

Mass Observation Archive

Day Survey Respondent 097
Day Survey Respondent 123
Diarist, MO/D/5285
Diarist, MO/D/5438
File Report 33, 'Music Halls', February 1940
File Report 143, 'North London Refugees', May 1940
File Report 184, 'Anti-Italian Riots in Soho', 11 June 1940
File Report 238, 'Refugees', 30 June 1940
File Report 291, 'Brick Shelters', July 1940
File Report 292, 'Note on the Hampstead Housewives Service', 20 July 1940
File Report 392, 'Evacuation and Other East End Problems', 10 September 1940
File Report 403, 'The Effect of Air Raids on the Isle of Dogs', 15 September 1940
File Report 431, 'Survey of the Activities of Official and Voluntary Bodies in the East End, during the Intensive Bombing September 7–27, 1940'
File Report 1648, 'Recent Trends in Anti-Semitism', 10 March 1943?
File Report 2121, 'V1. A Survey on the Pilotless Planes from data collected June 16th to July 3rd [1944] and compiled 18.4.45'
File Report 2199, 'The Flying-Bomb Evacuation', n.d., c. February 1945
File Report 2207, 'V2. A Report on South East London', February 1945
File Report 2267, 'Election Observations', June–July 1945
File Report 2268, 'A Report on the General Election. June–July 1945', October 1945
File Report 2282, 'Post-Mortem on Voting at the Election', September 1945

File Report 2415, '"It Isn't There." An interpretation of political trends based on Mass-Observation Material', 3 August 1946

Reform Club Archive

General Committee Minute Book, 30 October 1935–14 June 1945

The National Archives

AST 11/32
AVIA 10/267
HLG 7/561
HLG 7/608
HLG 71/694
HLG 71/706
HO 186/952
HO 186/2352
HO 199/394A
HO 205/231
HO 205/379
INF 1/292
MEPO 4/126 Pt 2
MEPO 4/127 Pt 1
MEPO 4/128
MEPO 4/129
MEPO 4/130
MEPO 4/131
MH 101/58

Unpublished Sources

Holl, W. E., 'Civil Defence Goes Through It: Paddington, 1937–1945', typescript, British Library, 1946

Woolven, Robin, 'Civil Defence in London 1935–1945: The Formation and Implementation of Policy for, and the Performance of, Air Raid Precautions (later Civil Defence) Services in the London Region', University of London PhD thesis, 2002

Newspapers and Periodicals

Aberdeen Evening Express
Chelsea News and General Advertiser

Daily Herald
Daily Mirror
East London Advertiser [Boroughs of Poplar and Stepney and East London Advertiser]
Estates Gazette
Fulham Chronicle
Hackney Gazette
Harrow Observer
Hendon and Finchley Times
International Women's News
Islington Gazette
Kensington Post
Lewisham Borough News
London Calling
London Library Magazine
Marylebone Mercury
Middlesex Chronicle
Middlesex County Times
Middlesex Gazette
Municipal Journal
News Chronicle
New Statesman and Nation
Norwood News
Penguin New Writing
Picture Post
Radio Times
South London Press
Stratford Express
Sunday Pictorial
The Times
Town and Country Planning
Tribune
Uxbridge & West Drayton Gazette
West London Observer
Yorkshire Post and Leeds Mercury

Published Sources

The place of publication is London unless specified and titles marked *
   are volumes in the *History of the Second World War, United Kingdom Civil Series*, and associated publications.

Abercrombie, Patrick, *Greater London Plan 1944*, 1945

Addison, Paul, and Crang, Jeremy A. (eds.), *Listening to Britain: Home Intelligence Reports on Britain's Finest Hour, May to September 1940*, 2010

Allison, George F., *Allison Calling: A Galaxy of Football and Other Memories*, 1948

Allport, Alan, *Browned Off and Bloody-Minded: The British Soldier Goes to War*, 2015

Amati, Marco, and Freestone, Robert, 'All of London's a Stage: The 1943 County of London Plan Exhibition', *Urban History*, Vol. 43, No. 4, Cambridge, 2016, pp. 539–56

An ABC for Special Constables and Police War Reserves, 1939

Anderson, Verily, *Spam Tomorrow*, 1956

Anon., *The Bells Go Down: The Diary of a London A.F.S. Man*, 1942

Anon., *Roof Over Britain: The Official Story of the A.A. Defences, 1939–1942*, 1943

Arbib, Robert S., *Here We Are Together: The Notebook of an American Soldier in Britain*, 1946 (Right Book Club edition, 1947)

A Warden [Adrian Bury], *Dusk to Dawn: Letters by a Warden*, 1941

Baker, Michael H. C., *London Transport in the Blitz*, Hersham, 2010

Balchin, Nigel, *Darkness Falls from the Air*, 1942

Barker, T. C., and Robbins, Michael, *A History of London Transport: Passenger Travel and the Development of the Metropolis*, Vol. II, *The Twentieth Century to 1970*, 1974 (1976 edition)

Barltrop, Robert, *Bright Summer – Dark Autumn: Part III Growing up in North East London between the Wars*, 1986

Bates, Doreen, *Diary of a Wartime Affair: The True Story of a Surprisingly Modern Romance*, 2016

Bates, L. M., *The Thames on Fire: The Battle of London River 1939–1945*, Lavenham, 1985

Bató, Joseph, *Defiant City*, 1942

BBC Year Book 1943

BBC Year Book 1945

Beardmore, George, *Civilians at War: Journals 1938–1946*, 1984

Bearman, Marietta, et al., *Out of Austria: The Austrian Centre in London in World War II*, 2008

Beaton, Cecil, *The Happy Years: Diaries 1944–48*, 1972

Beaton, Cecil, *The Years Between: Diaries 1939–44*, 1965

Bell, Anne Oliver (ed.), *The Diary of Virginia Woolf*, Vol. V, *1936–1941*, 1984

Bell, Reginald, *The Bull's-Eye*, 1943

Benney, Mark, *Almost a Gentleman*, 1966

— *Over to Bombers*, 1943

Beveridge, Peter, *Inside the C.I.D.*, 1957

Beveridge, Sir William, *Social Insurance and Allied Services*, 1942, Cmd. 6404

Bird, Stephanie, *Stepney: Profile of a London Borough from the Outbreak of the First World War to the Festival of Britain, 1914–1951*, Newcastle upon Tyne, 2011

Blake, Lewis, *Bolts from the Blue: S.E. London and Kent under V2 Rocket Attack*, 1990

— *Red Alert: The Story of South East London at War, 1939–1945*, 'New Enlarged Edition', 1992

Bosman, Suzanne, *The National Gallery in Wartime*, 2008

Bradley, Simon, and Pevsner, Nikolaus, *London 1: The City of London*, 1997

Briggs, Asa, *The War of Words: The History of Broadcasting in the United Kingdom*, Vol. III, 1970

Brinson, Charmian, and Dove, Richard, *Politics by Other Means: The Free German League of Culture in London 1939–1945*, 2010

Brittain, Vera, *England's Hour*, 1941

Brockway, Fenner, *Bermondsey Story: The Life of Alfred Salter*, 1949

Brome, Vincent, *J. B. Priestley*, 1988

Bruley, Sue (ed.), *Working for Victory: A Diary of Life in a Second World War Factory*, Stroud, 2001

Bryher, *The Days of Mars: A Memoir, 1940–1946*, 1972

Bullock, Alan, *The Life and Times of Ernest Bevin*, Vol. II, *Minister of Labour 1940–1945*, 1967

Bullock, Nicholas, 'Re-assessing the Post-War Housing Achievement: The Impact of War-damage Repairs on the New Housing Programme in London', *Twentieth Century British History*, Vol. 16, No. 3, 2005, pp. 256–82

Burlingham, Dorothy, and Freud, Anna, *Young Children in War-Time: A Year's Work in a Residential War Nursery*, 1942

Butler, A. S. G., *Recording Ruin*, 1942

Calder, Angus, *The Myth of the Blitz*, 1991

— *The People's War: Britain 1939–45*, 1969

Calder, Ritchie, *Carry on London*, 1941

— *The Lesson of London*, 1941

Campbell, Christy, *Target London: Under Attack from the V-Weapons*, 2012

Capstick, John, *Given in Evidence*, 1960

Cesarani, David, and Kushner, Tony (eds.), *The Internment of Aliens in Twentieth Century Britain*, 1993

Cherry, Bridget, and Pevsner, Nikolaus, *London 2: South*, 1983

Cherry, Bridget, O'Brien, Charles, and Pevsner, Nikolaus, *London 5: East*, 2005

Churchill, Winston S., *The Second World War*, Vol. II, *Their Finest Hour*, 1949

— *The Second World War*, Vol. III, *The Grand Alliance*, 1950

— *The Second World War*, Vol. V, *Closing the Ring*, 1952

Clapson, Mark, and Larkham, Peter J. (eds.), *The Blitz and Its Legacy: Wartime Destruction to Post-War Reconstruction*, Farnham, 2013

Clark-Kennedy, A. E., *The London: A Study in the Voluntary Hospital System*, Vol. 2, *The Second Hundred Years 1840–1948*, 1963

Cockett, Olive, *Love & War in London*, edited by Robert Malcolmson, 2008

Collier, Basil, *The Defence of the United Kingdom*, 1957*

Collier, Richard, *The City That Wouldn't Die*, 1959

Collingham, Lizzie, *The Taste of War: World War Two and the Battle for Food*, 2011

Collins, Norman, *London Belongs To Me*, 1945

Colls, Robert, *George Orwell: English Rebel*, Oxford, 2013

Constantine, Learie, *Colour Bar*, 1954

Cooper, Diana, *The Light of Common Day*, 1959

— *Trumpets from the Steep*, 1960

Cooper, Lettice, *Black Bethlehem*, 1947

Copeman, Fred, *Reason in Revolt*, 1948

Court, W. H. B., *Coal*, 1951*

Crisp, Quentin, *The Naked Civil Servant*, 1968

Dalton, Hugh, *The Fateful Years: Memoirs 1931–1945*, 1957

Darwin, Bernard, *War on the Line: The Story of the Southern Railway in War-Time*, 1946

Dash, Jack, *Good Morning Brothers!*, 1969

Davidson, Peter (ed.), *The Complete Works of George Orwell*, Vol. 12, *A Patriot After All 1940–1941*, 1998

— *The Complete Works of George Orwell*, Vol. 13, *All Propaganda is Lies 1941–1942*, 1998

— *The Complete Works of George Orwell*, Vol. 15, *Two Wasted Years 1943*, 1998

— *The Complete Works of George Orwell*, Vol. 16, *I Have Tried to Tell the Truth 1943–1944*, 1998

Day, Sidney, *London Born*, Beaminster, Dorset, 2004

Dean, Basil, *The Theatre at War*, 1956

Dear, I. C. B., and Foot, M. R. D. (eds.), *The Oxford Companion to the Second World War*, Oxford, 1995

Delderfield, R. F., *For My Own Amusement*, 1968

Demarne, Cyril, *The London Blitz: A Fireman's Tale*, 1980 (revised and enlarged edition, 1990)

Dent, H. C., *Education in Transition: A Sociological Study of the Impact of War on English Education 1939–1943*, 1944

Dickens, Monica, *The Fancy*, 1943

Donoghue, Bernard, and Jones, G. W., *Herbert Morrison: Portrait of a Politician*, 1973

Drake, David, *Paris at War 1939–1944*, 2015

Dunn, C. L., *The Emergency Medical Services*, Vol. I, *England and Wales*, 1952*

— *The Emergency Medical Services*, Vol. II, *Scotland, Northern Ireland and the Principal Air Raids on Industrial Centres in Great Britain*, 1953*

Dunne, L. R., *Report on an Inquiry into the Accident at Bethnal Green Tube Station Shelter on the 3rd March, 1943*, 1945, Cmd. 6583

Everard, Stirling, *The History of the Gas Light and Coke Company 1812–1949*, 1949

Faviell, Frances [Olivia Faviell Lucas], *A Chelsea Concerto*, 1959

Fennell, Jonathan, *Fighting the People's War: The British and Commonwealth Armies and the Second World War*, Cambridge, 2019

Ferguson, Sheila, and Marchant, Hilde, *Studies in the Social Services*, 1954*

Field, Geoffrey G., *Blood, Sweat, and Toil: Remaking the British Working Class, 1939–1945*, Oxford, 2011

Firebrace, Aylmer, *Fire Service Memories*, 1949

Fitzgibbon, Theodora, *With Love*, 1982

Fogarty, M. P., *Prospects of the Industrial Areas of Great Britain*, 1945

Forshaw, J. H., and Abercrombie, Patrick, *County of London Plan*, 1943

Fraser, Frankie, *Mad Frank: Memoirs of a Life of Crime*, 1994

Freeman, William (compiler), *War-Time Memories: A Brief Record of the Activities of Addressograph-Multigraph Ltd. in the Years 1939–1945*, 1946

Gallup, George H., *The Gallup International Public Opinion Polls: Great Britain 1937–1975*, Vol. One, 1937–1964, New York, 1976

Gardiner, Juliet, *The Blitz: The British Under Attack*, 2010

Gaskin, Margaret, *Blitz: The Story of 29th December, 1940*, 2005

Glass, Charles, *The Deserters: A Hidden History of World War II*, New York, 2013

Goble, Bill, *Life-Long Rebel*, 1984

Gorodetsky, Gabriel (ed.), *The Maisky Diaries: Red Ambassador to the Court of St James's 1932–1943*, 2015

Gosden, P. H. J. H., *Education in the Second World War: A Study in Policy and Administration*, 1976

Goymer, Maurice, *Bombs, Stinging Nettles and Doodlebugs*, 2006

Graham, Virginia, *Consider the Years 1938–1946*, 1944

Graves, Charles, *Champagne and Chandeliers: The Story of the Café de Paris*, 1958

— *London Transport Carried On: An Account of London at War 1939–1945*, 1947

— *Londoner's Life*, 1942

— *Off the Record*, 1942

— *The Home Guard of Britain*, 1943

— *The Story of St Thomas's 1106–1947*, 1947

— *Women in Green (The Story of the W.V.S.)*, 1948

Grayzell, Susan R., *At Home and Under Fire: Air Raids and Culture in Britain from the Great War to the Blitz*, Cambridge, 2012

Green, Henry, *Caught*, 1943

Greeno, Edward, *War on the Underworld*, 1960

Haapamaki, Michele, *The Coming of the Aerial War: Culture and the Fear of Airborne Attack in Inter-War Britain*, 2014

Haldane, Charlotte, *Truth Will Out*, 1949

Haldane, J. B. S., *A.R.P.*, 1938

Hammerton, J. A., *As the Days Go By ... Leaves from My War-Time Diary 1939–1940*, 1941

Hammond, R. J., *Food*, Vol. I, *The Growth of Policy*, 1951*

— *Food*, Vol. II, *Studies in Administration and Control*, 1956*

Hancock, W. K., and Gowing, M. M., *British War Economy*, 1949*

Hargreaves, E. L., and Gowing, M. M., *Civil Industry and Trade*, 1952*

Harrisson, Tom, *Living Through the Blitz*, 1976

Harte, Negley, *The University of London 1836–1986: An Illustrated History*, 1986

Hebbert, Michael, *London: More by Fortune Than Design*, Chichester, 1998

Hennessy, Elizabeth, *A Domestic History of the Bank of England, 1930–1960*, Cambridge, 1992

Henrey, Robert, *A Village in Piccadilly*, 1942

— *The Incredible City*, 1944

— *The Siege of London*, 1946

Herbert, A. P., *Independent Member*, 1950

The Hermitage Shelter Minutes December 1940, 1990

Hewison, Robert, *Under Siege: Literary Life in London 1939–1945*, 1977

Hibberd, Stuart, *'This – Is London'*, 1950

Hodgson, Vere, *Few Eggs and No Oranges: A Diary Showing How Unimportant People in London and Birmingham Lived Through the War Years 1940–45 Written in the Notting Hill Area of London*, 1976 (2010 edition)

Hodson, James Lansdale, *Home Front: Being Some Account of Journeys, Meetings and What Was Said to Me in and about England during 1942–1943*, 1944

— *Through the Dark Night: Being Some Account of a War Correspondent's Journeys, Meetings and What Was Said to Him, in France, Britain and Flanders during 1939–1940*, 1941

Holden, Inez, *It Was Different at the Time*, 1943

— *Night Shift*, 1941

Holmes, Colin, and Kershen, Anne J. (eds.), *An East End Legacy: Essays in Memory of William J. Fishman*, 2017

Hopkinson, Tom, *Of This Our Time: A Journalist's Story, 1905–50*, 1982

Hornby, William, *Factories and Plant*, 1958*

House of Commons Debates [HC Debates]

Howard, Norman, *A New Dawn: The General Election of 1945*, 2005

Howlett, Peter (text), *Fighting with Figures: A Statistical Digest of the Second World War*, 1995

Hurley, Alfred James, *Days That Are Gone: Milestones I Have Passed in South-West London*, 1947

Hutton, Robert, *Agent Jack: The True Story of MI5's Secret Nazi Hunter*, 2018

— *Of Those Alone*, 1958

Hyde, Douglas, *I Believed: The Autobiography of a Former British Communist*, 1951

Idle, Doreen, *War Over West Ham: A Study of Community Adjustment*, 1943

Ingham, H. S., *Fire and Water: An Anthology by Members of the NFS*, 1942

Inman, P., *Labour in the Munitions Industries*, 1957*

Isaacs, Susan (ed.), *The Cambridge Evacuation Survey: A Wartime Study in Social Welfare and Education*, 1941

Jackson, Stanley, *The Savoy: The Romance of a Great Hotel*, 1964

Jackson, W. Eric, *Achievement: A Short History of the London County Council*, 1965

James, Robert Rhodes (ed.), *Chips: The Diaries of Sir Henry Channon*, 1967

Jesse, F. Tennyson (ed.), *Trials of Timothy John Evans and John Reginald Halliday Christie*, 1957

Jesse, F. Tennyson, and Harwood, H. M., *London Front: Letters written to America (August 1939–July 1940)*, 1940

— *While London Burns: Letters Written to America (July 1940–June 1941)*, 1942

Jones, Helen, *British Civilians in the Front Line: Air Raids, Productivity and Wartime Culture, 1939–45*, Manchester, 2006

Kelly, Debra, and Cornick, Martyn (eds.), *A History of the French in London: Liberty, Equality, Opportunity*, 2013

Kent, William, *The Lost Treasures of London*, 1947

King, Cecil H., *With Malice Toward None: A War Diary*, edited by William Armstrong, 1970

Kinnear, Michael, *The British Voter: An Atlas and Survey since 1885*, 1981

Kohan, C. M., *Works and Buildings*, 1952*

Kushner, Tony, *The Persistence of Prejudice: Antisemitism in British society during the Second World War*, Manchester, 1989

Kynaston, David, *The City of London*, Vol. III, *Illusions of Gold 1914-1945*, 1999

Laite, Julia, *Common Prostitutes and Ordinary Citizens: Commercial Sex in London, 1885-1960*, Basingstoke, 2012

Laurent, Livia [Eva Maierhof], *A Tale of Internment*, 1942

Law, Frank W., *The History and Traditions of the Moorfields Eye Hospital*, Vol. II, *Being a Continuation of Treacher Collins' History of the First Hundred Years*, 1975

LCC, *Administrative County of London Development Plan. Statement*, 1962

LCC, *A Survey of the Post-War Housing of the London County Council 1945-1949*, 1949

LCC, *Interim Report of the County Medical Officer of Health and School Medical Officer for the Year 1940*, 1941

LCC, *Interim Report of the County Medical Officer of Health and School Medical Officer for the Year 1943*, 1944

LCC, *Interim Report of the County Medical Officer of Health and School Medical Officer for the Year 1945*, 1946

LCC, *London Statistics 1936-38*, Vol. XLI, 1939

LCC, *London Statistics*, Vol. 1, New Series, *1945-1954*, 1957

LCC, *The LCC Hospitals: A Retrospect*, 1949

London Council of Social Service, *The Communal Restaurant: A Study of the Place of Civic Restaurants in the Life of the Community. Prepared in the Spring and Summer of 1943*, 1943

Lees-Milne, James, *Ancestral Voices*, 1975

— *Prophesying Peace*, 1977

Lehmann, John, *I Am My Brother: Autobiography II*, 1960

Lehmkul, Dik, *Journey to London: The Story of the Norwegian Government at War*, 1945

Let Us Face the Future: A Declaration of Labour Policy for the Consideration of the Nation, 1945

Leutze, James (ed.), *The London Observer: The Journal of Raymond E. Lee*, 1972

Lewis, Chaim, *Of No Fixed Address*, 2009

Liebling, A. J., *The Road Back to Paris*, 1944

Linehan, Thomas P., *East London for Mosley: The British Union of Fascists in East London and South-West Essex, 1933–40*, 1996

Loewe, Camilla, *Just Like the End of the World: Stories of the Coronation Mansions Disaster*, 2012.

Low, David, *Low's Autobiography*, 1956

LWP, *Health and Housing: Report 4th Session London Women's Parliament*, 1943

LWP, *You Can Get a War-time Nursery in Your District*, 1942

Lyle, H. Willoughby, *An Addendum to King's and Some King's Men (London) Being an Added Record of King's College Hospital and of King's College Hospital Medical School to 5 July 1948*, 1950

Lyttelton, Humphrey, *I Play As I Please: The Memoirs of an Old Etonian Trumpeter*, 1954

McCullough, Art (ed.), *The War and Uncle Walter: The Diary of an Eccentric*, 2004

McDermott, C. L., *A Yank on Piccadilly*, New York, 1951 (Popular Library Edition, 1952)

Mackay, Robert, *Half the Battle: Civilian Morale in Britain during the Second World War*, Manchester, 2002

Maclaren-Ross, Julian, *Memoirs of the Forties*, edited by Alan Ross, 1965 (1984 paperback edition)

Maclure, Stuart, *One Hundred Years of London Education 1870–1970*, 1970

MacNalty, Sir Arthur Salusbury (ed.), *The Civilian Health and Medical Services*, Vol. I, *The Ministry of Health Services; Other Civilian Health and Medical Services*, 1953*

Magee, Bryan, *Growing up in a War*, 2007

Malcolmson, Patricia and Robert, *Women at the Ready: The Remarkable Story of the Women's Voluntary Services on the Home Front*, 2013

Malcolmson, Patricia and Robert (eds.), *A Free-Spirited Woman: The London Diaries of Gladys Langford, 1936–1940*, 2014

— *A Woman in Wartime London: The Diary of Kathleen Tipper 1941–1945*, 2006

Marchant, Hilde, *Women and Children Last: A Woman Reporter's Account of the Battle of Britain*, 1941

Marshall, W. A. L., *A Century of London Weather*, 1952

Martelli, George, *The Man Who Saved London: The Story of Michel Hollard, D.S., Croix de Guerre*, 1960 (Companion Book Club edition, 1961)

Maschwitz, Eric, *No Chip on My Shoulder*, 1957

Mass-Observation, *Britain*, 1939

Mass-Observation, *War Begins at Home*, 1940

Matthews, W. R., *Saint Paul's Cathedral in War-Time 1939–1945*, 1946

Metropolitan Borough of Shoreditch, *Abridged Report on the Health and Sanitary Condition of the Metropolitan Borough of Shoreditch ... for the Year 1945*, 1946

Middleton, Drew, *The Sky Suspended: The Battle of Britain*, 1960

Milne, Gustav, and the Thames Discovery Project, *The Thames at War*, Barnsley, 2020

Ministry of Health, *On the State of the Public Health during Six Years of War*, 1946

Minney, R. J., *The Two Pillars of Charing Cross: The Story of a Famous Hospital*, 1967

Modern, Klara, *My Dearest Family: An Austrian Refugee's Letters from London to America, 1938–1945*, Milton Keynes [privately published], 2017

Morgan, Guy, *Red Roses Every Night: An Account of London Cinemas under Fire*, 1948

Morris, Mary, *A Very Private Diary: A Nurse in Wartime*, 2014

Mountevans, Admiral Lord, *Adventurous Life*, 1946

Mr Churchill's Declaration of Policy to the Electors, 1945

Murphy, J. T., *Victory Production!*, 1942

Murrow, Edward R., *This is London*, New York, 1941

Nash, George C., *The LMS at War*, 1946

National Council of Social Service, *Dispersal: An Inquiry into the Advantages and Feasibility of the Permanent Settlement out of London and Other Great Cities of Office and Clerical and Administrative Staffs*, 1944

National Federation of Women's Institutes, *Town Children Through Country Eyes: A Survey on Evacuation 1940*, Dorking, 1940

Nava, Mica, *Visceral Cosmopolitanism: Gender, Culture and the Normalisation of Difference*, Oxford, 2007

Newens, Arthur Ernest, *The Memoirs of an Old East-Ender*, Harlow, 2006

Nicolson, Harold, *Diaries and Letters 1939–1945*, 1967

Nixon, Barbara, *Raiders Overhead*, 1943

Nock, O. S., *Britain's Railways at War 1939–1945*, 1971

O'Brien, Terence H., *Civil Defence*, 1955*

ODNB [*Oxford Dictionary of National Biography*, www.oxforddnb.com]

O'Leary, John G., *Danger Over Dagenham*, 1947

Olson, Lynne, *Citizens of London: The Americans Who Stood with Britain in Its Darkest, Finest Hour*, New York, 2010

Ostrowska, Wanda, and Garvin, Viola G., *London's Glory*, 1945

Our Towns: A Close-Up. A Study Made in 1939–42 with Certain Recommendations by the Hygiene Committee of the Women's Group on *Public Welfare (in Association with the National Council of Social Service)*, 1943

Padley, Richard, and Cole, Margaret, *Evacuation Survey: A Report to the Fabian Society*, 1940

Panayi, Panikos (ed.), *Racial Violence in Britain in the Nineteenth and Twentieth Centuries*, revised edition, 1996

Paneth, Marie, *Branch Street*, 1944

Panter-Downes, Mollie, *Good Evening Mrs Craven: The Wartime Stories of Mollie Panter-Downes*, 1999

— *London War Notes 1939–1945*, edited by William Shawn, New York, 1971

Parker, H. M. D., *Manpower: A Study of War-Time Policy and Administration*, 1957*

Perry, Colin, *Boy in the Blitz: The 1940 Diary of Colin Perry*, Stroud, 2000

Pile, General Sir Frederick, *Ack-Ack: Britain's Defence against Air Attack during the Second World War*, 1949

Piratin, Phil, *Our Flag Stays Red*, 1948

Pope-Hennessy, James, and Beaton, Cecil, *History Under Fire*, 1941

Postan, M. M., *British War Production*, 1952*

Postgate, John, 'Glimpses of the Blitz', *History Today*, Vol. 43, 1 June 1993, pp. 21–8

Powell, Anthony, *The Soldier's Art*, 1966 (Mandarin edition, 1997)

— *To Keep the Ball Rolling*, Vol. III, *Faces in My Time*, 1980

Pritchett, V. S., *Midnight Oil*, 1971

Prunier, Madame [Simone B.], *La Maison: The History of Prunier's*, 1957

Quennell, Peter, *The Wanton Chase: An Autobiography from 1939*, 1980

Raczynski, Count Edward, *In Allied London*, 1962

Radford, Frederick H., *'Fetch the Engine ...' The Official History of the Fire Brigades Union*, 1951

Ramsey, Winston G. (ed.), *The Blitz: Then and Now*, 3 vols, 1987–9

Rawlings, William, *A Case for the Yard*, 1961

Read, Simon, *Dark City: Crime in Wartime London*, Hersham, 2010

Reader, W. J., *Metal Box: A History*, 1976

Recommendations of Lord Horder's Committee regarding the Conditions in Air-Raid Shelters with Special Reference to Health; and a Brief Statement of Action Taken by the Government Thereon, 1940, Cmd. 6234

The Registrar-General's Statistical Review of England and Wales for the Year 1937, Tables Pt II, Civil

Report of the Commissioner of Police of the Metropolis for the Year 1939, 1940, Cmd. 6201

Report of the Commissioner of Police of the Metropolis for the Year 1940, 1941

Report of the Commissioner of Police of the Metropolis for the Year 1943, 1944, Cmd. 6536

Report of the Commissioner of Police of the Metropolis for the Year 1944, 1945, Cmd. 6627

Report of the Commissioner of Police of the Metropolis for the Year 1945, 1946, Cmd. 7156

Report of the Commissioner of Police of the Metropolis for the Year 1946, 1947

Report of the Committee on Housing in Greater London, 1965, Cmd 2605

Report of the Royal Commission on the Distribution of the Industrial Population, 1940, Cmd. 6513

Report ... on the Preliminary Draft Proposals for Post-War Reconstruction in the City of London, 1944

Reynolds, David, *Rich Relations: The American Occupation of Britain, 1942–1945*, 1995

Reynolds, Quentin, *A London Diary*, 1941 (Popular Library edition, New York, 1962)

— *Only the Stars Are Neutral*, 1942

Richards, J. M. (ed.), *The Bombed Buildings of Britain: A Record of Architectural Casualties*, 1942

Ripman, Hujohn A. (ed.), *Guy's Hospital 1725–1948*, 1951

Ritchie, Charles, *The Siren Years: Undiplomatic Diaries 1937–1945*, 1974

Robb, Nesca A., *An Ulsterwoman in England 1924–1941*, Cambridge, 1942

Roberts, C. E. Bechhofer (ed.), *The Trial of Harry Dobkin*, 1944

— *The Trial of Jones and Hulten*, 1945

Robson, William A., *The Government and Misgovernment of London*, 1939

Rogers, David, *Shadow Factories: Britain's Production Facilities during the Second World War*, Solihull, 2016

Roodhouse, Mark, *Black Market Britain 1939–1955*, Oxford, 2013

Rose, Sonya O., *Which People's War? National Identity and Citizenship in Wartime Britain 1939–1945*, Oxford, 2003

Royal Borough of Kensington, *Annual (Interim) Report on the Health of the Borough for the Year 1942*

St Loe Strachey, Celia, *Borrowed Children: A Popular Account of Some Evacuation Problems and Their Remedies*, 1940

Salvoni, Elena, with Fawkes, Sandy, *Elena: A Life in Soho*, 1990

Sansom, William, *Westminster in War*, 1947

Sansom, William, Gordon, James, and Spender, Stephen, *Jim Braidy. The Story of Britain's Firemen*, 1943

Saroyan, William, *The Adventures of Wesley Jackson*, 1947

Saunders, Ann (ed.), *The London County Council Bomb Damage Maps 1939–1945*, 2005

Saunders, Hilary St George, *Ford at War*, 1946

— *The Middlesex Hospital 1745–1948*, 1949

Sayers, W. C. Berwick (ed.), *Croydon and the Second World War: The Official History of the War Work of the Borough and Its Citizens from 1939 to 1945 Together with the Croydon Roll of Honour*, 1949

Scannell, Dorothy, *Dolly's War*, 1975 (1977 edition)

Schimanski, Stefan, and Treece, Henry (eds.), *Leaves in the Storm: A Book of Diaries*, 1947

Schneer, Jonathan, *The Thames*, 2005

Schweitzer, Pam, et al. (eds.), *What Did You Do in the War, Mum? Women Recall Their Wartime Work*, 1985

Scott, Ann, *Ernest Gowers: Plain Words and Forgotten Deeds*, Basingstoke, 2009

Scott, Harold, *Your Obedient Servant*, 1959

Sheridan, Michael, *Rowton Houses 1892–1954*, 1956

Slater, Eliot, and Woodside, Moya, *Patterns of Marriage: A Study of Marriage Relationships in the Urban Working Classes*, 1951

Smith, Harold L. (ed.), *War and Social Change: British Society in the Second World War*, Manchester, 1986

Smithies, Edward, *Crime in Wartime: A Social History of Crime in World War II*, 1982

Sparks, Ruby, *Burglar to the Nobility*, 1961

Spier, Eugen, *The Protecting Power*, 1951

Srebrnik, Henry Felix, *London Jews and British Communism, 1935–1945*, Ilford, 1995

Stannard, Martin, *Evelyn Waugh: No Abiding City 1939–1966*, 1992

Stansky, Peter, *The First Day of the Blitz: September 7, 1940*, 2007

Strachey, John, *Post D: Some Experiences of an Air Raid Warden*, 1941

Streatfeild, Noel, *Beyond the Vicarage*, 1971

— *Saplings*, 1945 (Persephone edition, 2000)

Streatham's 41, 1945

Summary Report of the Ministry of Health for the Year Ended 31st March 1945, 1945, Cmd. 6710

Summerfield, Penny, *Reconstructing Women's Wartime Lives: Discourse and Subjectivity in Oral Histories of the Second World War*, Manchester, 1998

— *Women Workers in the Second World War: Production and Patriarchy in Conflict*, 1984

Sweet, Matthew, *The West End Front: The Wartime Secret of London's Grand Hotels*, 2011

Sword, Keith, et al., *The Formation of the Polish Community in Great Britain 1939–1950*, 1989

Thomas, Donald, *An Underworld at War: Spivs, Deserters, Racketeers & Civilians in the Second World War*, 2003

Thompson, Wally, *Time Off My Life*, 1956

Titmuss, R. M., *Problems of Social Policy*, 1950*

Todd, Ruthven, *Fitzrovia & the Road to the York Minster*, 1973

Todman, Daniel, *Britain's War: A New World 1942–1947*, 2020

Turpin, Albert, *The East End: My Birthright*, 2017

Twenty Point Manifesto of the Liberal Party, 1945

Vale, George F., *Bethnal Green's Ordeal 1939–45*, 1945

Vaughan Williams, Ursula, *R. V. W.: A Biography of Ralph Vaughan Williams*, Oxford, 1964

Wallington, Neil, *Firemen at War: The Work of London's Fire-Fighters in the Second World War*, Newton Abbot, c. 1981

Warmington, E. H., *A History of Birkbeck College University of London during the Second World War 1939–1945*, 1954

Wassey, Michael, *Ordeal by Fire: The Story and Lesson of Fire over Britain and the Battle of the Flames*, 1941

Watts, Marthe, *The Men in My Life*, 1960

Waugh, Evelyn, *Unconditional Surrender*, 1961

Webster, Wendy, *Mixing It: Diversity in World War Two Britain*, Oxford, 2018

West Ham, County Borough of, *Annual Report on the Health Services for the Year 1945*, [1946]

Weymouth, Anthony [pseud. Ivo Geikie Cobb], *Journals of the War Years (1939–1945) and One Year Later*, 2 vols., 1948

Wheeler-Bennett, John W., *John Anderson: Viscount Waverley*, 1962

White, Jerry, *London in the Twentieth Century. A City and Its People*, 2001

White, Jerry, *Zeppelin Nights: London in the First World War*, 2014

White, Jerry, 'The "Dismemberment of London": Chamberlain, Abercrombie and the London Plans of 1943–44', *London Journal*, Vol. 44, No. 3, December 2019, pp. 206–26

Wilson, Charles, and Reader, William, *Men and Machines: A History of D. Napier & Son, Engineers, Ltd. 1858–1958*, 1958

Woolven, Robin (ed.), *The London Diaries of Anthony Heap 1931–1945*, Woodbridge, 2017

Woolven, Robin, 'The Middlesex Bomb Damage Maps 1940–1945', *London Topographical Record*, Vol. XXX, 2010, pp. 130–210

Wyndham, Joan, *Love Lessons. A Wartime Diary*, 1985

Yee, Chiang, *The Silent Traveller in Wartime*, 1939

Young, Ken, and Garside, Patricia, *Metropolitan London: Politics and Urban Change 1837–1981*, 1982

Ziegler, Philip, *London at War 1939–1945*, 1995

Zweiniger-Bargielowska, Ina, *Austerity in Britain: Rationing, Controls and Consumption, 1939–1955*, Oxford, 2000

INDEX

penguin.co.uk/vintage